The Mind of Modernism

CULTURAL SITINGS

Elazar Barkan, Editor

CULTURAL SITINGS presents focused discussions of major contemporary and historical cultural issues by prominent and promising scholars, with a special emphasis on multidisciplinary and transnational perspectives. By bridging historical and theoretical concerns, CULTURAL SITINGS develops and examines narratives that probe the spectrum of experiences that continuously reconfigure contemporary cultures. By rethinking chronology, agency, and especially the siting of historical transformation, the books in this series go beyond disciplinary boundaries and notions of what is marginal and what is central to knowledge. By juxtaposing the analytical, the historical, and the visual, this challenging series provides a venue for the development of cultural studies and for the rewriting of the canon.

The Mind of Modernism

Medicine, Psychology, and the

Cultural Arts in Europe and America,

1880–1940

EDITED AND INTRODUCED BY

Mark S. Micale

STANFORD
UNIVERSITY
PRESS

Stanford,
California

2004

Stanford University Press
Stanford, California
© 2004 by the Board of Trustees of the
Leland Stanford Junior University

Printed in the United States of America
on acid-free, archival-quality paper

Library of Congress Cataloging-in-Publication Data

The mind of modernism : medicine, psychology, and the cultural arts in
Europe and America, 1880-1940 / edited and introduced by Mark S. Micale.
    p.   cm. — (Cultural sitings)
  Includes bibliographical references and index.
  ISBN 0-8047-4577-3 — ISBN 0-8047-4797-0 (pbk.)
    1. Psychology and literature. 2. Modernism (Literature). 3. Motion
pictures—Psychological aspects. Psychoanalysis.   I. Micale, Mark S.
II. Series.
PN56.P93 M56   2004
809'.9112 — dc22   2003018430

Typeset at Stanford University Press in 10/13 Electra

Original printing 2004
Last figure below indicates year of this printing:
13   12   11   10   09   08   07   06   05   04

Preface and Acknowledgments

The origins of this book are most likely autobiographical: they trace to my efforts as a teenager during the early 1970s to chose between a career in the cultural arts—painting and drawing, to be specific—and a career in medicine. The path I eventually followed, a professional scholar's career in the cultural studies of science and medicine, was doubtless an attempt to reconcile these youthful, divergent pastimes. The same desire and drive to bridge "the two cultures" (as C. P. Snow famously dubbed them in the late 1950s) kept cropping up in my higher education, too: as a university undergraduate, the curricular division of knowledge among disciplines and departments seemed to me arbitrary and artificial, and as a graduate student and later a postdoctoral fellow during the 1980s the two historians whose work I was most drawn to—Peter Gay and Roy Porter—both united in their scholarship a great range of ideas and information about science, medicine, politics, literature, philosophy, and the visual arts. Both authors also routinely reach readers in the humanities and the sciences alike. Today, at mid-career, I teach university courses about both the cultural history of modern Europe and the history of medicine and psychiatry.

Not surprisingly, in light of this background, I have long hungered for a full-scale historical account of the interaction of the two cultures. It would be a fascinating study. Doubtless because of the enormous multidisciplinary knowledge the undertaking would require, no single work comes close to the task. The 1964 study *Saturn and Melancholy*, by the brilliant Warburg Institute trio of Raymond Klibansky, Erwin Panofsky, and Fritz Saxl, achieves the goal for a single medical category. Likewise, a sizable corpus of specialized scholarship, most of it British and North American in provenance, now probes the links among individual sciences and specific authors, texts, genres, styles, and movements in the cultural, especially the literary, arts. Another lively and discerning line of inquiry from the past twenty years explores the styles and structures of narrative storytelling shared by the sciences, including clinical medicine, and the arts. But a comprehensive mapping of the historical and conceptual interpenetration of the two cultural fields—even the sketch of such a map—remains unavailable in any language.

As I emphasize in my introductory essay below, the *sciences of the mind* in particular bear special affinities to the cultural arts, and arguably at no time were these affinities more intimate and intricate and consequential than during the late nineteenth and early twentieth centuries. In one domain of Western European culture and thought after another, these were decades of astonishing fertility and creativity, decades that witnessed both the burgeoning of psychological and psychiatric knowledge and the burst of creative energy in the arts and philosophy that we designate retrospectively as cultural and artistic Modernism. A premise of this book is that this coincidence of chronology is not happenstance. Only the Swiss polymath Henri Ellenberger, in his mammoth and magisterial study *Discovery of the Unconscious* (1970), has to date attempted to write a complete account of the linkages between these two cultural fields during the years 1870–1930, and my discovery of Ellenberger's historical writings in the late 1980s was revelatory.

During the 1990s, as I continued to study and to teach the history of this period, I became increasingly convinced that a series of conventional, discipline-bound "influence studies" was inadequate to account for the extraordinary range and depth of interactions between these different arenas of human inquiry and expression. Completing the present work has only confirmed that conviction. I now believe that a kind of comprehensive psychologization of culture, permeating virtually all branches of the creative life of the mind, occurred in the European West a century ago. To make this statement, however, is immediately to raise a host of related, more specific questions: Why did this psychologization take place when and where it did? How was it accomplished? What does cultural psychologization entail, and what deeper historical forces underpin the process? Were there contradictions within and resistances to cultural psychologization?

Since a global interpretative account of the subject, in the Ellenbergian tradition, was beyond my grasp, I decided to do the next best thing: in the spring of 1995, I organized a wide-ranging interdisciplinary conference at Yale University and invited a stellar group of internationally known scholars to help me explore the subject. *The Mind of Modernism* is the result. This book offers readers a suite of case studies in the historical and conceptual interplay between the psychological and artistic varieties of Euro-American Modernism. I want to acknowledge that the present volume cannot claim comprehensive coverage; an entire second volume could (and probably should) be devoted to topics such as comparative psychosexualities, the science and aesthetics of dream life, languages of primitivism, theories of the nonrational, styles of psychopathology, and concepts of consciousness and unconsciousness. Nevertheless, I believe that *The Mind of Modernism* represents more than the sum of its constituent essays, and in the Introduction I have attempted to draw out succinctly these larger implications, and to provide a sketch of that map of the history of the two cultures during the heady years of 1870–1940.

During this book's passage into print, I incurred several debts, which it gives me pleasure to acknowledge at this time. In its first incarnation, the project took the form of a two-day conference held at Yale University on October 12–14, 1995. David Marshall, who then served as director of The Whitney Humanities Center at Yale, kindly embraced my proposal for an ambitious conference on this topic and provided sage guidance. Sheila Brewer and Jesse Matz helped to stage the conference. Lawrence Rainey, who then taught in Yale's Department of English, proved a superb fund raiser for the event; although he later withdrew in order to work on other projects, our early conversations about this area of mutual and intense interest helped to shape the eventual volume. Several conference participants whose presentations are not included in the book — Carolyn Dean, Sander Gilman, Louis Sass, Michael Roth, and Elaine Showalter — contributed to this highly successful event. Likewise, Peter Gay's keynote address, on Flaubert and the French medical profession, launched the event memorably. Martin Jay's brilliant closing lecture first brought to my attention the crucial phenomenon of "Modernist anti-psychologism."

Pulling these essays together into a book required other forms of assistance. Jesse Wegman provided yeoman service in helping to compile the timeline, a true scholarly labor of love. Pierre-Henri Castel, the dean of French historians of hysteria, kindly sent me a copy of his *Querelle de l'hystérie* (1988), which includes his own detailed chronology. Bruce Mazlish of M.I.T. has long been bridging the two cultures in his scholarship; his encouragement was most welcome. I delivered draft versions of the book's introductory essay to engaged and intelligent audiences at the Harvard Center for Literary and Cultural Studies, the Calgary Institute of the Humanities, the New York/Cornell University Psychiatric Grand Rounds series, and the University of Illinois Department of History. Josh Esty, who teaches just down the quad from me in the Department of English at U of I, also supplied a highly perceptive reading of the Introduction. Jesse Matz kindly alerted me to the emerging field of cognitive literary criticism. And, during the project's later stages, David Areford provided various forms of commentary and companionship. Jan Langendorf did some indispensable typing on the manuscript. To all these individuals and organizations, I express my warmest thanks.

I also want to acknowledge several publications that appeared while this book was in progress and that helped me to hone my thinking: Jacqueline Carroy's articles and books from the past fifteen years have documented beautifully the elaborate interplay of the arts and psychological medicine in nineteenth-century France. In addition to its other virtues, Judith Ryan's 1991 study *Vanishing Subject: Early Psychology and Literary Modernism* confirmed my conviction about the need to include, but decisively to move beyond, Freudian psychology in the study of this subject. In 1994, Dorothy Ross's edited volume of essays, *Modernist Impulses in the Human Sciences, 1870–1930*, explored the network of linkages among the sciences, philosophy, and social sciences during this period. Daniel Albright's *Quantum Poetics: Yeats, Pound, Eliot, and the Sciences of Modernism*, which appeared in 1997, showed me that many of the same cultural developments occurring in early twentieth-century psychology and biomedicine extended to the physical sciences as well. And the following year Tim Armstrong's *Modernism, Technology, and the Body: A Cultural Study* boldly speculated on the connections between Modernist literary texts and nineteenth-century biology and psychophysics. Lynn Gamwell's catalogue for the art exhibition *Dreams 1900–2000: Science, Art, and the Unconscious Mind* (2000), with its intriguing opening essay "The Muse Is Within: The Psyche in the Century of Science," underscored for me how much remained to be explored beyond my own volume's subjects. Elazar Barkan, Norris Pope, and Kim Lewis Brown come last but hardly least in these Acknowledgments. This is my second time to work with this team at Stanford University Press, and my second time to find the experience immensely agreeable and gratifying. I continue to find Elazar Barkan's Cultural Sitings series a highly congenial intellectual venue. (Barkan's own coedited work in the series, *Prehistories of the Future: The Primitivist Project and the Culture of Modernism*, touches on terrain similar to *The Mind of Modernism*.) For the past two years, Norris Pope's interest, support, and vision sustained the project. And by efficiently guiding this handsome and substantial volume through production, the SUP staff again helped me, in some small way, to stave off the advent of the e-book.

M.S.M.

Chicago

Contents

Contents

Contributors

JOHN BRENKMAN is Distinguished Professor of English and Comparative Literature at CUNY Graduate Center and Baruch College. He is the author of *Culture and Domination* (1987) and *Straight Male Modern: A Cultural Critique of Psychoanalysis* (1993) and is author of the literary magazine *Venue*.

JACQUELINE CARROY is Research Director at the École des hautes études en science sociales in Paris. She is the author of many books and articles on the history of psychology and psychopathology in nineteenth-century France, and she has a particular interest in the historical interplay between creative literature and psychopathology. Her leading publications include *Le mal de Morzine. De la possession à l'hystérie (1857–1877)* (1981), *Hypnose, suggestion et psychologie. L'Invention de sujets* (1991), and *Les personnalités doubles et multiples. Entre science et fiction* (1993). With Nathalie Richard she is also editor of *La découverte et ses récits en sciences humaines* (1998).

RAE BETH GORDON is Professor of French Studies and Comparative Literature at the University of Connecticut. She is also author of *Ornament, Fantasy, and Desire in Nineteenth-Century French Literature* (1992) and *Why the French Love Jerry Lewis: From Cabaret to Early Cinema* (2001). She is currently working on two projects, *Sensation and Soul: From Hysteria to Aesthetic Theory* and *Primitivism, Pathology, and the Idea of Modernity*, a study of the influence of black entertainers in the Parisian café-concert and music hall between 1880 and 1925.

TOM GUNNING is Professor in the Department of Art History and the Committee on Cinema and Media at the University of Chicago. He is the author of *D. W. Griffith and the Origins of American Narrative Film: The Early Years at Biograph* (1991) and *The Films of Fritz Lang: Allegories of Vision and Modernity* (2000). He has published widely, in several languages, dealing especially with early cinema, including a series of articles on "the cinema of attractions." He is currently working on the convergence of aesthetic and scientific processes at the turn of the century that led to the invention of cinema.

IAN HACKING is Professor at the Collège de France (Chaire de philosophie et histoire des concepts scientifiques) and University Professor of Philosophy at the University of Toronto. His most recent books are *The Taming of Chance* (1990), *Rewriting the Soul* (1995), *The Social Construction of What?* (1999), *An Introduction to Probability and Inductive Logic* (2001), and *Historical Ontology* (2002). He is currently working on a study titled *Making Up People*.

MARTIN JAY is Sidney Hellman Ehrman Professor of History at the University of California, Berkeley, where he chaired the department from 1998 to 2001. Among his many publications are *The Dialectical Imagination* (1973; 1996), *Marxism and Totality* (1984), *Adorno* (1984), *Permanent Exiles* (1985), *Fin-de-siècle Socialism* (1989), *Force Fields* (1993), *Downcast Eyes* (1993), *Cultural Semantics* (1998), and *Refractions of Violence* (2003). During the 2001–2002 academic year, he was a member of the Institute for Advanced Study, and he is currently finishing a book on the discourse of experience in European and American thought.

DAVID JORAVSKY has taught at the University of Connecticut, Brown, and Northwestern, where he was Milton H. Wilson Professor of the Humanities before retiring in 2001. His major publications include *Soviet Marxism and Natural Science, 1917–1932* (1961), *The Lysenko Affair* (1970; 2002), and *Russian Psychology: A Critical History* (1989). His essay in this volume is part of a larger, ongoing study titled *Nation and Jew: Fictive Knowledge and Total War*.

JESSE MATZ, who taught at Harvard University from 1996 to 2001, is now Assistant Professor in the Department of English at Kenyon College. He is the author of *Literary Impressionism and Modernist Aesthetics* (2001) and *The Modern Novel: A Short Introduction* (2003). He is presently at work on a study of the therapeutic and pedagogical uses of narrative temporality.

STEVEN MEYER teaches modern and contemporary poetry and poetics, as well as nineteenth- and twentieth-century intellectual history, at Washington University in St. Louis. His book *Irresistible Dictation: Gertrude Stein and the Correlations of Writing and Science* appeared in 2001. He is currently completing an edition of Gertrude Stein's complete lectures.

Two additional projects—a general, interpretative study of modern poetry and a second volume on Stein and modern narrative—are underway.

MARK S. MICALE is Associate Professor of History at the University of Illinois in Urbana-Champaign, where he teaches courses in European cultural and intellectual history and in the history of medicine, including psychiatry. He is the author of *Approaching Hysteria: Disease and Its Interpretations* (1995). He has also edited and translated *Beyond the Unconscious: Essays of Henri F. Ellenberger in the History of Psychiatry* (1993) and coedited *Discovering the History of Psychiatry* (1994), *Enlightenment, Passion, Modernity: Historical Essays in European Thought and Culture* (2000), and *Traumatic Pasts: History, Psychiatry, and Trauma in the Modern Age, 1870–1930* (2001). A work on medicine and masculinity from the Renaissance to Freud is in preparation.

LAWRENCE RAINEY is Professor of Anglo-Irish Literary Modernism at the University of York. He is the author of *Ezra Pound and the Monument of Culture* (1991), *A Poem Containing History: Textual Studies in The Cantos* (1997), and *Institutions of Modernism: Literary Elites and Public Culture* (1998). He also is founding coeditor of the journal *Modernism/Modernity*.

JOHN E. TOEWS is Professor of History and Chair of the Program in the Comparative History of Ideas at the University of Washington. He is author of *Hegelianism: The Path toward Dialectical Humanism, 1805–1841* (1981), and he has written numerous substantial articles on modern German cultural history, contemporary historiography, the history of psychoanalysis, and historical theory. He has just completed *Becoming Historical: Cultural Reformation and Public Memory in Early Nineteenth-Century Berlin*.

The Mind of Modernism

The Modernist Mind: A Map

MARK S. MICALE

Psychology is the domain where the physician and the man of letters meet.
  —Hippolyte Bernheim, "L'organisme humain" (1892)

He who wishes to plumb and describe the mental cannot completely escape
the creative writer's methods of conceiving and describing, however rigorous
the will to cool, sober objectivity.
  —Freiherr von Berger, review of *Studies on Hysteria* (1896)

Creative writers cannot evade the psychiatrist nor the psychiatrist creative
writers, and the poetic treatment of a psychiatric theme can turn out to be
correct without any sacrifice of its beauty.
  —Sigmund Freud, "Delusions and Dreams in Jensen's *Gradiva*" (1907)

It is a commonplace to observe that the cultural transformation of Modernism produced the most radical and far-reaching changes in Western culture since the Renaissance. Less widely remarked is the fact that these
changes occurred precisely when the distinctively modern disciplines of psychology, psychiatry, and psychoanalysis began to establish their "scientific"
foundations and to achieve the intellectual, institutional, and professional
forms in which we largely know them today. To be sure, there have been
many efforts to detail the influence of psychoanalysis on the arts and, vice
versa, to trace the cultural influences at work in the thought of seminal figures in the psychoanalytic tradition, chiefly Sigmund Freud and Carl Gustav Jung. Yet the insights achieved by particular studies have had the curious
effect of only making it more apparent that there has been no general, sustained, and broadly conceived attempt to chart the intellectual traffic that
linked these different cultural fields, no attempt to unravel the dense web of
connections that joined the aesthetic and psychological domains in a common probing of sexuality, subjectivity, and self-identity or to consider the
reasons why a shared Modernist project took shape when, where, and in the
circumstances that it did.

1

The cultural affinities between aesthetic and psychological Modernism are in fact strikingly varied and detailed. Perhaps most importantly, both psychiatric medicine and the creative arts during the late nineteenth and early twentieth centuries were marked by a massive "turn inward" and a thoroughgoing psychologization of their methods, subjects, and intentions.[1] During these years, artists, philosophers, and scientists probed beneath the surface reality of reason in order to uncover deeper irrational or nonrational levels of human experience and cognition. Both the arts and the sciences studied the unconscious, subconscious, and subliminal levels of mental life. Both psychological medicine and the literary-artistic avant-garde centered, but then destabilized, the self, and both fields were responsive to the subjectivity of individual consciousness and its relations to the external world. Both fields also demonstrated a greatly heightened interest in the psychology of sexuality, in all of its permutations, and a fascination with psychopathological states, including the "dark" realms of unreason. Both areas of human effort were vitally concerned with the nature and structure of the individual personality, and both pioneered new techniques of narration to capture the inner workings of the human mind and the moment-by-moment experience of individual consciousness. During these decades, the so-called primitive or "savage" mind attracted enormous attention across the entire spectrum of human inquiry and expression, including in the nascent human sciences of psychoanalysis, anthropology, and sociology, as well as in painting, music, and photography. A century ago in Paris and Vienna, those epicenters of radical innovation in both the cultural arts and the mental sciences, philosophers, physicists, novelists, and painters alike struggled to respond to an epistemological challenge in which inherited positivist and naturalistic ways of knowing and representing the world came to be viewed as intensely problematic. And in all these fields of endeavor the creative, anti-realist responses to that crisis of representation were received by conservative contemporaries as subversive, obscene, or revolutionary, and at times they elicited violent and censorious reactions. The links between the arts and psychiatry are closer than those between the arts and any other branch of medicine; and arguably, in no period were they closer than during the turn of the last century.

Since the early 1980s, there has been a scholarly trend toward the systematic investigation of "the mind of Modernism."[2] At the present postmodern moment, modernity and Modernism, both as theoretical concepts and historical categories, are among the most actively debated subjects across a wide range of the humanities. Philosophical, literary, and artistic Modernism, in all its nationalistic and stylistic varieties, has continued to inspire an outpouring of scholarship. At the same time, the professional study of the histories of psychiatry, psychology, and psychoanalysis has made enormous strides. Furthermore, in the past twenty years, the new and overlapping scholarly pursuits of the cultural studies of science, literature and science studies, and the cultural history of psychiatry have emerged as fertile areas of interdisciplinary inquiry.[3] Three monographic studies from the 1990s— Judith Ryan's *The Vanishing Subject: Early Psychology and Literary Modernism* (1991), Daniel Albright's *Quantum Poetics: Yeats, Pound, Eliot, and the Science of Modernism* (1997), and Tim Armstrong's *Modernism, Technology, and the Body: A Cultural Study* (1998)—have demonstrated the promise of studying the interrelated histories of science, medicine, and the cultural arts during the Modernist era in particular.[4]

The present volume of collected studies seeks to build on these precedents by providing the first detailed, synthetic, and cross-disciplinary study of the complex cultural interface between aesthetic and psychological Modernism. The book, I want to make clear, is neither a collection of psychoanalytic readings of past cultural texts nor a series of psychobiographical studies of the private mental lives of Modernist novelists, poets, and painters. Likewise, it is not a study of the psychocultural homologies between Modernist culture and mental illness (along the lines of Louis A. Sass's brilliant *Madness and Modernism*) nor an analysis of representations of madness in past cultural texts.[5] These approaches have yielded highly interesting and impressive scholarship, but by now they are established analytical exercises and interpretative genres. I have chosen, rather, to focus on the formal ideas and systematic theories of mind held by Modernist thinkers, writers, and artists themselves and the significance of these beliefs for their creative work. If this emerging interdisciplinary project is to move forward, however, I believe it is crucial at the outset to reflect conceptually and analytically on the culture-psychiatry nexus and to avoid a number of simplifications and misapprehensions that have bedeviled past approaches to the subject. Specifically, in assembling this collection I have followed five basic guidelines, which, I want to propose, are vital for future investigation of the subject in general as well as for this book.

First of all, the twelve essays below insist on treating the art-science relation as *mutually originative* and *reciprocally enriching*. Examples of Modernist literary intellectuals who were knowledgeable about and influenced by the psychologies of their day are well known. Most immediately, we are likely to think of Robert Musil's dissertation about the psychological theories of Ernst Mach, Marcel Proust's reading of French medical literature on memory, C. G. Jung's introduction to the German edition of James Joyce's *Ulysses*, or the vast and varied influence of Freudian psychoanalysis on the imaginative literature of Europe and America. But these examples, it turns out, represent only half the historical story, and not necessarily the more interesting half.

If a full-scale history of "the two cultures" is ever written, the pre–World War I era will surely emerge as a unique historical moment.[6] The fin de siècle and *aube de siècle* were the last periods in which physicians routinely received both scientific and humanistic formations and in which scientists (with the exception of physicists and mathematicians) were still working with discourses available to their generally educated peers. During these years, the study of Greco-Roman culture—including a thorough grounding in Latin in secondary schools—continued to predominate in western European education. Scientists, physicians, philosophers, and creative writers were often schooled in the same educational settings—Oxford and Cambridge, the École normale supérieure—and philosophy and philology were required components of all doctoral studies. In a similar vein, as George Rousseau has noted, "it was not uncommon for Victorian and Edwardian doctors . . . to write prolifically throughout their careers: medical memoirs and autobiographies, biographies of other doctors, social analyses of their own time, imaginative literature of all types."[7]

During this same period, general population rates burgeoned in the major Western countries, and cities grew explosively, bringing with them an expansion of metropolitan cultural activities and institutions, including universities. Literacy rates climbed dramatically as well. International exchanges in the sciences and the cultural arts—the founding of journals, the organization of international congresses, the staging of exhibitions— grew correspondingly. As a consequence, the number of ideas, images, and opinions in circulation, and the speed with which they crossed national and disciplinary boundaries, accelerated greatly. The degree to which these circumstances fostered the formation of a common pool of cultural resources available to humanists and scientists alike a hundred years ago has often been lost to our own age of specialized knowledge and disciplinary compartmentalization. A result of this cultural interplay was that, around 1900, novels, poems, plays, and paintings did not simply and secondarily voice a language of the self, psyche, and pathology created elsewhere. Rather, on the eve of the emergence of modern dynamic psychiatry, physicians were as influenced by cultural representations and popular stereotypes as novelists and artists were knowledgeable about the findings of medical science.[8]

There are countless historical examples of this cross-fertilization. Most familiar by far is the case of Freud. Freud was trained medically and began his career as a laboratory neuroanatomist and clinical neurologist. He was first schooled, however, in the broad, central European tradition of the classical humanities, and he read deeply in the German literary and cultural traditions.[9] In creating psychoanalysis, he drew key ideas and terms—catharsis, cathexis, the Oedipus complex, narcissism—from Shakespeare and the Greek tragedians as well as from contemporary novels, such as Wilhelm Jensen's *Gradiva* (1903) and Carl Spitteler's *Imago* (1906).[10] In the mid-1890s, Freud felt the need to alert his readers to the "literary" aspects of his medical case histories.[11] Writing several years later in the preface to *The Interpretation of Dreams* (*Die Traumdeutung*), he insisted, somewhat defensively, that he was "not a poet but a natural scientist," "nicht Poet sondern Naturforscher," and later in life the city of Frankfurt awarded him the Goethe prize, for his German prose writing, whereas a Nobel Prize in medical science and physiology eluded him.[12]

Freud was not exceptional on this score. Carl Gustav Jung's grandfather was allegedly an illegitimate offspring of Goethe, and the family legend of the German genius hung over Jung's work and sense of himself.[13] While a medical student, Jung was led to his ideas about unconscious psychical processes less through his formal psychiatric training than through a close reading of Arthur Schopenhauer, Eduard von Hartmann, Friedrich Nietzsche, and Henri Bergson.[14] In particular, the Jungian concepts of the unconscious, dream life, archetypes, and the persona were crucially shaped by Nietzsche's *Thus Spake Zarathustra* (*Also Sprach Zarathustra*), a book about which Jung taught courses and wrote an elaborate multivolume commentary.[15]

A somewhat similar situation obtained in France, where until the early twentieth century the final year of lycée education was devoted mandatorily to philosophy studies. Théodule Ribot's *Hereditary Psychology* (*L'hérédité psychologique*) of 1873, written as the author's philosophy and literature dissertation, was an important popularization of degeneration theory that became a basic source for hospital psychiatrists. In his time and ours, Pierre Janet was regarded as the most sensitive and original thinker in early French depth psychology.[16] Janet boasted double doctorates, in philosophy and in medicine, and during the mid-1880s he published his groundbreaking arti-

5

cles on psychological automatisms not in a psychiatric journal, but in the *Revue philosophique*, France's most widely read and respected journal of philosophy. Likewise, the literary critic Paul Bourget's influential *Essais de psychologie contemporaine* (*Essays on Contemporary Psychology*) of 1883 synthesized the most au courant ideas of psychology, psychiatry, and literary commentary. In chapter 7 of this volume, Jacqueline Carroy notes the appearance of a cluster of "physician-littérateurs"—including Ribot, Hippolyte Taine, Charles Richet, Gabriel Tarde, and Henri Beaunis—who during the early French Third Republic comfortably integrated the activities and identities of psychologist, philosopher, imaginative writer, and public intellectual.[17] Indicatively, in France and beyond, the intellectual-historical background indispensable to the "new psychology" of the late nineteenth and early twentieth centuries[18] was provided less by physicians working in a traditional clinical-positivist mode than by a trio of "psychological philosophers," Nietzsche, Bergson, and William James.

Perhaps the most significant convergence of the psychiatric and the literary during these years involved form and genre. Modernism in poetry, the novel, painting, and music is typically associated with the rejection of traditional linguistic and aesthetic practices and experimentation with new artistic forms to achieve heightened expressivity. Less widely appreciated is the fact that a similar process took place at the same time in certain types of medical case history writing.[19] Before the final quarter of the nineteenth century, psychiatric cases published in medical textbooks and monographs tended to be short and mechanical recitations of hereditary background, symptom profile, diagnosis, and prognosis. Dynamic models of mental functioning, however, were centrally concerned with the *consciousness* and the inner mental life of the patient; accordingly, a new aim of psychiatric case histories beginning around 1890 became the representation of individual emotional experience and intrapsychic subjectivity.

This change in goal required new narrative strategies. Psychodynamic therapeutics used language, the spoken word (rather than, say, water, massage, electricity, drugs, or physical restraint), as its primary curative agent. Treatment took the form of clients using introspective and free associative techniques to tell their life story to a sympathetic listener (a hypnotist, psychotherapist, or psychoanalyst) who interpreted the story and offered verbal suggestions.[20] Resulting from this clinical encounter, therapists often produced a narrative of their own, a narrative directed at a medical readership and intended to convey the story of a single, ever-changing mental personality over time—a kind of psychiatric *Bildungsroman*. In short, during the late nineteenth and early twentieth centuries Western psychiatry's subject of study, method of inquiry, and case-historical style became much more "literary" and narrative. As a result, the period 1880–1940 witnessed the publication of a sequence of highly readable, individualized, and often book-length case histories—Eugène Azam's Félida; Janet's Irène and Madeleine; Josef Breuer's Anna O.; Jung's Hélène Preiswerk; Théodore Flournoy's Hélène Smith; Freud's Dora, Wolf Man, and Rat Man; Morton Prince's Miss Beauchamp; Ludwig Binswanger's Ellen West—many of which attracted an extensive nonmedical readership. Later in the new century, these cases often contributed to the formulation of entire new psychological theories that, in turn, provided new ways of reading cultural texts.

And what does the new genre of the novelistic case history owe to Modernist literary practices? It is a commonplace to note that William James provided the term for a new technique of narration in Modernist fiction writing and to comment that certain Modernist writers produced brilliant stylistic equivalents of psychoanalytic texts.[21] Yet, as the Spanish historian of medicine Laín Entralgo has insisted, therapeutic use of the spoken word began in ancient Greek culture.[22] Likewise, the interior monologue has a literary history that long predates modern psychiatry, and introspection and storytelling are the creative writer's methods.[23] Any reconstruction of the Modernist mind, this volume suggests, must abandon a simple popularization model of influence, which runs unidirectionally from the allegedly originative realm of science to literature and the arts, and in its place take up a more flexible, dynamic, interactionist model of cultural relations.[24]

A second desideratum of studying aesthetic and psychological Modernism, and therefore a second guideline in assembling this collection, is the need to move beyond Freud. An astonishing share of the scholarship about this subject continues to take the form of influence studies of psychoanalysis in which Freud—and occasionally Jung—are presented as the sole exemplars of psychological Modernism.[25] In contrast, this volume reflects a growing scholarly desire to explore the larger world of ideas, attitudes, and practices around Freud. Recent psychiatric historiography establishes unmistakably that, for all of its eventual cultural influence, which was immense, psychoanalysis was only one of many emerging models of mind that comprised the coming of early dynamic psychiatry and that contributed to the constitution of the modern psychological self. Carpenter, Maudsley, and Myers in Britain; James, Putnam, Hall, and Münsterberg in the United States; Liébeault, Azam, Charcot, Binet, Féré, Bernheim, Richet, Ribot, and Janet in France; von Hartmann, Fechner, Brentano, Mach, Krafft-

7

Ebing, Moll, Weininger, and Jaspers in Germany and Austria; Forel, Flournoy, Claparède, Dubois, and Minkowski in French Switzerland; Forel, Bleuler, and Jung in German Switzerland; Delboeuf in Belgium; and van Eeden in Holland—all of these figures, among others, were members of a gallery of physicians, psychiatrists, and psychologists whose work was known to and resonated with artists and intellectuals between 1880 and 1920.[26]

Until as late as 1920, many of these figures were in fact much better known than Freud in the world of science, ideas, and culture. Accordingly, Judith Ryan's *The Vanishing Subject: Early Psychology and Literary Modernism* (1991) takes as its subject the influence of the formal psychological ideas of Franz Brentano, Ernst Mach, and William James on the artistic vision of Franz Kafka, Hugo Hofmannsthal, Arthur Schnitzler, James Joyce, Virginia Woolf, and Robert Musil. In chapter 4, Tom Gunning argues that the stylized close-up of the human face in early European film was informed by psychiatric and psychological studies of facial physiognomy, and specifically by the work of Duchenne de Boulogne, Charcot, and Albert Londe in the 1870s and 1880s. In other words, what would become the most culturally resonant technology of the psyche in the new century was, at its moment of inception, influenced by *pre-Freudian* sciences of the mind. *A la recherche du temps perdu (In Search of Lost Time)*, the leading document in French literary Modernism, provides yet another example. Published between 1913 and 1927, Proust's sprawling and astonishing exploration of the psychology of human memory and the fluidity of consciousness was shared by contemporary depth psychologists. Scholarly specialists have busied themselves tracking down Proust's "sources"; they have concluded that his multivolume work was informed by Bergson on time and memory, Janet on psychological automatisms, Alfred Binet on fetishism, Théodule Ribot on maladies of the will, and Émile Egger on the stream of consciousness, a list as noteworthy for whom it does not include as for whom it does.[27] In a similar fashion, Steven Meyer finds in chapter 8 that Gertrude Stein's "psychology" of the 1890s was wholly non-Freudian.

To much the same effect, the opening three chapters of this book examine the cultural history of hysteria during the famous French belle époque. Rae Beth Gordon, Ian Hacking, and I demonstrate in our essays that fascination with hysteria, the paradigmatic malady of the European fin de siècle, was sparked above all by Jean-Martin Charcot's spectacular demonstrations at the Salpêtrière hospital during the 1880s, rather than by Freud's and Breuer's *Studies on Hysteria (Studien über Hysterie)* of 1895.[28] In 1928, when the Surrealist poets Louis Aragon and André Breton (both of whom had attended medical school as young men) celebrated hysteria as "the greatest poetic discovery of the end of the nineteenth century," they saluted, again, Charcot, not Freud and Jung.[29] Hysteria was the theoretical and clinical vehicle for some of the most brilliant psychological theorizing of the late nineteenth century. Yet *Studies on Hysteria* and the Dora case were only two of dozens of contemporaneous books and dissertations about "the great neurosis," several of which advocated a new, more psychogenic understanding of the disorder.[30] In the 1890s, not Vienna but Paris, followed by Zurich, Geneva, Berlin, Amsterdam, and Boston, were regarded as the leading centers of avant-garde psychological medicine.[31]

Analogously, the first wave of therapeutics that pursued a more psychological orientation emerged during the 1880s from the rival schools of hypnotic and suggestive therapeutics of Charcot in Paris and Bernheim in Nancy.[32] Marcel Prévost's *A Woman's Autumn* (*L'Automne d'une femme*) (1891) is the first known novel depicting fictionally a practitioner of the new, more sensitive psychological analysis; the story's protagonist is thought to be modeled on Janet, whose richly detailed case histories are at the center of today's revival of scientific interest in psychological dissociation.[33] Along the same lines, the two-volume *Dictionary of Psychological Medicine*, which was published in London during the mid-1890s and is arguably the first modern reference work of psychiatry in the English language, documents—without citing Freud's name—the coming of what Janet later called "psychological healing."[34] A decade later, an entry on "psychotherapy" in the 1907 edition of the *Larousse* dictionary makes no mention of Freud either, but it does include a lengthy discussion of James, whose psychological essays and books were then translated promptly into French.[35]

Nor was James's work the only influential foreign importation to continental Europe during these years. As Diana Faber has shown, Alfred Binet's *Contemporary English Psychology* (*La psychologie anglaise contemporaine*) of 1870 brought the ideas of Herbert Spencer, John Stuart Mill, Francis Galton, and Alexander Bain to France, where they remained in circulation until the century's end.[36] For his part, James believed that the Briton Frederic Myers was the greatest living systematizer of the notion of the unconscious mind and that Myers's subliminal theory of the self would provide a foundation for the most important psychology of the twentieth century.[37] In fact, at the turn of the century, the assumption that a part of human psychic life—what James termed "the hidden self" and Virginia Woolf described as the "hidden depths" of the psyche—escapes our conscious knowledge was shared by a great many theorists.[38] Similarly, as Sonu Shamdasani has recently emphasized, the most widely discussed work of psychology published in 1900 was not *The Interpretation of Dreams* but *Des Indes à la Planète Mars* (*From India to the Planet Mars*). Written by Théodore Flournoy, founder of the Genevan school of psychology, *From India to the Planet Mars* is a fantastical four-hundred-page case history of multiple personality that for two decades provided inspiration for poets, novelists, and medics alike.[39] And in the United States, as Eugene Taylor has long argued, a dynamic psychology of the subconscious, synthesizing American, French, and Swiss-French ideas, flourished well before Freud lectured at Clark University in Worcester, Massachusetts, in 1909.[40] Until after the First World War, the concepts of mind and consciousness in the work of Bergson, James, and Janet were hugely more influential than Freud's teachings.

My intention with *The Mind of Modernism* is not to underestimate the cultural diffusion of psychoanalysis. In the long run, Freud without a doubt became the single most powerful and influential psychological theorist of the new century. But, in light of recent scholarship, earlier Freudocentric accounts, which were typically written during the second and third quarters of the twentieth century by American and central European psychoanalyst-historians, now require revision. A much more rounded and variegated historical picture is emerging. For contemporaries of and participants in the Modernist revolution, particularly in its early phases, a remarkably rich and diverse pool of psychological ideas, theories, and vocabularies was available for cultural appropriation. Conversely, it should be added, our understanding of Freudianism as a historical formation is greatly enriched by placing it in this larger contemporaneous intellectual environment.[41]

A third guideline this book follows concerns the disciplinary origins and identity of these many psychological theories and practices. A hundred years ago, distinct intellectual and disciplinary counterparts to early twentieth-first-century psychiatry, neurology, psychology, and philosophy of mind did not exist. The ideas and insights that eventually combined to form both twentieth-century dynamic psychiatry and the mental sciences of our own time issued historically from many different fields of inquiry, including general medicine, physiology, neuropsychiatry, asylum psychiatry, experimental psychology, philosophical psychology, and religious psychology. Furthermore, it would be a mistake to exclude from historical consideration theories and practices that the medical sciences of our own day judge to be wrong, silly, unscientific. To be specific, hypnosis, somnambulism, psychical research, magnetotherapy, metallotherapy, dream interpretation, mediumistic psychology, automatic writing, faith healing, and spiritualism were all subjects of keen and widespread interest among many of Freud's and Jung's contemporaries—indeed, of interest to Freud and Jung—that contributed mightily to the constitution of modern psychological medicine. An enormous corpus of commentary was written on these topics but was subsequently excluded from presentist and progressivist accounts of the history of the mental sciences.

In the late 1870s, for instance, Charcot took up the clinical and experimental study of hypnosis, which had been condemned academically as long ago as the 1790s and that throughout the nineteenth century had an aura of charlatanry about it. Charcot's influential endorsement spawned what the historian of science Anne Harrington has dubbed the "neo-Mesmeric renaissance" of the late nineteenth century.[42] Fin-de-siècle researchers conceptualized hypnosis as an extraordinary psychophysiological condition that enhanced suggestibility and inhibited the critical, controlling faculties of the personality. It thereby provided a means to probe beyond the normal activities of the mind and to gain access to the unconscious mind. Accordingly, many of the experimental psychologies emerging from France and Germany during the last two decades of the nineteenth century used hypnosis as their primary method of investigation, a technique researchers at the time regarded as perfectly scientific.[43] The Premier congrès international de l'hypnotisme experimental et thérapeutique, staged in Paris in 1889, was widely regarded as the leading event in the world of psychological medicine that year; it attracted physicians, psychologists, and philosophers from across the Western world, including Bergson, Forel, Freud, James, Janet, Max Dessoir, and Cesare Lombroso.[44] Celebrated itinerant hypnotists, such as Donato, Hansen, and Lafontaine, crisscrossed Europe, further popularizing hypnotic ideas and practices.[45]

Inevitably, hypnosis became the subject of widespread interest outside the medical world, too. Charcot's hospital demonstrations on hypnotized patients attracted writers, critics, and artists as well as scientists and physicians.[46] In chapter 2 of this volume, Rae Beth Gordon finds that the jerky, zigzag movements of the classic Charcotian hysterical seizure were taken up as models in the theaters, cabarets, and café-concerts of Montmartre and Montparnasse.[47] With a quarter century's perspective, the French minister of public education proposed that Charcot and the French hypnotic school had inspired an entire generation of "littérateurs-psychiatres" that ushered in a new, more psychologically oriented literary sensibility, including the work of the Goncourt brothers, J.-K. Huysmans, Bourget, and Proust.[48] Similarly, Mesmerist ideas, themes, and practices pervaded British

11

Victorian culture, as Alison Winter has recently documented in great detail.[49]

Charcot used hypnotic techniques experimentally. In contrast, his provincial rival Hippolyte Bernheim, working at the Nancy Medical Clinic in northeastern France, explored hypnotism's therapeutic potential.[50] From the mid-1880s onward, a steady stream of doctors—Delboeuf from Liège, Moll from Berlin, Freud from Vienna, Forel and Jung from Zurich—traveled to Nancy for instruction in hypnotic techniques.[51] These visitors then brought word of what they observed back to their own medical cultures, where they developed hypnotherapeutics in different directions.[52] Time and again, these physicians later emerged as pioneers in early twentieth-century psychotherapeutics. In the 1890s, Janet primarily used various unmasking hypnotic techniques in his landmark exploration of the psychogenesis of posttraumatic symptoms. Likewise, between 1888 and 1893, Freud published several pieces about hypnotherapeutics, and he translated Bernheim's major text into German.[53] Freud's own early therapeutic technique, which was a key stage in his intellectual movement from neuropathology to psychopathology, was essentially Bernheim's method of suggestion under induced hypnosis. In Paris, Nancy, and Berlin, researchers also investigated the subtle psychological bonds, or "psychic transfer," that formed between a hypnotizer and a patient. In short, the techniques of modern psychotherapy originated in large measure with the hypnotic and suggestive therapeutics of the 1880s and 1890s.[54]

A related aspect of the fin-de-siècle psychological world that has since fallen out of scientific favor but was highly influential a century ago is the psychology of mediums. As Sonu Shamdasani has commented aptly:

At the end of the nineteenth century, many of the leading psychologists—Freud, Jung, Ferenczi, Bleuler, James, Myers, Janet, Bergson, Stanley Hall, Schrenck-Notzing, Moll, Dessoir, Richet, and Flournoy—frequented mediums. It is hard today to imagine that some of the most crucial questions of the 'new' psychology were played out in the seance. . . . What took place in the seances enthralled the leading minds of the time and had a crucial bearing on many of the most significant aspects of twentieth-century psychology, linguistics, philosophy, psychoanalysis, literature, and painting.[55]

Before this time, the performances of mediums tended to be viewed either sympathetically, as supernatural interventions, or dismissively, as out-and-out frauds. In the final quarter of the nineteenth century, a group of vanguard experimenters pursued a third approach and sought a naturalistic, specifically psychological, explanation of these phenomena.

Following Frederic Myers's lead in Britain, these observers believed that the strange utterances of mediums expressed forgotten memories, hidden capabilities, and suppressed subpersonalities of the medium.[56] Jung's medical dissertation of 1902, titled "On the Psychology and Psychopathology of so-called Occult Phenomena," was a study of the mediumistic productions of his cousin Hélène Preiswerk.[57] Jung retained a lively interest in the occult throughout his years of psychiatric practice at the Burghölzli hospital in Zurich, and, as Nandor Fodor has emphasized, the subject formed a significant component of Jung's mature psychological theories and psychotherapeutic praxis.[58]

Similarly, Flournoy's best-selling *From India to the Planet Mars* (1900) relates the extraordinary life of a gifted medium, known pseudonymously as Hélène Smith, who claimed under hypnosis to be the reincarnation of a Hindu princess from fifteenth-century India, of the French queen Marie Antoinette, and of an inhabitant of the planet Mars, whose language she claimed to speak and whose landscapes she painted.[59] Flournoy and many of his contemporaries were keenly interested in the creative abilities that might be released through these paranormal states. Later in her life, Hélène Smith took up painting and religious mysticism, and in 1932 some commentators interpreted a well-publicized posthumous exhibition of her paintings in Geneva as a study in "art and the subconscious."[60] In a radio interview in 1952, André Breton claimed that the character Nadja in his 1928 novel of that name was modeled in part on Hélène Smith, and he explicitly credited Richet, Myers, and Flournoy with providing a theoretical impetus to the creation of Surrealism. Modern art, Breton explained, was indebted to these psychologists' "systematic study of trance-like states," which had opened up the specter of a fertile subterranean mental life to be tapped as an imaginative resource and represented a profound dimension of human experience by the artist.[61]

Mediumistic psychology was part of a larger interest in the so-called parapsychological a century ago that was taken far more seriously in late Victorian Europe than today. At times, this interest reflected a desire to study "the irrational" with the methods of positivist science; in other instances, it was part of an effort to recover the spiritual in the face of what James termed "medical materialism."[62] Frederic Myers, who was trained as a clergyman, philosopher, and classicist, founded the Society for Psychical Research in London in 1882. The society's published proceedings of the following twenty years are chock full of systematic, "scientific" studies of occult phenomena, including somnambulism, animism, spiritism, telepathy, trance speech, glossolalia, cryptomnesia, automatic writing, faith healing, and crystal vision.[63] Publications such as the *Annales des sciences psychiques* and organizations like the Société du spiritisme scientifique were not understood to involve a contradiction in terms. Rather, like hypnosis, parapsychological conditions were believed to offer clues to the mysteries of unconscious mentation. Interestingly, dream psychology was another frequent topic of discussion among psychical researchers, and Freud and Jung were both corresponding members of the British Society for Psychical Research.[64] James devoted his 1896 Lowell lectures to these matters, and the membership of the American Society for Psychical Research, founded in 1884, reads like a who's who of early American psychology and psychotherapy.[65]

Not surprisingly, psychical research and its allied subjects also seized the contemporary cultural imagination. Helena Blavatsky, a Russian émigré to the United States, was the most influential personality in the occultist circles of her time and founder of the modern Theosophy Movement. By 1900, Blavatsky's movement included hundreds of thousands of adherents in North America, Europe, and India.[66] With their shared backgrounds in Russian religion, Vassily Kandinsky, Igor Stravinsky, and Alexander Scriabin were enthralled by theosophy and mysticism during their youths. Kandinsky's famous proclamation of abstract aesthetics—*Über das Geistige in der Kunst* (*Concerning the Spiritual in Art*) of 1912—was directly informed by the theosophy of Rudolf Steiner, whom Kandinsky had heard lecture in Berlin.

William Butler Yeats and his wife were, similarly, committed occultists who between 1917 and 1920 conducted hundreds of séances of which they kept detailed transcripts. Psychical research became an important part of the evolution of Yeats's art and mind, figuring particularly prominently in his strange "spiritual autobiography," *A Vision* (1925).[67] Tim Materer has argued further that a range of occultist interests—alchemy, astrology, tarot cards, Indian mysticism, and gnosticism—influenced a succession of twentieth-century English-language poets.[68] In the same vein, the interest of Proust, Joyce, and Woolf in epiphanies and "moments of vision" developed against a background of widespread scientific and popular fascination with mystical phenomena and ecstatic states.[69] Furthermore, as Nicole Edelman has demonstrated, the "spiritualist" and "mesmeric" novel was a popular genre both in Britain and on the European continent during the 1880s and 1890s.[70] Spiritualist broadsides, like *Psychische Studien* in Leipzig, *La revue spirit* in Paris, and *The Banner of Light* in America, proliferated. In the years following World War I, a widespread revival of interest in séance psychologies also developed as thousands of mourners sought contact with relatives, friends, and lovers killed in the war.[71]

Psychological automatisms of all sorts, or physical and mental activities performed without awareness of the conscious self, were also believed by physicians and their cultural peers a century ago to offer royal roads to the unconscious.[72] In chapter 3 of this volume, Ian Hacking discovers that a cluster of medical writings in Paris and Bordeaux between 1887 and 1909 brought to light the new phenomenon of "ambulatory automatism," a "modern" psychological malady that impelled its victims to walk mindlessly and involuntarily across large swaths of Europe.[73] One of Hacking's most memorable case histories of the affliction was published in 1896 by Dr. Adrien Proust, the novelist's physician-father; not coincidentally, the figure of the *fugueur* also appeared in popular French fiction during the 1890s and, later, in Proust *fils's* In Search of Lost Time.[74] In a somewhat similar fashion, Lawrence Rainey, writing in chapter 6, finds that the flamboyant Italian Futurist impresario Filippo Marinetti discovered in the practice of automatic writing with a planchette a new "technology of writing" that directly accessed the creative psyche and that Marinetti could draw on in fashioning the "words in freedom" program of Futurist poetics. In chapter 8, Steven Meyer highlights yet another example, this one heralding from America. Working at Radcliffe during the 1890s, young Gertrude Stein published neuropsychological articles about automatic writing, which, Meyer argues, later informed the development of Stein's mature style of "experimental writing."[75] An interest in these subjects, too, was an indispensable part of the Modernist mind.

A fourth basic point on which this book's essays converge concerns the nature of the historical interaction itself between aesthetic and psychological Modernism. *The Mind of Modernism* demonstrates time and again that the encounter between these two great cultural fields was creative, selective, and distortive. Above all, it was highly individual. The French pointillist painter Georges Seurat sought directly to apply Maxwell's and Helmholtz's physics of color in his paintings of the 1880s and early 1890s with his scheme of "chromo-luminarism," and several decades later the Spanish Surrealist painter Salvador Dalí attempted to transpose Freudian theories of the unconscious and sexual symbolism directly onto his canvases.[76] The relation between the new theories of mind and the cultural arts, however, was rarely so direct and transparent. Indeed, a series of conventional "influence studies" between the arts and sciences would impose a false and simplifying uniformity on the culture-medicine nexus and obscure the range and complexity of cultural relations between the two realms.

One merit of Ryan's *Vanishing Subject* is its insistence on the great variety of ways in which European and American literary elites, from Pater to Proust, engaged the psychological doctrines of their day. Modernist authors, Ryan emphasizes, alternately applied, parodied, plagiarized, played with, and misappropriated the new mental sciences. Below, Steven Meyer discusses Stein's original and iconoclastic usage of James's psychological ideas, to which Stein was exposed when she was a medical student working in the Harvard Psychological Laboratory.[77] In a similar pattern, Jesse Matz discovers in chapter 11, the English poet, critic, and philosopher T. E. Hulme borrowed a single aspect of Bergson's vitalist psychology—the theory of "intuition"—but only to remove it from its naturalistic context, making it part of a theory with very different cultural content and political implications. Only rarely did physicians or artists set out to provide a direct translation of a new psychological theory into their own disciplinary language or artistic medium; rather, imaginative and original adaptation was the rule. In all cases, Modernist intellectuals were vitally concerned with the ways in which new art and science might contribute to their own creative agendas by increasing personal expressive ability or analytical power.

At times, the relation between the two Modernist fields was competitive, even openly hostile. The fifth and final section of this volume chronicles a strand of intellectual resentment and resistance to modern psychologism that runs through the entirety of post-Enlightenment Western thought. The antagonism was sharpest between philosophy and psychology, no doubt because philosophy boasted a long and independent tradition of generating its own models of mind (i.e., the philosophy of mind).[78] As Martin Jay discusses in the book's closing chapter, philosophers such as Edmund Husserl and G. E. Moore, as well as the mathematician Gottlob Frege, responded to the new sciences of the mind as a rival discourse of the self, a set of paradigmatic but reductive ideas about behavior and self-identity that sought imperialistically to colonize as many areas of culture as possible. As Husserl, Moore, and Frege saw it, a psychological perspective was inimical to the essence of Modernist aesthetic culture with its characteristic belief in the autonomy of art.[79]

Nor was this belief limited to academic philosophy. Writers and painters as diverse as Kafka, T. S. Eliot, and Marcel Duchamp included a repudiation of the emergent mental sciences in their aesthetic worldviews. Especially within interwar Anglo-American poetry, a "classicist" reaction set in against the new high aesthetic of consciousness and its perceived hyper-subjectivity. In his landmark study *A Genealogy of Modernism* (1984), the literary historian Michael Levenson reads the antinomy between "psychological" and "anti-psychological" visions of art as the central divide in English-language literary Modernism.[80] Likewise, the remarkable drive toward non-representation that characterizes European painting from Kandinsky in the early years of the century to the Abstract Expressionists of the 1950s has been interpreted as a continuing quest to escape the suffocating Romantic/Modernist specter of the artist's individual psyche.[81] Despite the placement of Jay's essay at the end of this volume, it would be a mistake, I believe, to conclude that philosophical and aesthetic anti-psychologism represent the final word and that the effort to find common ground between art, philosophy, and psychology was fated to fail. Rather, like seismic cultural plates continually scraping together, the volatile and evolving encounter between aesthetic and psychological Modernism was at times positive and interactive, at other times negative and repulsive. Most importantly, in all the case studies presented in this volume the encounter between the two fields generated cultural change. The book documents time and again what Matz has characterized as "the necessarily eccentric, partial, and inharmonious way that the arts and the psychological sciences productively met at the turn of the century."

Fifth and finally, this book strives to move beyond narration and description. If one studies side by side scientific texts and artistic artifacts from the late nineteenth and early twentieth centuries, it proves relatively easy to locate descriptive similarities and "parallels." Striking as these homologies are, however, I believe that if this scholarly enterprise is to develop it must progress beyond these analogical exercises and move toward an analysis of *the actual dynamics of cultural interaction* between aesthetic and psychological Modernism. Only in this way can this field of inquiry achieve a historical and conceptual theory of the cultural relations among and within modernisms.

Accordingly, these collected essays pose and explore a number of broad cultural-historical questions, questions, I believe, with implications that extend well beyond one book: What, finally, was the nature of the cultural interface between psychological and aesthetic Modernism? In what ways can the two cultural domains be viewed as parallel and as competing discourses of the Modern? What deeper social and intellectual developments subtended this massive psychologization of culture? Can these two areas of endeavor be viewed as autonomous expressions of a single idea of The Modern? More specifically, in formulating contemporaneous notions of perception, memory, and subjectivity, did the arts and psychological sciences draw upon a kind of macrocultural matrix that was then somehow "reflected" or "expressed" in local generic, disciplinary, and discursive forms? How are we to understand the simultaneous emergence of certain shared metaphors—the dissolution of the real, visualizing the unseen, the primitive in the modern—across European culture during these years?[82] Were the psychological and aesthetic varieties of Modernism reactive to a set of common historical circumstances, such as the advent of mass democracy and industrial capitalism (that is, ironically, to political and technological modernity)? In what ways did the very different epistemological languages in which the arts and psychological medicine spoke (the objective/analytical/experimental versus the subjective/autobiographical/experiential) serve to shape their respective Modernist projects, and in what respects did they overlap (e.g., the Zolan idea of "the experimental novel," the *pointilliste* painting of Seurat and Signac, the ideologies of Futurism and Vorticism)? Can the very categories of "the scientific," "the psychological," and "the aesthetic" maintain their integrity in light of these studies? Why did these distinctive intermixtures of the medical and cultural imagination emerge when and where they did? And was this complex intertwining itself primarily epiphenomenal to the cultural history of the time, or, as John Toews and David Joravsky hint below in their studies of early Austrian and Czech Modernism, were these interconnections fundamentally constitutive of the nascent modernities of the late nineteenth and early twentieth centuries, a condition for the mutual creation of Modernism as we know it today?

The twelve essays in this volume explore these, as well as many other, lines of inquiry. The book's chapters take as their central subject the historical and theoretical intersection of the cultural arts and the psychological sciences during the years 1880–1940 in western Europe and North America, with particular attention to France, Italy, and German-speaking central Europe. The cultural modes and media under inspection range from poetry and the novel to theater, painting, montage, photography, film, and popular culture. Correspondingly, the working category of "psychological Modernism" encompasses psychiatry, neurology, psychology, psychoanalysis, the philosophy of mind, and parapsychology. Clearly the meeting of these two vast and heterogeneous discursive fields over such a long period of time and in multiple national cultures makes for a large and diffuse subject matter, and the specific topics of the essays range widely. The book's contributors form a distinguished and diversified group of scholars from the United States, Canada, and France, and they include historians of philosophy, literary historians and critics, social, cultural, and intellectual historians, historians of science and medicine, historians of the visual arts, film historians, and scholars of gender and cultural studies. The authors adopt a wide variety of analytical frameworks and approaches.

The constituent essays of this book are preceded by a detailed timeline. The timeline intercalates dates from the histories of the creative arts and the psychological sciences during these years under investigation. Conceived and compiled as a key companion piece to this introductory essay, the timeline should serve further to illustrate to readers the rich and highly suggestive concurrence of events and people in the two fields. The body of the book consists of five sections—Cultures of Hysteria; Technologies of the Psyche; Medicine, Literature, and Modernism; Transformations of the Self; and Modernism and Anti-Psychologism—each of which represents a theme that unites the interconnected histories of science, medicine, and the cultural arts between the years 1880 and 1940. Together, these parts form a volume that a wide spectrum of students interested in the history of modern culture will, I believe, find pertinent and provocative. For professional scholars, my additional goal is to open up and articulate a new site of comparative, cross-cultural study by offering the first collection of original and critical historical studies in the field. Lastly, it is my hope that the book might encourage dialogue between the arts and the sciences themselves by examining their interaction at a particularly fruitful and fascinating moment in the past.[83]

The Modernist Mind: A Timeline

compiled by
MARK S. MICALE
JESSE WEGMAN

1843   The Manchester physician James Braid publishes *Neurypnology, or the Rationale of Nervous Sleep*, which begins to arouse interest in the scientific study of hypnosis.

1844   Appearance of the first issue of *Allgemeine Zeitschrift für Psychiatrie.*

Arthur Schopenhauer publishes the second German edition of his philosophical classic *The World as Will and Representation (Die Welt als Wille und Vorstellung).*

The Danish thinker Søren Kierkegaard writes his "pre-Existential" work *The Concept of Dread (Begrebet Angst).*

Birth of Friedrich Nietzsche.

1845   Publication of the first modern psychiatric textbook, Wilhelm Griesinger's *Pathology and Therapy of Mental Diseases (Die Pathologie und Therapie der psychischen Krankheiten).*

1848   Karl Marx and Friedrich Engels write their fatefully influential "Manifesto of the Communist Party" ("Manifest der Kommunistischen Partei").

Political revolutions in various European cities.

1849   Kierkegaard's *Sickness Unto Death (Sygdommen til Doden).*

1854   Birth of Théodore Flournoy.

The English physiologist and psychologist William B. Carpenter advances the notion of "unconscious cerebration."

1855   Publication of *Principles of Psychology* by the British philosopher Herbert Spencer.

Claude Bernard is named to a professorship of experimental medicine at the Collège de France.

1856   Birth of Sigmund Freud and Emil Kraepelin.

1857   B.-A. Morel, a French asylum doctor, writes *A Treatise on Degeneration (Traité des dégénérescences physiques, intellectuelles et morales de l'espèce humaine)*, which becomes a hugely influential treatise in psychiatry, culture, and society during the second half of the nineteenth century.

Gustave Flaubert's novel *Madame Bovary.*

The first edition of Charles Baudelaire's poetry collection *Les fleurs du mal* (*Flowers of Evil*) is censored by the government of Napoleon III.

1858   Appearance of the first issue of *The Journal of Mental Science,* later renamed the *British Journal of Psychiatry.*

The German pathologist Rudolf Virchow publishes *Cellular Pathology* (*Die Cellularpathologie*), providing the foundation of modern models of disease.

Eugène Azam begins to bring the work of the Manchester physician and hypnotist James Braid to the attention of his Parisian medical colleagues.

1859   Alexander Bain, Scottish philosopher and psychologist, publishes *The Emotions and the Will.*

Charles Darwin completes *On the Origin of Species,* the single most influential text in nineteenth-century science.

Pierre Janet and Henri Bergson are born in Paris.

Oblomov, by the Russian novelist Ivan Goncharov, is a forerunner of the fin-de-siècle "novel of nerves."

1859   Baudelaire writes his essay "The Painter of Modern Life" ("Le peintre de la
–60   vie moderne").

1860   Founding in London of Queen Square Hospital for the treatment of nervous and neurological disorders.

The English physician Thomas Laycock publishes *Mind and Brain: or, the Correlations of Consciousness and Organization.*

The German physicist, philosopher of nature, and founder of experimental psychology Gustav Theodor Fechner publishes his two-volume *Elements of Psychophysics* (*Elemente der Psychophysik*).

Death of Schopenhauer, an immensely influential thinker who drew attention to the irrational driving forces in human nature, stressed the "will to live," and initiated the modern philosophy of existence. A major revival of interest in Schopenhauer's teachings will occur in the 1890s among continental intellectuals.

The Viennese physician Ignác Semmelweis publishes his controversial tract *The Etiology, Concept, and Prevention of Puerperal Fever* (*Die Aetiologie, der Begriff und die Prophylaxis des Kindbettfiebers*).

Florence Nightingale opens the Nightingale Training School for Nurses at St. Thomas's Hospital, London.

1861   Publication of Karl Scherner's *The Life of Dreams* (*Das Leben des Traums*) and L. F. A. Maury's *Sleep and Dreams* (*Le sommeil et les rêves*), two "pre-Freudian" studies in the psychology of dream life.

The French surgeon Paul Broca discovers the seat of articulate speech in the left frontal lobe, thereby providing the first proof of the localization of brain function.

Appearance of a second, revised edition of Griesinger's textbook of psychiatry, with translations into French and English later in the decade.

1861–65   The American Civil War.

1862   The French neurologist G. B. A. Duchenne de Boulogne publishes his
seminal study of the physiology of human facial expression.

Jean-Martin Charcot is appointed chief physician at the Salpêtrière hospital
in Paris.

The Russian novelist Ivan Turgenev writes *Fathers and Sons* (*Ottsy i deti*),
featuring the famous nihilist and scientific ideologue Bazarov.

Otto von Bismarck becomes prime minister of Prussia.

1863   Édouard Manet paints two provocative masterpieces of early Modernism,
Olympia and *Luncheon on the Grass* (*Le déjeuner sur l'herbe*).

1864   William Carpenter publishes *Principles of Mental Physiology*, which
remains in print until the century's end.

Fyodor Dostoyevsky's *Notes from the Underground* (*Zapiski iz podpol'ya*).

Jules and Edmond de Goncourt's *Germinie Lacerteux*, a novel about hysteria and nymphomania.

In London Karl Marx founds the International Labor Association known as
the "First International."

1865   Griesinger is appointed professor of psychiatry at the University of Berlin,
the first professorship in psychiatry anywhere in the world.

The English surgeon Joseph Lister begins to practice antisepsis to prevent
surgical infection.

Claude Bernard produces his manifesto of medical positivism, *Introduction
to the Study of Experimental Medicine* (*Introduction à l'étude de la
médecine expérimentale*).

Otto Liebmann publishes a work entitled *Kant and the Epigones* (*Kant und
die Epigonen*), which is key in sparking the German neo-Kantian revival
of the later nineteenth century.

1866   Ambrose Auguste Liébeault, a popular local doctor in Alsace-Lorraine, publishes *Sleep and Its Kindred States: Its Effects on Mind and Body* (*Du
sommeil et des états analogues, considérés surtout au point de vue de l'action du moral sur le physique*). The work inspires Hippolyte Bernheim,
an internist at the University of Nancy, and sparks the Nancy School of
hypnotic and suggestive therapeutics.

Alfred Russel Wallace, co-discoverer of the theory of evolution by natural
selection, publishes *The Scientific Aspect of the Supernatural: Indicating
the Desirableness of an Experimental Enquiry by Men of Science into the
Alleged Powers of Clairvoyants and Mediums.*

The English surgeon Eric John Erichsen publishes a series of case histories
of "railway spine."

The Hegelian philosopher Johann Eduard Erdmann coins the term "psychologism" in his *Outline of the History of Philosophy* (*Grundriss der Geschichte der Philosophie*).

1867   The English psychiatrist Henry Maudsley publishes *The Physiology and Pathology of the Mind*, a leading textbook of British psychiatry for a generation, with subsequent German and Italian translations.

Appearance of the first volume of *Capital* (*Das Kapital: Kritik der politischen Ökonomie*), Marx's principal work of economic theory.

1868   In Berlin the *Archiv für Psychiatrie und Nervenkrankheiten* is founded.

The Viennese neurologist Moritz Benedikt conducts experiments with hypnosis.

1869   Eduard von Hartmann publishes *The Philosophy of the Unconscious* (*Philosophie des Unbewussten*), which remains in print in multiple editions for the next two decades.

The British science journal *Nature* begins publication.

Francis Galton publishes *Hereditary Genius: An Inquiry into Its Laws and Consequences*.

John Stuart Mill publishes *On the Subjection of Women*, a bold call for legal, economic, and social equality between the sexes.

The New York neurologist George M. Beard first uses the term "neurasthenia" to describe a new form of nervous exhaustion.

Richard Wagner completes *The Rhine Gold* (*Das Rheingold*), the first of four operas in *The Ring of the Nibelung* (*Das Ring des Nibelungen*), which opens in Munich.

1870   The French philosopher and historian Hippolyte Taine publishes *On Intelligence* (*De l'intelligence*), a foundational work in modern experimental psychology advocating the application of scientific methods to the study of personality.

Théodule Ribot publishes *English Psychology* (*La psychologie anglaise contemporaine*).

The Austrian neurologist Moritz Rosenthal publishes his *Handbook of the Diagnosis and Treatment of Nervous Disorders* (*Handbuch der Diagnostik und Therapie der Nervenkrankheiten*).

Karl Westphal, a psychiatrist in Berlin, publishes an article on "contrary sexual instinct" (*die conträre Sexualempfindung*) in the *Archiv für Psychiatrie*, thereby launching the modern sexological study of homosexuality.

The Galician writer Leopold von Sacher-Masoch publishes his novella *Venus in Furs* (*Venus im Pelz*), featuring a male protagonist who yearns to be enslaved romantically and sexually by domineering women. In 1890, the Viennese sexologist Krafft-Ebing draws on Sacher-Masoch's literary work to formulate the clinical and diagnostic category of "masochism," a concept Freud later integrates into psychoanalytic psychology.

Charcot delivers his first lectures on hysteria at the Salpêtrière.

Henry Maudsley publishes *Body and Mind: An Inquiry into Their Connection and Mutual Influence.*

In "Mechanism in Thought and Morals," the venerated American physician Oliver Wendell Holmes expresses strong interest in unconscious mental processes.

Jules Verne publishes his prescient science fiction novel *Twenty Thousand Leagues under the Sea.*

John Ruskin becomes the first Slade Professor of Fine Arts at Oxford.

1870–71   The Franco-Prussian War.

1870–72   Second, enlarged edition of Spencer's *Principles of Psychology.*

1870–73   A young William James suffers a period of nervous depression.

1871   The American neurologist William Hammond publishes the first edition of his *Treatise on Diseases of the Nervous System,* which becomes a standard textbook for the next generation of American physicians.

William Crookes publishes *Psychic Force and Modern Spiritualism,* a defense of the psychological and scientific validity of spiritualist experiences.

The London Dialectical Society prepares a detailed report on spiritualism.

Darwin publishes *The Descent of Man,* offering his long-awaited thoughts on the evolution of the human species.

Hermann von Helmholtz becomes professor of physics at the University of Berlin.

Dostoyevsky completes *The Possessed (Besy).*

George Eliot begins serial publication of *Middlemarch.*

Émile Zola publishes *La fortune des Rougons,* the first of his twenty-volume *Rougon-Macquart* series in the style of literary naturalism. Later well-known volumes include *Nana, Germinal,* and *L'Assommoir.*

The Paris Commune.

Unification of the German states. William I, King of Prussia, is proclaimed German Kaiser.

1872   The British physician Daniel Hack Tuke writes *Illustrations of the Influence of the Mind Upon the Body in Health and Disease.* The book allegedly cites for the first time in English the term "psycho-therapeutics."

Darwin publishes *The Expression of the Emotions in Man and Animals,* including extensive reflections on the psychology of facial expression.

Friedrich Nietzsche, a gifted young classical philologist teaching at the University of Basel, publishes his first book, *The Birth of Tragedy (Die Geburt der Tragödie).*

Claude Monet paints *Impression, Sunrise,* thereby providing the label "Impressionism" for a new style of painting in France.

Thomas Edison discovers the telegraph.

1873 Théodule Ribot writes *Heredity: A Psychological Study* (*L'hérédité psychologique*).

Alexander Bain publishes *Mind and Body: The Theories of Their Relation.*

Posthumous publication of John Stuart Mill's *Autobiography.* The book's fifth chapter chronicles the story of Mill's youthful "mental crisis."

George Henry Lewes, the English philosopher, scientist, and critic, publishes the first of five volumes titled *Problems of Life and Mind.*

The British cultural and literary critic Walter Pater writes *Studies in the History of the Renaissance,* a highly influential text for fin-de-siècle aestheticism.

The precocious French poet Arthur Rimbaud publishes his "spiritual and psychological autobiography," *A Season in Hell* (*Un saison en enfer*).

A new writing machine that produces small printed characters on paper by a manually operated keyboard with a set of raised types (i.e., the typewriter) is introduced.

1874 Publication in Leipzig of Franz Brentano's *Psychology from an Empirical Point of View* (*Psychologie vom empirischen Standpunkt*), a basic text for a generation of German-language doctors, scientists, and intellectuals.

Appearance of *Principles of Physiological Psychology* (*Grundzüge der physiologischen Psychologie*) by the experimental psychologist Wilhelm Wundt.

The German neurologist Carl Wernicke publishes a study of the physiology of aphasia.

Translation of Spencer's *Principles of Psychology* into French.

Publication of the first issue of the *Journal of Nervous and Mental Disease.*

Publication of the first issue of *Psychische Studien,* a monthly journal that will devote much space to occultism, mediums, hypnosis, and parapsychology.

Ribot publishes a study of Schopenhauer, which launches a vogue for the German thinker among Francophone artists and intellectuals.

First exhibition of French Impressionist art, including paintings by Claude Monet, Pierre-Auguste Renoir, Camille Pissarro, Paul Cézanne, and Alfred Sisley. Seven other Impressionist exhibitions follow between now and 1886.

James McNeill Whistler paints *Nocturne in Black and Gold.*

The Russian symphonist Modest Mussorgsky composes *Pictures from an Exhibition.*

1875 Birth of Carl Gustav Jung.

The Russian-born occultist Helena Blavatsky founds the Theosophical
  Society in New York City.
William James begins teaching psychology and philosophy at Harvard
  University.
Charles Richet writes "On Induced Somnambulism," which begins to
  arouse Charcot's interest in experimental studies of hypnotism.
Appearance of *Dream-Phantasy* (*Die Traum-Phantasie*) by the German
  philosopher Johannes Volkelt.
Publication of Alfred Russel Wallace's *On Miracles and Modern
  Spiritualism.*
Thomas Eakins paints his masterpiece of American visual realism, *The
  Gross Clinic,* which contains life-sized figures observing a graphic surgi-
  cal operation.
Opening of the new Paris opera house designed by Charles Garnier.

1875 Wilhelm Wundt, the "founder of scientific psychology," is professor of
–1917 philosophy at the University of Leipzig.
1876 Appearance of the first issue of *Revue philosophique* founded by Ribot.
  Under the influence of Alexander Bain, the journal *Mind* begins publication, declaring itself "the first English journal devoted to psychology and
  philosophy."
  The Scottish neurologist David Ferrier publishes *The Functions of the
  Brain.*
  In his enormously influential text *Criminal Man* (*L'Uomo delinquente*), the
  Italian physician Cesare Lombroso applies the latest ideas of psycho-
  pathology to the new discipline of criminology.
  Centennial edition of Walt Whitman's collection of poems *Leaves of Grass,*
  which presents a naturalistic attitude toward sexuality.
  Renoir's canvases include *Le moulin de la galette.*
  The Symbolist poet Stéphane Mallarmé completes "Prélude à l'après-midi
  d'un faune." Mallarmé's poetry text is used by Claude Debussy in 1894
  for an orchestral work and by Vaslav Nijinksky in 1912 for a ballet.
  Inauguration of Richard Wagner's Bayreuth Festival Theater with the first
  complete performance of his opera tetralogy, including *Das Rheingold,
  Die Walküre, Siegfried,* and *Götterdämmerung.*
  Working independently, Robert Koch and Louis Pasteur demonstrate con-
  clusively that specific bacteria cause specific diseases. Modern bacteriology is launched.
  Alexander Graham Bell invents the telephone.
  Opening of the New York City subway.

1876–77 Eugène Azam publishes two reports in the *Revue scientifique* about the
  case of "Félida X.," among the best-known patients in the history of multiple personality theory.

James McNeill Whistler decorates the Peacock Room for the London house of a private patron.

1876– Pioneering psychiatric photography, Bourneville and Regnard publish the
80 *Iconographie photographique de la Salpêtrière*.

1877 S. Weir Mitchell publishes *Fat and Blood*, propounding his famous rest cure for nervous ailments.

The French psychiatrist Charles Lasègue produces the first psychiatric study of "exhibitionism."

Thomas Edison invents the phonograph.

1878 Founding of the British journal *Brain*.

William James delivers a paper at Johns Hopkins University entitled "Are We Automata?" that criticizes mechanistic notions of consciousness.

At Harvard, G. Stanley Hall receives the first doctorate in psychology awarded in the United States.

Hippolyte Bernheim is appointed professor of clinical medicine in Nancy, France.

Death of Claude Bernard.

First women's suffrage amendment introduced, unsuccessfully, into the U.S. Congress.

1879 In Leipzig Wilhelm Wundt establishes the Institute of Experimental Psychology, the first laboratory of its kind in the world.

Auguste Forel, the "father of Swiss psychiatry," is appointed professor at the University of Zürich.

Ribot writes *German Psychology Today* (*La psychologie allemande contemporaine*), a companion volume to his earlier study of British psychology.

Richard von Krafft-Ebing, professor at the University of Vienna, publishes the first edition of his *Textbook of Psychiatry* (*Lehrbuch der Psychiatrie*).

In Washington, D.C., John Shaw Billings begins the *Index Medicus*, the first comprehensive listing of the world's medical literature.

A Doll's House (*Et Dukkehjem*), by the great Norwegian playwright Henrik Ibsen, opens in Copenhagen.

Dostoyevsky writes the last of his major novels, *The Brothers Karamazov* (*Brat'ya Karamazovy*).

The French Symbolist painter Odilon Redon publishes the album of lithographs *In the Dream* (*Dans le rêve*).

August Bebel writes *Women and Socialism* (*Die Frau und der Sozialismus*).

Edison produces the first commercially practical incandescent electric lightbulb.

1879– A young Arthur Schnitzler, the future Austrian novelist and dramatist,
85 receives a medical education in Vienna and develops a special interest in nervous and mental illnesses.

1880 The New York–based neurologist George Beard publishes *A Practical Treatise on Nervous Exhaustion* (*Neurasthenia*). The book launches a popular and medical vogue for studying and treating neurasthenic invalidism.

The British novelist Samuel Butler publishes *Unconscious Memory*.

Publication in French translation of Henry Maudsley's *Physiology and Pathology of Mind* of 1867.

Prosper Despine writes *Scientific Study on Somnambulism* (*Étude scientifique sur le somnambulisme*).

Jacob Bernays, the uncle of Freud's future wife, publishes *Two Essays on the Aristotelian Theory of Drama* (*Zwei Abhandlungen über die Aristotelische Theorie des Drama*), a study of catharsis in ancient Greek theater. The book spawns a body of German scholarship during the 1880s and 1890s on the concept of dramatic catharsis.

The traveling hypnotist Hansen gives a series of dramatic demonstrations in Vienna.

Publication of the novel *The Somnambulist* by William Minturn.

Émile Zola pens "The Experimental Novel" in which he tries to apply the physiologist Claude Bernard's methods of observation and experimentation to novel writing.

Louis Pasteur introduces the germ theory of disease.

The sculptor Auguste Rodin completes *The Thinker* (*Le penseur*).

1880 –82   Josef Breuer, a respected general practitioner in Vienna, treats Bertha Pappenheim—later known as the celebrated "Fräulein Anna O."—for a bizarre series of severe nervous symptoms. Pappenheim suggests the term "talking cure" for a method of discussing painful emotional events from her past that makes her feel better.

1881   Wilhelm Wundt founds *Philosophische Studien*, devoted to psychology.

Victor Egger writes *The Inner Word* (*La parole intérieure*), an early formulation of the idea of stream of consciousness.

Ribot publishes *Diseases of Memory* (*Maladies de la mémoire*). The most important scientific study of the psychology of memory during the late nineteenth century, Ribot's book goes through twenty-nine editions by the 1930s.

Paul Richer publishes his voluminous medical dissertation *Clinical Studies on Hystero-Epilepsy or Grand Hysteria* (*Études cliniques sur l'hystéro-épilepsie ou grande hystérie*), a comprehensive exposition of the most dramatic forms of hysteria from the perspective of the Charcot School. A physician at the Salpêtrière hospital, Richer later becomes professor of artistic anatomy at the Paris École des beaux arts.

Paul Ladame's *Hypnotic Neurosis* (*La névrose hypnotique, ou le magnétisme dévoilé*).

S. Weir Mitchell's *Lectures on Diseases of the Nervous System, Especially in Women*.

George Beard's *American Nervousness: Its Causes and Consequences*.

The Parisian novelist and journalist Jules Claretie publishes *Loves of an Intern* (*Les amours d'un interne*), a novel featuring the sexual escapades of a Salpêtrière doctor and his hysterical female patients.

Henry James publishes the masterpiece of his middle period, *The Portrait of a Lady*.

The American painter John Singer Sargent completes his first full-length portrait of a male figure, the physician, aesthete, and society figure Samuel-Jean Pozzi.

Appearance of the first volume of *History of Woman Suffrage*, written by Susan B. Anthony, Elizabeth Cady Stanton, and Matilda Gage, chronicling the global women's rights movement.

1882   Charcot is awarded the first Chair in Maladies of the Nervous System on the Paris Medical Faculty. The same year he reads "On the Various Nervous States Determined by Hypnotism in Hysterics" to the French Academy of Science, arguing for the systematic scientific study of hypnotism.

Publication of the comprehensive *Treatise on the Neuroses* (*Traité des névroses*) by Alexandre Axenfeld and Henri Huchard.

Hippolyte Bernheim is converted to the ideas of the village hypnotist Liébeault and introduces hypnotic practices at the University of Nancy hospital.

Cesare Lombroso publishes *Genius and Insanity* (*Genio e follia*), in which he speculates about the links between intelligence and psychopathology.

The classics scholar Frederic Myers, the physicist William Barrett, and the Cambridge ethicist Henry Sidgwick found the Society for Psychical Research.

Manet paints *Bar at the Folies-Bergère*.

Ibsen's plays include *Ghosts* and *An Enemy of the People*.

A medical bureau is established at the Catholic Lourdes shrine in southwestern France in order to verify "miraculous" cures.

Passage in England of the Married Women's Property Act.

Death of Charles Darwin.

1882–   Robert Koch, the originator of scientific bacteriology, discovers the tuberculosis bacillus and the cholera virus.
83

1883   Publication of Emil Kraepelin's *Compendium der Psychiatrie*, the first of eight editions of his famous textbook.

Thomas Clouston publishes *Clinical Lectures on Mental Diseases*.

Francis Galton publishes *Inquiries into Human Faculty and Its Development*.

The *Proceedings of the Psychical Society* begins publication in London.

Paul Bourget publishes *Essays in Contemporary Psychology* (*Essais de psychologie contemporaine*).

Henri Legrand de Saulle, chief psychiatrist at the Paris Police Prefecture, publishes *The Hysterics* (*Les hystériques*), an account of hysterical criminality in the French capital.

James Braid's *Neurypnology* of 1843 is translated into French for the first time.

The London society doctor William Playfair writes *The Systematic Treatment of Nerve Prostration and Hysteria*.

Publication in three volumes of the first complete English translation, under the title *The World as Will and Representation*, of Arthur Schopenhauer's *Welt als Wille und Vorstellung*.

Maurice Rollinat's novel *The Neurotics* (*Les névrosés*).

Alphonse Daudet's novel *L'Évangéliste*, dedicated to Charcot.

J.-K. Huysmans's collection of Impressionist art criticism *L'Art moderne*, which concentrates on the subjectivity of sensory perception in painting.

Antoni Gaudí, the Catalan architect, begins to design the Church of the Sagrada Familia in Barcelona, judged a masterpiece of Spanish Art Nouveau architecture.

Opening of the Brooklyn Bridge in New York City, the first suspension bridge using steel wire cables. Design and construction by John and Washington Roebling.

Sargent paints *Madame X*, his brilliant and scandalous portrait of the celebrated beauty Madame Gautreau.

Maurice Barrès, the conservative French social critic and Catholic politician, pronounces decadence a leading artistic tendency of the age.

Death of Karl Marx.

1883– Publication of Nietzsche's *Thus Spake Zarathustra: A Book for Everyone and*
85 *No One* (*Also Sprach Zarathustra. Ein Buch für Alle und Keinen*), perhaps the single most influential text in late nineteenth-century German thought and culture.

1884 Founding of the American Society for Psychical Research.

Theodor Meynert, professor of psychiatry at the University of Vienna, publishes his textbook *Psychiatry: A Clinical Treatise on Diseases of the Fore-Brain* (*Psychiatrie. Klinik der Erkrankungen des Vorderhirns*), a proclamation for a purely somatic psychiatry.

Bernheim in Nancy first challenges the Charcotian theory of hysteria.

Charles Richet publishes *Man and Intelligence* (*L'homme et l'intelligence*).

The American physician Elizabeth Blackwell writes *The Human Element in Sex*.

Posthumous publication of George Beard's *Sexual Neurasthenia*.

Publication of J.-K. Huysmans's *A Rebours* (*Against Nature*). The novel draws extensively on the vocabulary of nerves and becomes a programmatic statement of the decadent movement.

The German logician and mathematician Gottlob Frege publishes *The Foundations of Arithmetic* (*Die Grundlagen der Arithmetik*), attacking philosophical attempts to reduce mind to psyche.

Névrosée, a novel of hysteria, perversion, and suicide, is published by the popular writer Madame Jeanne Lapauze.

After meeting the scientist personally, the French painter Georges Seurat studies the chemist Michel Chevreul's theories of chromatic light.

First exhibition of the Groupe des Artistes Indépendants, including the neo-Impressionist painters Seurat and Signac.

Publication of volume one of the first edition of James Murray's *Oxford English Dictionary* (1884–1929), one of the great reference works of the age.

Formation of the British Fabian Society by Beatrice Webb, Sidney Webb, and George Bernard Shaw.

Introduction of state health insurance in Germany.

1884 –86 Georges Seurat produces *A Sunday Afternoon on the Island of La Grande Jatte*, his masterpiece of painting in the pointillist style.

Auguste Rodin sculpts *The Burghers of Calais*.

1885 Establishment in Paris of the Société de psychologie physiologique.

Ribot's *Disorders of Personality* (*Les maladies de la personnalité*) reaches lay and cultural reading audiences.

Pierre Janet begins to study the patient "Léonie."

Frederic Myers begins to publish studies of hypnosis and automatic writing in the *Proceedings of the Society for Psychical Research*.

Oliver Wendell Holmes writes *A Mortal Antipathy*, the last of his three "medicated novels."

Paul Cézanne's paintings include *Mont Sainte-Victoire* and *The Bathers*.

H. H. Richardson designs the Marshall Field Wholesale Store in Chicago, marking the beginning of the Chicago School of architecture.

Louis Pasteur performs the first preventive vaccination against rabies.

1885 –86 A young Sigmund Freud spends five months in Paris studying with Charcot. Freud becomes interested in the hysterical neuroses and undertakes the translation into German of a text of Charcot's.

1885–87 Interest in male hysteria peaks within the French medical community.

1885 –1900 The *Dictionary of National Biography*, edited by Leslie Stephen, appears in sixty-three volumes. The work integrates lengthy and highly readable entries on scientists, physicians, politicians, philosophers, and artists.

1886 Publication by the Austrian physicist and philosopher Ernst Mach of the enormously influential *Contributions to the Analysis of Sensations* (*Beiträge zur Analyse der Empfindungen*), arguing that there is no such thing as a coherent, unitary self or ego.

Publication of *Psychopathia Sexualis: A Clinical-Forensic Study*

(*Psychopathia Sexualis: Eine klinisch-forensische Studie*), the landmark study of scientific sexology, by Richard von Krafft-Ebing. The author publishes eleven subsequent editions in his lifetime, each including more illustrative case histories.

Eugen Bleuler is appointed director of the Rheinau Mental Hospital in Switzerland.

Freud opens a private medical practice, specializing in the treatment of nervous disorders. He also delivers the presentation "On Male Hysteria" to a critical Vienna Society of Physicians.

The collected works of the mid-nineteenth-century German psychologist Johann Friedrich Herbart are published in Hamburg and Leipzig.

Publication of Bernheim's *Suggestive Therapeutics* (*De la suggestion et de ses applications à la thérapeutique*), codifying his ideas about hypnotherapeutics for a generation of practitioners.

Janet begins to publish clinical and theoretical papers in the *Revue philosophique*. He also successfully treats the patient "Lucie," allegedly the first psychological treatment using the cathartic method.

Alfred Binet, director of the laboratory of physiological psychology at the Sorbonne, publishes *The Psychology of Reasoning* (*La psychologie du raisonnement*), which extensively discusses hypnosis and the unconscious.

Charles Richet publishes a study of the psychology of fear in the general journal *Revue des Deux Mondes*.

The French philosopher Henri Bergson writes an essay on hypnosis and the unconscious for the *Revue philosophique*.

King Lugwig II of Bavaria—"the mad monarch"—is hospitalized in an asylum where he kills his physician and then commits suicide.

Arthur Schnitzler publishes an account of Freud's lecture on masculine hysteria in a Viennese medical publication.

William Gowers, the distinguished British neurologist, completes the first edition of his *Manual of Diseases of the Nervous System*.

The British physician Charles Creighton publishes *Illustrations of Unconscious Memory in Disease*.

In his novel *Roland Blake*, S. Weir Mitchell draws directly on his case histories of female neurasthenic patients.

Guy de Maupassant's short story "Le Horla" deals with hypnosis, possession, and insanity.

Auguste Villiers de l'Isle-Adam publishes *Eve Future* (*L'Ève future*), an early science fiction novel discussing spiritism and dual personality.

Robert Louis Stevenson publishes *The Strange Case of Dr. Jekyll and Mr. Hyde*, which relates the story of a drug-induced double personality. Stevenson claims he entered a dream state to write the novel.

Nietzsche completes *Beyond Good and Evil* (*Jenseits von Gut und Böse*).

The Austrian Expressionist Gustav Klimt paints the murals at the Vienna City Theater.

In Germany Carl Benz introduces the first "motor coach."

The first newspaper with lettering set by machine rather than by hand is printed in New York City.

1887 After visiting Bernheim in Nancy, Frederik Willem Van Eeden and Albert Van Renterghem open the Institut Liébeault in Amsterdam, the first psychotherapy clinic in the world.

Charcot publishes the third volume of his *Lectures on Diseases of the Nervous System* (*Leçons sur les maladies du système nerveux*), including many case studies of "traumatic hysteria" in adult men. Freud later translates the book into German.

Philippe Tissié's *The Traveling Insane* (*Les aliénés voyageurs*), the first scientific study of ambulatory automatism, features the case of the extraordinary compulsive traveler "Albert."

Janet publishes his first study using the term "dissociation."

Julian Ochorowicz, a leading Polish psychical investigator, publishes *On Mental Suggestion* (*De la suggestion mentale*).

Eugène Azam's *Hypnotism, Double Consciousness, and Alterations of the Personality* (*Hypnotisme, double conscience et altération de la personnalité*), with a preface by Charcot, further discusses the famous case of Félida.

Charles Chaigneau publishes a survey of recent "spiritualist novels and poems" in the *Revue spirite*.

Appearance of the first issue of the *Revue de l'hypnotisme expérimentale et thérapeutique*.

Appearance of the first issue of the *American Journal of Psychology*.

Death of Dorothea Dix, the American mental health reformer.

Founding of the American Society for Psychical Research. Early members include James, Royce, Hall, Bowditch, and Putnam.

Charcot and Richer write *Les démoniaques sur l'art*, retrospectively diagnosing hysteria in past works of art.

Alfred Binet's essay on the medical concept of sexual fetishism appears in the *Revue philosophique*.

Freud commences his famous correspondence with the Berlin physician Wilhelm Fliess.

Arthur Conan Doyle creates the great fictional detective Sherlock Holmes.

Samuel Gompers founds and becomes the first president of the American Federation of Labor.

Albert Michelson accurately measures the speed of light and later becomes the first American scientist to win the Nobel Prize.

1887 Charcot publishes two influential volumes of *Leçons du mardi,* or bedside
–89   clinical lessons, including many cases of hysteria and neurasthenia.
       Charles Epheyre—a.k.a. the physiologist and psychologist Charles Richet—
       publishes *Possession* and *Sister Marthe,* two popular novels of love,
       obsession, and somnambulism.

1888 Ribot graduates to a new chair of experimental and comparative psychology
       at the Collège de France.
       Henri Bourru and P. Burot's *Variations de la personnalité* relates at length
       the case of "Louis Vivé," who reveals six distinct personalities. The book
       will be judged by historians the most important study of multiple person-
       ality in the nineteenth century.
       In Berlin Max Dessoir publishes a *Bibliography of Modern Hypnotism,*
       recording more than eight hundred recent medical publications on hyp-
       nosis.
       The Danish critic Georg Brandes delivers the first lectures on Nietzsche,
       whose fame now begins to spread rapidly.
       George John Romanes, the British physiologist and Darwinist, writes
       Mental Evolution in Man.
       Ibsen writes *The Lady from the Sea (Fruen fra Havet),* which includes the
       description of a woman who suffers from unconscious, neurotic conflicts
       due to a "pathogenic secret."
       "A Clinical Lesson at the Salpêtrière," an enormous painting by André
       Brouillet depicting Charcot demonstrating on a hysterical patient in
       front of a group of medical students, hangs in the annual Paris Salon.
       Publication of Édouard Dujardin's *We'll to the Woods No More (Les
       Lauriers sont coupés),* an early novelistic use of the "monologue
       intérieur" technique.
       Vincent van Gogh moves to Arles in southern France. His paintings this
       year include *The Postman Roulin, Van Gogh's Chair, Sun Flowers,* and
       Café at Night, Arles.
       Erik Satie composes his popular *Gymnopédies.*
       The German physicist Heinrich Hertz discovers electromagnetic waves.
       Founding of the Pasteur Institute in Paris.

1889 In Paris the Universal Exposition commemorates the centenary of the
       French Revolution and inaugurates the Eiffel Tower, the tallest structure
       in the world.
       The First International Congress of Psychology is held in Paris with 160 par-
       ticipants. The First International Congress on Experimental and
       Therapeutic Hypnosis is also organized in Paris, with James, Lombroso,
       and Freud in attendance.
       Janet publishes his philosophy doctorate *Psychological Automatism*
       (*L'Automastisme psychologique*), relating the cases of some twenty male

and female hysterics and codifying his ideas about subconscious acts, psychological dissociation, mental disaggregation, and psychological automatisms. The book remains in print until 1919.

In Berlin the physician and psychotherapist Albert Moll publishes *Hypnotism, Including a Study of the Chief Points of Psychotherapeutics and Occultism* (*Der Hypnotismus*), the fullest defense of hypnotherapeutics in German medicine up to that date.

S. Weir Mitchell publishes "Mary Reynolds: A Case of Double Consciousness."

Freud visits Nancy in order personally to observe Bernheim's hypnotic methods and comes away favorably impressed. Later that year he publishes *Die Suggestion und ihre Heilwirkung*, a German translation of Bernheim's leading text.

Schnitzler produces his first scientific publication, a study of hypnosis, suggestion, and hysterical aphonia.

Bergson publishes his doctoral dissertation *Time and Free Will: An Essay on the Immediate Data of Consciousness* (*Essai sur les données immédiates de la conscience*), an immensely influential critique of mechanistic and rationalist notions of time and space.

Van Gogh enters a local asylum in St. Rémy, southern France. His paintings this year include *The Starry Night*.

Nietzsche suffers a mental collapse while in Turin and begins a decade-long period of hospitalization and convalescence.

Founding of the Socialist Second International.

1889 –92   Alice James keeps a journal of her nervous illness, which she sees in part as an autobiographical medical case study.

The Freiburg psychologist and philosopher Hugo Münsterberg publishes *Contributions to Experimental Psychology* (*Beiträge zur experimentellen Psychologie*).

1890   Appearance of William James's two-volume magnum opus *Principles of Psychology*, including the much-discussed chapters "The Stream of Thought," "Consciousness of the Self," and "The Perception of Time." The same year James publishes "The Hidden Self" in the popular magazine *Scribners*, which reviews the latest Anglo-French theories of consciousness.

Max Dessoir, secretary of the Berlin Society for Experimental Psychology, publishes *The Double Ego* (*Das Doppel-Ich*), positing two spheres of mental activity, the "overconsciousness" and "underconsciousness."

The Austrian critic, novelist, and playwright Hermann Bahr writes a review titled "The New Psychology."

The Norwegian novelist, dramatist, and poet Knud Hamsun publishes "From the Unconscious Life of the Mind."

Gabriel Tarde completes his study of mass psychology, *Laws of Imitation* (*Les lois de l'imitation*).

The Genevan psychologist Théodore Flournoy publishes his first book, *Metaphysics and Psychology* (*Métaphysique et psychologie*).

The Belgian doctor Joseph Delboeuf publishes *Magnetisers and Medics* (*Magnétiseurs et médecins*).

Alfred Binet's *On Double Consciousness*, written in English, reviews existing theories of the relation between primary and secondary consciousness.

Dr. Adrien Proust, father of the novelist, publishes a study of hysteria and ambulatory automatism in the *Bulletin Médical*.

Fernand Levillain's *Neurasthenia: Dr. Beard's Disease* (*La neurasthénie. Maladie de Beard*).

Ibsen's *Hedda Gabler*.

George Bernard Shaw's *The Quintessence of Ibsenism*, an exposition and defense of Modernism in the theater.

First two volumes of James George Frazer's *The Golden Bough* (1890–1915). This encyclopedic thirteen-volume work of religion, folklore, and comparative anthropology influences many intellectuals, including Jung.

The German lyric poet Stefan George emerges with the publication of *Hymns (Hymnen)* and begins to gather around him a group of young aesthetes.

Van Gogh dies by suicide.

Paul Cézanne paints *The Card Players*, *Bathers*, and *Still Life with Apples*.

Edison patents his kinetoscope, used for showing early movies.

1890   Publication of the first and second series of Emily Dickinson's poems.

−91   Louis Sullivan designs the Wainwright Building in St. Louis, the first of Sullivan's urban, modern, multistoried commercial buildings in the Chicago style.

1891   In the *Proceedings of the Society for Psychical Research*, Frederic Myers publishes three studies presenting his ideas about an "inner," "secondary," or "subliminal" self separate from normal, waking consciousness.

Albert Moll publishes *Perversions of the Sex Instinct* (*Die conträre Sexualempfindung*).

Liébeault publishes *Suggestive Therapeutics* (*Thérapeutique suggestive*).

Flournoy is appointed professor of psychophysiology at the University of Geneva.

Georges Gilles de la Tourette assembles the first volume of his *Clinical and Therapeutic Treatise of Hysteria* (*Traité clinique et thérapeutique de l'hystérie*), systematizing Charcot's teachings.

Bernheim publishes a revised compilation of his ideas, *New Studies in Hypnotism, Suggestion, and Psychotherapy* (*Hypnotisme, suggestion, psychothérapie. Études nouvelles*).

Marcel Proust hears Bergson lecture about time, memory, and sensory experience at the Sorbonne in Paris.

Publication in Berlin of Leo Berg's *The Sexual Problem in Modern Literature* (*Das sexuelle Problem in der modernen Literatur*).

Emil Kraepelin is appointed director of the psychiatric hospital at the University of Heidelberg.

The neurologist Adolph Strümpell founds the *Deutsche Zeitschrift für Nervenheilkunde*.

A young Adolf Meyer leaves Zürich and immigrates to the United States.

The popular novel *Peter Ibbetson* by George du Maurier utilizes Hervey de St. Denis's writings on dreams.

Maurice Barrès publishes his novel *Trois stations de psychothérapie*, indicating how culturally widespread the term "psychotherapy" has become.

Marcel Prévost publishes his novel *The Autumn of a Woman* (*L'Automne d'une femme*), featuring an empathetic physician who uses new psychological techniques in treating neurotic patients. The protagonist is allegedly modeled on Janet.

Founding of *La Revue blanche*, the chief publication for Symbolist writers and painters.

The painter Paul Gauguin moves to Tahiti for the remainder of his life.

Oscar Wilde publishes *The Picture of Dorian Gray*, widely misinterpreted as a manifesto of hedonism and aestheticism.

George Gissing's *New Grub Street*.

Thomas Hardy's *Tess of the D'Urbervilles*.

Huysmans's *Là-Bas*.

1892 Formation of the American Psychological Association.

James Sully publishes *The Human Mind*, a leading British textbook of psychology.

Publication under the editorship of Daniel Hack Tuke of the two-volume *Dictionary of Psychological Medicine*, which has been labeled the first modern psychological dictionary

Alfred Binet publishes *Alterations of Personality* (*Les altérations de la personnalité*).

Charles Féré publishes *Pathology of the Emotions* (*La pathologie des émotions*).

Charcot publishes a study of the psychology and physiology of amnesia.

Scipio Sighele publishes *The Criminal Crowd: A Study of Collective Psychology* (*La foule criminelle: Essai de psychologie collective*).

In a letter to Fliess, Freud coins the term "abreaction" (*Abreagieren*) to denote one of the ways in which emotion is discharged after a psychical trauma.

Freud translates a second book of Bernheim's under the title *New Studies on Hypnotism, Suggestion, and Psychotherapy* (*Neue Studien über Hypnotismus, Suggestion und Psychotherapie*).

Death of both Theodor Meynert and Ernst Brücke, two leading exponents of psychiatric somaticism and two of Freud's early professors.

Charlotte Perkins Gilman publishes her short story "The Yellow Wallpaper," providing a chilling account of her neurotic breakdown in the 1880s and her experiences with her physician S. Weir Mitchell.

The Norwegian Knut Hamsun's novel *Mysteries* (*Mysterier*) examines unconscious motivation.

The Hamburg cholera epidemic.

1892 Janet completes his medical dissertation "Contribution to the Study of
–93 Mental Accidents in Hysterics" ("Contribution à l'étude des accidents mentaux chez les hystériques"), which emphasizes the purely psychological symptoms and causes of hysterical neurosis.

Max Simon Nordau—physician, medical journalist, and cultural critic— publishes *Degeneration* (*Entartung*), which applies the language of psychiatric degenerationism to the Modernist cultural arts. Enormously influential, the work is rapidly translated into English, French, Italian, and Spanish.

1892 Monet paints his Rouen cathedral series depicting the moment-to-moment
–94 changes in the color and light perception of a single object.

The Italian poet and novelist Gabriele D'Annunzio engages in a systematic study of Nietzsche's writings.

1892 Hugo Münsterberg is visiting professor at Harvard University. He returns to
–95 join the faculty permanently in 1897.

1893 Death of Charcot.

Breuer and Freud publish "Preliminary Communication: On the Psychical Mechanism of Hysterical Phenomenon," the first distinctly psychoanalytic text.

In the *Revue de neurologie* Janet reviews several new psychological theories of hysteria, including his own and those of Freud, Breuer, Grasset, Gilles de la Tourette, Moebius, Pitres, Sollier, and Moll.

Azam completes *Hypnotism and Double Consciousness* (*Hypnotisme et double conscience*).

Paul Souriau publishes *Suggestion and the Arts* (*La suggestion dans l'art*).

Charcot publishes "The Faith that Cures" ("La foi qui guérit"), a scientific discussion of Catholic healing shrines.

Madame Blavatsky publishes *The Key to Theosophy*.

Endlessly reprinted, Thomson Jay Hudson's *Law of Psychic Phenomena* introduces ideas of hypnosis, spiritism, dual consciousness, and mental therapeutics to lay American readers.

The Berlin journalist Paul Lindau publishes *The Other* (*Der Andere*), a novel about a criminal second personality.

Arthur Schnitzler's early play *Anatol* relates the story of the love affair of a young man suffering from "sexual neurasthenia."

The Norwegian Edvard Munch paints *The Cry*, his most famous painting, which he describes as expressing "modern psychic life."

First retrospective exhibition of Van Gogh's paintings.

Oscar Wilde writes *Salomé*.

Stéphane Mallarmé completes his collection *Verse and Prose*.

The Chicago World's Fair.

1893–94 Mary Cassatt's paintings include *The Boating Party*.

1893–95 Publication of select letters between Van Gogh and his brother Theo.

1893 Gertrude Stein attends Radcliffe College, where she works in the psycho-
–97 logical laboratory of James and Münsterberg.

1893–98 William James teaches the first course at Harvard on mental pathology.

1894 The English physician Havelock Ellis publishes *Man and Woman*.

Binet and Beaunis begin publishing the journal *L'Année psychologique*.

Binet's *Introduction to Experimental Psychology* (*Introduction à la psychologie expérimentale*) popularizes the work of the Sorbonne Psychological Laboratory.

Gustave Le Bon's *Laws of the Psychological Evolution of Peoples* (*Les lois psychologiques de l'évolution des peuples*).

Moritz Benedikt, associate professor of neuropathology at the University of Vienna, publishes *Hypnotism and Suggestion: A Clinical-Psychological Study* (*Hypnotismus und Suggestion*).

Freud publishes his first essay on "the neuro-psychoses of defense."

George du Maurier writes *Trilby*, a best-selling novel featuring a young singer who comes under the influence of the sinister musician and hypnotist Svengali.

Aubrey Beardsley takes up editorship of *The Yellow Book*, a leading quarterly publication of the literary avant-garde in Britain. He also illustrates Wilde's *Salomé*.

Les déséquilibrés de l'amour, "a series of novels of the psychopathological passions" by Armand Dubarry, begins to appear in press.

1895 The Dutch physician and novelist Frederik van Eeden writes "The Theory of Psycho-Therapeutics" for a general medical magazine.

Publication of Breuer's and Freud's *Studies on Hysteria* (*Studien über Hysterie*), which maintains that hysterical symptoms are symbolically meaningful expressions of repressed traumatic memories. The book features the clinical cases of five pseudonymous female hysterics, including "Fraulein Anna O." and "Emmy von N."

Freud completes his *Project for a Scientific Psychology* (*Entwurf einer*

Psychologie), a speculative attempt to formulate a model of mind based on contemporary neuroscience.

In Leipzig Albert Eulenburg publishes *Sexual Neuropathy: Genital Neuroses and Neuropsychoses in Men and Women* (*Sexuale Neuropathie. Genitale Neurosen und Neuropsychosen der Männer und Frauen*).

Henri Beaunis, first director of the Sorbonne psychological laboratory in Paris, publishes *Physiological Stories* (*Contes physiologiques*) under the pseudonym Paul Abaur.

Louis and Auguste Lumière develop a machine to project a continuous picture through moving rolls of segmented celluloid film onto a screen, thereby inventing cinematography.

In Paris, Samuel Bing opens the Galerie de l'Art Nouveau, giving the movement its name.

The French physician and social psychologist Gustave Le Bon publishes *The Crowd: A Study in Psychology* (*La Psychologie des foules*), which launches the pseudoscience of "crowd psychology." By 1921 Le Bon's book has run to twenty-nine French editions and been translated into sixteen languages.

H. G. Wells publishes *The Time Machine*.

In London, Oscar Wilde is tried for homosexual sodomy, found guilty, and sentenced to two years of hard physical labor.

Hugo von Hofmannsthal's poem "A Dream of Great Magic" explores dreams and the unconscious.

Gustav Mahler becomes artistic director of the Imperial Opera in Vienna.

The German physicist Wilhelm Röntgen invents x-rays.

Alfred Dreyfus, a Jewish officer of the French General Staff, is falsely accused and convicted of espionage for Germany, thereby beginning the Dreyfus Affair.

1895
–97   Period of nervous breakdown for the young Swedish dramatist August Strindberg.

1896   Wilhelm Wundt comes out with his monumental *Outlines of Psychology* (*Grundriss der Psychologie*).

Freud first uses the word "psychoanalysis" in print. In his essay "Further Remarks on the Neuro-Psychoses of Defense" he begins to formulate a notion of psychological defense.

The Third International Congress of Psychology is held in Munich with more than five hundred participants.

William James delivers the Lowell Lectures on exceptional mental states, including lectures on dreams, hypnotism, hysteria, automatic writing, and multiple personality.

Janet begins treatment of "Madelaine," which will become his longest case history.

Bergson writes *Matter and Memory* (*Matière et mémoire*), presenting his psychology and philosophy of time, memory, and consciousness.

Performance of Alfred Jarry's drama *Ubu Roi*.

French Symbolist poet and critic Paul Valéry writes *The Evening with Monsieur Teste* (*La soirée avec Monsieur Teste*).

Appearance of the first issue of the weekly satirical German journal *Simplicissimus*.

Richard Strauss completes his symphonic poem *Also sprach Zarathustra*, inspired by Nietzsche.

The Viennese architect Otto Wagner publishes *Modern Architecture* (*Moderne Architektur*).

Theodor Herzl writes his famous tract "The Jewish State" ("Der Judenstaat"), with which he establishes political Zionism.

Discovery of radioactivity.

1896 –98   Gertrude Stein coauthors two articles—"Cultivated Motor Automatism" and "Normal Motor Automatism"—in Harvard's *Psychological Review*. They are her first publications.

1897   Havelock Ellis publishes the first volume of his classic *Studies on the Psychology of Sex*. Six additional volumes appear up to 1928.

James Sully establishes the first experimental psychology laboratory in England at University College London.

Appearance of Albert Moll's eight-hundred-page *Libido Sexualis: Studies in the Psychosexual Laws of Love Verified by Sexual Case Histories* (*Untersuchungen über die Libido sexualis*), which seeks to integrate normal and pathological sexuality into the emerging field of sexology.

Wilhelm Fliess publishes *The Relation between the Nose and the Female Sexual Organs* (*Die Beziehungen zwischen Nase und weiblichen Geschlechtsorganen*).

W. H. R. Rivers is appointed director of Britain's first experimental psychology laboratory at the University of London.

Freud discards his earlier "seduction theory" and begins to emphasize the role of sexual fantasies in the genesis of the neuroses. The same year he reads Sophocles' play *Oedipus Rex* and finds it a guide to the universal experience of a male child loving his mother and resenting his father.

Ribot finishes *Psychology of the Emotions* (*La psychologie des sentiments*).

Paul Janet, uncle of the psychologist Pierre, publishes *Principles of Metaphysics and Psychology* (*Principes de métaphysique et de psychologie*).

Dr. Adrien Proust coauthors *The Treatment of Neurasthenia* (*L'hygiène du neurasthénique*).

William James publishes *The Will to Believe.*

An outpatient "mental clinic," the first of its kind in America, opens at the Boston Dispensary.

The Russian physiologist Ivan Pavlov becomes director of the new Institute of Experimental Medicine in St. Petersburg.

Émile Durkheim publishes his landmark sociological study *Suicide.*

First exhibition of paintings by the Vienna Secession.

Opening of the Tate Gallery at Millbank, London.

Dracula, by Bram Stoker.

Hystérique, by Armand Dubarry.

Georges Méliès's film "Le Magnétiseur."

Theodor Herzl founds and becomes first president of the Congress of Zionist Organizations.

The British physicist Joseph Thomson discovers the electron.

Freud undergoes systematic, psychological self-analysis.

1897–1901 Gertrude Stein is enrolled at the Johns Hopkins Medical School.

1898 Eugen Bleuler, a pioneer in the psychological approach to the psychoses, is appointed professor of psychiatry in Zürich and director of the famous Burghölzli Hospital.

Freud writes his first essay on infantile sexuality.

Felix Gattel publishes *On the Sexual Origins of Neurasthenia and Anxiety Neurosis (Über die sexuellen Ursachen der Neurasthenie und Angst-neurose).*

Otto Weininger enters the University of Vienna, where his teachers include the psychiatrist Julius Wagner-Jauregg, the physiologist Sigmund Exner, and the sexologist Richard von Krafft-Ebing.

The Scottish physician T. G. Stewart publishes *Lectures on Giddiness and Hysteria in the Male.*

The Russian-born American Boris Sidis publishes *The Psychology of Suggestion: A Research into the Subconscious Nature of Man and Society.*

Charles Richet's novel *Soeur Marthe,* in which the protagonist is a doctor-hypnotist, is performed as a lyric drama in Paris.

Henry James's short story "The Turn of the Screw" probes the relation between thoughts and objects.

The German art theorist Theodor Lipps publishes a "psychological-aesthet-ic" study of humor and the comic.

Discovery of radium and radioactivity by Marie and Pierre Curie.

First major exhibition of French Impressionist canvases in Berlin.

Charles Ives completes his first symphony.

Zola writes "J'accuse" in defense of Alfred Dreyfus.

The German graphic artist and sculptor Käthe Kollwitz exhibits *Weavers*, her first set of prints. The subject of the exhibition is strongly influenced by the work of her physician-husband in a proletarian district of Berlin.

Richard Strauss becomes conductor of the court orchestra of Munich.

Beginning of the Spanish-American War.

1898 Hector Guimard designs station gates for the Paris metro in the Art
–1901 Nouveau style.

1899 Appearance of the influential sixth edition of Emil Kraepelin's *Clinical Psychiatry* (*Psychiatrie: ein Lehrbuch*), which first advances the concept of "manic depressive psychosis."

Magnus Hirschfeld begins to publish his *Yearbook of Sexual Intermediacy* (*Jahrbuch für sexuelle Zwischenstufen*), the first periodical about homosexuality and related sexual phenomena.

The German psychiatrist Paul Möbius writes *On Schopenhauer* (*Über Schopenhauer*).

The Viennese writer Karl Krauss launches his bitterly satirical journal *Die Fackel* (*The Torch*).

Publication of Kate Chopin's *The Awakening*, a classic of American feminist fiction.

Anton Chekhov's play *Uncle Vanya* (*Dyadya Vanya*) opens in Moscow.

Paul Signac publishes *From Eugène Delacroix to Neo-impressionism* (*D'Eugène Delacroix au néo-impressionisme*), a widely read exposition of modern painting.

The Austrian composer Arnold Schoenberg performs his experimental string sextet *Transfigured Night* (*Verklärte Nacht*), which arouses a violent reaction among audiences.

1899–1902 The Boer War.

1899; August Strindberg writes *To Damascus I* and *To Damascus II* (*Till*
1902 *Damaskus*), in which dreams become a means for exploring the interaction of reality and fantasy.

1900 In Geneva Théodore Flournoy publishes *From India to the Planet Mars* (*Des Indes à la planète Mars*), a remarkable book-length case of a single medium with multiple personality.

Sigmund Freud publishes *The Interpretation of Dreams* (*Die Traumdeutung*), which he judges his most important book. The book is reviewed in literary, philosophical, and theological as well as scientific journals.

Jung is appointed psychiatric assistant at the Burghölzli hospital in Zürich.

Binet publishes *Suggestibility* (*La suggestibilité*), a four-hundred-page study of the psychology of suggestion.

Ribot writes *A Study of the Creative Imagination* (*Essai sur l'imagination créatrice*).

Paul Sollier publishes *The Problem of Memory* (*Le problème de la mémoire*).
Bergson begins to lecture at the Collège de France, which rapidly spreads the philosophy of Bergsonism.
S. Weir Mitchell publishes the novel *Dr. North and His Friends*, centering on a character suffering from double consciousness.
The German metaphysician Edmund Husserl publishes *Logical Investigations* (*Logische Untersuchungen*), which includes a spirited logical critique of the new empirical sciences of psychology.
The German sociologist Georg Simmel writes his classic essay "The Metropolis and Mental Life."
Ferdinand von Zeppelin makes his first flight in a dirigible.
Oscar Wilde dies in Paris.
Nietzsche, who had been mentally deranged since 1889, dies at Jena.
The French poet and essayist Charles Péguy founds *Cahiers de la Quinzaine*, which will publish the writings of many Modernist authors.
The Exposition Universelle, the acme of the French Art Nouveau movement, is staged in Paris.
Rediscovery of Gregor Mendel's experimental work on heredity.
The quantum theory of energy is formulated by the German physicist Max Planck.
In London W. E. B. Du Bois and others organize the First Pan-African Congress.
Founding of the British Labor Party.

1901   Formation of the British Psychological Society.
Death of Frederic Myers.
Paul Sollier writes *Hysteria and Its Treatment* (*L'hystérie et son traitement*).
Bergson lectures on dreams at the Psychological Institute in Paris.
Working in French-speaking Switzerland, Flournoy and Claparède found the *Archives de psychologie*.
Nietzsche's sister Elisabeth Förster-Nietzsche publishes tendentious selections from her dead brother's philosophical notebooks under the title *The Will to Power* (*Der Wille zur Macht*).
The novelist Octave Mirbeau publishes *Twenty-One Days of a Neurasthenic* (*Les vingt et un jours d'un neurasthénique*), set in a nerve clinic.
Schnitzler's novella *Lieutenant Gustl* (*Leutnant Gustl*), written in the "stream of consciousness" style, is intended as a literary equivalent of the Freudian method of free association.
Chekhov completes *The Three Sisters* (*Tri sestry*).
Publication of *Buddenbrooks*, Thomas Mann's first great novel.
Richard Riemerschmid designs the Jugendstil interior of the new theater in Munich.
Founding of the Socialist Party in the United States.

Guglielmo Marconi transmits the first transatlantic telegraph message.

The first affordable camera, the Brownie Box, is introduced by Eastman Kodak.

Death of Queen Victoria.

1901–4   Pablo Picasso's Blue Period.

1902   Janet is appointed titular professor of experimental psychology at the Collège de France, where he lectures for the next decade to professionals, students, and interested laypeople.

Jung publishes his medical dissertation "On the Psychology and Pathology of So-Called Occult Phenomena" ("Zur Psychologie und Pathologie sogenannter occulter Phänomene: Ein psychiatrische Studie"), which presents experiments with his medium cousin Helen Preiswerk.

Alfred Adler and Freud become acquainted. Freud sets up the "Wednesday evening" discussion group.

The psychiatrist Willy Hellpach writes the popular tract *Nervousness and Culture (Nervosität und Kultur)*.

Pavlov begins to investigate the psychology and physiology of conditioned reflexes.

In Edinburgh William James delivers the Gifford Lectures, subsequently published as *The Varieties of Religious Experience*.

Joseph Conrad's *Heart of Darkness*.

André Gide's *The Immoralist (L'Immoraliste)*.

The German lyric poet Else Lasker-Schüler publishes *Styx*, her first collection of poems.

August Strindberg's *The Dream Play (Ett Drömspel)*.

Jules de Gaultier publishes his classic study of "le bovarysme" in the human character.

A brilliant performance of his play *The Lower Depths (Na dne)* at the Moscow Art Theater brings the Russian novelist and dramatist Maksim Gorky to international attention.

The Hamburg art scholar Aby Warburg founds the Warburg Library for Cultural Scholarship.

Alfred Stieglitz begins the Photo-Secession in New York City to promote the art of modern photography.

The *Times* of London begins publication, including its weekly *Times Literary Supplement*.

Voyage to the Moon, the first science fiction film, directed by Georges Méliès.

Edison's short film *Facial Expression*.

Mahler's Symphony No. 5.

Death of Krafft-Ebing.

1902–   Jung attends lectures by Janet in Paris during the winter academic
3   semester.

1902 The future German Existentialist philosopher Karl Jaspers attends medical
–8   school at the universities of Berlin and Heidelberg.

1903 Posthumous publication of Frederic Myers's magnum opus, the 1,300-page
      Human Personality and Its Survival of Bodily Death, in which Myers
      presents his final ideas about mediums, hysteria, hypnotism, somnambu-
      lism, automatic writing, the strata of the personality, and unconscious
      mentation.

      Death of Herbert Spencer.

      Appearance of Janet's two-volume *Obsessions and Psychasthenia* (*Les obses-
      sions et la psychasthénie*).

      Kraepelin is appointed professor of psychiatry at the University of Munich,
      where he remains until retirement in 1922.

      Otto Weininger, a brilliant but troubled young Jewish philosopher, publish-
      es *Sex and Character: An Investigation of Principles* (*Geschlecht und
      Charakter: eine prinzipielle Untersuchung*). The work integrates masses
      of psychological, biological, and clinical data with ideas that are sharply
      misogynistic and anti-Semitic. Several months after publication,
      Weininger commits suicide in the house where Beethoven had died.

      Wilhelm Jensen publishes the short novel *Gradiva: A Pompeiian Fantasy*
      (*Gradiva: Ein pompejanisches Phantasiestück*) about a young, introvert-
      ed, love-struck archaeologist. Freud later provides commentary on the
      text.

      The German jurist Daniel Paul Schreber publishes his *Memoirs of My
      Nervous Illness* (*Denkwürdigkeiten eines Nervenkranken*). Later made
      famous by Freud's 1911 analysis, Schreber's memoir is a literary and psy-
      chological work in its own right.

      Hugo von Hofmannsthal completes his tragedy *Elektra*, for which he used
      Breuer and Freud's *Studies on Hysteria* as a source. The play is set to
      music by Richard Strauss two years later.

      The German-Austrian poet Rainer Maria Rilke begins to publish his *New
      Poems*.

      Gertrude Stein moves to Paris, where she becomes the center of a group of
      expatriate artists and intellectuals.

      Stieglitz begins the magazine *Camera Work*, which publishes the work of
      leading American and European photographers.

      The Great Train Robbery, twelve minutes long, is the first American feature
      film.

      The first successful airplane flight takes place by the Wright Brothers near
      Kitty Hawk, North Carolina, ushering in the age of aviation.

      Sylvia, Emmeline, and Christabel Pankhurst found the British Women's
      Social and Political Union, which uses tactics of militant civil disobedi-
      ence.

Vladimir Ilyich Lenin founds the Bolshevik wing of the Russian Social-Democratic Workers' Party.

1903 Franz Kafka is a member of the "Brentano Circle," a group of Prague artists
−5 and intellectuals that discusses the new psychologies and philosophies of the day.

1903 The German aesthetician Theodor Lipps publishes the two-volume study
−6 *Aesthetics: Psychology of the Beautiful and Art* (*Ästhetik: Psychologie des Schönen und der Kunst*).

1904 Janet and Georges Dumas found the *Journal de psychologie normale et pathologique*.

The *British Journal of Psychology* commences publication.

Francis Galton, a cousin of Darwin, establishes the Eugenics Laboratory in London.

The Swiss psychotherapist Paul Dubois publishes *Psychic Treatment of the Nervous Disorders* (*Les psychonévroses et leur traitement moral*).

Janet takes the first of several trips to the United States, where he lectures widely on French psychological theory.

William James writes his essay "Does Consciousness Exist?"

Freud publishes *On the Psychopathology of Everyday Life* (*Zur Psychopathologie des Alltaglebens*), which quickly becomes a popular text.

Hermann Bahr publishes *Dialogue on the Tragic* (*Dialog vom Tragischen*), in which he employs the cathartic method of Breuer and Freud to interpret past dramatic works.

The German ethnologist Leo Frobenius begins research trips to Africa to investigate primitive African art.

The actor and director Max Reinhardt, along with Hofmannsthal and Strauss, organizes the Salzburg Festival Community.

Henry James's late prose masterpiece *The Golden Bowl*.

Chekhov's *The Cherry Orchard*.

Frank Lloyd Wright's buildings include the Larkin Building in Buffalo, New York, and the Cheney House in Oak Park, Illinois.

The International Congress of Women is held in Berlin.

1905 Freud's *annus mirabilis*. He publishes three classic texts: *Three Essays on a Theory of Sexuality* (*Drei Abhandlungen zur Sexualtheorie*), which offers his revolutionary theories of psychosexuality; *Jokes and Their Relation to the Unconscious* (*Der Witz und seine Beziehungen zum Unbewussten*); and the Dora case.

Auguste Forel publishes *The Sexual Question* (*Die sexuelle Frage*).

Janet delivers fifteen lectures at Harvard, which later appear under the title *The Major Symptoms of Hysteria*.

An abridgment of Frederic Myers's major work is translated into French as *La personnalité humaine, sa survivance après la mort, ses manifestations supranormales.*

Theodor Meynert, reputed for his hard-nosed medical materialism, publishes a collection of his own poems.

Albert Einstein announces his historic Special Theory of Relativity, encompassing the concept of a space-time continuum and the equation $E = mc_2$.

Claude Debussy composes *La Mer* consisting of three symphonic sketches in the Impressionist style.

Cézanne completes *The Large Bathers.*

Picasso paints the portrait of his friend Gertrude Stein.

E. M. Forster publishes his first major novel, *Where Angels Fear to Tread.*

The German dramatist and actor Frank Wedekind publishes "On the Erotic," concerning the literary exploration of human sexuality.

Béla Bartók and Zoltán Kodály begin collecting and transcribing folk songs.

Nickelodeon movie houses begin to open in the United States.

Fritz Schaudinn and Erich Hoffmann isolate the microscopic parasite for syphilis.

The British physiologist Ernest Starling introduces the term "hormones" for internal secretions of the endocrine glands.

1905 Formation in Dresden of Die Brücke (The Bridge), a group of German
–6 Expressionist painters, including Ernst Ludwig Kirchner, Max Pechstein, and Emil Nolde.

1905–7 Picasso's Rose Period.

1905 High point of the Fauvist movement in the visual arts, led by Henri Matisse,
–8 André Derain, and Maurice de Vlaminck.

1906 First volume of the French neurology journal *L'Encéphale.*

Appearance of the fifth volume of Ellis's *Studies on the Psychology of Sex,* dealing with erotic symbolism.

Camillo Golgi and Santiago Ramón y Cajal are awarded the Nobel Prize in medicine and physiology for their discoveries about the structure of nerve cells.

Virginia Woolf suffers a prolonged mental breakdown upon the death of her brother.

Freud and Jung begin their famous exchange of letters, and Jung begins publicly to advocate psychoanalysis.

The Boston neurologist Morton Prince founds the *Journal of Abnormal Psychology.* The same year Prince publishes *The Dissociation of Personality,* a five-hundred-page biographical study of "Miss Sally Beauchamp" that formulates his theory of "co-consciousness." The book remains in print until 1930.

Adolf Meyer opens the Henry Phipps Psychiatric Clinic at Johns Hopkins Hospital in Baltimore.

The future German novelist Alfred Döblin works as a psychiatric resident in the Buch asylum in Berlin.

Hofmannsthal writes *Oedipus and the Sphinx* (*Oedipus und die Sphinx*).

Publication by the Swiss-German novelist Carl Spitteler of *Imago*, relating the story of a man who creates an ideal, imaginary picture of the woman he loves. Jung later discusses the novel in his study *Psychological Types*, and Freud uses the book's title for a psychoanalytic journal devoted to cultural topics.

The Austrian-German novelist Robert Musil publishes *Confusions of Young Törless* (*Die Verwirrungen des Zöglings Törless*), which is strongly influenced by Ernst Mach's psychological system.

The Austrian architect Adolf Loos establishes the Free School of Architecture to promote architectural Modernism.

Drs. Augustin Cabanès and Lucien Nass apply ideas of abnormal psychology to French history in *The Revolutionary Neurosis* (*La névrose révolutionnaire*).

Firmin Terrien, a doctor in Brittany, publishes *Hysteria and Neurasthenia in the Peasantry* (*Hystérie et neurasthénie chez les paysans*).

Claude Monet begins the "Nymphéas" paintings, a cycle of huge murals depicting the water lily ponds at his home in Giverny. Continued up to the artist's death in 1926.

Émile Cohl directs "Le Miroir hypnotique."

First American radio broadcast.

1907 The First International Congress of Psychiatry, Neurology, and Mental Health takes place in Amsterdam.

Jung publishes *Psychology of Dementia Praecox* (*Über die Psychologie der Dementia Praecox*), the most important attempt to date to apply psychoanalytic ideas to the study and treatment of the psychoses.

Alfred Adler publishes *The Study of Organ Inferiority and Its Psychical Compensation* (*Studie über die Minderwertigkeit von Organen*).

A young Ludwig Binswanger, the future founder of Existential analysis, meets Freud in Vienna.

Freud writes his first extended study of a literary text, "Delusions and Dreams in Jensen's *Gradiva*."

Otto Rank publishes *The Artist: Approaches to the Psychology of Sexuality* (*Der Künstler. Ansätze zu einer Sexual-psychologie*).

Bergson publishes *Creative Evolution* (*L'Évolution créatrice*), his most widely read book.

Émile Magnin publishes *Art and Hypnosis* (*L'Art et l'hypnose*), exploring the creative capacities unlocked by the hypnotic trance.

Color photography is invented by the Lumière brothers in Paris.

Picasso paints *Les demoiselles d'Avignon*, a masterpiece of Cubism that
draws on primitivist motifs.

Matisse produces several of his most important early paintings, including
The Joy of Life, Le Luxe II, Harmony in Red, and *Dance*.

An influential retrospective exhibition of the works of Cézanne is held at
the Salon d'Automne in Paris.

Edmund Gosse writes *Father and Son*, his novel of intergenerational psychological tensions.

Mahler completes his *Symphony of a Thousand*.

1907 The Austrian Expressionist Gustav Klimt paints *The Kiss*. Strindberg
–8 writes *The Ghost Sonata (Spöksonaten)*.

1908 The future German novelist Robert Musil completes his philosophy dissertation *Toward an Evaluation of Ernst Mach's Theories (Beitrag zur
Beurteilung der Lehren Machs)*.

Freud writes "'Civilized' Sexual Morality and Modern Nervousness," a
sharp psychosexual critique of Victorian sexual ethics.

Establishment of the Vienna Psychoanalytic Society.

The first psychoanalytic congress takes place in Salzburg.

In America, Clifford Beers publishes *A Mind That Found Itself*, which becomes the best-known psychiatric autobiography in the twentieth century.

The English social reformer Edward Carpenter publishes *The Intermediate
Sex* about homosexuality. The book remains in print until 1930.

Georges Sorel's *Reflections on Violence (Réflexions sur la violence)*.

André Lorde's two-act play *A Lesson at the Salpêtrière (Une leçon à la
Salpêtrière)*, dedicated to Binet and featuring themes and personalities
from Charcot's medical circle, is staged at the Grand-Guignol Theater
in Paris.

Schnitzler publishes his best-known novel *The Road to the Open (Der Weg
ins Freie)*.

A brooding and wayward Adolf Hitler, age nineteen, is rejected for the second time by the Vienna Academy of Fine Arts.

Picasso and Georges Braque paint their first Cubist still lifes, marking the
beginning of analytical Cubism.

A large Matisse exhibition is staged in Berlin.

In Munich the art critic Wilhelm Worringer publishes *Abstraction and
Empathy: A Contribution to the Psychology of Style (Abstraktion und
Einfühlung)*, which will be translated into eighteen languages.

Mahler composes *The Song of the Earth (Das Lied von der Erde)*.

The Russian pianist and composer Alexander Scriabin completes his Sonata
No. 5.

Nietzsche's *Ecce Homo* is published posthumously.

1908 Marcel Proust writes *Against Sainte Beuve (Contre Sainte Beuve)*, a state-
–10 ment of his early aesthetic theory.

1909   At the Sixth International Congress of Psychology, the "subconscious" is the theme and Janet the main speaker. The same year Janet publishes *The Neuroses (Les Névroses)*.

Moll publishes *The Sexual Life of the Child (Das Sexualleben des Kindes)*.

Freud, Jung, and Sándor Ferenczi lecture about psychoanalysis at Clark University in Worcester, Massachusetts.

Jung leaves the Burghölzli and sets up a private practice in his newly built home in Küsnacht near Zürich.

The future German metaphysician Karl Jaspers publishes his medical dissertation titled *Nostalgia and Crime (Heimweh und Verbrechen)*.

Clifford Beers, William James, and Adolf Meyer establish the National Committee for Mental Hygiene, thereby launching the American Mental Hygiene movement.

Bergson publishes *Matter and Memory (Matière et mémoire)*.

The Dutch pioneer of psychotherapy Frederik Van Eeden writes *The Bride of Dreams (Mellie von Auw)*, a novel about dream life.

On a snowy January evening, Marcel Proust sips a cup of lime-flavored tea and tastes a piece of dry toast, which overwhelm his senses.

S. Weir Mitchell publishes his twelve-volume literary *Works*, including novels, short stories, and poems.

Filippo Tommaso Marinetti, principal theorist of the movement, publishes the first Futurist manifesto.

Umberto Boccioni produces the Futurist canvas *Riot in the Gallery*.

The Austrian Expressionist Oskar Kokoschka paints *Portrait of Adolf Loos*.

Frank Lloyd Wright completes the Robie House in Hyde Park, Chicago.

Arnold Schoenberg writes *Five Orchestral Pieces*, the first large-scale instrumental composition in an atonal style.

Sergei Diaghilev organizes the Ballets Russes in Paris, which for the next twenty years performs much of the most important work in modern ballet. The brilliant Russian dancer Vaslav Nijinsky joins Diaghilev's ballet company.

Foundation of the National Association for the Advancement of Colored People (NAACP) in America.

The French aviator Louis Blériot is the first to fly a "monoplane" over the English Channel.

Henry Ford begins manufacturing the Model T, the first mass-produced automobile.

The future Dada and Surrealist painter Max Ernst studies philosophy and psychiatry at the University of Bonn.

1909   Karl Jaspers works as a psychiatric research assistant in Franz Nissl's labora-
–15   tory at the University of Heidelberg.

1910   Freud, Jung, Bleuler, and Ferenczi found the International Psychoanalytic Association.

T. K. Oesterreich publishes *Phenomenology of the Ego* (*Phänomenologie des Ich*).

Binet and André de Lorde coauthor the three-act play *The Mysterious Man* (*L'homme mystérieux*).

Death of William James.

Adolf Meyer is appointed professor of psychiatry and director of the psychiatric clinic at Johns Hopkins University.

Bertrand Russell and Alfred North Whitehead collaboratively publish the first volume of *Principia Mathematica*.

Henri Rousseau paints *The Dream*.

Boccioni, Giacomo Balla, Gino Severini, Luigi Rossolos, and Carol Carra publish "Technical Manifesto of the Futurist Painters."

Completion in Central Park of the main building for New York City's Metropolitan Museum of Art. Design by McKim, Mead, and White.

The attorney general of the state of Kansas rules that women may wear trousers in public.

1910 –11　Appearance of the famous eleventh edition of the *Encyclopedia Britannica*.

1910 –12　Vasily Kandinsky completes a number of *Improvisations* and *Compositions*. These are believed to be the first fully nonrepresentational paintings.

1910 –13　Igor Stravinsky composes *The Firebird*, *Petrushka*, and *The Rite of Spring*, three revolutionary works written for the Paris performances of the Ballets Russes.

1911　Bleuler publishes his great monograph *Dementia Praecox and the Group of Schizophrenias* (*Dementia Praecox oder Gruppe der Schizophrenien*). The study popularizes the term "schizophrenia."

The Swiss-German physician Hermann Rorschach begins to publish his ideas about psychodiagnostic testing.

Flournoy publishes a compilation of his life's work on mediumistic psychology titled *Spiritism and Mediums* (*Esprits et médiums*).

Adler splits from Freud, starting the independent Society for Free Psychoanalysis, later called the Society for Individual Psychology.

First meeting of the American Psychoanalytic Society.

Freud becomes a corresponding member of the Society for Psychical Research.

Grete Meisel-Hess writes *The Intellectuals* (*Die Intellektuellen*), believed to be the first work of fiction featuring a psychoanalyst.

Picasso exhibits his first decorative Cubist collages.

Gustav Klimt paints *Death and Life*, and Marcel Duchamp paints *Nude Descending a Staircase, No. 1*.

Anna Pavlova, the most famous classical ballerina of her era, founds her own company, which begins to bring Modernist dance to international audiences.

Frank Lloyd Wright builds Taliesin, in Wisconsin, which becomes his architecture school and workshop.

1911 Jung comes out with *Metamorphoses and Symbols of Libido* (*Wand-*
–12 *lungen und Symbole der Libido*), in which he details his ideas about mythology, sexuality, and symbolism.

1911 Major exhibitions of *Der Blaue Reiter* group, including paintings by Marc,
–14 Kandinsky, Paul Klee, and Jean Arp, are organized in several European cities.

1912 Appearance of the thousand-page *Handbook of Sexual Science* (*Handbuch der Sexualwissenschaften*), edited by Albert Moll.

Adler publishes *The Neurotic Constitution* (*Über den nervösen Charakter*).

Rank publishes *The Incest Theme in Literature and Legend* (*Das Inzest-Motiv in Dichtung und Sage*), a large compilation on the incest theme in culture and folklore.

The psychoanalytic journal *Imago*, devoted to cultural issues, begins publication.

The psychoanalyst Wilhelm Stekel publishes a book on dreams and poetry.

Édouard Claparède founds the Institut Jean-Jacques Rousseau in Geneva.

Lou Andreas-Salomé comes to Vienna to study psychoanalysis.

Freud publishes in English "A Note on the Unconscious in Psycho-Analysis" in the *Proceedings of the Society for Psychical Research*.

Thomas Mann writes "Death in Venice" ("Der Tod in Venedig"), the best known of his long short stories.

Kafka composes his story "The Judgement," drawing extensively on Brentano's and Freud's psychological teachings.

The cultural impresario Herwarth Walden becomes founding editor of the avant-garde journal *Der Sturm*.

Kandinsky publishes his classic statement of abstract aesthetics *Concerning the Spiritual in Art* (*Über das Geistige in der Kunst*), which is much informed by the occultist and theosophical teachings of Madame Blavatsky and Rudolf Steiner.

The Bloomsbury art critics Clive Bell and Roger Fry organize the landmark Second Post-Impressionist Exhibition in London.

Founding of the African National Congress (ANC) in South Africa.

On the night of April 14, the *Titanic*, the largest moving man-made structure ever, sinks in the icy North Atlantic on its maiden voyage from Southampton to New York City. More than 1,500 people die.

1912 Deterioration and termination of the Freud-Jung relationship.

–14 Culmination of the Imagist movement in poetry with Ezra Pound as its central figure.

1913 Edmund Husserl publishes *Ideas: General Introduction to Pure Phenomenology* (*Ideen zu einer reinen Phänomenologie und phänomenol-*

ogischen Philosophie), the founding philosophical statement of modern phenomenology.

Karl Jaspers publishes his *General Psychopathology* (*Allgemeine Psychopathologie*), which attempts to bring the aims and methods of phenomenology to clinical psychiatry. The same year, he takes up a post as *Privatdozent* in psychiatry at the University of Heidelberg.

Appearance of A. A. Brill's English translation of Freud's *The Interpretation of Dreams*, the first of Freud's texts in English to attract general cultural attention.

Founding of the London Society for Psychoanalysis by Ernest Jones and David Eder.

At the Seventeenth International Congress of Medicine in London, Janet repudiates psychoanalysis.

At a psychoanalytic congress in Munich, Lou Andreas-Salomé introduces the poet Rilke, her lover, to Freud.

The psychoanalyst Theodor Reik publishes *Arthur Schnitzler as Psychologist* (*Arthur Schnitzler als Psycholog*).

Charlie Chaplin makes his film debut.

Appearance of *Swann's Way* (*Du côté de chez Swann*), the first volume of Marcel Proust's sprawling novel sequence *A la recherche du temps perdu* (*In Serach of Lost Time*). Later volumes appear to 1927.

Publication of D. H. Lawrence's novel *Sons and Lovers*, which contemporary psychoanalysts interpret as a penetrating study of the Oedipus complex.

The Irish poet, critic, and dramatist Yeats joins the Society for Psychical Research.

Kafka is awarded the Fontane Prize.

The psychophysiologist Henri Beaunis publishes his collected plays under the title *Théâtre composite*.

The French poet Guillaume Apollinaire publishes *The Cubist Painters* (*Les peintres cubistes*).

The landmark New York Armory Show introduces hundreds of pieces of experimental European art to American audiences.

Ernst Ludwig Kirchner paints his well-known depiction of Berlin city life, *The Street*.

Franz Marc paints *The Tower of Blue Horses*.

Boccioni exhibits *Unique Forms of Continuity in Space*, perhaps the best-known piece of Futurist sculpture.

Duchamp completes his first "ready made" sculptures.

Constantin Brancusi sculpts *Mademoiselle Pogany*.

Construction of the Woolworth Building in New York City, the first of the high-rise skyscrapers.

1914   Founding of the British Society for the Study of Sex Psychology.

At the University of Freiburg young Martin Heidegger completes his philosophy dissertation, "Die Lehre vom Urteil im Psychologismus," providing a neo-Kantian critique of psychological doctrine.

Magnus Hirschfeld publishes his major text *Homosexuality in Men and Women* (*Die Homosexualität des Mannes und des Weibes*).

Emmanuel Régis and Angelo Hesnard publish *Psychoanalysis of the Neuroses and Psychoses* (*La psychanalyse des névroses et des psychoses*), one of the first sympathetic texts about psychoanalysis written within the French psychiatric community.

Charles Blondel's *Morbid Consciousness* (*La conscience morbide*) develops the notion of cenesthesia or the internal perception of our own bodies.

Morton Prince publishes *The Unconscious*.

John B. Watson begins to formulate his ideas of psychological behavioralism.

Walter B. Cannon publishes *Bodily Changes in Pain, Hunger, Fear, and Rage*, which brilliantly elucidates the psychophysiological mechanisms that mediate emotional responses and the sympathetic nervous system.

Stein publishes her major work of experimental prose-poetry *Tender Buttons*.

Publication of *The Complete Poems of S. Weir Mitchell*.

Freud writes a study of Michelangelo's sculpture *Moses*.

Yeats indicates his interest in and experimentation with spiritualism with the essay "Swedenborg, Mediums and the Desolate Places."

The American-born poet, critic, and dramatist T. S. Eliot settles in London.

Publication begins of the literary magazine *The Egoist*, including the writings of H.D., Eliot, and Pound.

E. M. Forster completes *Maurice*, centering on the life of a young gay man, but does not publish the novel until 1972.

The Canadian-born painter, novelist, and critic Wyndham Lewis emerges as the leading voice of the London-based Vorticist movement.

The Danish physicist Niels Bohr postulates a new model of atomic structure, challenging classical Newtonian laws of mechanics and initiating modern quantum physics.

1914   Freud writes his "meta-psychological" essays—including "Introduction to
–15   Narcissism," "Instincts and Their Vicissitudes," and "The Unconscious"—thereby initiating a major restructuring of psychoanalytic theory.

1914   World War I, fought between the Entente nations (Britain, France, Italy,
–18   Russia, Belgium, and eventually the United States) and the Central Powers (Germany, Austria-Hungary, and Turkey). More than eight million soldiers are killed on both sides, twenty million are wounded, and

countless civilians are injured or killed. Many figures in the artistic avant garde lose their lives, while others are badly injured. At the battlefront, hundreds of thousands of soldiers from the combatant countries experience "shell shock," or posttraumatic psychopathology, from the stresses and strains of the fighting.

1915 In the *Lancet* the English physician Charles Myers coins the term "shell shock" to account for the strange cases of nervous and mental breakdown being observed in epidemic numbers among infantrymen along the Western Front of the war.

Freud writes "Thoughts for the Times on War and Death."

The English novelist Dorothy Richardson begins to write *Pilgrimage*, a series of novels using stream of consciousness techniques of narration. Volumes appear up to 1938.

Marcel Duchamp arrives in America, beginning the New York branch of Dada.

David Griffith directs the first feature-length film, the highly racist *Birth of a Nation*.

Einstein formulates the General Theory of Relativity, with its model of a non-Euclidean four-dimensional space-time continuum.

1915 Working in Ferraro the Italian Surrealist Giorgio de Chirico completes
–19 several of his most important paintings, including *The Great Metaphysician*, *The Disquieting Muse*, and *Great Metaphysician, Interior*. De Chirico's work is recognized by contemporaries for its eerie emotional and psychological starkness.

1916 Bleuler publishes his *Textbook of Psychiatry* (*Lehrbuch der Psychiatrie*), with many subsequent editions.

Publication in English of Jung's *Psychology of the Unconscious* (*Wandlungen und Symbole der Libido*), which begins to introduce his ideas to an English-language audience.

Founding of the Psychological Club in Zürich.

The German-American psychologist Münsterberg publishes *The Film: A Psychological Study*.

James Joyce publishes his semi-autobiographical novel *Portrait of the Artist as a Young Man*.

The German art critic Theodor Däubler publishes *The New Perspective* (*Der neue Standpunkt*), the first book-length explication of German Expressionist painting.

Gustav Holst composes the popular orchestral suite *The Planets*.

The first news reports are broadcast on radio.

1916– At a sanatorium in Lucerne, Switzerland, Hermann Hesse undergoes a
17 Jungian analysis with Dr. Josef Lang.

1916–19 High point of the Dada school in Zürich.

1917   Kraepelin founds the German Psychiatric Research Institute (Deutsche For-
       schungsanstalt für Psychiatrie).
       The French novelist Léon Daudet publishes *L'Hérédo. Essai sur le drame
       intérieur*, which propounds Daudet's idea of a "metapsychology." Jung
       claims to be much influenced by the novel.
       The young English poet Wilfred Owen enters the Craiglockhart psychiatric
       hospital outside Edinburgh. He is treated for war neurosis by Dr. Arthur
       Brock.
       Appearance of *De Stijl*, a periodical of Dutch avant-garde art.
       Diaghilev's ballet *The Parade* is performed in Rome. Story by Cocteau,
       music by Satie, and sets by Picasso.
       The German physician-poet Gottfried Benn publishes *Flesh* (*Fleisch*), a col-
       lection of his poems.
       Eliot publishes *The Love Song of J. Alfred Prufrock and Other Observations*.
       The Russian-born French artist Marc Chagall works for the Yiddish theater
       in Moscow painting murals and designing sets.
       Sergei Prokofiev completes his first symphony, the so-called *Classical
       Symphony*.
       Lenin writes *Imperialism: The Highest Stage of Capitalism* (*Imperializm:
       Kak noveyshy etap Kapitalizma*).
       The Russian Revolution leads to the overthrow of Czar Nicholas II, the
       installation of a Bolshevik government, and the initiation of the Russian
       Civil War.
       The United States enters World War I. By the end of the war, roughly
       51,000 American soldiers are dead.
1917   Hirschfeld publishes *Sexual Pathology: A Study of the Derangements of the
–18   Sexual Instinct* (*Sexualpathologie*).
1917   Yeats and his wife undertake an extensive series of psychical experiments,
–20   conducting hundreds of séances. They record the results of their
       researches in dozens of notebooks, which include automatic writing
       scripts.
1917   Bertolt Brecht, the future German poet, playwright, and theatrical produc-
–21   er, attends medical school in Munich.
1918   The British physician Lewis Yealland publishes *Hysterical Disorders of War*,
       arguing for harsh, physicalistic treatments of war neurotics.
       The German physician Ernst Simmel publishes *Psychological Trauma and
       the War Neuroses* (*Kriegs-neurosen und 'psychisches Trauma'*), advocating
       sympathetic psychotherapy for the treatment of shell-shocked soldiers.
       The fifth international congress of psychoanalysis, held in Budapest, focuses
       on the theory and treatment of the war neuroses.
       Freud publishes his case history of "the Wolf Man."

Apollinaire publishes his poetry collection *Calligrammes*.

Lytton Strachey writes *Eminent Victorians*, his popular set of blistering biographical studies.

While hospitalized, Siegfried Sassoon publishes *Counter-Attack and Other Poems*. One poem in the collection, titled "Repression of War Experience," draws on the therapeutic ideas of Sassoon's physician, W. H. R. Rivers.

First opening of one of Eugene O'Neill's plays at New York's Provincetown Theater.

Joseph Stella paints *Brooklyn Bridge*.

Equal voting rights are won, finally, for British women over the age of thirty.

1918 –19   Piet Mondrian executes his first paintings of juxtaposed primary color squares on a rectangular grid.

1919   Janet publishes *Psychological Healing* (*Les médications psychologiques*), a major clinical and historical study of psychological healing.

Freud writes "The Uncanny," which includes a reading of E. T. A. Hoffmann's short story "The Sandman."

Jung lectures in London to the Society for Psychical Research.

Yves Delage writes *The Dream: A Psychological, Philosophical, and Literary Study* (*Le Rêve. Étude psychologique, philosophique, et littéraire*).

Magnus Hirschfeld opens his famous Institute of Sexology in Berlin. Visitors to the institute's museum of sexual pathology include Sergei Eisenstein, Douglas Fairbanks, George Gershwin, André Gide, Christopher Isherwood, and Anita Loos.

Hans Blüher publishes *The Role of the Erotic in Human Society* (*Die Rolle der Erotik in der männlichen Gesellschaft*).

Frederick W. Mott publishes *The War Neuroses and Shell-Shock*.

Hermann Hesse publishes his novel *Demian*, in which contemporaries recognize many affinities with Jung's new analytic psychology. Jung reads the novel and writes to Hesse, beginning an occasional, lifelong correspondence.

Proust's *Within a Budding Grove* (*A l'ombre des jeunes filles en fleurs*), the second volume of his literary masterwork, wins the coveted Goncourt Prize.

Paul Valéry writes "The Crisis of the Mind" about the impact of the war on European intellectual life.

Max Reinhardt inaugurates the Grosses Schauspielhaus in Berlin.

In the city of Weimar the architect Walter Gropius becomes director of the Bauhaus School of Design, the primary institutional site for Modernist design in interwar Germany. Kandinsky, Klee, and Lyonel Feininger are members of the faculty.

Robert Wiene directs the masterly Expressionist thriller *The Cabinet of Dr. Caligari (Das Kabinett des Dr. Caligari)*. The film features a hypnotist-psychiatrist who uses a somnambulist to commit his murders.

Benito Mussolini forms the Fascio Italiani di Combattimento, spawning political and military fascism in Italy.

Establishment of the Weimar Republic, Germany's first experiment with political democracy.

1920　London's Tavistock Square Clinic opens under the direction of Hugh Crichton-Miller.

Ernest Jones founds the *International Journal of Psychoanalysis*.

Freud's *Beyond the Pleasure Principle (Jenseits des Lustprinzips)* advances the idea of two fundamental drives, the life and death instincts, in human nature.

James Strachey, Freud's future English translator, is psychoanalyzed by Freud in Vienna.

Alfred Adler writes *The Practice and Theory of Individual Psychology (Praxis und Theorie der Individualpsychologie)*, an exposition of his new system of Individual Psychology.

W. H. R. Rivers publishes *Instinct and the Unconscious*, which fosters the adoption of psychoanalytic perspectives in British psychiatry.

Death of Flournoy.

In "Tradition and the Individual Talent," T. S. Eliot criticizes the idea of expressing individual emotion and personal psychology in art.

In "Freudian Fiction," Virginia Woolf mocks the new scientistic psychologies as sources of self-knowledge and character representation.

Kandinsky stages a one-man show of his oils and watercolors in Moscow.

Erich Mendelsohn completes the Einstein Tower in Potsdam, a key statement of German Expressionist architecture.

The Russian novelist and critic Yevgeny Zamyatin publishes his prescient, dystopian novel *We*, in which he projects a futuristic society of communitarian totalitarianism.

Premier of George Bernard Shaw's *Heartbreak House* in New York City.

Anti-Jewish pogroms in the Ukraine.

Niels Bohr becomes director of the newly created Institute of Theoretical Physics in Copenhagen.

Daily scheduled airplane flights within Europe begin.

Ratification of the nineteenth amendment to the U.S. Constitution grants American women the right to vote in federal elections.

1921　Jung publishes his magnum opus *Psychological Types (Psychologische Typen)*, in which he introduces the concepts of introverted and extroverted character types.

The Swiss psychiatrist Hermann Rorschach introduces his well-known diagnostic inkblot test.

The Tübingen psychiatrist Ernst Kretschmer publishes *Physique and Character* (*Körperbau und Charakter*), a key text in psychiatric characterology.

The International Psychoanalytic Press in Leipzig publishes Georg Groddeck's *The Soulsearcher* (*Der Seelensucher*), a "psychoanalytic novel."

The Surrealist poet André Breton meets Freud in Vienna.

Breton and Philippe Soupault publish *Magnetic Fields* (*Les champs magnétiques*), which attempts to explain the creative possibilities of automatic writing.

D. H. Lawrence writes *Psychoanalysis and the Unconscious*, an airing of his differences with the Freudian view of the psyche.

Picasso's *Three Musicians*.

George Grosz's collection of scathing caricatures *The Face of the Ruling Class*.

Luigi Pirandello's plays *Six Characters in Search of an Author* and *Henry IV*.

The gifted Austrian philosopher Ludwig Wittgenstein publishes his magnum opus, the *Tractatus Logico-Philosophicus*.

Einstein wins the Nobel Prize for physics.

1922 Richet publishes his late work *A Treatise on the Metapsychical* (*Traité de métapsychique*).

The German psychologist and neurologist Hans Prinzhorn writes *Artistry of the Mentally Ill* (*Bildnerei der Geisteskranken*).

Jaspers publishes a book-length study of Strindberg and Van Gogh.

Publication of Eliot's "The Waste Land," a groundbreaking text in Anglo-American poetic Modernism.

Publication of *Ulysses*, James Joyce's seminal work of prose Modernism in which the author reconstructs in minute-by-minute detail the mental life of Leopold Bloom and Stephen Dedalus on a single day. For years the book is banned as obscene in the United States.

The International Dada Exhibition is staged at the Galerie Montaigne in Paris.

In a letter to the author, Freud dubs Schnitzler his "double" (*Doppelgänger*).

In the journal *Littérature*, Breton writes "Enter the Mediums," discussing Myers, Flournoy, and Freud as inspirations for Surrealist aesthetics.

The British philosopher G. E. Moore publishes *Philosophical Studies*.

D. H. Lawrence's *Fantasia of the Unconscious*.

First published poetry of e. e. cummings.

Bertolt Brecht completes his first play, *Baal*.

The botanist and chemist Margarethe von Wrangell becomes the first woman in Germany appointed to a university professorship.

The "March on Rome" by fascist Blackshirts leads to Benito Mussolini's assumption of political power in Italy.

1922　Otto Dix paints *Trench Warfare* in the style of the "new social realism."

−23　Completion of the Chicago Tribune Tower.

1923　Freud publishes *The Ego and the Id* (*Das Ich und das Es*), in which he presents a new tripartite, "structural" model of the psyche, consisting famously of the id, ego, and superego.

Georg Groddeck publishes *The Book of the Id* (*Das Buch vom Es*).

Jean Piaget publishes his first monograph, *Language and Thought of the Child* (*Le langage et la pensée chez l'enfant*).

W. N. Maxwell writes *A Psychological Retrospect of the Great War*.

Yeats is awarded the Nobel Prize for literature.

The Hungarian Marxist philosopher and literary critic Georg Lukács publishes *History and Class Consciousness* (*Geschichte und Klassenbewusstsein*).

The Italian novelist Italo Svevo writes his best-known novel, *Confessions of Zeno* (*La conscienza di Zeno*), an ironic study of a disillusioned bourgeois undergoing psychoanalysis.

The French architect Le Corbusier publishes *Towards a New Architecture* (*Vers une architecture*).

Louis Armstrong emerges in Chicago as a leading figure in jazz.

1924　Rank publishes his best-known book, *The Trauma of Birth* (*Das Trauma der Geburt*).

Sándor Ferenczi publishes *Thalassa: A Theory of Genitality* (*Versuch einer Genitaltheorie*).

Thomas Mann publishes his novel *The Magic Mountain* (*Der Zauberberg*).

Establishment of the Institute for Social Research in Frankfurt, which quickly becomes a leading venue for avant-garde left-wing social and cultural theory.

The British poet, critic, and philosopher T. E. Hulme completes *Speculations*.

Roger Fry, the Bloomsbury art critic, publishes *The Artist and Psychoanalysis*.

The Hogarth Press in London, founded by Leonard and Virginia Woolf, begins to publish Freud's writings in authoritative English translation.

Breton writes his first *Manifesto of Surrealism*, extolling dreams, psychic automatisms, and the free flow of unconscious thoughts.

Constantin Brancusi sculpts *Bird in Space.*
Premier of George Gershwin's *Rhapsody in Blue* for piano and jazz band.
1924–25 Alix Strachey is psychoanalyzed in Berlin by Karl Abraham.
1925 Alfred North Whitehead publishes *Science in the Modern World.*
Otto Rank publishes *The Double: A Psychoanalytic Study (Der Doppelgänger).*
Virginia Woolf hears Melanie Klein lecture. Woolf also publishes *Mrs. Dalloway,* her first major stream-of-consciousness novel, which includes a highly unflattering portrait of a fictional psychiatrist.
The first Surrealist exhibition is held at the Galerie Pierre in Paris.
André Gaucher publishes his play *L'Obsédé: Drame de la libido,* accompanied by letters from Janet and Freud.
Schnitzler's "Dream Novella."
Edward Hopper's painting *House by the Railroad.*
Dmitri Shostakovich's Symphony No. 1.
Charlie Chaplin writes, directs, and stars in *The Gold Rush.*
Battleship Potemkin, Sergei Eisenstein's groundbreaking film using montage techniques.
Adolf Hitler publishes a rambling and hate-filled autobiography in two volumes, titled *Mein Kampf.*
1925–
26 Publication of Franz Kafka's *The Trial (Der Prozess)* and *The Castle (Das Schloss),* both written a decade earlier.
1925–
35 The Austrian novelist Hermann Broch undergoes psychoanalysis with Hedwig Schaxel.
1926 First annual meeting in Baden-Baden of the General Medical Congress on Psychotherapy.
In Berlin Moll organizes the International Congress for Sexual Research.
Melanie Klein moves permanently to England.
Karen Horney questions "penis envy."
In *The Psychological Achievements of Nietzsche (Die psychologischen Errungenschaften Nietzsches),* Ludwig Klages interprets Nietzsche as a "philosopher-psychologist."
Death of Kraepelin.
The French dramatist H. R. Lenormand writes *The Love Magician (L'Amour magicien).* Inspired in part by Jung's medical dissertation about the medium Helen Preiswerk, the play relates the story of a medium's romance with a painter.
H. G. Wells's novel *The World of William Clissold* includes a scene depicting Jung.
Publication of *The Collected Poems of Ezra Pound.*
Yeats publishes *A Vision,* expounding a bizarre cosmology based on mytho-

logical, numerological, and astrological symbolism. The system derives
in part from his extensive psychical experiments.

Stein writes *Composition as Explanation*, the fullest statement of her theory
of writing.

Appearance in America of *Amazing Stories*, the world's first science fiction
magazine, edited by Hugo Gernsback.

Completion in the International style of buildings in Dessau for the new
Bauhaus school.

Alban Berg composes his *Lyric Suite*.

The black entertainer Josephine Baker brings a New Orleans–style orchestra to Paris and Berlin, signaling a new fascination with American jazz
music in France and Germany.

Fritz Lang directs the spectacular silent science fiction film *Metropolis*.

Debut of *The Jazz Singer*, the first talking film.

G. W. Pabst directs *Secrets of a Soul* (*Geheimnisse einer Seele*), a silent film
allegedly based on a case of phobia recorded and treated by Freud. The
melodrama, for which the psychoanalysts Karl Abraham and Hanns
Sachs were extensively consulted, includes a celebrated dream
sequence.

First wireless telephone conversation between London and New York.

1926 –28 Janet publishes *From Anxiety to Ecstasy* (*De l'angoisse à l'extase: Études sur
les croyances et les sentiments*), a two-volume account of his twenty-two-
year clinical study of "Madelaine," a Salpêtrière religious ecstatic.

1927 The Austrian psychiatrist Julius Wagner von Jauregg is the first psychiatrist
to win a Nobel Prize in medicine and physiology, for his development of
a malarial treatment for advanced syphilis.

Freud writes *The Future of an Illusion* (*Die Zukunft einer Illusion*).

Wilhelm Reich publishes *The Function of the Orgasm* (*Die Funktion des
Orgasmus*).

Martin Heidegger publishes *Being and Time* (*Sein und Zeit*), a foundational
text of modern Existentialism and a theoretical precondition for
Existential analysis.

Bergson receives the Nobel Prize for literature.

Woolf's *To the Lighthouse* and Hesse's *Steppenwolf*

Kasimir Malevich publishes *The Non-Objective World* (*Die gegenstandslose
Welt*) about abstraction in the visual arts.

Martha Graham founds the School of Contemporary Dance in New York
City.

Abel Gance directs the epic three-screen silent film *Napoléon*.

Charles Lindbergh makes the first nonstop solo airplane flight across the
Atlantic Ocean.

1928 First translation into English of Pavlov's *Lectures on Conditioned Reflexes*.

Sándor Ferenczi edits *The Psychoanalysis of the War Neuroses* (*Zur Psychoanalyse der Kriegsneurosen*), which emphasizes trauma, repression, defense, and dream life in understanding shell shock.

Freud writes "Dostoyevsky and Parricide" as well as a foreword to a new German edition of *The Brothers Karamazov*.

Posthumous publication of a collection of poems by Emil Kraepelin, the leading psychiatric clinician of his time, under the title *Werden. Sein. Vergehen*.

Parisian Surrealists celebrate hysteria as "the greatest poetic invention of the nineteenth century."

T. S. Eliot reviews Freud's *The Future of an Illusion* in his journal *The Criterion*.

The Belgian Surrealist René Magritte paints *The False Mirror*.

D. H. Lawrence publishes *Lady Chatterley's Lover*.

Eisenstein directs *Ten Days That Shook the World* (*Oktyabr*).

Salvador Dalí and Luis Buñuel produce *An Andalusian Dog* (*Un chien andalou*), a classic film of early Surrealism.

Alexander Fleming observes the accidental growth of penicillin molds in his Cambridge laboratory, eventually leading to the mass production of this antibiotic substance.

First transatlantic television broadcast.

1929   Janet publishes *The Psychological Evolution of the Personality* (*L'Évolution psychologique de la personnalité*).

Appearance of Alfred Döblin's monumental novel *Berlin Alexanderplatz*. Set in the working-class district of Berlin where Döblin had worked as a doctor, the novel includes an episode of two young psychiatrists using psychoanalysis with a psychotic patient.

Klages publishes *Der Geist als Widersacher der Seele*, a three-volume critique of philosophic rationalism.

Thomas Mann wins the Nobel Prize for literature.

Erich Maria Remarque publishes his antiwar novel *All Quiet on the Western Front* (*Im Westen nichts Neues*). The book quickly becomes an international best-seller.

Completion of the art deco Chrysler Building in New York City. Design by William Van Alen.

Publication by the American literary critic Joseph Wood Krutch of *The Modern Temper*.

Founding of the Museum of Modern Art in New York City.

Collapse of the American stock market and onset of the Great Depression.

1929   William Faulkner writes *The Sound and the Fury* and *As I Lay Dying*, both
−30   of which employ multiple instances of stream of consciousness narration.

1930   The city of Frankfurt awards Freud the coveted Goethe Prize for literary and cultural achievement.

Freud publishes his late essay in cultural criticism, *Civilization and Its Discontents (Das Unbehagen in der Kultur)*.

Salvador Dalí enters his most Freudian phase, drawing heavily on sexual symbolism and ideas of the unconscious.

Ludwig Binswanger writes "Dream and Existence," marking a shift away from Bleuler and Freud and toward Existential analysis.

Robert Musil publishes the first volume of his masterwork *The Man without Qualities (Der Mann ohne Eigenschaften)*. The third, unfinished volume, posthumously published in 1943, includes two chapters sketching Musil's psychology of the emotions.

Marlene Dietrich stars in the German film classic *The Blue Angel (Der blaue Engel)*, based on a novel by Heinrich Mann.

Hopper's paintings include *Early Sunday Morning*.

1930–33   Mies van der Rohe directs the Bauhaus School.

1931   Jung writes his popular book *Modern Man in Search of a Soul (Seelenprobleme der Gegenwart)*.

Melanie Klein publishes *The Psychoanalysis of Children (Die Psychoanalyse des Kindes)*.

Dalí paints *The Persistence of Memory*.

Woolf writes *The Waves*, her most experimental novel, based on a series of stream-of-consciousness monologues.

Hermann Broch publishes his novel trilogy *The Sleepwalkers (Die Schlafwandler)*.

Publication for the first time of the Marquis de Sade's *120 Days of Sodom (Les 120 journées de Sodome)*.

The social philosopher and critic Max Horkheimer takes up the directorship of the Frankfurt Institute of Social Research.

Henry Ford produces his twenty millionth automobile.

1932   The German internist and neurologist Viktor von Weizsäcker publishes his classic in psychosomatic medicine, *Körpergeschehen und Neurose*.

Jung receives a prize for literature from the city of Zürich. He also writes a cultural and psychological analysis of Picasso paintings on exhibit in Zürich and publishes an essay about Joyce's *Ulysses*.

Freud reads Breton's *The Communicating Vessels (Les vases communicants)*, which discusses the Surrealist theory of dreams.

F. Scott Fitzgerald publishes *Tender Is the Night*, which draws extensively on his wife Zelda's psychiatric experiences.

Aldous Huxley's *Brave New World*.

The German painter Otto Dix completes his massive *War Triptych*.

The French dramatist and theoretician Antonin Artaud publishes
"Manifesto of the Theater of Cruelty," calling for liberation of the
unconscious from the constraints of bourgeois rationality.

Charles Sherrington and E. D. Adrian share the Nobel Prize in medicine
and physiology for their work on the functions of the neuron.

1933   The French-Polish psychiatrist Eugène Minkowski publishes *Lived Time*
(*Le temps vécu*), a collection of phenomenological case studies of the
subjective, mental experience of time in psychopathology.

Wilhelm Reich publishes *Character Analysis (Charakteranalyse)*.

Thomas Mann publishes "Freud's Position in the History of Modern
Thought" in Eliot's journal *The Criterion*.

The U.S. poet, novelist, and critic Conrad Aiken publishes *Great Circle*,
which is much influenced by psychoanalytic theory.

Stein writes her fictionalized autobiography as seen through the eyes of her
secretary-lover Alice B. Toklas.

Franklin Delano Roosevelt is elected president of the United States.

Adolf Hitler assumes power as chancellor of Germany.

1933   The American Imagist poet Hilda Doolittle—H.D.—undergoes psycho-
−34   analysis with Freud.

1934   Founding of the International Society for Medical Psychotherapy.

Jung writes "Archetypes of the Collective Unconscious."

Käthe Kollwitz publishes eight lithographs under the title *Death*.

Maud Bodkin publishes *Archetypal Patterns in Poetry*, an early work of
Jungian literary criticism.

1934–39 Jung teaches a yearly seminar on Nietzsche's *Thus Spake Zarathustra*.

1935   Jung lectures at the Tavistock Clinic in London on the elements of his analytic psychology.

W. H. Auden writes "Psychology and Art Today" in a popular arts magazine.

Introduction of the first sulfa drugs, forerunners of antibiotics.

1936   Anna Freud, youngest child of Sigmund Freud, publishes *The Ego and the
Mechanisms of Defense (Das Ich und die Abwehrmechanismen)*.

As a tribute to his eightieth birthday, Stefan Zweig and Thomas Mann present Freud with a commemorative address signed by 191 artists and writers. Mann also writes his essay "Freud and the Future."

Broch publishes "Remarks on Psychoanalysis from the Point of View of
Value Theory."

The Nazis burn Freud's and Hirschfeld's books, as well as those of other
sexologists, and seize the psychoanalytic press's warehouse in Leipzig.

Robert Musil writes "Oedipus Threatened," criticizing psychoanalytic psychology as arrogant and deterministic.

Eliot publishes his *Collected Poems*.

Frank Lloyd Wright builds the Kaufmann House, Fallingwater, a breathtaking example of Modernist residential architecture, in Bear Run, Pennsylvania.

The Nobel Prize in medicine and physiology goes to Henry Dale and Otto Loewi for their research on the chemical transmission of nerve impulses.

1936–39 The Spanish Civil War.

1937 Karen Horney completes *The Neurotic Personality of Our Time*.

Picasso paints *Guernica*, his depiction of the bombing and destruction of the Basque town of Guernica by German planes in the service of Spanish fascists. Exhibited in the Spanish Pavilion of the Paris World's Fair, the painting becomes a major icon of twentieth-century art and society.

In Munich the Nazi government stages *Degenerate Art* (*Entartete Kunst*), a notorious exhibition of 650 works of avant-garde art intended to mock and persecute German Modernist artists.

Walter Gropius joins the faculty of the Harvard School of Architecture.

Jean Renoir directs the acclaimed war film *Grand Illusion*.

1938 Jaspers publishes his *Philosophy of Existence* (*Existenzphilosophie*).

The French philosopher of science Gaston Bachelard writes *The Psychoanalysis of Fire* (*La psychanalyse du feu*).

Stefan Zweig brings Dalí to visit Freud.

Freud flees Nazi-occupied Vienna for Paris and then London.

1939 Freud dies in Hampstead, England.

W. H. Auden writes "In Memory of Sigmund Freud."

1940 Adolf Hitler, the most destructive psychopath of twentieth-century Europe, invades Poland. Beginning of World War II.

PART I

Cultures of Hysteria

CHAPTER 1

Discourses of Hysteria in Fin-de-Siècle France

MARK S. MICALE

Scholars have generally cast what is called the history of hysteria in terms of medicine and science. They have tended to view the subject as the story of a literal disease entity that over the centuries generated a wealth of theoretical and therapeutic responses from physicians that were recorded in specialized medical texts. During certain periods and in certain cultures, however, hysteria has been not only a subject of clinical investigation among medical elites, but also a powerful, vibrant presence in the popular and cultural imagination. At these times hysteria has appeared in scientific texts, but also and simultaneously as an icon in the visual arts, a trope in novels and poems, a philosophical category, and a point of reference in social and cultural commentary.

What interests me in the pages below is the nature and extent of these different but contemporaneous discourses on hysteria. What causes an independent metaphorical history of disease to develop at particular times? Why has the medical idea of hysteria become culturally available in certain places and at certain historical moments, such as Enlightenment France and Britain, turn-of-the-century Paris and Vienna, and late twentieth-century America? What functions has the hysteria concept served in these nonmedical settings? And, perhaps most to the point of this volume, what is the historical and theoretical relation between these two contemporaneous textual traditions — that is, between hysteria as figure or metaphor in extrascientific texts and the nonmetaphorical, medical-historical study of the disorder?

This chapter explores these questions in four parts. In the first part, I sketch the descriptive history of hysteria in the creative arts during the fin-de-siècle period. In the second section, I narrate the metaphorical history of the concept in the social and political domain during this same period.[1] Against this backdrop, I examine in the third part some of the patterns emerging from this story and their implications for studying the past interaction of psychology and culture. Finally, in the fourth section, I analyze the social and political reasons for the formation of a "culture of hysteria" a century ago and speculate on the "metacultural" relation of hysteria discourses to the emerging Modernist movement. Throughout, I focus on the exceptionally rich French historical experience.

Strikingly, the founding years of European Modernism correspond to the "heroic period" of French hysteria.[2] During the 1870s, 1880s, and 1890s in particular, hysteria was at once an object of scientific investigation and of aesthetic contemplation. Beginning in the early 1870s, Émile Zola, in his epic cycle of novels of French national decline, the twenty-volume Rougon-Macquart series, traced the spread of the so-called nervous pathologies through six generations of two French families.[3] In Zola's dynasty of degeneration, the original neurological defect, or *tare nerveuse*, comes from Tante Dide, the progenitor of both the Rougon and Macquart lines, who suffered from semi-imbecility and attacks of nerves and convulsions. Zola, who was conversant with the writings of mid-century French psychiatrists, describes Tante's *crises* alternately as hysterical, epileptic, and cataleptic. In the greatest literary undertaking in France of the early Third Republic, which maintained a national readership for more than two decades, hysteria operates as one of two primal pathologies that generates a range of social pathologies, including alcoholism, prostitution, sexual perversion, criminality, and suicide.[4]

A decade later, in the writings of J. K. Huysmans, the hysteria concept adapted to changing cultural times. With Huysmans, the naturalistic degenerationism of Zola gave way to a highly self-conscious cult of sensual and aesthetic decadence. Huysmans's characters are men and women of the arts and aristocracy who morbidly pursue their tainted heredities as sources of social eccentricity and sensory gratification.[5] Huysmans's A Rebours (Against Nature) of 1894 provided the literary manifesto for the late nineteenth-century cult of decadence. The story of the debauched anti-hero Des Esseintes—the leading male hysteric of fin-de-siècle French literature—spawned an entire literary subgenre of its own.

A cast of what might be called aspiring, borderline hysterics, in whom nervous degeneration accompanies a morbid quest for sexual and aesthetic intensities, people the pages of French fiction during the final decade and a half of the century. In Huysmans's novel, we read that Des Esseintes craves artistic novelties, including "a few suggestive books . . . to shake up his nervous system with erudite hysterias." And from the musical world he seeks new harmonies that will leave him "choked by the suffocating *boule* of hysteria." The cultural historian Debora Silverman has discovered that Huysmans drew directly on two medical texts—the *Traité des névroses* of Alexandre Axenfeld and Henri Huchard and Camille Bouchut's *Nouveaux éléments de pathologie générale*, as guides to the depiction of Des Esseintes's nervous accidents.[6] These literary-medical linkages were not lost on readers at the time. In a review of *A Rebours* in 1887, the critic Barbey d'Aurevilly lamented the main character of the novel: "The hero of Monsieur Huysmans . . . is sick, like all the heroes of the novel of this sick era. . . . He is prey to the neurosis of the age—la névrose du siècle," intoned Barbey d'Aurevilly. "He is from the *Hôpital Charcot*."[7]

As Jacqueline Carroy shows elsewhere in this volume, Charles Richet provided other examples of "l'hysterie littéraire" in late nineteenth-century France. Best known today as a psychologist, physiologist, and collateral member of the Salpêtrière circle, Richet first aroused in Charcot an interest in hypnosis. He subsequently won the Nobel Prize in physiology and medicine for his research on the concept of anaphylaxis. However, Richet also wrote poetry and novels under the pen name Charles Epheyre. Among his many novels, *Possession* of 1887 and *Soeur Marthe* 1889, written at the peak of the Nancy/Salpêtrière controversy over the nature of hypnosis, interweave the themes of love, hysteria, hypnotism, and somnambulism.[8]

A generation later, in 1906, a disciple of Zola's, Henri Céard, published his own "roman à l'hysterie," titled *Terrains à vendre au bord de la mer*. Céard's book relates the story of an entire province in Brittany in which the inhabitants, due to chronic drunkenness and consanguineous marriage, succumb to "hereditary hysteria." The novel was intended as a critique of the Zolan notion that the source of regeneration for the French people was interbreeding with healthy peasant stock and as a literary rendition of a text by a Breton physician that appeared earlier that year, Dr. Firmin Terrien's *Hystérie et neurasthénie chez les paysans*.[9]

Yet another pertinent work from this period that extended the metaphorization of hysteria into new areas is Augustin Galopin's *Les hystériques des couvents, des églises, des temples, des théâtres, des synagogues et de l'amour* of 1886.[10] Galopin's is a weird and whimsical book that recounts in farcical terms the story of an outbreak of hysteria in the imaginary Convent of the Repentant Women in northeastern France while also presenting the author's rambling but pungent observations about hysteria as it currently gripped the big cities. The fifteenth chapter of the work details the different categories of "love hysteria," including "l'hystérique érotique," "l'hystérique de jalousie," "l'hystérique tendre," "l'hystérique ovarienne," and "l'hystérique de l'envie."

A decade later, Galopin's book was surpassed by Armand Dubarry's series *Les déséquilibrés de l'amour*, which combined the literary representation of hysteria with the emergent medical sexology of the late nineteenth century. Each novel of the series, a kind of lowbrow blend of Zola and Krafft-Ebing, explores unblushingly some perceived excess or perversion of emotional and sexual life in contemporary French society. Eleven volumes of Dubarry's series, including books on sadism, incest, fetishism, flagellation, and her-maphroditism, titillated Francophone readers. The fourth novel in the set was titled *Hystérique*. In it, Dubarry presents the hysteric as a universal character type. He interprets the disease as a variant of "erotic insanity" and a manifestation of female degeneracy. After a series of increasingly tragic *chagrins d'amours*, and a final fall into craven nymphomania, each character in the novel ends up either dying of disease, being committed to an asylum, or killing himself or herself. By 1900, Dubarry's set had gone through more than twenty printings. The popularity of the books suggests that by the close of the century, the language of hysteria had become a generic terminology for the vagaries of human sexual and emotional life.

As the remark of Barbey d'Aurevilly indicates, cultural discourses on hysteria during the belle époque drew inspiration not only from earlier literary texts (Rousseau, Flaubert, Baudelaire), but also from the famous hysteria physician Jean-Martin Charcot. To a degree surpassed by no other figure in the history of the disease, Charcot inspired paintings, novels, and plays as well as extensive commentary in the popular press.

The best-known visual representation of the fin-de-siècle hysteric is Andre Brouillet's "Une leçon clinique à la Salpêtrière." Brouillet was an established painter who specialized in epic historical, military, and scientific scenes. His painting hung in the Paris Salon of 1887, where it was viewed by *le tout Paris*. Brouillet's canvas portrays Charcot as the great *maitre d'école*, professing to a serious and attentive gathering of medical students, while a hysterical female patient faints dramatically and voluptuously into the arms of a medical resident. Artistically rather undistinguished, the painting is remarkable for its dimensions, the figures being nearly life size; Brouillet obviously deemed hysteria a suitable subject for monumental presentation. Contemporary reviews of the canvas reveal that the painting rapidly became a familiar popular icon and was reproduced endlessly in black-and-white etchings, one of which famously hung on the wall of Freud's consulting room in Vienna.[11]

Novelistic representations of Charcot-style hysteria were also common in France during the closing decades of the nineteenth century. Charcot personally was closely acquainted with many figures in the Parisian literary world who were as likely to appear at his formal hospital lectures as in his celebrated Tuesday soirées. French literary intellectuals seem simultaneously to have been attracted to and repelled by Charcot, often using their novels as a means to settle personal and professional disputes with the great man.

Jules Claretie's *Les amours d'un interne*, published in 1881, relates the story of the young Salpêtrière intern Vilandry and his secret nocturnal *liaisons amoureuses* with hysterical patients in the wards of the hospital.[12] Along the same lines, in 1894, a year after Charcot's death, Léon Daudet (son of the novelist Alphonse Daudet, a former medical student, and later cofounder of the right-wing royalist Catholic organization Action française) published *Les morticoles*.[13] Daudet's novel conjures up a kind of medical anti-utopia in which authoritarian physician-scientists rule over an oppressed patient-citizenry. Daudet provides acidulous caricatures of the senior medical personnel on the Paris Faculty, including Dr. Foutange (Charcot), described as "the doctor of hysterics and somnambulists" who demonstrates on the patient "Rosalie" in a domed amphitheater of the "Hôpital Typhus." Daudet's book became a national best-seller.[14]

Other works of fin-de-siècle fiction drew less on the personal image of Charcot and his hospital than on individual aspects of his teachings. In an essay appearing in 1987, Emily Apter studied the past figural representation of a single hysterical symptom.[15] Specifically, Apter examines Charcot's clinical writings on hysterical disorders of vision, including hysterical scotomas, or visual defects in which perception is absent or impaired in an isolated area of the visual field. She then reconstructed the history of a medical symptom as cultural symbol. In one nonmedical field after another in the late nineteenth century, Apter finds, the idea of hysterical blind spots functioned metaphorically as a way of describing dulled or disordered or destroyed perception in the social, moral, and aesthetic worlds. She tracks these usages through a remarkable diversity of French sources, including colonialist propaganda, anti-Semitic posters, literary presentations of the Dreyfus trial, and art criticism of the Impressionists. Apter focuses on the novel *Le Jardin des supplices* (1889), published by one of the leading younger naturalist writers, Octave Mirbeau. Mirbeau's novel concocts a fantastical botanical allegory in which a Chinese torture garden doubles as both an erotic floral paradise, modeled on Monet's Giverny, and a medical microcosm along the lines of the Salpêtrière. At the center of the story is a detailed description, with almost textbook fidelity, of a hysterical attack *à la Charcot*.[16]

Nor was Charcot the only medical figure to inspire literary intellectuals during this period. Henri Ellenberger has brought to notice Marcel Prévost's *L' automne d'une femme*, published in 1893.[17] Prévost's novel, too, is set at the Salpêtrière. It tells the story of one Dr. Daumier, a gifted young physician who conducts long and sensitive psychological analyses with several neurotic patients beset by depression, lovesickness, and various hysterical stigmata. Ellenberger believes that Daumier is a portrait of the psychologist and philosopher Pierre Janet, then at the outset of his career. Prévost was one of the major originators of the Modernist "psychological novel" in France, and, artistically speaking, *L'automne d'une femme* is arguably the finest *roman à l'hystérie* of its generation.[18] During the centennial celebrations of Charcot's birth in 1925, the minister of public instruction cited more than a dozen authors, including Zola, the Goncourts, Maupassant, Huysmans, Mirbeau, Bourget, and Proust, who were indebted to Charcot. With a quarter century's perspective, he proposed, it was clear that Charcot's teachings had inspired an entire generation of "littérateurs-psychiatres" who ushered in a new, more psychologically oriented literary sensibility.[19]

Hysteria proved more adaptable to the theater than any other art. The late nineteenth century witnessed a flowering of European drama, and numerous stage actresses achieved fame portraying many memorable female characters. The hysterical heroine flourished, and it is easy to see why: the theater is a public and highly performative artistic medium, and hysteria is the most extroverted of psychopathologies, its own act and audience. In the contemporary popular press, an analogy was commonly drawn between the amphitheater of the Salpêtrière and the theater stage. In his weekly demonstrations, Charcot hypnotically induced localized hysterical symptoms that were then literally "acted out" by patients before an audience, and Charcot's pedagogical technique, employing posters, photographs, and illuminated projections, was based on a kind of theatricalization of symptoms. It was not inappropriate, then, that a decade after its appearance in book form Richet's novel *Soeur Marthe* was rewritten and performed in Paris as a lyrical drama. Similarly, when in 1884 Sarah Bernhardt, the most celebrated stage actress of her age, wished to perfect a performance of an attack of hysterical insanity in the play *Adrienne Lecouvreur*, she repaired for practice to a cell in the *quartiers des aliénées* at the Salpêtrière.[20]

One of the most entertaining sources in the French theatrical history of hysteria is "Une leçon à la Salpêtrière," a two-act play written by André de Lorde and performed in the spring of 1908 at the Théâtre du Grand-Guignol in Paris.[21] The play is a mishmash of ideas and images from Brouillet's canvas, Claretie's *Les amours d'un interne*, and Daudet's *Les morticoles*. Again, viewers get a pastiche of the bygone medical world of Paris with fictionalized caricatures—Professor Marbois as Charcot, Suzanne as Blanche Wittmann, and a coterie of obsequious medical students—situated in an amphitheater.[22] Lorde, the son of a physician, dedicated the piece to the respected Sorbonne psychologist Alfred Binet. Plainly, hysteria occupied a prominent place in the cultural imagination of turn-of-the-century France.

Hysteria's pervasiveness during the fin de siècle was by no means confined to the world of the arts. During the late nineteenth century, the disorder also furnished a set of popular and highly serviceable images to many areas of cultural, social, and political commentary. Use of the hysteria concept in these contexts was caught up with the larger phenomenon of "medicalization," the process by which medical assumptions, practices, values, and vocabularies penetrate traditional, prescientific attitudes, institutions, and practices. In late nineteenth-century Europe, medicalization was proceeding apace and included among its facets the application of descriptive disease imagery to the social and political world. The use of the language of nervous and mental pathology in particular became a common feature of French public discourse between 1870 and 1914.

Consider Max Nordau, whose best-selling *Entartung*, or *Degeneration*, influentially combined the hysteria and degeneration paradigms of the later nineteenth century.[23] By birth a Hungarian Jew, Nordau received a medical degree in Germany, and for most of his adulthood practiced medicine in Paris. In addition, he found time to write voluminously as a cultural critic and medical journalist. Nordau's book appeared in German in 1892–93 and was translated with fanfare into French the following year.

The framework of Nordau's *Dégénérescense* is explicitly medical. The long opening section presents a chapter-by-chapter presentation of the "symptoms," "diagnosis," and "etiology" of Europe's current cultural malaise, while the concluding section offers disquisitions on "prognosis" and "therapeutics." Throughout the work, Nordau's main diagnostic categories are hysteria and degeneration, which run in close, if wholly confused, relation to one another. Nordau takes as established fact "the enormous increase of hysteria in our time" as well as the correspondence between individual hysteria and the features of fin-de-siècle European society as a whole.[24]

References to the publications of French physicians, including Charcot, Richer, Binet, Axenfeld, Huchard, and Gilles de la Tourette, litter the bottom of his pages.

Nordau's book is essentially an extended anti-Modernist diatribe in which hysteria serves as the metaphor of choice for cultural innovation and experimentation of all sorts. Artists as diverse as Ibsen, Zola, Wilde, Tolstoy, and Nietzsche and movements such as Pre-Raphaelitism, Naturalism, Impressionism, and Symbolism receive the author's disapprobation. Nordau uses the term "hysteric" to describe the artists themselves, the works they produce, and the cultural styles they manifest.

The medical literalness of Nordau's analyses is bracing. In one passage the author discusses the latest medical literature on hysterical amblyopia (dullness of vision) and dyschromatopsia (distorted color perception) and applies it directly to the Impressionist art of the day. Artists in this camp, Nordau declares flatly, are "hysterical painters." They misperceive color, and their vision breaks up from an integrated field into isolated spots over the retina. How else to explain "the whitewash of a Puvis de Chavannes," "the screaming yellow, blue, and red of a Besnard," and "the violet pictures of Manet and his school." The canvases of avant-garde artists, Nordau adds, become "at once intelligible to us if we keep in view the researches of the Charcot school into the visual derangements in degeneration and hysteria."[25] Nordau was no less excoriating toward literary Modernism. Huysmans, he charged, was "the classical type of the hysterical mind without originality who is the predestined victim of every suggestion."[26] Despite its hyperbole, Nordau's *Degeneration* was one of the most widely read pieces of cultural criticism in western and central Europe during the late nineteenth and early twentieth centuries.

Hysteria also made its way during these years into French political and historical criticism. Since the late eighteenth century, French asylum doctors had commented upon catastrophic political events as potential causes of mental disturbance. Beginning in the 1870s, this line of reasoning was reversed, and a descriptive psychopathology of the right emerged in which violent group political activity was interpreted as the manifestation of a prior latent state of mental or nervous instability. This new counterrevolutionary historiography focused on the French Revolution of the 1790s and the Paris Commune of 1871. Most notably, in his monumental account of modern French history, Hippolyte Taine trotted out the vocabulary of "collective madness," "group hysteria," "mass suicide," and "political paroxysm" to describe the actions of the *sans culottes* and the events of the Revolutionary

Terror.[27] Taine conceptualized the history of the French nation as a study in the social and political psychology of a people, a kind of pre-Freudian psychohistory.[28] Like Zola's Rougon-Macquart series in the literary sphere, Taine's *Les origins de la France contemporaine* was the most popular and ambitious historical project of its age.[29]

In a parallel development, the nightmare of *l'année terrible* of 1870–71 had barely passed before conservative political critics formulated a theory of "morbid psychology" to account for the gruesome events. Some authors specifically presented their political critiques as applications of contemporary medico-psychological theories.[30] In 1882, the writer Guy de Maupassant characterized the Commune as "pas autre chose qu'une crise d'hystérie de Paris" (nothing else than Paris having an attack of hysteria).[31]

A second wave of historical writing in this genre appeared around the turn of the century. Spurred by the Dreyfus Affair, this work fused reactionary political conservatism with contemporary ideas about hysteria, hypnosis, and group psychology. The most conspicuous author in this camp was Lucien Nass. A practicing physician, Nass was struck by the periodicity of political upheavals in France during the preceding one hundred years. With this pattern in mind, Nass developed a theory of the "national revolutionary neurosis."[32] According to Nass's scheme, the sorry sequence of events in 1789, 1792, 1830, 1834, 1848, and 1871 represented the political spasms of an incipiently and inherently hysterical people who, like epileptic or hysterical patients, were prone to convulsions at regular intervals. To Nass's thinking, not only individuals but also collectivities—Paris, the working classes, the French nation—could suffer from bad hereditary characteristics and, with the appropriate agents provocateurs, could lapse into violent attacks of hysteria.

I have found textual instances from the 1880s and 1890s in which the hysteria label has been applied to the outpouring of emotion during the public funeral of Victor Hugo in the spring of 1885, idolatrous demonstrations among royalists and army officers in support of General Boulanger in 1889, reactions to the stabbing death in 1894 of the president of the Republic Sadi Carnot, right-wing newspaper attacks on Alfred Dreyfus, and xenophobic outbursts against the Germans during the Fashoda incident of 1898.[33] Hysteria also figured metaphorically in the emergent social sciences, including social psychology and criminology, of the fin de siècle. The concept of crowd psychology was a disciplinary novelty of late nineteenth-century France and Italy.[34] The most influential of these publications were a trio of texts written by Gustave Le Bon in the five years following Charcot's death:

La psychologie des peuples (1894), *La psychologie des foules* (1895), and *La psychologie de socialisme* (1898). Like Nordau and Nass, Le Bon was trained medically but made his career in social commentary. While a young man, he worked as a military doctor during the Paris Commune revolt, an experience that affected him deeply. Le Bon was strongly nationalistic, fearful of the new social egalitarianism, and rabidly antisocialist. He was also highly impressed by recent scientific research on animal magnetism, somnambulism, hysteria, and hypnosis.

In "The Mind of Crowds," the opening section of *La psychologie des foules*, Le Bon asserts that collectivities lose the faculties of will and ratiocination possessed by individuals. The mental mechanism operating between the crowd and its demagogic leader, he reasoned, has been elucidated by the latest medical research. He likens the excitability of crowds to a spreading disease infection, to electrical and magnetic radiation, and to outbursts of hysteria and somnambulism. He characterizes modern mass political activities as epidemic contagions and mental illnesses. And he claims that the psychological features of the individual in the crowd are those of the constitutional hysteric: immorality, impulsiveness, susceptibility to suggestion, and emotional excitability. Le Bon drew the building blocks of his psychology from Lamarck's evolutionary biology, Charcot's theory of hysterical pathology, and Hippolyte Bernheim's ideas about hypnotic suggestion. He was personal friends with Richet, and he attended Charcot's lectures.[35]

The fledgling field of criminology was yet another discipline that appropriated the fin-de-siècle idea of hysteria. The self-appointed expert in this field was Cesare Lombroso, whose *Criminal Man* appeared in the original Italian in 1893. The book was hugely influential in France. In *Criminal Man*, Lombroso attempted to found the discipline of criminal anthropology, which studied the physical and mental typologies of criminality.[36] For his new science, Lombroso, too, drew on the most up-to-date medical ideas, images, and terminologies. In his elaborate characterology of criminality there appears the ludicrous category of "the hysterical criminal."[37] In Lombrosian criminal anthropology, the hysterical criminal, invariably female, was willful, deceitful, egotistical, and often sexually promiscuous. Moreover, she combined an illegal act of some sort with social and sexual insubordination, especially in her relations with male authority figures, such as employers, doctors, or policemen. In Lombroso's mind, the most common crimes involving hysteria were theft and slander, but the disorder could also accompany arson, assault, false accusation, infanticide, and murder.

In Le Bon's crowd psychology and Lombroso's criminal anthropology, hysteria was deployed to characterize and control groups deemed threatening to the bourgeois professional classes. Ruth Harris, however, has demonstrated how subtle and complicated the social and legal applications of the diagnosis could be at this time.[38] Harris has discovered that between 1880 and 1910 hundreds of women were brought to trial in the Paris Cour d'assises for committing violent crimes against their husbands and lovers and that the diagnosis of hysteria played a key part in the court proceedings. These cases, she finds, were strikingly stylized. Defendants, typically middle- or lower-middle-class women, had been abandoned by their fiancés, left pregnant and unprotected by lovers, or subjected to infidelities by their husbands. Desperate pleadings, love letters, and suicidal threats had proven ineffective, and so, frustrated by official social and legal channels, these women acted. Most commonly, the *criminelle passionnelle* sought out her victim/lover in public—in a café, for example, or on the street—and then threw vitriol in his face or shot at him with a pocket revolver. In a majority of cases, the men survived unscathed or suffered only superficial wounds. After the deed, the perpetrators were usually horrified by the violence of their actions and oftentimes gave themselves up to the police. In almost every case, they were acquitted.

Plumbing the pretrial judicial dossiers compiled by the magistrates and physicians who interviewed these women, Harris finds that the hysteria diagnosis appears routinely. A few defendants experienced sensory stigmata or minor hysterical fits, but by and large the conception of the disorder was behavioral. In the French forensic context, hysteria was a medical metaphor for willfulness, erratic behavior, and a lack of emotional self-control. Harris speculates further that *crimes passionnelles* became "accepted" forms of female criminality in the late nineteenth century because they involved prescribed gender roles. According to the judicial mentality of the time, these crimes merely carried normal female behavior to an unacceptable extreme. Constitutionally volatile, women were unable to control their emotions and lashed out in this childish manner when their matrimonial and sexual lives were threatened. As a result, the courts responded protectively, while the press reacted with sympathetic sensationalism. Harris also implies that there was an unspoken collusion between all the parties involved. The ritualized crime of passion was a means for male professionals to administer justice, for bourgeois women to maneuver through patriarchal society, and for the two sexes to negotiate tensions.[39]

A related attempt at maintaining the sexual status quo during these years appeared in the first generation of writings directed against the women's movement. Daniel Lesueur's novel *Névrosée*, published in 1884, is an antifeminist yarn with a hysterical heroine.[40] *Névrosée* is a latter-day version of Flaubert's *Madame Bovary* that is set, somewhat improbably, in the world of Parisian academe. Maxime Dulaure is a brilliant professor at the Collège de France, and Étiennette an exceptionally intelligent young women who at the age of eighteen advances to the study of the biological sciences. A notorious misogynist, Dulaure nonetheless falls in love with Étiennette, who, unlike the other masculine Amazonian women attending his lectures, is slight, blond, and beautiful. Maxime and Étiennette court and marry, and the union is hailed by the Parisian intellectual community. However, things begin to go awry almost immediately. Étiennette gets pregnant, but she soon becomes frail, sickens, and miscarries. Later, depressed and bored by her life with Maxime, she is increasingly thrilled by the idea of an extramarital affair. She devours questionable literature and eventually gives herself over to a lecherous cousin. (In one scene, Maxime discovers his wife reading *Autour de l'adultère: Psychologie d'une névrosée* and then lectures her about the treatment of sex-obsessed, novel-reading women at the Salpêtrière hospital.)[41] In the end, desperate at having destroyed her marriage, Étiennette swallows an overdose of morphine and drifts melodramatically to an early death. For its compression of contemporary cultural anxieties into one text, *Névrosée* is unsurpassed. In Lesueur's novel we find hysteria linked to the national preoccupations with depopulation, sin, suicide, sexual perversion, and the new idea of the *femme savante*. The interest of the book heightens when we learn that Lesueur was a nom de plume of Madame Jeanne Loiseau Lapauze, a popular novelist and playwright who in 1910 was the first women to be awarded the Légion d'honneur for literature.

During the later nineteenth century, the hysteria diagnosis also made its way into French medical commentaries on specialized sociological problems. The overwhelming majority of cases of hysteria published in France during these years were set in the modern metropolis. Paris in particular was the usual mise-en-scène, conveying the idea that the pathology was a kind of natural outgrowth of the noxious urban environment. A choice document on this score is Henri Legrand du Saulle's *Les hystériques* (1883).[42]

Legrand du Saulle was trained at the Salpêtrière during the 1850s and began his career in the 1860s as a degeneration theorist. During the 1870s and 1880s, he worked as senior admitting psychiatrist at the Central Police Prefecture of Paris. Every criminal case brought into city police headquarters, day or night, that was suspected of psychiatric complications passed under his scrutiny. Legrand du Saulle was an important and powerful man, the official interface between the French psychiatric profession and daily Parisian street life.

The most heavily prescriptive commentary about hysteria from the later nineteenth century comes from French and German legal psychiatry. Legrand de Saulle's four-hundred-page *Les hystériques* offers a compendium of urban criminality, including thefts, slanders, arsons, poisonings, abductions, infanticide, sexual crimes, and murders.[43] All of these, Legrand du Saulle argues, reveal an underlying hysterical neuropathology. Although the purely medical aspects of hysteria were currently being studied exhaustively, Legrand du Saulle comments, "the medico-legal study of hysteria" remained to explore. He urges his colleagues to study the disease sociologically, in its "thousand relations with civic life." Furthermore, based on his unique institutional placement, he estimated that at present there were "around 50,000" hysterics in Paris, including 10,000 suffering from convulsions.[44]

Finally, hysteria during these years merged with what were regarded as the most destructive and deadly of social and medical pathologies. Syphilis became a grave threat in many European cities during the late nineteenth and early twentieth centuries. Since syphilis and hysteria were both then regarded as neurodegenerative in nature, neurologists, psychiatrists, and venereologists pondered the possible causal links between the two diseases.[45] Did syphilitic infections provoke hysterical attacks? Was hysteria an incipient form of venereal disease? Or was syphilis the result of hysterically promiscuous behavior? One physician warned of a new and virulent hybrid pathology, "hystero-syphilis."[46] The hysteria diagnosis was associated similarly with alcoholism.[47] Along these same lines, the conservative medical press of the late nineteenth century posited connections between hysteria, degeneration, and prostitution.[48] Lombroso, for instance, reviewing the data in Legrand du Saulle's book, calculated that 12 percent of the hysterical female population of Paris were prostitutes.[49] And Alain Corbin, Charles Bernheimer, and Jann Matlock have found that the image of "the hysterical prostitute," often afflicted simultaneously with syphilis or alcoholism, appeared recurrently in French novels and short stories of the second half of the century.[50]

The cumulative impression from this summary of sources is that hysteria was nearly ubiquitous in French culture and society a century ago. To contemporaries, the impression was not far off the mark. In 1880, Richet observed that "as for mild hysteria—hystérie légère—one finds it everywhere," and two years later, a bemused Guy de Maupassant confirmed that "we are all hysterics."[51] The clearest statement, however, came from the journalist Jules de Claretie, who, in addition to his novel writing, published popular yearly chronicles of social and cultural life in the French capital. In March 1881, Claretie devoted half a chapter to his favorite disease:

The illness of our age is hysteria. One encounters it everywhere. Everywhere one rubs elbows with it. . . . Studying hysteria, Monsieur Lassegue [sic], the illustrious master, and Monsieur Charcot have put their finger on the wound of the day. It is not only enclosed within the gray walls of the Salpêtrière; this singular neurosis with its stupefying effects, it travels the streets and the world.

Reflecting at the close of his chapter on his Parisian contemporaries, with their extravagant, feverish, and self-absorbed lives, Claretie proclaimed "Hystériques! hystériques! tous hystériques!" (Hysterics, hysterics, all hysterics!).[52]

Many features of these passages could be commented upon. I want now to take up several points about the metaphorics of hysteria in fin-de-siècle French culture that bear directly on the themes of this volume. Most obviously, there is the almost endless extension of the arena of application of the hysteria concept a century ago. From its origins in medicine, hysteria—as word, image, theory, and diagnosis—penetrated one cultural area after another, including fiction, poetry, dramaturgy, historical writing, social and political criticism, sociology, criminology, and anthropology. Indeed, during the height of the French fascination with the subject in the late 1880s and early 1890s, there seems scarcely to have been an area of social and cultural activity that was not at one time or another described as hysterical.

The sheer accumulation of meanings of hysteria a hundred years ago is extraordinary. In France during the late nineteenth century, hysteria was employed as a metaphor for: artistic experimentation, collective political violence, radical social reformism, and foreign nationalism. It became shorthand for the irrational, the will-less, the uncontrollable, the convulsive, the erratic, the erotic, the ecstatic, the female, the criminal, and a host of collective "Others." It was a synonym for everything that seemed excessive, or extreme, or incomprehensible about the age.

In the arts, where its great expressive potential was recognized clearly from mid-century onward, establishment and avant-garde writers alike exploited the hysteria concept. It was integrated into Realist, Naturalist, Decadent, and Symbolist aesthetics. And it was used by writers across the political spectrum. In sociologically oriented narratives, it was applied equally to the individual body and collectivities, and up and down the social scale. It was used to signify women, socialists, workers, alcoholics, prostitutes, syphilitics, crowds, *les classes dangereuses*, city life, the French people. It served sometimes as a primary pathology, at other times as a complicating secondary reaction, a behavioral gloss, or a rhetoric. On the eve of the origins of psychoanalysis, hysteria was as likely to appear in novels, plays, social science textbooks, and newspaper editorials as at the bedside, in the medical lecture hall, or in the physician's study, and with a multifarious spectrum of meanings.

Another notable feature of hysteria's cultural history a hundred years ago is the striking degree of interconnectedness between different authors and texts. In 1894, Nordau, a physician who wrote cultural criticism, lavishly dedicated his book, *Degeneration*, to the criminal anthropologist Lombroso. Lombroso in return dedicated *Le crime: causes et remèdes* of 1899 to Nordau. Richet, scientist and Salpêtrian, wrote novels about hysteria and nymphomania and penned the preface to the French edition of Lombroso's *L'homme de génie*. Claretie, the cultural journalist, also wrote a six-volume history of the 1871 Paris Commune, attended Charcot's lectures, authored *Les amours d'un interne*, and directed the Théâtre français. And Brouillet's canvas of the School of the Salpêtrière pictures two novelists (Claretie and Paul Arène), a politician (Alfred Naquet), and an Impressionist art critic (Philippe Burty).

The above survey of sources suggests, furthermore, the need to rethink the dynamics of the relation between the scientific and cultural discourses of hysteria. In the sciences and humanities today, we are in the habit of projecting the direction of influence between these two domains in one direction only. It is typically assumed that, at least since the seventeenth century, ideas have originated in the realm of the sciences and then spread out concentrically to various nonscientific arenas. In this view, cultural sources are seen as applications or misapplications of concepts and terminologies that originated in the worlds of medicine and science.

In the present case, however, such a unidirectional model of influence is glaringly insufficient. It is inaccurate to write separate, isolated historical accounts—one medical-scientific, the other cultural-popular—of hysteria in late nineteenth-century France. The chronology of texts cited above, as well as the multiple professional activities and identities of many of their authors, indicates that, at least in nineteenth-century France, novels, plays, and works of criticism did not simply and secondarily voice a language of pathology created elsewhere. Rather, doctors were as influenced by literary representations and popular stereotypes as novelists, painters, and social theorists were knowledgeable about the findings of medical science. The standard distinction between scientific and fictional texts dissolves, and the traditional division between professional theory, enlightened lay opinion, and popular belief is untenable. The imaginative worlds of physicians, novelists, poets, painters, historians, and social and cultural critics continually interpenetrated. Ultimately, I think, it is more accurate and interesting to conceptualize hysteria's history as a set of discourses that alternately converge and diverge over time. France in the late nineteenth century was clearly a period of dramatic cultural convergence. During these decades, medical, literary, theatrical, visual, and religious theories and images of the disorder became inextricably caught up with one another. In Paris in particular, this crisscross of ideas, information, and associations formed a single, integrated sociocultural milieu from which all authors could draw in the formation of a common "culture of hysteria," a culture that contributed powerfully to the formation of early Modernist thought and culture.

The major remaining question, of course, is why? Why did medicine, psychology, and culture coalesce around hysteria in France during the penultimate decades of the nineteenth century? I believe that two historical contexts—one social and political, the other broadly cultural—are key to answering these questions.

First, hysteria's belle époque, and the birth years of European Modernism, occurred at a distinctive and difficult moment in French history. The concept of the belle époque is a postbellum idealization, a retrospective creation that emerged only after World War One. In reality, the early Third Republic was a period of rapid social, economic, and political modernization during which France underwent sudden and profound internal changes associated with the processes of industrialization, urbanization, and democratization.[53] In the final third of the century, the rural and artisanal economy of France finally began to give way to a more industrially and technologically based society. The explosive growth of cities brought to urban areas a host of new and newly visible social problems. The concentration of workers in the cities led to organized socialist and syndicalist movements; growing and raucous left-wing political parties organized the first workers' strikes. New social problems arose and old problems were magnified in the cities, which concentrated seemingly menacing subpopulations in one place for observation and analysis. A large and alarmist literature indicates that in the eyes of many contemporaries crime, alcoholism, prostitution, homosexuality, tuberculosis, and venereal disease were proliferating dangerously and uncontrollably. In Paris, an active and voluble feminist movement, led by Hubertine Auclert, made its first legislative gains in the late 1870s and early 1880s, providing a sharp challenge to middle-class professional males. Violent anarchist acts terrorized politicians and the public.[54] All the while, the world of the cultural arts was being convulsed by a dizzying succession of new aesthetic movements and theories—Impressionism, Postimpressionism, Fauvism, Pointillism, Symbolism, Primitivism, Cubism—that rejected age-old aesthetic theories and practices. In sum, the twentieth-century Western world—open, mass, secular, heterogeneous, economically dynamic, socially egalitarian, and culturally experimental—was coming into being.[55] Many French people a century ago found these transformations to be startling, incomprehensible, and enormously anxiety producing.

These social and political dislocations were accompanied by changes in popular mentalities. Among the educated middle classes, older religious mental habits were decisively on the decline. With the advent of the Republic in 1870, the waning of superstitious and religious worldviews was accelerated by the new republican government. The secularization of French thought and society greatly enhanced the intellectual prestige of medicine and science in this self-consciously positivist and progressivist period. The popular medical press burgeoned, and readers increasingly conceptualized social life in terms of health, sickness, and disease.[56] The expansion of knowledge concerning the structure and function of the central nervous system led to the rapid growth of the mental sciences and the emergence of neurology as a clinical specialty. Correspondingly, new academic "sciences of society," such as sociology and anthropology, which sought to study society as a natural organism with its own laws of operation, were appearing. By the turn of the century, these factors had conspired to elevate physicians and "social scientists" into the arbiters of normality and abnormality for both individual and social behavior.[57]

The links between new scientific knowledge and social, political, and cultural ideology in France during this period are manifest and extensive. Robert Nye has shown that this concatenation of occurrences in France during the 1870s, 1880s, and 1890s gave rise to the distinctive notion of "the social pathologies."[58] Nye has established that one area of social and political thought after another was medicalized during this period, a process that entailed the use of images of neuropathology and psychopathology to account for many of the most disturbing changes and conditions of the day. According to Nye, the main projected social pathologies in the late nineteenth century were alcoholism, prostitution, homosexuality, criminality, venereal disease, and suicide.[59]

My essay suggests that the hysteria concept played an important role in the social pathologizing impulse of the period. The height of interest in hysteria coincided chronologically with the early decades of the Third Republic. I believe that in large measure hysteria's great metaphoric appeal at this time, especially in the social and political realms, lay in the fact that it helped to make sense of the new conditions of modern urban life emerging suddenly and uncontrollably. Time and again, the application of the diagnosis centered on what were perceived to be the most threatening social problems of France during the late nineteenth century. In the troubled, traumatized sociopolitical world of the early Third Republic, hysteria joined in turns with the discourses of national decline, alcoholism, antifeminism, prostitution, criminality, sexual perversion, and venereal disease. Hypothetical disease etiologies served to project and to rationalize widely held social values and moral attitudes. Moreover, by cloaking normative social and moral judgments in the terminology of contemporary neuropathology and psychopathology, authors sought to increase their explanatory power and cultural authority by embracing the new and prestigious sciences. The age and elasticity of the hysteria label further increased its applicability.

If I am correct in this analysis, then the interrelated medical-scientific and popular-cultural histories of hysteria at this time involve a fundamental paradox. Jan Goldstein has demonstrated that, within the French medical community of the 1870s and 1880s, hysteria was linked with liberal, republican causes.[60] Likewise, hysteria was the "founding neurosis" of Freudian psychoanalysis and contributed to the establishment of other new psychologies and psychiatries at the turn of the century. Nonetheless, in contemporaneous French commentary on society and politics the idea of hysteria was habitually pressed into the service of conservative, reactionary, and anti-Modernist programs and points of view. Simultaneously, fin-de-siècle hysteria played a key role in the birth of psychological modernism and provided a wide-ranging critique of social and political modernity.

A second line of explanation I call metacultural.[61] The arrival of artistic and philosophical Modernism brought a crucial shift in Western epistemologies. In the visual arts, Modernism initiated a revolution in the conception and perception of the artistic object: painting ceased to be an attempt to imitate or represent natural objects and events, becoming instead either an expression of the artist's intimate, subjective experience of the sensory world or a representation of the formal pictorial qualities of painting itself. Impressionism, for instance, dissolved form into separate dabs of color that were perceived by the individual spectator's eye and that shifted through time; Cubism discarded conventional Renaissance notions of perspective by presenting objects from multiple angles against skewed dimensional backgrounds; and abstract painters from Kandinsky to Mondrian sought to create images that represented pure form, line, shape, and color.[62] In parallel fashion, composers such as Debussy, Stravinsky, and Schoenberg rejected compositional techniques that had dominated Western music for centuries and experimented with dissonant harmonies, violent rhythms, and new systems of tonality. In imaginative literature, novelists and playwrights turned away from theories of realism and naturalism that attempt to describe an objective, natural world through a single, omniscient observer speaking in a linear narrative. Instead they explored new techniques for narrating the rich evolution of individual consciousness through time, memory, and circumstance. And Nietzsche, Bergson, and James, among other philosophers, critiqued the deterministic and rationalistic heritage of nineteenth-century thought. In its place, they emphasized the power of intuitive modes of apprehension, the mediation of all perceptions by consciousness and language, and the subjectivities of knowledge and self-knowledge. Even theoretical physics underwent transformation: the stable world of classic Newtonian physics gave way to new models of the universe as waves and particles in perpetual motion. Against commonsense understanding, the Einsteinian worldview advocates a vision of an unsolid and unstable universe composed of temporary masses of randomly circulating energy. In all these disparate cultural domains, Modernism involves the same type of reorientation in understanding the world: a comprehensive questioning of inherited positivist certainties about human nature and the external environment; a recognition that all categories of thought and culture are relational; and, in the words of one scholar, an appreciation of "the subjectivity of perception and cognition, a subjectivity that calls into question the unity of the observing subject as well as its relationship with the outside world."[63] Stated succinctly, the revolution of Modernism entailed an increasing separation of representation from "the real."[64]

Standing wholly outside these radical challenges to traditional beliefs was medicine. In fact, the medical sciences in Europe and North America experienced their high, positivist period precisely during the later nineteenth century. In France, the 1870s, 1880s, and 1890s were the heroic age of Claude Bernard and Louis Pasteur, an era during which the causes and courses of one infectious disease after another were discovered. The intellectual prestige of the *homme de science* reached a historic high point. Throughout the period, the orthodoxies of medical positivism remained firmly intact: in sickness and health, the human body and mind were to be studied, understood, and eventually mastered through precise and detailed observation by a community of experts. Pathology was seen to have rational causes, subject to immutable and ascertainable patterns or laws. Conversely, nonempirical methods of investigation and sources of insight were to be rejected as corrupting, contaminating forces in the quest for objective, value-neutral knowledge.[65] Positivist medical science was the ultimate "discourse of the real," seeking to produce an authoritative account of an unproblematically real world of the human body and mind.

The place of hysteria within the epistemology of nineteenth-century medical science, however, was intensely problematic. Construed as an object of knowledge, as a site of scientific representation, hysteria had no coherent and fixed identity of its own.[66] As most commonly understood by nineteenth- and twentieth-century medicine, hysteria is a "neuromimetic" affliction.[67] It is the masquerading malady that has no essence but rather emerges, chameleon-like, by aping the symptomatological forms of other organic diseases, most often neurological diseases. It is an image made in the image and likeness of other images. Furthermore, hysteria is not a simple copy or imitation of another "real" pathological type. Rather, its form and meaning change radically and erratically over time, from individual to individual, and culture to culture. Its appropriate metaphor is less the mirror than the hall of mirrors or echo chamber. Indeed, the synthesis of shifting, elusive symptoms that is hysteria has always been discussed by medics in metaphorical language, as a *sign* of something more fundamental: a detached and mobile womb, sexual and maternal deprivation, demonic possession, pathological femininity, defective heredity, clinical exhibitionism, a dysfunctional doctor-patient relationship.[68] Even its basic ontological status was (and remains) deeply in question: Is it a disease, a reaction, or a syndrome? A physical or a mental malady? Is it a real pathology at all or a gestural language of social protest? Shapeless and ever-changing, unfixed and indefinable, endlessly open to interpretation, a signifier without a signified, hysteria *is* Modernism.

These qualities, I believe, are central to explaining why, for both physicians and artists a century ago, hysteria became the paradigmatic psychological malady. In the 1870s and 1880s, neurologists and "nerve doctors," trained in the methods of mainstream organic medicine, grappled with the so-called "functional nervous disorders" that filled their private and hospital practices. Charcot in particular, drawing on new technologies of representation such as medical photography, attempted to construct a fixed *tableau clinique* of hysterical symptoms and a scheme of the laws of periodicity for the hysterical fit. But Charcot failed famously. The "founder of neurology" was in a real sense defeated, intellectually and professionally, by hysteria.[69]

This failure was crucial for the founding of modern dynamic psychiatry, which to a significant extent began as a theory and therapy of hysterical illness. Resisting positivization, hysteria for fin-de-siècle observers represented the limits of organic medicine's ability to explain human behavior. A kind of Kuhnian "anomaly" in the reigning positivist paradigm, it opened up the possibility of alternative, nonorganic conceptualizations of mind and body. Like Modernist culture at large, the theories of the mind that emerge in Charcot's wake question the explanatory adequacy of the nineteenth-century materialist-scientific worldview. From early Janetian psychology and Freudian psychoanalysis in the 1890s to existential psychiatry and Lacanian psychoanalysis at mid-twentieth century, the dynamic and neo-dynamic psychological traditions lavished attention on hysteria. But for all their doctrinal differences, these new psychologies shared a number of key features in their conceptualization of the disorder: they all emphasized mental experiences over the actual phenomenal world of the hysteric; they acknowledged the centrality and subjectivity of individual consciousness; they appreciated the crucial intersubjectivity of the doctor-patient relationship; and they construed hysteria metaphorically, casting the therapist in the role of clinician-semiotician who must decode a set of individual symptom-symbols.[70] The late nineteenth-century encounter with hysteria was at once the sign of a crisis of positivist medicine and an attempted solution of that crisis.[71]

It should be clear that the psychological modernism emerging from this generation-long engagement with hysteria shared many features with the Modernist movement in the arts. In closing I want to suggest that this fact provides a final reason for the formation a century ago of an integrated culture of hysteria that cut across the worlds of art and science. As Louis Sass has shown in intricate detail, what disease a culture chooses to privilege is not a matter of insignificance.[72] We have seen that during the decades associated most decisively with the advent of Modernism, French neurologists, psychiatrists, psychologists, novelists, poets, and dramatists were deeply and equally preoccupied with the subject of hysteria. The commonality of their interest, and the rich representational history that resulted during this period, is linked, I claim, to the larger cultural resonances of hysteria's unstable epistemological identity. The kaleidoscope of behaviors that is hysteria represented the limits of representation itself within positivist medicine, a fact that was keenly appreciated by observers outside the sciences.[73] Destabilizing organic medicine, hysteria opened up a cognitive space that by the beginning of the new century was filled by the depth-psychological ideas of the psyche, the unconscious, mind-body conversion, and psychological automatism and symbolism. As this volume of essays demonstrates, these new psychological models of reality were powerfully deconstructive of traditional theories of perception and knowledge in other, nonscientific areas of thought and culture. It is no coincidence that hysteria's "revolt against positivism" is precisely coincident in time and place with the heyday of Impressionist painting, the great vogue for Bergsonian vitalist philosophy, and the formative artistic years of Proust.[74] If from Baudelaire in the 1860s to the Surrealist poets in the 1920s, and from Janet in the 1880s to Lacan in the 1950s, French literary and scientific intellectuals were forcefully drawn to "the elusive neurosis," it was at least in part because hysteria expressed an ongoing crisis of knowledge and representation that transcended disciplinary boundaries and that formed perhaps the most crucial intellectual condition for the possibility of early Modernism.[75]

CHAPTER 2

From Charcot to Charlot: Unconscious Imitation and Spectatorship in French Cabaret and Early Cinema

RAE BETH GORDON

It is certain that today, primarily in the cities, hysteria is the illness in vogue. It is everywhere. . . . The instinct to imitate comes from the unconscious parts of the nervous system.
— Paul-Max Simon, *L'Hygiène de l'esprit*, 1881

A good half of the hit songs of this period belong to the jiggling pit of the late Charcot. . . . They have gesticulatory hysteria.
— Georges Montorgueil, *Les Demi-Cabots*, 1896

Film is nothing but a relay between the source of nervous energy and the auditorium. . . . Chaplin has created the overwrought hero. . . . a synopsis of . . . photogenic neurasthenia.
— Jean Epstein, "Magnification," 1921

Experimental psychology, clinical observations, and psychiatric theory in late nineteenth-century France furnished the Parisian cabaret and early film comedy with a new repertoire of movements, grimaces, tics, and gestures. At the same time, scientific experiments in the physiology of stimulus response lent themselves to new ways of looking at the way that spectators reacted to certain performance styles. These are the important components in the history of the two forms of mass culture that I want to reconstruct here. Notions and, especially, images from medical science must be included alongside images from the wax museum, pantomime, puppet shows, and precinematic devices in the cultural series that contributed to the genesis of performance styles in the Parisian cabaret, the café-concert, and early film comedy. This chapter, then, proposes and examines a previously unnoticed relation between a significant cultural and aesthetic style and the extraordinary upsurge of concern with and diagnosis of hysteria and epilepsy in late nineteenth-century French medical practice and theory. Parallel studies of sug-

93

gestion and unconscious imitation, similarly, have considerable pertinence for spectatorship in the same period.[1]

Is there a relationship between ways that movement was staged in early cinema and corporeal pathologies—contractures, tics, catalepsy, and convulsive movement—related to hysteria and epilepsy? I believe that hysterical gesture and gait were important inspirations for the style of frenetic, anarchic movement that is so often present in early French film comedy, and that many spectators recognized this source, thanks in large part to the emphasis that had been placed on nervous pathology in cabaret and café-concert performance styles before they were carried over to film. I also argue here that there are correlations between filmic movement and induced gesture in public exhibitions of magnetizers in the 1890s.

In addition, it seems plausible that café-concert performers provided models for potential hysterics who couldn't resist imitating the tics, grimaces, and convulsive movements that later came to characterize the medical journal *Nouvelle iconographie photographique de la Salpêtrière*. The enormous prestige that this entertainment venue had among the working classes—the same classes that populated the Salpêtrière and Charenton—forces us to ask whether the remarkable increase in cases of hysteria wasn't due in part to mimetic behavior. This was, at the very least, a fear frequently expressed by those who warned of the cabaret's pernicious and contagious atmosphere. Even a great fan of the café-concert like Georges Montorgueil wrote that the person who prophesied that his generation would end up in the same "bag of disarticulated subjects" as Charcot's patients was probably coming out of a café-concert at the time he made his pronouncement.[2] Conversely, many psychiatric patients were keenly interested in the theater; one of Jacques Roubinovitch's patients who barely knew how to read and write composed a play in five acts. An 1878 case observation describes a woman with partial epilepsy and a memory that is "practically nil": she can't count or read, but she can remember the melody of any song.[3] More than one of Charcot's patients, "cured" or not, went on to make a living as a street singer or, in the case of Jane Avril, as a Moulin Rouge dancer, when he or she left the hospital. Although it is perhaps impossible to trace the crisscross of influences with perfect assurance, what is certain is that, as early as the 1870s, a number of café-concert and cabaret artists borrowed gestures and movement from asylum inmates and that the enormous popularity of epileptic performers and of songs about nervous pathologies in the café-concerts contributed to the furor of attention paid to nervous disorders in the 1880s and 1890s.

The expectations that spectators took with them to film screenings, knowledge about science that was common currency, and the inevitable associations in the minds of spectators around 1900 with other forms of entertainment—magnetizers' shows and cabaret performance, as well as Grand Guignol theater, the stereoscope, and wax museums—are all crucial factors in tracing what the audiences of 1895–1910 experienced.[4] A new genre, "le théâtre médical," created by André de Lorde for the Grand Guignol, was immensely successful. The theater staged *Obsession, The Horrible Experiment, The Laboratory of Hallucinations,* and *A Crime in an Insane Asylum,* plays written (in collaboration with de Lorde) by one of France's most important experimental psychologists, Alfred Binet, to whom de Lorde dedicated the horrific but oftentimes hilarious *A Lesson at the Salpêtrière* in 1905. Not only did Binet write five, and possibly eight, plays for the Grand Guignol, but Joseph Babinsky himself (in collaboration with Pierre Palau) contributed *The Mad Ones (Les Détraquées)* to the "Theater of Fear." Weekly columns in *Le Figaro* magazine and other widely read publications were written by popularizers of medicine like Dr. de Fleury, and the contentious debate on hypnotism between the Salpêtrière and Nancy schools, as well as the attempt to outlaw public exhibitions by magnetizers in the 1880s and 1890s, were closely followed in the press. Notions about hysteria, somnambulism, hypnosis, and physiology, popularized in the press, were at work in the imagination of the period.

Interest in spectatorship is not of recent vintage. At the beginning of the twentieth century, tests were conducted in which spectators were monitored as they watched films, the exact intensity of their sensations (which were then interpreted as emotions) measured at dramatic or comic moments. According to late nineteenth-century physiology, successive stages of intensity in aesthetic emotion corresponded to changes in the body.[5] When Drs. Édouard Toulouse and Raoul Mourgue published their analysis of physiological responses (specifically, respiratory changes) to the avant-garde filmmaker Abel Gance's *Mater dolorosa* (1917), they wrote that "film acts more powerfully on the affective life of individuals than other modes of experience . . . because 'the feeling of reality, due to movement in the three dimensions of space, is so intense.'"[6] Several years earlier, in a similar vein, Yhcam had underlined that the impression on the film viewer was far more vivid than on the theatergoer. However, he ascribed this to a very different cause: "the spectator's attention is caught and concentrated on the luminous projection, without possible distraction."[7] Is the impact of film due to an intense feeling of reality or to an equally intense state of hallucinatory hypnotic trance? That is a question that this essay tries to answer.

Physiology of the Spectator

The relation of shock and nerves to modern life was a recurrent theme in French newspapers, scientific journals, and fiction from the 1860s on. Thérésa, who rose to stardom in 1864, "acts out her song as much as she sings it. . . . The shock is violent"; Polaire, in the 1890s, "mimes all sorts of shocks";[8] the spectator "lives only for shocks and the big reason for the success of certain 'artists' is that they give a stronger shock. It passes quickly; the *habitué* falls back into his usual state of torpor" (*CC*, 51). "There came a day when a new and urgent need for stimuli was met by the film." "Perception in the form of shocks was established as a formal principle" quite naturally, albeit with an awe-inspiring new bag of technical possibilities:[9] this understanding of spectatorship had already proved to be immensely popular and profitable in café-concert, cabaret, circus, and fairground entertainments.

Louis Haugmard and Georges Duhamel voiced the anxiety that in such spectatorial experiences at the cinema moving images replace thought. The intensely physical experience of perception in watching a film forces one to abandon conscious mental processes. Film is experienced in the body, and if body is seen as distinct from (conscious) mind in the nineteenth century, it is because the body is the site of the unconscious. Benjamin wrote that "tactile appropriation is accomplished . . . by habit" and "reception in a state of distraction . . . finds in the film its true means of exercise."[10] What is habit according to late nineteenth-century physiologists and philosophers? Habit is equivalent to the automatic responses exemplified by nervous reflex and by unconscious mental processes. The importance of physiological response in the production of affect in aesthetic experience cannot be overemphasized in the context of the fin de siècle. Clearly, it is not only *visual* shocks that are involved in cabaret and film spectatorship. To begin with, perception and mental images do not take place in the mind or eye alone; they are linked to their motor component. Moreover, psychophysiologists of the 1880s and 1890s proposed that the dynamic infrastructure of perception had to include not only a motor component, but also a component that was governed by the forces of instinct.[11]

Physiological aesthetics tried to measure and analyze the impact of form, movement, and color not only on the eye, but also on the body. Research in psychophysiology ascribed specific emotions to certain gestures and forms, a mechanics of emotion that could then be used by painters, actors, and filmmakers. Charles Henry, director of the Sorbonne laboratory of physiology, applying Gustav Fechner's psychophysical formulas of stimulus response,[12] established that directional movements were either inhibitory or dynamogenous. Discontinuous lines and downward movement, for example, inhibit movement in the body according to Henry, while continuous lines and upward movement stimulate it; they are dynamogenous. Correspondingly, perceiving the former causes sadness and anxiety while perceiving the latter causes calmness and happiness. Henry's theories were tested on hysterical patients at the Salpêtrière hospital: "the dynamometric experiments of Dr. Féré, and the expressions [on the faces] of hypnotized subjects that characterize all the states of pleasure and pain in response to the different directions of the arm of the experimenter," demonstrated to Henry the validity of the relation between the direction of line and emotion.[13] His research informed the work of neo-Impressionist painters like Georges Seurat and Paul Signac as well as that of poets Gustave Kahn and Jules Laforgue.[14] Pursuing the application of psychophysics to aesthetics (specifically in the context of pain and pleasure), the American Henry Rutgers Marshall wrote that it was "probable that, in the future, one will tend to limit the use of the word *emotion* to the description of those states determinable by the content of their muscular sensations."[15] From Théodule Ribot and Pierre Janet in France to Marshall and James in America, scientific psychologists were busy looking for the somatic basis of emotions.

Moreover, at the same time as we *perceive* an object, our "internal machinery" *re-creates* it. Charles Henry wrote that thanks to eye movements, to phenomena in our vascular and muscular systems, and to our breathing, "there is no idea without virtual, then real, movement." "One can consider the sensation and the idea as virtual exercises of our 'mécanique naturelle.'"[16] This notion comes to Henry from Charles Richet, who concisely stated "there is no perception without movement."[17] Some doctors in the 1880s even believed that women, children, and nervous males could contract epilepsy merely by watching an epileptic seizure (more on this below). There is a physiological basis for this belief: when a movement is directed to a particular organ or limb, the latter *remembers* and tends later to repeat this movement. When Nietzsche wrote in 1881 that "all nerves, for example in the leg, remember their past experiences. . . . What the nerves have assimilated continues to live in them," he was drawing on Ribot (*Les Maladies de la mémoire*, 1881) and Henry Maudsley (*The Physiology of Mind*), as Marcel Gauchet has pointed out.[18] For Ribot, the personality is formed by the sensations received from the organs and tissues and by movements—all the bodily states represented in the *sensorium*. Thus, the personality varies with these sensations. Pathologies like doubling (*le dédoublement de la personnalité*) are directly tied to changes in bodily sensations "and are but an extreme example of the phenomenon" described by Ribot.

In his 1887 *Sensation et mouvement,* Charles Féré showed that all sensation was accompanied by an augmentation of muscular force, measurable on the dynamometer. This augmentation, however, is not perceived by the conscious mind. The acuteness of joy, pain, desire, or shame results from the automatic movements that these feelings engender. Virtual movement, set in motion from the outside (stimuli and sensation) *and* from the inside (ideas and internal sensations), if it can be gauged by the dynamometer and other instruments, make possible a scientific aesthetics.[19]

To summarize, psychophysical experiments originating with Gustav Fechner in 1860 that purported to measure sensation led to experiments for gauging aesthetic emotion (beginning in Germany in the 1870s, in France in the 1880s, and in America in the 1890s). These correlations between physical response and aesthetic emotion were combined with Henry's theory that perceiving the aesthetic object not only produces specific sensations, but also corporeal reactions that retrace the form and movement of that object. According to Henri Bergson, we "may not be able to consciously comprehend an emotion that an artist tries to express but we can be made to *feel* it; artists set down those outward manifestations of their emotion *that our body will mechanically imitate, however lightly,* so as to place us in the indefinable psychological state that caused them."[20] The barriers between the artist's consciousness and ours disappear thanks to unconscious imitation.

Unconscious imitation and other forms of automatic response had strong links to the pathology of hysteria, a connection I develop below. Henry had noted that when the "hypnotizable subject" perceives the movements of another subject, he or she first re-creates them virtually as ideas, then as acts. We know that hysterics are eminently hypnotizable; thus their bodies will always be solicited by this form of internal mimicry.[21] But many normal people are hypnotizable—*all people,* according to Hippolyte Bernheim and the Nancy School of psychology—so the reverberations of what everyone sees are mirrored in and by the body. The mimetic tendency due to corporeal automatism that is so marked in hysterics is inherent to aesthetic experience. Applying the "scientific aesthetics" to cinema, Toulouse and Mourgue wrote that "since it is proven by science that the perception of movement gives birth to the beginnings [*l'ébauche*] of the corresponding movement, 'a phenomenon would take place on the screen akin to hypnotic suggestion being practiced on a subject placed in a given pose.'"[22]

In 1923, Sergei Eisenstein was certain that he had found the perfect vehicle for measuring the emotional effects of art. "Attraction . . . is every aggressive moment of the theater performance, that is, every element subjecting the spectator to a sensory or psychic action *verified by means of experiment and mathematically calculated to produce in the spectator certain emotional shocks* [in a proper order within the totality]."[23] Eisenstein's concept of the "montage of attractions," worked out in 1922–23 in the theater before being applied to film and published in *Lef* 3 (1923), is yet another example of the impact of psychophysics on aesthetics. Eisenstein's ideas for his Acrobatic Theater emerged from Vsevolod Meyerhold's theory of biomechanics (the biological component based on Pavlov's work on conditioned nervous reflexes). In this theater, as in that of Artaud, every movement of the body corresponds to and expresses an emotion. Eisenstein stressed the power of circus performers, music hall performers, and mimes to produce physical and emotional reactions in the spectator, "bridg[ing] the 'chasm' separating the actor from the spectator" and uniting them in such a way that the spectator would identify with the action.[24] Eisenstein offers an example of the attraction in film: it is communicated "by the mechanics of [Chaplin's] movement."[25] (Two years earlier, the avant-garde filmmaker Jean Epstein had identified Chaplin's "photogenic neurasthenia"; his "entire performance consists of the reflex actions of a nervous, tired person.")[26] One has only to look at Chaplin's gait to understand that the "mechanics of his movement" is the actor's signature. And that will be true of nearly every great comic star in France from Dranem and Boireau to Jacques Tati. Further, one has only to compare Chaplin's gait to that of the psychiatric patients filmed at Salpêtrière between 1910 and 1912 to see that there is but a small step to take from Charcot to Charlot. And, in the context of spectatorship, is it possible to leave a screening of a Monsieur Hulot film without wanting to imitate Tati's gait? I believe that the fascination that pathological gait and gesture held for spectators, greatly intensified by the echoes in their own bodies, played a considerable part in the rise to stardom of these actors. Eisenstein's conception of the attraction was, of course, brilliantly taken up by Tom Gunning and André Gaudreault. Continuing his work on the concept and characterization of the "cinema of attractions," Gunning has considered Benjamin's "perception in the form of shocks" in the context of an aesthetics of astonishment. The cinema of attractions foregrounds "the role of the spectator, [addressing him or her] in a specific manner."[27] It is a "series of visual shocks" that exerted an "uncanny and agitating power . . . on audiences."[28] To understand this power, I believe that we must see it in the context of contemporary notions about the body and the unconscious. When one considers not only the visual but also the corporeal shocks, recourse to physiology and psychiatry explains *why* the shocks, the jolts in the viewer, occurred and how they are linked to the unconscious, instinct, hysteria, or—in the shorthand of the period—the "lower orders."

What exactly were bodies doing in the music halls, sideshows, and circus and cabaret acts? Because of the spectator's incorporation of what he or she sees (whether one takes this dynamic to be a function of biomechanics, psychophysics, or unconscious imitation), it is important to reflect on the *kinds* of movement reproduced. And since the majority of performers in film came from the cabaret, one of the primary forms of spectacle that inspired the concept of the montage of attractions and, later, the "cinema of attractions," that is where I propose to start.

Epilepsy as Performance Style

The artistic representation and popular spectacle of the body as a collection of nervous tics, dislocations, and mechanical reflexes, with the accompanying implications of medical pathology, began in the cabaret. There are good reasons that the cabaret should have been the principal site for a radically new aesthetic and ethos that would later be recognized as typifying modernity. One reason was the carnivalesque atmosphere of raucous audience participation, with its vital exchange of energy between performer and spectator; another was the unique mingling of classes to be found there.

The Parisian cabaret and café-concert between 1865 and 1907 were characterized by a convulsive body language made up of frenetic, angular, and "mechanical" movements accompanied by tics and grimaces (fig. 2.1). Late nineteenth-century cabaret performance was very much influenced by the medical discourse surrounding hysteria and epilepsy and by popular depictions of the nervous disorders in newspapers and magazines.[29] Hysteria was conflated with epilepsy in the popular imagination, and the term "hystero-epilepsy" remained in medical use up until the end of the nineteenth century. The most popular performers of the café-concert and cabaret between 1875 and 1900 jerked and twisted their bodies in bizarre contortions and dislocations, kicking, hopping, and gesticulating like a marionette or an epileptic, their faces alive with grimaces and mechanical tics.[30] One of the seminal literary-artistic groups in the early 1880s called themselves the Epileptic Red Herrings. The adjective "epileptic" was used frequently in newspaper reviews, and a new genre came into being with *la chanteuse épileptique.*[31] Joris-Karl Huysmans praised Degas's pastels and prints of café-concert singers bleating and twisting their hips in "those inept convulsions responsible for the quasi-celebrity of that epileptic doll, la Bécat."[32] Émilie Bécat "invented" the genre of epileptic singer in 1875 according to Paulus, the

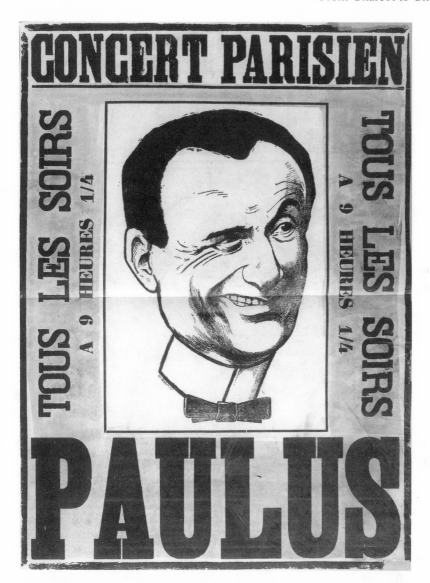

Fig. 2.1. Poster of Paulus at the Concert Parisien in 1882

biggest male star of the 1870s and 1880s.[33] The genre emerged at precisely the same time as the rise in cases of hysteria, feeding into and capitalizing on a popular phenomenon that was just getting underway (figs. 2.2–2.3).

The most famous epileptic singer was Colette's "twin," Polaire. "Polaire! The agitating and agitated Polaire . . . hops around, trembles, quivers . . .

Fig. 2.2. "Mademoiselle Bécat aux Ambassadeurs," lithograph transferred from three monotypes, by Edgar Degas, 1877–1878

mimes all forms of shocks and shaking, twists, leans over backward in the form of an arc."[34] Colette wrote that she "applauded Polaire in her epilepsy,"[35] and singers routinely used the term to describe their style, as Mistinguett did when she wrote, "I was tired of the daily epilepsy."[36] Maurice Vaucaire called the women who belonged to this genre "female Pauluses."[37] Paulus, who erupted on the Paris stage in 1871, was indeed a precursor of the epileptic singer. The mechanical tics of the extraordinarily popular Paulus

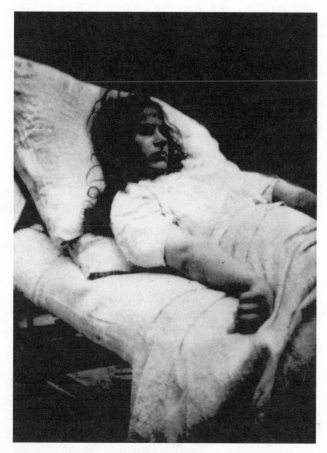

Fig. 2.3. Patient with partial epilepsy, *Iconographie photographique de la Salpêtrière*, 1878

were syncopated with his hops and leaps. He sang "with the gestures of someone being exorcized,"[38] and was "a veritable electric battery." The "Comic Trooper" Ouvrard was also "a seeker of mechanical tics . . . a packet of nerves" (CC, 139–40). An epileptic observed by Féré could easily have been a stand-in for Paulus or Ouvrard. "He possesses an extreme mobility of the face and members; his mouth deviates to the right . . . as his eyes wink or close. The head rotates . . . while his members flex and extend themselves in all directions."[39] These movements could be seen nightly on cabaret and café-concert stages; mechanical tics, angularity, and jerky, frenetic gesture were the keys to stardom and the essential characteristics of the cabaret and café-concert aesthetic. There is a cipher for these characteristics: the zigzag.

The angularity of the zigzag expresses pain, the violence of cutting wit, and the anarchy of epileptic gesture in the cabaret well before the form appears in art and literature. The body of a black-suited, fin-de-siècle Pierrot traces zigzags across the pages of the *Chat Noir* journal, while Jean Richepin's 1886 novel *Braves gens: Roman parisien* informs us that gestural arabesques are passé and that modern pantomime must consist of "convulsive" gestures: "Zig, zag, paf!" explains the mime as he describes the startlingly new show of the mime troupe The Happy Zigzags. For Charcot, the zigzag was a form symptomatic of hysteria. It is found not only in the gestures of hysterics but in the "dazzling scotoma" that erupt in their field of vision, in their drawings, and in their handwriting. The hysterics in some of Maupassant's short stories (for example, "Le Tic") are also afflicted with an uncontrollable arm movement in the form of a zigzag.

Movement in the performance style of the cabaret, like that of early French film comedy, was, as I have said, explicitly directed toward the production of shocks, as dozens of journalistic and literary accounts that contain the words "des secousses" attest. Thus, an electric jolt is communicated by the performer to the spectator. And who composed the greatest number of male hysterics, according to Augustin Galopin? Actors. Moreover, they "communicate to their fellow citizens an electro-magnetic spark from their electrified imagination, the incandescent foyer that consumes and devours them so quickly."[40] Add to this the internal repetition of nervous, convulsive, mechanical movement in spectators and one has an atmosphere that journalists of the period often characterized as "Charentonesque," as pathological. "It is the Bicêtre asylum where the public's madness is free to express itself."[41]

The first two stages of an attack of major hysteria, as codified by Charcot, were convulsive, epileptoid movements followed by the acrobatic contortions of "clownism." Trembling, contractures of the hands and feet, facial asymmetry, tics and grimaces, and constant agitation were also frequent symptoms. Pierre Janet describes a patient who suffers from akathisia, or the inability to remain seated. After a few minutes of being seated, he desperately contorts himself, spreads his legs, and becomes rigid on the left side as the rest of his body shakes.[42] Commentators of the fin de siècle did not fail to notice the parallels between performance style and hysteria. "A good half of the hit songs of this period belong to the jiggling pit [*le trémoussoir*] of the late Charcot. These songs vibrate and stamp [*elles trépident*]. They have gesticulatory hysteria" (*DC*, 14). A decade earlier, in 1886, Maurice Vaucaire clearly perceived that performers were borrowing from hysterics in the asylum: the "nutty refrains [are] sung by subjects who indulge in spewing out the cries of a hysteric."[43] Limping was a pathology of movement linked to epilepsy and hysteria, and Paulus was known for imitating people with a limp or with other pathologies of movement (for example, in *The Limping Girl*). Montorgueil explained that Paulus's "success was largely due to his . . . prancing, his imitations of various forms of infirmity, of the crippled and of the invalid. *This was an entirely new art that had to be learned*" (DC, 15, 17; emphasis mine). Even the posters plastered all over Paris "glorify the gestures of a cretin, make one laugh at physical deformities, celebrate a famous ham's cachexia of the brain."[44] A hit song of 1899 and 1900 was Alice de Tender's "La Parisienne épileptique." By 1906, self-conscious references to nervous disorders were commonplace: Dalbret's song "Neurasthenia" followed Dranem's "I'm a Neurasthenic," and Mugette de Trévy sang "Don't tickle me like that, I'm a little woman who's excessively nervous. . . . In reality, the blood of a turnip runs through my veins. But the fashion today, le grand chic, is to appear neurasthenic."

In *L'Art de dire le monologue*, Ernest Coquelin gives the following advice: "You come on stage with the physiognomy of one who is a bit overwhelmed, the body slightly *automatic*; . . . be concentrated, *obsessed*, very *anxious* and worried, but not hallucinated: you are a theatrical subject, not a medical subject. You belong to the stage, not to Dr. Charcot."[45] Evidently, comics needed to hear this warning or admonition (yet, the very traits that Coquelin recommends to the apprentice monologuist are symptoms of neurasthenia). Coquelin *cadet* was himself an offender; he made the public "dizzy" with his "terrifying grimaces, insane capers, and extravagant gestures."[46] The very definition of the monologue emphasizes pathology: "a kind of one-person vaudeville, mixed with fantasy and satire . . . but with a *modern* twist, which, precisely in what it contains of madness corresponds to the state of our nerves."[47] The same audiences who applauded Coquelin also applauded "a starving madman who recited . . . a hysterical sonnet, a macabre ballad, an idiotic monologue."[48] Maurice Rollinat, author of *Les Névroses* and *L'Abîme*, attended Charcot's lessons for two years, incorporating what he observed into his own style, just as Sarah Bernhardt visited the wards of the Salpêtrière in 1884 in order to study hysterical movement. Rollinat's performances of macabre songs at the Chat Noir, accompanied as they were by convulsive grimaces and corporeal twitches, caused Barbey d'Aurevilly, author of *Les Diaboliques*, to write, "And so it is that we have one more modern poet."[49] "Modernity" in the cabaret is, to an astonishing extent, another word for "pathology."

Figs. 2.4–2.5. Hysterical male patient with ambulatory automatism, from a medical film made ca. 1910–1912

Figs. 2.6–2.7. Dranem, "Le 5 O'cloc," (top) and "Jiu-Jitsu" (bottom), from Gaumont *phono-scènes*, ca. 1905

The analogy I've drawn between hysteria and cabaret or café-concert performance style is visually documented by a 1911 Gaumont film by Jean Durand about an epileptic singer, *Dancing Girl*, and by two films made circa 1910–12 at the Salpêtrière hospital that recorded the various tics, grimaces, gesticulations, and gaits of the patients paraded before the camera. These are the same movements and expressions described in dozens of newspaper reviews and posters of café-concert performers. Even more striking visual proof of the mutual influence of hysteria and movement in cabaret performance is found in two 1907 *phono-scènes* (postsynchronized sound films) of the famous "comique idiot" Dranem, interpreter of the hit song "I'm a Neurasthenic." His movements correspond exactly to those of one of the hospital inmates (figs. 2.4–2.7).

High and Low, Charcot and Charlot

Janet wrote that the hysteric almost always claimed to feel mechanical, like an automaton; he or she is ruled by the lower, automatic, and instinctual level of life, the level that Binet and Janet labeled the unconscious. This is the corporeal unconscious, a notion that arose from the study of automatic reflexes and from repeated gestures in hysterics under hypnosis or in spontaneous somnambulism. Poses communicated under hypnosis could be held for as long as an hour and twenty minutes, a fact that caused Binet and Féré to reflect, "[i]t seems as though the [anesthetized] member doesn't belong to the Subject."[50] They also noted that their patients had lost consciousness of the movements suggested by the psychiatrist, but that "this loss of consciousness is not absolute. . . . Another personality, so to speak, exists in him and is conscious of these movements; it receives the suggestion and executes it. . . . This is an episode of major hypnotism that one can encounter in the waking state in certain predisposed individuals." What constitutes this "other personality"? Pure sensation and nerves. "The sensation [erased from consciousness] is registered in the nervous centers of the patient, and it is this physiological registering that allows him to reproduce the movement without being conscious of it" (R, 332, 348–49, 352). Binet made the capital discovery that this doubling of the personality isn't successive but simultaneous. Up until then (1887), the second personality was perceived to be in alternation with a normal waking state and equated with a somnambulistic state. Binet was the first to suggest that it coexists with the conscious personality. The self, then, was not a Dr. Jekyll and Mr. Hyde, but two very different selves always copresent. Doubling of the personality, or double consciousness, one of the most dramatic symptoms of hysteria, was common to *all* hysterics and had been studied from the 1840s on, for example, by Drs. Landouzy and Moreau de Tours.[51] Now, at century's end, the second personality, identified with automatisms, could clearly be seen as the unconscious. This revelation regarding the unconscious was thus the result of Binet's and Féré's experiments in cataleptic plasticity, automatic and repeated gestures, contractures, and the sensation of dismemberment, all aspects of the pathologized body that are at the center of performance style in the cabaret and in early cinema. Janet underlined that all his patients use the same language; the words *machine, automaton,* and *mechanical* return again and again.[52] Bergson based his extremely influential theory of comedy on the concept of automatic gesture and word: "the comic is unconscious"; "gesture escapes us; it is an automatism." I feel certain he did so because he wrote *Le Rire* at the height of the cabaret's popularity.[53]

An idea that preoccupies philosophers, psychologists, psychiatrists, and physiologists alike from the mid-nineteenth-century on is the radical division between the higher and lower faculties: reason, judgment, choice, and will as opposed to sensation, motor response, automatisms, and instinct. Lodged in the opposition between high and low was the specter of insanity and hysteria; hysterics were precisely those people in whom the higher faculties were totally subservient to the lower faculties. In his 1889 *L'Automatisme psychologique: Essai sur les formes inférieures de l'activité humaine,* Janet developed this notion more fully than anyone had up until then. In addition, from around 1870, a capital new way of envisaging high and low had been joined to the psychiatric views: Darwinian and Spencerian theories of biological and social evolution. The kind of performance I'm describing quite deliberately appeals to the lower faculties. Thérésa, after all, "sang the flavor of the gutter," and her public, "seeking strong shocks [*de grandes secousses*], vibrate[d] passionately as she produce[d] a shock wave with her unadulterated gut twisting."[54] T. J. Clark has discussed the link between this new "primacy of the body" and other forms of violence and terror.[55] The Goncourt brothers were horrified by the public's delirious, "unhealthy" laughter in response to a singer's "epileptic gesticulations," prophesying that blood would have to flow in order to "cleanse" their laughter (*CC*, 42). (The Paris Commune was only six years away; we know that the association in the press of the female leaders of the Commune with hysterics was immediate.) And, while the domination of the higher faculties by the lower was seen to lead to hysteria, hallucination, and split personalities, it also generated an absolutely new aesthetic, an aesthetic that was described by innumerable observers as "magnetic." The concept of high and low culture takes on new meaning in light of nineteenth-century psychiatric and physiological theory.

The spectator's physical experience is exciting and stimulating, yet anxiety producing; the experience of the body involuntarily imitating the convulsive movements, cataleptic poses, and facial contortions that characterize epilepsy and hysteria could not help but remind the viewer of the all-too-common attacks of epilepsy and hysteria that found their way into the popular press. Performance style could be modeled on medical discourses and iconography because the latter were so widely recognizable by the general public. "Epileptic performers" cause anxiety and hilarity, and the latter is a response to the former. This is why deformity, dismemberment, dislocation and contortion, grimaces, tics, and epileptic convulsions are so funny to so many spectators.[56]

The aesthetics of performance style that I'm describing was carried over into cinema thanks to the number of cabaret and music hall performers who moved to film in the first two decades of the new art form. The actors who composed Pathé's repertory troupes in Nice, La Comica and La Nizza, responsible for some of the most anarchical comic chaos imaginable, came from the café-concert, from the circus, and from the fairground; many were acrobats, ensuring that dislocations and contortions of the body would continue to occupy a central place in popular entertainment. That is why the first comic films owe so much to the themes of cabaret comedy style (deformity, scatology, pathology), and especially to their rhythms. The performers in these films were "mostly wild, inhuman creatures, animated comic strips."[57] "The level of the majority of Pathé-Zecca's comic productions are of a surprisingly low, base nature. . . . The unforgettable sidekicks of Charlot [Charlie Chaplin] are the direct descendants of the types that Zecca and his followers went looking for in the residues of the 'caf'conc.'"[58] The overlap between cabaret and film ensures that the performance codes are carried over into the new art and that the messages conveyed by gestures (certain tics, contractures, movements, and grimaces) are read as pathological and are transmitted to the spectator as before.[59]

The privileged relationship between pathology and café-concert performance style also existed between pathology and cinema, and not simply films with explicit pathologies in their title, like Roméo Bosetti's Le Tic and Le Matelas épileptique (The Epileptic Mattress) and Méliès's The Escapees from Charenton. Jean Mauclaire (the founder of Studio 28) categorized a large number of films from the turn of the century as "the spectacle of 'automatic comedy' . . . and sentimental-epileptic dramas."[60] The disputed term "primitive cinema" then takes on a different cast; it signifies an over-whelming emphasis on movement, sensation, visual pathologies, and the unconscious, including the biological evolutionary connotations that were attached to this paradigm in the late nineteenth century. We can then appre-ciate more fully the impact that these images had, as well as their uncanny nature.[61]

The continuing discourse on film reception between 1895 and 1910 that turns on the idea of madness is also linked to the preoccupation with automatisms and the lower orders. We can look at Maksim Gorky's first film experience—his visit to the "realm of Shadows/Spirits" on July 4, 1896—in this light. "You forget where you are. *Strange ideas invade your mind; you are less and less conscious.* . . . This is a strain on the nerves. . . . Our nerves are getting weaker and weaker, are growing more and more unstrung . . . and [they] thirst more and more eagerly for new, strong, unusual, burning and strange impressions. The cinematograph gives you them."[62] The effect of shock on audiences was explicitly linked to the onset of mental illness in an article by the American comedian Sidney Drew, who warned, in 1917, of "mental upheaval" due to the "rapidity" of comic action, incidents, and "ill-timed" facts in certain films.[63] The public nonetheless expects to have this experience and derives pleasure from it. There is a continuous line and directing force running from the cabaret and café-concert performances of the last quarter of the nineteenth century, through the films of Méliès and the musicals of Ernst Lubitsch in the 1930s, and, finally, to the films of Jerry Lewis.[64] The uniting element is hysterical gesture and gait.

Cinematic Illusion and Pathology

In numerous films of Méliès, Émile Cohl, and others, doctors, surgeons, and psychiatrists are busy at work on their patients; consider Méliès's *The Doctor's Secret, Fin-de-siècle Surgery, The Chevaliers of Chloroform, Dr. Soufflamort, The Doctor and the Chimpanzee, Roentgen Rays,* and *An Indigestion;* and Cohl's *Brains Repaired* and *Nothing Is Impossible for Man* (fig. 2.8: "through hypnotism, he scrutinizes the hidden thoughts and reads the depths of consciousness").[65] *Calino Eats Horsemeat* (Calino played by Paul Bertho) is an allegory of filmic incorporation: Calino is transformed into a horse due to his gluttonous ingestion of too much horsemeat and gal-lops out of the house on all fours, creating havoc. Like the spectator, he has incorporated the movements and identity of a foreign being; too much hors-ing around on the screen has a direct impact on the viewer's body. He is

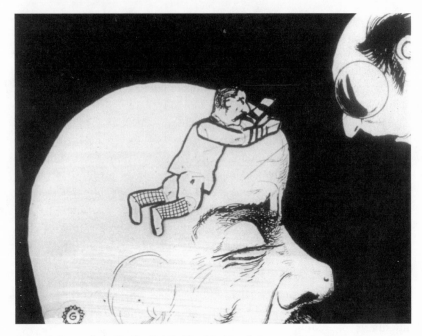

Fig. 2.8. Scene from Emile Cohl's film *Nothing Is Impossible for Man*, 1910

finally captured and taken to the hospital, where surgeons remove a toy horse from his body; he is cured. In the same period, there is a proliferation of mise-en-scènes of doctors, mesmerists, magnetizers, and hypnotists. These representations of medical penetrations of the body and brain were accompanied by the cinematic technologies that made it possible to reproduce the corporeal sensations in hysteria. And there was no scarcity of physical anomalies for cinema's medical practitioners to study. There were short films of dislocation acts, and comic films capitalized on the fascination that grotesque dislocations of the body held for audiences. One example is Méliès's 1905 *Dislocations extraordinaires*, with André Deed (the funniest man in early French cinema, star of Pathé's Boireau series and of the Cretinetti series in Italy). Corporeal dislocations apparently reminded one of marionettes or automatons and thus evoked the mechanical, automatic life of the hysteric. A 1911 Gaumont film called *L'Automate acrobate* was advertised with the following text: "Is it an acrobat? Is it a dummy? This is the question that arises before this curious attraction." Extraordinary motor capability is astonishing, can be hilarious, and was considered an "essentially pathological phenomenon" by Drs. Binet and Féré because of its links to feats that, thanks to altered sensory functioning, only a hysteric with partial

Fig. 2.9. Scene from Georges Méliès's Le "Cake-Walk" infernal, 1903

anesthesia or a subject under hypnotic suggestion could perform. Dislocation is joined to madness in Méliès's 1903 Cake-Walk infernal, in which little devils hop over each other frenetically while Satan dances the cakewalk at an accelerating pace. A vaudeville couple (dancers from the Olympia music hall) appear and easily surpass Satan in the wild frenzy of their movements. Not to be outdone, Mephisto pops out of a cake with his legs twisted and distorted like a stuffed doll's. As he dances with his arms flailing about like an epileptic's, his legs and arms detach themselves from his body and continue to dance separately (fig. 2.9). At the end, all the little demons "dance like madmen" (comme des fous, in the scenario): dislocation, epilepsy, madness.

As physiology had shown, the spectator's body was jolted by the amazing pratfalls and the disconcerting contortions and grimaces of acrobatic screen comics. If one's body was unconsciously solicited to imitate the movements in film comedies, there was a danger in viewing these thrilling feats. Some of Janet's patients suffered not from symptoms but from the fear of having them, from the neurotic anxiety surrounding the impulse to imitate what one sees. A thirty-three-year-old woman, for example, felt dizzy from the powerful "emotion of fear that she might have an epileptic attack, become insane, have convulsions of the face if she look[ed] up."[66] The fantasy of corporeal amputation is a prevalent hallucination in hysteria,[67] and the hallucinatory power of the cinematic image conveys this sensation to the body of the spectator. Filmic examples of decapitation and dismemberment are legion and have been profitably considered from a psychoanalytic point of view,[68] not from the perspective of high (reason, will) and low (motor automatisms, instinct). Take, for example, Méliès's *The Terrible Turkish Executioner*, or *Le Mélomane*, in which the bandleader repeatedly decapitates himself, using the heads as musical notes tossed up onto a suspended staff. Decapitation is definitely an affair of high and low in *Turkish Executioner*, with the body representing automatic movement and loss of control. The executioner's body is chopped in two at the waist, and even when he fits himself back together, he is shown still kicking on the floor before rising. Similarly, in the final scene of *L'Éclipse du soleil en pleine lune* (1907), Méliès (as the gesticulating astronomer) falls from a second story head first into a barrel of water (only the bottom half of his body is visible, with legs convulsively kicking). He is pulled out and held on either side by two assistants; the group advances toward the camera with the astronomer's legs kicking automatically to each side. (These frames bear an uncanny resemblance to Walter Chase Greenough's "Epileptic Seizure #5" in the *Epilepsy Biographs* shot in 1906.) Cut to the observatory, where the astronomer is placed into an armchair, but then, in response to his students' attempts to help (by smothering him with blankets), he falls to the floor, legs kicking wildly as in an epileptic seizure. His students lift him up onto the chair, where he becomes rigidly cataleptic. The title of the lost film *The Nuts of the Omnibus, or The Escapees from Charenton* (*Les Toqués de l'Omnibus ou Les Echappés de Charenton* [the mental hospital]) is explicit enough; the passengers of a bus turn into aggressive clowns who fuse into one personality and then break apart into "a thousand" pieces, according to the scenario. Doubling and multiplication of the self are rampant in Méliès's films: doubling in *Dédoublement cabalistique* (1898) and *L'Illusioniste double* (1900), tripling in *Homme de têtes* (1898), multiplication of the head in *Le Mélomane* (1903), and seven exposures of the entire body in *L'Homme orchestre* (1900). In *Illusions extraordinaires* (1903), Méliès takes the separate body parts of a dummy—legs, torso, head—out of a box and tosses them onto the floor, where they form a living woman. As he demonstrates, her head is still detachable. She is then transformed into confetti, only to become a woman, a monkey, and again a dummy, whose dismembered body is thrown into the air, ending the film. This type of metamorphosis figures in the hysteric's repertoire; Charles Richet treated the hysterical personality disorders of a somnambulist who "became," one by one, a peasant, actress, general, priest, nun, sailor, old woman, and little girl. Yet one can come even closer to Mélièsian metamorphoses in psychiatric lore: "one encounters people every day who . . . believe themselves changed into lions, bears, fountains, or fish . . . *neurotics!*" (*H*, 137).

Méliès referred to his illusions as "the entire arsenal of fantastic, magical compositions *amazing enough to drive the most intrepid spectator crazy.*"[69] And while viewers could be "driven crazy" by trick shots, Méliès the actor could be perceived as a madman by his audience because, in his films, the dizzying metamorphoses of the images orchestrated behind the camera are matched by the furor of Méliès's movements in front of the camera. An American fair impresario, in Paris to buy films, met the filmmaker and was astonished that he was normal: "he probably figured that I was . . . off my rocker, demented, the completely insane person . . . [that] he had seen on the screen."[70] When Méliès reminisced about "le cinéma primitif" at the Gala Méliès on December 16, 1929, he again emphasized the effect on the viewer of "this enormous accumulation of unexpected *trucs* that struck the spectator of the time with stupor. . . . Incomprehensible images where I executed the wildest cavorting and pirouettes to amuse [them]."[71] Méliès referred to his films as his "crazy productions" in a letter to Maurice Druhot.[72] Should we take these references to madness seriously? Was the filmmaker consciously drawing on medical science for his images of dismemberment, multiplication of the self, and convulsive movement? His first persona in the cabaret was, after all, "Dr. Melius."

"Spectators experienced near total identification" with the "dreamlike fantasies, hallucinatory colors, and antirational . . . photography" in films like those of Méliès, as Donald Crafton has so justly noted.[73] Henri de Parville wrote in *La Nature*, "The cinematograph is marvelous. It's unimaginably true. The power of illusion! When you find yourself before these moving pictures, you wonder if you're not hallucinating and if you're a simple spectator or, instead, an actor in these astonishing scenes of realism."[74] This is the most prevalent reaction to film screenings in the first decade of cinema, and identification with and incorporation of the screen image were studied by early commentators on film such as Wagenknecht and the Harvard psychologist Hugo Munsterberg. The nature of film's powerful impact on the body and on the unconscious is summarized in Jules Romains's lyrical pronouncement "All of the inner reality [of the crowd] trembles on the screen."[75] Blaise Cendrars wrote that film was:

Automatism. Psychism. And it is the machine that . . . at last uncovers the sources of feeling. . . . The brain is profoundly shaken, overwhelmed [*bouleversé*]. . . .

Everything is rhythm, word, life. . . . The image lies at the primitive sources of emotion. . . . The spectator is no longer immobile in his armchair; [he is] ripped out of it, done violence to, participates in the action, [and] recognizes himself on the screen among the convulsions of the shouting, protesting, and frantically agitated crowd [*qui se démène*].

The link with the lower orders, with primitive forces, was, moreover, not lost on the poet Cendrars: he writes of "the crowd who leaves the cinema, who flows out into the street like black blood, who *like a powerful beast* extends its thousand tentacles and . . . smashes the palaces and prisons."[76] He spoke from his privileged vantage point as both Gance's assistant (scripting, directing, and editing) on *La Roue* and *J'accuse* and as author of his own film scenarios.

Imitation and Contagion

Around 1900, public demonstrations by magnetizers were causing considerable controversy, not only because they seemed a parody of serious medical practice by charlatans, but also because they were dangerous.[77] The effect they had on their audiences aroused grave concern and apprehension; many spectators had recurrent experiences of catalepsy, hallucination, or other hysterical symptoms long after the magnetizer and his somnambulist had left town. In *Névrose hypnotique*, Ladame described a *manie hypnotique active* in the wake of these demonstrations around 1880.[78] Several people in France and Switzerland had to be admitted to psychiatric hospitals as a result of these shows. An army officer who nearly became insane was thereafter fascinated and put into a trance state by the sight of any brilliant light. (Could he later go to film screenings?) Ladame describes the effect on both the spectators and the hypnotized subject: the latter "is delivered up as a spectacle to the crowd, which is alive with unhealthy emotions, . . . abruptly put under a spell of fascination, [and] hallucinated to complete madness . . . at the risk of compromising his mental health" (*MM*, 40). It is particularly in this period "of outrageous realism in novels [that the] representation of clinics of mental pathology in novels is no longer enough [for those] who are thirsty for pleasures and morbid emotions: *they want to see this clinic on the stage*" (*MM*, 42). Had this statement been made a few years later, Ladame might well have added "and in the cinema." The goal is to "amuse and entertain the public [by the] display of symptoms of insanity and of major neuroses *whose comic character is exploited*." The comical can also be terrifying: these phenomena are surrounded "with a frightening and mysterious atmosphere suitable to . . . throw terror into weak brains" (*MM*, 41; emphasis mine). Many who did not become hysterics were thought now to be predisposed to hysteria, since spectacles like this "open the door" to alienation in individuals with "weak brains."[79] Worse, there was an effect of contagion. Doctors, like Paul-Max Simon and Paul Grellety, vociferously warned of the danger of the contagion of somnambulism from magnetizers' shows, along with the danger of hallucinations from prestidigitators' shows in fairs and of epilepsy from the mere sight of an epileptic attack. "There is no doubt that [epilepsy] can be engendered by imitation," and in fact this cause is more frequent than one might think; "as a result one must pay the most careful attention to preventing children, adolescents, and impressionable women from witnessing epileptic attacks."[80] Only ten years later, these very groups of people would comprise a good number of filmgoers. But, of course, the quintessentially contagious affliction was hysteria.

Imitation is one of the privileged domains of hysterics, wrote Pierre Briquet, one of the first to emphasize this clinical observation. Imitation is the means by which hysteria is spread, since a hysteric has only to see a gesture in order to unconsciously imitate it.[81] As Simon wrote, "sometimes hysterical attacks due to imitation [occur] in such a great number of subjects that the word *epidemic* has been used with some justification" (*HE*, 18). Hysterics imitate other hysterics—in fact, everyone they see—and normal subjects unconsciously imitate the convulsive movements that they witness. In addition, an "all too frequent cause of convulsions and subsequent forms of nervous illness" are spectacles that strike the imagination too vividly—for example, shows put on by fairground performers in which "the usual tricks with goblets, the bottomless bottle, and other phantasmagoria" are followed by the "apparition of devils, skeletons, and specters" (*HE*, 3, 4).[82] Other theatrical spectacles are breeding grounds for hysterical contagion. For doctors in the 1880s, "hysterical contagion is demonstrated and proven by science" (*H*, 391), and the spread of nervous illness is "more noticeable every day" (*HE*, 18).

Somnambulism and imitation, like automatisms, were inseparable from definitions and diagnoses of hysteria in the nineteenth century. Gilles Deleuze described light and somnambulism as typical of German expressionist film and an excess quantity of movement as typical of French cinema. "The robots, puppets, and automatons emphasize an [excess] quantity of movement."[83] This is a useful generalization; movement is the key to understanding not only French cinema, but also performance style in the cabaret, as I've argued here. Nonetheless, somnambulism is very present in the less well-known films of French cinema's first two decades. What is more, movement is not absent in somnambulists; it is simply internalized. The somnambulist only *appears* anesthetized; in reality the body is super-sensitive or *hyperesthetic*.

At the beginning of this study, I asked whether the impact of film on spectators during film's first decades was due to an intense feeling of reality or to an equally intense state of hallucinated hypnotic trance. It is now possible to propose the following answer: the *feeling* of reality is in fact the physical stimulus and the response of internal bodily movement, and this feeling state in no way contradicts the somnambulistic trance.

In the mid-1880s the celebrated sociologist Gabriel de Tarde, in a calmer register than Simon and Ladame, but with far greater ramifications, was situating the theme of imitation and contagion in a broader context. This work was collected and published in 1890 under the title *Les Lois de l'imitation*. Suggestion and its corollary, unconscious imitation, is a universal phenomenon, according to Tarde. Bernheim and other psychiatrists furnished convincing support for his thesis, and by 1890 "there [was] no more commonplace knowledge than this point of view."[84] If imitative behavior in response to unconscious suggestion is a universal phenomenon, then the paradigmatic figure of the individual in society is the somnambulist. This is exactly what Tarde says: the somnambulistic state *epitomizes* social behavior. "Society is imitation, and imitation is a form of hypnosis." "To have ideas only suggested and to believe them spontaneous, such is the illusion of the somnambulist." "Why should we be astonished, after all, by the unilateral and passive imitation of the somnambulist? A given act performed by any one of us gives those who witness it the more or less unconscious [*irréfléchie*] idea to imitate it" (*L*, 95, 83, 86). Note Tarde's qualification: "more or less unconscious." Whereas emphasis is placed on unconscious imitation in Tarde's text, as well as in Simon's and Gustave Le Bon's (and in mine), one cannot exclude a conscious desire to imitate those in power . . . or in the spotlight. Certainly, the fashionable aspect of hysteria, as depicted in society or on stage, provided an impetus for conscious imitation.[85] Tarde acknowledges his debt to theories of automatic reflex in physiology. And, citing Maudsley, Tarde notes that "the somnambulist is perhaps capable of unconsciously reading the mind [of the person who is exercising the hypnotic suggestion] *by an unconscious imitation of the pose and expression of the person whose muscular contractions he or she copies instinctively and precisely*" (*L*, 85). These concepts are, to my mind, central to late nineteenth-century spectacle and, as I've indicated, not only to public shows of hypnotism and

Fig. 2.10. Scene from Émile Cohl's film "The Hypnotic Mirror," sequence 1. The thief, under hypnotic trance, is reenacting the crime. 1910

magnetism. Descriptions of the most famous somnambulists of the nineteenth century could easily be mistaken for descriptions of the most famous actors, and hypnosis and acting talent were often compared. Tarde wrote that the hypnotized subject is "an excellent actor [since he or she] incarnates the personality suggested to him or her so profoundly that it enters into the heart, the character, and is expressed by his or her poses, gestures, and language" (L, 216n).[86] In his 1893 La Suggestion dans l'art, Paul Souriau underlined the two principal traits of the actor: doubling and imitation. These traits are present in the spectator as well, according to Hugo Munsterberg in America and to Louis Haugmard in France. Two decades after The Laws of Imitation, Haugmard wrote that film "launch[es] imitation, for the image excites naïve souls."[87]

It is no coincidence that somnambulism is omnipresent in French films and film criticism between 1895 and 1935, from Méliès's 1897 Le Magnétiseur to Jean Vigo's 1933 Zéro de conduite. Somnambulism easily shifts from comedy to melodrama, as in Émile Cohl's Le Miroir magique (1909) (fig. 2.10), Max Linder's Max hypnotisé (1910), Nick Winter et le voleur *somnambule* (1911), André Deed's *Cretinetti hypnotizzatore* (1912), and Louis Feuillade's *Les Vampires* (1915) and his comic *Bébé hypnotiseur*. As can be seen from the list here, it was not only theorists, scientists, and poets (like André Breton and Robert Desnos) who thought that film was "magnetizing." In 1908, arguing for the prohibition of looking directly into the camera, a journalist wrote that "when an actor looks at the camera . . . it is like a hypnotist snapping his fingers to bring a subject out of a trance."[88] In fact, the look into the camera can tend to induce trance as well; the most striking example in early cinema is the character of Dr. Mabuse in Fritz Lang's *Mabuse der Spieler*, parts 1 and 2. I want to underline the fact that the very respectable cover identity of Mabuse, the gambler, hypnotist, and omnipotent head of the underworld, is that of psychoanalyst. Director of the underworld (or unconscious) thanks to hypnotic suggestion, Mabuse is also he who knows most about hysteria. The presence of a character in the role of mesmerist or hypnotist training his gaze out into the audience underlines the film spectator's tendency to mime hysterical or somnambulistic gesture, and this is enhanced by the often-noted hypnotic power of the flickering light on a luminous screen in a darkened room.[89] It is the filmmaker who controls the magnetizing gaze out into the room. As Epstein wrote, "the director suggests, then persuades, then hypnotizes. . . . The film is nothing but a relay between the source of nervous energy and the auditorium which breathes its radiance. That is why the gestures which work best on screen are nervous gestures" ("M," 2: 238).[90]

According to Tarde, the sight of any gesture makes us want to imitate it. Arm and leg movements are especially contagious. One immediately grasps the pertinence of this notion for the spectator of early cinema, where (as Pascal Bonitzer puts it) "the only currency is that of gesture."[91] Diction and pronunciation, according to Tarde, are also "eminently imitative." Psychiatrists observed that "this instinct of imitation . . . seems to come from . . . the unconscious parts of the nervous system" (*HE*, 37). "It is certain that today, principally in the cities, hysteria is the illness in vogue: it is everywhere. And the essential trait of this sickness is the predominance of the nervous system [*la vie spinale*] over the life of the mind [*la vie cérébrale*]." "One became, without fail, hysterical and sometimes mad" as a result of putting "one's nervous system in unison with the anxious vibrations [*trépidations*] of the music of Offenbach" (*HE*, 98).

The unconscious tendency—not to say, irresistible urge—to imitate another's gestures or movements is often used to comic effect in French cinema, and the frequent presence of the double in early cinema is related to this urge. The double functions as a paradigm for unconscious imitation, somnambulism, automatisms, and the "lower order," and, indeed, for the film experience itself. In *Onésime contre Onésime* (Jean Bourbon, made between 1912 and 1914), doubling, joined to dismemberment and incorporation, is clearly designated as the division between the higher and the instinctual, lower order; the first intertitle reads "The good Onésime knew how to conduct himself in society, but the second one behaved like a hoodlum." The second Onésime always emerges, through superimposition, from the body of the first. Knees bent, posterior high in the air, the grotesque figure of the clown, the double grimaces to the camera. Disgusted by his alter ego, Onésime, "angry, separates himself from the other"; he does this by rolling out of bed and leaving the other (somnambulistic, instinctual) self behind. But the "bad Onésime took advantage of the new situation by behaving worse yet." By imitating his "better self's" gestures, he becomes indistinguishable from his respectable double. Division and incorporation, up until now staged through filmic superimpositions, are again enacted in the film's (missing) final scene, and here incorporation is literal. Driven to distraction, the once-civilized, "good" Onésime dismembers the bad Onésime and *eats him*.

The 1909 film *La Bous-Bous Mie* (credited to Émile Cohl but probably directed by Étienne Arnaud and written by Cohl) offers a compelling exploitation of imitation and viewer contamination. In addition, in this film one sees a slippage from the spectator's unconscious imitation of dance movements seen on stage to his or her conscious identification and repetition of the performance. Like Méliès's *Cake-Walk infernal, La Bous-Bous Mie* illustrates the contagion of extravagant dance movements. A stout Parisian concierge goes to the music hall (the Casino des Tourelles, where Maurice Chevalier is said to have made his professional debut in 1901) to applaud the new dance, La Bous-Bous Mie. The dancer performs a mixture of the undulations of Arabian belly dance and African jerking of the hips and buttocks, with arms raised akimbo and waving from side to side. After the dancer leaves the stage to enthusiastic applause, a comic comes onstage, only to be upstaged by Madame Ducordon, the concierge, who has risen from her seat and is dancing the Bous-Bous Mie (fig. 2.11). The gendarmes force her back into her seat, but, seconds later, she uncontrollably begins dancing again. This time she's firmly escorted out onto the sidewalk, where she starts to dance again; now the gendarmes are irresistibly caught up in the movement. Suddenly, they realize what has happened to them and, turning on their heel, they march back into the music hall with rigidly controlled

Fig. 2.11. Scene from Étienne Arnaud and Émile Cohl's *La Bous-Bous Mie*.
Madame Ducordon is imitating the cabaret dancer. 1909

steps. We then see her back in her *loge* (a word denoting both a concierge's
apartment *and* a theater box), where the dance has gotten such a hold on
her that—ignoring the calls of the occupants of the building—she stands on
a stool in front of the mirror doing the Bous-Bous Mie. (She is now both
spectator and entertainer.) When a resident comes in to complain, he, too,
is caught up in the movements. In the last scene, there is a reception for
friends in the *loge*. Here Madame Ducordon's transformation from spectator to performer is fully realized. Her husband, acting as master of ceremonies, taps three times as Madame Ducordon makes her entrance (in ori-
ental costume). Soon everyone present is imitating the movements of the
Bous-Bous Mie, faces ecstatic or convulsed with laughter (fig. 2.12). In the
meantime, unheard in the commotion, a group of well-heeled residents are
impatiently pulling on the cord outside the front door. They finally break in,
and they, too, are disarmed by the erotic, anarchic, and highly contagious
movements of the dance. In these scenes we see that the concierge, the half-
involuntary performer of hysterical movement, clearly uses these movements to fascinate, entrance, and disarm others; her audience is put into a

state resembling hypnotic trance, and they are helpless to resist imitating the movements they see before them. If one is not a performer exercising this power over others, then one is in the position of the spectator, in whose body these "uncivilized" movements take root. The spectator, whose body—like a second personality or an unconscious—is an expression of explosive sexuality and anarchy, is not in control of herself. (For example, the initial confrontation with the police is superseded by their conversion; a policeman who figures among the friends at the party takes center stage at one point, imitating the bumps and grinds in a totally lewd, uninhibited fashion; and there is a collapse of class distinctions between the concierge and the bourgeoisie at the end of the film.) Arnaud and Cohl's film, for all its gaiety and hilarity, is an illustration of the dangers of the music hall's and cinema's propagation of frenetic movement.[92]

If it is true, as Charles Keil believes, that "reflexive films . . . can indicate how the nature of the actual reception situation in this period might inflect our understanding of the operation of psychic mechanisms traditionally

Fig. 2.12. Scene from *La Bous-Bous Mie*. Another performance by Madame Ducordon. 1909

held to be transhistorical,"[93] then we should look very carefully at these films in which spectatorship is represented in relation to unconscious imitation and in which somnambulists, doubles, and popular entertainment are juxtaposed. In a 1907 article in *Le Cri de Paris*, we read that "the cinematograph . . . is in the process of turning into, like appendicitis, the national malady."[94] And in 1913, Haugmard wrote that because of the cinema,

the charmed masses will learn to combat all will to reason . . . they will only know how to open their big and empty eyes, and look, look, look. . . . The cinematograph will be [the only mode of] action for neurasthenics. And we will progressively reach those threatening days when universal illusion will reign in universal hamming [*cabotinage*].[95]

The suggestive power of gesture and movement takes on an unsuspected dimension in popular entertainment. Shaking, corporeal agitation, convulsive laughter: all are signs of the lower orders, the body dominating reason, hysteria—in short, loss of control. Aragon and Breton called hysteria "the greatest poetic discovery of the end of the nineteenth century." Their definition of hysteria, in 1928, perhaps best summarizes the aspects of cabaret and early film comedy that I've described here: "Hysteria is a mental state . . . characterized by the subversion of the relationships established between the subject and the moral world. . . . It can, from every point of view, be considered as a supreme means of expression."[96] The considerable legacy of what I've called the cabaret aesthetic and the central place played by physiological spectatorship in the period extend from popular culture to the major artistic movements of the early twentieth century. We see it in the zigzagging shapes of Karl Schmidt-Rottluff's, Max Pechstein's, and Egon Schiele's expressionist paintings as well as in Robert Wiene's film *The Cabinet of Dr. Caligari*. We see it in the "constant invention of new elements in stupor," the "profound analogies between humanity and the mechanical world [with the] contortions and grimaces of future humanity" that Marinetti conceptualized as a Theater of Stupor and Psychofolie in the 1913 Futurist manifesto entitled "Music Hall." We see it in the corporeal anarchy and hilarity of Dada and in the automatons and somnambulists of early cinema. The pain and liberation of the hysterical body indeed played a major role in making the term "pathology" nearly synonymous with "modernity."

CHAPTER 3

Automatisme Ambulatoire: Fugue, Hysteria, and Gender at the Turn of the Century

IAN HACKING

In 1891, the Bordeaux-based physician André Pitres observed that:

By the term ambulatory automatism is understood a pathological syndrome appearing in the form of intermittent attacks during which the patient, carried away by an irresistible impulse, leaves his home and makes an excursion or journey justified by no reasonable motive. The attack ended, the subject unexpectedly finds himself on an unknown road or in a strange town. Swearing by all the gods never again to quit his penates, he returns home but sooner or later a new attack provokes a new escapade.[1]

Ambulatory automatism, by whatever name—*dromomanie, poriomenie, Wandertrieb, determinismo ambulatorio,* psychogenic fugue, or, in the parlance of the current *Diagnostic and Statistical Manual* of the American Psychiatric Association, dissociative fugue—is an exemplar, even a caricature, of late nineteenth-century madness. It is also a distorting mirror of one of the obsessions of the modern middle class, the world of Thomas Cook and Son, the world of the comfortable traveler. For *les aliénés voyageurs*—to use the title of the first medical thesis about these men—were compulsive travelers, solid artisans or honest men of the laboring classes who, on hearing the name of a distant place, would set out on foot or by fourth-class carriage, not knowing why they went. So far as casual passers-by could tell, they behaved quite sensibly en route, yet they knew not what they were doing or, in some cases, who they were. That is the prototype.[2] Rich men had fugues, and so did knaves, but the central examples of nineteenth-century *fugueurs* were humble, decent men, who remained humble and decent on their deliberate yet unwanted trips, of which they later had almost no memory. Hysteria has been called the body language of female powerlessness. Fugue was a body language of male powerlessness.

Fugueurs did not wander. They traveled with perseverance, in a straight line, so to speak. At the end of 1899 a Swiss psychologist published *From India to the Planet Mars*, a once-famous book about a middle-class medium, hysteria, and multiple personality.[3] The book captured the imagination of a public already dedicated to spiritualism and Thomas Cook. *Fugueurs*, who were usually men of a humble station in life, did not get to Mars, but they got to India, to Moscow, to Algiers, or to Constantinople, although most were more modest in their simultaneously purposeful and meaningless expeditions. *Fugueurs* felt compelled and were fixated on a single idea or destination, a variant, as would once have been said, of an *idée fixe*. They had but one idea, and yet when we look back at them a century later, a whole cornucopia of ideas tumbles out. I shall manage to discuss, under the single heading of fugue, not only hysteria but also multiple personality, epilepsy, hypnosis, the military, the vagrancy scare (or homeless men in the 1890s), the police, anti-Semitism (wandering Jews), photography, art collectors, archaeology, the bicycle, the Olympic Games, and Proust. People have always gone on strange unmotivated trips, but when fugue became a medical entity, we had truly become modern.

Ambulatory automatism is not quite extinct; it is an extreme example of a modern malady. It is parlous to identify any clinical diagnosis of current psychiatric medicine with a mental illness from times gone by. Who will say which complaints today match the florid hysteria of the late nineteenth century? But plainly the official American definition of dissociative fugue in 1994 was a lineal descendant of Pitres's slightly more colorful characterization cited above:

A. The predominant disturbance is sudden, unexpected travel away from home or one's customary place of work, with inability to recall one's past.

B. Confusion about personal identity or assumption of new identity (partial or complete).

C. The disturbance does not occur exclusively during the course of Dissociative Identity Disorder (the new name for multiple personality disorder) and is not due to the direct physiological effects of a substance (e.g., a drug abuse, a medication) or a general medical condition (e.g., temporal lobe epilepsy).

D. The symptoms cause clinically significant distress or impairment in social, occupational, or other important areas of functioning.[4]

The 1992 guidelines of the World Health Organization often sound more sensible to the layperson than those of the American Psychiatric Association. There we find a greater emphasis on amnesia. "For a definite diagnosis," we are told, there should be:

(a) the features of dissociative amnesia

(b) purposeful travel beyond the usual everyday range (the differentiation between travel and wandering must be made by those with local knowledge); and

(c) maintenance of self care (eating, washing, etc.) and simple social interaction with strangers (such as buying tickets or petrol, asking directions, ordering meals).[5]

ICD–10 further explains that "although there may be amnesia for the period of the fugue, the individual's behaviours during this time may appear completely normal to independent observers."

A first respect in which dissociative fugue is exceptional is that almost no psychiatrists in the world today maintain that it is an autonomous, free-standing mental illness. "Fugue episodes" are taken to be symptoms or behaviors associated with other psychological or neurological problems. Yet if you turn to the appropriate page in the up-to-date American *DSM–IV* or European *ICD–10*, there it is, as if dissociative fugue were something you could simply have, like the measles. This modern diagnosis is a curious historical relic, grandfathered from a past that psychiatrists have forgotten, the fugue epidemic of the 1890s.

Ambulatory automatism really was an independent diagnostic entity in its homeland, France, in a precisely defined period, 1887–1909. I am content to posit a precise date range in order to highlight how specific the ailment was. The first celebrated case of fugue as a complaint in itself was written up in Bordeaux in 1887.[6] Albert was an extraordinary compulsive traveler, who, like the other men in his family, was employed by the local gas company. The last extended discussion of fugue was at a psychiatric conference held in Nantes in 1909. The conference had two themes: fugue and desertion from the army.[7] This combination of the two topics in a single meeting was no accident. In order to gain acquittals for some of the hapless conscripts who deserted in peacetime, military doctors would diagnose them as *fugueurs*.

We see from the *ICD–10* definition that fugue is, among other things, a curious special case of the topic so well studied by Michael Roth—forgetting.[8] We may even wonder why fugue is not simply a species of amnesia—amnesia with traveling. The distinction is enforced at present, by both *ICD–10* and *DSM–IV*, not because fugue is somehow an independent disorder, but because of how fugue and ambulatory automatism emerged as a distinct disorder in the late nineteenth century. And here we have to note another remarkable fact, that the psychiatric profession itself exhibits a kind of collective amnesia. There is now a distinct diagnosis, fugue, only because of what happened a century ago. Dozens upon dozens of cases of fugue were published in France alone between 1887 and 1909, and there have been excellent survey articles in the psychiatric literature, running through past cases. Yet in the present-day medical literature all but two of the nineteenth-century studies have been lost, forgotten, abandoned.[9]

For the primarily European *ICD–10*, the main problem for people with dissociative disorders is amnesia. For the American *DSM–IV*, the main problem is multiple personality.[10] *DSM–IV* reminds us that fugue was not only a disorder of forgetting but also, to a lesser extent, a disorder of personal identity: "Confusion about personal identity or assumption of new identity (partial or complete)." A definition is used to keep dissociative fugue distinct from dissociative identity disorder (multiple personality), but a mere definition cannot draw a sharp line between the two types of behavior, either now or a century ago. Although complete identity confusion was rare, *fugueurs* of the 1890s tended to have at most a foggy sense of who they were. In particular, the *fugueur* tended to lose touch with exactly those facts that bureaucrats use to identify us: his proper name, his place of birth, where he lived, whether he was married or single, the name of his relatives, his educational history, his job. Compulsory identity cards had not yet been introduced. *Fugueurs* crossing borders would commonly carry some sort of passport, but, it seems that is was used simply as a means to cross the border, not as a token of identity.

Yet there is a fundamental difference between fugue and multiple personality. You seldom find it stated explicitly in summaries of clinical experience, although it might be smuggled in under the discreet heading of "Epidemiology." The fact is that those with multiple personalities are women. *Fugueurs* are men. Today there is a great cry among those who treat the dissociative disorders: "Where are the men with multiple personalities?"[11] This is because nine out of ten diagnosed multiples are women. Why is this a question at all? Is a disorder stigmatized by being "female"? Or is it rather that practitioners fear that the fact that nearly all recent multiples have been women will be used as grounds for arguing that the disorder has been suggested to their patients? Or that multiple personality, like hysteria long ago, is less a mental illness than a confused expression of female powerlessness? At any rate, there has for some years been a popular explanation for the missing male multiples. They are, it is claimed, not in the mental health system, but in the criminal justice system—they are in jail. It is also true that most persons diagnosed with multiple personality one hundred years ago were women. But there is an easy answer to the question "where were the men?" The male multiples were out on trips. According to my count, almost exactly nine in ten *fugueurs* were men. The 1907 presidential address to the American Neurological Association stated the matter more strongly. In the course of arguing that ambulatory automatism was a type of hysteria, the speaker observed that:

Early on in my investigations I was struck by the enormous preponderance of men. In the very considerable number of reported cases, I have found only two women. . . . Why no ambulatory automatism in women? . . . It is quite natural that a hysterical woman should not go off on a long and complicated journey but, for her attack, should have one of the "regular" manifestations of the disease.[12]

Quite natural, indeed. Fugue is here seen as a male expression of hysteria, a type of expression that would be improper or dangerous for a woman to adopt. It is no literary trope to say that fugue is the body language of male powerlessness: here our neurologist implies the same thing. Fugue was at the cutting edge of clinical and theoretical thinking about hysteria. A chief diagnostic issue in 1890 was whether ambulatory automatism was a type of hysteria or a type of epilepsy. The hyphen in the then-common diagnosis "hystero-epilepsy" needed to be removed. A case of fugue had to be either hysterical or epileptic. "Hystero-epilepsy" was replaced by "hysteria/epilepsy," with a sharp divide between them. This is in itself a remarkable tale in the history of psychiatry. It is well known that although Charcot by no means originated the notion of male hysteria, he did legitimate and popularize it. He is also the man who gave us the label "ambulatory automatism." So we might expect him to say that his men who took irrational journeys confirmed the idea of male hysteria. Not at all. Charcot fiercely and firmly diagnosed latent epilepsy. Even when there were no seizures, and no family history of the disease, the trips of a man afflicted with *automatisme ambulatoire* were "epileptic equivalents." I will mention just a couple of his arguments here.

Charcot was a neurologist. He believed that hysteria was part of a structure of hereditary defects, which could also include epilepsy and alcoholism. It was produced by occasioning causes. In women these could be emotional or moral, but in men the causes were physical trauma, typically injury to the head, neck, or spinal column; poisoning by industrial or artisanal use of lead, mercury, or silver; or the consumption of alcohol. Charcot's *fugueurs* had no history of physical trauma, ergo, they were not hysterical. He confirmed that fact by clinical questioning, a practice that today we believe could at his hands incite or remove symptoms of hysteria based on the dictates of theory. In addition to his clinical analysis, Charcot also claimed that his men stopped traveling when given large doses of sodium bromide, which was effective for epilepsy but largely worthless for hysteria. He was in fact wrong about that: his classic patient wandered off, never to be seen again, when stuffed full of bromide. Whatever the merit of his arguments, he established a little paradigm: ambulatory automatism is latent epilepsy.

According to *DSM–IV*, dissociative fugue by definition cannot be frontal lobe epilepsy. *ICD–10* states more carefully that:

> Differentiation from post-ictal fugue, seen particularly after temporal lobe epilepsy, is usually clear because of the history of epilepsy, the lack of stressful events or problems, and the less purposeful and more fragmented activities and travel of the epileptic. (*ICD–10*, 155)

Hence my claim that today's diagnosis of dissociative fugue is the lineal descendant of ambulatory automatism looks suspect. Charcot, after all, argued that ambulatory automatism is latent epilepsy (although the travels of his own favorite patient were, contra *ICD–10*, thoroughly purposeful).

However, there was another, anti-Charcotian paradigm established in Birdhouse the year before Charcot invented the very phrase "ambulatory automatism." The Birdhouse *fugueurs* had many of the florid symptoms of hysteria, such as restricted fields of vision, partial anesthesias, inexplicable headaches, trance preceded by the *globus hystericus* sensation, and exceptional suggestibility. Above all, although they usually could not remember where they traveled, they could recall many specific details under hypnosis. Hypnosis and hysteria had been firmly joined by Charcot himself. The recovery of lost itineraries by hypnosis was standard and striking. This proved—in the second paradigm—that fugue was a type of hysteria.

So two stories were in circulation about *fugueurs*. One claimed that they were epileptics, and the other that they were hysterics. Examples of both types of men were described by rival parties. After Charcot died in 1893, all but his most faithful acolytes climbed on the hysteria bandwagon. Sage opinion had it that there were two types of fugue, but that most *fugueurs* could be expected to be hysterical rather than epileptic.[13] That opinion did not last long. Fugue was found among an extraordinary range of mental illnesses, and finally was associated with that new German diagnosis, *dementia praecox*. Fugue ceased to be a type of hysteria or a type of latent epilepsy and became simply a symptom or manifestation of a superordinate disorder.

The above is a snippet from the French story. Fugue powerfully illustrates the role of national tradition and spheres of influence. Whereas Italy had its spate of mad travelers directly after the disorder erupted in France, there was no such diagnosis in Germany until 1898, when a doctor declared that German psychiatry was derelict in its duty: it reported no clinical studies of ambulatory automatism. The golden age of this disorder in Germany began a decade after the one in France and stopped only with the Great War. The same is true in Russia. The Germans and Russians were faithful Charcotians: fugues were epileptic equivalents. Italians, on the other hand, inclined to the hysteria opinion.

Why were German-speaking doctors Charcotian, believing *Wandertrieb* to be epileptic in nature? This question leads us to our next subject, the military. A number of military doctors all over Europe were repelled by the swinging punishments handed down for conscript deserters during peacetime. As a result, army and navy physicians fastened on automatism as a way of getting men off. Male hysteria never had the prominence in the German- and Slavic-speaking worlds that it had in France and Italy. By 1905, when fugue really caught on in central Europe, hysteria was dying, for reasons so well described by Mark Micale.[14] Hence latent epilepsy was the best hook on which the military could hang *Wandertrieb*.

Incidentally, fugue never did catch on in the English-speaking world, despite the fame of Ansel Bourne. Bourne was a preacher who was reborn as someone else, a grocer named Brown.[15] He was described by contemporary physicians as a multiple personality, not as a *fugueur*. William James and other spiritualists interviewed him. In his Lowell lectures in 1896, James went so far as to take ambulatory automatism as the central idea of dissociation, with multiple personality as peripheral—precisely the opposite of what was done, then or now, by every other theorist of dissocation.[16] Charcot's lecture on ambulatory automatism was widely reported in Britain and America, and a few cases did attract brief attention, but aside from William James few took the disorder seriously.[17] A few instances of what would in France have been reported as classic ambulatory automatism were described as multiple personality. Two phrases readily explain why fugue was unimportant in America: no conscript army, and "Go West, young man." Fugue requires, as the 1994 *DSM–IV* puts it, a home or customary place of work. But there is also a third reason. Hysteria, epilepsy, and hystero-epilepsy all fell under the sign of hereditary degeneracy, which was an especially French-Catholic obsession.

In the nineteenth century, different mental illnesses were prevalent at different times. At the beginning of the century, suicide, madness, crime, and prostitution attracted the greatest social and medical attention, because they helped to keep down the French birth rate relative to that of Germany or Britain. After 1870 vagrancy—*vagabondage*—began to be recognized, and by 1885 it was deemed a major social problem. To exaggerate, it became the "universal of mental pathology, the prism through which all the categories of madness and abnormality could be distributed."[18] Vagrancy was thus medicalized straightaway. Vagrants were degenerates, sure enough. And many must have suffered from *automatisme ambulatoire*. Jean-Claude Beaune has gone so far as to describe the medicalization, and medical incarceration, of tramps and hobos as a species of "genocide."[19] The population was not literally killed, but it was extinguished in asylums and jails. Enter the police. In fact, Charcot's first and classic case of ambulatory automatism had been subject to police harassment. He was a deliveryman for a company that manufactured brass ornaments. On his first fugue, he was on a train crossing the Seine when the ticket collector approached. Having no ticket, he jumped out of a window into the river. He could not swim, but he was fished out and taken to a hospital. Within an hour he was reached by the long arm of the railway police, who demanded the fare. On his next fugue he got to the seaside, and there he was detained for some days. Because of these events Gilles de la Tourette proposed that every person diagnosed with *automatisme ambulatoire* should have a medical tag with clear instructions about his disease and his home physician.[20] That was the way in which innocent deviants could be fitted into the growing system of surveillance of an increasingly mobile public. Notice, incidentally, how Charcot's patient was, in terms of social class, a prototypical *fugueur*, a hard-working deliveryman, who, in his fugue state, was so shocked to find that he was traveling without a ticket that he risked drowning over dishonor.

Those were early days, when philanthropy and concern for the patient were paramount in the minds of the physicians. At the end of the ambulatory automatism period we find a very different political philosophy of fugue. It was stated by the head doctor at the Paris Police Prefecture and an alienist at a mental hospital who served regularly as an expert witness in prosecutions: "Fugue," the two men insisted, "is an anti-social act."

> Every individual has obligations under which he lives. From the moment that he breaks the social contract, be it instinctively or voluntarily, he puts himself outside legality. That is the case of the *fugueur* who abandons his domicile, and that is why fugue is an anti-social malady.[21]

Then they gave a brisk distinction of fugue from the problems that had perplexed the clinicians. Fugue is to be distinguished from "procursive epilepsy, automatic somnambulism, alcoholic and all other displacements which *are not accompanied by the disappearance of the subject.*"[22] In short, the police don't care about the medical niceties. If a person stays at home or at work, that's fine, no matter what ails him. But if he flees, for any reason it is anti-social and subject to detention and punishment.

Our strange topic seems to touch upon every issue of the day. The 1890s is the decade of the Dreyfus case, but Jews were also deemed to be a pressing problem at a much lower stratum of society. The great pogroms in the east sent Jews all over Europe. Albert, the first Birdhouse *fugueur* of 1887, had been casually compared to the Wandering Jew (he was not Jewish). Charcot's students, working in a public hospital, saw many poor Jewish refugees.

Charcot and his assistants were fascinated by what they called the iconography of the mad. They were delighted to compare representations of the insane in medieval art with photographs prepared in their clinic. One thesis from Charcot's clinic is rich in copies of mostly seventeenth-century woodcuts of the Wandering Jew. "The Wandering Jew of the old prints is indeed a true wandering Jew, none other than the wandering Jew of the Salpêtrière."[23] A French medical thesis consisted of an opening discussion, some general description, a number of cases presented in clinical detail, and a conclusion. In it we find five detailed cases, four men and a woman. Several of them have standard hysterical symptoms of partial anesthesia and restricted vision. The overall diagnosis is hystero-neurasthenia. (Beard's American diagnosis, neurasthenia, had recently become prominent in the clinic.) This being Charcot's clinic, these patients could not suffer from ambulatory automatism, which was a species of epilepsy. There is an odd twist here, because in the course of surveying the literature, Charcot's student decided that the patient closest to the wandering Jews was none other than Albert, the original *fugueur* of Bordeaux. By implication Albert did not suffer from Charcotian ambulatory automatism, although for Pitres, quoted at the opening, the hysterical Albert was the very model of ambulatory automatism. All of which reminds us that you can't retain ownership of the names that you invent.

The wandering Jews in Charcot's ward were duly photographed, although the photographs were not reproduced in the thesis. Photography is a modern art. The very first multiple personality in history—that, is, with more than two distinct and diagnosed personalities—was photographed in some ten supposed distinct personality states. Albert, the first *fugueur*, appeared only as a drawing in a thesis about him. (Medical theses had only drawings, not photos, which explains why the thesis on wandering Jews merely refers to the photographs taken at the Salpêtrière, but includes many reproductions of old woodcuts.) For published photographs of Albert we must turn to the textbook by Pitres.[24] There we see Albert as normal, as natural somnambulist, as hypnotized, and as *fugueur*. Thus the very first case of fugue was presented to the world with what was called an iconography. I should say a little more about the medical culture in which Albert made his way.

The first French double personality to be studied in depth was Felida X, known to hospitals in Bordeaux from 1858 but presented as a double personality only in 1876.[25] Her doctor was Eugène Azam. Philippe Tissié, who wrote up Albert, was a protégé of Azam's. For twenty years Bordeaux, *point d'origine* of the double personality, also produced almost half the written-up cases of fugue, or ambulatory automatism, in France. The doctors there were true bourgeois. Azam had a notable collection of paintings, objects from the ancient world, and local archaeological discoveries. Azam and Tissié knew each other best not as senior and junior doctor, but because Tissié was honorary secretary of the Bordeaux archaeological society, over which Azam presided. It was these thoroughly modern figures, the small bourgeois collectors, who gave us multiple personality and fugue.

It may seem a large jump to another modern instrument, the bicycle. The bicycle has for too long been crushed between the steam locomotive and the automobile in accounts of the modern world and its machinery. In the 1890s the bicycle was the thoroughly modern middle-class sporting instrument of choice. Tissié was able to discover *fugueurs* on bicycles. His *fugueurs* on foot often did eighty kilometers a day; we have no distance for the bicyclists. But, possibly because he was fascinated by these feats of endurance, Tissié made physical education rather than psychiatry his forte, not that he saw these as being distinct. He devised a remarkable cure for severe hysteria, which involved riding endlessly on a bicycle.[26] It worked. Another great product of modernism is the Olympic Games. There was once a real question, fought out in the 1890s, about the nature of sport. The Swedish system opposed competition and favored individual development through gymnastics. Pierre de Coubertin famously took the opposite view, that the English (and ancient Greek) model of competitive sport should rule. Coubertin nearly lost.

Tissié was dead set against what he saw as the excesses of competitive sport, the very elements of enthusiasm, liberty and schoolboy association that Coubertin so vigorously endorsed. Their rivalry grew, until, by the early '90s, they were implacable enemies, and when Coubertin again pleaded for athletic games at a conference of the French Association for the Advancement of Science at Caen, in 1894, Tissié strenuously attacked him and carried the day. The conference resolved "to encourage physical exercise, but to make war on sports in school establishments."[27]

Tissié, as we all know, may have won the battle, but he lost the war, terribly. He did, in a way, have the last, if forgotten, word. Having trained as an alienist, he could name the mental illness from which his opponents suffered. They were afflicted by "ludomania."[28] Middle-class travel, photography, the bicycle, and the Olympic Games are all parts of the idea of the modern that have been too much neglected in our concern with, for example, painting and the novel.

But I had better return to stories. Here is one about a man more prosperous than your typical *fugueur*. Émile, a Paris lawyer aged thirty-three, "present[ed] all the manifest signs of hysteria." He was "almost instantaneously hypnotizable"—he had only to be asked to fixate on a point in space, or to hear a sharp sound (the clap of a hand), and he would fall into hypnotic sleep. He even went into a trance when he caught himself looking into a mirror in a café by the Bourse. It is perhaps not too surprising that every once in a while he lost his memory. "A new life, a new memory, a new me, begins. He walks, takes the train, makes visits, buys things, gambles, etc." Some of the events in Émile's second state were not altogether unrelated to events in his normal state. Thus he visited his stepfather, with whom he had a fight, before changing state on September 23, 1888. He returned to his normal state in the middle of October. Meanwhile he had visited one of his uncles, a bishop in Haute-Marne. There he had broken furniture and torn up books and even manuscripts. He also incurred five hundred francs of debt during his peregrinations, which led to a charge of swindling. Since no one knew exactly where he was, he was tried and convicted in absentia. The decision was reversed once medical evidence had been heard. He repeated the offense, and this time he also stole a small sum of money. He was again apprehended. Two well-known expert witnesses made a favorable deposition, and the charge was again dismissed.

The man recalled under hypnosis that, during the first incident, he had borrowed five hundred francs to gamble, and he described in detail the games he had played and how he had lost. The second incident furnished even more compelling evidence of the power of hypnosis (and hence of the hysterical nature of the case). Émile knew that he had possessed in his normal state, before he lost consciousness, a wallet containing 226 francs. It disappeared during his second state, although he had no idea where or how.

Six months later, under hypnosis, he recalled the hotel in which he had left it. Upon awakening from the hypnotic state, he was told to write to that hotel, and the next day he received his wallet in the mail.

Here we find what was to become the central criterion for hysterical fugue: amnesia or confused memory regarding the trip, which could be resolved under hypnosis.[29] This story was presented to the Académie des Sciences Morales on January 20, 1890, as a case of ambulatory automatism in a hysteric. It was thereby an anti-Charcotian case. Émile had been treated by an eccentric Parisian alienist and magnetizer, Dr. J. B. Luys, but it was the highly respectable professor of medicine and hygiene Dr. Adrien Proust who reported the case. Henri Ellenberger, that exemplary student of the history of dissociation with an encyclopedic knowledge, recalls "idle talk in Madame Verdurin's salon" about a double personality, and writes, "It is noteworthy that this very story had been published by Marcel Proust's father, Adrien Proust, as a significant psychopathological case."[30] That may be pushing things, because ambulatory automatism, the very point (and title) of Proust's report, is not mentioned by Marcel Proust, and the disorder had, indeed, disappeared in France by the time Marcel Proust published his great cycle of novels. For the passage occurs in *Le Temps retrouvé*, in the voice of Dr. Cottard, who, "with the delicacy which reveals the man of distinction," is changing the course of conversation from a disagreeable subject. He "relates in more philosophical terms than most physicians can command" how the trauma of a fire changed Madame Verdurin's footman into a new man, with new handwriting and an intolerable character that led to his being dismissed. Then, as they move from the dining room to the Venetian smoking room,

Cottard told us that he had witnessed actual doublings of the personality, giving as example the case of one of his patients whom he amiably offers to bring to see me, in whose case Cottard has merely to touch his temples to usher him into a second life in which he remembers nothing of the other, so much so that, a very honest man in this case, he had actually been arrested several times for thefts committed in the other during which he had been nothing less than a disgraceful scamp.[31]

Is this the specific story of Émile, reported in 1890 by Adrien Proust, or is it more of an amalgam? No matter. Émile himself is not a prototypical *fugueur* because he was of the middle class, a lawyer. And in his fugue he was dishonest, a swindler. The prototypical *fugueur* was an honest craftsman, artisan, clerk, or regularly employed laborer—or a conscript. He was not a Paris lawyer, nor was he a tramp. In his fugue state he never stole unless it was out of necessity, a piece of food or clothing.

Hence I return to my opening remarks. The *fugueur* is a distorting mirror of the classier stuff that we call modern, for the modern is assuredly bourgeois, and when modern men and women traveled compulsively, they hired Thomas Cook and Son to make the arrangements. After a fugue the prototypical *fugueur* does not ask, am I far from home? He does not ask, where am I? When he wakes up he knows where he is, and he wants to go home to family, unless compulsion strikes again, and he moves on. We do not find this humble man in the impeccably controlled Proust, who at most frames a man, possibly Émile, in a conversation. The *fugueur* is more a figure of popular culture. His descendant appears in trashy stories as the man who wakes up in a strange town, with no idea how he got there and a train ticket in his pocket. In television thrillers his descendant is run together with amnesiacs, contrary to the intentions of the ICD–10. I should expect *fugueurs* to occur in the ephemeral popular writing of the 1890s, but I do not know of any. I should be grateful to any reader who can direct me to examples.[32]

My first and favorite *fugueur*, Albert of Bordeaux, figured not in Proust but in a popular book, complete with illustrations.[33] He was well worth the tale. On his greatest trip he was arrested in Moscow as a nihilist. (How right the police of Moscow were: what is a *fugueur* but the ultimate unwitting nihilist?) After several months of incarceration, he was released with some three hundred others (the remainder of his fellow nihilists were executed or sent to Siberia). He and his gang, mostly Gypsies, were force-marched to the Bosphorus. That is a story to tell elsewhere. I should like to conclude not with Albert, the first *fugueur*, but with another man, the last of the French mad travelers.

The last *fugueur*, as I think of him, was a compulsive deserter; the military doctor who examined him called him a *deserteur voyageur*.[34] I take him to be my own mirror image, because his routes were ones of which I am deeply fond. His first desertion was from the barracks at Perpignan. From there he walked over the smugglers' trails between France and Spain, a network of glorious rocky walks in the Alberes, the foothills of the Pyrénées. There on a flowery slope or on a windblown outcrop you may still encounter a nervous man who is hoping not to be seen. Today he is more likely to be a confused Moroccan making his way gingerly through to France than a dazed French conscript heading for the safety of Spain.

PART II

Technologies of the Psyche

CHAPTER 4

In Your Face: Physiognomy, Photography, and the Gnostic Mission of Early Film

TOM GUNNING

Béla Balázs, writing in the 1920s, declared "At present a new discovery, a new machine, is at work to turn the attention of men back to a visual culture and give them new faces."[1] This claim exemplifies an almost forgotten utopian tradition of film theory, one that saw cinema not only as a new art form or a new language, but also as a new instrument of knowledge. For theorists such as Balázs, the motion picture camera had the ability not only to capture reality, but also to penetrate it as a new instrument of the visible that had a revelatory mission. We could call this potential for uncovering new visual knowledge the gnostic (from gnosis, knowledge) mission of cinema. For Balázs and other utopian theorists, the gnostic potential of the cinema was especially evident in the conjunction of the cinematic device of the close-up and the subject of the human face: "It is the "microphysiognomics" of the close-up that have given us this subtle play of feature, almost imperceptible yet also so convincing. The invisible face behind the visible has made its appearance."[2]

One could find parallel quotes from other utopian theorists of the 1920s (as well as parallel ideas in Benjamin's somewhat later essay "The Work of Art in the Age of Mechanical Reproduction"), such as Vertov ("a shot of the banker will only be true if we can tear the mask from him, if behind the mask we can see the thief") or Jean Epstein ("I am sure . . . that if a high speed film were made of an accused person during his interrogation, then beyond his words, the truth would appear, unique, evident, written out").[3]

I would like to use this detour into film theory to highlight something about the origins of cinema and this overdetermined fascination with the close-up and the human face. In earlier canonical accounts of film history, the close-up transformed cinema from a mere means of reproduction into a unique art form, a transformation often attributed to D. W. Griffith. Not only is this account discredited on factual grounds (Griffith did not invent the close-up, and in fact it occurs rather infrequently in the films he made for the Biograph Company, which are generally seen as the foundation of his later film style), but it also obscures the complex archaeology of the facial close-up in early cinema.[4] A close examination of this archaeology underscores the key role that the gnostic view of cinema played in both the invention and the form of early cinema.

Behind the gnostic impulse that motivates the invention and the practice of early cinema lurk ambiguous relations woven among visuality, technology, knowledge, representation, and entertainment in modern culture. Uncovering the role that capturing the face played in both cinema and its antecedents traces a saraband between seeing and knowing within the new visual terrain opened up by photographic technology, which could not only reproduce human eyesight but exceed it. At the center of this figure lies the expressive human face whose relation to knowledge and communication forms a central preoccupation of Western culture, serving as a pivot between individuality and typicality, expression and destiny, body and soul. The attempt to bring photography, and especially motion photography, to bear on this most polysemous of human objects reveals a crisis in understanding visual representation beneath a proclaimed confidence.

It is well known that close framings of human faces appear at the origin of cinema. The early Edison kinetoscope films *Fred Ott's Sneeze* (shot in 1894) and *May Irwin Kiss* (1896) frame figures at the waist in a manner that clearly emphasizes the transformations of their faces as they perform simple biological actions. Even earlier, one of the first cinematic or protocinematic apparatuses was fashioned by George Demenÿ in 1891 precisely to obtain a moving image of the human face (and especially the mouth as it spoke) to use as an aid in teaching deaf children to speak.[5] The Edison and Demenÿ motion pictures may seem to diverge sharply in purpose and audience (education versus entertainment; a small, specialized audience versus a mass one), but I would claim that they are in fact dialectically interrelated. Early cinema, whether designed as entertainment, pedagogical tool, or instrument of scientific investigation, maintained an important relation to the gnostic impulse, although it often operated as parody.

The gradual perfection of still photography stimulated the pursuit of visual phenomena that might otherwise slip below the threshold of conscious observation and opened up new possibilities of visual knowledge. The desire to make photography ever more sensitive to the ephemeral and instantaneous events of physical nature was a major motivation for cinema's

Fig. 4.1. Close-up of Mae Marsh from D. W. Griffith's film *Intolerance*, 1916

invention and perfection. Early cinema owes its gradual technical realization to this gnostic impulse driving the work of Eadweard Muybridge, Étienne-Jules Marey, Albert Londe, Georges Demenÿ, and others. Beyond the
technical invention of photography, the origin of this impulse lies in a rede-
finition of the role of visual evidence and new methods for investigating the
visual world. The successive ways the human face was categorized, investigated, and visualized in the pursuit of knowledge provides one way of tracing this gnostic impulse through to the cinema (see fig. 4.1).

But the study of the face possesses its own history, as well as its own
ambivalent relation to systems and methods of knowledge. Balázs's term
"microphysiologies" invokes (with the added precision of "micro") the
somewhat antiquated term "physiognomy," a science of facial classification
that had basically been discredited by the twentieth century.[6] In many ways
the decline of this pseudo-evidence paralleled the growth in new methods
of visual observation, such as photography. Physiognomy has its roots in texts
from antiquity attributed to Aristotle and Pythagoras that trace the relation
between physical appearance and character, a practice that ultimately
derives from magical forms of interpretation and divination such as chiro-

mancy. It found its most influential formulation in the work of Giovanni Battista della Porta at the end of the sixteenth century, in which the shape of the elements of the human face was interpreted by a series of analogies to animals, the elements, and the stars within a Neoplatonic cosmic system. In this system of resemblances and affinities, the human face took on meaning by a series of metaphors that joined man's physical appearance to the powers that rule his soul and destiny via emblematic animals (e.g., facial resemblance to a lion indicates strength and hot temper) as well as the astral and planetary influences of astrology. As an exemplar of magical thinking, physiognomy worked on the basis of visual resemblance, tracing, as Foucault describes it, similitudes as "visual marks of invisible analogies."[7]

At the beginning of the modern age (and under the direct influence of Descartes), physiognomy became reinterpreted as a guide to visual representation in the arts, detouring from a means of knowing man's destiny to a system of aesthetic signification. The work *Conférence sur l'expression générale et particulière* (1688) by Charles Le Brun, first painter to Louis XIV, which assembled physiognomic principles as a method for the proper way for painters to portray emotion and character through facial expression, dealt both with facial structure, the traditional domain of physiognomy, and the more transient passions, the domain of facial expression rather than type. His discussion of the passions is modeled on Descartes's last work, *The Passions of the Soul* (1649), and provides drawings for each of the simple and complex passions as Descartes had outlined them. Le Brun understood his task in terms of Cartesian relations between mind and body: "Whatever causes passion in the soul creates also some action in the body. It is necessary to know which are the actions of the body that express those passions and what action is."[8] In doing this, however, he placed himself in unacknowledged opposition to Descartes's own declaration that facial expressions are difficult to discern as signs of the passions and, being easily feigned, are often misleading.[9] Le Brun's discussion of physiognomy, the structure of the face as a sign of character rather than as expression of passion, further developed traditional analogies between human faces and those of animals and the qualities they represented (see fig. 4.2). As Patrizia Magli says, "In his links with ancient traditions, and in his merging them with more innovative trends, Le Brun both fell behind and preceded his own times."[10]

Physiognomy entered into the age of reason and sensibility (and strongly influenced both Realist and Romantic aesthetics of the nineteenth century) through the famous *Physiognomische Fragmente* of the Swiss theologian Johann Caspar Lavater, first published in 1775.[11] Basically a further system-

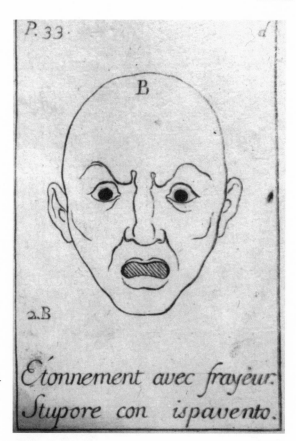

Fig. 4.2. Charles Le Brun's drawing illustrating a typical expression of astonishment, 1668

atization of the ancient tradition, Lavater's work no longer approached physiognomy as divination, but, developing Le Brun's understanding of body as the expression of the soul, it presented the science as a means of deciphering the mysterious inner world through bodily signs.

Existing on the other side of Descartes's split between the mind and body, the Romantics believed Lavater's physiognomy reunited mind and body in an act of symbolic reading, as Novalis's notes on physiognomy reveal: "The religious essence of physiognomy. The divine and infinitely meaningful hieroglyphs of each human body. . . . The way in which these hieroglyphs have their occasional moments of revelation."[12] The Romantics also recognized Lavater's method as revealing the unique qualities of each individual physiognomy, analyzing each face as a combination of individual elements rather than as a master table of analogies. Lavater's physiognomy exerted as much influence on aesthetics as on scientific discourse, and was directly

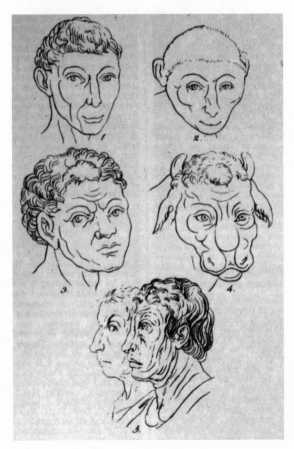

Fig. 4.3. Johann Casper Lavater's illustration of diverse physiognomies, circa 1775

responsible for the increased popularity of the silhouette as a mode of representation. Not only did the silhouette accurately capture the facial profile so important in Lavater's method, but its indexical process of production—directly tracing the shadow of its subject—announced the importance of new visual technologies in sciences of observation, directly anticipating photography (see fig. 4.3).[13]

Although the tradition of physiognomy is complex, one can see a consistent drift in its conceptions as it moves from traditional systems of occult knowledge to a modern discourse with at least pretenses to being a science. Physiognomy became less of a system by which one reads an individual's fate inscribed in facial features through cosmic and symbolic analogies than a means of observation in which the face is mobile and expressive, revealing a person's accumulated history as much as predetermined fate (Lavater emphasized that a person's way of life could affect his physical appearance).[14] Features no longer embodied the coded writing of destiny. They spoke the language of emotion conveyed through expressions, the changeable signifiers of varying moods. The facial traits that reflected character served less as predictions of a person's future than as traces left by their profession or way of life, less occult symbols than the residue of a scientific logic of cause and effect. For instance, the French editor of Lavater, Dr. Moreau de la Sarthe, described the physiognomies of professions as a reflection of habitual behavior:

Skillful and very experienced surgeons have in their physiognomy a particular dominant trait, which comes from a habitual movement of raising the upper lip—which can be attributed to the effort they make to resist the impression caused by the sight of suffering and pain which they have before their eyes during major operations.[15]

But however systematized and rationalized, physiognomy still carried a promise of knowledge that verged on the occult. Since our reactions to faces seem immediate and untutored, physiognomy exemplified the Romantic concept of universal hieroglyphic language, more intuitive than analytical, a signifier that, far from being arbitrary, still carried the surplus value of visual similarity. It is no coincidence that one of the few attempts at film theory that preceded Balázs's, that of Vachel Lindsay, declared cinema to be a "hieroglyphic" art.[16]

Physiognomy became a popular social science in nineteenth-century Paris, where it provided a visual means to order the diverse and anonymous masses that surrounded the urban dweller. These typologies of observation greatly affected the novels of Balzac and the caricatures of Honoré Daumier and Jean Grandville.[17] It was suggested that choosing a wife or hiring a servant should never be undertaken without the aid of physiognomic analysis. The physiognomic studies of Lavater and his disciples became transformed into the "physiologies" that appeared as a sort of literary fad in the 1840s. Somewhat broadening the physiognomies into descriptions of specific manners and lifestyles, these physiologies outlined the various "types" of Parisians, through a somewhat ironical "scientific" observation.[18] As Walter Benjamin has indicated, these physiologies attempted to reduce classes and professions to stable and recognizable stereotypes, reassuring to a petty bourgeois worldview:

The long series of eccentric or simple attractive or severe figures which the physiologies presented to the public in character sketches had one thing in common: they were harmless and of perfect bonhomie. Such a view of one's fellow man was so remote from experience that there were bound to be uncommonly weighty motives for it.[19]

Weighty indeed. The physiologies were the last gasp of confidence in one's ability to sort people into types that were not only stable but also easily recognizable, an attempt that gained urgency as the fluid contours of a modern world made such methods of classification increasingly difficult. Balzac, who authored several physiologies, nonetheless was aware of the new precariousness of sorting people into general types. He bewailed the fact that whereas previously "the caste system gave each person a physiognomy which was more important than the individual; today the individual gets his physiognomy from himself."[20]

The Illegible Face: Photography, Individuality, and Madness

We owe to M. Londe, the chemist of Salpêtrière, the following anecdote. . . . [Blanche] Wit[man] was in a state of [hypnotic] somnambulism, and [Londe] showed her a photograph of a view of the Pyrenees with donkeys climbing one side, and told her, "Look, this is your portrait; you are absolutely naked." On coming out of the trance the patient saw by chance the photograph and, furious to see herself there represented in a "state of nature," threw herself upon it and destroyed it.
                                        —Alfred Binet, *La psychologie du raisonnement*

If the future of such social physiognomy as social science was doomed by the dissolving of the visual signs of caste, profession, and type (or their slipping below the threshold of the immediately recognizable), the extremely individualizing processes of photography allowed for a new positivist science of observation of the face and its expressions. The physiologies were accompanied by growth in the art of caricatures, which were frequently used to illustrate them. But with the advent of photography the human face became less a realm described in generalities (such as Moreau's description of surgeons) than a zone of intense scrutiny on an individual basis. An anonymous British author writing on physiognomy in 1861 saw the progress of the science as lying precisely in its use of photographs:

It is equally true that with such portraits and engravings of portraits as we have had, it has been utterly impossible to get beyond the nebulous science of a Lavater. We required the photograph. . . . It must be remembered that to give a general likeness is one of the easiest strokes of art. With a half-a-dozen lines the image is complete, as anyone may see in the million wood-engravings of the day; while at the same time it would be difficult to gather from these rough sketches, where two dots go for eyes and a scratch for a mouth, what is the precise anatomy of any one feature. So while we can accept as in the main truthful the portraits that have come down to us, it is impossible to place perfect reliance on any particular lineament.[21]

In this new method of investigation of the face, rooted in individual faces and their transient expressions, photography served as the optimal tool. From this new empirical perspective, physiognomy no longer served primarily as a guide to aesthetic representation, but it demanded the accuracy of new mechanical modes of image making.[22]

A seminal figure in this research was G. B. Duchenne de Boulogne. Duchenne was a founder of neurology in France, and the teacher and master of Jean-Martin Charcot.[23] Duchenne's pioneering work in the classification of neurological disorders was often based on his innovative use of electricity to stimulate directly muscles and nerves. His use of new technology for medical purposes also extended to photography, as he began in the 1850s to photograph the debilitating results of neurological diseases. He combined electricity and photography in his investigation of the mechanism of human facial expression that was published in 1862. Duchenne wished first of all to accurately map out the muscles of the human face that created the common expressions of emotion. Direct application of electrodes to the faces of human subjects allowed Duchenne to cause involuntary contractions of facial muscles. In this way Duchenne actually sculpted expressions and grimaces on the faces of his subjects. Photography could fix these momentary contractions and allow them to be studied at leisure, to be scrutinized and compared (see fig. 4.4).

Duchenne's distance from the earlier physiognomies came from both his positivist scientific ambitions and his use of modern technology. Instead of seeking a permanent physical imprint of fate or character he sought to understand the face in motion, describing facial expressions as a mobile muscular phenomenon. This interest in motion set him apart from Le Brun, who, as Duchenne stated, "represented the diverse aspects of facial expression produced by the emotions but without worrying about their laws of motion," as well as from Lavater who "entirely omitted the study of facial expression in movement" (*MHFE*, 4).[24] This interest in the phenomenon of motion and the belief that the physical effects of motion had laws indicate Duchenne's place within a modern line of scientific investigation that would lead directly to the invention of the cinema. What had seemed contingent and below the threshold of knowledge for the earlier physiognomists was precisely suited to the possibilities of new technology. The electrode could affect a facial muscle in isolation, while photography could capture a facial contraction that was much too brief to be otherwise recorded (see fig. 4.5). As Duchenne put it:

Skillful artists have tried in vain to represent the faces of my subjects; for the contractions provoked by the electrical currents are of too short a duration for an exact

Fig. 4.4. Duchenne de Boulogne demonstrating his electrode-induced expressions, 1862

reproduction of the expressive lines that develop on the face to be drawn or painted. Only photography, as truthful as a mirror, could attain such a desirable perfection. (*MHFE*, 36)

Since Duchenne's major goal was to identify the muscles and motor nerves in the face and their role in a variety of expressions, he tried to reveal the "invisible face behind the visible." Yet for Duchenne, following the Cartesian tradition, facial expression had another interior—the spirit. "The

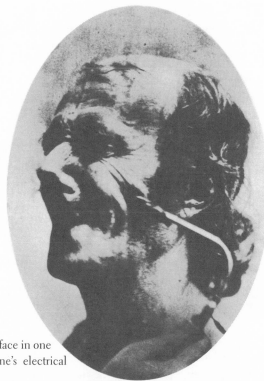

Fig. 4.5. Close-up of male face in one of Duchenne de Boulogne's electrical demonstrations, 1862

spirit is thus the source of expression. It activates the muscles that portray our emotions on the face with characteristic patterns" (*MHFE*, 1). But in Duchenne's experiments the spirit as the motive force of facial expressions was replaced by the electrode that caused the face involuntarily to "speak the language of emotions and the sentiments" (*MHFE*, 1). However artificial such expressions might be when electrically induced for purposes of demonstration and investigation, Duchenne had no doubt that he was investigating a language that was universal and God-given:

In the face our Creator was not concerned with mechanical necessity. He was able in his wisdom or—please pardon this manner of speaking—in pursuing a divine fantasy, to put any particular muscles into action, one alone or several muscles together, when he wished the characteristic signs of the emotions, even the most fleeting, to be written briefly on man's face. Once this language of facial expression was created, it sufficed for him to give all human beings the instinctive faculty of always expressing their sentiments by contracting the same muscles. This rendered the language universal and immutable. (*MHFE*, 19)

But if Duchenne represents a modern scientist devoted to empirical observation through the use of modern technology rather than a traditional physiognomist tracing mystical signatures and resemblances; the strong tie between the study of the face and the codes of aesthetic representation continued to compel aspects of his work. Duchenne hoped to reformulate Le Brun's work and provide artists with documentary proof of the visual language of the human emotions.[25] He divided the photographic plates that illustrated his theses into "Scientific" and "Aesthetic" sections. In place of the predominantly male models imaged in the scientific section, the aesthetic section makes use exclusively of a female model, and the close framing of the face frequently gives way to dramatic tableaux in which the female model is posed in costume with props.

Duchenne glosses these images with narration that describes situations that might explain or specify the emotions he evokes with his electrode. If somewhat less aggressive in their framing and less agonized in their facial contortions, these images seem even more bizarre, the electrode and its manipulator incongruously visible among the stage sets and poses of genre painting. The photographs display disturbing tensions between the conventional sentiments and narrative of the poses and scenarios and a nightmarish scene of a metanarrative of control and technological manipulation that the intervening electrode indicates. Further complicating his simple narratives, Duchenne deconstructs the unified effect of the facial expression by attempting to create distinct expressions within different zones of the face. For instance, he describes plate 80:

The young lady photographed in this figure is visiting a poor family; we recognize, from her tender laughter (cover the left side of the face) or from her kind smile (cover the right side of the face) that she is touched by the misery and suffering of this unhappy family and that this sentiment has inspired an act of charity. (MHFE, 118)

Although Duchenne frequently apologizes for the lack of physical beauty of his older male model who appears frequently in the scientific section of the work, he never explains why he uses a female model exclusively (whom he describes as neither pretty nor ugly and mentions was nearly blind) in the aesthetic section.[26] Undoubtedly a belief that a female model would be more pleasing to viewers corresponded with his desire in this section "to please those who possess 'a sense of beauty'" (MHFE, 102). However, more deeply embedded cultural conceptions of gender clearly operate here, relating the female model not only to the aesthetic but also to an atmosphere of drama and mystery created by the use of the fictional settings and narrative scenarios in this section. Although his experiments in electrically creating different expressions on each side of the face appeared in the scientific section as well, here it becomes a nearly constant practice, as if the conjunction of a woman model and drama led naturally into a succession of facial expressions and moods. For instance, his gloss on plate 77 describes not only diverse expressions but also a typology of female desire: "Earthly love at right and celestial love at left. Ecstasy of human love, by covering the left half of the face; gentle rapture of divine love (ecstasy of St. Teresa), by covering the opposite side" (*MHFE*, 104–5).

This division of the sides of the face into separate expressions became for Duchenne a means of expressing the ambivalence of a dramatic scene, as in his extraordinarily revealing discussion of plate 78, which he elaborates with a complete drama:

> In Plate 78 I wanted to show a little comedy, a scene of coquetry, a gentleman surprises a lady while she is dressing. On seeing him, her stance and her look become disapproving (cover the bottom half of her face). Nevertheless, we note her nudity, which instead of covering she seems to reveal with a certain affectation. It is the mannered pose of her hand, which supports a rather overtly revealed bosom. All this betrays her coquetry. The young man was becoming more audacious, but the words "get out," pronounced in a scornful way by the girl, stop him in his enterprise (see only the left side of the lower half of her face). The mocking laughter that accompanies the amorous rejection (see the right side of the lower half of the face) we believe to mean, "Conceited ass." Perhaps she says also, much lower: "The fool, if he had dared." (*HFE*, 111–12)

For Duchenne the face was an extremely flexible medium on which the spirit writes a translatable message of emotions in a language created by God himself. However, his investigation via an arbitrary stimulation of the diverse muscles of the face could also produce the face as a sort of collage in which contrasting emotions occupied different zones of the face. Duchenne also found that he could produce nongrammatical expressions that he termed grimaces "where it was hard, sometimes nearly impossible, to make any meaningful interpretation" (*MHFE*, 17). Such grimaces serve only as the background noise within his system of facial expression in which a mask of muscles sculpts the invisible impulses of the spirit. But the very bizarre nature of Duchenne's aesthetic section may betray anxiety about the arbitrary expressions he has induced on the face by substituting electrical impulses for the passions of the soul. Narrative scenography imposes itself as a means of containing (though not dispelling) his own intervention, as if familiar situations and cultural clichés of feminine roles provided a context of ideologically reassuring recognizability necessary to allow the viewer to see these shocking demonstrations of the human face as the play of muscles as part of a visible "natural language." In any case, it would seem that Charcot learned the effectiveness of staging a scenography of female performers under the dominance of a male "operator" from his master.

Charles Darwin drew heavily on Duchenne in his 1872 study *The Expression of the Emotions in Man and Animals.* He particularly praised the use of photography in the investigation of facial expression: "I have found photographs made by instantaneous process the best means, as allowing more deliberation."[27] However, he strongly rejected as contrary to the principles of his theory of evolution any claim that expressions were a language designed by the Creator in order to allow humans to communicate, as Duchenne had believed. Darwin tried to explain the communicative aspects and the forms of expressions through recourse to a deeper history than the personal one of habit or profession. Expression provided a link between men and animals. "With mankind some expressions, such as the bristling of the hair under the influence of extreme terror, or the uncovering of the teeth under that of furious rage, can hardly be understood, except on the belief that man once existed in a much lower and animal-like condition" (*EEMA*, 12).

Darwin was probably unaware of the irony of this return to the most ancient form of physiognomy, the comparison between humans and animals. However, Darwin's method was historical and evolutionary rather than analogical, discovering, like most nineteenth-century systems of thought, the traces of the *longue durée* of history on the forms of nature, rather than the timeless semantic tables of resemblance that guided della Porta's and even Le Brun's physiognomy. But Darwin also sought the survival of this evolutionary past in the present through a different sort of analogy. If the investigation of expression led directly to the extensive evolutionary past of man, he felt it essential to investigate not only man's animal ancestors, but also human subjects whom he believed might be closer to this ancestry due to their distance from civilizing influences, such as infants, the insane, and different races of man (Darwin, *EEMA*, 13). Darwin's investigation sought to strip the face of its civilized mask of convention and reveal a language of expression that derived from the struggle for survival and various forms of adaptation to environmental or physical forces. But to understand the laws of the human face a new importance had to be accorded to faces that were somehow alien to "normal" human behavior. A science of deviant faces took on a new importance, in contrast to physiognomy's traditional search for the typical and ideal.

Facial photographs held a special place in the treatment of the insane, with Hugh W. Diamond pioneering the use of photographic portraits in both the study and the treatment of the insane. The photographs that Diamond took at the Surrey County Lunatic Asylum in the 1850s were used not only in his public lectures on mental illness but also in the therapy of patients using "the effect they [the photographs] produced upon the patients themselves" to help the progress of their cure (*FM*, 21). Diamond's associate Dr. John Conolly discussed these photographs in 1858 in an article entitled "Case Studies from the Physiognomy of the Insane" in which he portrayed these faces as traces of a battle between original character and the physical effects of mental aberration. The idea of a physiognomy of the insane had already been described in 1838 by J. E. D. Esquirol, who made drawings of mental patients in order to trace similarities between them (*FM*, 25–72). As Conolly's essay shows, this was a system of description still indebted to the ancient forms of analogy and metaphor, but it was inflected by a modern concern for individual case history and clearly showed the influence of Lavater.[28] Describing a pathetic case of what he termed "suicidal melancholy," he portrayed the face as a battleground of emotional struggles:

The features are unrefined; but the wide and high head indicates intellectual qualities that cultivation might have improved; so as to control perhaps a now dominating ideality. The copious and disheveled hair, which we feel sure must be black mingled with grey, is parted with no care, but straggles in sympathy with the tortured brain. Those many and curved wrinkles in the brow are not wrinkles of ordinary trouble. The raised and equally curved eyebrows; the large melancholy, and the uplifted eyes, declare that the sense is fixed on some image of fear, which no other eye can detect; and the intensity of the prevalent emotion is forcibly expressed in all the other parts of the face. The upper eyelids disappear; the lower are strongly depressed; the muscles of the cheeks are drawn down, the lower lip being, as it were, spasmodically acted upon, showing nearly all the front teeth of the lower jaw. The chin has been scratched and scarred by her own fingernails. The very ears seem starting forward. Everything bespeaks terror. (*FM*, 37)

The face photographed becomes a text to be read by the male doctor employing a bewildering variety of interpretive means, ranging from deviation from norms of behavior (the unparted hair), to traces of past behavior (the scarred chin), through a range of analogies (the hair that "straggles in sympathy with the tortured brain"), to a general sort of allegorical method that sees the face as "bespeaking terror." These faces stand primarily as deviant faces, horrifying visual evidence of the mental sufferings the subjects have undergone. Diamond underscored these aspects in assembling in one plate four photographs of a woman in different stages of illness and

Fig. 4.6. Engraving from photographs by Hugh Diamond of stages in a woman mental patient's cure, 1858

cure, in which the variety of expression seems perhaps less remarkable than the variety of clothing that clearly differentiates the deviant expressions from the controlled face of convention (see fig. 4.6).

Succeeding decades saw a general adoption of photography for medical and scientific purposes (the *Revue photographique des hôpitaux de Paris*, for instance, was established in 1869), and toward the end of the century increasingly short exposure time allowed the recording of motion for scientific purposes to move asymptotically toward the invention of cinema.[29] Undoubtedly the most famous and complex use of photography to record facial movement and expression came from Jean-Martin Charcot and the medical periodical *Iconographie photographique de la Salpêtrière*. In 1878 Charcot, the head physician of the Salpêtrière, a Parisian charity hospital for women, had installed there a photographic service complete with a glass-roofed studio and a photographic laboratory (*IH*, 47).[30] Albert Londe, who was placed in charge of the photographic service in 1884, lauded the gnostic possibilities of photography, describing the latest photographic plate as "the true retina of the scientist," a means of seeing that could, in fact, be more sensitive than the human eye (*IH*, 35). Charcot's greatest fame came from his description and treatment of hysteria. Documenting the behavior of hysterics was especially important since this elusive disease was characterized by a set of behaviors rather than clearly isolable physical symptoms (which lead frequently to the claim that hysterics were simply malingerers who "mimicked" the symptoms of others to gain attention) (*IH*, 36, 39).[31] Charcot claimed to have discovered predictable patterns to this behavior (such as the succession of different physical actions in a consistent order that made up the hysterical fit), which gave the disease a character that could be analyzed and diagnosed.

Observation was essential to the diagnosis of hysteria, and photography increases the power of this observation as well as provides its faithful record. Charcot had actually compared his method to that of photography, declaring "in truth I am absolutely nothing but a photographer; I inscribe what I see."[32] In diagnostic use medical photography mediated between the patient's individual body and the general characteristics of the disease. Determining this general aspect, or *facies*, of a disease called for a specific use of photography. As Londe explained:

To determine the *facies* belonging to each disease, to each illness, to place it before the eyes of all, this is what photography is capable of. In certain doubtful or uncertain cases, comparing photographs taken in diverse places or at quite different times allows one to be sure of the identity of the illness of diverse patients whom one has not had under one's care at the same time. This has been accomplished with great success by M. Charcot and the *facies* belonging to this or that illness of the central nervous system is now well-known.[33]

Visual demonstration as well as diagnosis played a key role in Charcot's investigation of hysteria. Both were evident at his famous public "Tuesday

Lessons" in which female patients and their symptoms were paraded before an audience made up of interns, doctors (such as the Viennese physician Sigmund Freud—who later overturned Charcot's theory of hysteria—attending the lectures on a travel grant), and invited members of high society (including such luminaries as Henri Bergson, Émile Durkheim, Guy de Maupassant, and Sarah Bernhardt).[34] In these sessions Charcot not only displayed the symptoms of his female patients, but experimentally influenced their behavior through hypnosis, drugs, or various forms of physical manipulation (including, during photographic sessions, sudden exposure to a magnesium flash, as Ulrich Baer has stressed).[35]

But the *facies* revealed by these means of investigation and observation was the paradoxical typicality of the deviant. Charcot used hypnosis to provoke effects similar to those his teacher Duchenne had induced by electrical current, occasionally invoking contradictory impulses within a patient so that "the subject found herself in some way divided in two" (*IH,* 228). Charcot also on occasion used electrodes to affect his hysterics, but he found that such force was unnecessary to provoke facial contractions. Slight pressure from a simple metal rod would produce the same sorts of facial contractions Duchenne had induced by more powerful means.[36] Sudden loud noises, flashes of electrical light, or dramatic gestures on the part of the doctor could produce extraordinary physical results, from cataleptic postures to violent seizures.

The extremely theatrical nature of Charcot's demonstrations and treatments, as well as his use of hypnosis, led to widespread suspicion and criticism of his methods and conclusions. Charcot's critics portrayed him as the histrionic impresario of his mimicking hysterics, inducing symptoms through suggestion and training his subjects (knowingly or unwittingly) to perform for himself and his invited audiences.[37] The collapse of Charcot's view of hysteria led to alternate scenarios, most obviously that of psychoanalysis, and one can see Charcot's highly visualized and dramatic performances as an attempt to give this paradoxical disease a recognizable visual face, an attempt, on the cusp of modernity, to once more tie the act of seeing to the act of knowing. The role of photography in all of this is perhaps more complex than previous treatments, such as that of Didi-Huberman, have indicated, as insightful as they have been. Charcot's patients and their symptoms were paraded before the camera as well as before interns and the public. These photographs were published in the three volumes of the *Iconographie photographique de la Salpêtrière* in 1876, 1877, and 1879. After a significant hiatus, the photographic series reappeared in a new format in 1888 as *Nouvelle iconographie de la Salpêtrière*. These photographs include a number of facial close-ups, although framing including the posture and contortions of the full body predominates. However, in contrast to Diamond and other earlier photographers of mental illness, there is no attempt to create a physiognomy of madness here.

The *facies* of hysteria demands a specific etiology of an elusive disease. The contorted faces of women were fit into a pattern that made hysteria conceivable as a disease and visibly recognizable. Londe described the importance of facial close-up photography in capturing the characteristics of the disease:

Certain modifications of the face that by themselves were not recognized as constituting in isolation a clear indication of a particular illness took on a very great importance when they were found over and over in similar sufferers. Unless one happened by chance to have patients show the same expressions at the same time, they might go unnoticed. However, with close-up photographs of them, one can make comparisons between a number of examples and deduce the typical modifications of different aspects. (*IH*, 52)

Londe here perhaps knowingly recalls Bertillon's system of criminal photography that allowed the photographs of suspects and convicts to be compared in terms of physical characteristics and the identity of malefactors to be established. However, as in the case of Bertillon, we see that the satisfaction of pure visual recognition remains elusive. No one photograph could finger the guilty party or portray the *facies* of the disease. The act of recognition relies on comparison, and knowledge resides not in the single photograph but within vast photographic archives, cross-indexed by systems of classification.[38]

The recent biographers of Albert Londe, Denis Bernard and André Gunthert, have questioned Charcot's personal devotion to photography as a method of medical investigation. They point out that the *Iconographie* was instigated by Désiré Bourneville and that its hiatus coincided with Bourneville's departure from Salpêtrière for Bicêtre in 1879.[39] They also claim that Bourneville rather than Charcot was the driving force behind photography at Salpêtrière and that the photographic service as well as the *Iconographie* stagnated until Londe took charge in 1888.[40] From this perspective, Charcot's self-identification with the photographer may indicate he felt that his own gaze was more useful as a device of visual investigation than the photograph. As Bernard and Gunthert indicate, "The gaze [*regard*] and the image are not synonymous."[41] Photographic sessions at Salpêtrière took place without Charcot present, and the "most serious rival of the photographic plate remained the clinician's gaze."[42]

Londe, a devoted advocate of medical photography (whose book on the subject was published in 1893), understood that in order to become scientific a photograph had be placed within a system.[43] Each photograph had to find its place within a series. In addition to the comparisons that a physician could make by rummaging through the *Iconographie*, Londe also explored the possibilities of serial photography to indicate the succession of actions typical of hysterical attacks. The need to obtain successive photographs led Londe to photographic inventions that brought him to the cusp of cinema, including a number of multilens cameras capable of taking a series of separate images in rapid succession. His crowning apparatus possessed twelve lenses and was therefore able to take at brief intervals twelve images of an ongoing action.[44] Such images inscribed a temporal progression onto photography. Still photography in the late nineteenth century had gained a scientific and gnostic role not only through its iconic resemblance and indexical reliability, but also through its increasing mastery of the increments of time and its ability to freeze an instantaneous event, such as a sudden facial expression or the convulsions of a hysteric's limbs. The ambition of nineteenth-century science to discover not only the characteristic lineaments of the face as interpreted by physiognomy, but also the laws of motion and the temporal processes of the body and the face, led directly to the technical invention of the cinema.

As a leader in bringing photography (and especially scientific and medical photography) to the attention of the public, Londe knew the motion analysis photographs of Eadweard Muybridge and the chronophotography of Étienne Jules Marey very well. A pioneer in the development of instantaneous photography, Londe was enthusiastic about the scientific possibilities of new photographic techniques.[45] Not only chronophotography (the taking of a series of still photos in rapid succession to analyze the phases of a motion) but stereoscopic three-dimensional photography was employed by Londe to capture the symptoms of medical patients.[46] In his drive to master the analysis of space and time through photography Londe seems to have created a counterforce to his subjects' lack of bodily control; he attempted to master through technology behavior that otherwise defied order. But, like Marey, Londe, at least initially, found the *cinématographe*, the device for projecting motion pictures to create an illusion of movement, a mere novelty bereft of scientific interests.[47] Unlike photography, which could be used to fix and analyze temporal processes, revealing phenomena otherwise difficult to perceive, motion pictures were seen to simply to reproduce the experience of the normal eyewitness.[48]

For Londe, scientific photography mastered its visual subject, moving beyond the simple resemblance and illusion of motion that Lumière's *cinématographe* offered. Through still photography's control of time, the hysteric fit was frozen, delivered to the physician's gaze with movement tamed. We find here, at the moment of the invention of cinema, a dilemma that thwarts any simple tracing of a linear progression in film's genealogy. The gnostic impulse pushes toward cinema's control of time and motion, but it also expresses suspicions of its illusory potential. At this critical point, the bifurcation between cinema as a device of mass entertainment and its use as a scientific tool becomes evident, as the conflict between Marey and his assistant Demenÿ dramatized. However, one should not assume too quickly an absolute separation. The two impulses continue to infect each other, indicating less a parting of the ways based on principle than a crisis of representation based on the illusory power of technological imagery and a new mimesis of time. This conflict influenced the development of cinema for at least its first decade and is responsible for its eventual development into a technological popular medium.

How, then, are we to understand Londe turning his experimental photography on nonscientific subjects, photographing acrobats from the Hippodrome in stereo in 1887 and the tightrope-walking act of Mlle. Barenco of the Nouveau Cirque in 1893 (see fig. 4.7)?[49] Clearly such subjects were ideal for demonstrating the new powers of photography to capture action. The twelve images of Mlle. Barenco demonstrate her delicate control of balance in a manner that the naked eye, absorbed in the ongoing moment-to-moment drama of her act, might not catch. But the sequence also anticipates the strong link that early cinema, as a popular art, will forge with vaudeville, circus, and the attractions of popular culture.

If Marey and Muybridge stand as the best known and most influential of cinema's scientific progenitors, the focus of chronophotography on the face owes more to the experiments of Marey's assistant Georges Demenÿ, whose attempt to bring the motion picture into the realm of show business (even before the Lumière brothers) led to the loss of his position as a researcher. Discussing his cinematic work some years later, Demenÿ still presented himself as a savant rather than a showman, claiming that for him, "the cinema was only a means of study momentarily rendering me the same service that a microscope provides for the anatomist."[50] Demenÿ had served as

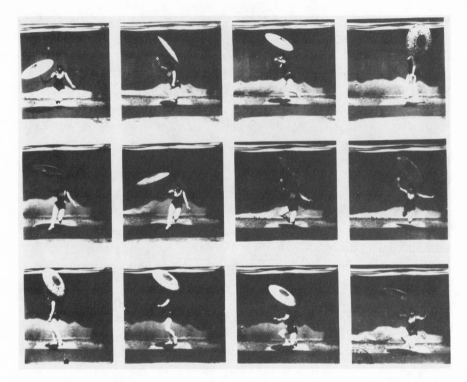

Fig. 4.7. Albert Londe's chronophotographs of Mlle. Barenco's balancing act, 1893

Marey's *préparateur* and trusted assistant from 1881, when he had approached the renowned physiologist and investigator of the science of movement about the application of Marey's methods to a system of gymnastic training Demenÿ had been perfecting.[51] Demenÿ oversaw the construction and subsequent functioning of Marey's Station Physiologique. In 1891 Marey turned over to him a project brought to the physiologist by the director of the National Deaf Mute Institute to study the physical mechanics of speech. The director hoped that a series of chronophotographs showing the positions of lips and tongue during speech might aid deaf mutes learning to lip read and, hopefully, to speak.[52]

For this project Demenÿ placed the camera much closer to the subject than had been customary for Marey's chronophotographic studies of the body in motion, framing speaking subjects above midchest. However, since the aim was not only analytical but synthetic—helping deaf mutes to imitate the processes of speech as well as observe them—devising a means of presenting these photographs in such a manner as to reconstitute their motion

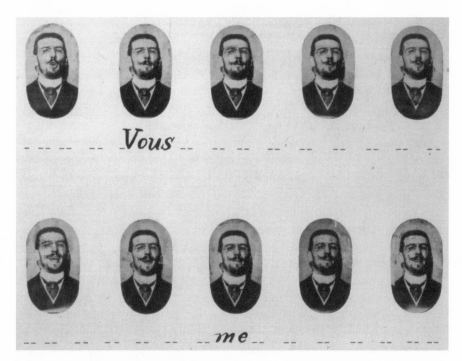

Fig. 4.8. George Demenÿ's series of photographs, 1893

became a primary issue in a way that it had not been for Marey's earlier motion studies. The attempt to create the illusion of a human face in motion, speaking, brought Demenÿ even closer to the cinema than Londe had ventured. Although both Muybridge and Marey had also employed various means of reconstituting motion from their analytical photographs, Demenÿ was certainly a pioneer in the production of motion pictures, even if his technology was heavily indebted to his mentor. He cut and pasted the images captured on the chronophotographic strips around the edge of a wheel based on an earlier "philosophical toy" for the production of the illusion of motion, the phenakistiscope.[53] Two initial series of images were produced, both with Demenÿ himself (his eyes closed because of the blinding light necessary for the brief exposure) speaking the emblematic phrases "I love you" and "Vive la France!" (see fig. 4.8). When this device was presented to the public in 1892 (three years before the cinématographe and a year before the first public demonstration of Edison's kinetoscope), it generated a fervent interest that overwhelmed the pedagogical purposes for which it was designed.

Demenÿ, long concerned about financial security, hoped that this interest in his moving photographs could be exploited commercially. He patented his apparatus, which he called the "phonoscope," demonstrated it at the 1892 Photographic Exposition and was approached by carnival operators with offers to exploit it as an entertainment device. For Demenÿ, however, the possibilities of the phonoscope were firmly linked to the image it provided of the human face in motion. He described his new invention as a "living portrait," saying "The future will replace the static photograph, fixed in its frame, with the animated portrait that will be given life with the turn of a wheel. The expression of physiognomy will be presented as the voice is preserved by the phonograph."[54] The living portrait, Demenÿ believed, would rescue the traditional family portrait from the effect of mummification, allowing it "to live again like a veritable apparition."[55]

Although the device that presented the moving image was of Demenÿ's design (although based on the traditional phenakistiscope), the chronophotographic camera that took the images was Marey's invention, and a growing conflict over the commercial exploitation of the phonoscope led to a bitter rupture between the savant and his protégé. Although the conflict revolved around what Marey perceived as Demenÿ's appropriation of his work, the prospect of marketing chronophotography as a fairground attraction undoubtedly further annoyed Marey. Marey's deep and abiding suspicion of the fallibility of human vision was even more intense than Londe's, and his lack of interest in the illusion of motion strongly expresses the scientific disdain of motion pictures as a betrayal of the possibilities of scientific photography.[56] Demenÿ continued to attempt to make a commercial success of his invention and, adapting it to flexible film, designed both a camera and a projector. He set up his own studio, where he filmed living portraits as well as other subjects. After approaching the Lumières about a partnership and getting a cold response, Demenÿ eventually sold the rights to his patents to Louis Gaumont and returned to his first passion, gymnastic and physical training.[57]

We find among the films that Demenÿ shot before dissolving his company, catalogued by Laurent Mannoni, one that Mannoni entitles "Demenÿ making a grimace." Mannoni adds this brief speculative description: "An illustration perhaps intended to represent two different human expressions, as Le Brun had done in the 17th century in his work *The Expression of the Passions*."[58] Demenÿ's interest in the motion picture of the face clearly embraced not only the "living portrait," but also the investigation of expression that extends from della Porta to the facial expression films to come.

The Grimace of Curiosity and Motion Pictures

Take this kinetoscopic record of a sneeze, a topic intended to excite a smile,
and let us rise higher.
  —Barnet Philips, "The Record of a Sneeze," *Harper's Weekly* (Mar. 24, 1894)
  (see fig. 4.9)

Given the seeming interruption of the scientific tradition with the tri-
umph of actual motion pictures, can we assert that early cinema still owes
something to the gnostic impulse? Although the cinematic devices of
Edison and the Lumière brothers owe a great deal to the technical path
traced by their scientific predecessors, does the illusion of cinema invert and
betray their own anti-illusionary impulse, as Marey and Londe suspected? Is
the simulation of motion nothing but a parlor trick limited to dubious entertainment value, bereft of scientific interest because it relies on a simple visual mimesis rather than scientific analysis and manipulation of time and
motion? Although the road in the development of cinema does fork here,
the interchanges between the gnostic impulse and entertainment continue
to assert themselves, something that becomes clearer if we maintain our

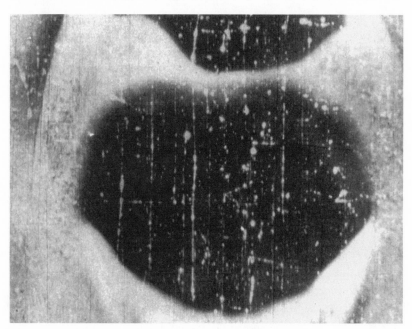

Fig. 4.9. The penultimate moment from James Williamson's film *The Big Swallow*,
1901

broader view of the gnostic impulse as preceding modern science and inherent in such metaphor-based systems as physiognomy.

The scientific impulses that gave birth to modern science derive from a more primal curiosity, that *curiositas* that was condemned as a sin against the faith by St. Augustine in the third century, a fascination with the unusual that the theologian saw as the root of both a sideshow theatricality and an unseemly concern with the nature of God's universe, in other words, the root of both popular entertainment and scientific investigation.

Because of this disease of curiosity monsters and anything out of the ordinary are put on display in our theaters. From the same motives men proceed to investigate the workings of nature which is beyond our ken — things which it does no good to know and which men only want to know for the sake of knowing.[59]

The monumental work of Hans Blumenberg has traced the gradual overturning of this theological stricture and the eventual validation of curiosity as a positive force and power of man in the sixteenth and seventeenth centuries, supplying one of the major transformations in the legitimation of a modern secular world.[60] In the more modern era, the nineteenth and twentieth centuries, the exploiting and exercising of such curiosity outside the disciplines of actual science constituted a major impulse of popular entertainment, and they operated explicitly in the presentation of motion pictures as a show business novelty. Although the pseudo-educational and scientific claims of Barnum's nineteenth-century museum of curiosities were partly a response to American puritanical suspicion of entertainment, they also tapped a growing popular curiosity about scientific and technological innovations. While claims of scientific value could serve as camouflage for simple forms of popular entertainment, a peculiarly modern exploitation of curiosity may also introduce new regimes of aesthetic appreciation, ones that conflict sharply with traditional modes of contemplation and absorption, revealing parallels with modernist attacks on traditional aesthetics. Therefore, we need to question how thoroughly illusionistic the earliest exhibition of motion pictures was, and in what ways they may have continued the scientific probing of illusionistic coherence, but now for the sake of curiosity rather than coherent knowledge. Londe and Demenÿ found their photographic experiments intersecting with the world of popular entertainments. And certainly part of the fascination with Charcot's "Tuesday Lessons" came less from their scientific demonstrations than from the complex scenography of attractions — erotic, sadistic, and simply curious — that Charcot evokes from his female patients. In fact, one of Charcot's critics,

Leon Daudet, even described the sessions as Grand Guignol.[61] But more is at issue here than an unmasking of the motivations behind scientific display. Curiosity indicates audience members that remain skeptical, capable of devising their own explanations of the phenomena before them.

It was precisely this skeptical but curious spectator that Barnum wished to attract to his museum, employing what Neil Harris has called an "operational aesthetic."[62] According to Harris the operational aesthetic draws viewers who want not only to see a marvel, but also to understand and to speculate about how it works. An impresario technique tailored to an age of technology and its fascinations, this aesthetic both excites and satisfies curiosity and supplies a very different aesthetic experience from that of traditional art forms. It was precisely such curiosity that drew the first spectators to the premieres of motion pictures devices. They came to see a new technology demonstrated, and they received it with discussions of how it was achieved. Thus the first exhibitions of the *cinématographe*, the Vitascope, and the Biograph, although certainly part of modern show business, were not as divorced from their scientific progenitors as it might first appear. It is as though the two aspects of Augustine's *curiositas*, the investigation of nature and the fascination with novelties, had been rejoined in a peculiarly modern gnostic impulse.

It should come as no surprise, then, that motion pictures of faces, films consisting entirely of facial close-ups, formed an important genre of early film, dating, as I indicated earlier, from the very first attempts at motion pictures undertaken by Edison and Demenÿ. These experiments became in cinema's first decade a genre known as "facial expression" films, which display very clearly this early motion picture aesthetic founded on curiosity.[63] In line with the operational aesthetic, such films demonstrated to early audiences cinema's ability to capture complex and detailed motions. Although Fred Ott's sneeze and May Irwin and John Rice's kiss were ordinary, everyday actions, captured on film they became subjects of curiosity. The close framing of these brief films endowed them with a sense of physical proximity that was particularly startling given the actions portrayed, inviting scrutiny and delivering surprise. Although the ideology of the close-up in later narrative cinema invited emotional intimacy, the physical closeness of these early images seems rather confrontational and comical. Once these images had emerged from the confines of Edison's kinetoscope (a peepshow device into which each viewer peered to see small moving images through a magnifying lens) and were projected on the screen, the new possibility of gigantism added to their unfamiliarity. The huge enlargement of the close-up was

advertised as an attraction of facial expression films, as in this announce-
ment from 1902 by the English film company Hepworth for their film *Comic
Grimacer*: "A human face shown the full size of the screen is always a comic
and interesting sight."[64]

If this sort of novelty satisfied the curiosity of a popular audience, it could
stick in the throats of a traditional genteel audience whose modes of aesthetic representation seemed to be upset by such unsublimated attention to
the human face. The editor of the Chicago literary journal *The Chap Book*
in 1896 sputtered after seeing the May Irwin–John Rice Kiss projected on
the screen, "When only life size it was pronounced beastly. But that was
nothing to the present sight. Magnified to Gargantuan proportions and
repeated three times over it is utterly disgusting."[65]

The Rabelaisian reference here may be more significant than the author
intended. Early facial close-ups, whether in single shot facial expression
films or serving as emblematic shots in early multishot films, frequently
show the mouth in action, eating, slobbering, kissing, guffawing, and generally partaking of the carnivalesque pleasure of the open orifice in a most
unseemly manner. As with Charcot, the camera once again aimed at bodies
out of control, but with a very different viewing perspective. Rather than supplying the intimate moments that furnish narrative emphasis or reveal psychology, as is typical of close-ups in later cinema, close-ups in early cinema
display monsters and giants, their mouths swallowing and chewing, before
viewers who are fascinated (and sometimes repulsed) by the new revelations
of such unusual sights. In their very physicality and lack of aesthetic sublimation, such images are closer to the images of scientific facial photography
than to the romantic close-ups of shimmering movie stars in later cinema.
Thus the simple illusionism that motion pictures seemed to afford could
also be experienced as a new mode of perception, as motion reconstituted
and defamiliarized by the technology of enlargement. Clearly, motion pictures breached new modes of representation. But if such images seem to
subject the human face to an enlargement that relates more to scientific
scrutiny than to enraptured absorption, we must not lose sight of the comic
nature of these close-ups, quite at odds with the sober discourse of scientific
investigation. The popular curiosity that delights in these odd and marvelous expressions and facial behavior does part company with the use of
photography as a means of investigation and operates more like a parody of
the gnostic impulse. In their delight in the ridiculous and nonsensical, the
uncivilized aspects of the body, and the contortions rather than the expressions of the face, early facial expression films derive from a long clowning

tradition of grimaces that stretches from medieval jesters through circus traditions to nineteenth-century vaudeville. Seen within this tradition, we can understand the way these early close-ups not only denied access to the psychology of characters but also celebrated the very meaninglessness of their swiftly changing grimaces, overturning the gnostic attempt to endow the face with meaning, whether through occult resemblances or photographic scrutiny of its phases.

The grimaces that Duchenne exiled from his system become in these films the major motivation for the facial play. Enlarged enormously, such grimaces became more grotesque than those any performer in the circus or the café-concert could manage, a true carnival of flesh heightened visually through modern technology. In these films the face cavorts on an open playing field, freed from any relation to narrative or drama or any labor of conventional signification. The performer faces the camera and viewer directly and goes through a succession of expressions dazzling in their range and rapidity.

Of course the evolution of popular traditions of grimace humor and of scientific investigations in the era of modernity did not take place in hermetically separated realms. Daudet could compare Charcot's demonstration to the Grand Guignol, while at that Parisian theater of horrors André de Lorde took the *Leçons du mardi* as the subject for his grim drama *Une leçon à la Salpêtrière*, in which a hysteric patient tosses acid in the face of an intern who has been sadistically torturing her, after her accusations have been dismissed as hysteric symptoms.[66] And as Rae Beth Gordon has shown, the performance styles that were used by such turn-of-the-century *caf' conc'* *grimaciers* as Paulus were compared by fans such as J. K. Huysmans to the hysterics of Charcot, who may even have served as models for such performers.[67] In tracing the intersections between scientific investigation and the curiosity of popular culture in the emergence of cinema at the end of the nineteenth century, I want not only to relate these two traditions, but to uncover a dialogue between them, centered on the semantically loaded and unceasingly ambiguous representation of the human face. In this encounter, the popular tradition has something to say to the scientific, as well as vice versa.

Unlike his predecessor Duchenne (who rested secure in his belief in a God-given language of facial expression from which grimaces were excluded), Charcot did investigate facial contortions (and perhaps this is why he strikes us as so modern), seeking behind their chaos for the *facies* of hysteria. Within the amphitheater of his clinic and in the studio of the photographic service, his female patients' facial gymnastics were presented to the public. His patients were doubly victims, subject both to the symptoms of their disease and the control and manipulation of their doctors, who provided, as Didi-Huberman and others have shown, the mise-en-scène of both the Tuesday lessons and the photographs of the *Iconographie*. But in the early facial expression films such grimaces explode any framework of interpretation, seeking only the curiosity and the laughter of onlookers. Films such as Edison's 1902 *Facial Expressions* and his 1903 *Goo Goo Eyes* seem to fulfill Didi-Huberman's fantasy about Charcot's "star" patient Augustine, in which her impulse toward "making a scene" might subvert Charcot's effort to create a mise-en-scène. In her performances, Didi-Huberman declares, Augustine shows "the mastery not of an autocrat, but of an acrobat" (*IH*, 247–48).[68] Similarly, in Edison's films the female performers contort their faces endlessly in a dazzling display of dexterity and absurdity, invoking amusement, curiosity, occasional revulsion, and ultimately a certain admiration for their novel skill as facial performers.

Clearly, we must resist the impulse to see the images presented by such early films simply as fulfillments of a utopian desire that defies narrative order and scientific symptomatology in pursuit of an ethos of pure play and physical transformation, a mode of representation using mimesis to subvert cultural logic. As products of popular culture, these films are deeply complicit in the stereotypes of patriarchal, racist, and economically exploitative ideologies, and the marks of these systems are clearly legible in their imagery. However, they also contain, like the dream world of commodity culture evoked by Walter Benjamin, the seeds of utopian urges.[69] Utopian possibilities are opened by early cinema's non-narrative configurations of time and its direct confrontation of the viewer with images that seem familiar and yet are also uncanny. If the history of the close-up ultimately extends to the nearly religious absorption in the mystery of the human countenance, the sort that Roland Barthes expresses in his rapture over the face of Garbo, we can see the close-up's origins in a very different gnostic impulse, a curiosity about the meanings of the face and an attempt to assert mastery over it through the analysis and classification of its muscle structure, its evolutionary derivation, and its forms of deviance.[70] The desire to know the face in its most transitory and bizarre manifestations was stimulated by the use of photography; but that desire, in turn, also stimulated the development of photography itself, spurring its innovators to increasing technical mastery over time and motion and prodding them toward the actual invention of motion pictures. Paradoxically, once the illusion of motion was technically feasible, emphasis could shift from the dominating eye of the scientist to the skill of the performer as the facial close-up became an arena for grotesque grimaces and goo-goo eyes, a delightful facial play.

The face had formerly served as a guarantor of meaning and significance, a mode of communication that exceeded any conventional or cultural system of exchange; but modern science and medicine dissolved this guarantor into pure physical materiality or a welter of chaotic symptoms. Yet as the techniques of photography attempted to penetrate this apparent chaos and discover new patterns of regularity, the popular art of early cinema again allowed this investigation to dissolve into curiosity and amusement, rehearsing an encounter with representation that the techniques of aesthetic modernism would replay on a different level, borrowing, as Surrealism in particular acknowledged, a great deal from its popular predecessors.

CHAPTER 5

Freud the Modernist

JOHN BRENKMAN

Psychoanalysis and Modernism

In what sense was Freud a modernist?

First, psychoanalysis takes up cultural works from diverse traditions and turns them into ciphers of personal destiny. Freud's theoretical writings and therapeutic sessions are filled with fairy tales, the humanist canon from *Oedipus Rex* to *Faust*, modern dramas and realist novels, popular fiction and humor. Whatever social origins or purposes animated the works themselves, they became an immense vocabulary and flexible grammar for elaborating the self, its benchmarks of identity, its desires, its aspirations. The modernist interprets freely. Stories and symbols become meaningful if they can illuminate—or are illuminated by—the individual's ongoing, continually revised life story. One's personal life-history grounds cultural receptivity and learning; traditions loop through individual contingencies.

Second, Freud's thought, like that of Nietzsche, Bergson, and Heidegger, stylizes the large-scale, invisible forces at work within society and the uncertain, largely unpredictable trends of historical change, distilling them down to a drama of forces and trends within individual experience. The unsettling recognition that no overarching principle determined the actual patterns of historical change distinguished these modernists' response to modernity from that of their immediate predecessors. They embraced nothing like Hegel's Absolute Spirit or Marx's History. Between the 1870s and the 1920s, various modernist thinkers lost faith in the notion that modern ethical, political, and aesthetic ideals were destined to fuse with scientific, technological, and economic advances and lift humanity into a new life. Perhaps only European Marxists originally inspired by Lenin and the Russian Revolution and American pragmatists bewitched by national prosperity and expansion kept the faith. As Carl E. Schorske first showed, Freud's personal crises of profession, nationality, and class stamped his thought with the habit of recoding political conflict as intrapsychic conflict.[1] The conflicts that had become unmasterable on the political stage of troubled Austrian liberalism were remounted on the psychic stage. Freud's thought stylizes in the sense that it scans the conflicts within society and transposes them to family life, whose conflicts are in turn transposed from the politics of the family to the individual's intrapsychic representations of the family.

Third, Freud's most concrete invention, psychoanalytic therapy itself, is corollary to significant strands of modernist art and literature. Like other modernists, Freud responded to the double imperative of newness and mastery, that is, expressive newness and expressive mastery. The drive to *make it new* certainly derived much of its force from two of art's sometimes antagonistic, sometimes complementary counterparts: fashion and technology. But the imperative of newness ultimately demanded that artworks measure up as a response to the *unprecedentedness* of modern life itself, its continual transformations and dislocations. A century after *The Interpretation of Dreams* and Freud's first case studies, we easily forget how unprecedented psychoanalytic therapy was. Freud invented an utterly new form of expression: an autobiographical project carried out in an asymmetrical dialogue via an amalgam of free association, dream, and transference continually reworked by constructions, rememberings, and interpretations. A dialectic of fragment and totality, Freudian psychoanalysis promised its initiates a new mode of mastery at the level of individual self-narration.

All three features of Freud's modernism—the interpretive transformation of cultural traditions into ciphers of personal destiny, the intellectual transformation of social crisis into individual drama, and the therapeutic transformation of the self through expressive experiment and mastery—place an ultimate value on the individual, even on individualism. At the same time, they seem to erode the moral and ethical claims that tradition, religion, and community make on the individual. Modernity's morality problem—are there any legitimate, unarbitrary moral values and ethical ideals?—is a question on which Freud, like other modernists, vacillates.

Modernity is variously credited with and blamed for inventing the individual: the rights-bearing individual with the freedom to pursue a chosen course of life, as well as the alienated individual deprived of community and living in the world spiritually homeless, abandoned, exiled (metaphors that gained their weight from the waves of wars and pogroms, housing crises, unemployment, and recessions that afflicted Europe). Sovereign and free or exiled and abandoned—both views seem true. The contradictory impact of modernity on the individual can best be discerned in modern thought's obsession with the theme of alienation.

Individuals in the modern world experience a three-way estrangement. They do not directly control, and seldom even indirectly influence, the processes of their material existence. They are uprooted from any predictable or permanent place within their social world, increasingly becoming instruments of the impersonal forces regulating social life. They live history neither as divine providence nor as rationally controlled change but rather as the unmasterable flow of time. These were the great themes, respectively, of Marx, Weber, and Heidegger. According to their visions, the modern individual is estranged and uprooted, manipulated and exposed.

Nevertheless, this same individual is heralded as an end in him- or herself in all the humanistic strands of thought that take shape in the modern era. Those strands are themselves rich in contradiction because so much depends on which aspect of personhood gets foregrounded. For classical liberalism, the setting of individuality is the capitalist economy. For the republican tradition, revived in the context of the French Revolution, it is citizenship that bestows dignity and power on the individual. In various educational, aesthetic, and therapeutic trends, it is the individual's self-enrichment that counts, as the civilizing process gives rise to modern secular ideals of soul and mind. Our modern efforts at self-designation pit these archetypes of individuality—beautiful soul, cultivated mind, property owner, citizen—against the archetypes' alienation.

In Freud's own formative historical moment, Austrian liberalism encountered the limits of its extraordinary achievements and the erosion of its values. With the emergence of anti-Semitism in Austrian politics, racial identity began to displace the universalist ideology of Austrian modernization, and the revolt of the working class exposed liberalism's failure to integrate all strata of society into a democratic political order. As Schorske and others have shown, this fin-de-siècle crisis informed the birth of psychoanalysis and certainly gave Freud his critical and cautious attitude toward the achievements and possibilities of modern society. By the same token, Freud's career and therapeutic practice did thrive through the first decades of the twentieth century, blossoming into a movement whose associations, journals, and credentialing procedures firmly established his ideas, gave him a public, and drew patients to him and his followers.

Freud's clients were decidedly middle-class, and frequently wealthy. He occasionally lamented that his movement could not address the mental health of the lower classes, but he never doubted that the theoretical insights he gained from his clinical practice were universal in their scope. He saw himself treating the mind, not tending to the lifeworld of the bourgeoisie. I have argued elsewhere that Oedipal theory, the cornerstone of Freud's thought, is not, as he believed, a universally valid account of intrapsychic representations. Rather, it is a theoretical stylization of the construction of masculinity and heterosexuality in modern patriarchy. Unlike the patriarchalism that modernization overthrew, modern patriarchy invests power in the individual male insofar as he takes up his expected roles in the bourgeois lifeworld. Men's identity hinged on career, citizenship, and marriage, and it was the promises and pathologies of this threefold role that shaped Freudian theory. Freud made the tacit assumption that a man's ability to synthesize these roles defined the "psychic" norm, an assumption that skewed the psychoanalytic understanding of gender and sexuality.[2]

My focus in this chapter will be on one facet of Freud's modernism: analytic therapy, in particular in the work he did between 1910 and 1920. Oedipal theory was firmly in place. It informed every aspect of his reflections on therapy in the *Papers on Technique* (1911–15) and related writings. Those reflections led him to give a rich account of analytic technique, to ponder the ethical framework and moral import of psychoanalysis, and to wrestle with the most basic questions of sexuality and gender.

Therapy as Expressive Form

Lou Andreas-Salomé put her finger on the ethical core of psychoanalysis when she declared, in a draft she enclosed in a letter to Freud on June 30, 1916, that psychoanalysis "established as the principle of its scientific method the absolute integrity of each individual."[3] I take her to mean that there was to be nothing coercive in psychoanalytic treatment. One ventured into the dialogue of the "talking cure" voluntarily, and the power to heal, to alleviate symptoms and suffering, ultimately rested on the patient's own insight and understanding as much as the analyst's.

This parity between therapist and patient was implicit in many of Freud's assumptions and practices. He followed the same principles in treating severely neurotic patients as he did in his own self-analysis and the training analyses of his students. His work on dreams led him to question any hard-and-fast distinction between the neurotic and the normal mind. As he tells his audience in the *Introductory Lectures on Psycho-Analysis* (1916–17), "the dreams of neurotics do not differ in any important respect from those of normal people; it is possible, indeed, that they cannot be distinguished from them at all." He wryly concludes "We must therefore say that the difference between neurosis and health holds only during the day; it is not prolonged into dream-life."[4]

Although therapy aimed to make patient and analyst equals, they began on the uneven terrain where a troubled person was seeking help from an expert. The analyst's consulting room, with its couch and armchair, has become the emblem in popular culture for the patient's need and dependency and the analyst's calm and aloofness. But Freud also saw the analyst-patient relationship from a more material standpoint. Analysis was a business. The analyst's practice was a small enterprise organized according to a professional ethos. Analysts should emulate surgeons, Freud advised, and base their fees on their skills and the value of their time.

Freud himself found intellectual as well as professional independence by hanging a shingle, creating a career that was relatively protected from the anti-Semitism and discrimination he faced from the medical and psychiatric establishment. He maintained a no-nonsense attitude about his livelihood. In "On Beginning the Treatment" (1913), he even recommended that the analyst use the discussion of fees to introduce patients to the proper therapeutic attitude by "treat[ing] money-matters with the same matter-of-fact frankness to which he wishes to educate them in relating to sexual life." He further advised analysts "not to allow large sums of money to accumulate, but to ask for payment at fairly short intervals—monthly perhaps"; not to charge too small a fee; and to "refrain from giving treatment free," including to "colleagues or their families."[5] Unlike the shaman supported by the tribe, the priest by the Church, or the rabbi by the congregation, the Freudian healer survived on cash—payment for services rendered. Secularized healing enlisted the cash nexus to aid in the treatment: "The absence of the regulating effect offered by the payment of a fee to the doctor," Freud warned, "makes itself very painfully felt; the whole relationship is removed from the real world, and the patient is deprived of a strong motive for endeavouring to bring the treatment to an end."[6]

Freud insisted that "psycho-analytic treatment is founded on truthfulness. In this fact lies a great part of its educative effect and its ethical value."[7] He introduced the patient to this ethic through the famous "fundamental rule of psycho-analytic technique," which was to be imparted at the very beginning of treatment, indeed, to be elicited from the patient as a pledge:

You will notice that as you relate things various thoughts will occur to you which you would like to put aside on the grounds of certain criticisms or objections. You will be tempted to say to yourself that this or that is irrelevant here, or is quite unimportant, or nonsensical, so that there is no need to say it. You must never give in to these criticisms, but must say it precisely *because* you feel an aversion to doing so. . . . Finally, never forget that you have promised to be absolutely honest, and never leave anything out because, for some reason or other, it is unpleasant to tell it.[8]

The rule had derived from Freud's self-analysis and the interpretation of dreams. Free associations were spontaneous but not random. To follow the fundamental rule the patient needed to adopt an attitude that Freud described by means of a modernist archetype, the train ride: "'So say whatever goes through your mind. Act as though, for instance, you were a traveller sitting next to the window of a railway carriage and describing to someone inside the carriage the changing views which you see outside.'"[9]

As an expressive form, the analytic dialogue tapped into streams of thought, from the trivial to the shameful, which would be withheld in ordinary conversation. It differed markedly from other innermost explorations known to European culture. It was neither a reverie, nor a trance (whether induced by hypnosis or hashish), nor an act of contemplation (religious or philosophical), nor a confession (to inquisitor, priest, police, or reading public).

Analysis is an *expressive form* in a double sense. It is the medium in which the patient's inner reality gets expressed, from his or her wishes, feelings, and involuntary memories all the way to a persuasive version of his or her life-history. Second, analysis is an expressive form because its actual shape and the know-how to make use of it are the product of techniques and practices that must be developed and learned by the practitioners (analysts and patients). Like other expressive forms, especially artistic ones, analysis derives its shape from the contradictory materials it assembles. I am here presupposing the insight we owe to the tradition of modern aesthetic theory from Hegel to Adorno that the formative or constructive power of an artwork lies in its capacity to draw contradictory contents, imperatives, and modes of representation into some new form.

The contradictory pull in analysis is between spontaneity and reflection, contingency and causality. Free association has the élan of spontaneity and chance—saying whatever comes into your mind—but the consciousness thus reporting whatever flashes by the window is in turn inevitably surprised by the unconscious linkages between the associations, linkages that have the force simultaneously of contingency and necessity. Life's random happenings turn out to possess psychical causality. The psychoanalytic dialogue, as an expressive form, has to oscillate between these poles until it takes shape as the patient's inner history.

Psychoanalytic technique was forged in the effort to master this rhythmic alternation. Free association made spontaneity the rule of analysis, and this spontaneity also characterized the role of dreams and of transference. Dreaming is involuntary, churning images before the mind's eye at the speed of the landscape outside the railway carriage. Dreams also seemed to contribute to the interpretive work of psychoanalytic therapy, for Freud found that the images that the patient's inner dream machine manufactured at night would pick up on themes from that day's session and give direction to the next day's. In other words, the dreamwork itself melded the spontaneity of dreaming with the purposiveness of interpreting. The resulting form is more a collage than a synthesis, a Cubist rather than a Dutch portrait: "in the course of the treatment one must endeavour to lay hold first of this, then of that, fragment of the symptom's meaning, one after another, until they can all be pieced together."[10]

Transference: Technique or Ethic?

The other spontaneous event in psychoanalytic therapy, besides free association and dreaming, was the transference. In contrast to dreams, however, transference arose not so much as an effort of the unconscious to meet the analysis halfway but rather because of the patient's resistance to the developing interpretations themselves. Unconscious thoughts or desires that might at a given moment advance those interpretations would, instead of being acknowledged, hide themselves in the minute particulars of a passion for, and a wish to be loved by, the analyst.

The *Papers on Technique* contains two essays on transference. The first, "The Dynamics of Transference" (1912), provides the premise behind Freud's understanding of transference: "each individual . . . has acquired a specific method of his own in his conduct of his erotic life—that is, in the preconditions to falling in love which he lays down, in the instincts he satisfies and the aims he sets himself in the course of it. This produces what might be described as a stereotype plate (or several such), which is constantly reprinted afresh—in the course of the patient's life," though it can undergo changes "in the face of recent experiences."[11] Freud believed the transference was just such a fresh printing; its "stereotype plates" or "prototypes" were the repressed or inhibited impulses that the analysis threatened to bring to light. The analyst would become the object of passions and "anticipatory ideas" that originally attached to the patient's "father-imago," "brother-imago," "mother-imago," and so on.

The key to the transference's role in therapy, however, was not that it proved a false love, but rather that it "emerge[d] as *the most powerful resistance* to the treatment*," marking a stoppage of the patient's free associations. Because the transference was "a compromise" between the contrary demands of the resistance and the "work of investigation," the challenge to the analyst was not to convince the patient of the difference between true love and false, but rather to use the transference as a signpost of resistance and guide to the very interpretive work its appearance momentarily blocked. In the terminology of "Remembering, Repeating and Working-Through" (1914), the patient wants to repeat the repressed impulse in relation to the analyst, while the analyst wants the patient to work it through in memory: "The doctor ties to compel him to fit these emotional impulses to the nexus of the treatment and of his life-history, to submit them to intellectual consideration and to understand them in light of their psychical value."[12]

The technique of psychoanalytic therapy, the skill or art required of the analyst, hinged for Freud on the "handling" of the transference. From the moment the transference emerged in the analysis, the dialogue began to give shape to—that is, take the shape of—a struggle between repeating and remembering. Rather than letting the work of investigation be undone by the spontaneity of a passion, itself contradictorily formed by impulse and resistance, the analyst had to let the interpretive work be directed by the patient's passions, just as the patient had to be guided into "working-through" the resistance itself.

In the second essay on transference, "Observations on Transference-Love" (1915 [1914]), Freud took up the ethical as well as technical dilemmas of transference. The particular situation he chose to discuss occurred often in psychoanalytic therapy. It "is the case in which a woman patient shows unmistakable indications, or openly declares, that she has fallen in love, as any other mortal woman might, with the doctor who is analyzing her." The essay is written from the viewpoint of an experienced analyst advising his colleagues. It is one male analyst speaking to other male analysts. There were scarcely any women practicing psychoanalysis in 1914, and "the Committee," Freud's inner circle of six loyal disciples after the break with Jung and Adler, were all men. The essay has its share of male-bonding tics, as Freud infantilizes the "class of women . . . who tolerate no surrogates" once they fall in love and refers to them as "children of nature who refuse to accept the psychical in the place of the material, who, in the poet's words, are accessible only 'to the logic of soup, with dumplings for arguments.'" Describing the usual result of trying to treat such women, Freud uses, whether coyly or unwittingly, the image of an analysis interruptus: "One has to withdraw, unsuccessful."[13]

Freud nevertheless exhibits considerable tact and sensitivity in the essay as a whole, being quite aware that his topic was difficult for his fellow analysts and their patients and potentially explosive for a suspicious, moralistic public. He unqualifiedly makes the case that the analyst must neither return the patient's advances nor repudiate them as illusory, immoral, or irrelevant. The case he builds consistently entwines technical and ethical arguments about how the male analyst should handle transference-love. To get a feel for Freud's style of argument, it's worth quoting the following paragraph in its entirety:

> It is, therefore, just as disastrous for the analysis if the patient's craving for love is gratified as if it is suppressed. The course the analyst must pursue is neither of these; it is one for which there is no model in real life. He must take care not to steer away from transference-love, or to repulse it or to make it distasteful to the patient; but he must just as resolutely withhold any response to it. He must keep firm hold of the transference-love, but treat it as something unreal, as a situation which has to be gone through in the treatment and traced back to its unconscious origins and which must assist in bringing all that is most deeply hidden in the patient's erotic life into her consciousness and therefore under her control. The more plainly the analyst lets it be seen that he is proof against every temptation, the more readily will he be able to extract from the situation its analytic content. The patient, whose sexual repression is of course not yet removed but merely pushed into the background, will then feel safe enough to allow her preconditions for loving, all the phantasies springing from her sexual desires, all the detailed characteristics of her state of being in love, to come to light; and from these she will herself open the way to the infantile roots of her love.[14]

What is the significance of this mixing of technical and ethical arguments? It could be the way a wily scientist, steeped in the ethos of the fact-value distinction and acutely aware of the public's antagonism to objective discussions of sexuality, keeps his entire argument firmly grounded in the factual conditions of illness and treatment while coincidentally — luckily — satisfying the public's mind on the ethical question. If so, fact finesses value in Freud's rhetoric. Alternatively, thinking back to Andreas-Salomé's assertion, Freud's argumentation may suggest that psychoanalytic procedures as a whole, intellectual and therapeutic, scientific and medical, essentially *are* an ethics. There is certainly ample evidence that Freud saw the analyst-patient relation and the very possibility of therapy as determined by truthfulness, care, trust. If so, value suffuses fact. It's not all that easy to distinguish these two attitudes toward therapy in Freud's writings. It was quite likely a problem he considered philosophical and therefore not all that interesting. Let's come back to it later.

Therapy as Mastery

I have been making the case that Freud the therapist responded to modernism's twin imperative of newness and mastery. He created an unprecedented expressive form in response to the unmasterable changes of modern everyday life, and he made the patient's mastery the aim of this new mode of expression. What was the nature of the mastery that the psychoanalytic dialogue promised and sought? What was the patient to master? Here too the nagging question Freud preferred to finesse will reappear: What is the ethic in psychoanalytic technique?

The promise or goal of psychoanalytic therapy Freud saw as a process of enlightenment. The patient's neurotic symptoms had originally formed because of "an obstinate conflict . . . between a libidinal impulse and sexual repression, between a sensual and an ascetic trend." While it was true that "in neurotics asceticism has the upper hand," the goal of analysis was not to lead the patient toward "'living a full life' sexually." Once again letting moral questions take a back seat to psychological ones, Freud insisted that the aim was merely to put the sensual and the ascetic trends "on the same psychological footing," leaving the patient with "a normal struggle between mental impulses": "To make this possible is, I think, the sole task of our therapy." Moreover, there was no question of serving as a mentor when the time came for the patient to weigh the conflict between libidinal impulses and moral or practical considerations: "there is nothing we would rather bring about than that the patient should make his decisions for himself."[15]

Nevertheless, a key factor in this enlightened independence was the patient's ability to learn from the analyst's "unprejudiced consideration of sexual matters," an attitude that itself casts "a critical eye" on society's "conventional sexual morality," whose normal "proceedings," in Freud's view, "are not based on honesty and do not display wisdom." Freud's was always an attenuated criticism of the bourgeois lifeworld and the norms of the bourgeois household. He did not promote sexual liberation, merely a reduction in the neurotic suffering fostered by his society's hypocrisy and asceticism. So long as patients "decided on their own judgment in favour of some midway position between living a full life and absolute asceticism, we feel our conscience clear whatever their choice." His faith lay in the idea that psychoanalytic knowledge would demystify prevailing moralities without over-turning the patient's mature, self-regulating morality: "We tell ourselves that anyone who has succeeded in educating himself to truth about himself is permanently defended against the danger of immorality, even though his standard of morality may differ in some respect from that which is custom-ary in society."[16]

From within this framework, then, mastery lay in the taming of instincts and the strengthening of the self that deals with reality. The *taming of instinct* Freud understood in the sense of overcoming an impulse whose power to influence one's behavior, feeling, or thought lay in the mere fact that it was unrecognized, unconscious because repressed. The self's *dealing with reality* he understood in the sense of answering to those practical and moral demands of everyday life that were rationally acceptable. He saw neu-rosis as a depletion of the psychical energy available for erotic gratification, for sublimated activities of the mind, and even for social change. By hewing to a quantitative explanation of neurosis in terms of the economy of psychi-cal energies, Freud once again finesses the moral or moral-political account of repression. In his own words, "The distinction between nervous health and neurosis is thus reduced to a practical question and is decided by the outcome—by whether the subject is left with a sufficient amount of capaci-ty for enjoyment and of efficiency."[17]

The mastery promised by the new expressive form was secular, utilitari-an, and hedonistic—an Apollonian rather than Dionysian hedonism: enjoy-ment and efficiency. Freud saw therapeutic success in a patient's relatively sober resumption of everyday responsibilities coupled with an ability to weigh the importance of newly recognized impulses relative to the limits of the life he or she had already made. He dismissed the idea that the recogni-tion of long-repressed desires could lead to immoral, antisocial behavior. The objects and circumstances that had occasioned the repressed impulses were themselves long past, and the mature self, however damaged by repres-sion and neurosis, had in the intervening years built up and adapted to its lifeworld. The practical and rationally acceptable moral demands of that lifeworld would assert themselves at the end of therapy.

The Moral of Psychoanalysis

There have of course been many significant reassessments and revisions of Freud's concept of the therapeutic promise of mastery. Left Freudians, beginning with Wilhelm Reich, radicalized Freud's own tendency to take the incapacity for sexual enjoyment as the benchmark of neurosis and advocated a programmatic attack on repressive society for the sake of liberating sexuality. Herbert Marcuse eventually declared "the obsolescence of the Freudian concept of Man." He argued that industrialized, consumer society's increased capacity to meet human needs had overtaken Victorian asceticism and undermined the material foundations of the severe father figure and the cautious, calculating, self-preserving ego.

More recently, Richard Rorty has inflected the ethic of pleasure seeking with yet another significance. He ignores the political intent of Reich or Marcuse as well as the more recent challenges that feminist and gay thinkers have mounted against prevailing understandings of the boundary between private and public in the social regulation of sexual life and gender relationships. Rorty, instead, credits Freud with giving modern individuals a new self-conception and hence a new approach to private *as opposed to* public morality:

> Freud, in particular, has no contribution to make to social theory. His domain is the portion of morality that cannot be identified with "culture"; it is the private life, the search for a character, the attempt of individuals to be reconciled with themselves (and in the case of some exceptional individuals, to make their lives works of art).
>
> . . . Freud, by helping us see ourselves as centerless, as random assemblages of contingent and idiosyncratic needs rather than as more or less adequate exemplifications of a common human essence, opened up new possibilities for the aesthetic life. He helped us become increasingly ironic, playful, free, and inventive in our choices of self-descriptions. . . . It has helped us think of moral reflection and sophistication as a matter of self-creation rather than self-knowledge.[18]

Rorty readily admits that his playful ironist is nothing like the moral character-type projected by the stoical Freud's writings. Rorty simply gleans from some unspecified selection of Freud's concepts the idea of selfhood that happens to suit his own philosophical project and cultural outlook. It would no doubt be rather pedantic to object to such a free interpretation were it not for the fact that in the process Rorty lets the therapeutic origins of Freud's thought drop from view. He sheds no light on, draws no insight from, the ability of society to produce or intensify the debilitations and agonies that Freud's patients suffered. Ignoring the social mainspring of psychoanalysis, he can assert that Freud "has no contribution to make to social theory." In Rorty's fable, we postmoderns have somehow just opted for ludic joy and irony. Were that the case, there would likely be nothing to discover about the human mind and moral reflection, private or public, from any psychoanalytic or psychiatric project.

Another permutation on Freud is found in the work of Jacques Lacan. Couching his theoretical project as a "return to Freud," and organizing his seminars and writings as oblique, allusive commentaries on Freud, Lacan reworked the classical psychoanalytic vocabulary into the idiom of postwar philosophy and structuralism. He offers a very different view of the therapeutic process from Freud's, even though his clinical reference points are Freud's case histories more often than his own. According to Lacan, therapy neither tames the instincts nor strengthens the self. It first and foremost displaces the self. The patient's initial discourse—the explanation of his or her troubles to the analyst and the spontaneous narrative of his or her life—is, Lacan argues, the *parole vide*, the empty speaking, the vacant speech, the vacuous talk, of a self guarding its image, making its appeal to the analyst by making itself appealing. The free associations and dreams that ensue interrupt this *parole vide*. The analytic dialogue creates the conditions for the unconscious to puncture the patient's self-presentation. Lacan calls the unconscious the discourse of the other to stress its power to exceed the self's strategies and habits. It is not the discourse of another, since the unconscious thoughts and imagery are your own; yet it comes to you—in dreams, slips, free associations—as though from elsewhere, as though from another. As you accept these encrypted impulses as your own, you are displaced from, have to let go of, the self-regarding discourse through which you normally present yourself to others and to yourself.

The early Lacan called the ultimate self-narrative that the subject achieved through analysis a *parole pleine*—a full or fulfilled speaking—in which the hitherto unconscious elements were fully articulated in the patient's narrated life-history. Lacan backed off this phrase in the mid-1960s in the atmosphere of the radical criticism of the very idea of meaning-filled speech carried out by Althusser, Derrida, and Foucault. After his lectures went public in 1964 and as his audience became predominantly university students rather than analysts, he gave a less utopian, increasingly ironic account of the outcome of therapy. The discovery that your desire and identity are the effect of the unconscious (structured like a language) yields a heightened awareness of chance in the formation of your personality, of the errancy of desire, its whimsy and cruelty. A bit like Rorty's aesthete, you acquire an ironic awareness that your desire is capricious and your identity aleatory.

Like Freud, Lacan saw analysis leaving the patient with a question to answer without the analyst's mentoring or monitoring: Now that I know what I desire, what do I want? *Do I want what I desire?* Unlike Freud, Lacan construes *jouissance* (enjoyment) as ineluctably transgressive. If you want to "come" (*jouir*), you must submit to errant desire, you must cross a barrier, exceed a limit, defy a law, in your "enjoyment of" another (*jouir de*: to enjoy, get pleasure from, enjoy the use of). Whereas Freud saw treatment terminate with your difficult but lucid readjustment to the less-than-gratifying routines of the bourgeois lifeworld, Lacan expected you, newly decentered and invigorated, to scan your desires, reconnoiter your boundaries and barriers, assay your chances, in order ultimately to decide which barriers and boundaries to brave for the sake of a desire.

It's difficult to avoid a strictly ad hominem assessment of the Lacanian versus the Freudian prognosis. The Parisian ladies' man (to borrow Jane Gallop's definitive ad hominem formulation, though she used it to take aim at the ladies, the women who embraced Lacanian theory, more than the theory) versus the Viennese paterfamilias, cannily amoral but unwilling to overturn a life of respectability, so mindful of respectability, in fact, that he chose sexual abstinence, it has been speculated, to control his passion for his wife's sister.

The appeal of ad hominem explanations here actually points to a larger question. These various accounts of the moral import of psychoanalysis all express not merely the theorists' personal penchant but more importantly the specific cultural formation and social movement undergirding their thought. A mosaic of twentieth-century intellectual life emerges in the psychoanalytic reflections on sexuality and social life. Reich covertly drew on the rich sexual subcultures of Berlin in the 1920s and early 1930s, converting the rebellious sexualities we would today call queer into a decidedly male-centered, heterosexual philosophy of the bedroom. Marcuse was a harbinger of the counterculture of the 1960s, articulating a moral imperative for the urge to reject middle-class suburban life on account of its hypocrisy, shallowness, and functionalism. Rorty turns the Marcusian critique of affluence inside out by reaffirming the *private* possibilities afforded by "education, leisure, and money" and erects the miniature utopia of a suburban, professorial aestheticism that echoes more than it challenges the mainstream values of the 1980s and 1990s.

Freud made less radical—and less optimistic—moral claims for psychoanalysis than any of these revisionist commentators, largely because he believed that the actual success of modern individuals in conducting their lives in enlightened independence was extremely limited. Although he presupposed a capacity for enlightenment and independence in the very aims he set for analysis, he was at the same time struck by how thoroughly the modern promise of individual autonomy was thwarted by the very conditions that created it: "Only very few civilized people are capable of existing without reliance on others or even capable of coming to an independent opinion. You cannot exaggerate the intensity of people's inner lack of resolution and craving for authority. The extraordinary increase in neuroses since the power of religion has waned may give you a measure of it."[19]

The challenge Freud saw in modern life was twofold: to lessen the asceticism of modern "civilized" morality, and to replace the authority of religion with individuals' enlightened independence. The modern individual was compelled to replace the lost authority of tradition and doctrine with moralities dependent on persuasion and personal conviction. However much Freud doubted whether humanity was up to the task, he never wavered from his commitment to the idea that morality was the province of the individual rather than the community and of moral argument and personal conviction rather than authority and obedience. That commitment is visible even in the texts where he shied away from moral questions, for his psychological claims nonetheless tacitly evoked the various secular value frameworks of modern thought. His arguments are by turns utilitarian, hedonistic, libertarian, and universalist, but at every turn moral value enters his discourse as argument rather than authority.

Freud's commitment to a secular, individualistic conception of morality has dissatisfied his critics from the left and the right. The former want psychoanalysis to furnish a vision of social change; the latter want assurances against the anarchy of the drives and the amorality of values like enjoyment and autonomy. Is the purpose of therapy to undo repression or, on the contrary, to tame the instincts? Freud seems to vacillate between the two. But to get beyond the impasse it's necessary to reframe the question. For there is in fact a dimension of moral (or moral-political) reflection missing in psychoanalysis. It concerns the place of moral relations in the *genesis* of psychological complexes and pathologies.

Although Freud, as we will see, considered this question moot in light of Oedipal theory, it nevertheless agitated his discussions of the limits of therapy. Psychoanalysis was caught in a conceptual bind. On the one hand, the supreme value placed on individuality bolstered the critical, therapeutic attitude toward the moral strictures of religion and the sexual hypocrisy of bourgeois society: psychoanalytic therapy thus entrusted the patient with responsibility for his or her own desires, however aberrant, archaic, or asocial. On the other hand, the theoretical concepts that supported this tacit ethic of enlightened autonomy removed the mind or psyche from the web of social relationships in which individual identity and desire are actually shaped: psychoanalytic therapy thus tended to remove social, political, and moral contexts from its account of psychogenesis. This theoretical gap becomes apparent in two themes Freud considered decisive in limiting the success of therapy: the "negative therapeutic reaction" and the "repudiation of femininity." I will take them up one at a time.

Negative Therapeutic Reaction

Freud frequently demarcated the external limits of psychoanalytic therapy in his writings between 1910 and 1919. Although analysis could successfully treat the "transference neuroses" (anxiety hysteria, conversion hysteria, obsessive-compulsive disorder), so called because the patient readily formed a transference vis-à-vis the analyst, it proved ineffective with schizophrenia, paranoia, melancholia, and other disorders in which the patient did not form such a transference. He also occasionally referred to another limit that could interrupt even a properly conducted analysis. Some patients exhibited a "negative therapeutic reaction" because their unconscious sense of guilt and need for punishment caused them to evade successful treatment for the very reason that it would stop their suffering. Freud first noted this kind of reaction in "half-recovered" patients who short-circuited their treatment when some mistake or misfortune in their lives suddenly suspended their symptoms because it gratified their need for punishment. "By a foolish choice in marriage they punish themselves; they regard a long organic illness as a punishment by fate and thereafter often cease to keep up their neurosis."[20]

In one of his last published essays, "Analysis Terminable and Interminable" (1937), Freud took a more systematic look at the internal limits of therapy. He revisited the negative therapeutic reaction, now using the new theoretical perspective he had introduced in *Beyond the Pleasure Principle* (1920) and *The Ego and the Id* (1923). The "sense of guilt and need for punishment" were now understood as an unconscious conflict or breach between the ego and the superego, a conflict that satisfied the need for punishment and gave evidence of the death drive. Masochism, the negative therapeutic reaction, and the neurotic sense of guilt were all "unmistakable indications of the presence of a power in mental life which we call the instinct of aggression or of destruction according to its aim, and which we trace back to the original death instinct of living matter."[21]

Classical psychoanalysis was faced with a fundamental challenge, since it had previously assumed that the whole therapeutic dynamic was driven by *eros*: repressed impulses sought gratification; the self wanted to overcome the suffering caused by its symptoms; even resistance took the form of love in the transference. The inner violence of a breach between ego and super-ego ran counter to all of that. Faced with evidence of "free aggressiveness" within the human psyche, analysts had to realize that "we shall no longer be able to adhere to the belief that mental events are exclusively governed by the desire for pleasure."[22]

Even though the negative therapeutic reaction manifested a moral torment thwarting the individual's very desire for recovery, Freud did not look to the moral relations between self and others to find the origins of the torment. Instead, he stayed with the explanation provided by Oedipal theory. The answer was firmly in place as early as the *Introductory Lectures on Psycho-Analysis* of 1916–17. So essential are "the two wishes—to do away with his father and in place of him to take his mother to wife"—that "even if a man has repressed his evil impulses into the unconscious and would like to tell himself afterwards that he is not responsible for them, he is neverthe-less bound to be aware of this responsibility as a sense of guilt whose basis is unknown to him. There can be no doubt that the Oedipus complex may be looked upon as one of the most important sources of the sense of guilt by which neurotics are so often tormented."[23]

Oedipal theory gave moral sentiments a singular origin: "Originally this sense of guilt was a fear of punishment by the parents, or, more correctly, the fear of losing their love; later the parents are replaced by an indefinite number of fellow-men."[24] The true prototype of parental punishment is the threat of castration. When Freud made the claim in *Totem and Taboo* (1913) that "the beginnings of religion, morals, society and art converge in the Oedipus complex," which itself "constitutes the nucleus of all neuroses,"[25] he sealed the idea that conscience originated in the *fear* of castration as punishment for masturbatory fantasies of incest with the mother or for the wish to kill the father.

The dogmatism of Oedipal theory lies just here. Freud did not entertain the possibility that conscience or a sense of guilt and responsibility could *originate* intersubjectively in one's experience with others (including non-parental fellow beings), for example, in the experience of injuring and being injured, in doing and suffering harm. Nor did he explore the implications of the fact that even the Oedipal fear arises from a *threat* of punishment, not from a punishment—that is, from what Lacan would later identify as the dis-cursive-symbolic order in which the parent-child relation takes place. Nor did he seek out a more variegated typology of infantile fears and threats that might have included disapproval, abandonment, humiliation, invalidation, shame, mockery, or repudiation. Nor did he ask whether a betrayal of trust in the earliest self-other relations could, by analogy with "primal repression," impair the very formation of the self, fracturing its relation to the world of others. All such questions were moot (or derivative) because of the explanatory scope granted the Oedipus complex as the "nucleus of all neuroses."

However, psychoanalysis had not penetrated all neuroses, only the transference neuroses. Freud's reasoning was based on them alone: No neurotic symptom could form unless sustained by the unconscious. Since the unconscious itself knows no "No" and forms no judgments, it cannot be the seat of any moral sense. Rather, it is the seat of impulses, libidinal or aggressive, and these impulses form a symptom only after coming into conflict with the interests of the ego. Among these ego interests is avoiding punishment. Therefore, conscience is the result of the conflict between the (incestuous or patricidal) impulse and the fear of punishment. In this way Oedipal theory created a perfect fit between the theory of conscience and the theory of neurosis. But weren't the limits of Oedipus at issue once Freud began taking account of phenomena that did not fit the transference neuroses at all?

Occasionally the inadequacy of Oedipal theory did push Freud to give more ample scope to his reflection on moral relations, as in "Some Character-Types Met with in Psycho-Analytic Work" (1916). There Freud explored how every patient's style of resistance provided an intensified form of his or her "peculiarities," "attitudes," "traits of character." To illustrate some significant character-types met with in analysis Freud turned not to his own cases but rather to a series of literary characters from Shakespeare and Ibsen (Richard III, Macbeth, Lady Macbeth, and Rebecca in *Rosmersholm*). Without going into Freud's rich, richly troubled readings of the plays, I want simply to stress that all three of the "character-types" he discusses are defined by complexities or paradoxes rooted in their moral experience. There are the *exceptions*, who live as though exempt from everyone else's moral norms because they themselves have been wronged in the past. There are *those wrecked by success*, who show a determination beyond good and evil to achieve what they desire and then, once it is achieved, begin to disintegrate from a guilt that must have antedated the offense they committed with such single-mindedness. And there are the *criminals from a sense of guilt*, whom Freud associates with the Pale Criminal denounced by Nietzsche's Zarathustra, who commit a crime in order to justify a mysterious preexisting "feeling of guilt."

Each of these types exhibits what Freud would later identify as the condition for the negative therapeutic reaction, namely, that inner violence that bespeaks an *unconscious* breach between ego and superego. The essay goes as far as he ever went in suggesting that the source of later pathologies might come from some primal rent in the individual's relation to others. When Lacan offered an intersubjective model in place of Freud's intrapsychic model, he took another step in that direction, especially by stressing the role of trust or good faith in the discursive relation between self and others. But only a few analysts in the Freudian-Lacanian tradition pursue the question on its own terms. Marie Balmary, for example, reassesses Freud's earlier seduction theory of neurosis to show how, not only in formulating the theory but also in repudiating it, he failed to appreciate how a breach of trust in the child's relation to his or her parents could generate symptoms. Maud Manonni, who has produced one of the most detailed and imaginative records of clinical work in the Lacanian tradition, gives fuller attention to disturbances in the moral or intersubjective fabric of the primary relationships that form the child's identity and desire.[26] The negative therapeutic reaction, in sum, had theoretical as well as therapeutic implications for psychoanalysis; it was an unheeded signal to rethink whether the Oedipus complex could truly explain all that it was called upon to explain.

The "Repudiation of Femininity"

Oedipal theory also distorts Freud's interpretation of the other relevant theme of unfinished analyses, the so-called "repudiation of femininity." The final three pages of "Analysis Terminable and Interminable" are a blur of Oedipal logic run amok. Freud discusses "two themes" that "give the analyst an unusual amount of trouble" and that have "an obvious correspondence" to one another though "different forms of expression" in accordance with "the difference between the sexes." Right from the start, the asymmetry he posits between the sexes suggests something other than a correspondence: "The two corresponding themes are, in the female, an *envy for the penis*—a positive striving to possess a male genital—and, in the male, a struggle against his passive or feminine attitude to another male." Creating symmetry where there is none, Freud calls both themes a "repudiation of femininity."[27]

Whenever Freud raises the theme of penis envy he refers to women who cannot, or refuse to, reconcile themselves to what is denied them in life because they are women. Nowhere does he provide clinical material compelling or detailed enough to demonstrate that women typically or inevitably represent their rage or disappointment as an unacceptable lack of penis. That women feel such rage and disappointment, that many find it intolerable, that they might represent what society denies them via their body image, that they might incorporate society's overvaluation of masculinity into their symbolic body image, that a revolt against the status of inferiority can take the form of rage-filled, distorted images of oneself—all of these hypotheses would find much to support them in the literature, memoirs, and, presumably, psychoanalytic sessions of twentieth-century women. But none of it adds up to penis envy. Even though some feminist theorists have embraced the psychoanalytic concept of penis envy or accepted its psychological truth while revising its social meaning, I vote with the more radical skeptics, for it seems to me that the symbolic equation *deficiency = castration* is too crude to account for the ways in which women's social subordination finds subjective expression within their individual body image, identity, and desire. Consider the simple historical and political fact that from before Freud's time until our own feminists have expressed an extraordinary range of attitudes toward women's roles, values, lifestyles, and modes of self-presentation, all the while refusing to reconcile themselves to what is denied them in social life. It is impossible to reduce their repudiations of inequality to a "repudiation of femininity," whatever significance "femininity" may acquire. Freud's tacit *social* interpretation of women's repudiation of inequality as a "repudiation of femininity" lay behind and propped up his *psychological* interpretation of the "repudiation of femininity" as penis envy.

What about the male "repudiation of femininity"? Freud applies this term to a phenomenon—a man's "struggle against his passive or feminine attitude toward another male"—that suggests the power of homophobia to deplete men's relations with one another. Such a phenomenon might have led Freud to dissect the fragility of masculine identity in a society that banned and denigrated homosexuality or to investigate the murky ties between homophobia and misogyny in heterosexual men. But Oedipal theory deflects those inquiries because it presupposes, however covertly at times, that the heterosexual couple and unambiguous gender identity are an inherent *psychical* norm as opposed to a variable social norm with untold psychological consequences.

Although Freud frequently disputed the norms of heterosexuality and gender identity—from his ideas about the bisexual nature of the human psyche to his refusal to pathologize homosexuality—those same norms kept inserting themselves into his most central theoretical constructs. Telltale signs of his uncertainty are scattered throughout his writings. When he tries to clarify the exact meaning of the "repudiation of femininity" in "Analysis Terminable and Interminable," he does not use his own words but cites a passage from Sándor Ferenczi that, in furnishing a definition of the goal of a truly terminated analysis, baldly asserts the most sexist and heterosexist of psychoanalytic assumptions:

Every male patient must attain a feeling of equality in relation to the physician as a sign that he has overcome his fear of castration; every female patient, if her neurosis is to be regarded as fully disposed of, must have got rid of her masculinity complex and must emotionally accept without a trace of resentment the implications of her female role.[28]

Even as he distances himself from Ferenczi's therapeutic expectations—"speaking from my own experience, I think that in this Ferenczi was asking a very great deal"—Freud incorporates these normative definitions of gender and sexuality into his own discussion, leaving no doubt as to the nature of the female role: "Normally, large portions of [a woman's masculinity] complex are transformed and contribute to the construction of her femininity: the appeased wish for a penis is destined to be converted into a wish for a baby and for a husband, who possesses a penis."[29] A woman's "masculinity complex" has but two possible fates; either penis envy is transformed into the gratifications of marriage and motherhood or it is "retained in the unconscious and, from out of its state of repression, exercises a disturbing influence." Freud considered these vicissitudes of penis envy to be "purely psychological." To maintain that thesis he had to relegate the moral-political question of sexual inequality to the margins, first by reducing the social phenomenon of women's struggles against inequality to the little girl's penis envy and then by reinterpreting the grown woman's dilemmas and choices as the inner drama of her masculinity complex: would her primordial penis envy undergo a pathogenic repression or would it be transformed into the socially acceptable role of passivity, subordination to a man, and satisfaction with motherhood as a substitute for other gratifications in life?[30]

Freud's own account of the force of the "repudiation of femininity" in interrupting the therapy process is as follows:

At no other point in one's analytic work does one suffer more from an oppressive feeling that all one's repeated efforts have been in vain, and from a suspicion that one has been "preaching to the winds," than when one is trying to persuade a woman to abandon her wish for a penis on the ground of its being unrealizable or when one is seeking to convince a man that a passive attitude toward men does not always signify castration and that it is indispensable in many relationships in life. The rebellious overcompensation of the male produces one of the strongest transference-resistances. He refuses to subject himself to a father-substitute, or to feel indebted to him for anything, and consequently he refuses to accept his recovery from the doctor. No analogous transference can arise from the female's wish for a penis, but it is the source of outbreaks of severe depression in her, owing to an internal conviction that the analysis will be of no use and that nothing can be done to help her. And we can only agree that she is right, when we learn that her strongest motive in coming for treatment was the hope that, after all, she might still obtain a male organ, the lack of which was so painful to her.[31]

The supposed correspondence between the male and female "repudiation of femininity" now issues into a scarcely disguised asymmetry: a man's "passive attitude toward men does not always signify castration" while a woman's aspiration for anything beyond her female role invariably signifies penis envy. From there the asymmetries simply proliferate: women's "severe depression" versus men's "rebellious overcompensation"; women's rage against inferiorization versus men's repudiation of emotional reciprocity; women's resentment over their social role versus men's fragile prestige; women's longing for equality versus men's denial of indebtedness. Thanks to the various waves of feminist theory and practice and the accompanying experiments and changes in everyday life, we discern psychosocial patterns of sexual politics in these oppositions more readily than did Freud.

He disclosed the patterns but eclipsed the moral-political relations that affected his patients' experience of sexuality and gender. Eschewing the moral-political dimension, he made do with a confusing dichotomy between the "psychological" and the "biological":

We often have the impression that with the wish for a penis and the masculine protest we have penetrated all the psychological strata and have reached the bedrock, and that thus our activities are at an end. This is probably true, since, for the psychical field, the biological field does in fact play the part of the underlying bedrock. The repudiation of femininity can be nothing else than a biological fact, a part of the great riddle of sex.[32]

Contrary to Ferenczi's aspiration to solve the riddle, Freud did not presume that the whole of gender identity is "psychological"; Ferenczi's total gender therapy implied that the patient could adequately uncover his or her inner representations of masculinity and femininity (whatever their origins) and then emotionally accept the "proper" set once the contingent barriers to such acceptance were identified and overcome. In too many cases, according to Freud, the individual's inner representations simply did not permit such acceptance. What then was the source of the misfit between the representations and the patient's desire and identity? Freud's theoretical habits led him to consider the source to be "biological," by which he meant either "constitutional" factors (innate peculiarities or inherited tendencies below the level of psychical representations) or the death drive (the unmasterable rhythm and strife of organic life).

I certainly do not want to suggest that there is no biological substratum of psychological life; science continues to explore the whole realm of physiological, chemical, neurological, and genetic determinations of gender and sexuality. I am arguing, rather, that the kinds of misfit that Freud identified in gender and sexuality have a large cultural, social, and moral-political component that lies hidden behind the psychology/biology polarity. Freud reached not so much bedrock as a limit—or hole—at the heart of analysis that touched on the political as well as the biological conditions of gender and sexuality. He recognized that the socialization to heterosexuality and gender role more often than not remained unfinished; that is why he rejected Ferenczi's assumption that heterosexuality and unambiguous gender identity were normatively secured in society and normally achieved in the lives of men and women. Individuals' sexual experience and identity did not obey the dictates of modern patriarchy, and Freud frequently emphasized that the supposedly normal outcome of the Oedipus complex was rare, an exception rather than a norm. The psyche's recalcitrance to patriarchal or Oedipal norms is the unacknowledged theme of "Analysis Terminable and Interminable," but the moral-political questions that press against Freud's reflection are ultimately evaded and their import for psychoanalysis unexplored.

The tracks left by those evasions are what give Freud's texts their unique power as a drama of the mind grappling with the mind. To reiterate, the tracks I have tried to follow here are: Freud's suggestive equivocations when it came to distinguishing the technique and the ethic of transference; his undeveloped hints, drawn from literature, of a primal rent in the moral relations to others; and the stubborn return of modern patriarchal and heterosexual norms in a thinker who distrusted all norms.

Freud the therapist was modernist in his impulse to separate the analytic dialogue from morality. The personal transformation that therapy offered had nothing to do with acquiring a code of conduct or embracing particular values. Freud thereby kept religion at an arm's length and conveyed to his patients a deeply secular morality, which called upon them to follow their individual moral convictions in making ultimate choices. At the same time, he did not embrace Kant's conception of moral autonomy, which provided the modern age with its surest alternative to religious and communal sources of the moral self. Instead, he demystified the indwelling autonomy of Kantian individuality by exposing the impulses and rages that traverse the ego. As Lacan argued in his great essay "Kant avec Sade," psychoanalysis sees a violence, even a delight in torment, at the very heart of the self-regulating self's conscience.[33] In sum, Freud rejected the comforts of the cradling, coercive community of religious morality *and* the transcendental certainties of universalistic individual morality. In that sense, he unflinchingly affirmed that moral experience is ungrounded in its origins and uncertain in its outcomes.

Freudian therapy also kept moral-political reflection at bay, in part with the aim of not influencing or contesting the patient's personal convictions and beliefs. But what comes to light in "Analysis Terminable and Interminable" is that Freud and other analysts brought to therapy their society's moral-political determinations of the meaning of gender identity and sexual orientation and in turn failed to investigate those determinations in their own theories of gender and sexuality. What remained crucially unaddressed was not so much the origins of our moral capacity as the consequences of the ruptures in our moral and moral-political relations with each other. By moral-political rupture I mean the violence or exploitation woven into modern institutions. Gender identity cannot be understood without reference to women's subordination and inequality; sexual orientation cannot be made intelligible without reference to the severe moral and legal barriers imposed on homosexuality. Freud left a crucial gap in his psychoanalytic reflection on modernity because he could not overcome the heterosexism of his own theory when it came to the riddle of gender and sexuality or unveil the workings of homophobia in modern life, including in psychoanalysts' own procedures and concepts.

Let us not, however, congratulate ourselves for surpassing Freud. The theoretical obstacles he encountered are not that easy to overcome. Psychoanalysis rests on the seam between an aesthetic-psychological and a moral-political attitude toward sexuality. The two attitudes are simultaneous and yet incommensurate. They are not amenable to theoretical synthesis. The moral-political dimension of sexuality and gender, no matter how critical and progressive the elucidation of it, will never disclose all that determines sexuality and gender in psychic life. The critique of modern patriarchy and homophobia in the social construction of sexuality and gender reaches only so far; it can overturn the assumption that Oedipal norms legitimately guide the aim of analysis, and it can bring to light the role of homophobia and misogyny in psychosexual life, but it cannot explain the psyche by means of anti-norms or alternative norms any more than Ferenczi could explain it by the prevailing norms. Moral-political reflection is a crucial and, I have argued, largely missing element of psychoanalytic theory. Nevertheless, when it comes to psychoanalytic practice, Freud was right to separate therapy from morality. The analytic space—starting with the consulting room, the couch, and the armchair—is a realm of radically individual freedom. In this space one is free to unfold one's life-history in a dialogue untouched by the demands of the state, society, community, or family, even as the very possibility of such a material and psychic space, and of such a freedom, is created by modern social and political institutions. The lapses in Freud's theory, and perhaps in his practice, occurred when he did not see how the covert power of social and political institutions like sexual inequality or the proscription of homosexuality returned *within* the analytic space. Those flaws in his social thought are most significant, however, because they compromised the hallmark of his therapeutic ethic: the absolute integrity and radical freedom of each individual.

CHAPTER 6

Shock Effects: Marinetti, Pathology, and Italian Avant-Garde Poetics

LAWRENCE RAINEY

The "Technical Manifesto of Futurist Literature" (published in May 1912) begins with a narrative vignette that precedes the manifesto proper, depicting the speaker as he sits astride the fuel tank of a biplane that is soaring over the city of Milan.[1] As he glances at the urban panorama below, the speaker announces his ambition to destroy "the Latin period," a type of sentence he goes on to characterize with metaphors of the body that playfully allude to ancient rhetorical terminology, in which the periodic sentence had been said to be composed of "members."[2] The classical period has "a head, a stomach, two legs and two flat feet, but," he adds proleptically, "it will never have two wings" (*LMM*, 92; *TIF*, 46). No sooner has this been said, however, than the speaker's discourse abruptly changes direction: he disavows his own authority, ascribes his statements to another source, and then enigmatically vanishes altogether: "This is what the swirling propeller told me as I sped along at two hundred meters above the smokestacks of Milan. And the propeller added . . ." (*LMM*, 92; *TIF*, 46). The ellipsis gives way to the manifesto proper, with its formulaic listing of instructions and interdictions, a text that has been the subject of many discussions assessing its form, contents, and historical precedents.[3] Though such studies have enhanced our sense of the manifesto's interplay of argument and rhetorical form, their neglect of the opening vignette has deflected attention from a complex of metaphors that not only inform the opening sketch of "The Technical Manifesto," but also recur throughout Marinetti's early manifestos and link together a series of motifs central to the Futurist project. Encompassing images of mediums and automatic writing, analogies between the body and language, and a metaphorics of shock, trauma, and pathology, this complex of metaphors owes much to debate among psychologists and psychiatrists in the decades prior to the creation of Futurism, and as assimilated and mobilized by Marinetti, it poses a series of anxious questions about identity and authority, the self and technology, language and the possibilities of representation within the expanding regime of modernity.

The opening vignette sketches a scene not normally associated with the rambunctious persona elsewhere adopted by Marinetti: the speaker, rendered utterly passive and devoid of will, is taking dictation from an equivocal source, in this case an object of the latest technology, the "swirling propeller" of the biplane. It is true, of course, that the scene alludes to Homeric accounts of the poet who receives dictation from the muses, an allusion reinforced by explicit reference to "the old syntax inherited from Homer" (*LMM*, 92; *TIF*, 46). No less plainly, however, Marinetti is also invoking another paradigm of textual production that was considerably more recent in origin and the subject of intense discussion during the decades that straddled the turn of the century: the practice of automatic writing. Nor was Marinetti alone, during the decade 1910–20, in probing the implications of automatic writing. In the spring of 1912, just when Marinetti was composing the "Technical Manifesto," William Butler Yeats was having his first encounters with Elizabeth Radcliffe, a young medium whose automatic writings revealed hidden knowledge and mysterious powers; and only five years later, in 1917 (just a few days after his marriage), Yeats would discover that his wife Georgie could also produce automatic scripts, prompting a program of experimentation that lasted three years, yielded 3,600 pages of material, and furnished the basis for *A Vision*, Yeats's intricate system of symbolic psychology, philosophy, and history.[4] In France, meanwhile, André Breton and Philippe Soupault, during a period of some three weeks in April 1919, would write *Champs magnétiques*, widely considered the first "literary" achievement of automatic writing.[5] During the years 1910–20, automatic writing offered a paradigm of graphic practice and a metaphorical field that mobilized, articulated, and modified the resources of signification in ways that resonated with the era's deepest fantasies, myths, and fears.

Automatic writing could appeal to such diverse writers in part because it was not a single entity with well-defined features that could be readily listed or cataloged: it was not a genre, a style, or a recognizable form, though at times it took on dimensions of all three. Its hybrid status derived from its origins and early development. In early 1848 Margaret and Kate Fox of Rochester, New York, announced that they had been conversing with spirits from the afterlife by a system of signs that consisted of rapping noises. To answer "yes" or "no" to their questions, the spirits would rap once or twice, respectively; to respond to more complex inquiries, they would purportedly rap at the appropriate moment as the sisters called out the letters of the alphabet.[6] The Fox sisters began to attract public attention when they acquired two accessories to their "natural" talents: a press agent and business manager, and, as a result, they gained a capacity to produce public spectacles through their finding that spirits could relocate furniture and levitate tables and other objects with ease. In late 1849 they staged a public exhibition in Rochester (admission 25 cents); in the summer of 1850 they journeyed to New York, where they were "discovered" by the contemporary press. The movement that would soon acquire the name of spiritualism was born. The result was predictable: "The phenomenon," as one contemporary noted, "began, as it were, to propagate itself, and to be witnessed in other families."[7] Already in 1850 the Davenport brothers, also from Rochester, reported that their house had been the site of similar rappings for years, but that it was only after reading about the Fox sisters that they had understood its significance; when they staged a séance of the sort described by the newspapers, they discovered that they too were in contact with spirits, one of whom seized the hand of "Ira, the elder boy," and left "messages [that] were written by an invisible scribe."[8] Two years later Mrs. Hayden and Mrs. Roberts became the first American spiritualists to go to England, and soon the new spiritualism was being reported in Germany and France, with séances being held in Strasbourg, Bourges, and Paris.[9] It was in September 1853, for example, that Victor Hugo attended his first séance on the island of Jersey, an experience that would lead to two years of colloquies with an amiable group that included Aeschylus, Shakespeare, Cervantes, and Molière.[10]

From the outset, automatic writing flourished in an ongoing rapport with changes in contemporary communications and transcription technologies. It is no accident that the first reports of "rappings" took place in Rochester, a city whose leading citizens were pouring their capital into the development of early telegraph companies, their enthusiasm sparked by Henry O'Reilly, editor of the city's principal daily.[11] In the mid-1840s they were backing lines built across Pennsylvania and throughout the Ohio Valley, then another series crisscrossing New York State. In 1848 O'Reilly's partners bolted to form the New York State Telegraph Company, reorganized two years later as the New York and Mississippi Valley Printing and Telegraph Company in order to indicate its goal of westward expansion. Five years later, when it joined forces with the firm of Ezra Cornell, it drew virtually all the interior lines into a vast monopoly under the new name of Western Union.[12] As had been the practice elsewhere, the firm's lines were laid out to follow the rapid expansion of railroads.[13] (An analogous linkage between transportation and communications technologies is presupposed in the rapport between the biplane and the new "words-in-freedom" to be announced in the "Technical Manifesto.")

The spread of spiritualism was fueled by contemporary newspaper accounts, and the link between new religion and new technology was epitomized in the title of "the most widely circulated spiritualist newspaper of the period," the *Spiritual Telegraph*.[14] The technology of automatic writing itself, as if imitating the vertiginous pace of change in other fields, was also rapidly modified. The "rapping" procedures that the Fox sisters had first announced, for example, were soon supplanted by others associated with table moving or levitation: séance participants would attach a pencil or crayon to a table's leg, then place a sheet of paper beneath it and wait for the desired message to appear.[15] A tedious process, this too was rapidly supplanted by yet other technologies. On the one hand there were new and increasingly elaborate machines for automatic writing, some of them almost fantastic in nature, as if made to parody contemporary fascination with the marvels of engineering. On the other hand there were devices that were much simpler, cheaper, and more susceptible to mass production, such as the planchette, which first appeared in France between 1853 and 1856. The planchette consisted of a small, triangular piece of wood that was supported by rolling casters under two corners and a pencil at the third, a structure that enabled it to move under the slightest impulse from two or more séance participants. By 1868 it was said to be on sale at bookshops throughout the United States, and in 1899 an ambitious businessman named William Fuld designed a variant of it that he called "OUIJA, the MYSTIFYING ORACLE," a product he launched three years later with great success.[16] To be sure, many mediums preferred to dispense with devices and machines altogether, electing to write directly on paper. Machines, after all, merely duplicated the activity of the mediums; they were transcription machines, a metaphor that contemporaries often invoked and that further underscored the link between spiritualism and technology that had been implicit from the outset. In the words of Allan Kardec, the French author who became the chief spokesman for French *spiritisme*:

Mediums are simple electrical machines that transmit telegraphic dispatches from one point that is far away to another that is located on earth. Thus, when we wish to dictate a communication, we act upon [*nous agissons sur*] the medium just as the telegraph employee does upon his apparatus.[17]

Or, as one historian of spiritualism has put it:

Spiritual journals were full of mechanical images. The telegraph was a favorite choice of those trying to explain how something once considered marvelous might be reduced to a completely understandable accomplishment. A symbol of long-distance communication as well, it suggested a model of how spirit communications might take place.[18]

The point needs to be taken much further. For its followers, spiritualism may well have offered the promise of messages and consolation from another world; but in reality its communications were always uttered in the silent syntax of capital, murmured to the rhythms of its machines.

Automatic writing might have remained only a footnote in the history of spiritualism had it not been integrated into contemporary discussions about the mind and human identity, discussions that were laying the foundations for the so-called "dynamic" psychologies taking shape between 1875 and 1900. The medical history behind these debates is complicated. Individual components of the history have been treated by several monographic studies, but a cursory sketch can indicate its basic contours. A starting point might be the famous case first publicized in 1876 of Félida X, a woman who would spontaneously lapse into a cataleptic state in which she exhibited a curious array of symptoms, chiefly anesthesia or hyperesthesia and enigmatic pains that had no discernible cause. Félida was found to have two distinct and alternating personalities, a condition that was soon characterized with the term *dédoublement*, doubling of the personality.[19] At it happened, Félida was "discovered" just when there was a revival of scientific interest in the subject of hypnosis and the nature of hypnotic states, and from the beginning it was urged that "magnetic somnambulism" or "induced somnambulism" (the state of hypnosis) presented important analogies with the "natural" or "spontaneous somnambulism" into which Félida lapsed, raising similar questions about the nature of memory, amnesia, and will.[20] Contemporaneous with these developments was the wave of scientific interest and public fascination inspired by Charcot's famous studies of hysteria; Félida, in fact, would have been classed by her contemporaries as having hysteria, a term that was expanding to encompass ever more symptoms throughout the period 1850 to 1910.[21] Finally, there was the notion of trauma, a concept that was assuming its characteristically modern sense during the same period as a direct result of the social experience of new technology. Whereas trauma had previously designated purely physical lesions, it now began to undergo a process of psychologization, acquiring, as the Swiss historian Esther Fischer-Homberger has shown, its modern sense in the late 1860s in connection with injury claims that stemmed from railroad accidents.[22] It soon became the term of choice to designate a cluster of symptoms that evidently indicated genuine illness yet failed to correspond with discernible injuries or physical lesions, symptoms that included amnesia and the kinds of mysterious pains found in the case of Félida. Trauma, in other words, seemed to offer suggestive analogies with multiple personality as well as with hysteria, whose puzzling etiology remained an open question. Thus, the same period also witnessed a new taxonomy of hysteria that now included the category "traumatic hysteria," a hybrid term that indexes the resonant chain of analogies late–nineteenth-century psychiatrists and psychologists discerned across a spectrum of disturbing and perplexing phenomena.[23] The outcome of this vast and variegated discussion was the gradual formation of what Ian Hacking has called "a free-floating sequence of associations," a sequence in which vague yet haunting similarities could link the notions of multiple personality, dissociation, hypnosis, amnesia, shock, and trauma— an overlapping set of descriptive habits that established a field of associations, a metaphorics.[24] The missing link that would connect these diverse pathologies to one another, and thence to a potential aesthetics, would turn out to be writing—automatic writing.

Of all the early psychologists who worked on these questions, perhaps none was more influential than Pierre Janet.[25] "No one wrote more about the hysterical personality than Janet," one medical historian has claimed; and few, it might be added, have written more about mediums or automatic writing.[26] Just when psychologists and psychiatrists were seeking a paradigm, a matrix in the sense made famous by Kuhn, that would weave together the strands of debate surrounding hysteria, trauma, amnesia, and doubling of the personality, Janet provided one with the notion of automatism, a descriptive concept that he developed through his clinical encounters with automatic writing.[27] In a celebrated essay that he published in 1886, "Unconscious Actions and the Doubling of Personality during Hypnosis," Janet reported his experiments with Lucie.[28] His starting point was an observation already noted in previous studies of hypnotism: when in a posthypnotic state, Lucie would execute commands that he had given her while hypnotized. But Janet pushed his inquiries further. He began to give Lucie tasks that required her to execute complex mathematical calculations, actions that demanded not just passive or rote obedience, but forms of intelligent reflection. When she proved successful at these tasks, he commanded Lucie to write letters, a task that she also performed with ease, though without knowing that she had done so. Finally, he began to ask Lucie to answer in writing, while in her waking state, questions that concerned the traumatic events whose repressed memory was the source of her hysterical fits. When he showed a sample of her script to a colleague, he was surprised to learn that it resembled that of spiritualist mediums. Janet, in short, had discovered an experimental counterpart to the automatic writing of the spiritualists, writing governed by a mysterious and hidden self that existed independently of normal consciousness, a "second state" as Janet would term it, that was produced "by a certain doubling [*dédoublement*] of consciousness."[29] The effect of this discovery was to turn automatic writing into a crucial filament in the web that connected multiple personality, hysteria, dissociation, somnambulism and hypnosis, and shock and trauma. Three years later Janet published *L'automatisme psychologique*, a work that further articulated the concept of automatism and endowed the practice of automatic writing with importance for discussion about the nature of consciousness.[30] Devoting an entire chapter to a synthetic discussion of spiritualism, he concluded that mediums were "almost always" what he termed "*névropathes*" (suffering from a neuropathological condition), if not "simply hysterics."[31] The moment when the medium was possessed represented a hysterical convulsion, and at the core of the séance was "a violent nervous crisis" (*une violente crise de nerfs*).[32] The medium's ability derived from a morbid state analogous to conditions that could generate hysteria or insanity ("*un état morbide particulier analogue à celui d'où peuvent sortir plus tard l'hystérie ou l'aliénation*").[33] And he detailed at length "more precise analogies between the states of mediumism and hypnotism."[34] What Janet had done was create a resonant chain of analogies that crystallized in the notion of automatism, strands of identity and repressed memory that were a response to traumatic experience and that functioned like machines, evidently independent of consciousness, the self, or the ego.

The significance of Janet's work was recognized immediately. In February 1887, only two months after the appearance of the pioneering essay on Lucie, Frederic W. H. Myers, an English scholar who had been working for some time on a study of automatic writing, published the third and concluding essay in a series synthesizing the fruits of his researches.[35] In contrast to his previous essays, Myers now took an approach that directly followed the lead of Janet, focusing on the "formation of a secondary chain of memories, linking together . . . periods of altered consciousness into a series of their own."[36] He drew an analogy to dreams, which could exhibit sufficient continuity with one another to suggest the formation of "a secondary memory, a secondary manifestation of the Self,"[37] and he urged that a similar formation was readily discernible in hypnotism or somnambulism, intoxication with drugs or alcohol, epilepsy, cataleptic hysteria, and—most important—the state of possession in which mediums produced automatic writing. He also cited the case of Lucie at length,[38] comparing both Lucie and his own subjects with the famous descriptions of Félida.[39] Such studies, he concluded, rendered it impossible to "draw a broad line between the conscious and the unconscious"; they dissolved the everyday sense of a "true self" or "true identity"[40] and suggested, as Myers expressed it elsewhere, the "profound" and "disquieting . . . change, which at the touch of Science, is stealing over *ourselves*" (italics mine).[41] A similar sense of the urgency and significance of Janet's discoveries was felt by William James: "As soon as I read M. Pierre Janet's admirable account of the double personality of his somnambulist, L., I resolved to look for this symptom in ordinary writers."[42] James, of course, found what he was seeking: "Here, as the reader will perceive, we have the consciousness of a subject split into two parts."[43] And as James summarized the implications of his initial studies, "the great *theoretic* interest of these automatic performances, whether speech or writing, consists in the questions they awaken as to the boundaries of our individuality."[44]

The two decades that followed Janet's synthetic account of automatism did little to alter the intellectual context for the assessment of automatic writing. The stability was the result of several factors. One was Janet's growing reputation—upon the death of Charcot in 1893, he was named Director of the Laboratory of Psychology at the Salpêtrière, and in 1902 he was elected to a chair at the Collège du France—which retrospectively enhanced the prestige of his earlier studies on automatic writing. Another was Janet's continued productivity: during the period 1890 to 1905 he wrote a series of impressive works that further elaborated his understanding of spiritualism and displayed his mastery over almost every aspect of contemporary debate about hysteria.[45] Yet another consisted in the reciprocity between Janet's approach and the imperatives of clinical practice: Janet's accounts were more suggestive than rigorously theoretical, more amenable to the working world of most psychologists and psychiatrists. Early psychoanalytic theory, in contrast, not only demanded assent to a highly specific and internally coherent corpus of theory, but it also required a substantial investment of time in therapeutic techniques whose promise was hardly self-evident.[46] Anglo-American culture would prove especially responsive to Freudian theory, as illustrated by Freud's triumphant visit to Clark University in 1909; but in France and Italy the situation was notoriously different. The first article on Freud to appear in French was published only in 1907, in Italian in 1908.[47] The first book by Freud to be translated into French was not issued until 1921, and the first to be translated into Italian did not appear until 1927.[48] And whereas the London Society of Psycho-analysts was founded in 1913, both the Société psychanalytique de Paris and the Società psichoanalitica italiana were not established until 1925.[49] Prior to World War I, in short, the intellectual paradigm of automatism established by Janet was unchallenged and widely diffused across the spectrum of well-educated cultural life. For someone such as Marinetti, whose residence in the decade 1899–1909 alternated between Paris and Milan and whose education was more Franco- than Italophonic, knowledge of automatism would have been part of his general horizon of thought, loosely assimilated to ongoing popular discussion about hysteria, trauma, and the turbulent world of spiritualism.

The semiotic chains that had been constructed by previous psychological discussion, sequences that were also in ongoing dialogue with contemporaneous newspaper accounts of mediums and séances, furnish a stage on which Marinetti rehearses the critical motifs of Futurism throughout the early manifestos, on which, indeed, he assimilates and mobilizes the metaphorics of hysteria, trauma, and spiritualism to produce an aesthetics of shock that restages the traumatic encounter with technology. It is no accident, in other words, that the famous "Foundation and First Manifesto" of Futurism begins with a brief narrative that recounts an accident, the overturning of a car that is the traumatic birth scene that gives way to the recitation of the manifesto proper. Significantly, before the Futurists set out upon their drive, we are told that Marinetti and his companions have stayed up all night, as if watching at a wake, presiding over the spirit of a corpse who is never named. They are noctambulists, "alone" in the dead of night "with the black specters who grope in the red-hot bellies of locomotives"—a statement that situates the ensuing narrative within a genealogy of trauma, placing the proto-Futurists alongside shadowy beings who have already been transformed into mechanical "specters" by their subjection to the engines of modernity (*LMM*, 47; *TIF*, 7). As the protagonists go outside to commandeer the automobile that will take them to the scene of their traumatic experience, the narrator lies "stretched out on my car like a corpse on its bier" (*LMM*, 48; *TIF*, 8).

In a famous passage at the beginning of *Beyond the Pleasure Principle*, an attempt to reconsider the notion of trauma in the wake of World War I, Freud urges that the principal characteristic of traumatic neurosis is a type of repetition compulsion that indexes a failure of symbolization, an incapacity to render experience into the symbolic language of dreams or mentation. By this logic, perhaps it is only inevitable that the traumatic automobile accident leads Futurism to declare a historical end to symbolism in the oft-reprinted manifesto, "We abjure our Symbolist Masters, the Last

Lovers of the Moon." What ensues from trauma is not symbolic production but compulsive repetition: manifesto after manifesto is issued with a formulaic, obsessive sameness, each designed to recreate for writer and reader the traumatic sense of shock. The notion of the author, a figure of conscious selection, deliberate order, and control, is replaced by an indifferent and empty machine that repetitively produces its graphic quotas, the countless manifestos that are the uniform products of the new trauma-machine.

In the "Technical Manifesto" and its related supplementary texts, the "Responses to Objections" and the more famous "Destruction of Syntax— Words Without Wires," Marinetti extends the language of trauma into new terrains that encompass the microlevels of textual production. The rules that constitute the manifesto proper become an impersonal machine for the infinite reproduction of shocking experience, and its principal components (specific injunctions concerning syntax, diction, etc.) turn out to replicate many of the features basic to automatic writing. But to create the trauma-machine requires the destruction of the self, a task that is implicitly enjoined in the very first rule. Trauma, we recall, was thought by early psychologists to be characterized by a dissociative process of the self or the ego, which undergoes a process of dissociation (*desagrégation*) that generates multiple strands of independent selves functioning automatically; the clinician's task, in this context, was to reintegrate the dissociated entities with everyday consciousness, with the "I" as ordinarily understood. Yet Marinetti urges a process that is just the reverse, almost a form of resistance to therapy: the new literature of Futurism must "destroy the I," eliminate the ego, and so dispense with any authority or principle of organization. "Art," writes Marinetti as he explains the culminating eleventh rule, "is a need to destroy oneself and scatter oneself" (*LMM*, 97; *TIF*, 54). Which leads to the syntactic counterpart to this precept, the first rule spoken by the chattering propeller: "One must destroy and scatter one's nouns at random, just as they are born" (*LMM*, 92; *TIF*, 47).

Since the noun is the syntactical unit that most often occupies the position of the subject, and since the destruction of the subject and subjectivity is a paramount aim of the Futurist program, much of the manifesto revolves around the proper treatment to be accorded the noun. Indeed, the manifesto offers not a single or definitive precept for the noun, but three different injunctions that progressively displace and ultimately destroy the subject altogether. Just as traumatic experience was thought to initiate a process of psychological *dédoublement*, the creation of a "second self" that exists independently of the subject or his will, so the manifesto enjoins its own syntactic *dédoublement*: "Every noun must have its double, that is to say, must be followed immediately by another noun to which it is related by analogy" (*LMM*, 92; *TIF*, 47). Yet this initial formulation is inadequate, insofar as it suggests a residual survival of the original self (the first term or noun) and still adumbrates a principle of relatedness and cohesion (analogy) that seemingly gainsays the notion of traumatic dissociation. As a consequence, it is rapidly supplanted by a second injunction to "deliberately confound the object with the image that it evokes" (*LMM*, 92; *TIF*, 47), a principle that more effectively blurs the boundary between the primary noun/self and the secondary one. Yet even this injunction still evokes a faint survival of the original term as a component within the process of fusion, and therefore it too is supplanted by a third and much harsher imperative, "to suppress all the first terms of our analogies and render no more than an uninterrupted sequence of second terms" (*LMM*, 97; *TIF*, 53). At the level of syntax, the original noun/self has now been wholly effaced by the creation of a second self, a haunting specter that uniformly signifies the absence of its original referent, the destroyed self.

The propeller's treatment of verbs is much briefer, but it too turns upon the same thematics of self and syntax. "The verb should be used in the infinitive form, because the infinitive adapts itself elastically to the noun and doesn't subject it to the ego of the writer who observes or imagines" (*LMM*, 92; *TIF*, 47). Here again the object of suspicion is consciousness and the distance that it marks between the subject and reality, whether that reality be external (observed) or internal (imagined). The infinitive, in short, is a form of speed, the Futurist archetypal metaphor for whatever can bridge the gap between reality and the self, or, more accurately, the new dissociated self that traumatic experience has created. The verb in the infinitive is a means of bypassing consciousness altogether, a strategy to endow the verb with autonomy that renders it independent of the noun or the self that accompanies it.

Apart from its treatment of nouns and verbs, the manifesto's most notorious injunctions concern the insistent use of onomatopoeia. In another manifesto published in early 1914, "Geometric and Mechanical Splendor and the Numerical Sensibility," Marinetti presents his fullest defense of onomatopoeia, one that explicitly links it with the thematics of shock and offers it as an alternative to the verb in the infinitive.

Our growing love for matter, our will to penetrate it and know its vibrations, the physical sympathy that links us to motors, push us to the *use of onomatopoeia*.

Noise, after all, is the result of solids, liquids, or gases that are in rapid motion and

are either in friction with one another or crashing against each other. Onomatopoeia, which reproduces noise, is necessarily one of the most dynamic elements of
poetry. As such it can substitute for the verb in the infinitive form, especially when
one onomatopoeia is opposed to two or more others. (*LMM*, 109; *TIF*, 105)

Onomatopoeia, in this account, is the primal language of shock. It epitomizes and restages the principle of matter itself, which is now envisaged as
animating a universe of indifferent objects in perpetual collision, a continuous concussion that lends "natural" sanction to the mechanical jolts and
vibrations of modern technology, even as it simultaneously recapitulates and
replicates them. Onomatopoeia can substitute for the verb in the infinitive
because both are the syntactic counterparts of technological violence that
has been turned into an attribute of nature, because both epitomize a common refusal of the human and a regression to the state of inorganic matter
itself.

Nowhere is the primal scene that underlies the graphic program of Marinetti more clearly delineated than in a passage in the manifesto "Destruction of Syntax—Words Without Wires," in which Marinetti gives his principal example of how words-in-freedom are meant to function:[50]

Now imagine that a friend of yours, gifted with this lyrical ability, should find himself in a zone of intense life (revolution, war, shipwreck, earthquake, etc.) and would
come, immediately afterwards, to recount his impressions. Do you know what your
lyrical friend will instinctively do while he is still shocked [*commosso*]?

He will begin by brutally destroying the syntax of his speech. He wastes no time
in constructing periodic sentences. He could care less about punctuation or finding
the right adjective. He disdains subtleties and shadings, and in haste he will assault
your nerves [*vi getterà nei nervi*] with visual, auditory, olfactory sensations, just as
their insistent pressure in him demands. The rush of steam-emotion will burst the
steam pipe of the sentence, the valves of punctuation, and the regular clamp of the
adjective. Fistfuls of basic words without any conventional order. (*FM*, 98; *TIF*, 70)

Here is a perfect depiction of the trauma victim who is compelled by over-
whelming events—and Marinetti explicitly links them with technological
mishaps and war—to repeat the auratic experience of violence; who, unable
to integrate his experience into the temporal orders of narrative and memory, is subject to a form of repetition compulsion that obliges him to assault
his auditor with the violent sensations of the traumatic occasion, sensations
that simultaneously acquire talismanic significance even as they acknowledge their resistance to ordered structures of meaning. Images will now be
scattered about with "a maximum of disorder" (*TM*, rule 10), creating what
Marinetti calls "a net of images," or one in which every image stands in an

equal status, creating a discursive counterpart to the dissociated psyche from which the ego has been expelled. Not surprisingly, this imperative corresponds to the stylistic requirement that there be no punctuation, which has the effect of leveling different syntactic units into an equally centerless net. The absence of punctuation, of course, is one of the most common features of automatic writing, inherent not only in the use of the planchette but in every type of automatic writing in which the scribe would not lift the pen, but write in one continuous motion. And that, too, is what Marinetti recommends: "an uninterrupted succession of images."

It is at this point, now, that we can return to where we began, to the analogies that Marinetti draws in the initial vignette between syntax and the body. In "Multiplied Man and the Reign of the Machine," an essay written perhaps as early as 1910, Marinetti offers a vision of Futurist man that derives directly from the world of spiritualist séances in which automatic writing had originated. Man, he urges, will soon "externalize his will and make it into a huge invisible arm. . . . [H]e will be endowed with surprising organs" such as "a prow" that will emerge directly from the breastbone and be "more marked the better an aviator the man of the future becomes."[51] Indeed, he declares, "We believe in the possibility of an incalculable number of human transformations, and without a smile we declare that wings are asleep in the flesh of man." To explicate these images, Marinetti turns to the world of automatic writing and spiritualism: "You can easily understand these seemingly paradoxical hypotheses by studying the phenomena of externalized will that continually reveal themselves at spiritualist séances" (LMM, 99; TIF, 299–300). Marinetti, of course, is referring to a phenomenon, largely forgotten today, that was receiving significant media attention at the time. From the bodies of some mediums a strange foamy, frothy, or filmy substance, dubbed ectoplasm, would seem to condense and form mysterious limbs: twisted hands, oddly shaped arms, distorted heads. The most widely reported phenomena were a "second" head that would appear just above or behind the medium's own, and a hand that would seem to emerge from the medium's chest or bosom. These are the phenomena that Marinetti cites as a prototype for the production of the new "multiplied man," who will display the same sort of "externalized will" as that of mediums, and who will now create new "organs adapted to a world of ceaseless shocks" (LMM, 99; TIF, 299); these are the members of the new syntax, the new linguistic body, that correspond to "all the brutal sounds, all the expressive screams of the violent life that surrounds us" (LMM, 97; TIF, 53). The techno-body of the immanent future is identified with the somatic language of the hysterical medium whose performances issue in the creation of ectoplasmic limbs (hands, heads, etc.), and it is precisely this hysterical and largely female language of the body that he invokes as a metaphor for the program of "words-in-free-dom"—an automatic writing of shock in which the normalized, expressive subject of liberal humanism is replaced with a collective writing of dissoci-ated, traumatic selves that appear only as dispersed and scattered fragments spread across the page in disorder.

To be sure, this image of textual production is not without elements of paradox. When Marinetti praises the medium who transcribes automatic writing and generates the somatic language of ectoplasmic limbs, he does so by urging that these new organs exhibit the force of her "externalized will." This is paradoxical, of course, because the one trait that is consistently held to characterize automatic writing is the lack of volition involved in its pro-duction, the absence of will. But in the metonymic chain that Marinetti establishes, will vanishes only to be reinscribed in the figure of the machine. "You surely must have heard the remarks that owners of automobiles and factory directors commonly make: motors, they say, . . . seem to have per-sonalities, souls, or will" (*LMM*, 99; *TIF*, 298). This reinscription, to be sure, is attenuated, hesitant: Marinetti doesn't actually assert that machines have will; he merely transmits the report that they "*seem* to have . . . will" (*sembra che abbiano*).

This is not to say that one could not demonstrate other ways in which will is reinscribed in the figure of the machine. Jeffrey Schnapp, in an especial-ly probing assessment of the "Technical Manifesto," calls attention to its reappearance in the figure of the aerial gaze that ranges above the earth and encompasses everything with totalitarian power: "words in freedom, the imagination with outspread wings, analogical synthesis of the earth em-braced by a single gaze and wholly gathered together in essential words" (*TIF*, 53).[52] Schnapp deftly traces the network of associations that connect this gaze with practices of contemporary advertising, air meets and similar spectacles organized by contemporary newspapers, aerial reconnaissance for military purposes, and even "crude experiments with aerial bombardment" that Marinetti had observed in Tripoli.[53] Yet even when seemingly caught within its web of historical connections, the idea of a sovereign subjectivity proves elusive, evanescent. The "single gaze" captures "nets" or "networks of images," a metaphor whose structural model suggests loss and dispersion as much as connection or gain.[54] As Peter Nicholls notes, drawing on Umberto Eco, a net lacks any center or periphery, entrance or exit, because it is a figure of potentially infinite repetition. "Subjectivity drains through its holes," dispersed through uniform sectors of emptiness.[55]

Marinetti himself seems to recognize the vertiginous and paradoxical nature of this enterprise in one of the most telling passages from the "Response to Objections" that he published three months after the "Technical Manifesto." Describing the experience of writing words-in-freedom works, or automatic writing, he observes:

It is impossible to identify exactly the moment in which unconscious inspiration comes to an end and lucid will begins. . . . The hand that writes is seemingly dissevered from the body and its activity is prolonged in [a state of] freedom from the brain, a brain which itself has become detached from the body in some way or other and become airborne, observing from on high, with frightening lucidity, the unforeseen sentences that issue from the pen.

Does this domineering brain passively contemplate, or does it actually control the leaps of imagination that excite the hand? It is impossible to know. In moments such as these, I have observed, from a physiological standpoint, nothing more than a great void in the stomach.[56]

The unresolved tensions disclosed by such a passage are partly a consequence of a certain ambivalence that stems from Marinetti's circumstances during this period. The words-in-freedom stage was an evanescent moment in the trajectory of Futurism's development, scarcely lasting more than two years from 1912 to 1914, and the automatic writing that was invoked as its prototype was deeply, perhaps irreconcilably, inimical to the ethos of will and power that was always central to Marinetti's thought. Further, though Marinetti possessed a genuine lyrical talent that has yet to win due recognition among Anglophonic readers, a result of poor translations and the limited availability of his poems, he was also driven by an impulse toward narrative that would increasingly come to the fore in the years that followed Italy's entry into the Great War in 1915 and would lead to the major novels that appeared from 1918 to 1925. Narrative, with its highly mediated and distanced symbolic orders, is a form inimical to the aesthetics of traumatic immediacy cultivated by the "words-in-freedom" project. It typically presupposes a voice that is already detached from the experience it recounts, one that in the very act of narration already discerns significance, coherence, and development in its selection and sequencing of incidents. Narrative represents the de-auraticization of experience, while automatic writing presupposes a self that is still possessed by traumatic experience, an event so endowed with the aura of the unique and unrepeatable that it can find expression, paradoxically, only in compulsive repetition, in resistance to narrativization, in verbs that forever cling to the infinitive form, so refusing integration into temporal and hence human orders.

Yet more, and plainly much more, than just the trajectory of Marinetti's development is at stake in the nagging persistence of such unresolved tensions at the core of the "words-in-freedom" project. Marinetti's attempt to turn the metaphorics of trauma into an aesthetics, a poetics of shock, represents a disturbing project in many regards. Though Marinetti, famously, calls for the destruction of art in the "Technical Manifesto," he simultaneously aestheticizes the dissolution of the self under the impress of the machine. His program celebrates the immolation of the rational subject in its identification with the very sources of violence against it, demanding that the self now be turned into a mechanical register, a writing machine that passively transcribes the perpetual shocks of modernity. Marinetti's subject is haunted by the very machines he has created, specters that now dictate his every utterance, with speech itself reduced to the regressive stammer of onomatopoeia, an inarticulate groan that simultaneously expresses and conceals the sources of its agony. Lacking any form of solidarity with other humans and blindly subjected to images of power, he becomes a specter who exists only in his identification with the powers that stifle him.

It is here, perhaps, that we can best discern Marinetti's relationship to the complex and heterogeneous body of practices that we have come to call Modernism. For Modernism, whatever else it did, mounted a series of sustained and unprecedented interrogations of representational codes that had long been viewed not as conventions constructed by social orders, but as "discoveries" of "real" orders that offered transparent access to realities no less stable, no less grounded. Yet in order to formulate its interrogations of representation, Modernism was obliged to engage in a paradoxical endeavor, to find a way of representing nonrepresentation. That is what automatic writing embodied. By seeming to bridge the gap between experience and language, to fuse together the dissociated self and pure matter, to close the spatio-temporal distances that are preconditions for figuration and metaphor, automatic writing became the most vertiginous metaphor of all: the metaphor for not having metaphors, the figure for an end to figuration, the language that would be a form of not-language, only "an uninterrupted succession of images." That paradox, in turn, may well stem from another, more important contradiction at the heart of the avant-garde or Modernist project. Automatic writing and the words-in-freedom program that it inspired were a response to a basic contradiction within Modernism itself, a contradiction between that logic in the practice of Modernism that constantly directs it toward the human field of the sign and its dissolution, with its recurrent drive toward a dismantling of the kind of individual and individualist practice that typifies elite bourgeois culture (one thinks of its notions of expression and individualism); and that equally insistent drive toward an ethics and an aesthetics of individualism, an equally insistent impulse toward a reinscription of a sovereign and even heroic subject. The perennial equivocation that appears in the claim to collectivity jostling alongside the reinscription of narcissism or in the oscillation that places plebeian realities side by side with claims about the purity of art—that basic contradiction is the site to which Modernism returns time after time. That is also the motor that drives the machine of automatic writing.

PART III

Medicine, Literature, and Modernism

CHAPTER 7

Playing with Signatures:
The Young Charles Richet

JACQUELINE CARROY

Early in the Third Republic, Ernest Renan was at the height of his glory, a figure emblematic of *le savant*. The appearance of a new work by Renan was an event in itself. In 1883, he published *Souvenirs d'enfance et de jeunesse*. Taking Goethe and Chateaubriand as his models, he evoked the "vanished Atlantis" of his childhood and youth in an idyllic Celtic world dominated by women. He described himself as an amalgam of contradictory identities. His own intellectual itinerary had, he felt, an iconic value; speaking of "man"— a term to be understood here as the male human being whose brain has been "parched by reasoning"—he declared, "Nearly all of us are double. The more a man develops intellectually, the stronger is his attraction to the opposite pole: that is to say, to the irrational, to the repose of mind in absolute ignorance, to the woman who is merely a woman, the instinctive being who acts solely from the impulse of an obscure conscience" (Renan 1883: 4). Renan's expression "Nearly all of us are double" probably glances at the latest developments in the psychology of his time, which directed his attention to multifarious experiments with "doublings"; it had concluded, in the wake of Taine and Ribot, that the self was not unitary, but double, multiple, divided. In 1887, Renan himself took the initiative of creating a professorship at the Collège de France for Ribot, bestowing an official imprimatur on the new psychology. Renan thus offered his contemporaries the model of a man of science turned man of letters to announce that objectivity in research came at the price of a divided self. He also stated that his more strictly literary productions should be considered an integral part of his oeuvre, on a par with his scientific publications. Three years later, Robert Louis Stevenson had, in a manner no longer nostalgic but thoroughly disturbing, made famous in his *The Strange Case of Dr. Jekyll and Mr. Hyde* the story of a doctor dramatically divided between two contradictory identities. These two examples will serve as an Ariadne's thread in what follows.

This study extends the range of a recent work (Carroy 1993a) in which the consideration of the personality and works of Charles Richet was subsumed into a more general analysis of the origins of French psychology. In this perspective, Richet was one of a number of psychologists, including Henri Beaunis, Gabriel Tarde, and Alfred Binet, who were also littérateurs. The perception that they formed a series seemed to me to raise questions of historical epistemology. For one account tirelessly repeated in polemical rather than analytical spirit by the pioneers of scientific psychology in the nineteenth century has been widely adopted in certain contemporary histories (Boring 1929; Reuchlin 1957); it states that a "modern," objective psychology came into being only through the rejection of a philosophical and literary psychology, which it stigmatized as "archaic." Against this reductive vision, I felt the need to take seriously the fact that many of the founding fathers of French psychology were scientific Dr. Jekylls whose doubles were literary Mr. Hydes. "Doctor" is to be understood here in a general sense as "man of science," since neither Tarde nor Binet were doctors of medicine. These double identities belong to a social and cultural context illustrated — to take one example — by the flamboyant Charcot, scientific grandee and artist. The humanities and literature stood on an equal footing with science; the poet was no less esteemed than that privileged representative of science, the doctor of medicine. The first works published by Tarde in 1879 and, as we shall see, by Richet in 1874 were literary and poetic. Beaunis and Binet, by contrast, published "physiological" tales and horror plays, respectively, late in their careers. Instead of dismissing these double or multiple careers as anecdotal, I have attempted to relate them to one another, and to analyze the links that rive and unite the identities of authors, literary and scientific narratives, and psychologies. Once this Pandora's box has been opened, it becomes possible to draw a more complex portrait of the French turn-of-the-century psychologist, rather than a caricature reducing him to his scientism or the struggle to construct his professional identity (Carroy 1993a; Carroy and Plas 1996). In the perspective of a cultural history, the psychologist–man of letters forms an integral part of modernity, which can itself, as Renan's example shows, be based on the ambivalent resurrection of archaic worlds. Some of these perspectives are close to those of a recent book by Tony James (1995). Of course, this approach is not exclusive of other kinds of analysis, and it should be tested through a comparative study of other countries.

In this chapter, I shall consider in depth the highly significant example afforded by Charles Richet (1850–1935). In contrast with Stewart Wolf's interesting book of 1992, I shall show that the literary and political careers of

Richet are not mere curiosities; I shall also analyze some interactions between his psychological, literary, and political works. In addition to my analysis of unpublished Richet manuscripts, I felt it was of interest to interrogate another aspect of modernity, one that is, no doubt, more specific to turn-of-the-century France. In his groundbreaking work, Christophe Charle (1990) showed that the Dreyfus Affair marked the advent of a group of avant-garde men of letters and pioneering scientists for whom scientific and artistic modernity was linked to political commitment.

I shall consider three facets of Charles Richet that relate to his three careers as a French psychologist, littérateur, and intellectual. I shall neither highlight nor ignore the other aspects of this extraordinary man; Richet, after all, not only broke new ground in his chosen profession, but he also saw himself as a pioneer in aviation and "metapsychics." But my intention is not to write an exhaustive monograph on Richet. Instead, I wish to capture him at the critical and mold-breaking moments of his life, when, between 1874 and 1900, he was coming to grips with modernity in a variety of different ways. He was then a physiological psychologist; he was also a writer of short stories and novels presenting heroes and heroines with multiple and sometimes extraordinary personalities. And his narrative works raised such questions as the different roles of the sexes and the identity of the scholar/scientist. Lastly, he was one of those who invented a mode of self-presentation for the French intellectual at the turn of the century.

I shall attempt to follow each of his three careers in turn, and to discern what they have in common. I shall also try to situate them in their historical context. The Ariadne's thread in my analysis will be the multiple signatures and identities of Charles Richet. One might think there is a contradiction between his careers, between his identification with a split personality and his commitment to science. How did Charles Richet resolve this dilemma?

Richet's Backgrounds

Let us first, in the wake of Stewart Wolf (1992) and Pierrette Estingoy (1992–93), remind ourselves of the origins and descent of Charles Richet. His father, Alfred Richet, was appointed professor of surgery at the Faculty of Medicine in Paris in 1865 and became a member of the Académie des Sciences in 1883. Charles Richet, therefore, found himself from the very first at the center of the scientific and medical worlds and was destined to carry on a dynasty created by his father's elevation to high social rank.

For Alfred Richet, born of a family of Burgundian locksmiths and merchants, had carved himself out a prestigious career by dint of hard work and tenacity. His marriage to Eugénie Renouard, daughter of Augustin Charles Renouard (1794–1878), no doubt contributed to his social advancement, as his father-in-law was a pupil of the Ecole Normale and a lawyer who was public prosecutor at the Cour de Cassation before being elected senator. Unlike the Richet family, the Renouards had a long-standing tradition of cultivation and political activism. Charles Renouard's father was Antoine Augustin Renouard. A member of the Commune de Paris in 1793, he was a bibliophile and journalist who directed a printing press that carried his own name.

Alfred and Eugénie Richet gave their son his maternal grandfather's first name (Wolf 1992: 7). The latter became a model for his grandson: "His grandfather, who was above all a liberal, taught the young Charles those great moral values—truth, justice, and liberty—in which the voice of the Enlightenment could still be heard. With his grandfather, Charles learned to love the poetry of Virgil but to hate Napoléon and war" (Estingoy 1992–93: 8). In 1879, the young Charles Richet published a note on the life of Charles Renouard, who had died the previous year; he described him as a sage and "philanthropist" for whom he had felt a "tender and profound affection." Recalling his "family talks" with his grandfather, he described them as "one of the fondest memories of [my] childhood and youth" (Richet 1879: 48). Eugénie Richet, herself a cultivated woman, probably helped to confirm her son's taste for literature, books, and reading, a taste that he incidentally shared with his sister Louise. The latter, for whom he felt great affection, married Charles Buloz, editor of the prestigious magazine *Revue des deux mondes*, a literary and general magazine. The marriage was to prove an unhappy and ultimately a ruinous one, but for Charles it opened up the possibility of publication outside the more specialized scientific and medical world.

Eugénie Richet was a highly religious woman; Charles made his first communion with real devotion and fleetingly promised to enter the priesthood, but he abandoned his childhood faith during his adolescence. As an adult, he became an agnostic, a freethinker and a Freemason, who was nonetheless fairly tolerant of his wife Amélie's continued faith (Wolf 1992: 7, 43). Charles Richet was thus confronted with various kinds of heritage: social, cultural, political, and psychological. On the paternal side, there was the requirement to found a dynasty; ambition and hard work in the professional and scientific departments were imperative. On his mother's side, there was the taste for literature and books, a concern for humanity and politics, and nostalgia for a form of knowledge that transcended science.

How did he manage this diverse heritage? Charles Richet loved play and playacting; he was a great gambler and had a passion for the theater. With his friends, he invented a card game similar to whist, "Gobefiche," which involved, he felt "in the right proportions, an element of chance and an element of talent or method" (Richet n.d.: 6). One of the subtleties of Gobefiche was knowing how and when to raise the bid. One might say, as Estingoy has (1992–93: 25), that Richet made play with his origins and "bet on" his heritage, that he staged and played both for all he was worth. Certainly, this is the attitude implied when he glances over his shoulder at his own story in *Souvenirs d'un physiologiste*, published two years before his death.

There he describes how in 1868 he chose to study medicine:

When I left the Lycée Bonaparte, I had a strong predilection for literature and philosophy but was uncertain what career I should choose. Though my father had never formally made his wishes known, I was aware that he secretly desired me to study medicine. So I said to myself: "Why not?" My father's eminent position as professor of the faculty and a highly reputed surgeon might prove useful to me in this noble profession of medicine. So I decided to enter the Ecole de Médecine as a student. (Richet 1933: 9)[1]

It is difficult to know whether "this noble profession of medicine" is serious or deadpan. Its gravity certainly contrasts with the playful and lighthearted question he poses when he considers this career choice—"Why not?"

Estingoy and Wolf suggest that in this "Why not?" we may overhear "oedipal" conflicts between Alfred and Charles Richet and disagreement within the family. Charles's maternal grandmother Adèle is thought to have disapproved of her grandson's decision to study medicine (Wolf 1992: 9).[2] Whatever the truth of this, Charles Richet followed his father's behest, but he chose to differentiate himself on both professional and scientific levels (Estingoy 1992–93: 10). He also chose to enter first one and then several other careers, as we shall see.

Charles Richet's "Physiological Psychology"

Both as a schoolboy and as a medical student, Charles Richet seems to have been something less than diligent (Wolf 1992: 8). To cite the title of two of his collections of short stories, he seems to have been "in search of happiness" rather than "glory." He describes himself as "not particularly taken with surgery" and "not liking anatomy very much at all" (Richet 1933: 11). Enthusiasm and hard work were reserved for sciences peripheral to medical studies or areas of medicine remote from his father's specialties. In his first year of medicine, he took a practical course in the laboratory of the chemist C. A. Würtz, where he met men who, like Edouard Grimaux, showed "a love of science." "I acquired a passion for chemistry that has never left me," he subsequently wrote (Richet 1933: 10). In 1874, he entered the physiological laboratory of E. J. Marey and decided to take a degree in science. From then on, his interests were clear: they were physiology and research. He quickly emerged as a young research scientist who regularly published in technical journals. Thereafter he made a brilliant career. He was still less than forty years old when, in 1887, he became a very young professor of the Faculty of Medicine in Paris; he was made a member of the Académie de Médecine the following year. His crowning achievement was the 1913 award of the Nobel Prize for Medicine for his research on anaphylaxis.[3]

In his *Mémoires*, he presents himself as much more a researcher than a practitioner of medicine. He was, he says, an extern (in 1872, at the Hôpital de l'Hôtel-Dieu), then an intern (in 1873 at Beaujon and in 1875 at the Salpêtrière).[4] By the standards of the average student, his concerns were, he states, discrepant if not depraved. This he links with his interest in hypnotism, an interest that he was not afraid to make public as early as 1875. Indeed, his first scientific publication, signed "Charles Richet, intern," concerned induced somnambulism.[5] Several years later, after Charcot and Bernheim's work of 1878–84 had made hypnotism scientifically respectable, Richet's article came to seem a pioneering study.

Charles Richet's later account of his youthful passion for hypnotism is as follows. As a first-year student, he was fascinated by an experiment performed on him by thè mesmerist Caunelle during a private entertainment. He subsequently set about mesmerizing a young friend of his sister's, whom he was unable to wake from her trance (*Mémoires*, III, 215–16). At the Hôtel-Dieu and above all at Beaujon he had a supply of subjects for such experiments, and he spent most of his time conducting induced somnambulism experiments on his patients. In France, animal magnetism had been condemned by the Académie de Médecine in 1784 and again in 1837. In the eyes of a member of the medical establishment such as Alfred Richet, an interest in these phenomena could only ruin a serious medical career; it was the height of folly to attempt to prove, in light of the 1837 conclusions, that such phenomena were not simulations. In his *Souvenirs* (150) and in his *Mé-*

moires (III, 218), Charles Richet recalls his father's warnings about the temerity of publishing on this subject.

In his *Mémoires*, he introduces and summarizes the history of his scientific interest in hypnotism thus: "It is a peculiar story, and one that demonstrates better than any theory how bizarre and inextricable is the entanglement of cause and effect" (III, 214).[6] Though Richet experienced it as peculiar, it was in some respects merely banal. Over the course of the century, professional mesmerizers had elicited not inconsiderable scientific interest, and many medical students had mesmerized hospital patients, especially women patients. This was done out of curiosity, as a joke, or as an initiatory rite, and was generally concealed from superiors (Carroy 1991: 40, 60, 86–96). Moreover, we should not make too much of the taboo on hypnotism in scientific circles, and more particularly among French physiologists in 1870. True, animal magnetism had been condemned. But the work of James Braid, the "inventor" of hypnotism (hypnotism was sometimes referred to as Braidism at this time), was beginning to be known in France. His findings had been summarized by the physiologist Edward Carpenter in the article "Sleep" of volume four of *The Cyclopaedia of Anatomy and Physiology*, published by Robert Bentley Todd in 1852. In 1857, Dr. Antoine Béraud had reported his experiments with hypnotism in the *Elements de physiologie* as revised by Charles Robin (the editor of the *Journal de l'anatomie et de la physiologie*, in which Richet published while an intern). In 1859, Broca gave a short talk to the Académie des sciences on the subject of an operation conducted under hypnotism. Above all, Taine's epoch-making *De l'intelligence*, published in 1870, legitimated hypnotism as an important subject in "physiological psychology," as the field was then called (Carroy 1993b: 180–85). Whether or not it was perceived as a recrudescence of animal magnetism, hypnotism was already an avant-garde theme when Charles Richet first seized on it.

Richet's audacity lay in taking Braidism seriously; he considered it a subject suitable for experimentation and even for a first publication. He was fortunate enough to interest Charcot in hypnotism, though this was to prove a mixed blessing. Charcot was then at the height of his glory as the man who had discovered *la grande hystérie*. Around 1878, the Salpêtrière physician began to present experiments in hypnotism during his public lectures; in doing so he gave his scientific imprimatur to his colleague's son, who thus acquired the status of a precursor. But Charcot arrogated to himself the prestige of the discovery of *le grand hypnotisme*. In his *Mémoires*, Richet records that he was not alone in introducing Charcot to hypnotism, citing one

Ruault. Charcot's role, Richet insists, was exclusively one of "populariza-tion" (III, 221).

Richet made it clear from the beginning where he disagreed with Charcot. He avoided polemics but presented different theses nevertheless. For example, in "Les démoniaques d'aujourd'hui" (The possessed of our time), he refers to the theory of the *grande crise hystérique*, and defines som-nambulism as a neurosis pertaining to pathological psychology (Richet 1880). But he more or less directly contradicts the Paris School's dogmas when he states that hypnotizability is not confined to hysterics. Unlike Charcot, he was more interested in somnambulism than in its "simple" forms such as lethargy and catalepsy. And he insisted that somnambulists have an "overexcited and very lively intelligence." In 1884, Richet's first prominent book, *L'homme et l'intelligence*, was published by Félix Alcan.[7] It represented Richet as an independent researcher and quickly established itself as a classic of physiological psychology. In *Les médications psy-chologiques* (1919), Pierre Janet defined Richet as the leader of a third school, alongside those of Nancy and Paris.

According to the *Mémoires*, Richet's 1873 experiments at Beaujon were decisive:

To come back to Beaujon, my experiments with hypnotism decided my career. We have seen that I was hesitating between medicine and surgery. Having once had a taste of experiment, I realized that this was the road for me; and I resolved, if not actually in early 1873, but eventually in late 1873, to be a physiologist. (224)[8]

This impressive statement makes it clear that we should not dismiss Richet's interest in hypnotism as a sort of youthful hobby. From today's perspective, this may seem difficult to comprehend. But it must be remembered that hypnotism was considered a state-of-the-art department of neurology in the years around 1870. Since Thomas Laycock, Carpenter, and Braid (or at least Braid as reread by Laycock and Carpenter), hypnotism had been the locus par excellence for testing "unconscious cerebration" and the idea of a reflex unconscious (Gauchet 1992: 44–48). At the same time, the idea was taking root in France that hypnotism was a means of experiment, if not *the* means of experiment, in physiology and physiological psychology (Carroy 1991: 158–59; Carroy and Plas 1996). Indeed, this was to become a scientific com-monplace within a few years. Charles Richet and his colleague Beaunis were then to describe hypnosis as a means of "psychological vivisection."

Richet sought a compromise, something that departed from and tran-scended a strictly orthodox career as a physiologist. It was a compromise that he found partly in the new psychology and philosophy developed by Taine and Ribot. Under the terms "physiological psychology" and "pathological psychology," the attempt was made to institutionalize a new discipline. It was created by an alliance of philosophers with a passion for science, and physiologists, alienists, and neurologists with a passion for philosophy. For example, Richet, like Beaunis, was one of a group of physiologists with a strong interest in literature and philosophy who contributed assiduously to the *Revue philosophique* founded by Ribot in 1876 (Thirard 1976). Richet was also the general secretary of the Société de psychologie physiologique. This body was founded in 1885, and in 1889 it organized the first International Congress of Psychology in Paris. The congress's president was Charcot, and its vice presidents were Ribot and Paul Janet, Pierre Janet's uncle. In 1887, Richet's second book published by Alcan was an attempt to erect a "general psychology" on the model of the reflex. Today this attempt seems excessively reductionist. However, an attentive reading of *L'homme et l'intelligence* reveals that the reflexological paradigm is often duplicated (deconstructed?) by theatrical metaphors (Carroy 1993a: 121–23).

The psycho-physiological compromise pointed to a different dimension, a dimension artistic and (this was the term used) "moral." In this perspective, it is interesting to analyze the contradictory positions adopted by Richet in three articles. These articles dealt with the "pathological psychology" of "Les démoniaques d'aujourd'hui," the "psychology of fear," and the "general psychology" of love, and they appeared in the *Revue des deux mondes*, a periodical that represented a crossover between literature and scientific popularization. In 1880, Richet followed Charcot in viewing art as equivalent to a scientific document. But Richet went substantially further, suggesting (in relation to *Madame Bovary*) that science could learn from art (Beizer 1994; Micale 1995). He also sketched out in passing a description of the human psyche as dominated by the conflict between "two contradictory forces: feeling and will" (Richet 1880: 348). But this theory was to some extent conventional in the philosophical psychology then taught at secondary level.

In 1886 and 1891, by contrast, he was promoting an evolutionary physiological psychology of fear and love. In this perspective, human behavior was continuous with animal behavior and had to be understood on the basis of biological functions. The approach is well suited to fear but less satisfactory for love. Taking up the theme in 1891, Richet began by criticizing the "convoluted" descriptions of psychologists and dramatic authors; "true naturalism" he states, "is in natural history and not in the history of human aberrations" (Richet 1891a: 136). After a description of the sexual behavior of animals, he sets out to speak of love and its reproductive function in the human animal. Humans are subject to "an unconscious sentiment that prompts all beings towards love" (147). But the article ends with two affirmations that to some extent undermine the declarations of principle with which it began. Richet gives a description—consistent, he states, with the animal model— of a bellicose young man encountering a languid and submissive young woman. The latter, it would seem, is "biologically" somewhat hysterical, though Richet avoids this term. He then rejects this account as "schematic" and appeals to novelists and poets to do better (160); whether the writers should be "naturalists" or not he does not specify. Finally he notes that many forms of human love (paternal and filial love, marital love, the love of humanity, and even to some extent those more "natural" forms, sexual and maternal love) obey social rather than natural laws. He simply hopes that, via the Lamarckian principle of hereditary acquired traits, these "artificial" passions may in the long term become an integral part of human nature (166). Thus literature returns to save us from schematic science, while a conflict between physiology on the one hand and morality and political commitment on the other is patched up somewhat hypothetically by a Lamarckian *deus ex machina*. Why should one be a good father and a good husband, or indeed a pacifist, if the natural law for the male is to be led by his sexual and warlike instincts? By the end of "L'amour" there is a clear implication that physiological psychology must be supplemented on the one hand by a new and different psychology, and on the other by activism and moral will.

The further dimension that Richet sought he found soon enough in his interest in scientifically inexplicable phenomena such as somnambulism, which some then believed to pertain to the supernatural, the spirit world, or the occult. Richet states that he took part in spiritualist séances near the Panthéon during his early years as a medical student; he found them "idiotic" (*Mémoires*, 216). By contrast, he took much more seriously certain extraordinary phenomena that the former mesmerizers had connected with induced somnambulism, such as mental suggestion (with no verbal command) and remote suggestion. In the year in which he published *L'homme et l'intelligence*, he attempted to make mental suggestion a scientific subject by the use of probability calculations (Richet 1884b). He thus set himself up as a pioneer in both "psychic science" (a term approximately equivalent to today's "parapsychology") and a psychology of scientific aspiration. Richet's 1884 experiment was indeed one of the first occasions that the method of probability calculation had been applied to psychological phenomena

(Hacking 1988: 437–40). Richet was also one of several researchers much taken with the somnambulist Léonie, who had been "discovered" by Dr. Gibert and made famous throughout Europe by the young Pierre Janet. Richet brought her to Paris in December 1886 and performed remote suggestion experiments on her that, both at the time and in retrospect, he considered disturbing but not conclusive (Richet 1889: 14–15; *Mémoires*, 220). Much later, in his *Souvenirs*, avoiding any reference to her subsequent role in the Dreyfus Affair, he recalled the remote vision she had apparently had from Le Havre of the 1885 fire in his Paris laboratory (Richet 1933: 66; Carroy and Plas 1995).

In his *Mémoires*, he also recalled with some "emotion" the "daughter of a petty umbrella merchant" whom he had met in the Hôtel-Dieu in 1872; she was an exceptional somnambulist whose gifts, he states, he would not have dared to acknowledge at that time. When speaking of her, the elderly Charles Richet assumes the vocabulary and theories of the mesmerists of the early nineteenth century, men such as Joseph Deleuze, for example, who spoke of an individual fluid emanating from the "operator" (hypnotist), and of a somnambulistic "clairvoyance" (Richet 1933: 148; *Mémoires*, 216–17). At the same time, in 1922, he published (still with Alcan) the *Traité de metapsychique*, in which he again presented himself as the pioneer or inventor of a new "science."

The Career of Charles Epheyre

A further dimension of the psychologist Charles Richet was his career as a man of letters, which he assiduously pursued throughout his life. In 1874, a year before his first scientific publication, he essayed what was then the noblest literary genre: poetry. To do so he adopted a pseudonym that he was ultimately to abandon. But between 1878 and 1896, he revealed himself as a prolific novelist and *nouvelliste* (with a sideline as a playwright) under the name Charles Epheyre. Published by Paul Ollendorff, Epheyre enjoyed not inconsiderable success; several of his works went into second editions.[9] Only the endpaper of the 1887 volume *Possession* indicated that Charles Epheyre had also written poetry. Previous and subsequent volumes published by Ollendorff, and *a fortiori* those from Alcan, drew a veil of silence over this.

In 1891, the year in which Alfred Richet died, Charles Richet gave up his pseudonym and for the first time signed a literary text with his family name. The text was *Fables* and was dedicated to his son. That the author "Charles

Richet" had also written novels was first announced in 1892, in the futurist narrative *Dans cent ans* (In a hundred years' time). Indeed, under the heading "By the same author" were listed the works he had published with Ollendorff *and* those he had published with Alcan. In 1896, in *La douleur des autres*, Charles Epheyre in the same way laid claim to the works published by both houses.[10]

The identity of Charles Epheyre was thus made common knowledge. But it seems that it had not been a complete secret to Richet's friends. In the epilogue of *Poésies*, the authors state that their work is intended much more for their friends than for the public (P. C. Epheyre 1874: 158). And Charles Epheyre dedicated his first collection of short stories to his philosophy professor, Henri Marion:

Like any other author, I might write page after useless page about my book. The best thing is to avoid doing so, and to leave to my readers the business of interpreting or understanding me. Besides, in declaring myself your student, I give sufficient notice that I love truth more than anything else in this world, and that I hate, as I hate death, whatever is conventional and banal. (Epheyre 1878: i–ii)[11]

By revealing the identity of his master in this proud introduction, the author allows his own identity to be guessed by a chosen elite of initiates. By 1887, it would seem that the secret had come out to some extent, as *La revue spirite* suggests that "a man of science" might lie behind the author of *Possession* (Chaigneau 1887: 31).

To my knowledge, the signature of Charles Epheyre was to appear only twice after *La douleur des autres*: in 1898, for the republication of *Soeur Marthe* in the form of a *drame lyrique* (opera) in collaboration with Octave Houdaille, and, lastly, in 1903, for a short Christmas story signed "Charles F.-R. Epheyre." Later, in 1933, Charles Richet publicly answered a riddle to which he had already given a clue by signing "F.-R. Epheyre" in 1903:

I took the pseudonym of Charles Epheyre because when my dear friend Paul Fournier and I were still both students, we together published a volume of poetry (1874), which has fortunately disappeared without trace, and which bore the first letters of our two names, F. and R. (Epheyre). (Richet 1933: 138)[12]

In doing so, he gives the key to the riddle but maintains a degree of equivocation, whereas in the corrections to his manuscript he sought to be more explicit on certain points.[13] It is as if the collection had to be made to "disappear" by leaving the uninitiated reader to choose between two possible signatures, "F. and R." and "Epheyre." For the author of the 1874 volume did indeed have two initials, but they were those of the two first names Paul and Charles. Over the course of the book, each author respectively signed his poems "P." or "C.," while the book was collectively signed "P. C. Epheyre," as if it were by a single author with a double first name (this is not unusual in France). Moreover "Epheyre" may be a French transcription of "epheure," which means in Greek "he invented, he imagined."[14]

Subsequently, in 1879, Paul Fournier took another pseudonym (Palefroi) and published *Théâtre bizarre*. Then he wrote unpublished plays with his friend.[15] Charles Richet appropriated the collective pseudonym for himself by bestowing his own first name on it. He thenceforth used "Charles Epheyre" as his standard literary pseudonym, but he probably signed his work "F. and R." at least once more before his 1903 use of the pleonastic "F. R. Epheyre." In the Académie de médecine Richet collection, there is an offprint of the *Revue philosophique* of 1880 on "the chemical philosophy." In a clear exception to the magazine's normal procedure for original articles, the piece is signed "F. and R."[16] Paul Fournier was a magistrate; he is unlikely to have been interested in chemical philosophy. It is much more likely that Ribot, the editor of the journal, made an exception for Charles Richet, one of his regular contributors, and allowed him to hide behind these discreet initials because of the fact that, though he was passionate about philosophy and devoted to chemistry, he was a specialist in neither field. Thus a single name could hide two others (P. C. Epheyre), or recall a previous duality (Charles Epheyre), while a double name could refer to a single author (F. and R.).

A later twist to this story is that the Nobel laureate was stimulated to new literary endeavor and sent a poem on Pasteur to the Académie française. In 1914, the Académie, still unaware of his identity, awarded him the poetry prize (Richet 1933: 140). Despite this award, Richet never succeeded in being elected to that organization.

This web of complex identities and anonymities suggests that Charles Richet played with many half-secret, half-public masks, as Maurice Laugaa has noted (Laugaa 1986). In common with many French psychologists of the time, he staged himself by playing with his signatures, like some scientific Dr. Jekyll attended by a literary Mr. Hyde. Let us consider in outline the oeuvre of this "Mr. Hyde" and focus on his works' male characters, especially on the scientists, the lovers, and the committed men who haunt Epheyre's literary world.

In the epilogue to the *Poésies*, the authors humorously summarize the themes of what they present as youthful poetic endeavor:

We have brought ourselves before you
we were wrong to do so.
We have sung of love and war, of fate, spring, and death.
Well! Honestly! We might just as well have kept quiet!

(P. C. Epheyre 1874: 157)[17]

The first poems, on pages 5–37, are a reaction to the national humiliation of France's 1870 defeat by Germany: the tone is not yet one of pacifism but one of shame, expiation, and revenge. Though the collection contains some idylls and love poems, many of C.'s pieces are of a darker hue and speak of illness and death. The longest poem, dated 1873, is "Deux destinées" (73–97), a sort of orientalizing philosophical story. In it, C. contrives both to tell an adventure story in a distant and rather detached fashion, and to meditate on the differing fates of two brothers. One is sedentary, poor, and free of passions, the other a rich traveler disappointed in love. When both stories end in death, the concluding moral is delivered as it might be in a fable:

No anger, if you please; everyone must die
To solve the unknown problem up there. (97)[18]

"Regrets" (49–51) is dated 1872 and speaks of the conflict between pleasure and study. The poet C. presents a "philosopher" who has regretfully resigned love in order to make Truth his "only mistress." This theme recurs in 1878 in two short stories of Charles Ephyre. In "L'expérience du professeur Rothbein" (The experiment of Professor Rothbein), Lucius, a student of Sanskrit, is torn between two personalities: the wise and studious Lucius and the amorous gambler Lucien. Fortunately, Lucius wakes up and finds that Lucien was just a dream. This short story is thus a lively variation on the theme of the scientist afflicted with a double personality, a theme that Stevenson gave a blacker turn in his *Strange Case of Dr. Jekyll and Mr. Hyde* of eight years later. By contrast, "Le docteur Rüderich" is an anguished fable about the passion for truth and science, that "chimera" that makes the scientist its "slave" and "victim" (Carroy 1993a).

Other narratives from the 1878 collection are short studies in physiological and pathological psychology. They are often full of verve and exhibit a rather dark sense of humor; subjects include hypnosis, a missed vocation, expectation, hypochondria, and love. Others are philosophical novels in miniature, in which themes of obscure wisdom, destiny, guilt, and choice of vocation recur. The epilogue takes the form of an Indian story that offers a conclusion and a moral that might have found favor with Charles Renouard: men are "not yet wise," and one must continue to amuse oneself with "houses of cards." In these short stories, the young Charles Epheyre presents himself as psychological storyteller, a moralist, and a philosopher. He offers his reader a gallery of male characters who are negative or positive models or types: the man who has missed his vocation, the sage, the scientist with a split personality or who is enslaved by science, the spiritualist philosopher whose theories are contradicted by his destiny, the poet who sells himself to the Devil for wealth, and the lover.

The lover stands at the center of the three narratives published by Charles Epheyre in quick succession between 1887 and 1889, just after Charles Richet had precociously established his professional and scientific reputation.[19] *Possession, Une conscience d'homme,* and *Soeur Marthe* are love stories that end badly, in death, humiliation, or the hero's renunciation of his love. They feature pairs of male friends and love triangles: a man caught between a real woman and her somnambulistic incarnation in *Possession* and *Soeur Marthe,* a woman between two men in *Une conscience d'homme.* In *Théâtre bizarre* by Palefroi, alias Paul Fournier, we find similar themes transposed to a fantastic Greek background. Richet appropriated their common pseudonym, but the intertextuality of Palefroi and Epheyre continued.

Possession, set in Russia, is probably loosely inspired by Turgenev's short story "Après la mort" (After death), which was published in 1883 in *La nouvelle revue.* Epheyre's hero Stéphane, like Turgenev's, is madly in love with a dead lover who drags him down into death. In Epheyre's novel, the dead woman is revenged by taking possession of Stéphane's wife while the latter is in a somnambulistic trance. The theme of hypnotic objectification developed in *L'homme et l'intelligence* brings the venerable theme of possession up to date. At the time, a critic in the *Revue spirite* attempted to harness the novel to the spiritualist cause; he even suggested that the soul of Turgenev had returned to haunt the scientist concealed beneath the pseudonym Epheyre. Subsequently, Charles Richet was to lend some credibility to this conclusion; in *Suite de mes mémoires* he referred to *Possession* as a spiritualist novel. *Soeur Marthe* might similarly be said to be a "mesmeric novel," a fairly popular genre in the nineteenth century; Alexandre Dumas's *Joseph Balsamo* of 1848 is the most illustrious example of the genre (Carroy 1993a).[20]

Moreover, *Possession* and *Soeur Marthe* belong to a genre specific to the nineteenth century, a genre that, in deference to Maupassant's 1883 article, we might call the *fantastique.* Citing Hoffmann, Poe, and Turgenev, Maupassant characterized the genre in terms of the reader's hesitant response; his definition is incidentally very close to that given by Todorov in

1970. In Maupassant's view, the reader of the fantastic narrative loses his footing "as if in water where he constantly finds himself out of his depth, grasping at the real only to go under again at the very next instant, and again struggling for foothold in a confusion painful and exciting as a nightmare" (Maupassant 1883: 257). The reader of *Possession* and *Soeur Marthe* remains uncertain about the somnambulistic personalities incarnated by their heroines. Are these alternative selves dream or supernatural reality? Do they call for occult or psychological explanation? The two novels are quite as much evocations of enigmatic incarnations as they are descriptions of heroes madly in love with creatures who may be their own creations. Rather than induce (or reinforce) a belief in either spirits or exceptional clairvoyance, Charles Epheyre sought to disturb the reader, who is left "on the threshold of mystery." Indeed, the latter is the title of a collection published much later, in 1934, by Charles Richet.

In *Une conscience d'homme*, Charles Epheyre sought to introduce his reader into the mind—the consciousness and conscience—of a man in love. The narrator, Charles, speaks in the first person at the beginning of the story. He presents himself as a school friend of two inseparable but utterly different friends, Georges Dessemon and Léon Desroches. The three sit together in class as their alphabetical proximity requires. Georges is an orphan, poor, studious, and thoughtful; Léon is rich, lazy, and absent-minded. The story concentrates on Georges, the dreamy poet figure who nevertheless loves discipline. The narrator interrupts his portrait to remark, "This meeting in one and the same individual of two different tendencies will perhaps be found very abnormal. But is it not generally recognized that humans are complex beings?" (Epheyre 1888: 12).[21] Georges becomes a seemingly austere magistrate; the plot begins when he is thirty-six years old and falls in love with Louise, Léon's wife. The novel repetitively details the amorous magistrate's forensic soliloquies; he is torn by the conflicts between love and profession and between love and friendship, and he is haunted by the dilemma "Honest man or scoundrel?"[22] At each step of the plot, despite Georges's determination not to declare himself, then not to become Louise's lover, then not to continue their liaison, he gives in, "as if some unknown person spoke for him" (46). Georges is described as if he were a somnambulist or medium who does not forget the hypnotic state or séance but hears and observes himself speak:

The words came to his lips, independent of his will, as if a magical power were dictating them. Strange as it seems, another personality appeared in him, listening to his own words, realizing that they went too far, but without the power to stop them. He was not speaking; he was letting himself speak. (61)[23]

Two episodes are central to the plot. One, a theatrical performance, brings the protagonists' feelings into being; the second, a nightmare, brings them to an end. Georges and Louise, playing Lucidor and Angélique (the lovers in Marivaux's play *L'épreuve*) become the characters they portray (83–90). They are overcome by their roles, like somnambulists objectifying a personality in *L'homme et l'intelligence*: "It is as if an actor were suddenly overcome with madness and imagined that the drama in which he is acting was reality, and that he had been transformed body and soul into the character he is supposed to be playing" (Richet 1884a: 237).[24]

The borders between theater and reality fade. In defiance of Diderot's views on acting, Georges-Lucidor and Louise-Angélique lose the distance from their roles necessary for performance; they *recreate* Marivaux by inventing new dialogue. The protagonists throughout read and recount novels to the point of being "possessed" by them. Here man *and* woman emulate Madame Bovary, as in Richet's 1880 article for the *Revue des deux mondes*. Their Bovarysme is associated with dreams. Georges's internal monologues are peopled with waking dreams. After several "real" episodes with Louise or Léon, he repeatedly wonders whether these were not a dream. The love story is experienced as a real fiction or real dream, which turns to nightmare in the third part of the book.

The epilogue to the second part is an account of a nightmare, which prefigures the end of love and the fall of the hero. Thereafter, he is increasingly bogged down in guilt and morose procrastination. Before delivering the summing up of the prosecution case in the trial of a man who has murdered his mistress's husband, Georges has a strange dream, which brings together several different scenes. He sees himself as a child with his mother, who forbids him to pluck a rose:

His mother turned away; he snatched at the rose; but then, from the stem, there flowed something red, like blood; his mother gave a great cry, and suddenly he found himself, a dagger in his hand, his hair all white and standing on end with horror, before the corpse of a woman into whose breast were scored dagger blows. The judges, seated in a circle around him, pointed their fingers at him. On the table, beside the corpse, was a rose. And behind the circle of judges resounded the great mallet blows as the guillotine was raised. (232–33)[25]

The following morning, his plea for the prosecution is devastating.

The dream might lend itself to Freudian interpretation. But this would be to forget that we are here in very carefully constructed and highly dramatized literary narrative; the novelist offers an implicit interpretation. If the text seems "Freudian" it is because Freud was able to pick up and systematize what was coming to the surface of the medico-literary culture of his time.

The narrator, entering his protagonist's state of mind, offers his own compassion, exclaiming (for example) "Poor Georges!" or "Alas!" Such is his identification with Georges that at times he defies the rules of punctuation and, without warning the reader by quotation marks or dashes, moves from indirect to direct speech: "Louise is there, beside him! And there is no one around to spoil our fun. No one will come and force us into feigned indifference" (167).[26]

The narrator often records Georges's meditations but rarely enters into the mind of Louise. She is, for the most part, laconically presented as a somewhat indistinct figure who changes as required by the progress of the plot, in contrast with the figure of Georges, frozen into his repetitive internal monologues. Louise appears successively as a giddy coquette, a nervous woman, an observer curious about Georges's absurd love, an actress disturbed by the play in which she is acting, a woman in love who gives herself entirely, and a pious old lady to be. It is only at the end of the novel that she acquires any conviction. The hero, abasing himself to her, is given his marching orders, and in the final *coup de théâtre*, the roles are reversed. "The spectacle has gone on too long," she concludes after revealing herself capable of an implacably lucid "psychological vivisection":

No! You never gave yourself unreservedly, and even in the early days, you thought more about Léon than about me. You were afraid that you would be compromised. Afraid, you were always and always afraid. Afraid of everything, afraid of scandal, afraid of remorse. . . . Your hesitations and your weakness eventually made you pitiful in my sight. (314–15)[27]

Behind the love story there was a male friendship story.

From this point on, the narrator's "Poor Georges!" is imbued with a rather condescending and mocking pity. In the novel's epilogue, Charles Epheyre again adopts the identity of a distant narrator who has spoken about a love story now in the past. "These events, whose history I have scrupulously recounted, took place two years ago. Today, oblivion has set in, and its thick shroud entirely covered this old story" (321).[28] He thus incidentally reveals (is this a wink to the informed reader of the time?) that his hero was, in 1888, exactly the same age as Charles Richet and Paul Fournier. But Charles

Epheyre, though he has at times identified with Georges's narrative of two years ago, is ironic about the fate of his old school friend. The magistrate's fall from grace, which should have made him more merciful, has made him more severe.

The novel thus rests on a contradictory duality, internalized in Georges's conscience and externalized in the characters of the two friends Georges and Léon. The novel doubles this duality in self-referential fashion, in the narrator Epheyre's alternating distance from and identification with his main character, and in Charles Richet's similar relation to his own pseudonym. This novel places the reader in a position of indecision analogous to that of the fantastic narratives. Throughout the plot, the author-narrator Epheyre tends to coincide with the main protagonist, and the narrative thus becomes almost autobiographical. At the dénouement, the confusion is cleared up, but the author, under the mask of his pseudonym, proffers another autobiographical clue in passing. This game of transformation and evasion is somewhat reminiscent of the protean and mysterious identity of the narrator of *A la recherche du temps perdu*: now author, now narrator, and sometimes protagonist. Comparison between Richet and Proust ends there. *Une conscience d'homme* remains in certain respects a rather classical novel.

The hero of *Une conscience d'homme* is a magistrate, like Paul Fournier; he was succeeded, in *Soeur Marthe*, by a protagonist (Laurent) who, like Charles Richet himself, is a doctor and hypnotist. "Georges" becomes the first name of the hero's friend. The author who signed himself "Charles Epheyre" is no longer present as a first-person narrator. Unlike *Une conscience d'homme*, which is a novel of psychological analysis pure and simple, *Soeur Marthe*, a mesmerist novel, belongs to the genre of the fantastical. In contrast with the ductile figure of Louise, the heroine of *Soeur Marthe* has an extraordinary dual consciousness. Her psychology remains opaque. Angèle, the amorous woman whom Marthe incarnates, can only disappear and/or die. The narrator has access only to the mind of Laurent, whom he treats empathetically, exclaiming "Poor Laurent!" and moves without warning between direct and indirect speech (Epheyre 1889: 406, 423; 1890: 84–85, 153–54). The hypnotist is still divided by his love, but he finds the strength to order Angèle, a depersonalized other, never to appear again. Rather than a masculine problem, duality now seems a feminine enigma.[29]

We might now reread the "general psychology" of love that Charles Richet put forward in 1891 in the light of the three love stories by Charles Epheyre. The two psychologies do overlap, but only in part; the novelist's is subtler than that of the scientist. In retrospect, for someone who has read the three previous novels, the difficulties and patchings of the 1891 article might seem to suggest an underlying conflict between the "schematic" psychologist and the "complex" novelist who was about to quit the literary scene.

In that same year, 1891, Charles Epheyre reworked his magistrate-in-love character from *Une conscience d'homme* for the stage. The action is transferred to the eighteenth century. The plot's master of ceremonies is an indulgent and mischievous doctor who wishes to put to the test not (like Marivaux's Lucidor) the love of a woman, but the virtue of a man: his friend the magistrate. Charles Richet's theatrical version of *Soeur Marthe* in collaboration with Houdaille similarly puts the plot back into the eighteenth century: Laurent has become a young doctor and mesmerist. But the plot, instead of simply being rewritten for the stage, is injected with heroism and Christianity for the purposes of the opera. Soeur Marthe implores the Virgin to save her from hell, and *she* dies, whereas in the novel it is only Angèle, the somnambulistic incarnation, who dies. Laurent brings down the curtain with an emotional alexandrine: "Morte! Je suis maudit! Ah! Ma raison chancelle!" (She is dead! I am accursed! Oh! Madness descends!) (Epheyre and Houdaille 1898: 48).

In the 1892 collection of short stories, love is sidelined. In the first story ("Why bother?"), Charles Epheyre humorously identifies with a rich, idle, disillusioned dilettante; this character is trying to write a collection somewhat coincidentally entitled *A la recherche de la gloire* (In quest of glory), but he falls asleep dreaming of "the vanities of glory . . . and the glory of being able to demonstrate them in the eyes of man" (17).

The two most prominent characters of these short stories are scientists. Hermann Backermann, a ridiculous, naive, and alarming German scientist, invents a microbe that triggers a vast epidemic to which he then finds a remedy; this leaves him to dream of a still more deadly and invincible microbe. "Le Mirosaurus," the longest story, relates the tale of Georges, a young Norman fossil hunter.[30] After a great Parisian professor brazenly steals his discovery, he chooses to renounce love in favor of friendship and academic glory and decides to live a sheltered life as a provincial researcher. In what remains of the story, Georges finds that he cannot help daydreaming. Sometimes "he has made a great discovery that has stood science on its head and opened up a new world"; sometimes he is a great explorer and colonizer in Africa. "At other times he sees himself as an all-powerful minister" and righter of wrongs. "Often again [he envisions] a brilliantly lit theater. The most beautiful women in Paris, the most attractive actresses, gather attentively round him, the curtain goes up, his voice is heard, and his audience is overwhelmed with admiration" (Epheyre 1892:, 221–22).[31]

La douleur des autres (The pain others feel), the last important work to be signed Charles Epheyre, was written between May 1891 and October 1895 and is a novel of adventure and a *bildungsroman*. The story takes up a theme much favored by Epheyre: the destiny of one man, in this case a young American blessed with the fateful name "William Will." He inherits a huge fortune from his uncle, who in his will directs him to use it as best he can for humanity. William Will goes from country to country and is confronted in various ways with causes to support; he moves, too, from one love affair to the next, and these are diversions from and obstacles to his mission. The story presents him with a gallery of different kinds of women in the countries that he visits. Eva, his American fiancée, is a spoiled and selfish heiress. Ida, the Swedish woman, is an unsatisfied wife who wishes to die with William after giving herself to him. This is reminiscent of the heroine of Paul Bourget's *Le disciple* (1888), which itself drew on the Chambige Affair, a famous court case that also inspired Bernheim and Tarde. Jeanne, the amorous French woman, bears him a son but eventually bores and tires him. Olga, the Russian revolutionary, wishes to be an activist and a free woman, but she realizes that she is not cut out for this and confesses her love for him. After many adventures William, freed of all his emotional entanglements, dreams of his uncle, and he sets up an international court of arbitration that averts a Franco-German war. His task accomplished, nothing remains for him but to die under the guns of the Russian revolutionaries he has refused to finance. The adventure- and love-story hero gives way to the activist hero passionate for progress and justice. The novelist Epheyre gives place to the moralist. There is no further need to write novels; *La douleur des autres* is both a farewell to youth and the novelist's literary testament. "I gave up the novel, though I did not give up literature," Charles Richet was to write in his *Suite de mes mémoires*.[32]

This was the last appearance of the pseudonym Epheyre, to the best of my knowledge, except for a naive short story of Christian inspiration. The soul of an old woodcutter from the Black Forest is seen to rise above his body after death and reach a paradise worthy of the edifying dreams of a child taking its first communion (F. R. Epheyre 1903). It is as if the pseudonym had allowed the freethinker to rediscover, in fond and playful fashion, the imaginary world of the pious child.[33]

With this exception, the career of Charles Epheyre ended with the century. Charles Richet no doubt felt freer after the death of his father to sign nonscientific texts with his family name. From this point on, in defiance of certain of Charles Epheyre's youthful declarations, in which science seems a tyrannical mistress, Charles Richet sought to reconcile art and science. He now insisted on the continuity or link between poet and researcher (Richet 1896b: iii–iv). The scientist who discovers and creates, with whom Richet identifies, has an eye for the unexpected and the nonconformist (Richet 1923).

The novelist gave way to the journalist, essayist, fabulist, poet, writer of memoirs, and playwright who signed all these works with his patronymic. The culmination of Richet's career as a dramatist was *Circé*, a play in verse that premiered on April 3, 1905, at the Theatre of Monte-Carlo. The great actress Sarah Bernhardt played the central role. In 1910, Richet published a further verse-play, *Socrate*. But a large proportion of his dramatic output remained unpublished. In 1920, in his *Suite des mémoires*, he declared good-humoredly that he had in his possession "a terrifying list" of fourteen unpublished plays.

Having recounted and contemplated the destiny of heroes novelistic and theatrical, Charles Richet now rehearsed his own destiny. At times he made use of the narrative themes and patterns of his fiction. In 1920, considering whether he would make the same choices again, he recalls the dreams of Georges, the hero of "Le Mirosaurus": "Often, looking for what would most have attracted me, after the role of explorer or adventurer entering lands unknown, it would have been that of the playwright" (*Suite de mes mémoires*, 45).[34]

In his untiring production of novels, short stories, plays, and memoirs, he often felt the need to imagine himself through the looking glass of often contradictory personalities (family and friends, scientific colleagues, novelistic or theatrical characters) whose lives were similar to his own in some ways and yet different in others. He seems ultimately to have vacillated between two conceptions of acting and thus of his relationship with himself; one of these was playful and distant, the other intense and objective and modeled on somnambulistic or amorous "personifications."

The Politically Committed Scientist and the Emancipated Young Woman

Certain stylistic and literary innovations aside, Charles Epheyre is a relatively classical writer; his modernity lay more in his subject than in his style. One text—we cannot know what signature he would have used had it been published—takes up a theme that was, before 1914, highly topical and emphatically modern. *Katia*, a three-act play in the collection of the Bibliothèque de l'académie de médicine, deserves careful analysis.[35] Like *La douleur des autres*, *Katia* seems to bring together and dramatize a number of questions that recur throughout Charles Epheyre's novels and short stories, in particular the relation of man and woman to love, and the relationship between science and political commitment. The relevance of these two themes was particularly clear at the turn of the century. In *Katia*, the male choice of activism and the female choice of liberty are presented as parallel and antithetical.

Katia is a young Russian woman who resembles the character Olga in *La douleur des autres*. In the first act Katia refuses the customary fate of women, that of becoming "a little doll" (36) and marrying, which her father, a general, wishes to impose. She has educated herself by reading the books in her father's library, "Tolstoy, Michelet, Victor Hugo" (51), and runs away with Alexis, her brother's tutor, who goes to work in the chemistry laboratory of Professor Hermann. In the second act, set in Iena, these two pass themselves off as husband and wife but are living as brother and sister. Two parallel debates take place, between Alexis and Hermann (scene two) and Katia and Marguerite, the German professor's daughter (scene three). Hermann, the old master, criticizes the young Alexis in gruff, paternal tones:

Hermann: . . . A chemist should know nothing but his formulas. Do you think I've read Bakunin, and Tolstoy, and Spencer, and Nietzsche? . . . Outside his laboratory, a chemist should know nothing but his home and family. If that! . . . In politics he should have no other opinion than that of his government. In that way he can be sure of avoiding mistakes. And as to big words about society and humanity, he should leave those to the ignorant. . . .

Alexis: Well, and what about the great problems the world is facing? . . .

Hermann: Science is a jealous person. She wants to be loved exclusively and won't be having any rivals. On which note, let us go and have a look at our alembics!" (72–74)[36]

Hermann here appears as a good-natured double of the Germanic professors in the short stories, Rüderich and Hermann Backermann.

Another debate, this one on the destiny not of the scientist but of woman, subsequently takes place between Katia and Marguerite. Marguerite believes that a woman must seek love and marriage, and that she should adopt her husband's ideas. Katia says that a man is always a tyrant, and goes further still: "Mark my words, Gretchen, and remember this sad truth, on which I have often meditated: even the man that we love is a stranger to us. . . . Indeed, he above all!" (79).[37]

In the third act, while Alexis pursues his ideal of becoming a politically committed scientist, Katia's feminism collapses. She discovers that Alexis loves Marguerite and decides to marry a man whom she respects but does not love. At the play's conclusion, she reproaches Alexis for his failure to perceive her love, much as Louise reproaches Georges in *Une conscience d'homme*. This is Katia's farewell to Alexis:

Adieu! . . . Wait! One more thing! I believe in your future! And you mustn't let a woman hold you back. . . . Women understand only love. Nothing else counts! Nothing! Nothing! In the past I thought that higher ideas . . . Well, I was wrong. For us, there is nothing but love. (133–34)[38]

Katia and Olga represent a kind of woman familiar to professors of medicine at this time. From 1885, despite the resistance of their male colleagues, some young women worked as interns. Russian and Polish women came to study medicine and science in France: the most famous of these was Marie Curie. The young, emancipated Slavic woman was a figure whose currency had been revived by news of terrorist attacks in Russia. In 1908, Lorde and Binet's drama *Une leçon a la Salpêtrière* had represented a Slavic woman with liberated manners among the students attending the lectures of Professor Marbois (alias Charcot).

The question of the free woman, like that of the hysterical woman, became an obsessive theme and gave rise to an abundant if not excessive literature given the limitations of women's social advancement and the very moderate feminist claims advanced at the time. Richet belonged to a generation of men who had progressive political ideas (he campaigned in favor of Dreyfus, for example) but who, like the novelist Octave Mirbeau, believed that a woman "is not a brain box" or, like Émile Zola, that women should be confined to the function of childbearing (*Fécondité*). In 1891, Richet similarly attempted to prove, as we have seen, that young women were physiologically destined for love. Katia and Olga were, of necessity, just deluding themselves.

But Richet connected this position with a symmetrical choice on the part of men. Like Katia and Olga, Epheyre's heroes, whose desire for love is doomed to fail, are sympathetically presented. For the young man must in his turn give up love and the ideal of love in order to become a scientist or an activist. It is as if the physiologist-moralist Epheyre-Richet believed that neither sex could achieve acceptance of its destiny without sacrifice and nostalgia. This morality, already present in the poem "Regrets" of 1872, is no doubt expressive or symptomatic of the late ninteenth-century "crisis of masculine identity," to cite the title of Maugue's excellent historical survey (Maugue 1987).

The Career of an Intellectual:
From Pacifism to the Dreyfus Affair

In his *Suite de mes mémoires*, Richet refuses to be considered an amateur in any subject and presents himself as the "universal specialist." He concludes the manuscript thus: "My conscience is clear that I have never written anything other than what I thought and that I have only ever been inspired by love of truth, justice, and mankind."[39] The reference to truth, omnipresent in his scientific and literary work, is combined with reference to justice and humanity.

From 1884, when Charles Richet joined the Société de la paix, he took up many different causes that seemed to him just: pacifism (probably his most constant commitment), an increased birth rate, Dreyfusism, the struggle against anti-Semitism, eugenics, support for Poland, and the defense of Esperanto. From 1891, he placed his literary talent at the service of his pacifism in certain of his fables. In the year in which *La douleur des autres* appeared, he published his first campaigning article, taking up the cudgels on behalf of an international court (Richet 1896a). He was probably unwilling to publicize his opinions in this way before he had acquired a degree of fame. From then on, a corpus of campaigning articles was added to his scientific and literary production. The literary texts that he signed with his family name were sometimes secondary to the political lessons he wished to impart, and he also signed opuscules, essays, books, and journal and magazine articles in support of various causes.

It seems likely that the Dreyfus Affair legitimated his campaigning activities, and that Richet could then identify himself wholeheartedly with the role of the intellectual and universal specialist, the friend of justice and truth. This is why it seems to me important to grasp the position occupied by Richet at this crucial moment in French political and cultural history.

After Esterhazy's acquittal and the appearance of Zola's article "J'accuse," two protests appeared in the Dreyfusard papers *Le Siècle* and *L'Aurore*, on January 14 and 15, 1898, respectively.[40] Both demanded a review of the Dreyfus trial. The first two lists of signatories included persons both known (for example, Zola) and unknown (Proust at that time, for example). Many of them specified their social position. Among the scientists, Émile Duclaux signed himself "membre de l'Institut Pasteur, membre de l'Académie des sciences" for the January 14 protest, known as the "first protest." Edouard Grimaux identified himself as "membre de l'Institut, officier de la Légion d'honneur" for the "second protest" on January 15.[41] Charles Richet had sent a congratulatory card to Zola (Wolf 1992: 100ff.), and he signed the second protest in *L'Aurore* of January 17: "Charles Richet Professeur à l'Académie de Médecine."[42] He was thenceforth one of the most prominent Dreyfusards, and his name regularly appeared in the petitions and appeals that proliferated in the press. In June 1898, he took part in the Assemblée générale constituante de la Ligue des droits de l'homme (Constituent general assembly for the League of Human Rights), which was founded in February 1898, during the trial of Zola, who was found guilty and sentenced to a long prison term after the publication of "J'accuse."

Clémenceau christened the January and February signatories *intellectuels*. The term had been in circulation since 1870. In Dreyfusard texts, its overtones were "scholar, literary figure, teacher, writer, talent, culture, intelligence, elite, science, reason," while in anti-Dreyfusard texts it was associated with "intellectualism, intellectuality, Protestant, Jew, Freemason."[43]

The promotion, negative or positive, of a noun (such as *intellectuel*) is, says Charle, linked to the appearance of a new social group that will thereafter play an important role in political and cultural history (Charle 1990). In his *Mémoires*, Richet emphasizes that almost all biologists campaigned as he did.[44] Today's historians confirm that the majority of biologists and Pasteurian doctors (who were primarily researchers) were, in contrast to practicing doctors, Dreyfusards at the time (Duclert 1994: 77). Richet, who was president of the Société de biologie in 1898 and an admirer of Pasteur, was thus in tune with the social group and scientific network with which he professionally identified. His pacifist commitments probably also led him to distrust a verdict handed down by the military establishment, and predisposed him to become one of the first signatories.[45]

The Dreyfusards of 1898 saw themselves as belonging to a republican ideal inherited from the Revolution. They were for the most part freethinkers or Freemasons. But for many of the signatories, taking a public stance in favor of a judicial review was not really a political act. They committed themselves, they said, in the name of the science that they practiced. The old chemist Edouard Grimaux testified in the Zola case on February 12, 1898. He explained that he had a common cause with those who "had come out of their laboratories, their offices, and their workshops" because an ideal of science and the experimental method had been brought into contempt by the Dreyfus indictment (*Le procès Zola* 1898: 535). Grimaux, a model of scientific rectitude in Richet's view, presented himself in his testimony at the Zola trial as a "Professor Hermann" who could, in terms of the debate in *Katia*, no longer confine himself to his alembics.

Richet's motivations for becoming a Dreyfusard were probably analogous to those of his old master, with the difference that Grimaux professed himself a Catholic, whereas Richet was agnostic and freethinking. At the height of the Dreyfus Affair, when more and more people were taking up the cause of judicial review, Richet twice wrote to Joseph Reinach, the Dreyfusard politician with whom he was to write a pacifist history. In these letters, Richet referred to a piece of gossip that had been circulating in his laboratory and concluded, "Since you rightly love the scientific method, *this does not count*" (Jan. 24, 1899). Thus, in his view, it went without saying that a person who loved the scientific method would be a Dreyfusard. But Richet's originality in these letters lies elsewhere. He characteristically focuses on the contradictory psychology of the honest anti-Dreyfusard, on something inexplicable that escaped the rationality that he perceived in his own Dreyfusism: "I cannot understand how it is that these honest people are not with us. —Alas! There are many very honest men among our adversaries! How can this be? What a strange and mysterious thing" (Jan. 23, 1899).[46]

The use of petitions, which after 1898 became increasingly popular and widespread, appeared at the time a real innovation. Each signatory on the list was one among many, yet was also distinguished by name and title. It thus involved two contradictory strategies of number and distinction (Charle 1990). Distinction is subverted by this treatment, as the anti-Dreyfusard Ferdinand Brunetière remarked, ironically inquiring what competence a professor of Syriac or Chinese brought to a judicial matter. A universalist philosophy or ideology was required to justify the authority and legitimacy of the signatory whose public stance was made outside the scientific or literary domain for which he was known. The possibility of parading his commitment as an intellectual signatory perhaps offered Charles Richet an opportunity to play with his family name and titles.

Richet did not merely sign petitions. In his *Mémoires*, he prides himself on having organized a demonstration in favor of Grimaux at the Société de Biologie (Reinach 1903: vol. 3, 511). Grimaux, who was a member of the Société, had just been officially dismissed for having testified at the Zola trial. On February 27, 1898, page two of *L'Aurore* offered its readers a first report of the previous night's meeting of the Société de biologie, entitled "Due Homage":

Right at the start of the meeting, M. Richet, professor of physiology and a member of the Académie de médecine, stood up, and spoke these words to a hushed audience:

"Whenever one of our members receives an honor or a distinction, is it not the Society's habit to congratulate him? One such member, M. Grimaux, has been honored by measures whose nature I am not required to specify. What we can do is assure M. Grimaux of our affection and esteem."

In the midst of the applause of all the Society members and members of the public present at the meeting, M. Grimaux, obviously much moved, thanked his colleagues in a trembling voice for the mark of esteem that they had conferred on him:

"The law has been broken," he stated, "in my case; witnesses are not to be prosecuted. In my testimony, I listened to nothing but the voice of my conscience; I swore to speak the truth, and speak the truth I did."

The audience again broke into applause and almost all the members signed a letter of congratulation to M. Grimaux, that victim of his own honesty.

Dr. R.[47]

One wonders whether the "Dr. R." who so diligently provided the newspaper with this report was the president of the Société himself, with his confirmed taste for publishing in journals and papers. Whoever the author and however different the versions of the meeting, Richet created and staged an homage both theatrical and, as it were, pictorial. In the accounts we have of it, the scene is ripe for a theatrical tableau or an engraving; it is performed with dignity for the spectators and for the papers (read by intellectuals) who were to make an event of it. The intellectual Grimaux "clad himself in the magistracy of heroism," to cite the words of another Dreyfusard, Péguy; and the scene pertains to what André Daspre describes as a Dreyfusard "heroification" (in Leroy 1983: 149–57).

Richet showed his dramatist's touch in paradoxically transforming the standard reaction to a sanction—keeping it secret, considering it an object of shame—by making it the occasion of a public congratulation. Several months later, the opera *Soeur Marthe* was performed at the Théâtre des Variétés. It seems likely that in February Richet created a successful *coup de théâtre* at the Société de biologie.

The art of *coups de théâtre* was no doubt linked to a capacity to think antiphonally and even against himself, a capacity that was of particular service in his discovery of anaphylaxis. As Pierrette Estingoy (1993–94) very interestingly shows, Charles Richet was able to recognize the importance of unexpected data that ran counter to the Pasteurian notions about immunology that prevailed in his time. He made these data the subject of experiments.

This fascination for the unknown and his express nonconformity also led him, after 1900, increasingly to publicly present himself as a researcher in "metapsychics." In doing so he put his scientific reputation at stake and resumed the audacious pioneer's stance that he had taken in 1875 in relation to hypnotism. He did not hesitate to face ridicule and discredit when coming to the defense of mediums such as Eusapia Palladino and Marthe Béraud who were subsequently discovered to have (to a greater or lesser extent) practiced deception and hoaxes.

Throughout his life, Charles Richet was often at the forefront of modernity in various forms: he was an inventor, explorer, defender of justice, and man of letters. Inevitably, he ran the risk of dissipating his energy. His career was that of a discoverer; above all, he sought a new role for the scholar/scientist that might involve many different identities. This new role he himself incarnated in two different modes, as a psychologist-novelist and then as a public political intellectual.

Pseudonyms allowed the young Charles Richet to lead a double life, to take risks and to publish—behind a mask that protected his family name from disapproval and ridicule—poetry, love stories, philosophical speculations, and narratives halfway between the genre of the marvelous, in the Christian or spiritualist traditions, and the fantastical. In his adoption of other authorial identities, he was able to rely on a very old literary tradition. But he was also able to play at being one of the somnambulists who fascinated the scientists of his time, by assuming one or several personalities under different names. Thus able to stage himself as a multiple self, he could also evoke, if not indeed theorize, a complex and contradictory subjectivity that in some measure transcended the physiological notions of his scientific environment.

For the physiologist Charles Richet publicly defended a form of psychology that sought to minimize all reference to a hidden psychological interiority. But he was also irresistibly attracted by strange and complex psychological phenomena that ran counter to his notions and that led him in other directions. Alongside the scientist, the novelist Charles Epheyre created a literary oeuvre in which he attempted to explore the gulfs and labyrinths of the individual consciousness while he playfully sought to disturb his readers.

In pursuing this double career, Charles Richet-Epheyre formed part of a generation of researchers. At the end of the nineteenth century, he, like Janet and Freud, set off in pursuit of a new model of the psyche, which they presented as divided and under the control of unconscious forces.

In his maturity, Charles Richet disposed of his pseudonym (and of his contradictions?). He affirmed himself under a single authorial name. He took quite new risks with his signature in publicly presenting himself as a French intellectual involved with many different causes. He sought to be an actor in relation to the problems arising from a new social and political scene, problems that he also dramatized in his literary work. He thus asserted himself as a man of science and letters unified by campaigning actions. In similar fashion, in his career as a "metapsychist," he turned away from the psychological questions that had fascinated him in his youth. He turned instead toward the "objective" exteriorizations of the unknown forces produced by mediums, such as remote movement of objects and ectoplasm.

Thus, starting from similar issues and research work, Richet, Freud, and Janet followed divergent paths in the early part of this century. In contrast with Freud, Richet chose to abandon his exploration of the psyche more or less completely and to turn toward political activism and the investigation of external or exteriorized phenomena. Janet prudently kept his own counsel over the Dreyfus Affair and politics in general and followed a traditional career path as scientist and university teacher. He, too, left behind him his initial research; in contrast to Richet, he took up not political action, but a psychology of action.

Bibliography

Charles Richet's Works

PUBLICATIONS

[P. C. Epheyre, pseud.] (with Paul Fournier). 1874. *Poésies*. Paris: A. Derenne.

[Charles Epheyre, pseud.]. 1878. *A la recherche du bonheur*. Paris: Ollendorff.

———. 1887. *Possession*. Paris: Ollendorff, 2d ed.

———. 1888. *Une conscience d'homme*. Paris: Ollendorff.

———. 1889. "Soeur Marthe." *Revue des deux mondes* (May 15): 385–431.

———. 1890. *Soeur Marthe*. Paris: Ollendorff.

———. 1891. *Il n'est si bon marinier qui ne risque de se noyer. Proverbe en un acte*. Paris: Typographie A.-M. Baudelot.

———. 1892. *A la recherche de la gloire*. Paris: Ollendorff.

———. 1896. *La douleur des autres*. Paris: Ollendorff.

[Charles Epheyre, pseud., and Octave Houdaille]. 1898. *Soeur Marthe. Drame lyrique*. Paris: Ollendorff.

[Charles F.-R. Epheyre, pseud.]. 1903. "Conte de Noël pour les grands enfants. Hans Winter (Légende de la forêt Noire)." *La revue du bien dans la vie et dans l'art*, (Jan. 1) 3° année: 1–3.

[Charles Richet]. 1875. "Du somnambulisme provoqué." *Journal de l'anatomie et de la physiologie*: 348–77.

———. 1879. "Notice sur la vie de Charles Renouard." In C. Renouard, *Discours prononcés à la Cour de Cassation. 1870–1877.* Paris: Ollendorff.

———. 1880. "Les démoniaques d'aujourd'hui. Étude de psychologie pathologique." *Revue des deux mondes* (Jan. 15): 340–72.

———. 1884a. *L'homme et l'intelligence.* Paris: Alcan.

———. 1884b. "La suggestion mentale et le calcul des probabilités." *Revue philosophique* 18: 609–74.

———. 1886. "La peur. Étude psychologique." *Revue des deux mondes* (July 1): 73–117.

———. 1887. *Essai de psychologie générale.* Paris: Alcan.

———. 1889. "Expériences sur le sommeil à distance." *Bulletins de la Société de psychologie physiologique* IV (1888): 1–18. Paris: Alcan.

———. 1891a. "L'amour. Étude de psychologie générale." *Revue des deux mondes* (Mar. 1): 135–67.

———. 1891b. *Pour les grands et les petits. Fables.* Preface by M. Sully Prudhomme. Paris: Hachette, 1893, 2d ed.

———. 1892. *Dans cent ans.* Paris: Ollendorff.

———. 1895. "Préface. L'alimentation et le luxe. Réponse à L.Tolstoï." In L. Tolstoï, *Plaisirs cruels.* Paris: Charpentier et Fasquelle.

———. 1896a. *L'idée de l'arbitrage international est-elle une chimère?* Paris: V. Giard and E. Brière. Originally published in *Revue internationale de sociologie* [May 1896]: 5.

———. 1896b. "Préface." In O. Houdaille, *Possessions.* Paris: A. Lemerre.

———. 1905. *Circé. Drame en deux actes en vers.* Paris: J. Gamber.

———. 1910. *Socrate. Pièce en vers en quatre actes et six tableaux.* Paris: G. Ficker.

———. 1922. *Traité de métapsychique.* Paris: Alcan.

———. 1923. *Le savant.* Paris: Hachette.

———. 1933. *Souvenirs d'un physiologiste.* Joigny: Peyronnet.

———. 1934. *Au seuil du mystère.* Paris: Peyronnet.

———. N.d. "Introduction." In *Règle du jeu de Gobefiche.* Paris: Maison Quantin.

PUBLICATIONS ATTRIBUTABLE TO CHARLES RICHET

[F. et R., pseud.]. 1880. "Considérations sur la philosophie chimique." *Revue philosophique* 1: 601–31. This attribution is almost certain: there is a copy in Charles Richet's collection of off-prints in the *Académie de médecine*, Richet collection.

[Dr. R., pseud.]. 1898. "Hommage mérité." *L'Aurore* 27 (Feb.): 2. Possible attribution.

MANUSCRIPTS

Bibliothèque de l'Académie de médecine, Charles Richet collection (Boxes III and IV). In addition to a few manuscripts of scientific articles, which I have not listed, the collection contains literary texts that are for the most part undated, writ-

ten in Charles Richet's and other hands (secretaries or collaborators?), or type-written; the latter seem to be more recent. Some have been published, others not.
L'auberge de Panitzoff (play).
La douleur des autres (see Charles Epheyre 1896, above).
L'honneur et le roi (play).
Katia (play).
Mémoires sur moi et les autres (ca. 1916).
La naissance d'un monde (play).
Souvenirs d'un physiologiste (see Charles Richet 1933, above).
Suite de mes mémoires sur moi et les autres (Nov. 1–5, 1920).
Le testament de Michael Will (play, after 1912).
Bibliothèque nationale, Département des manuscrits, Letters to Joseph Reinach, NAF 13556, folios 41–56.

General Bibliography

Beizer, Janet. 1994. *Ventriloquized Bodies: Narratives of Hysteria in Nineteenth-Century France*. Ithaca, N.Y.: Cornell University Press.

Boring, E. G. 1929. *A History of Experimental Psychology*. New York: Appleton, 2d ed., 1950.

Carroy, Jacqueline. 1991. *Hypnose, suggestion et psychologie. L'invention de sujets*. Paris: Presses Universitaires de France.

———. 1993a. *Les personnalités doubles et multiples. Entre science et fiction*. Paris: Presses Universitaires de France.

———. 1993b. "Magnétisme, hypnotisme et philosophie." In *Importance de l'hypnose*, ed. Isabelle Stengers, 169–92. Paris: Synthélabo.

Carroy, Jacqueline, and Régine Plas. 1995. "Dreyfus et la somnambule." *Critique* (Jan.–Feb.): 36–59.

———. 1996. "The Origins of French Experimental Psychology: Experiment and Experimentalism." *History of the Human Sciences* 9, no. 1: 73–84.

Chaigneau, C. 1887. "Le spiritisme dans la littérature." *Revue spirite*: 26–31.

Charle, Christophe. 1990. *Naissance des "intellectuels," 1880–1900*. Paris: Minuit.

Duclert, Vincent. 1994. *L'affaire Dreyfus*. Paris: La Découverte.

Edelman, Nicole. 1995. *Voyantes, guérisseuses et visionnaires en France 1785–1914*. Paris: Albin Michel.

Estingoy, P. 1992–93. *Charles Richet (1850–1935)*. Mémoire de DEA (Diplôme d'Etude Approfondie) d'histoire sous la direction de M. le Professeur Régis Ladous, Université de Lyon III Jean Moulin.

———. 1993–94. *Charles Richet (1850–1935) et la découverte de l'anaphylaxie*. Mémoire de médecine pour l'A.E.U. d'histoire de la médecine, sous la direction de M. le Professeur Normand, Université de Lyon I Claude Bernard.

Gauchet, Marcel. 1992. *L'inconscient cérébral*. Paris: Seuil.

Gauld, Alan. 1992. *A History of Hypnotism*. Cambridge: Cambridge University Press.

Hacking, Ian. 1988. "Telepathy: Origins of Randomization in Experimental Design." *Isis* 79: 427–51.

James, Tony. 1995. *Dream, Creativity and Madness in Nineteenth-Century France*. Oxford: Clarendon Press.

Janet, Pierre. 1919. *Les médications psychologiques*. Paris: Société Pierre Janet, 1986.

Julliard, Jacques, and Michel Winock, eds. 1996. *Dictionnaire des intellectuels français*. Paris: Seuil.

Laugaa, Maurice. 1986. *La pensée du pseudonyme*. Paris: Presses Universitaires de France.

Le procès Zola. 1898. Paris: Aux bureaux du *Siècle*, Stock.

Leroy, Géraldi, ed. 1983. *Les écrivains et l'Affaire Dreyfus*. Paris: Presses Universitaires de France.

Marivaux, P. de. 1740. "L'épreuve." In *Théâtre complet*. Paris: Gallimard, 1949.

Maugue, Annelise. 1987. *L'identité masculine en crise au tournant du siècle*. Paris: Rivages.

Maupassant, Guy de. 1883. "Le fantastique." In *Chroniques II*. Paris: 1950.

Micale, Mark S. 1995. *Approaching Hysteria: Disease and Its Interpretations*. Princeton, N.J.: Princeton University Press.

Milet, J. 1970. *Gabriel Tarde et la philosophie de l'histoire*. Paris: Vrin.

Palefroi, R. (pseud. of Paul Fournier). 1879. *Théâtre bizarre*. Paris: Ollendorff.

Pitman, C. B., trans. Ernest Renan. *Recollections of Childhood and Youth*. London: George Routledge and Sons, 1929.

Plas, Régine. *Naissance d'une science humaine: la psychologie, les psychologues et le "merveilleux psychique."* Rennes: Presses Universitaires de Rennes, 2000.

Reinach, Joseph. 1903. *Histoire de l'Affaire Dreyfus*. Paris: Charpentier et Fasquelles.

Renan, Ernest. 1883. *Souvenirs d'enfance et de jeunesse*. Paris: Folio, 1993.

Reuchlin, Maur"trainice. 1957. *Histoire de la psychologie*. Paris: Presses Universitaires de France, 1969.

Richet, Gabriel. 1993. "Charles Richet: l'anaphylaxie." *Histoire des sciences médicales* 27, no. 3: 1–7.

Rigoli, Juan. *Lire le délire. Aliénisme et littérature en France au XIXe siècle*. Paris: Fayard, 2001.

Thirard (Carroy), Jacqueline. 1976. "La fondation de la *Revue philosophique*." *Revue philosophique* (Oc.t–Dec.): 401–13.

Todorov, Tzvetan. 1970. *Introduction à la littérature fantastique*. Paris: Seuil.

Tourguénieff, I. 1883. "Après la mort." *Nouvelle revue* 20: 255–314.

Wolf, Stewart. 1992. *Brain, Mind and Medicine: Charles Richet and the Origins of Physiological Psychology*. New Brunswick, N.J.: Transaction Publishers.

CHAPTER 8

Writing Psychology Over: Gertrude Stein and William James

STEVEN MEYER

As a student at the Harvard Annex—rechristened Radcliffe College at the end of her freshman year—Gertrude Stein worked closely with William James and Hugo Munsterberg at the Harvard Psychological Laboratory. This early exposure to the new science of psychology was supplemented by a summer at the Woods Hole Marine Biological Laboratory in 1897, followed by four years, and part of a fifth, of further study at Johns Hopkins Medical School. This thorough training in experimental science played a crucial role in Stein's subsequent development as perhaps the twentieth century's preeminent "experimental" writer. The few critics who have addressed the nature of her scientific background mistakenly argue, however, that in her writing practice Stein accepted the "mechanistic conception of life" uncritically.[1] In the course of the following pages, a broad reevaluation of Stein's career, I propose a very different view of her relation to the biological and psychological sciences of the last hundred years. Not only was she much more critical of mechanistic science than has generally been supposed, but her criticism, constructive as well as deconstructive, emerges principally in her experimental writing, her *literary* compositions.[2]

It is not just that Stein's ideas of writing were influenced by science: she reconfigured science *as* writing and performed scientific experiments *in* writing. Initially her understanding of science was thoroughly mechanistic; thus in *The Making of Americans*, written between 1902 and 1911, she attempted to describe the precise mechanisms of human personality in great detail. Yet with *Tender Buttons*, composed the year after she completed her monumental novel, she embraced a nonmechanistic outlook. In this collection of prose poems—and in hundreds of pieces, large and small, written over the next twenty years—Stein endeavored to portray consciousness in terms of the experience of writing, as she moved to a more "organic" sense of writing, a perspective that corresponded both to Alfred North White-head's "philosophy of organism"[3] and to Ralph Waldo Emerson's "natural-ism."[4] Like Emerson and Whitehead, she did not strictly distinguish be-tween the literary and the scientific, and the science she rejected was a sci-ence devoted exclusively to what James, in *The Principles of Psychology*, called "knowledge-about" or descriptive knowledge.

The "one thing," Stein remarked in her 1934 lecture, "The Gradual Making of the Making of Americans," that she had "completely learned" from James was that "science is continuously busy with the complete description of something, with ultimately the complete description of any-thing, with ultimately the complete description of everything."[5] To the prac-tical question of the extent of such "complete[ness]"—"if this can really be done, the complete description of everything, then what else is there to do"—she responded that one might try to stop "continuing describing every-thing."[6] This seeming tautology is easier said than done. When some lines later Stein rewrote her question in the form of the more brutal and rhetor-ical, "If it can be done why do it," she was offering a motive both for dis-continuing the "scientific" project of *The Making of Americans*—which she now felt sure could be accomplished—and for beginning the new project of "stop[ping] describing everything," about which she was not certain at all.

The shift from writing in her "first manner" to the mannerism of *Tender Buttons*—from "It is a simple thing to be quite certain that there are kinds in men and women. It is a simple thing and then not any one has any wor-rying to be doing about any one being any one" to "Suppose it did, suppose it did with a sheet and a shadow and a silver set of water, suppose it did"—occurred because the project of William James, as she understood it, had ceased to interest her.[7] "Being at last really convinced that a description of everything is possible it was inevitable that I gradually stopped describing everything."[8] Description was replaced by portraiture, or more exactly by what James termed "knowledge of acquaintance."[9] "I am acquainted," James proposed in *The Principles of Psychology*, "with many people and things, which I know very little about, except their presence in the places where I have met them. . . . [A]bout the inner nature of these facts or what makes them what they are, I can say nothing at all. I cannot impart acquaintance with them to anyone who has not already made it himself. I cannot *describe* them."[10] Stein in her writing attempts to do what James says can't be done: imparting acquaintance to someone who hasn't already experienced it, and so replacing James's acquaintance *without* description with what she would call, in 1926, "an acquaintance with description."[11] The story of the "gradual making" of *The Making of Americans* was consequently the story of Stein freeing herself from James's beneficent influence—that is, from the dictates of his descriptive psychology, the limits of his science.[12]

Experience as a Kind of Writing

By 1904 James could observe in the essay "Does 'Consciousness' Exist?" that "for twenty years past I have mistrusted 'consciousness' as an entity; for seven or eight years past I have suggested its non-existence to my students."[13] Stein, his student from 1893 to 1897, would have witnessed this pedagogical shift.[14] Experience, he had come to believe, "had no such inner duplicity" as that between content and consciousness. Divisions along these lines resulted from "the addition, to a concrete piece of [experience], of other sets of experience," which caused the same "piece" to be taken in two different ways. This could be illustrated with some paint, as James explained:

In a pot in a paint shop, along with other paints, it serves in its entirety as so much saleable matter. Spread on a canvas, with other paints around it, it represents, on the contrary, a feature in a picture and performs a spiritual function. Just so, I maintain, does a given undivided portion of experience, taken in one context of associates, play the part of knower, of a state of mind, of 'consciousness'; while in a different context the same undivided bit of experience plays the part of a thing known, of an objective 'content.'

Dualism, he observed, "is still preserved in this account, but reinterpreted, so that, instead of being mysterious and elusive, it becomes verifiable and concrete. It is an affair of relations, it falls outside, not inside, the single experience considered, and can always be particularized and defined."[15]

James's was a "radical" empiricism because it required that both content and consciousness be recognized as epiphenomena and as essentially relational.[16] At the cost of denying substantiality to either form of substance, material or mental, he was thus able to counter reductive monisms with a "pluralistic universe."[17] Dualism was not all that was reinterpreted in this account of experience, however. James also reinterpreted the experience of estrangement that Emerson had so powerfully expressed in the essay he chose to call "Experience." "We fancy," Emerson had written,

that we are strangers, and not so intimately domesticated in the planet as the wild man, and the wild beast and bird. But the exclusion reaches them also. . . . [They too] are just such superficial tenants of the globe. Then the new molecular philosophy shows astronomical interspaces between atom and atom, shows that the world is all outside: it has no inside.[18]

Yes, James responded, there is no inside per se; but that does not empty us and our categories of all meaning.

James proposed to treat pieces of experience the way the literary critic William Empson would later treat pieces of writing: as meaning different things in different "contexts of associates" and as such becoming "an affair of relations." (The resemblance to Empson is not arbitrary; Empson's mentor, I. A. Richards, was trained as a psychologist and like James was fascinated by the mechanics of reading.) Rather than defining consciousness in terms of, for example, categories that could either be filled or emptied—a model in which all activity occurred within the categories—James reinterpreted it here as one way of contextualizing "undivided" bits of experience, which had necessarily to be taken up from the outside. This pluralism, enabling him as it did to equate the "state of mind" of the knower with the "thing known," would form the rationale for Stein's project (and projection) of a portraiture that "recreated" the object instead of merely describing it. But, as James would have been the first to recognize, his conception of representation remained inadequate for so ambitious a project.

As a second example of the pluralism he had in mind, James described an experience he could be sure all his readers shared: "let him [the reader] begin with a perceptual experience, the 'presentation,' so called, of a physical object, his actual field of vision, the room he sits in, with the book he is reading at its centre."[19] Aside from the insistent "he"—and the unlikely event that anyone reading *The Journal of Philosophical, Psychological and Scientific Methods*, where the article first appeared, would be lying down or out of doors—this would seem to define James's common reader, who could be defined with certainty only in terms of the experience of reading the article James was currently writing. The book or journal that contained the article would simultaneously be at the center of the room and in the reader's mind (not to speak of all of this also being in James's mind and in the center of the room he was sitting and writing in). Typically, however, James did not address the Pandora's box of self-reflexivity he opened here with his gesture to the very words he was writing as he was imagining the reader reading them. He left it up to the reader to make the connection between the reading of the article and its writing. All that really mattered, as far as James was concerned, was the reading. For him, and certainly for most of his readers as well, books may often have been the objects closest to hand; yet he did not consider, as Emerson would have, what effect this was having on his phi-losophy.[20] (The effect of this curious failure of curiosity, or nerve, on his writ-ing was obvious: the famous clarity of style survived intact.) He left it for Stein to ponder the effect on his thought.

Part of the inadequacy of James's theory of representation lay in its over-simplification. "A given undivided portion of experience," he had written, "taken in one context of associates, play[s] the part of a knower, of a state of mind, of 'consciousness'; while in a different context the same undivided bit of experience plays the part of a thing known, of an objective 'content.'" But in writing, as even more obviously in his example of painting, the content is not unidimensional. There is the physical paint and there are the objects painted; there are the words and there is what the words are about. Yet it would seem that in the analogy with painting James had only the material—the paint on the canvas, the words on paper—in mind as "content." "There is no self-splitting," he would say a few pages later of "experience per se," "into con-sciousness and what the consciousness is 'of'"; but the "of" here self-splits.[21] In a painting of a person reading a book, or in a written description of such a per-son, is one not conscious of the person as well as of the words and paint?

The same nonmaterial item that would seem so readily to operate as con-tent—the representation of someone reading, for example—can also be taken as performing a further "spiritual function." The viewer of the painting might, and in all probability would, begin to contemplate what "state of mind" of the painter's was represented in the figure of the reader. Thus, at least in the experience of writing and painting, a third item appears to par-take of the double-edged nature that James attributed to experience general-ly. James was so concerned to stress the "undivided" nature of experience that he quite radically oversimplified the doubleness of ordinary experience. If, for example, one were to take literally his comments about the pot of paint, one would have to attribute to the paint on the canvas the part of a knower, of "consciousness." This could only be asserted within a much more complicated story than the one he was prepared to tell.

Even if this oversimplification were corrected, James's representational scheme would still remain inadequate. Although writing certainly counted as a representational act for him, it was wholly reducible to the act of read-ing. He was always ready to mistake the act of writing for all the acts of read-ing that followed from it, as neither Emerson nor Stein was. The account of representation he relied on was essentially interpretative: representation involved different "contexts of associates" whereby "undivided" pieces of experience appeared in different forms, with different meanings. The writing, pragmatically speaking, was what one made of it, not what went into its composition; in itself it was assumed to be just another undivided piece of experience. The enemy was opacity of meaning, whether the experience in writing of inspiration—of the writing running ahead of consciousness, of one having meant more than one could know—or the experience of indeterminacy, of the impossibility of getting down to the bottom of what something might mean. Either all such opacity was interpretable, or there was nothing interesting one could say about it.[22] Ultimately this model of representation depended on an unexamined notion of "undivided." In exposing the ill-considered "divisions" of experience, James too readily assumed that actual experience could not be examined directly. "The instant field of the present," as he called the domain of undivided experience, was by definition inaccessible to any kind of analysis, although one continually acted in response to it.[23]

Emerson provided a contrary model for Stein: although he, too, refrained in his lectures and essays from directly talking about his experience of writing, he nevertheless faced up to it in the act of composition. (When he discussed writing per se, he stood at some remove and retreated into either an idealized or a demonized version of it—writing as originality or threats to originality.)[24] Whereas James talked about "undivided" pieces of experience and let them go at that, Emerson elaborated, as in the lines quoted above from "Experience": "undivided" meant that "betwixt atom and atom" there were "astronomical interspaces." It was these "astronomical interspaces," only between word and word, that James left out of his picture; Stein would spend her career, most concentratedly the period between 1912 and 1932, examining them with what she called in *The Autobiography of Alice B. Toklas* "the intellectual passion for exactitude in the description of inner and outer reality."[25] This was the same passion that she attributed to Emerson in a 1935 interview when she observed that he "might have been surprised if he had been told that he was passionate. But Emerson really had passion; he wrote it; but he could not have written *about* it because he did not know about it."[26] The passion he wrote, but could not write about, was, like Stein's, a passion for writing.[27]

James, as it happened, left unrepresented in his theory of representation the exacting form of "concentration" that Stein practiced: the kind of concentration—the word is Stein's, from the *Autobiography*, and harkens back to Emerson's concentric "circles"—that consists in exploring the inter-, not inner, spaces of words.[28] He accepted too uncritically the notion that representation was always in some manner a *re*-presenting, and thus that the "present" lay beyond examination. Although for both Stein and Emerson it was impossible to get behind the present (there was nothing "behind" the present or inside it, it was all outside) or beyond it (the present was always present in our experience of everything as "outside," in our estrangements), it was certainly not itself beyond examining: in one's acts of writing it was what was most immediately there to have its measure taken. It was the writing as it was being written. Stein, like Emerson, might exult in this fact; she might despair of it. James, by keeping his distance from his own writing— keeping a hands-off attitude toward it, even as he was so hands-on with respect to the reader—allowed himself no such direct experience of it.

It is here too that William Empson stops looking so much like William James. To be sure, Empson was most concerned with the effects that "pieces of writing" had on readers—hence his elaborate mapping of the ways words themselves self-split and, through the lines of force he alternately called "ambiguity" and "equation," produce significance, or as he preferred to think of it, impose doctrines on readers. He insisted nonetheless that there was more to writing than these effects; thus, early in *Seven Types of Ambiguity*, he made room for "the poet's sense of the nature of a language," which was to be distinguished from a poet's or anyone's sense of language. The latter determined how successfully one achieved the effects one was after; it was one's way with words, one's ability to have one's way with words. The sense of a language was nothing like that. It involved recognizing any word "as a member of the language" rather than as "a solid tool" for the production of meaning.[29] The examples Empson gave, in 1930, of writers with this sense "of language as such" were Racine, Dryden, and "Miss Stein." It is probable that Empson was in the audience at Cambridge in 1926 when Stein presented the first of her public lectures, "Composition as Explanation." Writing like hers was not susceptible, as Empson noted, to his method of analysis, for it was not "about" something the reader was supposed to be convinced of. "The mode of action" of the language was not directed toward the reader; rather it was directed toward the language, toward the writing itself.[30]

Automatic Writing

The difference between James and Stein on the subject of writing, and particularly on the relation writing bears to consciousness, is perhaps exhibited most clearly in their attitudes toward automatic writing. While an undergraduate at Harvard, Stein conducted experiments in automatic writing under James's supervision.[31] "The first automatic writing I ever saw," James recalled in 1909, the year Stein's *Three Lives* was published, "was forty years ago." "I unhesitatingly thought of it as deceit," he continued, "although it contained vague elements of supranormal knowledge. Since then I have come to see in automatic writing one example of a department of human activity as vast as it is enigmatic. Every sort of person is liable to it, or to something equivalent to it."[32] Stein, in contrast, some thirty-five years after her first encounter with automatic writing in her Harvard experiments, would insist that it did not exist, that it was a delusion. This is how she put it in a letter she wrote in mid-December 1932, a month or so after she completed *The Autobiography of Alice B. Toklas* ("Solomons" is Leon Solomons, a graduate student and close friend at Harvard with whom she conducted the initial set of experiments and whose account of the results was published under both their names in the nascent journal *Psychological Review*, then only in its third year):

The xperiments that Solomons reported were not cases of automatic writing, they were xamples of a certain amount of distraction of attention entered into deliberately to ease the act of creation. That is as I understood it. He and I did not agree in this matter. Later on I carried on xperiments of my own in automatic writing with students and I came to the conclusion that there are no real cases of automatic writing, there are automatic movements but not automatic writing. Writing for the normal person is too complicated an activity to be indulged in automatically.[33]

Yet Stein's disagreement was with James as well as with Solomons. Everyone, James said, wrote automatically or did something like it; for Stein, nobody did, least of all herself.

In this comment and others like it Stein was responding to accusations that culminated in a 1934 article by B. F. Skinner called "Has Gertrude Stein a Secret?" Stein, Skinner asserted, was trading on techniques of automatic writing that she had learned as a psychology student and passing them off as literary innovations. His argument was twofold: first, she had become accomplished in automatic writing in the series of experiments at the Harvard Psychological Laboratory. Second, in her later "experimental writing" she used these techniques to construct a secondary personality, the "hypothetical author" of these works, as he phrased it—although a singularly immature one, "intellectually unopinionated," "emotionally cold," with "no past" and "unread and unlearned beyond grammar school."[34] The writing, then, rather than being the significant construction of art that it was sometimes taken for, merely entailed the construction of a "superficial" author. If it seemed meaningless, this was because the "inferential author" had an inadequate conception of meaning, not because the meaning was difficult; it was not a reflection on any inadequacies of the reader.[35] Skinner offered his analysis ingeniously as nothing more than a diagnosis of the failure, in his eyes, of Stein's experimental writing to mean anything. It was not directed at Stein or at, as he put it, "the finer work of a very fine mind."[36] The writing was only as superficially related to Stein as its "hypothetical" author was and as easily and painlessly removed. It was a mistake, perhaps, but not a very serious one.

Skinner's argument was itself premised on a series of factual and interpretative mistakes. Stein and Solomons, he would have read in the *Autobiography*, "together worked out a series of experiments in automatic writing under the direction of Munsterberg." "The result of her own experiments," the passage continued, "which Gertrude Stein wrote down and which was printed in the *Harvard* [sic] *Psychological Review*, was the first writing of hers ever to be printed."[37] Skinner took this publication to be a piece entitled "Normal Motor Automatism," which appeared in the September 1896 issue of the *Review*. In fact the first publication that Stein composed herself, and the one she was referring to, was "Cultivated Motor Automatism; A Study of Character in Its Relation to Attention," published in May 1898. The earlier study had been written entirely by Solomons, although Stein was credited as coauthor. Stein had assisted and with Solomons served as one of the two subjects, but she had not written a word that was not "automatic." Indeed, as she later noted, she had her doubts about whether any of the writing was genuinely automatic.

Both sets of experiments were designed to test the extent of what could be considered "automatic" actions in "normal" persons. In the first series, with Solomons, the aim was to show that actions that in hysterical patients were usually taken as having been performed by "secondary personalities" could, nonetheless, be performed by "ordinary people" as automatic actions, that is, performed without consciousness of the action. Hysterics, suffering from a particularly extreme form of neurosis, often exhibited what was called an "anaesthesia" in the sensibility of parts of the body. From no apparent physical cause, the hysteric would lose sight in an eye, for example, or sensation in an arm. Emerson's hysterical blindness during his months at the Harvard Divinity School took this form; often the anaesthesia would persist much longer than it did in his case. It had been observed by clinical psychologists in the late 1880s that such lack of consciousness or sensibility was often accompanied by a distinct "sensibility to the anaesthetic parts," as William James put it in his *Principles of Psychology*, "in the form of a secondary consciousness entirely cut off from the primary or normal one, but susceptible of being tapped and made to testify to its existence in various odd ways."[38] If, however, it could be shown that the "normal subject" could write automatically or unconsciously, as the hysteric did, then the hypothesis of some kind of split in consciousness—the hypothesis upon which the notion of a "secondary personality" was premised—would be superfluous. Solomons's experiment was thus meant to disprove the construct of the kind of secondary personality to which Skinner wanted to attribute the writing of works like *Tender Buttons*.

In the experiments Stein conducted on her own, she shifted the emphasis of inquiry from this earlier concern with the different kinds of actions that "normal" persons could be shown to perform automatically—in which the normal, nonhysterical, subjects were assumed to be a homogeneous mass—to the differing capabilities of individuals to perform particular automatic actions. As Stein observed in *Everybody's Autobiography*, she had been led to doubt the validity of the original experiments. This was not merely because there had only been two subjects, self-proclaimed as normal, but because of the artificiality of the experiments and the extreme self-consciousness of the experimenters:

Solomons reported what he called his and my automatic writing but I did not think that we either of us had been doing automatic writing, we always knew what we were doing how could we not when every minute in the laboratory we were doing what we were watching ourselves doing, that was our training.[39]

In her own article Stein still talked in terms of automatic writing, but the writing consisted of "circles, the figure eight, a long curve, or an m-figure," movements "of a decidedly rhythmic character."[40] The so-called automatic writing of the Solomons experiment—with Stein coming up with, for example, "When he could not be the longest and thus to be, and thus to be, the strongest"—was, on the contrary, never automatic.[41]

It should be added, all the same, that Skinner's hasty indictment of Stein was not entirely a trap of his own making. In *The Autobiography of Alice B. Toklas*, unlike in her other statements on the subject, Stein did not explicitly dissociate herself from Solomon's description of their experimental writing as automatic. She spoke of the "series of experiments in automatic writing" and "the result of her own experiments" without observing that the point, and interest, of her work was the way it illustrated that if movements were automatic they would not produce writing and if, on the other hand, they did produce writing they were not automatic. Moreover, when she noted in the *Autobiography* that "the method of writing to be afterwards developed in Three Lives and Making of Americans already shows itself," she unhelpfully conflated her writing in the Solomons piece (the examples of so-called automatic writing) with what she actually had in mind: the *mode of analysis* that she used in writing up her later experiments.[42] Skinner, however, chose to interpret each ambiguity in such a way as to prop up the weak, uneducated secondary personality he had unearthed, a personality that he hastened to add was not "a true second personality" but "a literary second personality," not a conscious self but little more than an arm that Stein periodically set in motion.[43]

Stein never denied the obvious link between the writing in her work with Solomons and the experimental writing she began to compose after *The Making of Americans*; thus in describing the writing produced in the Harvard Laboratory as "xamples of a certain amount of distraction of attention entered into deliberately to ease the act of creation," she deliberately left room for the later acts of "creative" writing as well. What she objected to was the characterization of any of this writing as "automatic" and hence — this is the crux of the matter — both unconscious and meaningless. No writing was meaningless, she countered, and her writing was certainly not unconscious. On the contrary, she insisted that her writing, no less in the experiments with Solomons than in works like *Tender Buttons*, be recognized as conscious and the product of a rational mind; that it not be taken, as Skinner had, as a simulacrum of the unconscious writing of an hysterical woman — as little more, and perhaps much less, than the work of female hysteria.[44] This consideration made all the difference. To Ellery Sedgwick, the editor of the *Atlantic Monthly*, which between May and August of 1933 had published four large excerpts from the *Autobiography*, Stein wrote in response to Skinner's piece (also published by Sedgwick): "No it is not so automatic as he thinks. . . . If there is anything secret it is the other way. . . . I think I achieve by xtra consciousness, excess."[45]

There are two equally valid ways of understanding Stein's categorical rejection of any attempt to explain her writing as somehow "tapping" her unconscious — as James might have said had he found the notion of an unconscious, or even subconscious, useful in relation to normal life, which he did not. The distinction "between the unconscious and the conscious being of the mental state," James argued in *Principles of Psychology*, was not required to explain the "great class of experiences in our mental life which may be described as discoveries that a subjective condition which we have been having is really something different from what we had supposed."[46]

This is not the place to engage Freud's strikingly different conclusion, but it should be noted that in *The Psychopathology of Everyday Life*—Freud's central text on the relation of the unconscious to the same class of common experiences—he does not make an especially convincing case for his claim that the unconscious is the determining factor in the parapraxes he marshals. To be sure, as he himself observed in a 1924 footnote, "this book is of an entirely popular character; it merely aims, by an accumulation of examples, at paving the way for the necessary assumption of *unconscious yet operative* mental processes, and it avoids all theoretical considerations on the nature of this unconscious."[47] Not only is Freud's tendentiousness here suspect, however—his success in providing explanations for every parapraxis he meets only shows that he could reduce them all to equations with one unknown, the unconscious—but he was puzzlingly untroubled by the existence of alternative explanations. "It remains an open question," he wrote, "whether there are, within the range of normality, yet other factors that can—like the unconscious motive, and in place of it—create parapraxes and symptomatic acts along the lines of these [physiological and psycho-physical] relations. It is not my task to answer this question."[48] Yet it is this very question that challenges the strict determinism of his "psychology of the unconscious."[49] The possibility that the experiences of "everyday life" are overdetermined has as its corollary the underdetermined state of his own determinism. This is a matter that Stein, following James, deliberately kept open.[50]

In the first place, she quite reasonably associated unconsciousness with hysteria. The experimental psychology of her college days would have confirmed her in this, and just as she later observed that abnormal psychology "frightened" her, she shifted the emphasis in her experiments at Harvard from the psychology of the abnormal hysteric—which was what intrigued Solomons—to that of the normal college student.[51] "The subjects used in this experiment," one reads in "Cultivated Motor Automatism," "were members of Harvard University and Radcliffe College . . . 41 male subjects . . . and . . . 50 female subjects."[52] "She always says she dislikes the abnormal," Stein would have Toklas comment about her in the *Autobiography*. "It is so obvious. She says the normal is much more simply complicated and interesting."[53] This insistence on normality extended to Stein's characterization of herself as an "everybody" in the second installment of her life story, which was concerned primarily with the reception of the first. *Everybody's Autobiography* was thus offered as the autobiography of an ungendered everyman instead of as the life of a particular woman. The same refusal to make a public issue of her personal negotiations with gender—and in so refusing, making it all the more an issue for any serious consideration of her writing—entered as well into her delighted self-identification with the middle class, whose ways she flaunted but never rejected. Clearly her embrace of what she called in the first draft of *The Making of Americans* the "material middle class" derived in part from a fear of losing control, or, more precisely, of her control—her ability to call her life and writing her own—being taken away from her.[54] Within a page of expressing a decisive interest in the "simply complicated," she might confess that "Dickens had always frightened her," and note, without missing a beat, that "as she says anything can frighten her."[55] Yet if she could so readily acknowledge the fear, she already had it well under control. The middle class, which provided protection and a certain camouflage, at the same time presented the greatest threat to a person's independence; the refuge in normality has to be understood as a response to the common labeling of nonconformist tendencies in women as signs of "hysteria." The best disguise, as Poe—favorite of Stein's and an important early theorist of hysteria—spelled out so clearly in "The Purloined Letter," was one that looked like no disguise at all.[56]

In addition to this political explanation of Stein's refusal to accept a role for the unconscious in her writing—the unconscious thus representing a mode of putting, or keeping, women and others who challenge the dominant social order in their place—one can also observe a second, less partisan motive. The unconscious was not merely situated on one side of a dividing line: it was itself divisive. In addition to being, by definition, invisible, it could at any time prevent what one saw in the normal course of things from being accurately registered. Stein, like contemporaries as different from her and from each other as William Carlos Williams, Robert Frost, and Marianne Moore, chiefly concerned herself in her writing with possible (possibly impossible) constructions of the ordinary, what was normally seen and heard and said and done. She aimed to remove all distortions from the writing and thereby rid it, as she said of Picasso's similar art, of "the things everybody is certain of seeing, but which they do not really see."[57]

The notion that some form of dynamic unconscious was unavoidable implied, on the contrary, a skepticism that put all perceptions, and any supposed relation of the self and world, into question; and Stein's experimental project of portraiture from late 1910 on served to counter, if not exactly refute, a comparable skepticism that had informed her previous work. Thus the elegiac ending of *The Making of Americans*, of 1911, is among other things a representation of the death that this skepticism, embodied in the melancholy of David Hersland, drives inexorably toward. At the same time, in allowing Hersland actually to die, Stein can be said to have freed herself from her own skeptical frame of mind. The skepticism—what Stein referred to in the lines cited above from "A Long Gay Book" as "any worrying to be doing about any one being any one"—had operated in conjunction with a desire, indeed a faith, that "the complete description of everything" was possible; thus "it is a simple thing to be quite certain that there are kinds in men and women." With the shift from description (of kinds) to portraits (of individuals, and occasionally of collections of individuals), the skepticism, at least its force, dropped out of the picture. It had to be overcome, or "transcended," as one might say, for the shift to be possible at all. Yet it could only be overcome in the course of the move itself; hence the back-and-forth movement, the extended period of transition, which was carried out "in," as well as carried over "into," so many different works of Stein's between 1910 and 1913. With the shift in her career that the turn to portraiture marked, and with the change in style that followed from it, the unconscious was good and buried—at least so far as the writing of the next twenty years was concerned.

When, in an anthology of American writing called *Americans Abroad* that appeared in 1932, Stein proposed that "I take things in and they come out that way independent of conscious process," she was distinguishing such independence from any kind of dependence on an unconscious process. "All this foolishness," she continued, "about my writing being mystic or impressionistic is so stupid. Every word I write has the same passionate exactness of meaning that it is supposed to have. Everything I write means exactly what it says."[58] She was not claiming to have absolute control over her writing, but she was not willing to acknowledge any other entity as possessing such control over her. She was not, in other words, willing to divide herself up into a consciousness and an unconscious of any kind. Skinner in his expose might talk unconcernedly about "the two Gertrude Steins"; Gertrude Stein was having none of that.[59]

Nonautomatic Writing

"There is no good nonsense without sense," Stein concluded in the 1932 letter in which the Harvard experiments were discussed, "and so there cannot be automatic writing."[60] She agreed with Skinner that the only sign of automatic writing in nonhysterical cases was its meaninglessness. There was no other way of registering that the required degree of disengagement had been achieved. Skinner was too hasty, however, in attributing such meaningless-ness to her own work. "I found out very soon," she observed in 1946, con-cerning her writing at the time of *Tender Buttons*, "that there is no such thing as putting [words] together without sense. I made innumerable efforts to make words write without sense and found it impossible. Any human being putting down words had to make sense out of them."[61] Automatic writ-ing was impossible, this meant, for anyone who was not clinically hysterical.

Stein's dismissal of automatic writing, and more generally of the notion that an unconscious was somehow necessary to human life and writing—her "refusal," as she said in *The Autobiography of Alice B. Toklas,* "of the use of the subconscious"—was not a gesture of repression but on the contrary a lib-erating act for her.[62] Any attempt to ally her with the subconscious, she insist-ed, was nothing other than a repressive gesture itself. She could even cite William James on this. "Gertrude Stein," begins an account in the *Auto-biography* of what emerges as an attempt to deny her her individuality, and her conscious participation in it,

never had subconscious reactions, nor was she a successful subject for automatic writing. One of the students in the psychological seminar of which Gertrude Stein, although an undergraduate was at William James' particular request a member, was carrying on a series of experiments on suggestions to the subconscious. When he read his paper upon the result of his experiments, he began by explaining that one of the subjects gave absolutely no results and as this much lowered the average and made the conclusion of his experiments false he wished to be allowed to cut this record out. Whose record is it, said James. Miss Stein's, said the student. Ah, said James, if Miss Stein gave no response I should say that it was as normal not to give a response as to give one and decidedly the result must not be cut out.[63]

Part of what being normal meant for Stein was that it legitimated responses of hers that were exceptional: she might or might not be the exception that proved the rule, but she *was* the rule that proved to be an exception. No mat-ter how far out of line she appeared, she still had to be taken seriously.

In *Everybody's Autobiography* some of the details of the experiment in question are given:

Sidis was interested in studying sub-conscious reactions but being a Russian he nat-urally expected us to do things and we did not do them. He would have a table cov-ered with a cloth and one of us sat in front of it and then when he pulled off the cover there was a pistol underneath it, I remember I naturally did nothing after all why should any one do anything when they see a pistol uncovered and there is no dan-ger of anybody shooting. We all of us were somewhat discouraging to all of us.[64]

Instead of acting automatically or, as one might say, emotionally and starting at the sight of a gun, Stein acted with equanimity. She quite reasonably
refused to delude herself and forget the context of the experiment. She was
not in the Wild West or a Dostoevsky novel but in the Harvard Psychological
Laboratory.

The unconscious might be, in Emily Dickinson's pointed phrase, "a
Loaded Gun," but in certain contexts its potential for good or ill, destruction
or defense, makes no difference; or rather, the fact that this makes no difference makes all the difference.[65] Sidis, like Solomons, tried to ignore the laboratory context of their experiments. Stein distinguished herself from them
by her self-consciousness, her awareness of what she liked to call the "training" that went into the work, which, for example, enabled her to recognize
that a gun in a laboratory no longer functioned as a gun: that it was as good
as painted and perhaps even less effective than a painting might be.
Moreover, a refusal to attend to something, such as the actions of one's writing hand, required a great deal of concentrated attention. Stein may well
have only just begun to appreciate this in the early experiments, but by 1932,
after thirty years of writing with precisely that degree of concentrated attention, she knew that any attempt not to credit her claims of rigor and "passionate exactness of meaning" was, however innocently, an attempt on her
life and on her life's work. "Automatic" writing produced in a laboratory
context required the same degree of attention that one needed to write a
book that, like *Three Lives*, contained long stretches that reworked the broken English of German immigrants as well as the dialect of American
English spoken in the African-American community of Baltimore. Stein's
critics, of course, would still insist that the transcendence of her own habitual, highly educated patterns of speech was merely a matter of inattention
or even ignorance. In her writing through *The Autobiography of Alice B.
Toklas* Stein responded to these accusations with increasingly novel examples of her powers of inattention.

Ultimately dictating the experiments with automatic writing at the
Harvard Laboratory was William James himself, who made the initial proposal to Stein and Solomons that they work with a planchette, the kind of
small, mobile board with a pencil attached that spiritualists used to spell out
messages from the spirit world.[66] "William James added a planchette," Stein
recalled in *Everybody's Autobiography*, "he liked a planchette."[67] More than
that, he liked automatic writing, and when he went "on record" in his 1909
essay, "The Confidences of a 'Psychical Researcher,'" "for the common-

ness" of such phenomena as automatic writing, he explained that

> there is a hazy penumbra in us all where lying and delusion meet, where passion rules beliefs as well as conduct, and where the term "scoundrel" does not clear up everything to the depths as it did for our forefathers. . . . [W]hoever encourages it in himself finds himself personating someone else, either signing what he writes by a fictitious name or spelling out, by ouija-board or table-tips, messages from the departed. Our subconscious region seems, as a rule, to be dominated either by a crazy 'will to make-believe,' or by some curious external force impelling us to personation. The first difference between the psychical researcher and the inexpert person is that the former realizes the commonness and typicality of the phenomenon here, while the latter, less informed, thinks it so rare as to be unworthy of attention.[68]

The automatic writing that Stein and Solomons were looking for in their experiments was writing that had nothing behind it, neither the person whose hand wrote it nor the "secondary consciousness" in hysterics that, as James noted in *Principles of Psychology*, was "susceptible of being tapped" and thereby "made to testify to its existence." No such writing was found; there really was no writing without consciousness. The automatic writing that James examined as a psychical researcher was something entirely different: a piece of writing produced by a medium—a human agent—writing for, or in the name of, another person. By definition, there was always someone or something behind the writer, whether "a crazy will to make-believe" or "some curious external force impelling us to personation."

Not so curiously, this *external* force matches up with the "initiative from *within*" to which Stein, in a celebrated notebook jotting written about the same time as James's essay, credited her first literary innovations and which she also characterized as "a propulsion" that she neither "control[led]" nor "create[d]."[69] The middle figure, or medium, in which James and Stein come together is the Emerson who counseled his reader to "place yourself in the middle of the stream of power and wisdom which animates all whom it floats, and you are without effort impelled to truth, to right, and a perfect contentment."[70] Stein in fact recognized in her career a movement from an early excessive concentration on "the inside," which was still operative at the time of the notebook entry, to some relatively middle ground, as in the observation in *The Autobiography of Alice B. Toklas* that during the summer of 1912 Stein's "style gradually changed": "Hitherto she had been interested only in the insides of people, their character and what went on inside them, it was during that summer that she first felt a desire to express the rhythm of the visible world."[71] This shift is elaborated some pages later: the manuscripts written in Spain, among them a substantial part of *Tender Buttons*, "were the beginning, as Gertrude Stein would say, of mixing the outside with the inside. Hitherto she had been concerned with seriousness and the inside of things. In these studies she began to describe the inside as seen from the outside."[72] In so doing, she heeded the call to "place [her]self in the middle." Although Emerson was careful not to delineate the impediments to actually getting into the middle—once there one would "without effort" be "impelled to . . . a perfect contentment"—reading him made these clear enough. So too would the effort, in acts of one's own composition, of seeing how and if the thing could be done. The difficulty lay in convincing oneself that one actually was in the middle or even knew exactly where the middle was. At the same time one could not say just what the difficulty was or if there really was any. "It was a long tormenting process," Stein recalled; "she always was, she always is, tormented by the problem of the external and the internal."

In describing herself and her work thus, Stein added that among contemporary painters it was Picabia who had most deliberately confronted the same insoluble problem of inside and outside. In his case it took the form of the paradox, for a painter, that "the human being essentially is not paintable"—is, in William James's terms, composed of "consciousness" as well as "content."[73] Picabia, she observed,

had conceived and is still struggling with the problem that a line should have the vibration of a musical sound and that this vibration should be the result of conceiving the human form and the human face in so tenuous a fashion that it would induce such vibration in the line forming it. It is his way of achieving the disembodied.

This tenuous "vibrant line" echoes, even vibrates with, the "hazy penumbra" that James perceived "in us all" as he imagined the disembodied speaking through us.[74] Stein, however, immediately distinguished her work, and Picabia's, from any kind of mysticism. She did this by invoking Juan Gris—the only painter, she claimed, whom Picasso felt threatened by and consequently "wished away"—and the passion for exactitude she shared with Gris. Hers was an "intellectual passion," she proposed, whereas in Gris "exactitude had a mystical basis." "As a mystic it was necessary for him to be exact. In Gertrude Stein the necessity was intellectual, a pure passion for exactitude."[75]

This distinction was vital for Stein; clearly William James set less stock by it. He was willing to "go on record" for some kind of "cosmic consciousness" and to identify himself with "psychical research."[76] For Stein the crucial thing about James's position was that he still found it necessary to characterize the "larger psycho-physical world" in terms of writing.[77] He might use as an example automatic writing or, as often happened, have recourse to the figuration of writing in such details as his twice-repeated gesture of "going on record," but it seemed that the only thing he could say with any certainty about the "cosmic consciousness" was that it took the form of written language. In fact whenever James talked of consciousness, large or small, he framed it in similar "graphic" terms. He is often criticized, for example, for the apparent naivete of his introspection, the way he talked about his own motives and feelings.[78] It only appears naive, however, in light of the most schematic Freudian analysis. Instead of dwelling on what was going on inside him, James preferred to locate himself on the interface of inside and outside, in the perceptual and grammatical realm of the stream of consciousness. John Dewey, in his celebrated essay "The Development of American Pragmatism," called attention to the "reinterpretation of introspective psychology" that James accomplished in *The Principles of Psychology*: "James denies that sensations, images and ideas are discrete and . . . replaces them by a continuous stream which he calls 'the stream of consciousness.'"[79] The key element in the reinterpretation was the continuity; and although James certainly used the empiricist terminology Dewey invoked, often and with much greater originality he described such continuity in grammatical terms.

The transitions we feel between thoughts, he insisted, are quite as much states of consciousness as those elements we choose to consider substantive. (Indeed James preferred to speak of thoughts or feelings rather than "states of consciousness," because with his emphasis on action he wanted nouns with cognate verbs.) Such "bare images of logical movement" both designate mental states and call them forth.[80] "There is not a conjunction or a preposition," he noted,

and hardly an adverbial phrase, syntactic form, or inflection of voice, in human speech, that does not express some shading or other of relation which we at some moment actually feel to exist between the larger objects of our thought. . . . We ought to say a feeling of *and*, a feeling of *if*, a feeling of *but*, and a feeling of *by*, quite as readily as we say a feeling of *blue* or a feeling of *cold*. Yet we do not: so inveterate has our habit become of recognizing the existence of substantive parts alone, that language almost refuses to lend itself to any other use.[81]

Indeed, so inveterate is the habit that James, in alerting us to it, falls into it himself: turning conjunctions and prepositions (*and, if, but, by*) into substantive parts of speech ("a feeling of *and*," etc.). It was precisely this habit that Stein set out to break in her writing after 1903, first by simplifying "speech" and then, after *The Making of Americans,* by mixing it up and in the process mixing inside with outside. Her preference for the relational parts of speech—she especially liked, as she said in her 1934 lecture, "Poetry and Grammar," to write "with prepositions and conjunctions and articles and verbs and adverbs but not with nouns and adjectives"—was a literary prejudice that James, framing his psychological hypotheses in grammatical terms, had confirmed her in.[82] "It is this," she insisted in another lecture, "that makes the English language such a vital language that the grammar of it is so simple and that one does make a fuss about it."[83]

James also made the following observation, equally fundamental to Stein, in his discussion of "the stream of thought" in *The Principles of Psychology.* Suppose one were formulating a sentence: if the stream could be frozen at a particular moment and that slice of time examined, one would discover that the thought thus isolated contained both the word being uttered just then and the whole sentence—the whole thought, so to speak—of which the word was a part. Over time the emphasis would change, moving from word to word, and the state of consciousness with it, but the same sentence will have remained present to consciousness all along. This does not mean that the echoes in a moment of consciousness are restricted to the surrounding words, any more than that consciousness has to take the form of sentences. One may feel thunder even if one is deaf; and as one feels it, one will feel a thousand other things as well, including what one might initially describe as a sudden absence of silence. But if one is speaking, that is, expressing in words what one feels and thinks, then the bare minimum present at any moment is the sentence. This is, to be sure, inadequate as anything more than a bare-bones description of the state of mind of either reader or writer. In the first place, the sentence is likely to change in the course of its being written, as the writer's sense of the completed sentence, the sentence to be completed, changes—as it is rewritten. Even so, the writer will have some sentence in mind at any given moment. Nor can one know, as a reader, how a written sentence will end until the full sentence has been registered. Yet if one is to make sense of the part that one has read, one must have some idea of the whole sentence. So there will be a sentence in the reader's mind even if it differs from the sentence on the page. No doubt one may read with a limited sense of the "sense" as well. James discusses in *The Principles of Psychology,* for example, how a "foreboding of the coming grammatical scheme combined with each successive uttered word" may enable "a reader incapable of understanding four ideas in the book he is reading aloud" to "read it with the most delicately modulated expression of intelligence."[84] This is the kind of reading, indeed, that Stein's writing demands—at least on a first reading, whether of *The Making of Americans* or *Tender Buttons*.

Stein may be understood as refining this picture of the sentence swimming in the stream of thought, first in *The Making of Americans* and then, very differently, from 1912 on. She kept the sentence, whatever sentence, in front of her when she was writing and deliberately dulled the echoes, the associations that would naturally come with the sentence and distract one from it. Here, for example, is a paragraph from *The Making of Americans* that illustrates a relatively early, and straightforward, mode of such refinement. Rather than making changes in the sentence by varying the syntax, Stein substitutes one similarly functioning phrase for another:

Some have virtuous feeling in them from having in them concrete and generalised virtue *always* really in them. Some have virtuous feeling in them from having in them concrete and generalised virtue *almost always* really in them. Some have virtuous feeling in them from having in them concrete and generalised virtue *very often* really in them. Some have virtuous feeling in them from having in them concrete and generalised virtue *sometimes* really in them. Some have virtuous feeling in them from having in them concrete and generalised virtue *sometime* really in them.[85]

The sentence on which Stein works her variations has as its basis the near-tautological proposition that persons feel virtuous because they are virtuous. Feeling and being are thus intimately connected, and it is this intimacy that the sentence details. A person's feelings, for instance, do not just happen to exist but are the result of something that causes one to feel a certain way. This is something that exists inside one, not outside. It is, Stein writes, both concrete and generalised. Does she mean, then, that it feels both concrete and generalised? Or has she simply chosen not to determine its exact nature? Perhaps the virtue of this "virtue" is precisely its inexactness? Although the etymon of "virtue" is *vir*—Latin for "man"—here the gender, and much else, is left indeterminate.

In fact Stein is not explaining how particular feelings (in this case, one's feeling of being virtuous) actually get produced. Instead she describes how different people define virtue (namely, their own virtues) differently. What they all share is an emphasis on the virtue's existence "in them," an emphasis that Stein's sentence quite literally repeats: some have virtuous feeling *in them*; they have *in them* concrete and generalised virtue; it is really *in them*. If there is no special emphasis on the phrase in its first appearance, in the second it is notably wrenched out of place and squeezed between the verb and the all-encompassing object. In the end it becomes the focus of the writer's, and the reader's, attention. This is a sentence, and paragraph, designed to convey "the insides of people, their character and what went on inside them" and nothing else. The analysis of character takes the form of an equation with one variable and hinges entirely on the relative frequency, ranging from always to rarely, that different persons feel "concrete and gen-eralised virtue" to be "in them." The result is a "vibration" not unlike that which Stein described Picabia as aiming for, only in reverse. Instead of "con-ceiving the human form and the human face in so tenuous a fashion," she conceives human "insides" with the utter specificity of her substitutions. There is nothing tenuous about the way her vibrating sentence, at once con-crete and generalised, expresses the variety of disembodied "characters" and "insides."

Although James limited his own analysis of thought to the sentence removed from its "original halo of obscure relations," he still insisted that to "feel" the full "idiosyncrasy" of any sentence, the entire "horizon" that "bathe[d]" the sentence would have to be reproduced.[86] Joyce and Proust, for instance, among Stein's contemporaries, might be said to have worked in different ways for this more idiosyncratic, comprehensive horizon, but Stein took the alternative route of removing every association from the sentence and thereby limiting the range of likely echoes. The less "obscured" the sen-tence was, however, the more idiosyncratic it became, as it ceased to resem-ble its less self-enclosed, and more typical, cousin. Stein did not want an idiosyncratic horizon, she wanted idiosyncratic words and sentences and paragraphs: words without echoes that functioned as their own echoes.

For portraying, among other things, the "innumerable consciousnesses of emptiness"—"no one of which," as James observed, "taken in itself has a name but all different from each other"—Stein developed two distinct sets of techniques.[87] Both did away with acquired associations. The first method, partly achieved in "Melanctha"—which depends for many of its effects, however, on local details of the invented speech—and then more thor-oughly in *The Making of Americans* and the first set of portraits of 1910–11, consisted in repeating sentences that resembled one another but that were, in some important respect, not repetitions.[88] Stein would try to catch or por-tray the process of someone working something through; thus in the para-graph above on "virtuous feeling"—which, all the same, is less a portrait than an abstraction of one, as Stein was only just beginning to substitute the portrait of a person for the description—the logical and diminishing movement from sentence to sentence of the adverb of frequency ("always," "almost always," etc.) was both the point and carried the point across.

The opening paragraph of Stein's 1911 portrait of Picasso, to cite another example, consists of four strikingly similar sentences:

One whom some were certainly following was one who was completely charming. One whom some were certainly following was one who was charming. One whom some were following was one who was completely charming. One whom some were following was one who was certainly completely charming.[89]

The only elements in these sentences that vary are the adverbs "certainly" and "completely." The second and third sentences are identical to the first except that in the second "completely" has been removed, and in the third "certainly." Both terms are then joined in a single phrase in the fourth. In effect, the initial sentence is a composite of the two that follow it: *One [whom some were certainly following was one who was charming]* plus *One [whom some were following was one who was completely charming]* equals *One [whom some were certainly following was one who was completely charming]*. The "sum" of one and one is still one.

Moreover, just as the first sentence is broken down analytically into the second and third, the terms "certainly" and "charming" themselves function as composites. "Certainly" can be taken either as an editorial comment on the part of the person making these observations—it is all quite certain to this observer—or as characterizing the actors themselves, who, certain that they are following someone "completely charming," follow with certainty. Similarly, the adjectival use of "charming" is combined with its participial use ("one" is not only a charming individual but is also in the process of charming "some") with the result that the reader—here "following" the writer—may, with some justice, feel "completely" certain that the term is "certainly completely" in play. While holding in each of these sentences to the strict formal constraints of the stripped down "One whom some were following was one who was charming," Stein thus uses the adverbial forms of "completeness" and "certainty" to convey the partiality and uncertainty of any particular assertion one might make. If the combined followers-and-charm of Picasso is the first thing that strikes one about him, it is not enough just to assert the existence of this interesting combination. Like Picasso in his own work, one is furthermore obliged to break one's impression into its elements; and those that Stein has chosen to focus on in this paragraph are the apparent certainty and completeness themselves. Surely Picasso's charm is the principal imponderable here, but his is not the only one as Stein weaves her sentences—each "following" from the others—into a charm of her own.[90]

The vocabulary of these sentences and paragraphs is of the simplest kind, rather like the Basic English of Ogden and Richards: words meant to be used and not weighed, calling minimal attention to themselves and maximally free of personal association.[91] The vocabulary is as unpoetic, as anonymous, as possible. Conversely, the second technique that Stein developed carried association to the point where even the most elementary associations were almost impossible to follow.[92] Beginning in 1912, the words called maximum attention to themselves, and a line such as "Dirty is yellow"—from "A Piece of Coffee" in *Tender Buttons*—might, as late as 1946, be criticized for the dirt it brought with it. "Dirty has an association and is a word that I would not use now. I would not use words that have definite associations."[93] This is not prudish posturing on Stein's part. She rejected all "definite associations," and those of "dirty"—whether in the common expansion of "dirt" to cover all manner of uncleanliness (as in "soiled") as well as in the application of the term to erotic matters—happened to be especially difficult to wash out. That her own phrasing merely inverted, however parodically, the even more obvious "yellow is dirty" only made things worse. In fact, Stein had stopped writing this rigorously almost fifteen years earlier, and here was just trying to sanitize herself for public consumption. But the principle still held.

She objected to association, whether lexical or syntactical, on two counts. First, it distracted from the writing by removing one's attention from the object on the page and breaking one's concentration. Second, and still more damning, it was entirely habitual. One had no control over one's associations—it was hardly possible to stop them—and as such they were a sign of one's dependence on habit. By contrast, the writing in Stein's experiments with Solomons could not have been less automatic. It showed her how one might, with training, overcome the habit-forming habit. Beginning with those first experiments, and through the writing of *The Autobiography of Alice B. Toklas*, she was continually in training: training herself to break with her training.

In her experimental writing Stein continued a line of anti-associationism that extended from Coleridge, in his numerous refutations of David Hartley's psychological doctrine of the association of ideas, through James, who proposed "purely *physiological* principles of association" in place of associations of *ideas*.[94] Instead of Coleridge's "organic imagination,"[95] or James's physiological scheme, or Freud's materialistic one (in which the dynamic machinery of "concealed purposive ideas"[96] supplants the surface mechanism of Hartleian association), Stein produced, in her laboratory, experiments that were designed to test the organic nature of writing itself: as the medium, the middle ground, of body and idea.[97] No doubt much writing is mechanical, little more than a vehicle for communicating information. Yet might not some compositions operate along the lines of "organic mechanisms"—to apply Whitehead's distinction from *Science and the Modern World*—rather than as "mechanisms of matter"?[98] Stein's own example demonstrates that writing can serve as a legitimate medium for scientific experimentation; perhaps literary composition may prove a fit subject for a more truly self-conscious organic science as well.[99]

PART IV

Transformations of the Self

CHAPTER 9

Between Science and Art:
Freud versus Schnitzler, Kafka, and Musil

DAVID JORAVSKY

I

Interpretation of Dreams (1900), the foundational work of psychoanalysis, opens with a defensive claim of medical science, a rebuttal in advance of the charge that analysis of dreams has taken Dr. Freud from neuropathology into imaginative literature. "The author," he insists, "is not a poet but a natural scientist [*nicht Poet sondern Naturforscher*]."[1] That contrast has bedeviled arguments over Freudian psychology ever since. Is it science or art—or both, as Freud claimed, explaining scientifically what artists sometimes understand by intuition? Or is it both in the sense that palm reading and horoscope casting are hybrids of pseudoscience and trashy storytelling? Philosophical questions seem unavoidable: Are the arts as well as the sciences forms of knowledge, diverse approaches to different kinds of truth?[2] And are there standards that can be used to distinguish genuine science from pseudo sciences, authentic art from trash? Historians should not pretend that their discipline avoids such questions, or resolves them. At best we historicize them, that is, illuminate shifting contexts and changing responses, and maybe help that way to map evolving fields of tension among beliefs that can never be reconciled. If that vision implies a philosophical stance, call it modernist, the historians' belated adaptation to a revolution in the arts that challenged all claims of knowledge.

Observe, then, Franz Brentano (1838–1917) changing his mind. His initial expression of the scientific longing in psychology is especially significant, for he published it in 1874, when Freud was a medical student preparing to experience "academic bliss" in Professor Brentano's course at the University of Vienna:

It is not so much abundant and many-sided theses that we need most in the psychic realm as it is unity of conviction [*Einheit in der Überzeugung*]. We must strive to achieve here what mathematics, physics, chemistry, and physiology have already accomplished, some earlier, others later: a nucleus of generally recognized truth to which, through the combined efforts of many forces, new crystals will adhere on all sides. In place of *psychologies* we must seek to create *a psychology*.[3]

Brentano was a profound critic of modern knowledge, and sufficiently *self-critical* to retreat later on from his own dream of a single psychological science unified on the model of physics or physiology. He came to acknowledge a basic difference within knowledge of ourselves between expressive understanding and scientific explanation, between "I understand self-expressive persons" and "I explain objective law-bound processes."[4]

Freud would never consciously retreat from the positivist faith in a single, reductive science of the mind, though his own approach constantly regenerated the split between expressive understanding and reductive explanation. He ignored scientific criticism—it was a mask of "resistance"—and dipped into avowed fiction and other forms of expressive self-knowledge, such as jokes or sculpture, only for intuitions of truths that his science would clarify and explain. Thus, I will argue, Freud created *unwitting* fiction, which illuminated concrete issues in knowledge of ourselves—such as the ethnic and sexual components of personal identity—less effectively than some avowed fictions by modernist masters of Freud's time and place. I will focus my argument on Freud's case studies rather than his abstract theorizing, since clinical reports read like stories, and therefore oblige the reader to ask: How does one form of storytelling differ from the other?

Positivist ideology in the broadest sense was not the major difference; clinical realism (or dogmatism) was. In the exchange of stories between patient and doctor Freud took it for granted that the doctor knows what the patient is fumbling to discover. By that "alienation of the patient within the fantasmatic character of the doctor" Freud created fantasmatic stories that resembled Surrealist fiction.[5] It was his insistence on the privileged factuality of the doctor's imagination that distinguished his case reports from avowed fiction; it was not the underlying assumption that human beings are objects in nature, to be explained as such. Many storytellers shared that assumption—call it naturalism—which is the common metaphysical ground of diverse philosophies, including positivism. The grand positivism of the nineteenth century was not so much overthrown by antagonists as it was strangulated by believers: philosophers failing in their efforts to define "the method of science" that would be the single way to genuine knowledge, and psychological scientists splitting into warring schools while seeking a unified science of mind. Literary artists who shared the naturalistic vision undermined the positivist quest more powerfully, for their fictions reached more minds more deeply, with expressive knowledge of ourselves that revels in tumultuous multiformity, and in irony.

Ideology, as I understand the term, points accusingly to claims of universal knowledge that serve the interests of particular groups, and may serve them poorly. It can be tested and corrected by a rival ideology or by scientific inquiry, but the fictive imagination is the most vivid way to test the ideologies we absorb from our social groups. A made-up story can be a thought experiment, testing our experience of life to see in what sense we may be persons, not just socially conditioned neuroglandular mechanisms. The interaction of storytellers and audiences builds an endlessly changing, multiform collective awareness of who we are — as man or woman, "our" nationality or "theirs," authentic person or mechanical performer of prescribed roles.

Freud claimed to disprove the rule that science gives way to ideology and/or fiction in knowledge of ourselves as persons. He was the self-styled scientist of the mind who has been most widely accepted as such — the only one whose influence on knowledge of ourselves is comparable to the influence of avowed storytellers. But the exception, closely examined, proves the rule. When Freud's stories of personal identity are compared with those of Schnitzler or Kafka or Musil, Freud's are seen to be scientistic fiction, reinforcing faith in the doctor who knows better than the other characters in the stories. During the modernist upheaval in imaginative literature Freud stood as a clinical realist (or dogmatist) on the stage of let's pretend, the professor solemnly lecturing among fictive artists playing characters, among illusionists who call in question every person's authenticity, the author's included.

Arthur Schnitzler (1862–1931) compares interestingly, for he was also an Austro-German-Jewish physician, about the same age as Freud. Both served as assistants in the laboratory of Theodor Meynert, the famous brain scientist, and both studied hypnosis and dream analysis as ways to self-knowledge; Schnitzler even reviewed Freud's translation of Charcot, the French pioneer in neuropsychiatry. Schnitzler was above Freud in social origin — his father was a distinguished physician — and that probably encouraged the daring turn in his self-seeking career, from the supposed certainty of science to the riskier mysteries of art.[6] In public he and Freud expressed mutual respect; in private Schnitzler offered criticism, which Freud characteristically ignored, as he did the much more significant disagreement implicit in Schnitzler's stories.[7]

Robert Musil (1880–1942) — Ph.D. in experimental psychology and philosophy of science and supreme master of modernist fiction as a way to knowledge of ourselves—also repays comparative analysis in his unique joining of science and art. His judgment of Freud—that he was a "pseudo-poet" (*pseudo-Dichter*)—was on target, as I will show. He overlooked the genuine *Dichter* in Freud, the fictive artist in spite of himself who pushed clinical realism to Surrealist extravagance. The art/science nexus was apparent to avowed Surrealists, such as André Breton, who tried to extract from Freud some acknowledgment that his stories embody the fantastical nature of the author as well as the persons he claims to know by inventing stories about them.[8] Kafka had analogous but more vivid and painful objections to Freud, including the issue of the Jewish ethnicity that he shared with Freud, and that he probed more deeply.

I I

Freud's Jewishness—his sense of it, its significance in the development of psychoanalysis—has provoked many studies of dazzling diversity in their interpretations. Discord is essential to this issue. Jewishness has long provoked multiple viewpoints, both among Jews and in their relation to others, and it was never more wildly disputed than in Freud's lifetime, especially in his native land, which encouraged Jewish assimilation to German identity as Freud began his career, and turned to murderous exclusion as he ended it. This chapter is in debt to previous scholars both for the factual record they have dug out and for the discordant views on Jewish identity that they express. Their great diversity on the essence of Jewishness supports Musil's fictive image of national character as the "color and shape" of the hollow space at the core of our imagined selves, or Benedict Anderson's historical analysis of nationalism as the political creation of "imagined communities."[9]

The *problem* was by no means imaginary. Conflicting beliefs about national identity inflamed murderous passion precisely in the imperialist era that generated both psychoanalysis and modernist art, and passions were particularly inflamed in the Austrian Empire, which produced Hitler along with Freud—and also the Austro-German-Jewish ideologist who worked out the Marxist vision of a multinational federation to replace the polyglot monarchy governed by a German minority. (That was Otto Bauer, who happened to be the brother of "Dora," one of Freud's most famous patients.)[10] Ideologies of peaceful equality among nations were overwhelmed by exaltation of dying for "us" while killing "them" as the ultimate proof of who "we" are. In that mobilization of millions for the mass murder and mass suicide

of "the Great War" (1914–18), racist scientists and artists reinforced nationalistic ideologies, including a new kind of anti-Semitism: politically organized
hatred of "the Jew" as the enemy within "our" nation, the masked alien who
lives among "us" and pretends to be as "we" are, whether French, German,
or Russian.[11]

Freud's views on these poisoned issues were not the same in public as in
private, and they changed over time. His publications, while offering deep
analyses of personality, mostly ignored ethnic identity, tacitly reinforcing the
sense that it hardly mattered. Private comments to his disciples, who were
mostly Jewish, sometimes indicated a contrary belief, that Jewish and gentile minds are inherently different. In 1908, for example, he asked Karl
Abraham to be forbearing with Jung, since

you are closer to my intellectual constitution because of racial kinship, while he as
a Christian and a pastor's son finds his way to me only against great inner resistance.
I nearly said that it was only by his appearance on the scene that psychoanalysis
escaped the danger of becoming a Jewish national affair.[12]

The case study of the Wolfman (1918) also showed a mild infection by the
racist epidemic of the era. This Russian patient was closer to "the psychic
life of primitive races" than "we" Germans.[13] But the quoted phrase is from
a private letter; the published case report only implies that the Wolfman is a
typical Russian primitive.

In the case study of himself that is central to *Interpretation of Dreams*
Freud reports on his own Jewishness, which made him seem an exceptionally bold scientist. His treatise on wit (1905) reinforced that reputation by
analyzing some Jewish jokes. But the Jewish distinctiveness that he put on
display in those early works was largely the pride of a thoroughly assimilated
German rebuffing the insults of anti-Semites. That public stance changed
as Freud passed eighty and the Nazi takeover drove him into exile. Then he
published "an historical novel," as he originally called *Moses and Monotheism* (1938). It is actually less a novel than a fantasy on the innate moral
superiority of the Jewish people within the gentile nations, soothing the out-
rage of a German rejected by his own nation, as Peter Gay remarks.[14] The
book took up the basic assumption of "race science"—distinctive national
characters are transmitted genetically through centuries—and reversed the
emotional thrust: Jewish "we" are superior to gentile "them" in the restraint
of instinct, the repression that fosters civilized progress. If racist ideology
were extinct, I would attempt a sympathetic appreciation of Freud's wild
imagination getting even with the anti-Semites by turning their ideology

against them. But space is short and racism is still virulent, so I will draw the veil on *Moses and Monotheism*.[15]

In his greatest work, *Interpretation of Dreams*, Freud put himself on display as a German scientist of Jewish descent, calmly superior to the Jew haters who tried to obstruct a career of epochal discovery. Freud portrayed his father as a proper father for a great scientist—a cultivated German who resisted Jew hatred, but meekly, retrieving his hat and going his silent way when a bully knocked it off—rather than as shady businessman with a Jewish accent and an intense interest in the Hebrew Bible, as Jakob Freud was in all likelihood. The implicit formula for German Jewish identity—a stereotype that came down to Freud from Moses Mendelssohn and G. E. Lessing—is hardly one of the startling innovations that made *Interpretation of Dreams* a landmark book. Nor is the portrait of the author as an ambitious professional—another formulaic type, as Alexander Welsh has shown.[16] Nor is the picture of the author as a sexual being, trapped in the frustrations of the superior man who renounces instinct to work at *Kultur*, stoically enduring the withering away of sexual pleasure within marriage. Those were all conventional formulas of middle-class ideology, mingling self-satisfaction and self-pity as middle-class ideology still does, with somewhat different formulas—thanks in considerable part to Freud. (He helped to legitimate the "pleasure principle" within disciplined labor for *Kultur*, and for status, and for money.) What was startling was to find confession of any kind in a scientific treatise, a violation of the impersonal voice of objective discovery.

Freud was not the first to offer a scientific treatise on dreams and purport to bring them within the explanatory framework of modern medicine. He cites predecessors, however grudgingly and one-sidedly, and Ellenberger has carefully excavated their actual achievements.[17] They had all unavoidably relied on subjective reports of self-observation. A dream can be known in no other way than the report of the person who experiences it, or the storyteller who performs variations on the process.[18] The person who reports a dream makes the fictive leap twice, within the dream itself and again in the waking account of it, each time shaping subjective experience to express a sense of self and others in reciprocal construction of ourselves. Ellenberger credits Freud with a synthesis of dream studies, but he uses synthesis in a loose sense; he does not show that Freud actually squared the circle of reductive science and expressive art.

Freud's predecessors in the scientific analysis of dreams had tried to do that by chopping dream reports into discrete bits, presenting each bit as characteristic of common human experience, not just of one particular life experience. Freud did that too, but he also insisted that such chopping up requires reintegration into the particular life history of the dreaming individual, using symbolist interpretation to do so, offering indeed pyrotechnical displays of fantastical symbolist interpretation. He moved quite obviously into fictive art, while denying that he was doing so. His preface insists that "the author is not a poet but a natural scientist [*nicht Poet sondern Naturforscher*]," incapable of invention, though modesty forces him to make some "omissions and substitutions."[19] Such an art, which must deny its name, is the ultimate mask through which the author presents himself. He is not only a calmly self-assured German Jew, a professional who has risen above the petty concerns of careerist ambition, and an authentic person, which is to say, a stoically repressed male, self-sacrificing creator of *Kultur*; he is the ultimate of such authentic persons, the scientist who strips away fantasies of the expressive self to expose the creature within as an object determined by natural processes.

Thomas Mann saw here the self-mocking psychology of Schopenhauer and Nietzsche: our cerebral understanding is observer and agent of the visceral will that governs us. Mann neglected to observe the repression of self-mockery that inheres in Freud's clinical realism (or dogmatism).[20] The doctor's claim to know the psyche as the patient does not turn aside Nietzsche's challenge to the doctor's self as well as the patient's: can you conceive of yourself as an authentic person, as author of the roles that biological and social processes oblige you to perform? Serious fictive artists have thrust that question on audiences for centuries, but never with such vivid reminders of unavoidable pretense, as in the artistic revolution that we call modernism. Freud stands in the midst of the revolution insisting that he stands apart, not inventing self-knowledge but discovering it, as medical scientists discover glands and hormones, their functions, disorders, and cures. His supreme fiction is the elimination of fiction, as he takes off his own masks to show the knower of objective truth.

The ethnic mask is the most obviously a stereotype and therefore the easiest to pull away some more, more than Freud's modesty permitted. He lifts the edge when he tells his dream of "Myops," provoked by a play he had seen, *The New Ghetto*. He withholds the author's name—Theodor Herzl— and ignores the turmoil that followed, when Herzl turned to Zionist segregation, away from the integrationist ideology that the play still clings to. Freud notes that his dreaming mind was absorbed in "the Jewish problem," but he grows evasive as he tells what the problem meant to him: "Concern for the future of the children, whom one cannot give a fatherland; concern to raise them in such a way that they could become unbounded, free spirits [*die Sorge, sie so zu erziehen, dass sie freizügig werden können*]."[21]

After that vague gesture toward ideological strife that he prefers to ignore, Freud moves to intensive analysis of the nonsense words in his dream. He traces one to Hebrew—with the help of a linguist, he specifies, for Freud presented himself in public as completely ignorant of the religious language, though his father had recently given him the Hebrew-German family Bible with a long, flowery inscription in Hebrew. His dream analysis moves to "the use of that [Hebrew] word in the jargon," and the analyst does not pause to ask how a bit of Yiddish came into the dream of a cultivated German, or to wonder why he always calls it jargon, never Yiddish. In telling another dream Freud reports a joke that came to him in his sleep concerning a Jew in Paris without a knowledge of French who must ask his way to the Rue de Richelieu. Freud refrains from telling the joke, and Grinstein has dug out the reason why. The punch line is in Yiddish—not a single word but a whole sentence, too idiomatic to translate, with self-mockery as the comic barb.[22]

Sander Gilman has shown that Freud knew much more Yiddish than he allowed in public. In his letters to Fliess Yiddish expressions became frequent only after close intimacy had been established.[23] Freud's mother and father probably embarrassed Sigmund by *mauscheln*, that is, speaking like Moishe or Mausche, a German nickname for the archetypical Jew. To say that Freud escaped that problem by training himself to speak "pure German" is to evade, as he did, the painful question that Schnitzler and Kafka confronted. Within the urge to overcome *mauscheln* is there not some confession of shame in Jewish identity? Their response resembles the discovery of "second sight" in *The Souls of Black Folk* (1903), by W. E. B. Du Bois. "Second sight," he explained, is "no true self-consciousness, but . . . double-consciousness, this sense of always looking at one's self through the eyes of others, of measuring one's soul by the tape of a world that looks on in amused contempt and pity."[24] That is the thorniest part of self-knowledge within a low caste, and Freud evaded it while making a bold show of self-analysis, of discovering taboo wishes and attendant anxieties within the author's dreams.

Further evasion appears in *Jokes and Their Relation to the Unconscious* (1905). Freud includes some Jewish jokes, even a few with bits of Yiddish, bringing on stage a type of Jew different from his civilized German self, a type he calls "Galician." He dresses absurdly and speaks the comic jargon; he has bits of food in his dirty beard; he does not bathe. When the Galician near a bathhouse is asked if he has taken a bath, he replies, "Is one missing?" The comic punch, Freud explains, is the unconscious confession of habitual dirtiness—an explanation that is as comically obtuse as the joke is clever.[25] Imagine a learned analyst of jokes in our own time and place—a New York airport, let's say—pondering the wisecrack of a cabdriver with a dark face and a foreign accent. To the question, "Do you know where the Hilton is?" the cabbie replies, "Is it missing? Have they moved it?" Imagine the analyst attributing the comic effect to the cabbie's unconscious confession of confusion about English usage and the urban map. Doctor, we would say, analyze your own unwitting confession: of anxiety concerning the identity called in question by immigrants, by aliens doing imitations of the native self.

Freud's time and place gave powerful cause for such anxiety among cultivated German Jews. Approximately eight million of the "Galician" type were in motion, from east to west, from lower to higher status, with Vienna as a major center in the whirl of migration and social climbing.[26] The observer who looks on from a less explosive moment in a less confused culture should not be harsh with Freud's determined superficiality and evasiveness on ethnic or national identity. Nevertheless, however gently, one must note that evasive, superficial quality in contrast to the deep probing of Schnitzler, of Kafka, and of Musil.

Freud assumes that the comedy of Yiddish speech needs no more analysis than its breaking through repression, for example, in a cultivated woman giving birth. Her doctor sits idly waiting while she shouts her pain in French and German, and leaps to her side only when she shrieks at last "*Oi weh!*"[27] That is a comparatively feeble sample of jokes that mock the pretensions of Jews who rise in the gentile world. Funnier versions, which Freud did not use, expose anxieties closer to his condition. An example is the one about the Jewish mother on the beach, shouting, "Help! Help! My son the doctor is drowning!" Or the one about the Jewish doctor and his Mrs. telling Grandma to stay out of the parlor when company comes because she doesn't speak right (*sie mauschelt*). When the parlor is full of genteel guests, Grandma puts her head through the doorway and shouts, "*Leck mich am Arsch! Gut gesugt?*" (Kiss my ass! [in German] Did I say it right? [in Yiddish]). Such jokes, told by Jews to Jews, express their contradictory sense of identity in a time and place of rapid assimilation, a time when social climbers tried to resemble the hostile or sneering alien others—the upper class gentiles—who stood above.[28] (Let us seek painful precision in using the term "self-hatred." Let us avoid the pretension of easy self-assurance resting on an unexamined claim to know which form of Jewish identity deserves self-respect.)

Freud offers one joke that touches the sore but stops short of probing it. A Galician Jew, sprawled untidily in the compartment of a train, straightens up when a properly dressed man enters and sits down. The newcomer makes a remark that reveals the Jew within his gentile appearance. The Galician exclaims "A zoy!" (the Yiddish equivalent of "Ach so!") and slumps down again, his feet on the seat facing him. Freud explains the comedy as usual — a tiny thing has revealed a big thing — and does not ask what that big thing is.[29] Schnitzler used the same joke to ask the pointed question, Why does Jewish identity deprive a person of the respect owed to a gentile?

I I I

Schnitzler posed this question in Der Weg ins Freie (The Road to the Open) (1908), which may be the first novel in a gentile language to push examination of Jewish identity beyond such ideological stereotypes as one finds in Freud's Interpretation of Dreams — or in Conrad's Nostromo (1904), or Zola's Money (1891), or Chekhov's Ivanov (1889). The list could be greatly extended, and all the Jewish characters on it would fit within pat formulas.[30] Schnitzler's innovation was to go beyond the literary stereotypes and offer a realistic variety of Austro-German Jews, ranging from an empty-headed dandy who apes the German Catholic aristocracy at one extreme to a pair of politicized intellectuals at the other. The latter are a young brother and sister who vigorously affirm opposed versions of Jewishness, she as a Marxist preaching confederation of nationalities within a socialist state, he as a Zionist seeking to transcend the shame of a pariah caste by separation from gentiles. Brother and sister admire each other for lofty devotion to principle, and so does the author, though he is skeptical of both their solutions to the Jewish problem.

The novelist's greatest sympathy is for the types in between the extremes, especially for a young writer who represents the author's self. He tells the "A zoy!" joke to a friend, a gentile intellectual, and is nettled by the man's appreciative laugh. Gentile amusement at disrespect among Jews is not funny. Schnitzler's mouthpiece gives a long lecture on the subject, expressing along the way his exasperation at the Zionist solution: he feels at home in Austria, sometimes. Gentile hostility tells him he is a stranger in a hostile land, and that challenges his consciousness of self and others, of home and away, thus making him "even more at home than any of the self-styled natives [*sogenannten Eingeborenen*]" can be. The sense of homelessness is transcended (*aufgehoben*) by consciousness of the condition.[31] Novalis, the great German Romantic, echoes in that confession of discontent with the ideology of assimilation. Freud's colleague Josef Breuer expressed the ideology untroubled by soul searching in an open letter to a Zionist organization: he was glad to be of the "Stirpe Judaeus, Natione Germanus" (Jewish line, German nation), grateful to his father for abandoning Yiddish and assimilating to the superior culture of upper-class Germans.[32]

Schnitzler's fictive self shares that ideology but undermines it by dwelling on the tension it conceals: gentile scorn, internalized among Jews as disrespect for each other. "Envy, hatred, sometimes even admiration, in the end even love can exist between [Jews]; respect never."[33] The novel as a whole vivifies the discord inherent in Jewish identity by its diversity of Jewish types and viewpoints, all presented with some degree of sympathy—even for the empty-headed dandy who imitates the Catholic aristocracy. When his father shames him by deliberate use of Yiddish in mixed company, the reader smiles appreciatively; but then father slaps son's face in public for lifting his hat while passing a cathedral, and the storyteller's art makes the reader share the shame, and the pity.

It would be accurate but unfair to note that Schnitzler's Jews are a very incomplete sampling; the religious believer is entirely absent, and the "Galician" type flits by as a joke, as a few Yiddish words that briefly disturb the genteel drawing room of the arriviste minority. It would also be accurate but unfair to note that Schnitzler limited his analysis to the Jewish element among Germans, all of the comfortable classes, while taking for granted the German element of the gentiles; *their* national identity is not questioned. Novelists create out of their own experience of life. But such efforts to be fair to Schnitzler do finally bring one to see why he is persistently treated as a minor light of modernist fiction. His art probes deeply within his own experience, but he stops short of the point at which writers such as Kafka and Musil give a shock of recognition, of discovering themselves, to readers of any nationality. A qualification: readers of the world united by modernist fiction are a "high culture" minority, accused of sickness or degeneracy in Germany, of elitism in the U.S.—of sin against the culture of "the people" in any nation.

Schnitzler held back from the saddest laugh at Jewish identity, the joke that recalls Novalis's aphorism on philosophy teaching one to feel homesick everywhere in the universe. A Jew moving to a distant land provokes a fellow Jew to exclaim, "O, that is far away!" and responds, "Far from where?"

That's the whole joke: *Weit von wo?*[34] The sense of being forever on the move, of changing from one type of alienated being to another, achieves fearfully comic clarity in the fiction of Franz Kafka. The specific issue of Jewish identity appears only rarely in his fiction, though it is insistently present in the author's diaries and correspondence, most famously in the "Letter to Father." The most succinct summary of his views is in a letter of 1921 to Max Brod. *Mauscheln,* Kafka tells his Jewish friend, is inescapable and not entirely despicable. Standard German, a language of state and official culture, threatens to extinguish creative fire, which can be revived "when excessively lively Jewish hands rummage through the embers." The metaphor expresses some ethnic pride, but Kafka instantly takes it back, with analysis that combines history and psychology to fearful effect.

Emancipation of the Jews brought on "the frightful inner predicament of these generations of Jews eagerly taking up the German language and literature." Between fathers and sons conflict emerged, and it is *not* Oedipal:

> In this case psychoanalysis appeals to me less than the realization that this father complex, which is mental nourishment to many, concerns not the innocent father but the father's Jewishness [*Judentum*]. To get away from Jewishness, mostly with the father's fuzzy approval—that fuzziness [*Unklarheit*] was the revolting element—to get away, that's what most who began to write German wanted. They wanted it, but with their rear legs they stuck to the Jewishness of the father and with their forelegs they found no new ground. Despair over that was their inspiration.[35]

Excessively lively Jewish hands in creative fire have become forelegs seeking ground they cannot find. Nietzsche's famous maxim—"You must become the one that you are"—is turned away from tales of Superman as the emergent authentic person to the story of the white-collar worker, Gregor Samsa. The man who becomes a bug draws readers of any nationality into the Kafkaesque sense of ultimate shame, of failure to justify one's existence according to some universal rule or law.

Kafka's stories disclose that failure through characters as diverse as can be imagined. They show it in the man from "the country" waiting all his life for admission to "the law," and in Joseph K., who goes looking for "the law," with lethal result; in the Chinese historian endlessly waiting for the imperial message that would justify his nation's social project, and in the surveyor who tries to penetrate the castle of authority; in the executioner who seeks the approval of an anthropologist and, failing, condemns himself to execution; in modernistic fables of an ape, a dog, a mouse, some jackals, and a nameless animal hiding in a burrow. All express the manic self-questioning of an Austro-German-Jewish writer pressing "second sight" to a depth that is occasionally visible in Schnitzler, but not in Freud. Such depth begins to appear in Freud when scholars bring gifts of interpretive willfulness to the reading of his texts. Perhaps that is one reason why Freud was far more influential than the avowed storytellers of modernism, why his ideas could spread rapidly from high to middlebrow and even to mass culture. The avowed fictions of modernist writing require readers or theatergoers willing to engage in tragicomic soul-searching, while Freud offers diagnosis, a kind of self-knowledge that *can* be pondered by readers, but can also be dispensed to supplicants in the clinic, putting each in an appropriate case.

The basic difference between clinical diagnosis of personal identity and avowedly fictive inquiry into it has been widely obscured by amiable observation of their common concerns, evinced by Freud's tributes to certain writers, by the nice compliments he exchanged with Schnitzler and the two Zweigs, by the tributes that Thomas Mann and W. H. Auden addressed to Freud.[36] Such evidence, when critically analyzed, reveals latent discord. Substantial tributes by major artists are rare, and they transform Freud's doctrine beyond recognition, as I have indicated in Mann's case. Mere compliments are less rare, but they become empty smiles when set in context. The birthday greetings exchanged by Freud and Schnitzler, for example, omit Schnitzler's persistent objection, in his letters and diary, to the one-sided, doctrinaire view of the unconscious that he found in psychoanalysis.[37] More significant is the implicit orientation of his stories, which challenge readers to question themselves—whether as gentile/Jew, man/woman, or person/thing—in ways that are at odds with the diagnostic dicta of Dr. Freud.

Virginia Woolf put the central issue most simply and clearly in "Freudian Fiction," a brief essay of 1920 that mocked "the new key" to knowledge of ourselves as "a patent key that opens every door. . . . People of flesh and blood, in becoming cases, . . . have ceased to be individuals."[38] When she put a doctor of the mind in a novel (*Mrs. Dalloway*), her mockery grew angry: the clinician emerged as militant ignoramus, bullying a tormented patient, driving him to a suicidal leap out the window as the doctor hammers at the door. To be sure, the novel does not attach the monster psychiatrist to any specific doctrine of mental science. Evidently such distinctions hardly mattered to Virginia Woolf, who had especially harrowing experience of psychiatric medicine.[39] Other kinds of experience moved other writers to varied criticisms of psychoanalysis, as the reader can see in the quotations appended to this chapter. The large point here is the superficiality of nice-Nelly gestures toward a supposed harmony between Freud's science and avowedly fictive approaches to self-knowledge.[40] Discord is far more significant, especially in the case of Robert Musil, who acquired professional expertise in psychological science and worked out his own way of dissecting individuals in fiction.

Musil was a gentile but grew up, as Kafka did, speaking German among Czechs, whose leaders were organizing rejection of an Austro-German identity supposedly inherent in all subjects of Kaiser and König, K.K. for short, whence "Kakania" (Crapland), Musil's name for his native country. The inhabitants, as he perceived them, cherished a sense of self apart from nationality, occupation, or sex—the *Eigenschaften*, or characteristics that define a person in passports, in social rankings, and in conventional minds. But that sense of self as the inward author directing the external actor was a self-deception, Musil insisted, a passive fantasy rather than an active struggle for authentic personhood. Musil in his own life tried out many occupations—army officer, engineer, mathematician, philosopher of science, journalist and editor, civil servant—writing all the while, challenging the fictive imagination to find the autonomous person within the characteristics that define him—or her. His prewar fiction made an especially great effort to imagine the inwardness of women, with an emphasis on sexuality that was both naturalistic and mystical, a physiological drive and a yearning for completion of the self through union with another. (Note again the legacy of Novalis.)

When the Great War showed him another kind of imagined community, constructed by nation-states through mobilization for mass suicide of ourselves and mass murder of the alien others, Musil turned his inquiry to national identity. In essays and in *The Man Without Qualities* (*Eigenschaften*)—an essayistic novel—Musil subverted all sentimental pretense. The ideal "we" of the nation, he argued, conceals the real "we," who have in common only a condition of estrangement from each other, a sense of community generated by "everyone's natural resentment of everyone else's effort to get ahead." The fantasy of national community creates "a false 'we,' . . . a 'we' that does not correspond to reality." That judgment reached beyond the effort to justify a separate Austro-German identity. "'We Germans' is the fiction of a commonality among manual laborers and professors, gangsters and idealists, poets and film directors, a commonality that does not exist. The true 'we' is: We are nothing to each other."[41]

Musil portrays Jewish characters but no Jewish type. The Jews in his fiction are defined as the gentiles are, by the combination of *Eigenschaften*, or characteristics that give each one the outward appearance of a self-expressive person, however empty the internal reality may be. At the peak of the social pyramid Musil imagined Paul Arnheim, drawing in part on his acquaintance with Walther Rathenau, an eminent statesman in the Weimar Republic who was assassinated by right-wing anti-Semites. No such martyrdom wins the reader's sympathy for Arnheim in Kakania. He is a man of great wealth, of philosophical pretensions, of statecraft; he is grandly inauthentic in his manipulation of trendy phrases to drown issues in pretense — a master, as we say nowadays, of public relations. He entrances businessmen, diplomats, artists, and "journalists, who . . . were the first to make a great man of Arnheim by admiring him," without noticing that they have turned upside down the actual relationship between entrancer and entranced, messenger and media.[42] Near the bottom of the pyramid Musil imagined the lady's maid Rachel, who has "angrily forgotten" the "Jewish wisdom" taught to her in childhood, and worships the Kakanian hierarchy above herself, especially as embodied in the high-class gentile mistress whom she delights to bathe and dress. Whether statesman or body servant, gentile or Jew, man or woman, the individual abdicates its self to the collective mentality. As David Luft has shown, that was Musil's version of the intellectual tradition from which Freud drew his concept of the unconscious.[43]

The most intimate dramas of the bedroom are shaped that way. A woman of the Catholic gentry who married a Jewish banker in the liberal era, when it was fashionable to picture the banker as an agent of progress, comes in the time of rising anti-Semitism to see her bedfellow as a racial alien. Their grown-up daughter shares the racial newspeak, and brushes off her Jewish father's exasperation, telling him he doesn't get it: "It's symbolic." What it is symbolic of she does not try to show, but the author does. Dramas of family life express in miniature large forces of social interaction, and vice versa: the evolving social network is a vast summation of the miniature networks of changing relationships. We might speak of complex feedback loops; Musil draws on meteorology and engineering, biology and mathematics, for the compound metaphor that opens his novel. He pictures human beings as ants or bees, as vehicles and pedestrians in urban traffic, as molecules of air massed in cyclonic swirls. At one point he even draws on sanitary engineering, showing individuals moving past the portals of authority with no more understanding of the system that contains and directs them than drops of liquid have of the sewage system through which they flow.[44]

Surrender to the shaping influences of one's milieu, and the passive fantasy of a free agent active within, form the character (*Charakter*) shared by virtually all. At one point in an extended compound metaphor, all parts enlarging and intensifying the sense of hollowness, "national character" appears as the "color and shape" of the empty space within the psyche where a toy town, abandoned, represents the ultimate fantasy of ourselves as authentic persons.[45] The man without qualities (*Eigenschaften*) is the anti-hero of that absurd condition; his struggles against such inauthenticity give the author occasions to satirically represent a cross-section of Austro-German high society comically struggling for substantial identity.[46]

I V

All this on national identity and inauthentic personhood as defining elements of the modern self, you may say, is irrelevant to Freud, who chose a different approach. He sought the self on the gradient between mental sickness and health, not between the need to justify one's existence and the impossibility of doing so—where Kafka toiled, rejecting the Freudian notion that it was sick to question one's identity that way.[47] As for national identity, you may say that Freud's tendency to brush the issue aside is supported, not subverted, by the fictive inquiry of Schnitzler, Kafka, and Musil, who disclose various ironies of self-deceptive hollowness in national definitions of ourselves. And not only in Germanic "Kakania" on the verge of disintegration; in France and Russia the fictive probing of Zola and Chekhov, Proust and Babel, disclosed other versions of such self-deception in beliefs about "the Jew" as an alien limit that defines "our" nationality. Their discoveries of insubstantial fantasy in the "imagined communities" of nationhood may be said to support Freud's tendency to dismiss the problem.[48] But a poisoned implication lies within that defense of Freud. It is very like a common accusation, of escapism.

By shrinking knowledge of ourselves to little triangles of id/ego/superego he was escaping confrontation with the most powerful vectors that shape us, such as nationality, class, political system, cultural tradition, and stage or type of socioeconomic development. Musil's version of this widespread criticism—in the satirical essay "Oedipus Threatened" (1936)—pictures the Freudian believer as a person in retreat from the frightful complexities of the world at large, seeking refuge in a secluded room where one can shrink all troubles down to intimate recollections of childhood, of longing for comfort in mother's lap. The Oedipal dream of mother's lap, Musil argues, is now endangered, for the notion of womanhood that supports it is dissolving, as women take off the capacious skirts of old, showing their bodies, asserting themselves.

In short, changing social relations mocked Freud's views on sexual identity, but that is a large topic for a different essay. His views on national identity suffered ruder shocks, which prompted him to change his public stance on the subject. In 1930, writing a preface for a Hebrew translation of *Totem and Taboo*, he returned to the problem of Jewish identity within the German nation, which he had casually resolved in *Interpretation of Dreams*. Again he used authorial self-analysis, but this time to confess the problem unsolved. Estranged from "the religion of his forefathers and from the nationalist ideals of his people [*Volk*], the author nevertheless senses his character as Jewish [*seine Eigenart als jüdisch empfindet*]," and *that*, the sense of Jewishness, "is probably the essential thing [*Hauptsache*]. Though [the author] could not at present put this essence [*dieses Wesentliche*] in clear words, it will surely be accessible at some later time to scientific understanding [*wissenschaftlicher Einsicht*]."[49] I read that as Freud's confession that he had expressive knowledge of his ethnic identity but could not put it to the test of experimental fiction, or justify it in philosophical reasoning, or account for it in historical analysis, or reduce it to biological explanation. These are my distinctions among types of knowledge, implying a pluralist epistemology. Freud, as usual, lumped all knowledge in the single type that he called science (*Wissenschaft*). *Moses and Monotheism* (1938) was his subsequent claim to have achieved scientific understanding of Jewish identity.

At the beginning of this chapter I noted two fantastical premises of that work—a hereditary opposition of Jewish and non-Jewish mindsets since Moses, and the moral superiority of the Jews—and I refrained from criticism in deference to Freud's understandable urge to turn "race science" against the thugs who preached it. I must nevertheless note one more fantastical premise, for it appears repeatedly in Freud's claims to scientific knowledge of ourselves: the "biogenetic law"—ontogeny recapitulates phylogeny—in a psychoanalytic version.[50] What the analyst discovers in the individual unconscious is a recapitulation of the ancient experience of the race, which is also discernible in the characteristic myths of the race. Therefore the analyst is free to make intuitive leaps from one to another of all three. One might defend such anarchic sport as Surrealist fiction, which can achieve poetic truth by transcending the rules of evidence that hobble the disciplines of history or population genetics or literary analysis. That astonishment is evident in some of his writing on ourselves as sexual beings. But poetic truth can be found in *Moses and Monotheism* only by readers who are intent on claiming Freud for their own view of Jewish identity, as a religious or as a national community.[51] For readers who acknowledge the tensions of opposed views on Jewishness, and on ethnicity in general, the scientistic fantasy of *Moses and Monotheism* is less transcendent fiction than ideological tract, an embarrassing lapse rather than an astonishing achievement. Permit me once again to draw the veil on it—as Salo Baron did on its appearance.[52]

Freud's lifetime ideological tendency, like that of the avowedly fictive writers I have considered, was cosmopolitan rather than nationalist, subversive of belief in "our" superiority to alien "them." To be sure I have slighted evidence of conflicting tendencies expressed in the authors' lives, if not in their major writings. In World War I Freud favored the German cause; Musil served it in the Austrian army; Schnitzler confined his skepticism to private comment; Kafka, the furthest from any nationalism in his fiction, talked occasionally of joining the Zionist move to Palestine. But those sentiments expressed in their private lives are not supported in their enduring works. Such rifts between life and writing are further evidence of the intellectual scandal that nationalism has been. The most powerful political ideology of the past two centuries, molding virtually all lives and demanding many deaths, nationalism is celebrated in no monument of unaging intellect, that is, no literary work comparable to Virgil's *Aeneid* or Shakespeare's *Henry V* in its lasting hold on thoughtful educated minds. On the contrary, literary celebrations of this or that nation at the turn of century have been sinking into oblivion, while modernist works that subvert nationalism have become enduring classics.

In the run-up to World War I European culture was saturated with racist nationalisms. But the relentlessly skeptical, alienated, and ironical tendencies of modernist writers were preparing in high culture the mass disillusionment that would come to multitudes with the experience of total war. Of course there were some modernist masters who used "the Jew" as an emblem of utter loathsomeness, but they were few, and far less indicative of the main trend than, say, Joseph Conrad, who expressed in especially vivid ways the sense of being homeless everywhere in the universe, which tends to undercut national arrogance. That is a major reason why Conrad's *Heart of Darkness* (1899) has won generations of readers beyond the author's life, while Kipling's "The White Man's Burden" (1899) has lost them. They offer contrasting responses to the question, Who, after all, are "we," whose imagined national character is supposed to define the *summum bonum* of all humanity? No modern person can avoid entanglement in that sort of belief, that "our" people merit supreme devotion, not "theirs." It is a painful entanglement in falsehood and self-contradiction, as Conrad's narrator confesses and scholars abundantly demonstrate in their arguments over *Heart of Darkness.*[53] Knowledge of national or ethnic identity is shaped that way, on contested gradations of honor and shame, devotion and hostility. That is a type of knowledge that owes little to natural science, much to the metaphysical ground that modernist fiction shares with natural science.

Appendix

Schnitzler to Theodor Reik, Dec. 31, 1913, commenting on Reik, *Schnitzler als Psycholog* (1913):

Concerning my unconscious—my semiconscious, let us rather say—I still know more than you do, and into the obscurity of the mind there are more roads (I feel this ever more strongly) than psychoanalysts permit themselves to dream of (or to do dream interpretations of). And very often a path leads right through the illuminated inner world, where they—and you—believe much too soon you must bend off into the shadow world.

Über mein Unbewusstes, mein halb Bewusstes wollen wir lieber sagen—weiss ich aber noch immer mehr als Sie, und nach dem Dunkel der Seele gehen mehr Wege, ich fühle es immer stärker, als die Psychanalytiker sich träumen (und traumdeuten) lassen. Und gar oft führt ein Pfad noch mitten durch die erhellte Innerwelt, wo sie— und Sie—allzufrüh ins Schattenreich abbiegen zu müssen glauben.[54]

Schnitzler in 1914 to Henning, who had asked for a reaction to Reik's study of Schnitzler:

I have told Reik in our conversations—no more than two or three so far—that the Freudian methods of interpretation—from however deep a knowledge of human nature they may have emerged in their basic insights—will sometime signify to him not the one and the only saving way, but one among others, one that leads into the mystery of the writer's creativity, but also time and again leads past that into vagueness and error.

Dass ihm später einmal die Freud'schen Deutungsmethoden (aus einer so tiefen Kenntnis der menschlechen Natur in ihren Grundeinfällen sie auch entstanden sein mögen) nicht den einzigen und allein selig machenden Weg, sondern einen unter anderen bedeuten wird, der in das Geheimnis dichterischen Schaffens, zuweilen aber auch daran vorbei in Vagheit oder Irrtum führt.[55]

Kafka to Milena, November 1920:

You say, Milena, that you don't understand it. Try to understand it in that you call it a sickness. It is one of the many manifestations of sickness that psychoanalysis believes it has discovered. I do not call it a sickness and I see in the therapeutic part of psychoanalysis a helpless error. All these alleged sicknesses, sad as they may seem, are matters of faith, roots in some maternal ground for a person in distress. In the same way psychoanalysis also grounds religion on nothing other than alleged "sicknesses" of the individual. To be sure religious community is generally lacking among us; sects are countless, even limited to individual persons, but perhaps it only seems that way to vision imprisoned in present time.

Such roots, however, as take hold of real ground are not an individual exchangeable possession of the person, but are formed in his being and subsequently shape his being (and even his body) in the same direction. This they want to heal?

In my case one can imagine three circles . . . [a Kafkaesque diagram follows, of the inward person, the outer, and the in-between]

Du sagst Milena dass Du es nicht verstehst. Such es zu verstehn, indem Du es Krankheit nennst. Es ist eine der vielen Krankheits-ercheinungen, welche Psychoanalyse aufgedeckt zu haben glaubt. Ich nenne es nicht Krankheit und sehe in dem terapeutischen Teil der Psychoanalyse einen hilflosen Irrtum. Alle diese angeblichen Krankheiten, so traurig sie auch aussehn, sind Glaubenstatsachen, Verankerungen des in Not befindlichen Menschen in irgendwelchem mütterlichen Boden; so findet ja auch die Psychoanalyse als Urgrund der Religionen auch nichts anderes als was ihrer Meinung nach die "Krankheiten" des Einzelnen begründet, allerdings fehlt heute hier bei uns meist die religiöse Gemeinschaft, die Sekten sind zahllos und auf Einzelpersonen beschränkt, aber vielleicht zeigt es sich so nur dem von der Gegenwart befangenen Blick.

Solche Verankerungen aber, die wirklichen Boden fassen, sind doch nicht ein einzelner auswecheselbarer Besitz des Menschen, sondern in seinem Wesen (auch seinen Körper) noch in dieser Richtung weiterbildend. Hier will man heilen?

In meinem Fall kann man sich 3 Kreise denken . . .[56]

Musil in his notebook (1927):

[A childhood memory of watching a woman disembowel a fish leads to an ironic Freudian analysis of his feeling about women, thus to Schopenhauer's bitter view, thus to wonder how love appears to "the woman." He tests all this with his wife, Martha, who says she has nothing against Schopenhauer; his bitter disappointment describes woman's experience of love as well as man's.]

But against psychoanalysis M. showed herself to be very biased. She maintained that psychoanalysis is an ornate fabrication of men [*eine von Männern ausge-*

schmückte Erfindung]. Few women have actively participated in it; most only in the helpless role [*willenlosen*] of the sick. She cannot abide this arsenal of scissors and dreamed-up men with angry red heads. [*Sie kann dieses Arsenal von Scheren und geträumten Männern mit zornigen roten Köpfen nicht leiden.*] It would furthermore be not unnatural if these womanly fantasies were exposed as the fantasies of men concerning womanly fantasies, at least they have been screened, filtered, and colored through preponderantly masculine imaginative labor.[57]

Musil in his notebook (1938–39):

Psychologia phantastica: Sum up in this way [Ludwig] Klages, to some extent Freud, Jung . . . [*sic*]. My instinctive hostility: because they are pseudo-writers and deny to creative writing the support of psychology!

Psychologia phantastica: Fasse so Klages, z.T. Freud, Jung . . . [*sic*] zusammen. Meine instinktive Feindschaft: weil sie Pseudo-Dichter sind und der Dichtung die Stütze der Psychologie vorenthalten![58]

Refashioning the Masculine Subject in Early Modernism: Narratives of Self-Dissolution and Self-Construction in Psychoanalysis and Literature, 1900–1914

J O H N   E .   T O E W S

The publication of Otto Weininger's *Geschlecht und Charakter* (*Sex and Character*) in May 1903 evolved within a few months into one of those literary events that bring apparently disparate cultural trends into striking focus, that gather the inchoate anxieties and obsessions of an age (or its literate, self-styled spokespersons) into provocative, synthesizing outline. The book, which went through twenty-five editions in twenty years, quickly became an international best-seller and a reference point for countless diary entries, journal articles, and coffeehouse discussions.[1] The short and unhappy life of its twenty-three-year-old author, who shot himself in melodramatic fashion in October 1903 in the house in which Beethoven had died, added the celebrity of scandal as well as the seductions of a personal tragedy lived out in radical authenticity to the exemplary qualities of this mirror of the age. Reading Weininger's work in the early twenty-first century, however, it is difficult to imagine how such a cartoonishly hyperbolic, pretentiously philosophical, maniacally simplifying book, throbbing with uncontrolled misogynist and anti-Semitic feelings, could become the focus of intense, absorptive concern for a broad and sophisticated audience of artists, writers, and scholars. This audience included the Austrian modernists Arnold Schoenberg, Adolf Loos, Karl Kraus, Ludwig Wittgenstein, Oskar Kokoschka, Sigmund Freud, Georg Trakl, Franz Kafka, Heimito von Doderer, Hermann Broch, and Robert Musil, as well as modernists outside Austria and Germany such as August Strindberg, D. H. Lawrence, and the Italian Futurists.[2] Wonder at the Weininger phenomenon spurs historical questions and invites us to reexamine the connections between the three issues that were welded together in his work's distorting and simplifying mirror: the production of masculine identity out of universal bisexuality; the definition of the boundaries of community or "home"[3] through the projection of psychic division onto the relations between social and cultural groups; and the problematic resolution of the intractable polarities of historical existence in aesthetic or philosophical transcendence.

The most obvious and dominating of these three dimensions in Weininger's text was his conceptualization of sexual/gender polarization. *Sex and Character* was organized around the principled assertion that the difference between masculine and feminine natures did not arise as a generalization from observed attributes of male and female individuals but constituted a polarity of ideal-typical modes of being (or "characters") emerging from a duality of biological, "vital" substances unevenly distributed across the whole spectrum of plant, animal, and human life. "Living beings cannot be described bluntly as one sex or the other," Weininger wrote. "The real world from the point of view of sex may be regarded as wavering or oscillating [*schwanken*] between two points. No empirical individual being actually exists at either point, but somewhere between the two."[4] What began in the first part of the book as a scientific theory of biological bisexuality in which the relative ratios of "M" (masculinity) and "W" (femininity) in any individual could be quantified in mathematical terms was transformed in the second and major part of Weininger's study into a speculative, theoretical ("philosophical") construction of a dynamic dualism of essences. "Masculinity" designated the pole of conscious subjective agency, rational control, ethical individuality, freedom, and spiritual transcendence (all epitomized as "being"), and "femininity" designated the pole of unconscious objective passivity, sexual determinism, amorality, and material de-individualized immanence (summarized as nonbeing or "nothing").

The logical rigor of this polarization (essentially a pseudoscientific stylization of conventional sexual stereotypes) was combined with an ethical puritanism in which the feminine operated as that which needed to be expunged in order for the self to attain the essential, "human" ideal of pure masculinity. Conceptual femininity did not refer to actual women, Weininger insisted, but was a projection of the negative other constructed by the masculine within men as they struggled to overcome the effeminacy of sexuality within themselves. "Woman" existed only as long as "man's" guilt remained unexpiated, his sexuality unconquered.[5] Weininger denied that his theory was directed against actual existing women; the average bisexual woman was also presented with the existential possibility and moral task of vanquishing her femininity and attaining the ideal of pure masculinity. But his "scientific" theory of the relative bisexual ratios in men and women made his text appear like an attack on women in the contemporary battle of the sexes rather than a universalizable theory of ethical transcendence. The text moves with breathtaking ease from the analysis of abstract types to the critique of existing individuals and groups.[6] Masculine identity within any particular individual, though supported by quantitative ratios of biological substance, emerged as primarily a human construct, an ethical and cultural achievement. Femininity was also a construct, but always and only in a negative sense; it was not a true identity, not a goal of human achievement or a potential product of a process of self-determination, but "something that can be transcended [*aufgehoben*], which ought to be transcended."[7] Masculinity was also contingent, but only in the sense that its fulfillment was marked by its disappearance into the universal essence of humanity.

Sex and Character combined this radical polarization of masculine and feminine with a racial/cultural theory built on a parallel polarization of Aryan and Jewish "types." Jewishness in Weininger's theory was the collective form of "femininity" as it operated in the history of Western culture. The historical goal of constructing a community of autonomous, rational, self-legislating subjects (the Kantian kingdom of ends) was tied to the attainment of Aryan masculinity and the repudiation of Jewishness. Jewishness, as femininity's historical/cultural form, was also not identical with a particular biological population or nation, but presented as the ideal-type of a "psychological constitution, which is a possibility for all humankind but which has found its most grandiose actualization in historical Judaism."[8] Anti-Semitism as a cultural and political movement was thus grounded on a psychological displacement of the struggle against the Jewishness in everyone onto a struggle against a specific group of individuals whose relative quantity of Jewishness was particularly high; it emerged as an expression of the general human struggle to attain the goal of autonomous moral selfhood. To achieve the emancipated human identity of autonomous individuality was to repudiate the woman and the Jew in oneself. The true home for man was, by definition, an Aryan fraternity in which femininity and Jewishness had been repudiated and expunged. The sexual, moral, and political dimensions of this quest for autonomy were difficult to disentangle: Jewishness "was saturated with femininity."[9]

To achieve pure masculinity, to progress in the task of overcoming mere existence and attaining a genuinely human essence, to be a self-sufficient and autonomous human being—these goals were approached in the historical, human activities of art and philosophy. In both art and philosophy, at least as produced by the "genius"—the human exemplar who approached most closely the translucent autonomous self-consciousness of the purely masculine—attention was focused on the transcendent, on the timeless forms from which all existence in time derived its meaning. In Weininger's universe the realm of high culture was a product of higher beings who incarnated the highest in everyone, who educated their fellows in the moral task of repudiating their sensual being (femininity and Jewishness), and who interrupted the causal and functional networks of material/historical existence with epiphanies of timeless spiritual form. Such activities had been corrupted, become "decadent," in those fin-de-siècle artistic and philosophical movements that surrendered to the seductive pull of the sensually contingent. Drawing heavily on artistic heroes like Wagner and Ibsen, Weininger called for a purer and more autonomous art, an art that mirrored, articulated, and thus helped to achieve the redemptive goal of spiritual transcendence, of purified masculinity.

For Weininger the achievement of identity was not tied to the incarnation of meaning in time through narrative coherence, but through the repudiation of time in the achievement of timeless truths. Yet inevitably some of his contemporaries tended to see meaningful connections between Weininger's theories and his suicide. They thus turned his repudiation of existence in time into a story about a failed struggle for meaning in time. It became either a pathological "case" of identity shipwreck, or an exemplary story of a heroic and tragic struggle for masculine and national identity within the apparently intractable contradictions of a fallen world. In this chapter I will analyze the texts of a number of Weininger's Austrian contemporaries who were able to transform the polarities involved in this modernist crisis of identity into stories of the refashioning of masculine identity that were both diagnostic and exemplary, that found a problematic meaning in processes of constructing personal and cultural identity within the contingencies of embodied temporal existence. Weininger was not viewed as a "solution" in these writings (as he was at times in the works of August Strindberg and Karl Kraus) but transformed into a "case" whose conditions of possibility required critical analysis before its materials could be shaped into meaningful narrative form. In texts published by Sigmund Freud (1856–1939), Arthur Schnitzler (1862–1931), and Robert Musil (1880–1942) in the decade before World War I, Weininger's drive to achieve masculine identity and his search for a communal home were not in any way "resolved" through the "discovery" of true masculinity or of a satisfactory homeland. Literary art and systematic reflection on the conditions of experience were mobilized not as instruments for resolution or transcendence but as a means to portray, as the distinguishing core of the modernist identity itself, a conception of the interminable, experimental, contingent, conflicted processes of constructing gendered and communal identities. These exemplars of early Austrian modernism were thus not marked so much by a consciousness of the end of the story or the collapse of the narrative, the absence of meaning in time, as by the reconstruction of narrative coherence and meaning in time in a new "open" and self-reflexive form. Moreover, the construction of narrative meaning was not perceived as an act of transcendence, but placed in the service of a this-worldly, ethical task, the practical, interminable "work" of constructing autonomy.

The Freudian Case History as a Story of Masculine Identity Formation

The emergence and development of psychoanalysis as a distinctive theoretical perspective, therapeutic method, and scientific movement in the first decade of the twentieth century was inextricably entangled in the complex crisis of masculine identity so starkly portrayed in Weininger's book and played out in his life. Such entanglements involved both the psychopathological material that was the "object" of psychoanalytic diagnosis and therapy and the motivating intentions and organizing categories of this theory and practice. The problematic construction of human subjectivity as a construction of either masculine or feminine subjectivity was at the very center of the unconscious psychosexual structures, mechanisms, and conflicts that Freud presented as the discovery of a new continent mapped by psychoanalytic knowledge. The five "classic" Freudian case studies that Freud investigated and prepared for publication in the decade before World War I were, among all of the founding psychoanalytic texts of the early twentieth century, the most revealing of the ways in which the Freudian theories of the dynamic structures of unconscious mental life and convoluted pathways of sexual desire merged in the subjective problematic of constructing masculine and feminine identities. In these cases Freud not only worked out the conditions for the constitution of a workable or livable gendered identity within the psychopathological conflicts of his patients, but wrote out and worked out his own struggle to establish a satisfactory masculine identity as well. An investigation of three issues within these stories seems particularly relevant for a historical reconstruction of the relations between the psychoanalytic science of gender construction and modernist fictions of masculinity in crisis: the connections between biological bisexuality and the cultural construction of individualized gendered identities, the repudiation of femininity in the construction of masculine identity, and the repression of passive homoeroticism or effeminate "homosexual currents" in the production of masculine autonomy.

Freud's explicit encounter with the author and text of *Sex and Character* actually occurred before its publication in 1903 and became the center of a complicated controversy over scientific priority in the discovery of bisexuality, a controversy in which differing conceptions of the meaning of bisexuality played a prominent role.[10] In July 1904, Wilhelm Fliess, the Berlin sexual biologist who had been Freud's closest friend and confidante in the late 1890s, accused Freud of breaking confidence and passing on Fliess's theory of organic bisexuality to a friend of Weininger's (Hermann Swoboda), an indiscretion that resulted in the publication of *Sex and Character*, in which Weininger claimed Fliess's intellectual property as his own. Although Freud acknowledged that he might have provided Weininger with the "key" used to rob Fliess's house, his exchange with Fliess revealed the extent to which Freud differed from both Fliess and Weininger in his understanding of the significance of bisexuality. Freud seemed to think that the general biological theory of a constitutional, organic bisexuality was both widespread in the scientific literature (Fliess's originality was thus reduced to details and implications that others might themselves have been able to deduce from the principle without stealing his ideas) and not particularly relevant for explaining the ways in which the body's energies were lived out in the psychosexual conflicts of gendered identity formation.[11] Already in 1901 Freud had felt insulted by Fliess's insinuation that Freud's psychological analysis of the neurotic articulations of psychosexual conflict constituted subjective projections of Freud's own wishes and thoughts onto evidence that could be explained quite adequately through knowledge of the bisexual nature of vital processes, such as periodic biorhythms.[12] Although Freud began using the concept of bisexuality in his analyses as early as 1896, he persistently and increasingly relegated biological bisexuality to the category of an organic predisposition, a precondition of psychosexual conflict but not in any way a principle that could explain the particularities of that conflict. When Weininger presented Freud with an early version of his text in 1901, in the hope of gaining his support in finding a publisher, Freud criticized the work for the same kind of speculative and dogmatic reductionism he had discerned in Fliess.[13]

A decade later Freud would discern a similar reductionist tendency in

Alfred Adler's claim that an inherent "masculine protest" against the threat of feminization was the key to understanding psychosexual conflict. Any such masculine protest, he insisted, would have to be explained as itself a product of the complex conflictual relations of psychosexual wishing, contextualized within the history of desire.[14] In the claims of Fliess, Weininger, and Adler, Freud detected a simplifying reductionism that threatened to undermine the legitimacy of his own emerging science of unconscious psychic reality. At the core of these claims was a view of identity formation, a story of how humans came to be encultured men and woman, which submerged the historical contingency of the individual life story in the conflictual processes of vital substances or cultural essences. In each case, moreover, the theories had a tendency to become symptomatic, neurotically self-alienating, rather than analytical and reflexive, because they ignored the participation of the theorist in his theory.

Freud's own case histories can be construed as attempts to produce convincing stories of the struggle to construct gendered individual identities that would avoid the reductionism of his rivals. At the same time they were the textual sites on which he established his own identity as the knower of these psychic processes, an identity that was itself entangled in his battle to achieve masculine self-control and autonomy. The first properly psychoanalytic case study—"Fragment of an Analysis of a Case of Hysteria" (commonly known as "Dora")—was written during the first weeks of 1901, at the critical moment of Freud's decisive break with Fliess and his assertion of the autonomy of psychoanalysis, and it displays some of the distinctive components of the Freudian story of gendered identity formation in exemplary form.

In "Dora" the achievement of gendered identity is described not as an expression of biological nature, the fulfillment of a preordained metaphysical essence, or a socially imposed role, but as an "effect" constituted in a network of culturally conditioned relations. Although Freud assumes an organic bisexuality as a starting point, his analysis is focused on the ways in which Dora's conflicts are formed by her unconscious desires for, and identifications with, a multiplicity and overlapping confusion of relevant "others" of both genders. Dora's psychological conflicts relate to her difficulty in conforming to unconsciously assimilated cultural norms of femininity imposed through these desires and identifications, to her hostility to the repudiation of the "masculine" and homoerotic tendencies that prevented her from becoming a "normal" woman.

Freud's attempt to tell the story of Dora's struggle to achieve self-con-

sciousness and control of the unconscious conflicts concerning her gendered identity is entangled in the often inadvertent telling of his own struggle to impose his control (as a masculine, paternal, scientifically disciplined
subject) over her. The case history is a story of Freud's (failed) attempt to
assert his masculine identity by convincing Dora to take upon herself the
construction of a "normative" femininity as a self-conscious ethical task.
"Dora" is not just an account of Dora's illness but also a story of the therapeutic encounter, which is a story as much about Freud as about her.[15]

In writing "Dora" Freud was acutely self-conscious of the problems
involved in constructing a convincing narrative account of the psychological history of an individual subject. He differentiated the psychoanalytic
story, which reconstructs and examines the conditions of narrative coherence in its own telling, with those kinds of stories that simply assume an
unproblematic coherence in the representations of "external" biological or
social realities. Such glib and smooth accounts, unaware of the problematic nature of their own telling, were in fact symptomatic. They displayed a
disavowal of the unconscious psychic conflicts that underlay the construction of coherence. At the same time Freud was intent on distinguishing his
own construction of coherence from the fictions of novelists. The imaginative writer's need to create a coherent story, Freud insisted, involved censor-
ship, simplification, and abstraction. The complicated structural layering of
psychic life and the overdetermination of events within the realm of unconscious relations (the synchronic rather than diachronic relations between
pasts and presents) could be represented only through the analytic hypothetical models of the scientist. In the same way the impersonal, "dry" language of the scientist rather than the concrete language of the storyteller
asserted its superiority in the telling of stories that contained within themselves an analytic perspective on the conditions of their own story making.[16]

The analytic perspective that Freud saw as providing the necessary reflexive distance in constructing stories of identity formation, however, was itself
organized as a kind of metastory of various oedipal relations. By 1909 Freud
had begun to define the aggregate of complexes that came together at the
moment of the infantile enculturation of desire as the "nuclear complex" of
psychosexual development. It was from the perspective of the Oedipus complex that Freud, in 1909, was able to view Weininger's Sex and Character as
a symptomatic work of a "sexually disturbed young philosopher" and "neurotic." Weininger's uncontrolled hostility toward women and Jews, Freud
stated, was a product of his neurotic regression to the unconscious infantile
relations of the castration complex, in which circumcised Jews and penis-

lacking women both gave imaginary shape to the fear of castration. Weininger's text made sense within the story of a little Oedipus who felt threatened with the loss of his very existence if he did not renounce his sexual desires and submit to the "spiritual" authority of the father's law.[17]

In the decade after the publication of "Dora" there was one complex in the constellation of infantile sexual conflicts that seemed to draw Freud's particular attention and to arouse his narrative productivity—the unsuccessful working through of ambivalent relations to the father figure. This "father complex" produced a tendency toward obsessional neuroses, regression to the libidinal stage of anal eroticism, and the assumption of a passive "feminine" or "homosexual" position toward patriarchal authority. Freud's fascination with resolving the puzzles of such cases was a continuation of his attempts to work through his relationship to Fliess, as well as an expression of his desire to understand the unconscious dimensions in his problematic relations to the "sons" who gathered around him in the psychoanalytic movement after 1905. To attain a satisfactory masculine identity as an autonomous, law-abiding son was to work through the homosexual libido involved in the son's relation to the father in ways that did not encourage regression to the anal-sadistic stage and the formation of obsessional neuroses, but mobilized homosexual libido through the sublimated form of intellectual creativity and devotion to the "great common interests of mankind," or at least (within the context of the psychoanalytic movement) devotion to the "cause" of psychoanalysis. As a form of narcissistic love for individuals like oneself, homosexual impulses produced within the oedipal constellation formed the basis for social bonding, both between generations of fathers and sons and between "brothers," that is, they became the starting point for a human community or "mankind" defined as a masculine cultural form.[18]

In 1910 Freud extended his investigation of the "effeminate," emasculating seductions of homosexual libido to the construction of masculine subjectivities outside the therapeutic relations of his consulting room. He widened the scope of his attempts to understand the various experimental lives that could be constructed from a common "nuclear" constellation of psychosexual conflicts structured by the oedipal complex beyond his patients and disciples. In "Leonardo da Vinci and a Memory of His Childhood," Freud produced a speculative reconstruction, a "psychoanalytic novel," of the possible ways in which the working through of homosexual libidinal impulses, formed in the particular identifications and repressions that marked the transformation of the infant into "a civilized human being

[*Kulturmenschen*]," could lead to the self-consciously critical, investigative activities of the scientific researcher or to the sublimated eroticism of the creative artist, or, as in Leonardo's case, to a lifelong oscillation between the two.[19] Freud's Leonardo story was not simply the account of an "obsessional" neurosis or of the "transcendent" power of genius to rise above the common fate, but a reconstructed story of the particular way in which the structures of a common fate could be lived. It was not a model to be emulated or rejected, but a story that could contribute to a self-understanding of the potentialities and limits of living one's life as a masculine subject.

Freud's extended commentary ("Psychoanalytic Notes") on the published autobiography of a mental patient—the "Memoirs of My Nervous Illness" by the German judge Daniel Paul Schreber—would seem to lie at the opposite end of the spectrum of possible masculine identity formations from that portrayed in "Leonardo." But in this case as well Freud thought that his oedipal key had provided a method for unriddling the mystery of a particular life. And as in the case of Leonardo, Freud was drawn to Schreber's text at least in part because it exemplified for him one of the ways he might have lived out his own masculine identity crisis. In letters written on the same day (December 3, 1910) to Carl Gustav Jung and Sándor Ferenczi, Freud noted that as he worked on his interpretation of Schreber's case in the late evening hours, he experienced an almost total identification with his subject. "I am Schreber, nothing but Schreber," he wrote to Ferenczi.[20] Earlier in the year he had described Schreber to Jung as "our dear and ingenious Friend" who "should have been made a professor of psychiatry and director of a mental hospital."[21]

Working through the Schreber case, Freud claimed, revived the whole complex of issues that had come to a head in his break with Fliess. Moreover, his current difficulties with his ambivalent intellectual "sons," most notably the rebellious Alfred Adler and Wilhelm Stekel, but also the apparently "loyal" Ferenczi and Jung, were seen by Freud as repeating the tensions of the Fliess relationship. In psychopathological terms Schreber's illness was a "paranoia," a form of psychosis in which normal psychoanalytic interaction between patient and therapist was impossible due to the patient's unconquerable resistance to free association and transference. Paranoiacs, Freud claimed, only revealed what they wanted to reveal; they remained enclosed within their own private worlds. To reconstruct the story of a paranoiac thus required an empathetic reconstruction of his world. Like a voice from a foreign culture, the voice of the psychotic could only be construed from an understanding of his own language. During the period in which Freud was engaged in unraveling what he saw as the riddle of Schreber's world he also referred to Fliess and Adler as paranoiacs, as individuals who had constructed closed systems of meaning for themselves that were not open to critical analysis or communicative interaction. His own task was to show that he could grasp the conditions of this paranoid stance, that he could write the story of the paranoiac's story in a way that revealed the particular conditions of its construction.

The starting point, the originating "core" (*Kern*), of Schreber's pathological paranoia, Freud claimed, was a "feminine (passive homosexual) wish fantasy" that could be traced to the "familiar" or commonly shared father complex and castration complex of the oedipal constellation.[22] The unconscious infantile wish reenacted in Schreber's story was the wish to be the love object of the revered and feared father, to be the mother to the father. The fulfillment of this wish, however, implied an "unmanning" or emasculation articulated in the threat and fear of castration. What was at stake in the return of the infantile wish and its imagined consequences was the adult male ego's masculine identity. A resurgence and reexperiencing of the conflicting emotions of this infantile complex, Freud noted, was not uncommon among middle-aged men (in their early fifties, like himself), in whom the decline of heterosexual virility that characterized the male version of menopause often produced a resurgence of homosexual libido.[23] In severe cases of unmasterable homosexual impulse this crisis of sexual identity produced a regression to the stage of libidinal development in which the process of ego formation was in its embryonic stages, the stage of childhood narcissism[24] in which the scattered libidinal urges of the autoerotic stage were first integrated into a love of one's own embodied self, before being directed toward external objects, and thus before a recognition of the boundaries that defined the ego in relation to the world. In Freud's story of Schreber's story, therefore, the beginnings of paranoia lay in a response to the threat of the collapse of masculine identity through a virtual dissolution of the bounded ego and a return to the moment prior to the differentiation of the ego and the external world. Schreber's crisis moved from the fantasy of being transformed into a woman to the catastrophic collapse of the distinction between self and world, and a return to the archaic, primal moment of self and world differentiation. The familiar symptomatology of paranoid delusion could be understood from the "inside" (from the "native's point of view," we might say) as a defensive response to this experience of threat and dissolution and as a regression to the self-sufficiency and megalomania of the narcissistic stage. The specific originating cause of paranoid psychopathology was a traumatizing disavowal of the homosexual fantasy-wish of becoming a feminine love object of masculine desire. The defensive measures produced against this unconscious wish, however, were shaped by the particular stage of libidinal and ego development—infantile narcissism— within which they were originally constructed. The delusional world the paranoid created was an alternative to the real world, a self-contained world of imaginary (aesthetic?) objects that could be easily manipulated, and in which the wish for feminization could be artificially or symbolically mastered and thus given coherence and meaning.

As recounted by Freud, Schreber's construction of a delusional solution to the collapse of his masculine identity actually has two distinct elements. At the most obvious "paranoiac" level Schreber transforms the threat from within (the fantasy of becoming a woman) into a threat from without (the paranoid belief that he is the victim of a process of unmanning by external powers). Eventually Schreber finds a satisfactory meaning for this victimization. He transforms his humiliation and hostility into at least partial honor and acceptance by identifying his persecutor and "castrator" as God, by providing a cosmic theological framework and thus higher meaning and purpose for his suffering. However, in extreme psychotic forms of paranoiac delusion, which involve the collapse of the external world and regression to infantile narcissism, a further transformation is accomplished, which recreates the suffering victim as a messianic savior. The transformation into a woman who can only find her identity as the love object of a man is itself transformed into the identification with the mother who, as the primal origin of being, attracts to herself all of the "rays" of divine libido and gives birth to a new race of men and a new world.

For Freud, therefore, the story of Schreber exemplified two interrelated forms of delusional defensive formation against the threat to masculine autonomy: the story of the victim who defines himself as the object of the male ego, and the story of messianic election in which the dissolution of the individual ego becomes the condition for a megalomaniac and apocalyptic fantasy in which a new world and a new self is created out of the collapse into nothing. Both stories for Freud are signs of failure, exemplars of the construction of identities that ignore the real conditions of human finitude and the onerous tasks of achieved autonomy and identity. Demystification of these stories opens up the possibility for a recreation of the struggle for self-mastery and autonomy as an interminable work of self-construction in the context of a disabused knowledge of the limiting conditions of biological and historical fate.

In one sense Freud's Schreber story was a moral tale that allowed him to reconstruct the story of his own identity as *not* paranoid and *not* delusional. By working through and understanding the conditions of this kind of response to the threat of feminization as emasculation, Freud insisted, he had "succeeded where the paranoiac fails." By working through the "homosexual investment" in his relationship to Fliess he had succeeded in utilizing and controlling his femininity for the enhancement of his autonomy, for the "enlargement" of his ego.[25] But in the concluding paragraphs of his retelling of Schreber's story he raised the question, in an ironic but telling fashion, of whether or not his own self-conscious reconstruction of Schreber's narrative of feminization and masculine reconstruction might not itself be as much a "fictional" and delusional construct as Schreber's. Was the explanatory frame of the history of desire into which he had incorporated Schreber's world construction anything more than another delusional system, parallel to Schreber's own, and thus also a parallel defense against his own fears of feminization?

Schreber's "rays of God" which are made up of a condensation of the sun's rays, of nerve fibres and of spermatozoa, are in reality nothing else than a concrete representation and external projection of libidinal cathexes [*Besetzungen*]; and thus lend his delusions a striking similarity with our theory. His belief that the world must come to an end because his ego was attracting all the rays to itself, his anxious concern at a later period, during the process of reconstruction, lest God should sever his ray connection with him—these and many other details of Schreber's delusional formation sound almost like endopsychic perceptions of the processes whose existence I have assumed in these pages as the basis of our explanation of paranoia. I can nevertheless call a friend and a fellow specialist to witness that I had developed my theory of paranoia before I became acquainted with the contents of Schreber's book. It remains for the future to decide whether there is more delusion in my theory than I like to admit, or whether there is more truth in Schreber's delusion than other people are as yet prepared to believe.[26]

Freud thus recognized that Schreber's delusional creation of a private mythology and cosmology, in which gender identity was constructed and provided with meaning by the framing theory of the operation of divine invisible "rays" operating through nerves, sperm, and blood, was itself a kind of inadvertent parody of his own psychoanalytical framing of the process of gender differentiation through the transformations of libido. For a number of years he and Jung exchanged "Schreberisms," phrases derived from the private language Schreber had constructed to describe his delusional cosmos, in their private correspondence. This jargon humorously paralleled their use of the psychoanalytical jargon that had been created to gain a theoretical distance from, a scientific control of, similar processes of gender differentiation and identity construction.

Recent rereadings and commentaries on Freud's reading and retelling of Schreber's story do indicate that in at least two ways Freud's text constituted something like a competing fiction or myth about the processes of masculine identification, rather than a translation of delusions into controlled conceptual structures. In his reading of Schreber Freud chose to omit two elements that played a dominant role in Schreber's account. First, Schreber's "theory" clearly paralleled Weininger's in drawing analogies between his own feminization and his transformation into the "eternal Jew." In order to avoid the accusation (especially at the moment in which he was grooming Jung as his gentile crown prince) that psychoanalytic theory was less a universal science than a representation of the conflicts of a specifically Jewish experience, Freud narrowed his focus exclusively to the masculinity complex in the text. Second, Schreber's self-constructed messianic myth clearly transformed the negative definition of feminization as emasculation (threatening the collapse of masculine "being") into a positive identification with woman as mother and creator of being.[27] The "transformation" into a woman was ultimately interpreted by Schreber as a gain rather than a loss. His "unmanning" was not so much a loss of being as the assumption of a new form of being as the primal creative source of both masculine and feminine beings. Schreber's identification with the "feminine" was thus ambivalent, not just a taking of the passive feminine position vis-à-vis masculine agency, but also a merger with the maternal, originating ground of a world divided by subject/object, passive/active distinctions.

These critical elements in stories of the refashioning of masculine identity were not ignored in the more self-consciously fictional stories of masculine identity formation produced by Freud's Austrian contemporaries, Arthur Schnitzler and Robert Musil. Both Schnitzler and Musil were trained as scientists, specifically scientific psychologists; Schnitzler as a medical doctor and psychiatrist in the Vienna Medical School, Musil as an engineer and physicist in the Machian tradition. Unlike Freud, however, they eventually decided that it was the form of fictional narrative and the metaphoric language of art, rather than the analytical case study and the conceptual language of science, that was best able to portray the kind of self-reflexive narrative of identity construction that Freud described as the distinctive achievement of psychoanalytic science. Inverting the hierarchical distinctions Freud had constructed between art and science in "Dora," they judged the perspective of science as confined to the limiting one-dimensionality of surface phenomena and prone to a conceptual dogmatism (and thus to a recapitulation self-alienating myth) that crudely fixated the fluid dynamics of lived experience. They turned to experimental, aesthetic, fictional construction as the appropriate form for unveiling the multidimensionality of conscious and unconscious mental life, of psychic event and psychic structure, of memory and the present, in stories of self-dissolution and self-formation.

Schnitzler: The Problematic Entanglement of Emancipation and Masculinity in Der Weg ins Freie

Parallels in the generational, ethnic, social, professional, and educational experiences and cultural perspectives of Freud and Schnitzler have often been noted, as have the mutual recognition and admiration that prompted Freud to describe Schnitzler as his double (*Doppelgaenger*), and Schnitzler to remark on the way he found himself attracted by Freud's "total being" (*gesamtes Wesen*) and perceived himself as Freud's "psychological twin brother."[28] This acknowledged closeness, however, was matched by a mutual distancing and a marked attempt to avoid close social contact. Just as Freud separated his own work from the construction of narrative meaning by the fictional story teller in "Dora," so Schnitzler distanced himself from what he saw as the overly deterministic, schematic theorizing in much psychoanalytic writing.[29] Both saw a tendency toward self-deceptive closure and evasion of self-conscious reflectivity in the work of the other. Yet the parallelism in such mutual critique, often directed more vaguely at a category and genre (the psychoanalyst, the "Dichter") than at the person, only seems to make the "closeness" between Freud and Schnitzler more compelling.

Although Schnitzler's literary reputation in the early twentieth century was built on his short stories and dramas, the full-length novel he published in 1908, *Der Weg ins Freie* (*The Road into the Open*), was considered by Schnitzler himself as the culminating work of his literary career up to that moment. In early 1906, two years before the novel's completion, he imagined it as a representative epic of his age that would take its place in the line of great German novels from *Wilhelm Meister* to *Buddenbrooks*.[30] His emotional identification with his characters and his involvement in the depicted situations often became so intense that he experienced great difficulty separating his own existence from his work. Reading parts of the work in progress to his wife, he found himself choking back his tears, and when he was finished he noted not only his pride in accomplishment, but also his yearning to "return" to the novel, as if it were his only satisfactory home in a homeless world.[31] This identification with his subject, as in Freud's case studies, emerged from the attempt to work through and master his own experience. Schnitzler's autobiography and recently published diaries reveal remarkable personal analogies between the central plot of the novel and his own affair with Marie Reinhard in 1895–97.[32] The writing of the novel worked, again like Freud's case studies, as a process of both therapeutic self-understanding and self-construction.

Schnitzler's contemporaries, including close friends and admirers such as Hugo von Hofmannsthal and Georg Brandes, often appeared less impressed than Schnitzler by the alleged exemplary qualities of the novel, tending to interpret the psychological, social, and "philosophical" or theoretical dimensions of the novel as not fully integrated, as constituting separable stories that should have remained separate. Schnitzler, however, insisted that the connection between the three dimensions was precisely the "necessity" that had driven his work. Although *The Road into the Open* may not be the great modern German, Austrian, or even Viennese novel that Schnitzler had hoped it would be, it does provide an insight into the inner connections between becoming a man, finding a home, and being an artist in Schnitzler's particular version of early Viennese modernism.

The theme or problem of fashioning masculine identity is the most obvious and dominant of the centers around which the consciousness and existence of the novel's "hero," the aristocratic gentile composer Baron Georg von Wergenthin, his alter ego, the middle-class Jewish "Dichter" Heinrich Bermann, and their overlapping circles of friends and acquaintances is constructed. Developed as a cyclically arranged series of moments in the narrative of one year of Wergenthin's life, the novel begins shortly after the death of his father and ends shortly after the death of his (illegitimate) son in childbirth. Fatherhood and a version of the "father complex" are clearly at the center of Schnitzler's conception of the narrative of masculine self-making, and the discovery of the path to masculine autonomy (one of the possible meanings of the novel's title). Virtually every male character is first introduced through a description of the father/son relationship. The generational formation of masculine identity, the passing on of the powers and duties of fatherhood, is at issue. Examined through the lens of fatherhood, masculine autonomy is tied to the assumption of responsible freedom, the establishment of a character held in place by obligations and commitments as a "reliable" and "stable" center of order in time and space. Emancipation in this context means on the one hand emancipation from the determinations of unmastered desires, from passive surrender of the will to circumstance and the pull of the object of desire, and on the other hand, emancipation from the cul-de-sac of cynical, isolating egoism, in which self-consciousness of the constructed nature of personal identities leads only to directionless drift, to an inability to act out a program for the creation of any substantial identity.

In the opening scene, as Wergenthin muses about his recently deceased father, a memory drifts into his consciousness. A few months before his father's death he had been involved in a noncommittal, "free," self-indulgent love affair with an "emancipated" American woman (Grace) traveling in Italy. Trying to give aesthetic form to the emotional impressions of this "love," he had composed an adagio, swelling with harmonic richness but ultimately unable to sustain itself for any length due to a lack of systematic structure and clear overarching melodic narrative. His father had noted this failure of order and direction with a telling question posed as Georg's improvisations on the piano drifted toward aimless dissipation: "Where to? Where to?" (*Wohin? Wohin?*).[33] The inability to impose a satisfactory order on his experience, to make a commitment to a specific woman as the stable object shaping his sexual desire, to assume a tradition as his own past and to construct a "program" that would present beginnings and goals, pasts and future in clear narrative outline, the inability to take responsibility for the consequences of his actions and the effect of his self-defined personhood, define Georg's drift in a world where every definition and commitment appears open to constant renegotiation and only the moment and its immediate emotional content has recognizable value. Autonomy of the kind demanded by the father required a self-definition and substantial set of stable commitments that contradicted the open road of anchorless drift that Wergenthin would like to accept as his fate and the open road of infinite possibilities that he would like to avow as his chosen destiny.

In the novel, fathers represent the claims of independence as an achievement of disciplined responsibility, sustained work, and self-defined social obligation. Wergenthin constantly finds himself counseled to take responsibility for the social and moral consequences of his actions, to both affirm his subjective agency and recognize that his autonomy is regulated and affirmed under moral rules and social conventions. A series of fathers and father figures take on the position of enforcing the general law of the father, and thus intrude a voice of conscience and a reminder of transgression and guilt.

Wergenthin's inability to make himself into an adult person, a mature "man" according to the moral ideal of his real and symbolic fathers, is expressed in the vague guilt that always accompanies the recognition of his transgressions (despite all rationalizations about generational differences, historical change, and relative cultural values) and the insistent, repetitious assertiveness of a recent memory trace—the self-indulgent love affair with Grace whose "end" was also marked by the unexplained suicide of a young painter (Labinski) who had been traveling with them in Italy. While the memory of Grace keeps reappearing as an emotional sign of Wergenthin's faithless, self-indulgent, egoistic use of women as provisional objects of momentary desire, Labinski returns like a ghostly conscience revealing the dark underside (of transgression, disavowed guilt, punishment, and death) within his anchorless existence. In a dream near the end of the book, Labinski emerges as the "helmsman" of Georg's ship of life, the figure of death and guilt who steers his rudder. The persistent reemergence of "Grace" and "Labinski" in Wergenthin's memories, fantasies, and dreams also reminds the reader that his current affair is a repetitive acting out of an unmastered past that continues to frame Wergenthin's intrapsychic relations in the present. His "freedom" emerges as a repetitively enacted fate.

The failure of Wergenthin to achieve the kind of masculine identity designated by the personal autonomy and social responsibilities of fatherhood is most dramatically articulated in his relationship to the child whose conception and birth mark the boundaries of the novel's temporal narrative. Wergenthin is unable to commit himself to his offspring, to "remember" his part in its creation, to prepare or even imagine a "home" for its arrival, and its death in childbirth is at least partly recognized as an expression of these failures. The "son," Wergenthin allows himself to muse, refused to enter into a world where it would not be loved and sustained, where it could not hope to find a home.[34] Wergenthin's transgression and failure as a man lies in his unwillingness to work through his dependent sonship and to assume fatherhood, to take responsibility for the future, to define his identity in a way that would provide a moral framework for the reproduction of future generations.

Schnitzler situates the father/son thematic in Wergenthin's self-formation within a spectrum of analogous pairings in which similar tensions are played out in slightly different ways. Wergenthin's alter ego, Heinrich Bermann, suffers most dramatically under the burden of guilt and the consciousness of having betrayed his father's claims on him. Bermann's father is a former liberal lawyer and patriotic nationalist politician who suffered mental and physical collapse under the pressure of the crushing, disillusioning failure of all of his public hopes. His fall into incurable psychosis occurs at the same time as Wergenthin's father's death, and he dies near the end of the novel. Bermann projects his own creative work as a "monument" to his father's dreams and ideals, but he cannot go beyond imagining this monument as a tragicomedy that parodies his father's hopes as empty delusions, and that thus actually repudiates and kills him once again, adding to his sense of guilt. In the more peripheral father/son relationships of the Ehrenbergs, the Staubers, the Rosners, and the Eisslers, the sons range in their responses from violent repudiation to a resigned recognition of their failure to live up to paternal models and paternal claims. But the fathers in Schnitzler's novel are not simple representatives of a former world in which social conventions and roles affirmed secure gender identities and public callings: they already carry the seeds of their son's dilemmas within their own lives and careers. All are marked by disappointments in the public sphere that encourage with-drawal to scientific work, aesthetic enjoyment, domestic relations, or even dreams of exile and new beginnings. The dilemmas of the sons, as the elder Dr. Stauber suggests, are only quantitatively rather than qualitatively distinct from the conflicts that the older generation had experienced. Historical change may have made the tasks of achieving autonomous manhood more difficult, its conflicts more extreme, but it cannot absolve the younger gen-eration of the ethical demand to achieve a responsible freedom within the conditions in which they have been thrown by fate. The crises of sonship and fatherhood with which Wergenthin is surrounded are more extreme than his own, both in their repudiations and in their guilt-ridden anxieties, but they mirror back to him in revealing (though often disavowed) forms the patterns of transgression and guilt in his own consciousness and behavior. Only a few sons (all minor characters)—such as Wergenthin's brother Felician, who tends to assume his adult responsibilities almost as a "natural" role, or the social radical Leo Golowski, who experiments with future iden-tities by simply ignoring a father who has descended into hopeless impo-tence—attain even a semblance of "resolution." But even they are marked by the general tendency toward escape into ideological utopia, travel, or art.

The achievement of masculine identity as an assumption of the role of the father is tied to the disciplining and sublimating of sexual desire in com-plex ways. In Schnitzler's account of Wergenthin's struggle with his mas-culinity, the femininity in relation to which his masculinity jockeys for defi-nition is tied to the image and role of motherhood. Wergenthin's principal feminine other in the novel—his lover, Anna Rosner, who bears his child—

emerges as a potential maternal feminine figure that could mold his desire toward a responsible, paternal masculinity. From the beginning he experiences her not only as an object of sexual pleasure but as the psychosexual guide that might help him attain a secure consciousness of self within a stable sense of "home"; she is a woman who was "better suited than anyone else to counteract his tendency toward frivolousness and carelessness and to spur him on to purposeful and productive activities."[35] It is precisely her much-noted tendency to peaceful self-containment and bourgeois domesticity that first attracts him and then occasionally repels him as a restriction on his freedom of self-expression. Her gentle reproaches act in combination with "paternal" admonitions to impose a feeling of guilt for his failure to take responsibility for his own personal actions and social roles. During a long vacation in Italy during the late months of Anna's pregnancy, Wergenthin visits the site in Florence where he had watched his mother die when he was a young boy. As he tries to recreate the bedside scene in his memory he suddenly realizes to his amazement that the word "mother" no longer means "the long buried woman who had borne him; the word meant that other woman who was not a mother yet, but who would be in a few months . . . the mother of the child of whom he was the father. And now the word suddenly sounded as though it intoned something never heard before, never understood, as if accompanied by mysteriously singing bells in the distant future."[36]

But the image of the mother also operates in a rather different way in Wergenthin's psychosexual life. It functions as an image of transgressive, irresponsible sexuality, of dangerous surrender to unfettered desire. Just weeks before the birth of Anna's child, Wergenthin indulges in a wild, reckless affair with a married woman. This mystery woman also treats him like a mother, resting her hands on his head as he puts his head in her lap, and listening to and accepting his confessions without censure. However, she is also a maternal figure "created for every madness and ecstasy . . . the dark gaze of her eyes, the blue-black stream of her undone hair, the smell of her pale and naked body."[37] Wergenthin's passion also fills him with at least momentary self-confidence and a sense of power fueled by the vague forces of unconscious energies. Yet he returns to Anna and, crying in apparent contrition, lays his head in her lap, an experience that "seemed to him like a vague and sweet dream, as if he lay as a boy at the feet of his mother, and this moment was already a memory, remote and painful, as he was experiencing it."[38]

Wergenthin's struggle to define his masculinity in relation to this ambivalent maternal femininity is not offset by a correspondingly serious encounter with the femininity of emancipated younger, nonmaternal women. His flirtations in these directions all lead to problematic and unsatisfactory relations with persons who are caught in the same complex problems of self-definition that he is experiencing. In its extreme form, the fate of masculinity in relation to this "new" emancipated woman is represented by the tragic relations between Bermann and the unnamed actress who eventually chooses to take her life rather than continue to participate in the battle of power and submission between the sexes. This woman is constantly forced to submit to the identities imposed upon her, to exist only as a projection of Bermann's fear of feminization. Although Schnitzler continually reminds the reader that the women in the novel are themselves historical agents struggling with problems of gender and social identity that parallel those of the male protagonists, the male characters never themselves appropriate this understanding and continue to relate to individual women in terms of their own psychological needs and projections. Like Anna, the "emancipated" young Jewish women—Else Ehrenburg, Sissy Wyner, and Therese Golowski—all find themselves placed in positions in which it seems virtually impossible to avoid eventual resignation to the roles and types constructed for them by men. Neither Wergenthin nor Bermann is able to define his own masculinity in relation to the feminine as anything but an other that must be possessed. Just as Bermann refuses to recognize his lover as a responsible agent in her own right, and not just an affirmation of, or threat to, his own identity, so Wergenthin finds satisfaction with Anna only when he experiences her as a refuge in which he finally finds a home after a long journey, as "the only being who completely belonged to him,"[39] and as a kind of surrogate anchor for his own absent center. Neither Wergenthin nor Berman seems able to perceive the women in his life as individuals caught in the same conflicts as his own, as projects of identity formation that demand both an emancipation from maternal attachments and paternal domination and a free reshaping of the relations between feminine and masculine in their adult identities.

The narrative of masculine self-formation in *The Road into the Open* does not produce any clear resolution for the major characters. At the end of the novel, as Wergenthin abandons Anna to take on a temporary position as a conductor's assistant in a provincial German town, he is right back where he had begun a year earlier. He seeks the illusion of a freedom defined by mobility and lack of commitment and escape from the self-definition and responsibilities of fatherhood. The death of Bermann's lover leaves him as bound to the bitter resentments of being determined in his actions by the identities thrust upon him, and as stymied by his inability to forge relations of trust and intimacy, as he had been at the beginning of the novel. But in the telling of this unresolved "cyclical" story Schnitzler also told a story of its cultural and social contexts, of the conditions that made the ambivalences and apparent failures of his characters understandable.

The social dimension of *The Road into the Open* has often been perceived as disjoined from the "love story" because it seems so completely focused on questions of Jewish identity, a problem that apparently did not directly affect the non-Jewish principals, Georg von Wergenthin and Anna Rosner. Yet it seems clear that Schnitzler situated his story of personal identity adrift within the context of a world of Austrian Jews in a crisis of cultural assimilation, acculturation, and exclusion because he perceived the particular issues of anti-Semitism and Jewish self-identification as exemplary of a larger cultural process. This process determined, even if in less extreme and self-conscious form, the individual lives and the cultural worlds of Wergenthin and Anna as well. Throughout the novel it is clear that the oscillating attraction and repulsion that Wergenthin and Anna experience in their relations to their Jewish friends and acquaintances is indicative of the larger meaning that Schnitzler ascribes to Jewish experience and self-consciousness. The Jewish crisis is both exemplary of a general cultural crisis and an extreme form of that crisis. It can thus serve as an ideal-typical form that clarifies and articulates the determining structures and essential components of the larger cultural world. The particular experience of the dilemmas of Jewish emancipation and cultural identification forces an articulation and thinking through of a general cultural crisis of subjective autonomy and communal identity. In the novel it is the Jews who theorize, politically and philosophically, the meaning of fatherlessness and homelessness, the breakdown of responsible paternal masculinity, the inability to produce oneself objectively in art or society as a solid "essential" identity, and the ambivalence of "freedom" in a world without anchors where all are strangers within their own "homeland."

At the center of this story of the universalization of Jewishness is the friendship between Wergenthin and Bermann. From the beginning Wergenthin is drawn toward Bermann in part because of a curiosity about the alien and exotic, a desire to "peer into a world that until now had remained foreign to him."[40] Similarly, Bermann seems drawn to Wergenthin in part because he views him as somehow immune from the torturous conflicts of his own self-consciousness as a Jew. Attraction is mixed on both sides with distancing and occasional resentment at either the perceived smugness or hypersensitivity of the other. But Wergenthin does have moments in which he also recognizes himself in the other and envisions the tortured souls of Bermann and his other Jewish acquaintances as the cultural site on which "the future of humanity was preparing itself."[41] The elective affinity and disaffinity between Wergenthin and Bermann is given specific objectification in their attempted collaboration on an opera. Wergenthin was to provide the music to Bermann's story of a hero/son who ultimately is shattered in his attempt to take the father's place, to possess the primal object of desire and to inherit the kingdom, because of his inability to work through the guilt embedded in his fate and his unwillingness to construct a life in the context of the death that awaits him. Although Wergenthin and Bermann are both obsessively absorbed with the son's situation, neither can imagine a completion or third act for their story, just as their own mutual sympathies never find a satisfactory resolution in a stable, intimate, and loyal friendship.

The relationship between Wergenthin and Bermann as a relationship between insider and outsider, German and Jew, is mirrored from various perspectives in the personal relationships that surround them. Schnitzler follows up many possible ways in which Jewish experiments in identity formation could work as mirrors for a more universal understanding. Anna Rosner, for example, prior to her affair with Wergenthin finds herself attracted to two Jewish suitors. They appeal to her not only because of their understanding of the problems of constructing a home and a temporal identity (in generational continuity with parents and children) in a world in which such "homes" and "identities" are no longer simply "natural," but also because the choices they make from within this understanding recognize the need to discipline the autonomy of self-choice with social responsibilities. Although completely apolitical herself, she is drawn to men who define freedom as freedom in solidarity with others and take up public careers as political leaders. Although Wergenthin often runs away from the problematic self-consciousness of relations with Bermann and other Jews to the apparently unproblematic home of Anna's love and acceptance, Anna herself finds protection and consolation from Wergenthin's self-indulgent "freedom" in the support of Jews who recognize her unjust fate more readily than he does. In fact there is a sense in which Schnitzler does portray a kind of inner sympathy between women and Jews. Both are engaged in a battle for self-definition within a situation in which they can never escape the identities that have been thrust upon them by dominant masculine and/or Christian-German perspectives. Although both Bermann and Stauber have moments in which they assert their commitment to a Nietzschean ideology of self-sufficient self-making, their brave words seem like a spitting into the wind. And the women eventually end their brief experiments in self-making with resigned submission to conventional feminine identities.

Schnitzler constructs his fictional world in such a way that the gentile and Jewish positions are not presented as binaries, as closure and openness, as rootedness and homelessness, etc., but as distorting and illuminating mirrors of each other. The situation of temporal discontinuity and cultural exile envelops the whole society in which the Jews are situated. Wergenthin himself, although a member of a family in the service nobility whose aristocratic credentials reach back four generations, emerges from a rootless "hotel and wandering life" (*Hotel und Wandersleben*) as a child to a recognition that "he had no intimate relationship to any human being" despite his many acquaintances.[42] His homelessness does not carry the intense feelings of exclusion and involuntary identification experienced by the Jews—he wears his clothes with apparent elegant ease and can "fit in" less self-consciously than Bermann, who is always somewhat embarrassingly overdressed or underdressed. But Schnitzler does suggest that appearing awkward and out of place in public is not a problem confined to Jews, as indicated by the descriptions of Anna's brother's attempt to somehow fit in with the Christian nationalist right. In the dream that Schnitzler uses to portray the conflicts within Wergenthin's psyche, moreover, Wergenthin does appear to himself in the "Jewish" position of being awkwardly underdressed in a formal social gathering. Even among exemplars of a traditional privileged class whose public carriage and sense of self seem most "natural"—like Felician Wergenthin, or the Hungarian noble Demeter Stanzides—there are moments of social unease and cultural alienation that make participation in the Jewish social circles, exile, or a "hotel and wandering life" seem almost "natural" for them as well. As outsiders within, as foreigners in their own country, as experiments in self-construction whose emancipation has left them bereft of all "natural" identities, the Jews articulate the fate of the human. The illusory vision of a Palestinian fatherland parallels the delusions of German nationalists, anti-Semites and socialists, in which the split within the self experienced by all was projected into a division between a homogeneous "us" and an external "them." The problem of defining a "homeland" that would be neither an ancestral fatherland nor an emotionally exclusive motherland, but a space for the development of responsible freedom within the acceptance of realistic social obligation, was common to all, men and women, Germans and Jews.

Art's task for Schnitzler was to provide concrete shape or objectification, and thus ultimately self-conscious appropriation and understanding, of this human condition of identity dissolution and re-creation. Wergenthin the musical composer and Bermann the "Dichter" are artists who articulate two critical dimensions of this task. Wergenthin's art lives from the experience of the moment, expressing the experiential, only partly conscious movement of desire freed from conventional social discipline. His peak experiences emerge from moments of surrender to a primordial "maternal" sensuality in which conventional identities dissolve and he feels himself as pure potentiality. His characteristic compositions express rather than conquer the undisciplined drift of desire. He is most successful in the genres of the romantic song and brief, usually improvised, fantasias or tone poems for piano. Even in these genres, however, he is unable to "finish," to round off his creations as completed compositions with an internal structure. Even his most successful songs, Anna notes, tend to "drift" off at the end.[43] The quintet that represents his goal of accomplishing a fully formed and structured work goes nowhere during the course of the novel and becomes a sign of his failed promise, his incorrigible dilettantism, his inability to sustain the kind of disciplined work that would mark the achievement of an adult identity.

Wergenthin becomes self-confidently buoyant and creative when his unconscious feelings suddenly rise to the surface and find brief musical expression. During such moments Wergenthin feels inspired by a mysterious inner necessity, something "incomprehensible" that he simply needs to allow to "go its own way,"[44] and he dreams of future projects and endless possibilities. When Wergenthin allows his daydreams, memories, and half-understood desires free rein, he feels fully alive and is ready to turn back the persistent echoes of the paternal conscience that demand that he find a clear direction for his work, complete a fully formed composition, and fulfill his youthful potential.

Bermann seems acutely aware of Wergenthin's strengths and weaknesses as an artist. He recognizes with some envy that in his inspired moments Wergenthin can live in an "atmosphere" of aesthetic perception and feeling that does not demand the sense of creative accomplishment that comes from a fully articulated "work." Bermann himself cannot give himself over to his feelings and moods; he is unable to allow himself the sense of uncontrolled drift and surrender to memories, moods, and images in which Wergenthin indulges. Bermann's aesthetic tool is the word, his method incessant analysis. Everything must be articulated in consciousness, brought to full understanding. His own self-confidence comes from the conviction that he is "able to see into the human soul . . . deep inside, in everyone, honest or dishonest, men, women, or children, heathens, Jews, Protestants, even Catholics, nobles, and Germans."[45] The defensive and mistrustful position of the cultural outsider is for Bermann a position of superiority.

But like Wergenthin's surrender to the unconscious, Bermann's confident analytic self-understanding also produces aesthetic failure.[46] While Wergenthin can never find a systematic or teleological structure that will fully articulate his deeper feelings, Bermann finds that his words can never join together into a satisfying and coherent aesthetic whole. His creative conceptions dissolve into sentences, words, and finally isolated "letters on white paper," as if "a death's hand had touched it all."[47] When he tries to imagine a structure emerging from his method of analytical, self-conscious dissection he envisions a wildly spinning carousel moving upward to the top of a tower before plunging into the abyss.[48] Understanding does not produce a new meaning or create satisfactory self-conscious identities, but either dissolves everything or, in resigned irony and cynicism, leaves everything as it is. Even if all the lights on the various stories of the inner life were turned on, and the soul completely illuminated, Bermann laments, the self would remain a "mess," without coherence or continuity.[49]

Ironically it is precisely Bermann's self-conscious, critical, diagnostic, analytical obsessiveness that makes others dismiss his work as that of an outsider who doesn't really understand the actual worlds of the people he is writing about. Bermann himself recognizes that his analysis of half-understood moods, unconscious desires, and secret motives is not therapeutic, and that he therefore cannot really operate as Wergenthin's therapist:

My dear friend, understanding helps nothing. Understanding is a sport like any other. A very noble sport and a very expensive one. One can squander one's whole soul on it and be left a beggar. But understanding has nothing in the slightest to do with our feelings—almost as little as with our actions. It won't save us from sadness, from disgust or from annihilation. It leads to nothing. It's a blind alley, so to speak. Understanding only means an end.[50]

At moments like these, Bermann loses his sense of superiority over Wergenthin and wishes for a "capacity to perceive each experience as new and individual," for the strength to "endure in each moment" as if one stood in a "new world." The impulse to reduce all experience to words, he suggests, is just as cowardly, just as morally blind and defensive, as Wergenthin's refusal to face the full consequential logic of his surrender to the drift of unconscious desire and to assume self-conscious responsibility for his actions. The "diverse unity" of "life" will only appear in its "wondrous" and "true" form if knowledge can be turned back into feeling, the subjective aggression of analytical understanding into a shared consciousness of participation in and with the other.[51]

Although Schnitzler clearly imagines Wergenthin and Bermann as two variations on "modern" art, he does not condemn or promote either. His own art lies precisely in presenting the historical situation of their relation to one another. Wergenthin does not finally achieve self-understanding through his relationship to Bermann. After a brief moment in which he recognizes that the death of his child is a consequence of his moral failure in assuming the responsibilities of freedom, he returns to his persistent self-deceiving belief that his only true freedom lies in breaking all social ties and floating along "freely" on the sea of his moods and desires. Their collaboration on the opera falls apart as Bermann is unable to imagine a resolution of the son's quest for autonomy under the burden of his guilt, and, as Bermann loses the thread of his story, Wergenthin's musical inspirations cease as well. Neither is able to face the reality of the third act in which the "freedom" of self-construction in an anchorless world would be directly confronted with the moral responsibilities of selfhood and social obligation, in which the son would have to face the consequences of his patricidal and incestuous wishes. The revelation of Wergenthin's inner contradictions does not find its articulate shape in a libretto or in a critical diagnostic case study by Bermann. It emerges through the description of a dream that he cannot fully understand but whose keys are presented to the audience of readers by associations to the contradictory structures of the composer's world as created by the author. It is only within Schnitzler's fictional construction of the structure of psychic and social relations represented by the mutual entanglement of Wergenthin and Bermann that the differentiated "types" of the novel are seen as internal to the self and to the culture. Bermann and Wergenthin are not so much alternative models from which to choose as models of the mutual implicated polarities that define the cultural space in which stories of identity formation are lived, understood, and told.

Despite the many biographical parallels that have led critics to tie Schnitzler's own position in the novel to that represented by either Bermann or Wergenthin, Schnitzler did not simply mirror himself in these characters but rather constructed himself in their mutual relationship. He defined his modernism as a form of self-critical creativity in which the struggle to produce a satisfactory identity, to create a coherent narrative and a systematic though provisional "work" from the disjunctions of experience, became the story itself. Like Freud, Schnitzler might well have said that by articulating the conditions of the problem he "succeeded" where his patients (characters) failed. Unlike Wergenthin and Bermann, Schnitzler did complete a systematic work that revealed the consciousness of the modern not as a resolution of the struggle for identity in an essential masculinity, Germanness, Jewishness, or in aesthetic transcendence, but in the recognition of the open-ended processes of interminable identity construction and self-understanding. For Schnitzler the recognition of the other in oneself was the condition of a freedom that did not involve exclusion and repudiation.

But for both Freud and Schnitzler, this critical understanding remains a story of the male and his masculinity, a narrative of the struggle to achieve self-definition that occurs in the force field between the desire for surrender to the mother and the assumption of responsible "fatherhood." From this perspective the construction of femininity as a "free" act of self-creation remains a contradiction in terms. Schnitzler does imagine both women and Jews as engaged in exemplary struggles to construct new and experimental historical identities, rather than discover essential or natural ones. In order to assume the mantle of responsible autonomy, however, they must work their way through the stereotypical, culturally imposed identities of femininity and Jewishness that have been thrust upon them. The struggle to redefine a masculinity that will not so much repudiate as recognize, accept, and master its own femininity thus becomes in a sense the true exemplary "human" story of identity formation and reformation within Schnitzler's world. It is in the story of masculine identity formation that reflective self-understanding can become a generalized cultural critique.

Identity Dissolution, Identity Confusion, and the Processes of Masculine Self-Formation: Robert Musil's Young Toerless

The "confusions" of the teenage protagonist of Robert Musil's novella Confusions of Young Toerless (Verwirrungen des Zoeglings Toerless), published in 1906 and written at about the same time as The Road into the Open, are primarily and most obviously confusions of self-definition or identity. From the "carriage" of a story of adolescent psychosexual awakening, sadomasochistic homosexual perversion, and boarding school politics, Musil tried to provide a survey of the "landscape" that framed the "structuring of psychic relationships" (Gestaltung von seelischen Zusammenhaengen) in his culture. The particular materials Musil chose for this story, which drew heavily on his own traumatic adolescent experiences in an Austrian military academy during the 1890s, he claimed, were simply a "trick" (eine List) that made it easier for him to highlight, isolate, and simplify essential elements of the problem of self-formation.[52] The narrator characterizes the core of the dilemma fueling Toerless's confusions and self-reflections as pertaining to "what is felt to be the character or soul, the outline or timbre [*Klangfarbe*] of a person, that is to say, that something against which thoughts, decisions, and actions appear insignificant, contingent, and interchangeable . . . this ultimate, immovable background."[53]

At the beginning of the novel Musil describes Toerless as having "lost" this sense of a centered self, of subjective agency shaping perceptions and action in a characteristically individual fashion. But the problem is not that Toerless is simply without identity. Rather, he experiences himself as defined by an imposed, impersonal, and increasingly alien oppressive identity, through which his way of being who he is seems determined by forces beyond his control. Even in the sixteen-year-old student, the experience of imposed identity is already fairly complex and has at least three dimensions. There is first of all Toerless's identity as a son determined by the "unthinking, animal-like tenderness" of his parent's doting concern and the comfortable orderliness and refined, elegant manners of the society of middle-class social elites within which the warm nest of the parental home is situated, a society "of people whose lives moved in an orderly way between the office and the family, as though in a transparent and solid structure, a building all of glass and iron."[54] Second, at the boarding school, Toerless has come under the sway of a model of precocious, rebellious teenage masculinity purveyed by some of his classmates and expressed in typical forms of expressive debauchery and aggressive, though secret, hostility to the hypocritical moral formulas of the "masters." Two of the senior class leaders, Beineberg and Reiting, have become Toerless's mentors in the cultivation of this youthful manliness. In the novel's opening scene, a parental departure at the railway station after a brief visit, Toerless's father symbolically places his son under the protective care of these upperclassman, surrendering to them the role of masculine role model, much as he has surrendered Toerless more generally to the guidance of the schoolmasters for socialization into the moral order of society. This more general or universal discipline constructs the third, most pervasive and oppressive of Toerless's borrowed or imposed identities. Returning to the school after his parent's departure, Toerless places his feet in the dusty prints of the boy in front of him with the feeling of inexorable fate, of a "stony compulsion [*steinernen Zwang*] that captured his whole life and compressed it into this movement—step by step—along this one line, along this narrow band drawn out through the dust."[55]

Tensions among these imposed and passively absorbed identities provide the first openings for Toerless's experience of the absence or "loss" of that individualizing soul that might give shape to his personal character. The move from home to school had resulted in a brief but intense bout of homesickness in which feelings of abandonment, grief, and longing—feelings that expanded far beyond any attachment to his parents or his parental home, and that became a treasured object in themselves—emerged as the first revelation of a distinctive and personal inner life. During his first years at school, moreover, Toerless had developed a close attachment to a cultural outsider, a shy and sensitive young prince whose fragile individuality and religious consciousness were so entangled in his historically anachronistic "filigree habitation" of ancient custom and religious faith that they were unable to sustain themselves against the pressures of "the wooden yardstick of rationality" that Toerless applied to them.[56]

Memories of these moments, hinting at inner depths of experience and alternative modes of being a self, reemerge in Toerless's consciousness because of the unsettling powers of his emerging adolescent sexuality.[57] The structure of psychic relations that frame Toerless's existence are unveiled by the dissolving powers of sexual libido. For Toerless, the rough and precocious manliness of his school friends does not provide a satisfactory shaping, control, or disciplining of these vague, undefined feelings. Instead he is overwhelmed, as if he were falling through a trapdoor in the floor that held up the substantial and transparent relations of the everyday world defined by rational consciousness. While his friends display their teenage masculinity with lascivious comments about the peasant girls in the local village and in their puffed up bravado with the local prostitute, Toerless is overcome by fantasies of a shattering, blinding, ego-dissolving sensuality, by "some monstrous sight of which he could not form the slightest notion; something of a terrifying, beast-like sensuality; something that would seize him in its claws and rend him, starting with his eyes."[58] While his friends and student mentors use sexual transgression to prove their masculine identities, and test the limits of their power and the boundaries of their egos against the social conventions and moral rules of the adult world, Toerless is caught in regressive fantasies that lead him back to a primal childhood memory of total abandonment in an impersonal world, to that moment prior to the formation of any of the subject positions eventually imposed upon him in order to situate him within the world. While his peers test and establish the boundaries of their youthful selves in the world, the power of sensual urges and fantasies exposes Toerless to the threatening and exciting experience of a second dimension of existence. By undoing the weak defenses provided by his inherited identities, his libido leads him into a world of seething, boundary-effacing passion, of enigmatic darkness, of horizonless infinity.

Musil describes the collapse of Toerless's passively internalized identities, the dissolution of his ego boundaries and his descent into the world of unconscious desire, in gendered terms. Toerless's sensual passion seems relatively indifferent to the gender of its object, sliding easily from Bozena, the village prostitute, to Basini, a classmate. Both function as objectifications of desire more than objects of desire. What seems important for Toerless is the identification of the object of his lust with visions of degradation, shamelessness, humiliation. What attracts and frightens Toerless is the experience of falling through the trapdoor into the underworld where all the ego boundaries of the official daytime world are dissolved. Musil tends to describe the desire for, and identification with, the object of desire in terms of a passive, masochistic femininity. Toerless's hallucinations of nighttime abandonment to sensuality and absolute loneliness appear to him as both "the temptation of a woman and of something inhuman" and as something that he "experienced as a woman."[59] His visits to the village prostitute are described as an "awful rite of self-sacrifice" (*grausamer Kultus der Selbstaufopferung*).[60] His attraction to Basini develops only after Basini falls into a humiliating, degrading dependency on the sadistic whims of Beineberg and Reiting when he is caught stealing money from a student locker. In both cases Toerless's obsessions with "total humiliation" and shameless self-abandonment are inextricably, but also at first inexplicably, connected to images and memories of his mother. In his meetings with Bozena, Toerless cannot prevent the mental associations with this woman, who for him was a "tangle of all sexual lusts" and an exemplar of complete degradation, from occupying the same space as images of his mother. This unconscious association only increases his sense of the perversity of his actions, of the transgressive dimension in his surrender to his sexual fantasies.[61] In one of the episodes with Basini, the sudden emergence of the mother image is quickly repressed as if such thoughts were a "sacrilege."[62] Yet the holiness, the asexual purity, of mothers cannot be sustained. Toerless's fantasies and re-created memories persist in revealing his own mother as sexual being who has "betrayed" him with her image of refined transparency.

At the same time, Toerless's desire for Basini, as his earlier attraction to the prince, is imagined in terms of an attraction to a kind of prepubescent, feminine sensual beauty. Not only are Basini's facial features described as "effeminate" (*weibisch*), and his "soft, indolent" body movement as possessing a "coquettish agreeableness," but his naked body appears to Toerless as the "chaste slender leanness" of a "young girl," and lacks "virtually any trace of male development."[63] The moment of sensual abandonment to Basini arouses memories of Toerless's own childhood longing to be a girl, a longing that "had tingled all over his body and gone racing around on his skin."[64] For Toerless the feminine is not an image of what he wants to overpower and possess as a masculine subject, but an image of what he desires to be, or at least an image of a repressed and essential part of himself to which he must surrender in order to understand what his own individual character might be. Toerless's passion is described by Musil as "a flight" (eine Flucht) from the feelings and thoughts with which he had been "inoculated" in the everyday world and which "gave him nothing and oppressed him."[65] This "flight" is clearly directed regressively toward the mother, and it involves an identification with the feminine as the image of self-dissolution, of shameless abandonment to the power of unconscious desire, of degradation and humiliation. But Toerless's "love" for the prince and Basini also represents a recognition of the bisexual nature of the "soul" that emerges from the maternal womb. The dissolving of his ego defenses under the pressures of sensual desire brings to the fore the repressed feminine "other" of the "stony compulsion" of imposed masculine identities.

The confusions and contradictions in the psychic life of Toerless become concrete, become "things" in the world, through his homoerotic relationship to Basini. By transferring his enigmatic, incomprehensible feelings onto Basini, Toerless allows his own unconscious desire to emerge as a potential object of analysis and self-knowledge. His "affair" is described as a psychic disorder, a hysterical or even psychotic episode in which internal psychic conflicts are acted out and thus opened to the possibility of conscious understanding. By working through his relation to Basini, Toerless comes to understand the distinction between the reality of Basini as a thing in the world and as a figure of his desire and sexual fantasy. He learns to control his psychic projections and reappropriate them as elements of himself, distinct from the objective realities of the external world.

During this process of seeking therapeutic understanding, Toerless is placed in constant contrast to his two student mentors, Reiting and Beineberg, who are also engaged in turning Basini into an experiment for testing their present and future identities. Although Reiting and Beineberg are "rebels" against the master's rule and trenchant critics of the hypocrisy of conventional values in the adult world, both formulate their conceptions of masculine identity as a refashioning of the public roles of political domination and spiritual control over others. For them Basini represents a weak and contemptible object on which they can practice their method of controlling the irrational for personal power and egoistic gain. Unlike Toerless they do not recognize themselves in Basini; they do not fall "in love" with him, or identify with his humiliation. They use him as a means to assert their own masculine superiority over his feminine weakness. Their experiments in manipulation and torture aim at refurbishing traditional models of masculine autonomy as mastery over the feminine other, either as political domination or as spiritual purification.

Reiting and Beineberg are obsessed with their fathers and forefathers. They define their own identities in terms of a fulfillment of paternal claims and historical destinies, and their identities are described by Musil as essentially "modernizations" of inherited identities. Toerless, in contrast, seems virtually fatherless, even though he has a father. At least his weak and maladaptive father appears to make no claims on his future (other then giving him over to the control of schoolmasters and older peers) and thus allows him relative freedom to engage in the creative task of reformulating the relationship between unconscious desire and individualized character without overpowering historical baggage and guilt. Reiting and Beineberg are thus presented as the primary alternatives of father-oriented masculine identities to Toerless's innovative "confusions." Their strategies for dealing with Basini illuminate the particularity of Toerless's therapeutic refashioning of himself.

Reiting is the school demagogue who enters into the encounter with Basini with preformed political ambitions. Aspiring to be a Napoleon-like military officer and daydreaming "of coups d'état and high politics,"[66] he sees Basini's femininity and humiliating dependency from the standpoint of the manipulative strategies of the ego, as signs of a pathological weakness on which he can build the structures of his own power. Like Freud in his 1914 critique of the ego-oriented heresy of Alfred Adler, Musil interprets this stance as reductive, and, despite its revolutionary political posturings, as ultimately conservative, and perhaps dangerously reactionary.[67] Reiting provides the students who follow his leadership with an escape from their loneliness by creating a group identity formed around the objectification and projection of their inner demons onto the chosen outsider, and an identification of their potent, purified selves with his own person as their leader and father. This strategy not only disavows the reality of the inner psychic conflict, but it also raises the specter of a dangerous diversion and simplifying reduction of psychic confusion into politically organized mass identity and persecutory purification. Musil's Reiting and Freud's Adler disavow the feminine within themselves in their "masculine protest" against feminization. They thus continue to confuse internal and external conflicts, acting out their internal fantasies in relation to others. In Freud's terminology they reject the reality of the unconscious and build a world from the standpoint of the self-deceiving power of the ego and on the denial of "love."

In 1914 Freud paired Carl Gustav Jung's defection from the critical reflexive truth of psychoanalytic investigation with Adler's heresy. Freud considered both equally reductive systematizations of the signs of unconscious mental life into reconfigurations of religious myth and a traditional theological worldview. In Musil's novel Jung's position is played out by Beineberg. Like Freud's Jung, Beineberg approaches the realm that lies beyond the boundaries of rational knowledge with preconceived religious conceptions. From his father he has imbibed a powerful belief in the reality of transcendent spiritual forces infusing and controlling the world of surface phenomena. Toerless is attracted to Beineberg because of their common recognition of the two-dimensional nature of reality, but he ultimately rejects Beineberg's claim that the mysterious irrational powers he perceives are signs of a transcendent world of spiritual forces that must be liberated from their corrupt bodily habitations and mobilized to create a purified new world. Beineberg is in competition with Reiting as a self-styled prophet of a new cultural order and leader of youthful rebellion against the masters. He rejects Toerless's hesitating and unresolved ruminations about the double nature of psychic experience, rationalizes everything into a dogmatic system of supernatural essences, and trains himself for the imminent cultural collapse that will provide the opportunity for his prophetic religious leadership. Like Freud, Musil regarded such therapies of supranatural meaning and spiritual integration as both delusional and conventional, as a recycling of old religious intoxicants in new containers. In both cases as well, this stance leads to an opposition to the politics of identity as an appropriate model for human association. In fact, Freud, Schnitzler, and Musil all reject a type of political mobilization that involves a projection of the internal other onto a social group defined as the external other of the communal self. Basini might be construed as the symbolic "Jew" in the boarding school. Toerless separates himself from Beineberg and Reiting in recognizing Basini as the psychic projection of the other in himself, and thus also in seeing the real Basini as a victim of his peers' lack of self-knowledge and their consequent brutal acting out of their own psychic conflicts.

Both Reiting and Beineberg pursue the fulfillment of their fathers' claims and shore up conventional notions of masculine autonomy as mastery over the feminine other in their rush to resolve identity "confusions" with new therapies of meaning and commitment. By refusing to go along with their leadership, by insisting on thinking through the contradictions of his psychic life, Toerless, Musil suggests, is opening up a more innovative path. As Toerless works his way out of the crisis of self-dissolution with various experiments at self-understanding and self-construction, he does accept the validity of the existing parental order of law and convention, but only as a crude, contingent framework within which he can find working space to concentrate on the complex formation of his own soul (*Seele*) or spirit (*Geist*) as an individual person. Although he can find no rational or empirical grounds for constructing a general theory of "the nature of man," he remains stubbornly convinced that the construction of his identity must proceed from a disabused investigation of the immanent, natural origins of his enigmatic passions and internal confusions. This process of self-construction is guided, first of all, by a principled recognition and acceptance of the irresolvable difference between, on the one hand, the fantasies, dreams, and psychic projections that emerge from the never fully comprehensible life of boundary-dissolving passion and desire, and, on the other hand, acts and objects in the "daylight" world of clear boundaries, definitions and individuated identities connected with each other through rationally comprehensible functional and causal relationships. Both worlds are recognized as "real," and any non-repressive, nonillusory sense of subjective individual identity would have to be based on a consciousness of the fluid and porous boundaries between them. This double vision, however, also produces an ironic and detached stance toward the given identities of the apparently substantial and transparent external world, a knowledge that "it could all be otherwise, that there were fine and easily effaced boundary lines around each human being."[68]

Toerless must experience, accept, and come to understand the reality of his own "femininity" in order to work out and live a realistic, unrepressive, and undogmatic masculine identity. Autonomy based on possession or full mastery is illusory and thus no autonomy at all. Responsibility is not tied to fatherhood, in Schnitzler's sense of accepting the obligations of social interdependence and generational authority, but to the clear, disabused, and critical consciousness of responsibility for the individual self. This self must be constructed within the constant and irresolvable tensions between the powers of irrational desire and the necessities of social life.

In *Young Toerless*, the interminable construction of self-identity is tied to processes of self-narration, to the capacity to tell the story of one's own self-formation, to the ability to imagine one's own identity as an experimental and contingent possibility. Within the novel the attempts to attain clarity about the relationship between conscious rationality and the world of irrational desire and fantasy through philosophical comprehension are rejected as futile. For Toerless, Kant is no help in understanding Basini. But Toerless does reach a point at the end of the novel where he comes close to articulating his experience in words. He does not construct a synthesis that would make sense of his experience in some "total" or final sense, but produces an account that clarifies and makes intelligible, at least to himself, the dynamic structures that governed the sequence of events that produced the particular person he had become, or is in the process of becoming. Toerless's self-clarification occurs as he is confronted with the necessity of explaining his own actions to the schoolmasters. The attempts by the headmaster, chaplain, and mathematics teacher to appropriate his experience within their conventional discourses force Toerless to become more precise about his own particular perspective and the appropriate terms needed to describe it. For a brief moment Toerless is able to articulate what had been so vague and tormenting within him, so that his thoughts emerged like the extreme visible tip of his innermost being, rather than a lifeless system of words, or a wordless feeling.[69] He describes the double quality of his experience and connects it to the unconscious dimensions of his own inner life. He recognizes that the deeper dimensions, the something extra that allowed him to contextualize all of his experiences as simply contingent possibilities playing out against a background of unbounded chaos and infinite extension, emerged from within himself. In the world, "things just happen" (*Alles geschieht*), and "things are just things" (*Die Dinge sind die Dinge*).[70] The meanings we see in things, the words that define the identities of self and other, come from us and are contingent, "could be otherwise." This consciousness has two consequences. It allows him to see the other as simply another thing (either object or subject) in the world. Bozena and his mother, in the concluding scene, lose their terrifying auras as embodiments of his unconscious sexuality. Driving past Bozena's house on the way to the railway station after deciding to leave the boarding school, he perceived it as "utterly insignificant and harmless," and turning toward his mother, who is sitting at his side, he thoughtfully "considered" (*pruefte*) "the "faint scent of perfume that arose from her bodice."[71] At the same time, Toerless's own self has become more like a project than an iron cage of imposed identities. Recognizing the source of his fantasies in the never fully articulated power of his unconscious sensual desire presents the possibility of a future in which his own self will remain an always surprising and never closed story of aesthetic and critical self-fashioning and refashioning.

The narrator of *Young Toerless* participates with his subject in this process of self-fashioning and self-understanding. At the beginning of the novel the narrative voice is intrusive, authoritatively informing the reader of the later significance of particular events in his subject's life, constantly pointing to the ways in which Toerless's confusions will be absorbed into a life understood as fashioning its own self. By the end, the voice of the narrator and that of Toerless are in virtual harmony as Toerless learns to articulate himself in the words of the narrator. Toerless himself is described as developing in later years into an "aesthetically inclined intellectual" who can tell the story recounted in the novel in terms of its exemplary significance as a story of the fashioning of a person who is able to take his own life as an object for critical understanding and aesthetic stylization.[72] In this sense Musil's conception of the construction of self-identity goes a step further than that portrayed in the contemporaneous texts of Freud and Schnitzler. Unlike Dora or Dr. Schreber, Bermann or Wergenthin, Toerless internalizes the narrator's perspective as his own.

In a sense the achievement of masculine identity in Musil's novel, as in Schnitzler's *The Road into the Open* and Freud's early case studies, involves a mastery and disciplined control of femininity. Toerless's confusions arise from the release of his repressed femininity, from his surrender to the passive masochistic attraction of the ego-dissolving, boundary-effacing power of unconscious desire. But Toerless's solution is not to disavow this femininity and project it onto the other, as is the case with Beineberg or Reiting. Instead he learns to accept it. It is the deepest, ultimately never fully comprehensible source of his own subjective power to make and remake his self within the context of existing possibilities in a world in which things "just happen." But it is also one pole of that bipolar self for which a purified masculine or feminine identity could only mean a disavowal of the human project of making one's own self an object of critical examination and aesthetic work. Assuming a homogeneous masculine or feminine identity would entail a submission to the unrecognized and thus unmastered "other" within oneself.

Robert Musil was neither Jewish nor Viennese, and he was at least half a generation younger than Freud and Schnitzler. His participation in the cultural conflicts of prewar Austria and central Europe was certainly affected by the particular cultural perspectives and cultural baggage that he did not fully share with his older contemporaries.[73] Yet *Toerless* does display a focused concentration on a number of dilemmas and themes that are mirrored in and shared by the contemporaneous texts of Schnitzler and Freud, and could be construed as tentatively mapping out a particular dimension of the "mind" of early modernism. All of these texts take the ethical problem of autonomy as their object of diagnosis and experimental investigation, but construe and reformulate it as a problem of the construction of subjective identity rather than the emancipation of a natural or metaphysical essence. The generally recognized disintegration of conventional affirmations of centered, autonomous subjectivity—their unveiling as "illusions"—was interpreted as an opening to that dimension of psychic experience, the unconscious realm of psychosexual desire, that precedes the formation of identities, rather than as a liberation of already preformed identities. As a contingent product emerging from the shaping of undifferentiated or "bisexual" desire, the identity of the person, of "character," "soul," or "subjectivity," was portrayed as inextricably entangled in the processes of gender differentiation. From the standpoint of the individual's experience, gender difference was reimagined as an internal, psychic polarity. The articulation or enactment of masculine or feminine identity thus became a historical and ethical task, a process of self-fashioning within the limitations of natural and historical constraints. The conceptual language of science and its precise analytical distinctions, and the experimentally controlled playing out of particular programs, hypotheses, and "ideal-typical" models, were necessary tools for reconstructing the conditions and consequences of specific empirical determinations of identity within the real world in which the ethical task of self-fashioning was played out. As Musil noted in an interview with Oskar Fontana in 1926, his novels were to be interpreted as "contributions to the intellectual mastery of the world" in which "aesthetic qualities" were subordinate to the direction of the "will."[74] But in Musil, as in Schnitzler and Freud, the ideal of ethical self-mastery, of self-defining subjectivity, despite all attempts to disassociate it from an inherent basis in male or female natures, in biological, metaphysical, or historical determinations of gender, remained bound to an idea of "masculinity," for which "femininity" remained either the enigmatic, preverbal, never fully graspable ground of all differentiated, articulated identities (the maternal ground of being) or the negative "other" of the universal "human" ideals of autonomy, self-mastery, and creative potency.

PART V

Modernism and Anti-Psychologism

T. E. Hulme, Henri Bergson, and the Cultural Politics of Psychologism

J E S S E   M A T Z

Early twentieth-century models of mind influenced British modernist culture largely through the critical activity of T. E. Hulme. Hulme translated, explicated, and publicized the theories of Henri Bergson, Edmund Husserl, G. E. Moore, Gottlob Frege, Georges Sorel, and Wilhelm Worringer, and, as Michael Levenson has shown, Hulme applied those theories to the development of modernism's successive stages. His interpretations of Bergson inspired Ezra Pound's Imagism; his subsequent interest in Husserl and Moore helped to define modernism's classicist phase; and his late interpretations of French right-wing political writers and Worringer's theory of abstraction fed the anti-humanist strain in T. S. Eliot's version of high modernism.[1] He innovated, in Eliot's words, a "new attitude of mind." What Coleridge was to the nineteenth century, some argue, Hulme was to the twentieth—"the pioneer who helped to clear the frontiers of twentieth-century consciousness," the impresario of interdisciplinarity who helped modern theories of mind to transform modernist literature.[2]

Were Hulme simply our century's Coleridge, his career would interest students of the interrelations among psychology, philosophy, and modernist culture. But he is perhaps more important as an opponent to interdisciplinarity. As Hulme moved to each new phase of his theoretical development, he substantially repudiated the prior one, consequently defining each new stage of modernism through rejection of some prior belief. In this serial development, Hulme progressively eliminated psychological perspectives from his inquiries into social and cultural life. Therefore, while his career demonstrates the influence of philosophy and social science on modern art, it more strikingly shows how modernist culture also defined itself *against* contemporary psychology—how it developed through what Martin Jay has called the process of "negative exclusion," in which figures like Hulme implicitly branded psychology (science of mind and behavior) as psycholo-

gism (false reduction of mind to psyche) and thereby denied its compatibility with aesthetic, social, and philosophical theory.[3]

As Jay argues, *anti*-psychologism was a major force in the development of modernism's characteristic belief in art's autonomy. And Hulme gave force to anti-psychologism through his turn against Bergson. Bergson had been Hulme's first and greatest enthusiasm: *Time and Free Will* (1889), Bergson's first book, was for Hulme "a great influence and a great excitement." In his excitement, Hulme wrote a series of Bergsonian essays and articles, translated Bergson's *Introduction to Metaphysics* (1903), and, consequently, helped to make Bergson a popular sensation in England in the years preceding World War I.[4] But by 1912, Hulme had turned from Bergsonism to embrace an opposing position. Bergson, he came to think, mistakenly limited ethical and aesthetic value to human psychical processes. Opposed to that psychologism, and seeking an "objective" alternative, Hulme turned to the anti-psychologistic positions diversely held by Husserl, Moore, and Pierre Lasserre, a leader in the French right-wing group Action Française. Rejecting Bergson, Hulme led modernism's effort to exclude psychology from definitions of culture.

To explain this rejection, then, is to explain the largely unacknowledged conflict between psychology and culture in the years of Hulme's influence on British modernism. Critics have attributed Hulme's shift to the bracing critique of psychologism in Husserl's *Logical Investigations,* and to conversations in which Lasserre proved that Bergson's theories were incompatible with Hulme's Tory politics. I would like to suggest a different sociopolitical cause of Hulme's reaction against psychologism. In his 1911 essay "Bergson Lecturing," Hulme credits another source for his turn against Bergson, telling us that "the whole structure of [his] fixed beliefs, so laboriously constructed, was overturned by a trifle": the unsettling presence, at Bergson's lectures, of crowds of women (155). Upset by proof of Bergson's popularity with female audiences, Hulme reclassifies Bergson's theories. Once, Bergson's theory of "intuition" had helped Hulme define modern poetry; now, "intuition" becomes merely a female psychical talent. It was this transformation, in addition to that wrought by the influence of Husserl and Lasserre, that turned *psychology* into *psychologism* and consequently helped to shape literary modernism.

Hulme's interest in Bergson was part of a larger craze that widely animated European culture at the turn of the century. Writers as diverse as George Bernard Shaw, Marcel Proust, and D. H. Lawrence, as well as plastic artists and a wider public comprised of people less likely to follow theories of mind, made Bergson an international sensation.[5] The century's first pop psychologist (in spite of himself), Bergson provided the public with an enormously useful and appealing theory about the life of the mind. Bergsonian psychology holds that the authentic human mind exists beneath the surface of conventional thought and perception.[6] This psychology, the theory of the "two selves," aims at the liberation of authentic consciousness, thereby offering a model through which people across social and political spectrums could aspire to authentic selfhood. Bergson established this model in *Time and Free Will*, elaborated upon it in *Matter and Memory* (1896), and, in his *Introduction to Metaphysics* (1903), gave the name "intuition" to the process through which people might free their minds. But by the publication of *Creative Evolution* (1911), Bergson's most popular work, a reaction against him set in. So effective was that reaction that Bergsonism, so popular and notorious in its historical moment, is obscure in our own.[7]

Bergson began this mercurial career with an attempt to redefine psychological inquiry. In *Time and Free Will* he speaks against the ruling tendency, represented by theorists including Herbert Spencer and Gustav Fechner, to equate the mind with the physical and associative processes of the brain.[8] Psychology—or, more specifically, what Bergson calls "psychophysics"— had wrongly presumed that states of consciousness were distinct, quantifiable, and extensive. Interpreting consciousness in terms of space, Bergson claims, psychological materialists could not recognize the essentially temporal basis of mental life. Functioning not extensively but *intensively*, the mind is constituted by what Bergson calls "pure duration." Duration is its continuous mode of becoming, an interpenetration of heterogeneous mental states; and it "is the form which the succession of our conscious states assumes when our ego lets itself live."[9] But psychology had failed to discover this true durational basis of mental life because consciousness itself distorts it:

Consciousness, goaded by an insatiable desire to separate, substitutes the symbol for the reality, or perceives the reality only through the symbol. As the self thus refracted, and broken into pieces, is much better adapted to the requirements of social life in general and language in particular, consciousness prefers it, and gradually loses sight of its fundamental self. (128)

Facing practical existence, the mind increases its chances of real survival by developing an orientation toward action in space. In doing so, it develops a "second self" that "obscures the first," causing "our living and concrete self" to become "covered over by an outer crust of clear-cut psychic states" (167).

The true, "first" self is not determined by the material world; it has immediate insight into an essential reality beyond that world, but its insights are blocked by its "secondary" alter ego. For Bergson, the goal of psychology and human endeavor more generally must be "to go back to the real and concrete self and give up its symbolical substitute" (139), to "recover possession of oneself, and get back into pure duration" (232). Psychology, which had erred by defining the mind in terms of its superficial self, could not enable this recovery; Bergson's alternative defines the psychological orientation through which the real self could emerge.

Time and Free Will concludes that "there are finally two different selves, one of which is, as it were, the external projection of the other, its spatial and, so to speak, social representation" (231). This dualistic psychology proved irresistibly useful to many of the countercultural dispositions of Bergson's day, putting into highly assimilable terms the anti-dogmatic, anti-scientific, and anti-Victorian spirit of the moment. And as the theory of the two selves extended into meditations on metaphysics, evolutionary science, and ethics, an ever-widening public found inspiration in Bergson's effort to distinguish the truth of life from the falsifications of conventional intellect. In *Matter and Memory*, Bergson strengthens that distinction by explaining the necessary difference between memory and the perceptual processes that psychologists had mistakenly taken to be memory's basis. He also, however, begins to theorize a therapeutic link between the two selves, a possibility that becomes a focus of *An Introduction to Metaphysics*. The work that began to earn Bergson both significant popularity and significant criticism, *An Introduction to Metaphysics* explains how one might overthrow the control of the superficial self. What can restore consciousness to its natural freedom is the process of "intuition," defined as "the kind of *intellectual sympathy* by which one places oneself within an object in order to coincide with what is unique and consequently inexpressible."[10] Intuition, a kind of self-conscious instinct, conveys immediate experience, circumventing intellect's distortions; it entails "seizing [reality] without any expression, translation, or symbolic representation" (24). With it, Bergson develops a normative program, a means "to invert the habitual direction of the work of thought" (52). To supporters, intuition gave Bergson's philosophy a practical therapeutic dimension and a more emphatically countercultural use; to detractors, it pushed what had been a sound critique of scientific rationalism into the realm of irrationalism, making Bergsonism a questionable, sentimental attack on the basis of intellectual life.[11]

Controversy subsequently characterized the response to Bergson's most popular work, *Creative Evolution* (1911). *Creative Evolution* applies the distinction between the two selves to a critique of conventional perspectives on the way life develops. Human beings have not developed, Bergson argues, according to some mechanical or teleological scheme. Rather, a creative consciousness, a free "élan vital," develops life the way "pure duration" constitutes human consciousness.[12] Popular with the general public, *Creative Evolution* arrived at the moment in which a series of events began to ensure Bergson's exclusion from serious consideration. Bertrand Russell refuted his epistemology, drawing the kinds of boundaries that would also define the course of British analytic philosophy;[13] Pierre Lasserre's *Le Romantisme français* exposed the outdated romanticism in Bergson's dream of human progress; preparations for World War I distracted Europe from hopes of mankind's spiritual development; and, finally, T. E. Hulme, Bergson's great British disciple, rejected the beliefs that he himself had helped to make a modernist creed.

Hulme's interest in Bergson has been a persistent literary-historical problem. Until recently, confusion about the dates of Hulme's essays has made it difficult to see how Bergsonism could fit with Hulme's other, very different ideas. *Speculations*, the posthumous volume published by Herbert Read in 1924, arranges Hulme's writings almost exactly backwards: his latest theoretical position (anti-humanism) precedes the positions that in fact preceded it (his classicism and his interest in Bergson). The result of this confusion had been for many years a sense that Hulme's thought was embarrassingly eclectic and confused, and that it included Bergson only in error.[14] Bergsonism, it seemed, contradicted the spirit of Hulme's classicism, which holds that art and value must exist apart from man's subjective passions — apart from psychical acts like "intuition" and the generally romantic needs Bergson seemed to address. But Bergson's place in Hulme's career had only been obscured by editorial confusion. Recent work by Karen Csengeri and Michael Levenson has "restore[d] some of the lost coherence" to Hulme's writing, and enabled us to see that interest in Bergson preceded the development of Hulme's characteristic views.[15] Hulme discovered Bergson in 1907; he used Bergson to influence the cultural climate that prevailed roughly from 1908 to 1912; and wrote "Romanticism and Classicism," his famous explanation of the claim that "we are in for a classical revival" (59), in late 1911 or early 1912, at the moment in which he turned from Bergson to other, different influences.[16]

Distinguishing these stages in Hulme's intellectual development, Levenson and Csengeri clear ground for new insight into prewar intellectual activity. They make the contours of Anglo-American modernism emerge with unprecedented clarity: what had seemed more or less a consistent set of modernist impulses now appears, insofar as it parallels Hulme's development, a series: Bergson helped Hulme to theorize Imagism (circa 1908); rejecting Bergson encouraged the formalisms of the prewar moment (circa 1912); and further impetus away from romanticism led to anti-humanism (circa 1916) and, many believe, to the troubling affinity with reactionary politics that continues embarrass modernist aesthetics.[17] Because this progression so suggestively proves the significance of cross-disciplinary exchange in this period, it seems crucial to explain the great turning point that comes with the rejection of Bergson. With that rejection, Hulme reorients modernism's position with regard to the relation between art and psyche. Initially, Bergsonism led Hulme to a belief in the artist's unique psychological make-up; after Bergson, Hulme helped modernism to define the artist as someone able to transcend individual personality. To account for this shift is to explain how and why the anti-psychologistic impulse defined high modernism.

Hulme describes his discovery of Bergson in his "Notes on Bergson" (1911–12). Written at the moment of his theoretical shift, these notes briskly and precisely locate the source of Bergson's early appeal. Through Bergson, Hulme writes, he was "released from a nightmare" that he calls "the chess-board" (127). Victorian science and philosophy had explained all life in terms of the "mechanistic view"—the view, as Hulme puts it, that "the motion of every atom of your brain" is "subject to the same laws of motion as those which govern all matter," and that mental processes are therefore "completely mechanical and calculable" (141). Bergson dispelled the nightmare of determinism by making his distinction between the extensive world of matter and the intensive world of the mind, and by distinguishing the mental acts suited to the discovery of these different worlds. Hulme gratefully embraced Bergson's notion that the intellect may see the world as a "vast machine," but "intuition" knows it differently, freeing consciousness from mechanical determination (170–71). Hulme, then, found relief in Bergson's idea of "two different selves at two different levels" (176), and sought to develop it into an aesthetic method. That method, which Hulme called the "theory of intensive manifolds," became a way to distinguish the mind of the artist from the prison of matter that Victorian science had built around it.

More specifically, the theories of the "two selves" and "intensive manifolds" helped Hulme to determine the nature of modernist poetry. In Bergson's view, as Hulme puts it in "Bergson's Theory of Art," conventional intellect distorts reality by rendering it amenable to practical action, so that "human perception gets crystallized along certain lines . . . it has certain fixed habits, certain fixed ways of seeing things, and is so unable to see things as they are" (192). Not all minds, however, have this limitation: "From time to time in a fit of absent-mindedness nature raises up minds which are more detached from life"; there occasionally appear people "whose perceptions are not riveted to practical purposes" because "nature has forgotten to attach their faculty for perception to their faculty for action" (196). Nature, that is, sometimes produces natural "first selves"—people whose two selves are inverted so that intuitional capacities naturally dominate. Whereas ordinary people have ordinary perceptions and express them in conventional language, the artist's naturally intuitional perspective "breeds in him a dissatisfaction with conventional means of expression" (199), and he or she perpetually creates new language to convey immediate experience. "You could define art," Hulme writes, "as a passionate desire for accuracy," and a will to force language to convey reality immediately. Through this definition, he distinguishes conventional language, the "counters" that convey only the banalities of intellect, from the incisive metaphorical language of what would become Imagism.

Hulme, then, was able to discover in Bergson's theory of the two selves a privileged role for the literary artist. Bergsonian psychology, it seemed, appointed the poet its master practitioner. If Bergson's theory aims to liberate authentic, intuitional consciousness, the Hulmian artist—the genius who can provide the textual imagery through which the world discovers authentic reality—becomes a kind of supreme therapist. Personifying intuition therefore helped Hulme to define modern artistry; it also, however, rendered his relationship to Bergson necessarily unstable. For the personification of intuition *both embraces and rejects* psychological definitions of culture: in one sense, it defines art in terms of the personality of the artist; and yet it also defines the artist as one free from conventional personality. Hulme would ultimately come to believe in art's impersonality, and to discover, in other theorists, better and more decisive justification for that belief. What motivated that shift, I will claim, was a realization that tipped the scales so precariously balanced in Hulme's personification of intuition. Hulme realized that once Bergsonism was applied to exalt the personality of the artist, it could as easily exalt the psychological makeup of other kinds of persons, thereby threatening the very privilege that Bergson seemed to reserve for poetic language.

Ostensibly, Hulme lost interest in Bergson toward the end of 1911 because he came to see that Bergsonian psychology reduces the world to the psychical experience of it. In other words, "intuition" was a form of psychologism, although Hulme never uses that word to criticize it. In his latest writings (unpublished material that Csengeri entitles "A Notebook"), Hulme explains Bergson's psychologistic limitations and the "objective" alternative that he came to prefer. In general, Hulme writes, theories like Bergson's depend upon an "uncritical humanism" or "humanist idealism"—an anthropomorphic tendency always to place the human at the basis of the real. Wanting to subject that tendency to a "critique of satisfaction," Hulme determines that "the fundamental error is that of placing Perfection in *humanity*, thus giving rise to that bastard thing Personality, and all that bunkum that follows from it" (437). Opposed to this wrongheaded "humanist" view is what Hulme calls the "religious" attitude, which posits that "life is not the source and measure of all values," and that "ethical values are *not* relative to human desires and feelings, but absolute and objective." The religious attitude contradicts Bergsonism because while Bergson goes some way to distinguish the real from conventional human conceptions of it, he still locates truth in the determinations of some aspect of the human psyche. "Intuition" may remove the criteria of value from standard ideas, but it does so only to locate them more deeply in personal human discretion. Hulme therefore turns to those philosophers who offer guidance in the realm of determining objective truth, applying Moore and Husserl to begin to theorize his "anti-humanism." These philosophers, Hulme believed, enable "a complete reaction from the subjectivism and relativism of humanist ethics," establishing "the *objective* character of human values" and "an order or *hierarchy* among them"; they "free ethical values from the anthropomorphism involved in their dependence on human desires and feelings" (451–52); and they help Hulme to see the psychologism in Bergson's theory of the two selves.

Moore and Husserl, then, as critics have noted, are largely responsible for the anti-psychologistic turn through which Hulme helped to develop the theories of "impersonality" that drove modernist aesthetics. Husserl encouraged that turn through the explicit attack on psychologism in his *Logical Investigations*; Moore encouraged it less directly in the principles of his neo-realism, which sought to prove the objectivity of ethical values. But another influence, one more clearly political than theoretical, proves that Hulme's turn to "objectivity" resulted from a larger range of personal commitments. Most clearly responsible for Hulme's rejection of Bergson and its aesthetic consequences was Pierre Lasserre, who proved to Hulme, in his writings and in personal meetings in 1911, that Bergson's theories require a leftist belief in man's perfectibility. The conservative Lasserre attacked Bergson's faith in "continual progress for mankind," a faith that clashed with his political views, and, as he brought Hulme to see, with Hulme's own right-wing views as well.[18] As Sanford Schwartz notes, Hulme had always believed that there could be a "vitalism of the right," but "Lasserre and his compatriots persuaded him that Bergsonism actually promulgates a vitalism of the Left" (Schwartz 296). Lasserre's influence proves that sociopolitical distinctions helped to recast Bergson's psychology, and that psychologism emerged as a category at least partially through political views about what kinds of personalities ought to control human government.

That aspect of psychologism's provenance seems more significant in the face of proof that theoretical influence alone would not have changed Hulme's mind about Bergson. Certainly, Husserl and Moore make it harder to maintain enthusiasm about Bergson; moreover, Hulme often makes it clear that he never thought that Bergson had innovated any truly original theory, but had rather only dispelled the nightmare of the "mechanistic view" in language well suited to the times ("Notes on Bergson" 132). Now that times had changed, and Bergsonian language only confirmed a different form of determinism, that language could lose its appeal. But there are affinities between Hulme and Bergson that persist despite Hulme's rejection, and these make that rejection seem less than inevitable. Hulme in fact seems to have drawn his "critique of satisfaction" out of Bergson's opposition to the conventional, despite the apparent lack of fit between the skepticism of the "critique" and Bergson's alleged romanticism. Similarly, Patricia Rae has convincingly suggested that Hulme in fact develops his classical outlook through Bergson's often-overlooked resistance to "spilling the mystical into the realm of the human"; and, as Miriam Hansen notes, Hulme had until his death "a radical urge to promote the eclipse of the 'symbolic'" always relatable to Bergson's similar urge.[19] Until his last moments, Hulme did in fact hold to the first lesson that Bergson taught him: that the truth is other than that which human conventions determine it to be. This lesson is of course a general one, possible to distill from a range of philosophies, but its compatibility with Hulme's successive post-Bergsonian positions suggest that the break with Bergson needed extra-theoretical encouragement. Opposition to what Schwartz calls the "vitalism of the Left" is one such encouragement; another is opposition to another political development: the appearance of crowds of women in philosophers' lecture halls.

As suffragettes campaigned throughout London with increasing violence, parallel developments brought new successes to the struggle for women's equality in education and the professions, which were to culminate in Cambridge's 1920 decision, finally, to admit women. That trend, combined with Bergson's wild popularity among professionals and laymen alike, filled the lecture halls where Bergson spoke with an unprecedentedly diverse population. Women's political and cultural successes, however, produced considerable backlash: as Elizabeth Eschbach and Susan Kingsley Kent have recently noted, men found new ways to limit women's entrance into university and professional life, stepping up the "sex war" even as women seemed closest to achieving their victories in it.[20] That backlash expressed itself, with regard to Bergson, in mockery of the intellectual pretensions of the women who idolized him. In France, critics satirized Bergson's public lectures by making fun of the "pretty and frivolous Parisiennes" who so substantially comprised Bergson's audience; and one notorious cartoon, described in Mark Antliff's account of Bergson's influence, shows Bergson "inundated with flowers from female admirers, with the memorable caption: 'Mais . . . je ne suis pas une danseuse.'"[21] Women's interest in Bergson's teaching cemented the belief, common among Bergson's critics, that his philosophy had a "feminine" orientation—that it was, as Charles Maurras put it, a "feminine romanticism" that pitched feminine instinct over masculine reason (Antliff 99). In England as well, Bergson became the focus of an antipathy charged by new resistance to women's advancements and informed by old associations between women and irrational instinct.

Such antipathy spoiled Hulme's admiration for Bergson. It seems that his intellectual distaste for "anthropomorphism" was boosted by a more visceral distaste for what might be called "gynomorphism." In "Bergson Lecturing," Hulme tells of arriving at lectures given by Bergson at University College, London, in October of 1911. He had been led to believe that the lectures were "for advanced students only," but finds them crowded with consummate beginners. He encounters what seems to be a "harem": "nine people out of ten here are women, most of them with their heads lifted in that kind of 'Eager Heart' attitude, which resembles nothing so much as the attitude of my kitten when gently awaking from sleep" (154). In earlier writings, Hulme had noted the problem of this haremization: in an essay named "Bax and Bergson," Hulme admits that it has become increasingly difficult to get a seat at Bergson's lectures, and that "when you do get a seat you are distracted by what an exasperated student recently described as the 'blasphemous scents' of fashionable women" (119). Then, however, Hulme enjoyed some distance from the student's exasperation. Now, he is "suddenly struck down by a most profound fit of depression," and has "a most remarkable fit of the profoundest and blackest skepticism—a skepticism that cut right down to the root of every belief I had hitherto fancied I held as cer-

tain and fixed" (154–55). This, then, is the crucial moment of Hulme's transformation. Before, Hulme felt he had "finally found what I wanted in
Bergson. The beliefs I got there seemed to be of such character that I could
safely fix everything around them" (155); he had become "a disciple in the
dull sense of the word," and Bergson had given him "the spectacles through
which I have seen everything." What unfixed this belief was no "great
upheaval" in his intellectual life: "what did occur was something infinitely
more disturbing. The whole edifice of my fixed belief, so laboriously constructed, was overturned by a trifle." Seeing the crowds of women sharing his
enthusiasm for Bergson causes a "complete reversal of feeling" (156), a negative epiphany that compels him to believe first that "what these people
thought about Bergson was entirely wrong," and then ultimately "that
Bergson himself was wrong."

Hulme admits that this is "childish repugnance" (158), but its pettiness is
in fact what makes it so interesting a part of the history of anti-psychologism.
Explaining how his disciplehood could end with such a trifle, Hulme reveals
a basic temperamental incongruity between psychological theory and aesthetic culture. He notes that where he "ought to be pleased at the spread of
truth," he feels that "extraordinary distaste we feel for sharing even our most
cherished beliefs with a crowd" (157). Having to share beliefs in such a fashion invalidates those beliefs, for "it seems," Hulme writes, "as if ideas were
only valuable insofar as they distinguish one from the people we dislike"
(157). Hulme learns that psychology has a public scope that renders it unfit
for aesthetic and cultural use. Like fellow makers of modernist high culture,
he prefers theories of art that equate aesthetic and social superiority.[22]
Bergson's ideas had initially seemed to offer this kind of distinction, insofar
as they allowed Hulme to imagine a privileged sociocultural role for the
artist figure. But Bergson's manifest popularity with the female public suggests that women might practice Bergsonian psychology themselves; moreover, it suggests that they might even have a greater natural right to practice
that psychology than the Hulmian artist.

Hulme himself had earlier noted some such link between Bergson's
method and the female psyche. In "Searchers after Reality: Bax," Hulme
criticizes Ernest Bax for falling short of Bergson's rejection of logical philosophical method, and closes with a suggestive observation about Bax's
inability or refusal to arrive at his own version of Bergsonian intuition. "The
intellect," Hulme writes, "is still for [Bax] the only way of getting at Reality,
though we are always to remember that by its very nature we can never
reach it" (91–92). Mocking this peculiar "midway position," Hulme asks,

"What did he see in the promised land of the alogical which prevented him from wandering there?" (92). Hulme's answer to this question predicts his own conversion at Bergson's lectures two years later: "We can only surmise maliciously that somewhere in its pleasant valleys he saw a woman. Is not intuition too dangerous a process for an anti-feminist to suggest as the ultimate philosophic process?" (92). To promote "intuition," Hulme seems to suggest, is to promote a feminist category, due to some affinity—determined by pervasive gender caricatures—between women's minds and the capacity to know by instinct, to be productively irrational. As Bergson describes it, intuition has no normative affinity with female capacities, but Hulme's cultural application of the method requires a personification of intuition that leads ultimately to this one. What attracts Hulme leads to repulsion: he personalizes Bergsonism to glorify the artist, but then rejects the Bergsonian cult of personality once the category becomes too inclusive.

Intuition, then, became a kind of psychologism once Hulme discovered its relation to feminism. Defining modernism against this psychologism, Hulme participated in the kind of cultural negotiation that has increasingly become the focus of feminist criticism—the tendency, recently explored in Rita Felski's *The Gender of Modernity*, to define modernity through and against its apparent relation to the female psyche. As Felski notes, "the feminization of modernity" was a fact both celebrated and demonized by the male creators of high modernism.[23] On the one hand, women seemed to have the privileged relation to the goals of modernist aesthetics that Hulme notes when he considers the implicit feminism of intuition: femininity, Felski notes, "shares with the aesthetic a perfect integration of part and whole, as the utopian embodiment of a sensuous materiality which resists the tyranny of an abstract and one-sided reason" (48). At the same time, women represent the kind of threat to aesthetic culture to which Hulme's anti-psychologism responds, as "women and the masses merge as twin symbols of the democratizing mediocrity of modern life, embodying a murky threat to the precarious status and identity of the artist" (106). Insofar as it conditions the relationship between Hulme and Bergson, this double view of women's place in modernity turns psychology into psychologism; it associates the kind of mental process crucial to Bergson's psychology with the feminine mind, and then makes distaste for women's apparent privilege in this regard cause to distinguish psychology from definitions of culture.[24]

Resistance to this psychologism enables Hulme to reestablish the cultural boundaries that set the artist apart. He concludes "Bergson Lecturing" with the exhortation that we "re-establish the old distinction between the public and the esoteric doctrine," so that "the difficulty of getting into this hall" will be "comparable to the difficulty of getting into a harem, not only in appearance, but in fact" (158). That Bergson's psychology had become a "public doctrine" was proven by its appeal to the female mind; modernist culture had to define itself as an "esoteric doctrine" in order to reserve cultural power for the artist figure. Psychologism, it seems, at least partially developed out of this structural opposition between the public and the esoteric, proving that contrary to what interdisciplinary cross-currents might lead us to believe, psychology and aesthetic culture could not really collude. Moreover, this structural opposition explains the perpetual progression that characterizes Hulme's career and that of the culture of modernism his career reflects. As esoteric doctrines perpetually became public ones—as models of the poet's mind perpetually became popular—modernism's cultural producers perpetually had to redefine their endeavors against encroaching psychologies. For Hulme, this endless impulse toward what he called "disentangling" meant increasing exaggerations of the impersonality of art, in a progression that began with Bergson's distinction between the two selves, continued through the rejection of Bergson, and led to what some see as a proto-fascist distinction between human and absolute values.

Hulme's experience with Bergson's female audience helps to explain this trend in the response against psychologism because it draws our attention to the ways in which the local sociopolitical connotations of psychology condition culture's attitude toward it. Hulme may not have rejected Bergson had sociopolitical contexts not transformed Bergsonism from the kind of psychology that liberates consciousness into the kind of psychologism that degrades it. This is not to say, however, that culture capriciously demonizes psychology; in fact, the case of Bergson and Hulme suggests that psychology is consistently the ground against which aesthetic culture defines itself. For Bergson was himself a founder of modern anti-psychologism. He, too, had sought to oppose psychology's reduction of the mind to psycho-physical processes, having inherited that opposition from attitudes as old as the theories of empiricism that began to ground the mind in the body. The relationship between Hulme and Bergson, then, comes at a stage in a series of reactions against psychologism. A kind of infinite regress opens up around the modernism that Hulme helped to innovate, in which those who want to represent consciousness perpetually "disentangle" the mind from psychological determinations.

CHAPTER 12

Modernism and the Specter of Psychologism

MARTIN JAY

No genealogist of the complex and heterogeneous cultural field we have come to call aesthetic modernism can fail to acknowledge its multiple intersections with that other richly articulated field known as modern psychology. In both cases, an unprecedented preoccupation with the interior landscape of the subject, a no longer self-confident self functioning with increased difficulty in the larger world outside its threatened and vulnerable boundaries, led to voyages of scientific and artistic discovery whose endpoints have not yet been reached. Whether it be the empiricist tradition of Ernst Mach, Franz Brentano, and William James recently foregrounded by Judith Ryan in *The Vanishing Subject*;[1] Jean Martin Charcot's investigations of hysteria inspirational for such modernist movements as Surrealism; or Freudian psychoanalysis, whose importance for modernism is evident in such accounts as Carl Schorske's *Fin-de-Siècle Vienna*,[2] the story of aesthetic innovation has seemed impossible to narrate without reference to the no less radical developments in psychology happening at virtually the same time. What Ryan calls the "complex intertextuality"[3] between modernism and psychology has perhaps reached its zenith in Louis Sass's recent *Madness and Modernism*, which boldly seeks to understand such familiar aspects of the modernist temper as perspectivism, dehumanization, alienation, ironic detachment, hyperreflexivity, and spatialized form precisely by finding affinities with the workings of the schizophrenic mind, which was itself first labeled in the 1890s and quickly became, he tells us, "the quintessential form of madness in our time."[4]

Cultural fields, however, not only intersect and parallel each other, producing reinforcements, homologies, and elective affinities, but also sometimes interact through repulsions and negations, achieving their fragile definitions by means of abjecting the other. In the case of modernism and psychology, I want to argue, such a process of negative exclusion, a process that overlapped and sometimes interfered with the more positive interaction that has been explored by other scholars, did, in fact, occur. In particular, I want to show that what the philosophers of this period called "psychologism," and which many sought mightily to banish from their search for truth, also emerged as a source of anxiety at certain key moments in the genesis of aesthetic modernism as well.[5] My evidence will come from both literary and visual instances of this anxiety. Although I do not want to be understood as saying modernism was essentially a repudiation of psychologism, let alone unrelated to developments in the psychological sciences per se, no understanding of its emergence can afford to ignore the haunting presence of this stigmatized "ism" as a specter that refused to be effortlessly exorcised.[6]

The philosophical critique of psychologism can be traced at least as far back as Kant's claim that "in logic we do not want to know how understanding is and thinks and how it hitherto has proceeded in thinking, but how it ought to proceed in thinking. Logic must teach us the correct use of the understanding, i.e. that in which it is in agreement with itself."[7] His transcendental deduction thus explicitly distinguished between the fact of the "physiological derivation" of a priori ideas and the question of their validity. The most elaborate and influential development of the critique, however, appeared after a period in which psychologism gained ground among philosophers and the upstart discipline of experimental psychology had emerged to challenge philosophy as the royal road to unlocking the mysteries of the mind.[8] Although there were rumblings throughout the nineteenth century, only at the century's end did psychologism emerge as a primary target of a philosophical counterattack. In 1884, Gottlob Frege published *The Foundations of Arithmetic*, which vigorously criticized attempts by philosophers such as Friedrich Beneke, Jakob Fries, John Stuart Mill, and Franz Brentano to reduce the mind, in particular its logical function, to the psyche.[9] More radical psychologizers like Nietzsche were beneath Frege's consideration.[10]

Husserl, although himself initially indebted to Brentano, was putatively won over to Frege's position by a devastating review the latter wrote of Husserl's early work *Philosophy of Arithmetic* in 1894.[11] By his *Logical Investigations* of 1900, Husserl had come to see that the empirical science of psychology with its inductive laws of association could not provide a basis for a pure, deductive logic, which goes beyond mere probabilistic knowledge. In the 1890s, other philosophers, such as the neo-positivist Alexius Meinong and the neo-Kantians Rudolf Hermann Lotze and Hermann Cohen, also vigorously turned against psychologism, moving away from epistemological questions to logical and ontological ones.[12] In physics as well, a challenge to the radical associationism of Ernst Mach and the "energeticism" of Wilhelm Ostwald was launched by defenders of the reality of discrete atoms like Ludwig Boltzmann.[13] At the same time, sociologists like Émile Durkheim and Max Weber sought to avoid reducing social facts to their alleged psychological substratum, and historians like Wilhelm Dilthey gave up their search for underlying psychological types in favor of a hermeneutics of objective meaning.[14]

This is not the place to attempt a full-scale history of anti-psychologism, a task admirably carried out by Martin Kusch in a recent study on the sociology of knowledge.[15] Suffice it to say that shortly after Husserl's conversion, anti-psychologism became a fundamental principle of many influential twentieth-century philosophers in different camps, including such otherwise disparate figures as Heidegger, Cassirer, Russell, Moore, Carnap, Lukács, and Goldmann.[16] Even the early Wittgenstein, as Cora Diamond has recently shown, sought to banish psychology and follow the Kantian dictum that logic was in agreement only with itself, however much he may have ultimately come to question Frege's belief that logic might be freed of ordinary language as well and expressed in a pure, unequivocal "concept script."[17]

There were, of course, many variations in the alternatives to psychologism provided by these critics, and indeed their target was not always understood in precisely the same way, but the general complaint was as follows.[18] Reducing the mind to the psyche was problematic for logic and mathematics because it opened the door to relativism in which truth was merely a function of the specific thinking mind in which it appeared or of its cumulative experience over time. Even the concepts of a specieswide transcendental consciousness and innate biological capacities (of the kind later defended by Noam Chomsky) were insufficient to ward off the threat of psychological relativism. As Frege put it, "neither logic nor mathematics has the task of investigating minds and contents of consciousness owned by individual men."[19]

The philosophy of mind, in other words, was not reducible to the philosophy of actual human minds; the apodictic or a priori character of certain universal truths was not the same as the empirical and a posteriori character of contingent knowledge. The equation "$2 + 2 = 4$" and the law of contradiction were entirely independent of the minds that held them. The truth content of propositions had to be rigorously separated from the judgments made about them, judgments that would be better understood as "correct or incorrect."[20] The sense of a proposition, to put it slightly differently, had to be distinguished from its presentation or representation; confirmation and refutation were not the same as persuasion. Moreover, whereas psychological laws could never be more than vague and probabilistic, based as they were on inductive generalizations, the laws of logic and mathematics were valid, timeless, and pure; the latter could not therefore be derived from the former. Husserl, to be sure, ultimately paid more attention than did Frege to the links between disembodied, timeless mind and the actual cognition of real human beings; the ideal realm of logic and mathematics could, after all, manifest itself in the finite, but rational, consciousness of fallible mortals. If not, he reasoned, we could have no access to it. There is thus a possibility of eidetic intuition, Husserl claimed, which provided the immediate evidence of essential objects.[21] Achieving such intuition was, in fact, the point of his phenomenological rather than strictly logical method, with its continuing debt to Brentano's notion of intentionality. He thus returned to a variant of the transcendentalism that Frege scorned. Nonetheless, both he and Frege resisted the reduction of objective to subjective ideas, understood either as generalizations from empirical experience or the product of mere introspection into the individual self. They also shared a strong hostility to what they claimed was the psychologistic confusion of cause and justification, the genetic fallacy that understood validity in terms of origin. Whereas psychologism was determined to reduce logic and mathematics to a prior psychological disposition or the cumulative weight of successive experiences, they wanted to disentangle one from the other. As Frege admonished his readers, "never let us take a description of the origin of an idea for a definition, or an account of the mental and physical conditions on which we become conscious of a proposition for a proof of it. A proposition may be thought, and again it may be true; let us never confuse these two things."[22] Logic and mathematics had timeless validity, which meant their origins or causes were irrelevant to their intrinsic truth content.

How compelling these criticisms of psychologism may ultimately be cannot be decided here. There are, in fact, still heated disputes among philosophers, and defenses of psychologism have been mounted by positing alternative versions that allegedly escape its pitfalls.[23] What is important for our purposes is the remarkable extent of the critique's success in the very decades when aesthetic modernism was itself emerging, from the 1890s through World War I.[24] Indeed, its power remained strong well into the era after World War II. Its echo can still be clearly heard, for example, in one of the most powerful theoretical defenses of modernism made in the 1960s, Theodor W. Adorno's *Aesthetic Theory*. Speaking of the psychoanalysis of works of art in particular, Adorno writes, "it neglects to consider their real objectivity, their inner consistency, their level of form, their critical impulses, their relation to non-psychic reality and, last but not least, their truth content."[25]

For certain modernist artists as well, the threat to the integrity of the work of art and its timeless truth value posed by psychologism was also a palpable reality.[26] There was a modernist "mystique of purity," which, as Renato Poggioli noted many years ago, "aspires to abolish the discursive and syntactic element, to liberate art from any connection with psychological and empirical reality, to reduce every work to the intimate laws of its own expressive essence or to the given absolutes of its own genre or means."[27] A displaced variant of the time-honored struggle to maintain a boundary between the sacred and the profane, this aspiration can also be understood as yet another instance of what sociologists have seen as the uneven process of differentiating value spheres characteristic of modernization as a whole. At certain times, the dislocations produced by that process seem to have been especially acute, resulting in a struggle over boundary maintenance or reconfiguration that was particularly fierce. The late nineteenth century in Europe was by all accounts a period in which the cards, cultural as well as social, were being rapidly shuffled in new and threatening ways.[28]

The threats that resulted in the generalization of anti-psychologism beyond the confines of philosophy were multifarious: for example, the expansion of confidence in natural science produced a scientistic hubris that threatened the value of other approaches to reality; the extension of new forms of popular commodified culture appealing to the desires and fantasies of the masses menaced the allegedly disinterested nature of high art; and the challenge to traditional gender roles in the fin de siècle created anxieties about the domination of masculine conceptions of cultural value. Modernism, as Andreas Huyssen has shown, often defended itself against a feminized version of mass culture, which it stigmatized as debased kitsch.[29] Not surprisingly, one weapon in modernism's battle with these demons was the exorcism of psychologism in the name of a universalism that would, however, be based on nonscientific values.

Perhaps the most explicit manifestation of the struggle against psychologism appeared in the development of modernist literature in Britain around the time of World War I. In virtually all accounts of the evolution of British poetry from Yeats to Pound, Ford, and Eliot, the search for something called "impersonality" and the suppression of subjective expressivity has been duly recognized.[30] Although the tangled web of attitudes toward subjective expression and objective presentation in the history of British modernism has prevented the story from being a straightforward narrative of one-dimensional anti-psychologism, it is nonetheless clear that the anxieties we have traced in Frege, Husserl, and the neo-Kantians were given aesthetic voice in the work and theory of the major figures in that story.

In fact, the explicit importance of Husserl's critique of psychologism for the poetry and criticism of the influential critic and poet T. E. Hulme has been widely acknowledged. Although it took some time to disentangle Hulme's initial enthusiasm for Bergson's philosophy of flux and immediate experience from his later, very different position—an entanglement abetted by the ensemble publication of essays from his entire career in the collection entitled *Speculations*, posthumously appearing in 1924—there seems to be a consensus now that he shifted his opinion in the years directly before the war.[31] Partly due to the relentless critique of Bergsonism as hopelessly romantic and simplistically democratic, made by Pierre Lasserre, Charles Maurras, and other neoclassicist stalwarts of the right-wing Action Française, Hulme's change of heart also reflected a reading of Husserl's attack on psychologism in the *Logical Investigations*, which apparently allowed him to understand for the first time the implications of the anti-idealist realism he had encountered in the analytical philosophy of G. E. Moore and Bertrand Russell.[32] Liberally citing the German philosopher in the essay that opened *Speculations*, "Humanism and the Religious Attitude," a version of which had been already published in 1915, Hulme decried the entire trend of modern thought from the Renaissance on as distressingly anthropomorphic, based on the mistaken reduction of objective ideas to a merely human source, the confusion of pure philosophy with *Weltanschauung*.[33]

But Hulme went beyond Frege and Husserl's critique of psychologism in a crucial way: he applied their argument outside the realm of logic per se. Citing Moore's *Principia Ethica* of 1903, with its celebrated critique of the naturalist fallacy, Hulme argued that ethical values as well should be understood as irreducible to human construction.[34] It was possible, he contended (without bothering to demonstrate how), to arrange them in an objective hierarchy. A parallel argument loosely derived from Wilhelm Worringer's 1908 *Abstraction and Empathy* allowed Hulme to denounce aesthetic styles based on intersubjective empathy (or, more precisely, on a subject's pantheistic empathy with a beautiful object in the world) as inherently inferior to those, such as the Egyptian and Byzantine styles, that resisted naturalistic organicism in the name of impersonal, geometrical, nonvitalist abstraction.[35]

Modern art, exemplified by the sculpture of Jacob Epstein and the paintings of Cézanne and Wyndham Lewis, Hulme argued, promised a return to precision, austerity, and bareness, the anti-humanist values he so admired.[36] It would help clean up the mess produced by transgressing boundaries, that "pot of treacle over the dinner table" Hulme famously identified with the "spilt religion" that was romanticism.[37]

This is not the place and I am not the scholar to present a detailed and nuanced account of the complicated resonances of Hulme's ideas among the English modernists, especially the Imagist poets.[38] Nor can we pause to consider related developments in the modernist novel from Flaubert to Virginia Woolf, in which stylistic innovations like the *style indirect libre* helped create the effect of non-egocentric impersonality in ways that paralleled developments in the poetry of the modern era.[39] And we cannot open up once again the debate about spatial form in modern poetry and the novel launched by Joseph Frank, who acknowledged an explicit debt to Hulme and Worringer.[40] What, however, needs to be at least briefly underlined is the pivotal role of a figure of inestimable importance who acknowledged an explicit debt to Hulme and through him to Frege and Husserl: T. S. Eliot.

In his new journal, *The Criterion*, and elsewhere, Eliot energetically promulgated many of Hulme's ideas, aesthetic as well as political. In such celebrated essays as "Tradition and the Individual Talent" of 1919, he presented many of the same anti-psychologistic arguments we have already encountered. "Poetry," he contended in lines that quickly became canonical, "is not a turning loose of emotion but an escape from emotion; it is not the expression of personality but an escape from personality."[41] His influential notion of an "objective correlative" seems likely, in fact, to have been taken directly from Husserl, whom Eliot read when he studied philosophy at Harvard in 1914.[42] Although his obvious debt to F. H. Bradley, on whom he wrote his dissertation, has been widely acknowledged, Eliot also drew on the work of Meinong, Russell, and Moore and the other so-called "new realists" of the period.[43] According to Sanford Schwartz, "in his thesis he undermines the assumptions of the psychologist by reducing consciousness to its objects, and later used the same strategy in his critique of nineteenth-century poetry."[44] Eliot, Schwartz also shows, went on to criticize an equally abstract objectivism, which reified objects as a simple inverse of the romantic reification of the integral subject; he was clearly no naturalist seeing art as a passive reflection of an external world.[45] The poet's ability to fashion words from his immediate experience somehow overcame the very dichotomy between subject and object, challenging as well the infamous "dissociation of sensibility" that Eliot claimed had plagued the modern world ever since the English Revolution placed feeling above wit.

Through the dissemination of Eliot's ideas by the New Critics of the 1930s and 1940s, impersonality became a new dogma and the isolation of the poem from its contexts of production and reception an article of faith. Like the logic Frege had hoped to rescue from its psychologistic reduction and the ethical imperatives Hulme had sought to distinguish from the humans who followed or transgressed them, aesthetic value, often equated entirely with formal self-referentiality, became an end entirely in itself. The New Critics' dreaded genetic and affective fallacies and the fallacy of expressive form were all little more than redescriptions in poetic terms of the warnings against psychologism made by late nineteenth-century philosophy. Even when later champions of modernism like Charles Altieri sought to reintro- duce a notion of agency, they were careful to distinguish the structuring activity of the artist from the emotional interiority of the empirical, suffering subject lurking beneath its surface.[46]

All of this is by now well known and needs no belaboring. But what per- haps warrants some attention is the parallel process that can be discerned in the visual arts during this period. Not surprisingly, the value of hard-edged visual distinctness, which Hulme and the Imagists defended as a metaphor- ic antidote to the sloppy pantheistic continuities they saw in romanticism, could easily be adopted in literal terms by painters anxious to experiment with geometric abstractions and fields of color.[47] Despite the powerful sub- jectivist impulse in certain visual modernisms, most obviously German ex- pressionism, others manifested the same suspicion of psychological expres- sion that we have noted in literary modernists like Eliot.

The nineteenth century, to be sure, can be said to have been, by and large, a period of the increasing psychologization of the visual, the aban- donment of a geometric optics of representation based on the eyes' ability faithfully to mirror the world outside. The story of how, beginning in the sec- ond decade of the nineteenth century, scientists of perception undermined the classical observer modeled on the automatic functioning of a camera obscura has been masterfully reconstructed by Jonathan Crary in his recent *Techniques of the Observer*.[48] No longer a monological, punctual, mechani- cal eye coolly recording a world outside itself, the new spectator was embod- ied, binocular, and influenced by internal psycho-physiological processes such as afterimages, the presence of sensations without any simultaneous external stimulus. The psychologization of vision, the loss of confidence in the veracity of the eye and such systems of representation as Renaissance perspective, affected art history and criticism as well as practice. Thus, in his influential *Principles of Art History* of 1915, Heinrich Wölfflin would write of the oscillating pattern of classical and baroque styles he saw as a constant of visual representation: "There is no denying it—the development of the process is psychologically intelligible."[49]

The delayed artistic repercussions of the changes Crary details in the early part of the century can be found most readily in the "glancing," embodied, and dynamic—as opposed to "gazing," disembodied, static—eye of impressionism, to borrow Norman Bryson's well-known distinction.[50] It has thus been easy for commentators on the literary offshoots of psychological empiricism, such as Judith Ryan, to find compelling parallels between these offshoots and Impressionism.[51] Both psychology and Impressionism suggest a withdrawal from the world of stable objects and a new preoccupation with the perceiving subject, a subject in crisis, absorbed by its own dissolution, fascinated and sometimes bewildered by the flux of sensations flooding in from without.

It is, however, with the loose and amorphous body of work that has become known as Postimpressionism, including the painting of Cézanne in particular, that these parallels begin to break down. Indeed, it might be said that the famous "doubt" that Merleau-Ponty detected in Cézanne was directed not only toward the traditional perspectival order of the Renaissance frozen gaze, but also toward the adequacy of the Impressionists' glancing eye.[52] His attempt to return to objects and paint "nature" was not, however, a restoration of earlier representational realism; instead, it sought the real entirely on the surface of the canvas, where subject and object, perception and the perceived, were not yet distinct and separate.[53] Here a world of pure monstrance, of visual presence rather than representation, began to supplant the sensationalist psychologism of the Impressionists. Although Merleau-Ponty thought Cezanne had anticipated what later psychologists, such as the Gestaltists, were to realize in their laboratories, his description of the painter's achievement suggests a less psychologistic interpretation: "The lived object is not rediscovered or constructed on the basis of the contributions of the senses; rather it presents itself to us from the start as the center from which these contributions radiate."[54]

Cezanne's project to capture viewer and viewed together on the flat surface of the canvas and thus realize unmediated visual presence may have been utopian, but it provided a challenge to the psychologism that had come to dominate nineteenth-century spectatorship (a challenge, as Altieri has argued, that had an impact on modernist poetry as well).[55] Thierry de

Duve describes that challenge in terms of a difficult choice:

Modernity picked up Cezanne's heritage in the form of an alternative: either I actively destroy the object, the figure, and all the realism that goes along with it, in order to preserve that which remains of my subjective integrity—here I have no other choice than to destroy the represented real, but at least in destroying it I make myself master of it—or I agree to sacrifice my subjective unity and allow the plural significance of my self-image to appear, but to the benefit of an unalterable pseudo-object, the self-sufficient epiphany of a world that excludes me.[56]

At different times, different movements and figures opted for one or the other of these alternatives (and some, to be sure, sought to overcome them by somehow including a dispersed notion of subjectivity in the epiphany itself).[57] But it is perhaps legitimate to say that in the long run most modernist painting, at least as it became canonically described in the criticism of Roger Fry, Clive Bell, Clement Greenberg, and Michael Fried, took the second course. That is, it sought to purge painting of anything allegedly superfluous to it, any expression of the painter's interiority, any representational reference, decorative functionality, or theatrical appeal to the beholder. Instead, painting came increasingly to be understood as a quest to realize only the essential and immanent laws of painting themselves, a quest for an authentic, truth-telling art that would be ontologically "absolute." Even when that absolute was understood in spiritual terms, as it was by Kandinsky, it meant the extirpation of the psychological subject.[58] Very much in the spirit of Kant's defense of logic as understanding "in agreement with itself," high modernism became a game of purification and reduction in which formal pictorial qualities were their own ends.[59] Indeed, for Greenberg, Kant himself was "the first real Modernist" because he "used logic to establish the limits of logic, and while he withdrew much from its old jurisdiction, logic was left in all the more secure possession of what remained to it."[60]

Not surprisingly, the aesthetic variant of this strategy of *reculer pour mieux sauter*, most explicitly realized in the writing of Greenberg after his break with Marxism, often earned a comparison with the New Criticism that was the scholarly handmaiden of literary modernism at this time.[61] Greenberg's warm embrace of Eliot's banishment of personality from aesthetic judgment was also remarked, as was the similarity between his position and that of Adorno.[62] Although Eliot's later ruminations on culture and tradition suggest a more hermeneutic, contextual perspective, both he and Greenberg could be seen as championing self-reflexivity and self-absorption, in which the aesthetic object is rigidly segregated from anything outside its apparent boundaries.[63]

The anti-psychologistic impulse in the Greenbergian version of high modernism is thus not difficult to discern. More surprising is that something similar can be detected in the work of a modernist figure who fell entirely outside the canon established by Greenberg and the other champions of optical purity and self-sufficiency: Marcel Duchamp. What has been called his "pictorial nominalism," which perhaps became most explicit when Duchamp began fashioning his celebrated "readymades," meant foregrounding the constitutive power of the artist, who named an object an artwork through an act of enunciation ultimately valorized by the institutions of art rather than by his own genius or skill.[64] Eschewing the search for optical purity, indeed truculently indifferent to any optical values and hostile to the search for the "absolute" essence of the medium of painting, Duchamp was in many respects the antithesis of the artist who hopes for the epiphanic revelation of a self-sufficient world on the flat surface of his canvas.[65] Instead, he promoted the invasion of the realm of the visual by the textual and discursive, allowed the real world literally to appear through the surface of the "canvas" (the *Large Glass* was a transparent "window" mocking both the old metaphor of the canvas as window and the new celebration of its two-dimensional opacity), and foregrounded the persona of the artist, whose unstable identity registered the crisis of the genius model of creativity.

And yet, despite his radical problematizing of the mainstream modernist quest for pure visual presence and his deliberate mockery of its ontological pretensions, Duchamp was, I want to argue, equally suspicious of certain versions of psychologism in art. His famous dismissal of "retinal painting" was aimed at the positing of the painter's or beholder's eye, whether gazing or glancing, as the foundation of aesthetic value. His nominalism extended, we might say, to the perception of the artist, whose sensitively recorded act of ephemeral seeing was no less a questionable standard of veracity than the idealized representation of objects allegedly present in the visual field of a disembodied, camera obscura gaze.

Duchamp was even more antagonistic to an aesthetic of expressivity, arguing instead for an anti-romantic art of dehumanization. As Werner Hofmann has noted, "his act of choice consciously opposed the glorification of subjective creation and the principle which holds that the lowly object is ennobled by artistic 'expression.'"[66] Not surprisingly, in the 1950s Duchamp took to quoting T. S. Eliot's "Tradition and the Individual Talent," with its famous distinction between the "man who suffers" and "the mind who creates," and he told one critic in 1961 that "Eliot's essay presents his own feelings as well or better than he himself has ever done in writing."[67] In short,

even so maverick a figure in the pantheon of modernism as Marcel Duchamp felt obliged to distance himself from the lure of psychologism.
Duchamp and Eliot, to be sure, are certainly an odd couple and can only
remain together in a tense constellation for a short while before they begin
to drift apart. Duchamp, in fact, has emerged in the past few decades as the
quintessential critic of modernist pretensions to formalist purity, optical
essentialism, and the integrity of the medium. Although he may have called
into question expressive notions of genius and disparaged the empirical perception of the artist, his own role in dismantling the Greenbergian consensus has been increasingly written in heroic terms.[68] So too the personal, often
erotic traces in his work have come to the fore, in ways that invite the charge
of a renewed psychologism.[69]

The postmoderns, in their appropriation of Duchamp, in fact, would not
feel offended by this charge, for one of the most explicit dividing lines between modernism and its putative successor is precisely their differing attitudes toward psychologism. Indeed, in one sense postmodernism can be said
to be a "second psychologism."[70] Its return seems to have been prepared by
the widespread recognition that the modernist project of ruthless purification had reached a dead end, as there was little interesting left to write or
paint about once all contaminations were banished. The indifference to
human suffering that seemed too often to accompany the modernist differentiation of value spheres also made many uneasy, as the extent of the modernist entanglement with fascism became clearer. Similarly, the modernist
pretensions to disinterestedness have seemed increasingly hollow in the face
of multiculturalist and feminist critiques of its *soi-disant* universalism, as
well as the sociological claim that aesthetic value is really just another name
for "cultural capital."[71] And finally, the threat of a scientistic version of psychology seemed less pressing once the literary and hermeneutic dimensions
of psychoanalysis came to the fore. The recent return to some form of psychologism is, in fact, evident in philosophy itself, where a reaction against
the privileging of self-identical logic has taken many forms, among them a
new sensitivity to the impact of the institutional context of the discipline on
its subject matter.[72] The neopragmatism of Richard Rorty is a salient example of a renewed distrust of the fallacy that defenders of psychologism had
once mockingly dubbed "logicism."[73] In *Philosophy and the Mirror of Nature*, he notes with satisfaction that

seventy years after Husserl's "Philosophy as Rigorous Science" and Russell's "Logic
as the Essence of Philosophy," we are back with the same putative dangers which
faced the authors of these manifestos: if philosophy becomes too naturalistic, hard-

nosed positive disciplines will nudge it aside; if it becomes too historicist, then intellectual history, literary criticism, and similar soft spots in "the humanities" will swallow it up.[74]

Rorty's plea is to stop worrying in the face of these putative dangers and accept the inevitable blurring of the lines between philosophy and its scientific and historicist neighbors. Heeding his message, some of his pragmatist followers have reread the modernist tradition itself in the hope of resituating its figures in the new context; one has gone so far as to try to rescue even T. S. Eliot by turning him into a closet pragmatist, who ultimately came to believe in the virtues of historical tradition and practical wisdom over logical (or aesthetic) truth.[75]

Deconstruction has likewise taken aim at Husserl's attempt to use eidetic intuition to provide an avenue of entry into the timeless world of logical truth. Derrida's *Speech and Phenomena* begins with an attack on the confusions of a transcendental psychologism that seeks to exclude precisely those intrusions from without that any psychologism necessitates.[76] Gleefully extolling the very contamination and pollution that so troubled critics of psychologism, celebrating the temporal deferral and traces of the past that the fetish of spatial form in modernism hoped to keep at bay, restoring modified respect for the representation and mimesis that modernist self-reflexivity had banished, deconstruction transgresses many of the same boundaries that nineteenth-century psychologism had also violated.

Its effects on literary critical attitudes toward psychologism have been evident. Although eschewing any strong notion of the expressive subject and no less suspicious of humanist pieties than Hulme and Eliot were, deconstruction has reversed the New Critics' disdain for romanticism and reintroduced complicated notions of intentionality.[77] One need only mention New Historicism, reception aesthetics, the pervasive influence of Nietzsche, and the proliferation of psychoanalytically informed approaches to reinforce the same point: the taboo against psychologism now seems firmly laid to rest among literary critics. Or, more precisely, many have come to feel at home in a gray area between the absolute alternatives of a maximalist psychologistic reductionism, in which all mental activity and all cultural artifacts are merely an expression of emotional states, and an anti-psychologistic purism, in which everything of value must be protected against any pollution from without.[78]

Indeed, one of the reasons it may be meaningful to distinguish between modernism and postmodernism, however volatile that distinction may be, is the recent undermining of the taboo against psychologism, which operated so powerfully during the modernist era. As I hope is now evident, "psychologism," with all of its connotations of reductionism, contamination, and relativism, became one of the main anxieties of that era, a veritable "specter," as one recent commentator has called it, haunting the modernist mind.[79] Postmodernists, in contrast, seem more relaxed and untroubled by these dangers, having learned to live with the ghosts of the past rather than trying to exorcise them. Although they hold no brief for the notion of an integrated subject, whose individual psychology can be the genesis of art, they feel comfortable with a dispersed and decentered subjectivity whose impulses, desires, fetishes, and fantasies disturb the smooth workings of any cultural sublimation.[80]

But to give the screw one final turn, postmodernism may itself be haunted by a specter of its own, which refuses to die: the ghost of modernist anti-psychologism. Some contemporary philosophers of mind still struggle, after all, to produce a transcendental account of consciousness that will establish the autonomy of at least mathematics and logic.[81] Certain ethical theorists continue to balk at the "emotivist" reduction of moral imperatives to personal preferences.[82] And what Adorno liked to call the "truth content of art" stubbornly refuses to lose its fascination for those unwilling to level all aesthetic distinctions and reduce all judgments to matters of individual taste.

If Derrida is right in claiming that the specter of Marx still haunts our apparently post-Marxist world, the same might well be the case for the anti-psychologism that flourished during the heyday of modernism.[83] As the continuing wars over multiculturalism and the canon testify, it would be premature to believe that the pressures that produced the fear of psychologism have entirely subsided, or that the search for aesthetic value is entirely a thing of the past. Whatever the future of the debate, one thing is clear: it would be a serious mistake to ignore the creative energies unleashed by the effort to fend off psychologism during the previous era. For even if it now seems a losing battle, or its outcome at best a stalemate, the struggle was an indisputable ingredient in the making of that remarkable phenomenon we call modern art.

Notes

MICALE: INTRODUCTION

1. The classic discussion of this development in creative fiction is Leon Edel's *The Psychological Novel, 1900–1950* (Philadelphia, Penn.: Lippincott, 1955).

2. In *Modernism: 1890–1930* (Harmondsworth, England: Penguin Books, 1976), 71–93, Malcolm Bradbury and James McFarlane briefly discuss "the mind of modernism." Bradbury and McFarlane, however, use this term to designate the general mentality or outlook underlying the Modernist movement in the cultural arts. In contrast, I intend the term in this volume to denote, in a more specialized sense, the beliefs about human psychology and formal theories of mind to which Modernist intellectuals in both the arts and the sciences ascribed.

3. The most important voice in mapping the field of literature and medicine studies has been the American literary historian George Rousseau. From his many statements, see above all Rousseau, "Literature and Medicine: The State of the Field," *Isis* 72 (1981): 406–24, and Rousseau, *Enlightenment Borders: Pre- and Postmodern Discourses—Medical, Scientific* (Manchester: University of Manchester Press, 1991).

Anthologies of essays include Enid Rhodes Peschel, ed., *Medicine and Literature* (New York: Neale Watson, 1980); Joanne Trautmann Banks, ed., *Healing Arts in Dialogue: Medicine and Literature* (Carbondale: Southern Illinois University Press, 1981); J. A. V. Chapple, *Science and Literature in the Nineteenth Century* (Hound Mills, Hampshire: Macmillan, 1986); Christopher Fox, ed., *Psychology and Literature in the Eighteenth Century* (New York: AMS Press, 1987); George Levine, ed., *One Culture: Essays in Science and Literature* (Madison: University of Wisconsin Press, 1987); Frederick Amrine, ed., *Literature and Science as Modes of Expression* (Dordrecht: Kluwer Academic Publishers, 1989); Stuart Peterfreund, ed., *Literature and Science: Theory and Practice* (Boston: Northeastern University Press, 1990); and Marie Mulvey Roberts and Roy Porter, eds., *Literature and Medicine during the Eighteenth Century* (London: Routledge, 1992). See also Léon Binet and Pierre Vallery-Radot, *Médecine et littérature* (Paris: Expansion scientifique française, 1963); and Gérard Danou, *Le Corps souffrant—littérature et médecine* (Seyssel: Champ Vallon, 1994). For studies of individual figures, see Clarence P. Oberndorf, *The Psychiatric Novels of Oliver Wendell Holmes* (New York: Columbia University

Press, 1943); David M. Rein, *S. Weir Mitchell as Psychiatric Novelist* (New York: International Universities Press, 1952); Jean Theorides, *Stendhal du côté de la science* (Aran: Éditions du Grand Chêne, 1972); John B. Lyons, *James Joyce and Medicine* (Dublin: Dolman Press, 1973); Bernard Strauss, *Maladies of Marcel Proust: Doctors and Disease in His Life and Work* (New York: Holmes and Meier, 1980); John Wiltshire, *Samuel Johnson and the Medical World: The Doctor and the Patient* (Cambridge: Cambridge University Press, 1991); John Coope, *Doctor Chekhov: A Study in Literature and Medicine* (Chale, Isle of Wight: Cross Publishing, 1997); Robert L. Davis, *Whitman and the Romance of Medicine* (Berkeley: University of California Press, 1997); and Nicola Luckhurst, *Science and Structure in Proust's 'A la recherche'* (Oxford: Oxford University Press, 2001). The biannual journal *Literature and Medicine* was established in 1982—volume four, published in 1985, treats psychiatry and literature—and the Society for Literature and Science, which produces an annual newsletter and bibliography, was founded in 1985.

4. Ryan, *Vanishing Subject* (Chicago and London: University of Chicago Press, 1991); Albright, *Quantum Poetics* (Cambridge: Cambridge University Press, 1997); and Armstrong, *Modernism, Technology, and the Body* (Cambridge: Cambridge University Press, 1998). Albright argues that early twentieth-century theoretical physics, especially wave and particle models of matter, inspired literary savants in a search for the elementary components of poetry and language. See also Gillian Beer, "Wave Theory and the Rise of Literary Modernism," in *Open Fields: Science in Cultural Encounter* (Oxford: Clarendon Press, 1996), chap. 13.

5. Louis A. Sass, *Madness and Modernism: Insanity in the Light of Modern Art, Literature, and Thought* (New York: Basic Books, 1992). See also Lillian Feder, *Madness in Literature* (Princeton, N.J.: Princeton University Press, 1980); Soshana Felman, *La folie et la chose littéraire* (Paris: Édition du Seuil, 1978); and Allen Thiher, *Revels in Madness: Insanity in Medicine and Literature* (Ann Arbor: University of Michigan Press, 1999). Juan Rigoli's *Lire et délire. Aliénisme et littérature en France au XIXe siècle* (Paris: Fayard, 2001) is a recent signal contribution to this line of scholarship.

6. C. P. Snow, *The Two Cultures and the Scientific Revolution* (New York: Cambridge University Press, 1959). For a recent reappraisal, see Stefan Collini's lengthy introduction to the 1993 reissue of Snow's essay by Cambridge University Press.

7. G. S. Rousseau, "Literature and Medicine: Towards a Simultaneity of Theory and Practice," *Literature and Medicine* 5 (1986): 152–81. See also Michael Neve, "Medicine and Literature," in W. F. Bynum and Roy Porter, eds., *Companion Encyclopedia of the History of Medicine* (London and New York: Routledge, 1993), 2: 1520–35.

8. A note on usage: The term "dynamic" has complex and independent histories in several branches of science and medicine. In this introduction, I use the interchangeable terms "dynamic psychiatry" and "depth psychology" in a descriptive, his-

torical sense, to denote a cluster of theories of mind that emerged in Euro-American medicine during the period 1880–1940. Despite their differences, these psychologies all posited models of human mental functioning with multiple strata of consciousness and an interplay of energies and activities between the different levels. In exploring the conscious/unconscious duality, dynamic psychiatrists and depth psychologists were typically attracted to the study of the neuroses, dream life, psychosexuality, psychological primitivism, the structure of the psyche, psychological symbolism, the psychology of trauma, multiple personality formation, and the mythopoetic functions of the unconscious mind. The classic, comprehensive account is Henri F. Ellenberger's *The Discovery of the Unconscious: The History and Evolution of Dynamic Psychiatry* (New York: Basic Books, 1970). See, too, Josef Rattner, ed., *Pioniere der Tiefenpsychologie* (Vienna: Europaverlag, 1979), and Rattner, *Klassiker der Tiefenpsychologie* (Munich: Psychologie Verlag Union, 1990).

9. Ludwig Marcuse, "Die deutsche Literatur im Werke Freuds," *German Quarterly* 29 (1956): 85–96; Didier Anzieu, "The Place of Germanic Language and Culture in Freud's Discovery of Psychoanalysis between 1895 and 1900," *International Journal of Psychoanalysis* 67 (1986): 219–26; Ilse Grubrich-Simitis, "Reflections on Sigmund Freud's Relation to the German Language and to Some German-Speaking Authors of the Enlightenment," *International Journal of Psychoanalysis* 67 (1986): 287–94; Johannes Cremerius, "Der Einfluss der Psychanalyse auf die deutschsprachige Literatur," *Psyche* 41 (1987): 39–54.

10. Bennett Simon, *Mind and Madness in Ancient Greece: The Classical Roots of Modern Psychiatry* (Ithaca, N.Y.: Cornell University Press, 1978); Peter Gay, *Freud: A Life for Our Time* (New York: Norton, 1988), 100, 154, 313, 318–19, 323, 442.

11. In his clinical history of the patient "Elisabeth von R." in the *Studies on Hysteria* (1895), Freud commented further: "It still strikes me myself as strange that the case histories I write should read like short stories and that, as one might say, they lack the serious stamp of science. I must console myself with the reflection that the nature of the subject is evidently responsible for this, rather than any preference of my own. The fact is that local diagnosis and electrical reactions lead nowhere in the study of hysteria, whereas a detailed description of mental processes *such as we are accustomed to find in the works of imaginative writers* enables me, with the use of a few psychological formulas, to obtain at least some kind of insight into the course of that affection" (cited in James Strachey et al., eds., *The Standard Edition of the Complete Psychological Works of Sigmund Freud* [London: Hogarth Press, 1955], 2: 160–61, italics mine).

12. Freud, *The Interpretation of Dreams*, in ibid., 4: xxiv. For the most recent and comprehensive appraisal of the role played by literature in Freud's creation of psychoanalysis, see Graham Frankland, *Freud's Literary Culture* (Cambridge: Cambridge University Press, 2000).

13. Richard Noll, *The Jung Cult: Origins of a Charismatic Movement* (Princeton, N.J.: Princeton University Press, 1994), 20.

14. The influence of von Hartmann in German-speaking central European intellectual life has especially been forgotten. By 1890, Hartmann's *Philosophie des Unbewussten* (*Philosophy of the Unconscious*) (1869) had passed through no fewer than ten editions. For Schopenhauer and Bergson, see David Luft, "Schopenhaeur, Austria, and the Generation of 1905," *Central European History* 26 (1983): 53–75; and Pete Gunter, "Bergson and Jung," *Journal of the History of Ideas* 44 (1982): 632–52.

15. C. G. Jung, *Nietzsche's Zarathustra: Notes of a Seminar Given in 1934–1939*, ed. James L. Jarrett (Princeton, N.J.: Princeton University Press, 1988). See also Noll, *The Jung Cult*, 3–5, 29–30, 265–69; F. G. Crookshank, *Individual Psychology and Nietzsche* (London: C. W. Daniel Co., 1933); Paul-Laurent Assoun, *Freud et Nietzsche* (Paris: Presses Universitaires de France, 1980); and Ronald Lehrer, *Nietzsche's Presence in Freud's Life and Thought: On the Origins of a Psychology of Dynamic Mental Functioning* (Albany: State University of New York Press, 1995).

16. The best overview of Janetian psychology remains Ellenberger, *Discovery of the Unconscious*, chap. 6.

17. Medico-literary figures from these years outside France include S. Weir Mitchell, Oliver Wendell Holmes, William A. Hammond, Arthur Schnitzler, Moritz Benedikt, Theodor Meynert, Max Nordau, Gottfried Benn, and Frederik van Eeden.

18. "Die neue Psychologie" is the title of an essay written in 1890 by the Viennese dramatist, storyteller, and literary critic Hermann Bahr. See Gotthart Wunberg, ed., *Hermann Bahr: Zur Uberwindung des Naturalismus. Theoretische Schriften 1887–1904* (Stuttgart: W. Kohlhammer Verlag, 1968), 53–64.

19. On the medical case history as a narrative form of knowledge, see Kathryn Montgomery Hunter's pioneering study *Doctors' Stories: The Narrative Structure of Medical Knowledge* (Princeton, N.J.: Princeton University Press, 1991), as well as Hilde L. Nelson, ed., *Stories and Their Limits: Narrative Approaches to Bioethics* (New York: Routledge, 1997), and Tod Chambers, *The Fictions of Bioethics: Cases as Literary Texts* (New York: Routledge, 1999).

20. Jacqueline Carroy, "La psychologie de l'École de Nancy: Une psychothérapie de groupe par le langage," *Psychologie médicale* 19 (1987): 259–61. For a global history of "the talking cures," consult Stanley W. Jackson, *Care of the Psyche: A History of Psychological Healing* (New Haven and London: Yale University Press, 1999), chap. 5.

21. In a celebrated chapter titled "The Stream of Thought," William James writes of "the continuous flow of the mental stream" (*Principles of Psychology* [New York: Henry Holt and Company], 1: chap. 9). For the literary dispensation, see Robert Humphrey, *Stream of Consciousness in the Modern Novel* (Berkeley: University of California Press, 1954); Shiv K. Kumar, *Bergson and the Stream of Consciousness: A Study in Literary Method* (New York: New York Press, 1963); Dorrit C. Cohn, *Transparent Minds: Narrative Modes for Presenting Consciousness in Fiction* (Princeton, N.J.: Princeton University Press, 1978); and Erwin R. Steinberg, ed., *The Stream-of-Consciousness Technique in the Modern Novel* (London: National University Publications, 1979).

22. Pedro Lain Entralgo, *The Therapy of the Word in Classical Antiquity*, trans. and ed. L. J. Rather and John M. Sharp (New Haven, Conn.: Yale University Press, 1970). Cheryl Mattingly makes the same point in *Healing Dramas and Clinical Plots: The Narrative Structure of Experience* (Cambridge: Cambridge University Press, 1998).

23. Hence Freiherr von Berger's 1896 observation about Breuer's and Freud's *Studies on Hysteria* in *Morgen-Presse*, used as an epigraph above. Von Berger, who admitted to finding Breuer's and Freud's book artistically satisfying, was professor of the history of literature at the University of Vienna and director of the Vienna Burgtheater. See also the special issue of *Literature and Medicine*, vol. 11, no. 1 (1992), titled "The Art of the Case History."

24. For an elaboration of this point, see Mark S. Micale, *Approaching Hysteria: Disease and Its Interpretations* (Princeton, N.J.: Princeton University Press, 1995), 221–39; and Micale, "Littérature, médecine, hystérie: le cas de *Madame Bovary* de Gustave Flaubert," *L'Évolution psychiatrique* 60 (1995): 901–18.

25. A clear example of this practice is available in Peter Collier and Judy Davies, eds., *Modernism and the European Unconscious* (New York: St. Martin's Press, 1990). The library of book-length works on Freud and cultural Modernism includes Frederick J. Hoffmann, *Freudianism and the Literary Mind* (Baton Rouge: Louisiana State University Press, 1945); Sheldon Brivic, *Joyce Between Freud and Jung* (Port Washington, N.Y.: Kennikat, 1980); Michael Worbs, *Nervenkunst: Literatur und Psychoanalyse im Wien der Jahrhundertwende* (Frankfurt: Europäische Verlagsanstalt, 1983); Jeffrey Berman, *The Talking Cure: Literary Representations of Psychoanalysis* (New York: New York University Press, 1985); Leo Bersani, *The Freudian Body: Psychoanalysis and Art* (New York: Columbia University Press, 1986); Barry Richards, *Images of Freud: Cultural Responses to Psychoanalysis* (New York: St. Martin's Press, 1989); Elizabeth Abel, *Virginia Woolf and the Fictions of Psychoanalysis* (Chicago: University of Chicago Press, 1989); and Alexander Grinstein, *Freud at the Crossroads* (Madison, Conn.: International Universities Press, 1990).

26. In recent years, many of these theorists have begun to receive scholarly (and at times clinical) attention. See Theta Wolf, *Alfred Binet* (Chicago: University of Chicago Press, 1973); François Duyckaerts, *Joseph Delboeuf: Philosophe et hypnotiseur* (Paris: Les empêcheur de penser en rond, 1992); Pierre Castel, Jacqueline Carroy, and François Duyckaerts, eds., "Delboeuf et Bernheim: Entre hypnose et suggestion," *Corpus: Revue de philosophie*, special issue, no. 32 (1997); Joseph Delboeuf, *Le sommeil et les rêves et autres textes* [1885] (Paris: Fayard, 1993); Stewart Wolf, *Brain, Mind, and Medicine: Richet and the Origins of Physiological Psychology* (New Brunswick, N.J.: Transaction Books, 1993); Mireille Cifali, "Théodore Flournoy, la découverte de l'inconscient," *Le Bloc-Notes de la psychanalyse* 3 (1983): 111–31; D. P. Faber, "Théodule Ribot and the Reception of Evolutionary Ideas in France," *History of Psychiatry* 8 (Dec. 1997): 445–58; Sonu Shamdasani, "De Genève à Zurich: Jung et la Suisse Romande," *Revue médicale de la Suisse Romande* 116

(1996): 917–22; Christopher Goetz, Michel Bonduelle, and Toby Gelfand, *Constructing Neurology: Jean-Martin Charcot 1825–1893* (New York: Oxford University Press, 1995); Chandak Sengoopta, *Otto Weininger: Sex, Science, and Self in Imperial Vienna* (Chicago and London: University of Chicago Press, 2000); Allan Janik, *Essays on Wittgenstein and Weininger* (Amsterdam: Rodopi, 1985); Frank J. Sulloway, *Freud, Biologist of the Mind: Beyond the Psychoanalytic Legend* (New York: Basic Books, 1979), chaps. 5, 6, 8; Régine Plas, "La psychologie pathologique d'Afred Binet," in P. Fraisse and J. Segui, eds., *Les origines de la psychologie scientifique: centième anniversaire de L'Année Psychologique (1894–1994)* (Paris: Presses Universitaires de France, 1994), 229–45; and Carlo Trombetta, *Édouard Claparède: Psicologo* (Rome: Armando, 1989). Most dramatic has been the renaissance of studies of Janet, including the reprinting of Janet's major psychological texts. See Paul Brown, "Pierre Janet: Alienist Reintegrated," *Current Opinion on Psychiatry* 4 (1991): 389–95; J. C. Nemiah, "Janet Redivivus: The Centenary of *L'Automatisme psychologique*," *American Journal of Psychiatry* 146 (1989): 1527–29; and Henri Faure, "La réédition des oeuvres de Pierre Janet," *Bulletin de psychologie* 41 (1988): 477–81.

27. See, above all, Michael R. Finn, *Proust, the Body and Literary Form* (Cambridge: Cambridge University Press, 1999), chap. 1. Henri Ellenberger went so far as to assert that "it would be quite feasible to extract from his [Proust's] work a treatise on the mind, which would give a plausible picture of what the first dynamic psychiatry would have become had it followed its natural [i.e., non-Freudian] course" (*Discovery of the Unconscious*, 168).

28. See also Jacqueline Carroy, "Hystérie, théâtre, littérature au dix-neuvième siècle," *Psychanalyse à l'université* 7 (1982): 299–317; Micale, *Approaching Hysteria*, chap. 3; Sander L. Gilman, Helen King, Roy Porter, and Elaine Showalter, *Hysteria Beyond Freud* (Berkeley: University of California Press, 1993), passim; and Nicole Edelman, *Les métamorphoses de l'hysteriques: Du début du XIXe siècle à la grande guerre* (Paris: Découverte, 2003).

29. Aragon and Breton, "Le cinquantenaire de l'hystérie (1878–1928)," reproduced in Maurice Nadeau, ed., *Histoire du surréalisme: Documents surréalistes* (Paris: Seuil, 1948), 125. This point was also brought out by David Lomas in "Max Ernst: The Seductions of Hysteria," University of Manchester, Research Seminars in the History of Art, Dec. 5, 1995.

30. The clearest expression of Breuer's and Freud's own debt to the French psychological school is their footnotes and bibliography in *Studies on Hysteria*. On the new "psychological" theories of hysteria in France around the turn of the century, see Debora L. Silverman, *Art Nouveau in Fin-de-Siècle France: Politics, Psychology, and Style* (Los Angeles: University of California Press, 1989), chap. 5; and Martha Noel Evans, *Fits and Starts: A Genealogy of Hysteria in Modern France* (Ithaca, N.Y.: Cornell University Press, 1991), chap. 2.

31. Indicatively, Hermann Bahr's 1890 essay, coining the term "the new psychology," in the main discusses recent literature, philosophy, and psychology in France. See note 18 above.

32. See above all Jacqueline Carroy's *Hypnose, suggestion et psychologie: L'invention de sujets* (Paris: Presses Universitaires de France, 1991), which emphasizes the diversity of suggestive and hypnotherapeutic practices circulating during the late nineteenth century.

33. Marcel Prévost, *L'Automne d'une femme* (Paris: Édition Larousse, 1891); Henri Ellenberger, "The Pathogenic Secret and Its Therapeutics," *Journal of the History of the Behavioral Sciences* 2 (1966): 33–34; Onno van der Hart and Barbara Friedman, "A Reader's Guide to Pierre Janet on Dissociation: A Neglected Intellectual Heritage," *Dissociation* 2 (1989): 3–16.

34. Daniel Hack Tuke, ed., *A Dictionary of Psychological Medicine*, 2 vols. (London: J. & A. Churchill, 1893–95); Janet, *Psychological Healing: A Historical and Clinical Study* (1925), 2 vols. (New York: Arno Press, 1976).

35. Ryan, *Vanishing Subject*, 7.

36. Faber, "Théodule Ribot and the Reception of Evolutionary Ideas in France," *History of Psychiatry* (1997): 445–58. See also Robert J. Richards, *Darwin and the Emergence of Evolutionary Theories of Mind and Behavior* (Chicago: University of Chicago Press, 1987), chap. 8.

37. Myers's ideas first appeared during the 1880s and 1890s in a sequence of publications in the *Proceedings for the Society of Psychical Research*, and later appeared in his posthumously published synthesis *Human Personality and Its Survival of Bodily Death*, 2 vols. (London: Longman, Greens, 1903).

38. James, "The Hidden Self," *Scribner's Magazine* 7 (Mar. 1890): 361–73; Woolf, cited in Ryan, *Vanishing Subject*, 191. For historical surveys of this belief, consult Lancelot Law Whyte, *The Unconscious Before Freud* (New York: Basic Books, 1960); Mark Altschule, "The Growth of the Concept of Unconscious Cerebration before 1890," *The Roots of Modern Psychiatry: Essays in the History of Psychiatry* (New York: Grune & Stratton, 1957), chap. 4; and Ellenberger, *Discovery of the Unconscious*, passim.

39. Flournoy, *Des Indes à la Planète Mars* (1900) (Paris: Seuil, 1983), translated as *From India to the Planet Mars: A Case of Multiple Personality with Imaginary Languages*, ed. and introduced by Sonu Shamdasani (Princeton, N.J.: Princeton University Press, 1994). As Shamdasani notes, "Flournoy's successful combination of a literary and 'scientific' style led to extremely laudatory reviews in both the popular press and in psychological journals. It was read as both a treatise in psychology and as a novel" (xxvii).

40. Eugene Taylor, "The Boston School of Psychotherapy: Science, Healing, and Consciousness in Nineteenth-Century New England," Eight Lectures for the Lowell Institute (Feb.–Mar. 1982). See also G. E. Gifford, ed., *Psychoanalysis, Psychotherapy, and the New England Medical Scene, 1894–1944* (New York: Science History Publications, 1978); and Robert Fuller, *Americans and the Unconscious* (New York: Oxford University Press, 1986).

41. A case in point is the recent scholarly exploration—issuing simultaneously from the history of anthropology, Modernist literary studies, and postcolonial stud-

ies—of comparative Modernist primitivisms. In this work, Freud's model of the primitive psychic mind, as a repressed but ever-present animalistic unconscious, is presented as one of many metaphorizations of the primitive emerging during the early twentieth century, including in the new human sciences (anthropology, sociology, crowd psychology, psychoanalysis) as well as in Postimpressionist and Cubist painting, classical music, jazz, dance, and photography. See Elazar Barkan and Ronald Bush, eds., *Prehistories of the Future: The Primitivist Project and the Culture of Modernism* (Stanford, Calif.: Stanford University Press, 1995); Marianna Torgovnick, *Gone Primitive: Savage Intellects, Modern Lives* (Chicago: University of Chicago Press, 1990); and Marc Manganaro, ed., *Modernist Anthropology: From Fieldwork to Text* (Princeton, N.J.: Princeton University Press, 1990).

42. Anne Harrington, "Hysteria, Hypnosis, and the Lure of the Invisible: The Rise of Neo-Mesmerism in Fin-de-siècle French Psychiatry," in *The Anatomy of Madness*, ed. W. F. Bynum, Roy Porter, and Michael Shepherd (London: Routledge, 1988), 3: chap. 8. For the full neo-Mesmerist literature of the time, see Adam Crabtree, ed., *Animal Magnetism, Early Hypnotism, and Psychical Research, 1766–1925: An Annotated Bibliography* (White Plains, N.Y.: Kraus International Publications, 1988), and for a long-term history of hypnosis, see Alan Gauld, *The History of Hypnosis* (Cambridge: Cambridge University Press, 1993).

43. This point is well made by Jacqueline Carroy and Régine Plas in "The Origins of French Experimental Psychology: Experiment and Experimentalism," *History of Human Sciences* 9 (1996): 73–84. As Carroy and Plas observe, "the hypnotized subject in a state of cataleptic immobilization or lethargic subjection, to adopt Charcot's terms, was expected to realize an ideal, that of the decerebrated human laboratory animal reduced to a state of reflex-man or pure automaton" (79). See also Régine Plas, "De la vivisection morale et intellectuelle: L'hypnotisme comme moyen d'investigation psychologique en France au XIXe siècle," *Phoenix* 11–12 (1991): 41–44.

44. Léon Chertok, "L'Hypnose depuis le premier congrès international tenu à Paris en 1889," *La presse médicale* (1965): 1495–1500.

45. A study of these popular-medical troubadours, who reached audiences of thousands, would be welcome.

46. André Brouillet's famous canvas of Charcot displaying a hypnotized hysteric to a rapt group of medical students includes in its audience two novelists (Jules Claretie and Paul Arène), a politician (Alfred Naquet), and an Impressionist art critic (Philippe Burty).

47. On Charcot and the arts of his day, see also Silverman, *Art Nouveau in Fin-de-Siècle France*, chap. 5.

48. M. A. de Monzie, "Discours," *Revue neurologique* 41 (1925): 1159–62.

49. Winter, *Mesmerized: Powers of Mind in Victorian Britain* (Cambridge: Cambridge University Press, 1998).

50. Hippolyte Bernheim, *De la suggestion dans l'état hypnotique et dans l'état de*

veille (Paris: Doin, 1884); Bernheim, *Suggestive Therapeutics: A Treatise on the Nature and Use of Hypnotism* (1887), trans. C. A. Herter (New York: G. P. Putnam, 1889). For historical accounts, see Dominique Barrucand, *Histoire de l'hypnose en France* (Paris: Presses Universitaires de France, 1967), 103–34; Jacqueline Carroy, "L'École hypnologique de Nancy: Liébeault, Beaunis, Liégeois et Delboeuf," *Le pays lorrain* 2 (1988): 108–16 and 3 (1988): 159–66.

51. Hans H. Walser, "L'École hypnologique de Nancy: Berceau de la psychothérapie moderne," *Schweizer Archiv für Neurologie, Neurochirurgie und Psychiatrie* 685 (Apr. 28, 1965): 443.

52. For instance, see Richard von Krafft-Ebing, *Eine experimentelle Studie auf dem Gebiete des Hypnotismus* (Stuttgart: F. Enker, 1888); Moritz Benedikt, *Hypnotismus und Suggestion. Eine klinisch-psychologische Studie* (Leipzig and Vienna: Breitenstein, 1894); Boris Sidis, *The Psychology of Suggestion: A Research into the Subconscious Nature of Man and Society*, Introduction by William James (New York: D. Appleton, 1898); Albert Moll, *Der Hypnotismus* (Berlin: Fischer, 1889); and J. J. Déjerine, *Les manifestations fonctionnelles des psychonévroses, leur traitement par la psychothérapie* (Paris: Masson, 1911)—all of which are explicitly indebted to the Nancy School.

53. Hippolyte Bernheim, *Die Suggestion und ihre Heilwirkung*, trans. S. Freud (Leipzig and Vienna: Deuticke, 1896). Freud's writings on hypnosis, which include an essay, case history, book review, and book preface, are available in *Standard Edition*, 1: 63–128.

54. Auguste Forel's *Hypnotism; or Suggestion and Psychotherapy* (1889), trans. H. Armit (London: Rebman, 1906), provides a clear expression of the continuity between the practices of hypno- and psychotherapeutics, written by the so-called founder of Swiss-German psychiatry. The best contemporary study of the topic is, again, Carroy's *Hypnose, suggestion et psychologie*.

55. Sonu Shamdasani, "Encountering Hélène: Théodore Flournoy and the Genesis of Subliminal Psychology," in Flournoy, *From India to the Planet Mars*, 11.

56. On Myers, who awaits his biographer, see Gardner Murphy, "The Life and Work of Frederic W. H. Myers," *Tomorrow* 2 (Winter 1954): 33–39; and Adam Crabtree, *Magnetic Sleep: The Mesmeric Roots of Psychological Healing* (New Haven and London: Yale University Press, 1993), chap. 16.

57. C. G. Jung, *Zur Psychologie und Pathologie sogenannter occulter Phänomene: Eine psychiatrische Studie* (Leipzig: Mutze, 1902), available in translation in Herbert Read, Michael Fordham, and Gerhard Adler, eds., *Collected Works of Jung*, 2d ed. (Princeton, N.J.: Princeton University Press, 1970), 1: 3–88. See also F. X. Charet, *Spiritualism and the Foundations of C. G. Jung's Psychology* (Albany, N.Y.: State University of New York Press, 1993).

58. Nandor Fodor, *Freud, Jung, and Occultism* (New Hyde Park: New York University, 1971).

59. Flournoy, *Des Indes à la Planète Mars*. See also Flournoy's later study, *Esprits*

et Médiums: Mélanges de métapsychique et de psychologie (Geneva: Kündig, 1911). Indispensable for understanding Flournoy's work generally and this case in particular is Shamdasani, "Encountering Hélène," xi–li.

60. Foremost among these interpretations is Walter Deonna, *De la planète Mars en Terre Sainte: Art et subconscient. Un médium peintre: Hélène Smith* (Paris: De Boccard, 1932).

61. Breton, *Conversations: The Autobiography of Surrealism*, with André Parinaud, trans. Mark Polizzotti (New York: Paragon House, 1993), interview 6; Breton, *Nadja* (Paris: Gallimard, 1964); Breton, "The Automatic Message," in *What Is Surrealism? Selected Writings*, ed. Franklin Rosemont (New York: Monad, 1978), 97–109; Breton, "The Mediums Enter," in *The Lost Steps / Pas perdus*, trans. Mark Polizzotti (Lincoln: University of Nebraska Press, 1996), 89–95. See also Jean Starobinski, "Freud, Breton, Myers," *L'Arc* 34 (1968): 87–96; and Shamdasani, "Encountering Hélène," xliii–xliv.

62. William James, *The Varieties of Religious Experience: A Study in Human Nature* (1902) (New York: Modern Library, 1936), 14.

63. Frank Miller Turner, *Between Science and Religion: The Reaction to Scientific Naturalism in Late Victorian England* (New Haven and London: Yale University Press, 1974), chap. 5.

64. Fodor, *Freud, Jung, and Occultism*; Gay, *Freud: Life for Our Time*, 354–55, 443–45; Noll, *Jung Cult*, 76–80. See also Pierre Janet, "Le spiritisme contemporain," *Revue philosophique* 33 (1892): 413–42.

65. A large volume of scholarship of high caliber has now been devoted to this topic, including Eugene Taylor, *William James on Exceptional Mental States: The 1896 Lowell Lectures* (Amherst: University of Massachusetts Press, 1982); Taylor, *William James on Consciousness Beyond the Margin* (Princeton, N.J.: Princeton University Press, 1996), chaps. 2–5; Frederick H. Burkhardt and Fredson Bowers, eds., *The Works of William James: Essays in Psychical Research* (Cambridge, Mass.: Harvard University Press, 1986); Seymour H. Mauskopf and Michael R. McVaugh, *The Elusive Science: Origins of Experimental Psychical Research* (Baltimore, Md.: Johns Hopkins University Press, 1980); Marilyn Marshall and Russel Wendt, "William Wundt, Spiritism, and the Assumptions of Science," in *Wundt Studies*, ed. Wolfgang Bringmann and R. D. Tweny (Toronto: Hogrefe, 1980), 158–75; John Cerullo, *The Secularization of the Soul: Psychical Research in Modern Britain* (Philadelphia, Penn.: Institute for the Study of Human Issues, 1982); Edward M. Brown, "Neurology and Spiritualism in the 1870s," *Bulletin of the History of Medicine* 57 (1983): 563–77; and Janet Oppenheim, *The Other World: Spiritualism and Psychical Research in England, 1850–1914* (Cambridge: Cambridge University Press, 1988). For the French interest in the subject, see Régine Plas, *Naissance d'une science humaine: la psychologie, les psychologues et le 'merveilleux psychique'* (Rennes: Presses Universitaires de Rennes, 2000). Plas's emphasis on the occultist and spiritualist origins of French psychology nicely dovetails with my own interpretation.

66. Sylvia L. Cranston, *HPB: The Extraordinary Life and Influence of Helena Blavatsky, Founder of the Modern Theosophical Movement* (New York: G. P. Putnam's Sons, 1993).

67. W. B. Yeats, *A Vision* (London: T. Werner Laurie, 1925); W. B. Yeats, "Swedenborg, Mediums, and the Desolate Places" (1914), in *Explorations*, selected by Mrs. W. B. Yeats (London: Macmillan, 1962), 30–70. For the background to these writings, see the extensive introduction to George Mills Harper and Walter Kelly Hood, eds., *A Critical Edition of Yeats's 'A Vision' (1925)* (London: Macmillan, 1978), as well as George Mills Harper, ed., *Yeats and the Occult* (Toronto: Macmillan, 1975), xi–l.

68. Materer, *Modernist Alchemy: Poetry and the Occult* (Ithaca, N.Y.: Cornell University Press, 1995). Materer's projected tradition begins with Yeats and his wife, extends through Ezra Pound, T. S. Eliot, H.D. (Hilda Dolittle), Robert Duncan, Sylvia Plath, and Ted Hughes, and culminates in James Merrill.

69. Morris Beja, *Epiphany in the Modern Novel* (London: Peter Owen, 1971); Tim Cribb, "James Joyce: The Unconscious and the Cognitive Epiphany," in Collier and Davies, *Modernism and the European Unconscious* (1990), chap. 4.

70. Edelman, *Voyantes, guérisseuses et visionnaires en France 1785–1914* (Paris: Albin Michel, 1993).

71. Jay Winter, *Sites of Memory, Sites of Mourning: The Great War in European Cultural History* (Cambridge: Cambridge University Press, 1995), chap. 3.

72. Wilma Koutstaal, "Skirting the Abyss: A History of Experimental Explorations of Automatic Writing in Psychology," *Journal of the History of the Behavioral Sciences* 28 (1992): 5–27; Sonu Shamdasani, "Automatic Writing and the Discovery of the Unconscious," *Spring* 54 (1993): 100–131.

73. See also Jean-Claude Beaune, *Le vagabond et la machine. Essai sur l'automatisme ambulatoire: Médecine, technique et société en France, 1880–1910* (Seyssel: Champ-Vallon, 1987).

74. Christian Péchenard, *Proust et son père* (Paris: Quai Voltaire, 1993), esp. 200–211.

75. Gertrude Stein, "Normal Motor Automatism," *Psychological Review* 3 (1896): 492–512; Stein, "Cultivated Motor Automatism," *Psychological Review* 5 (1889): 295–306. For a full-scale treatment of this terrain, see Steven Meyer, *Irresistible Dictation: Gertrude Stein and the Correlations of Writing and Science* (Stanford, Calif.: Stanford University Press, 2001), as well as Daylanne English, "Gertrude Stein and the Politics of Literary-Medical Experimentation," *Literature and Medicine* 16 (Fall 1997): 188–209.

76. William Innes Homer, *Seurat and the Science of Painting* (Cambridge, Mass.: MIT Press, 1964).

77. See also Ryan, *Vanishing Subject*, chap. 15; M. J. Hoffman, "Gertrude Stein and the Psychological Laboratory," *American Quarterly* 17 (Spring 1965): 127–32; and Hoffman, "Gertrude Stein and William James," *The Personalist* 47 (Apr. 1966): 226–33.

78. A point well made by Martin Kusch in *Psychologism: A Case Study in the Sociology of Philosophical Knowledge* (London and New York: Routledge, 1995).

79. See also Roman Ingarden, "Psychology and Psychologism," *New Literary History* (Winter 1974): 215–23; John Fizer, *Psychologism and Psychoaesthetics: A Historical and Critical View of Their Relations* (Amsterdam: J. Benjamins, 1981); and Mark A. Notturno, *Perspectives on Psychologism* (Leiden: Brill, 1989).

80. Levenson, *A Genealogy of Modernism: A Study of English Literary Doctrine, 1908–1922* (Cambridge: Cambridge University Press, 1984), esp. chap. 1. My thanks to Jed Esty for clarifying this matter for me.

81. Jerrold Seigel, *The Private Worlds of Marcel Duchamp: Desire, Liberation, and the Self in Modern Culture* (Berkeley: University of California Press, 1995), chaps. 2 and 8.

82. This line of questioning was suggested to me by Mioara Deacs, who is researching a dissertation on cultural metaphors of the unconscious in late nineteenth-century England in the Department of the History and Philosophy of Science at the University of Notre Dame.

83. I should note in closing that at the outset of the twenty-first century we may well be passing through another fertile period of cultural interaction, but of a quite different order. Since the early 1990s, a new field of academic inquiry has emerged at the intersection of literary studies, cognitive theory, and the neurosciences. This line of research aims to apply the ideas, methods, and insights of the latest sciences of the mind—including linguistics, cognitive psychology, evolutionary psychology, sociobiology, artificial intelligence theory, computer modeling, and information processing theory—to the study of imaginative literature. "Cognitive literary studies" highlight the extent to which *The Mind of Modernism* provides only one case study in the historical and conceptual cross-fertilization of the arts and sciences. Viewed historically (that is, in light of the cultural histories of ancient humoral theory, physiognomy, and phrenology), this new body of scholarship should be regarded less as an unprecedented innovation than as an attempt to reground the understanding of artistic creativity in the materialist brain sciences of the day after the century-long hegemony of dynamic psychiatry. For an exhaustive bibliographical guide, see "Literature, Cognition, and the Brain" at http://www2.bc.edu/-richarad/lcb/bib/annot.html.

1. MICALE: DISCOURSES OF HYSTERIA

1. These sections of the chapter draw on my book *Approaching Hysteria: Disease and Its Interpretations* (Princeton, N.J.: Princeton University Press, 1995), 182–220.

2. "La période héroique de l'hystérie" is Fulgence Raymond's phrase in "Définition et nature de l'hystérie," in *Comptes rendus du Congrès des médecins aliénistes et neurologistes de France et des pays de langue française*, 2 vols. (Paris: Masson, 1907), 2: 378.

3. A. E. Carter, *The Idea of Decadence in French Literature, 1830–1900* (Toronto: University of Toronto Press, 1958), 69–79.

4. Proto-pathologies, that is, of female hysteria. On the male sides of the Rougon and Macquart families, the generative neuroses were imbecility and alcoholism.

5. Carter, *Idea of Decadence*, 80–87.

6. Debora Leah Silverman, *Art Nouveau in Fin-de-Siècle France: Politics, Psychology, and Style* (Los Angeles: University of California Press, 1989), 78, 332 n. 15.

7. Cited in Carter, *Idea of Decadence*, 86, Barbey d'Aurevilly's emphasis.

8. In addition to Carroy's chapter in this volume, see also Carroy, "Hystérie, théâtre, littérature au dix-neuvième siècle," *Psychanalyse à l'université* 7 (Mar. 1982): 311–12.

9. Carter, *Idea of Decadence*, 79–80.

10. Augustin Galopin, *Les hystériques des couvents, des églises, des temples, des théâtres, des synagogues et de l'amour* (Paris: E. Dentu, 1886).

11. Jean Louis Signoret, "Variété historique: Une leçon clinique à la Salpêtrière (1887) par André Brouillet," *Revue neurologique* 139 (1983): 687–701.

12. Jules Claretie, *Les amours d'un interne* (Paris: E. Dentu, 1881).

13. Léon Daudet, *Les morticoles* (Paris: Charpentier, 1894).

14. Toby Gelfand, "Medical Nemesis, Paris, 1894: Léon Daudet's *Les morticoles*," *Bulletin of the History of Medicine* 60 (Summer 1986): 155–76.

15. Emily S. Apter, "Blind Spots: Hysterical Vision from Charcot to Mirbeau," paper presented at the Thirteenth Annual Meeting of the Colloquium in Nineteenth-Century French Studies, Northwestern University, Evanston, Ill., Oct. 22–24, 1987, subsequently published with revisions as "The Garden of Scopic Perversion from Monet to Mirbeau," *October* 47 (Winter 1988): 91–115.

16. Octave Mirbeau, *Le jardin des supplices* (Paris: E. Fasquelle, 1899), 239ff.

17. Henri Ellenberger, "The Pathogenic Secret and Its Therapeutics," *Journal of the History of the Behavioral Sciences* 2 (1966): 33–34.

18. Leon Edel, *The Modern Psychological Novel*, rev. ed. (New York: Grosset & Dunlop, 1964).

19. M. A. de Monzie, "Discours," *Revue neurologique* 41 (1925): 1159–62.

20. This story is mentioned in Jules Claretie, *La vie à Paris: 1884* (Paris: Victor-Havard, 1885), 450–51, and enlarged upon by S. Veyrac in "Une heure chez Sarah Bernhardt," *La chronique médicale* 19 (Oct. 1, 1897): 614.

21. Carroy, "Hystérie, théâtre, littérature au dix-neuvième siècle," 303–4.

22. The text of the play may be found in André de Lorde, *Théâtre d'épouvante* (Paris: Charpentier et Fasquelle, 1909), 1–81.

23. Max Simon Nordau, *Entartung*, 2 vols. (Berlin: C. Dunker, 1892–93); *Dégénérescence*, trans. Auguste Kietrich, 2 vols. (Paris: Alcan, 1894). I cite from Nordau, *Degeneration*, translated from the second German edition, with an introduction by George L. Mosse (New York: Howard Fertig, 1968).

24. Ibid., 36.

25. Ibid., 27–29. Criticism of Impressionism as optical disease seems to have been common during the 1880s and 1890s. Huysmans, for instance, wrote of one exhibition in which "most of the paintings corroborate Dr. Charcot's experiments on changes in color perception which he noted in many of his hysterics at the Salpêtrière. . . . They had a malady of the retina" (quoted in Apter, "Blind Spots," 19).

26. Nordau, *Degeneration*, 302.

27. Hippolyte Taine, *Les origines de la France contemporaine*, 6 vols. [1876–93] (Paris: Hachette et Cie, 1877), 2: *La révolution — L'anarchie*, Part One.

28. See Susanna Barrows, *Distorting Mirrors: Visions of the Crowd in Late Nineteenth-Century France* (New Haven, Conn.: Yale University Press, 1981), chap. 3; and Jaap van Ginneken, *Crowds, Psychology, and Politics 1871–1899* (Cambridge: Cambridge University Press, 1992), chap. 1.

29. See also Jules Claretie, *Histoire de la révolution de 1870–71*, 6 vols. (Paris: George Decaus, 1875–76); and Maxime du Camp, *Les convulsions de Paris*, 4 vols. (Paris: Hachette et Cie, 1889).

30. J. B. V. Laborde, *Les hommes et les actes de l'insurrection de Paris devant la psychologie morbide. Lettres à M. le Dr. Moreau* (Paris: G. Baillière, 1872).

31. Guy de Maupassant, *Chroniques*, ed. Hubert Juin, 3 vols. (Paris: Union Générale d'Éditions, 1980), 2: 112.

32. Drs. Cabanès and L. Nass, *La névrose révolutionnaire* (Paris: Société française d'imprimerie de librairie, 1906); Nass, *Le siège de Paris et la Commune: Essais de pathologie historique* (Paris: Plon-Nourrit et Cie, 1914).

33. Raymond Rudorff, *Belle Époque: Paris in the Nineties* (London: Hamilton, 1972), 23; Nicholas Halasz, *Captain Dreyfus: The Story of a Mass Hysteria* (New York: Simon & Schuster, 1955); J. Kim Munholland, *Origins of Contemporary Europe, 1890–1914* (New York: Harcourt, Brace & World, 1970), 51; Roger Shattuck, *The Banquet Years: The Origins of the Avant Garde in France, 1885 to World War I*, rev. ed. (New York: Vintage Books, 1968), 14–15; Robert D. Anderson, *France 1870–1914: Politics and Society* (London: Routledge and Kegan Paul, 1984), 142.

34. Barrows, *Distorting Mirrors*, chap. 7; Y. Thiec and J. R. Théaton, "La foule comme objet de 'science,'" *Revue française de sociologie* 24 (1983): 119–36.

35. Robert Nye, *The Origins of Crowd Psychology: Gustave Le Bon and the Crisis of Mass Democracy in the Third Republic* (London: Sage Publications, 1975), 30.

36. César Lombroso, *L'homme criminel: Étude anthropologique et psychiatrique*, 2d French ed., 2 vols. (Paris: Félix Alcan, 1895).

37. Ibid., 2: chap. 6, esp. 412–17.

38. Ruth Harris, "Melodrama, Hysteria and Feminine Crimes of Passion in the Fin-de-Siècle," *History Workshop* 15 (1988): 31–63; Harris, *Murders and Madness: Medicine, Law, and Society in the Fin de Siècle* (Oxford: Oxford University Press, 1989), chap. 6.

39. For male crimes of passion, consult Harris, *Murders and Madness*, chap. 8.

40. Daniel Lesueur, *Névrosée* (Paris: Alphonse Lemerre, 1890).

41. Ibid., 191–92.

42. [Henri] Legrand du Saulle, *Les hystériques. État physique et état mental. Actes insolites, délictueux et criminels* (Paris: J.-B. Baillière, 1883).

43. Ibid., 329–513.

44. Ibid., 2, 5, 3. Legrand du Saulle's ideas were later elaborated upon in Théodor Andrev, "De l'irresponsabilité des hystériques en matière criminelle" (doctoral diss., Medical Faculty, University of Toulouse, 1905).

45. Georges Gilles de la Tourette, "Hystérie et syphilis," *Le progrès médical*, 2d series, 6, no. 51 (Dec. 17, 1887): 511–12; Alfred Fournier, "Influence de la syphilis sur les névroses et notamment sur l'hystérie," *Gazette des hôpitaux* 61, no. 96 (Aug. 23, 1888): 892–93; Lucien Bertrand, "Contribution à l'étude de l'hystérie dans ses rapports avec la syphilis secondaire" (doctoral diss., Medical Faculty, University of Lyon, 1892); Nicolas Kirkoff, "Contribution à l'étude de l'hystérie dans ses rapports avec la syphilis acquise et héréditaire" (doctoral diss., Medical Faculty, University of Paris, 1898).

46. M. Hudeyo, "Hystéro-syphilis," *Annales de dermatologie et de syphiligraphie*, 3d series, 3 (1892): 839–42.

47. Ferdinand Dreyfous, *De l'hystérie alcoolique* (Paris: Delahaye et E. Lecrosnier, 1888); Michael Guillemin, "Contribution à l'étude de l'hystérie alcoolique," *Annales médico-psychologique*, 7th series, 7 (1888): 230–35.

48. Alain Corbin, *Les filles de noce: Misère sexuelle et prostitution aux 19e et 20e siècles* (Paris: Aubier Montaigne, 1978), 439–40.

49. Lombroso, *L'homme criminel*, 2: 416.

50. Alain Corbin, *Les filles de noce*, 439–40, 440 n. 201; Charles Bernheimer, *Figures of Ill Repute: Representing Prostitution in Nineteenth-Century France* (Cambridge, Mass.: Harvard University Press, 1989), chap. 8; Jann Matlock, *Scenes of Seduction: Prostitution, Hysteria, and Reading Difference in Nineteenth-Century France* (New York: Columbia University Press, 1993).

51. Charles Richet, "Les démoniaques d'aujourd'hui," *Revue des deux mondes* 37 (1880): 342; Guy de Maupassant, *Chroniques*, ed. Hubert Juin, 3 vols. (Paris: Union générale d'édition, 1980), 2: 111.

52. Jules Claretie, *La vie à Paris: 1881* (Paris: Victor Havard, n.d.), 126, 135. In the prefatory notice to his *Les amours d'un interne* of 1881, Claretie observed similarly that "rien de plus fréquent, dans notre société moderne que ces névroses bizarres qui produisent soit les affolées du monde ou du théâtre, soit les exaltées de la politique et des réunions populaires: les déséquilibrées du foyer ou de la place publique. L'hystérie est un peu partout à l'heure où nous sommes."

53. Jean-Marie Mayeur, *Les débuts de la troisième république, 1871–1898* (Paris: Éditions du Seuil, 1973), and Anderson's *France 1870–1914* provide useful overviews.

54. Louis Chevalier, *Laboring Classes and Dangerous Classes in Paris during the*

First Half of the Nineteenth Century (New York: H. Fertig, 1973); Claude Willard, *Le mouvement socialiste en France (1893–1905)* (Paris: Éditions sociales, 1965); Steven C. Hause and Anne R. Kenney, *Women's Suffrage and Social Politics in the French Third Republic* (Princeton, N.J.: Princeton University Press, 1984); Paul Smith, *Feminism and the Third Republic: Women's Political and Civil Rights in France, 1918–1945* (New York: Oxford University Press, 1996); Michelle Perrot, "The New Eve and the Old Adam: Changes in French Women's Condition at the Turn of the Century," in *Behind the Lines: Gender and the Two World Wars,* ed. Margaret R. Higonnet et al. (New Haven, Conn.: Yale University Press, 1987), 51–60; Susanna Barrows, "After the Commune: Alcoholism, Temperance, and Literature in the Early Third Republic," in *Consciousness and Class Experience in Nineteenth-Century France,* ed. John Merriman (New York: Holmes & Meier, 1979), chap. 10; Alain Corbin, "La grande peur de la syphilis," in *Peurs et terreurs face à la contagion: choléra, tuberculose, syphilis, XIXe-XXe siècles,* ed. Jean-Pierre Bardet et al. (Paris: Fayard, 1988), 328–48.

55. For sociological discussions of modernity, see S. N. Eisenstadt's "Studies of Modernization and Sociological Theory," *History and Theory* 13 (1974): 226–52; Joyce Appleby's "Modernization Theory and the Formation of Modern Social Theories in England and America," *Comparative Studies in Society and History* 20 (1976): 259–85; and D. Dickens and A. Fontana's *Postmodernism and Sociology* (Chicago: University of Chicago Press, 1990), introduction.

56. Theodore Zeldin, *France 1848–1945: Anxiety and Hypocrisy* (Oxford: Clarendon Press, 1981), 59–64.

57. For a sense of the exceptional status accorded doctors at the turn of the century in France, see Jack D. Ellis, *The Physician-Legislators of France: Medicine and Politics in the Early Third Republic, 1870–1914* (Cambridge: Cambridge University Press, 1990).

58. Robert Nye, *Crime, Madness, and Politics in Modern France: The Medical Concept of Decline* (Princeton, N.J.: Princeton University Press, 1984), esp. chap. 5.

59. Ibid., 132–70.

60. Jan Goldstein, *Console and Classify: The French Psychiatric Profession in the Nineteenth Century* (New York: Cambridge University Press, 1987), chap. 9.

61. My thanks to Lawrence Rainey for helping me to clarify my ideas about this point.

62. George Heard Hamilton, *Painting and Sculpture in Europe 1880–1940* (Harmondsworth, Middlesex: Penguin Books, 1975), chaps. 1–5.

63. Dorothy Ross, "Modernism Reconsidered," in *Modernist Impulses in the Human Sciences 1870–1930,* ed. Ross (Baltimore, Md., and London: Johns Hopkins University Press, 1994), 6.

64. My discussion of intellectual Modernism as an ongoing epistemological challenge to the traditions of scientific and artistic realism, especially in its post-Enlightenment varieties, draws in general on the literature of postmodernism and specifically on three stimulating studies: Jonathan Crary, *Techniques of the Observer:*

On Vision and Modernity in the Nineteenth Century (Cambridge, Mass.: MIT Press, 1990); W. J. T. Mitchell, *Picture Theory: Essays on Verbal and Visual Representation* (Chicago and London: University of Chicago Press, 1994); and Ross, *Modernist Impulses in the Human Sciences.* See also Bernd Hüppauf, "Experiences of Modern Warfare and the Crisis of Representation," *New German Critique* 59 (Spring/Summer, 1993): 70–101.

65. W. F. Bynum, *Science and the Practice of Medicine in the Nineteenth Century* (Cambridge: Cambridge University Press, 1994).

66. Sander Gilman, *Disease and Representation: Images of Illness from Madness to AIDS* (Ithaca, N.Y.: Cornell University Press, 1988).

67. The term "neuromimetic" traces to an essay written by the English neurologist Sir James Paget titled "Nervous Mimicry" and published in *The Lancet* in 1873. The essay is reproduced in Stephen Paget, ed., *Selected Essays and Addresses by Sir James Paget* (London: Longmans, Green, and Co., 1902), chap. 7.

68. As Susan Sontag has perceived, it is precisely those diseases with murky causes and unknown cures that are most susceptible to this sort of symbolization (*Illness as Metaphor* [New York: Penguin, 1978], chap. 8).

69. Christopher G. Goetz, Michel Bonduelle, and Toby Gelfand, *Constructing Neurology: Jean-Martin Charcot 1825–1893* (New York: Oxford University Press, 1995), chap. 6.

70. Thus, in Freud and Breuer's *Studies on Hysteria* (1895), the twitches, phobias, and paralyses of patients are seen as complex bodily metaphors cast by the patient's unconscious into subjective, symbolic forms. The psychoanalyst's role is to interpret the meaning of these "materializations of psychic states" and to bring them to the conscious attention of the suffering individual.

71. This development extends well into the twentieth century. During the decades 1930–1960, when psychoanalysis dominated, hysteria remained an important diagnostic category in Western psychiatric thinking and practice. In 1980, however, the American Psychiatric Association, reflecting the decline of the psychodynamic tradition and the ascent of biological psychiatry, voted to exclude hysteria as a unitary diagnosis from the influential third edition of *The Diagnostic and Statistical Manual of Mental Disorders.* (See Steven E. Hyler and Robert L. Spitzer, "Hysteria Split Asunder," *American Journal of Psychiatry* 135 (1978): 1500–1504). This rejection may be seen as materialist medicine's most decisive response to hysteria's unrepresentability. Indicatively, the hysteria concept remained alive and well in French psychological medicine, with its independent clinical and theoretical traditions. Similarly, since the expulsion of the concept from the medical field by Anglo-American biopsychiatrists, academic humanists, working in a postmodernist mode, have enthusiastically picked up and explored the subject.

72. Louis A. Sass, *Madness and Modernism: Insanity in the Light of Modern Art, Literature, and Thought* (New York: Basic Books, 1992), introduction.

73. Gillian Beer has observed "the restiveness about representation in the later

nineteenth century—a restiveness shared, and crossing to and from, between physicists, philosophers, and poets" ("Wave Theory and the Rise of Literary Modernism," *Open Fields: Science in Cultural Encounter* [Oxford: Clarendon Press, 1996], chap. 13, 296–97). I am proposing that medical elites, too, experienced this intellectual anxiety.

74. The term "revolt against positivism" is associated with H. Stuart Hughes's classic study, *Consciousness and Society: The Reorientation of European Social Thought, 1890–1930* (New York: Alfred A. Knopf, 1958), chap. 2.

75. Alan Krohn, *Hysteria: The Elusive Neurosis* (New York: International Universities Press, 1978). For Baudelaire's (as well as Sainte-Beuve's and Flaubert's) interest in hysteria, which predates the period under study here, see Carroy-Thirard, "Hystérie, théâtre, littérature au dix-neuvième siècle," 311–16; Mark S. Micale, "Littérature, médecine, hystérie: le cas de *Madame Bovary* de Gustave Flaubert," *L'Évolution psychiatrique* 60 (1995): 901–18; and Micale, *Approaching Hysteria*, 187–94, 226–60. The key Surrealist statement is Louis Aragon and André Breton, "Le cinquantenaire de l'hystérie (1878–1928)," in *Histoire du surréalisme: Documents surréalistes*, ed. Maurice Nadeau (Paris: Seuil, 1948), 124–25. From a large scholarship on Proust and psychology, see Judith Ryan, *The Vanishing Subject: Early Psychology and Literary Modernism* (Chicago and London: University of Chicago Press, 1991), chap. 14. And on Lacan, see the sixth chapter of Martha Noel Evans, *Fits and Starts: A Genealogy of Hysteria in Modern France* (Ithaca, N.Y.: Cornell University Press, 1991).

2. GORDON: FROM CHARCOT TO CHARLOT

Unless otherwise noted, all translations are my own.

1. I first proposed the analogy between hysteria and performance style in the cabaret in a 1985 colloquium and have discussed physiological response and unconscious imitation in relation to film in two essays published in 1997. See Rae Beth Gordon, "Le Caf'conc' et l'hystérie," *Romantisme* 64 (1989): 53–67; "Les Pathologies de la vue et du mouvement dans les films de Georges Méliès," in *Georges Méliès: Illusioniste fin de siècle?* ed. Jacques Malthête and Michel Marie (Paris, 1997), 263–83; and "Laughing Hysterically: Gesture, Movement, and Spectatorship in Early French Cinema," in *Moving Forward, Holding Fast: The Dynamics of Nineteenth-Century French Culture*, ed. Barbara T. Cooper and Mary Donaldson-Evans (Amsterdam, 1997) 217–37.

2. Georges Montorgueil et al., *Les Demi-Cabots: Le Café-Concert, le cirque, les forains*, 3 vols. (Paris, 1896), 14; hereafter abbreviated *DC*.

3. Désiré Magloire Bourneville and Paul Regnard, *Iconographie photographique de la Salpêtrière* (Paris, 1876), 44.

4. See, for example, Vanessa Schwartz on the wax museum, the morgue, and the popular press in "Cinematic Spectatorship before the Apparatus: The Public Taste

for Reality in *Fin-de-Siècle* Paris," in *Cinema and the Invention of Modern Life*, ed. Leo Charney and Schwartz (Berkeley, 1995) 297–319; Jonathan Crary on the stereoscope in *Techniques of the Observer: On Vision and Modernity in the Nineteenth Century* (Cambridge, Mass., 1992); and Laurent Mannoni on the heritage of the magic lantern in *Le Grand Art de la lumière et de l'ombre* (Paris, 1994). Many of these forms of entertainment shared common elements: a visit to a wax museum, for example, may well have evoked the cataleptic poses in somnambulism and in hysteria. Alfred Binet, Charles Féré, A. Souques, Paul Sollier, and Paul Richer, for example, all point out the "waxlike catalepsy" of hysterics under their care. In *The Ciné Goes to Town: French Cinema 1896–1914* (Berkeley, 1994), Richard Abel writes that "the least examined area" in the history of early cinema, a history that he and others are now reconstructing, is the "historical reception of films . . . in France before the Great War." This space, "left open for further research" (p. xviii), is the one I am exploring here.

5. See Charles Féré, *Sensation et mouvement* (Paris, 1887).

6. Léon Moussinac, *La Naissance du cinéma* (Paris, 1983), 174. Theory based on physiological response in film spectatorship continued to be important in France (see, for example, Gilbert Cohen-Séat, *Problèmes du cinéma et de l'information visuelle* [Paris, 1961]) until the focus shifted to a Metzian semiotics of film language. I devote two chapters to psychophysiological and psychophysical measurement of sensation in *Sensation and Soul: From Hysteria to Aesthetic Theory* (Stanford, Calif., 2001).

7. Yhcam, "Cinematography," trans. Richard Abel, in *French Film Theory and Criticism: A History/Anthology*, ed. Richard Abel, 2 vols. (Princeton, N.J., 1988), 1: 69.

8. François Caradec and Alain Weill, *Le Café-Concert* (Paris, 1980), 50, hereafter abbreviated *CC*; Jean Lorrain, *La Ville empoisonnée: Pall-Mall Paris* (Paris, 1936), 279.

9. Walter Benjamin, "On Some Motifs in Baudelaire," in *Illuminations: Essays and Reflections*, trans. Harry Zohn, ed. Hannah Arendt (New York, 1969), 175. Ben Singer notes (as I've done as well in "Laughing Hysterically") that "Benjamin [and Kracauer] were tapping into an already widespread discourse about the shock of modernity," an experience that Singer aptly calls neurological modernity (Ben Singer, "Modernity, Hyperstimulus, and the Rise of Popular Sensationalism," in *Cinema and the Invention of Modern Life*, 73–74).

10. Benjamin, "On Some Motifs in Baudelaire," p. 240.

11. See Henri Ey, *Traité des hallucinations*, 2 vols. (Paris, 1973), 2: 1010–11.

12. Fechner, the inventor of psychophysics, held the chair in physics at the University of Leipzig and, like many other great nineteenth-century scientists, was many-faceted. He was a geographer, an art critic, and, under the pseudonym Dr. Mises, an author of satirical poems and plays. His psychophysical experiments involving the observation of the sun through colored glasses brought on hysterical

blindness and psychotic reactions that lasted for three years. I devote a chapter to Fechner in *Sensation and Soul*.

13. Charles Henry, "Correspondance," *La Revue philosophique de la France et de l'étranger* 29 (Mar. 1890): 334.

14. This is only one instance among several in which data garnered from experiments on hysterical patients became part of aesthetic theory.

15. "Revue des périodiques étrangers," review of Oct. 1889 issue of *Mind*, in *La Revue Philosophique de la France et de l'étranger* 29 (Jan. 1890): 110.

16. Charles Henry, *Introduction à une esthétique scientifique* (Paris, 1885), 2.

17. Charles Richet, *L'Homme et l'intelligence: Fragments de physiologie et de psychologie* (Paris, 1884), 520.

18. Marcel Gauchet, *L'Inconscient cérébral* (Paris, 1992), 208.

19. All of these notions are examined in Henri Bergson, *Essai sur les données immédiates de la conscience* (1888; Paris, 1988), 13–28.

20. Ibid., 13; emphasis mine.

21. Hospital wards housing hysterics and epileptics were spectacles of contagion. It seems, in fact, plausible that the convulsive movements of nineteenth-century hysterics were a result of their having been placed in the same ward as the epileptics at the Salpêtrière hospital. One patient's yawning would spread until the entire ward was transformed into an all-day yawning marathon. A 1909 Pathé comedy, *The Yawner*, illustrates this form of imitative disorder.

22. Quoted in Moussinac, *Naissance du cinema*, 174. The creator of the "theater of cruelty," Antonin Artaud, also believed that every movement of the body (including breathing) corresponded to an idea and an emotion and that this corporeal language was universally comprehensible. In the theater, the rhythmic repetition of certain syllables and the timbre of the voice "bypassing the processes of judgment involved in attaching meaning to words, act directly on the nervous system, creating a more or less hallucinatory state, and forcing the sensibility and the mind to undergo a kind of organic alteration" (Antonin Artaud, *Oeuvres complètes*, 26 vols. [Paris, 1961–94], 4: 145). Germaine Dulac's *La Coquille et le clergyman* is based on a film scenario by Artaud. The cinema, too, Artaud wrote, "acts on the brain matter directly" (quoted in Noureddine Ghali, *L'Avant-garde cinématographique en France dans les années vingt* [Paris, 1995], 346).

23. Quoted in Jacques Aumont, *Montage Eisenstein*, trans. Lee Hildreth, Constance Penley, and Andrew Ross (Bloomington, Ind., 1987), 47; emphasis mine.

24. Sergei Eisenstein, *Notes of a Film Director*, ed. R. Yurenev (New York, 1970), 134.

25. Marie Seton, *Sergei M. Eisenstein* (New York, 1952), 62.

26. Jean Epstein, "Magnification," trans. Stuart Liebman, in *French Film Theory and Criticism*, 1: 238; hereafter abbreviated "M." Also see Epstein's book-length essays *L'Intelligence d'une machine* (Paris, 1946) and *Le Cinéma du diable* (Paris, 1947). Epstein, who studied medicine before becoming a filmmaker, is particularly remem-

bered for his extraordinarily beautiful Impressionist film *La Chute de la maison Usher* (restored in 1996 by the Cinémathèque française).

27. Tom Gunning, "Now You See It, Now You Don't: The Temporality of the Cinema of Attractions," *Velvet Light Trap* 32 (Fall 1993).

28. Gunning, "An Aesthetics of Astonishment," in *Viewing Positions: Ways of Seeing Film*, ed. Linda Williams (New Brunswick, N.J., 1994), 116. See also Gunning, "The Cinema of Attractions: Early Film, Its Spectator, and the Avant-Garde," *Wide Angle* 8 (Fall 1986): 66, and note 53, below.

29. See Gordon, "Le Caf'conc' et l'hystérie." As Mark Micale points out, "Around 1878, the name of the Salpêtrière invaded even the popular magazines and newspapers" (*Approaching Hysteria: Disease and Its Interpretations* [Princeton, N.J., 1996], 198).

30. The public "took great pleasure in seeing marionettes in [Paulus's] person" (*DC*, 15).

31. A precursor to the epileptic singer was the "eccentric comic or dancer," a type of performer that persisted into the twentieth century and whose movements were similar to the epileptic singers'. Méliès portrays an eccentric comic in his 1904 *Le Roi du maquillage*.

32. Joris-Karl Huysmans, "L'Exposition des Indépendants en 1881," in *L'Art moderne / Certains* (1882; Paris, 1975), 203.

33. "Epileptic performers" were not, of course, epileptics themselves. Despite the "electricity" and "nervousness" of performers that doctors and journalists alluded to, these artists were miming epilepsy, not experiencing it.

34. Lorrain, *La Ville empoisonnée*, 279.

35. In Romi, *La petite histoire des café-concerts parisiens* (Paris, 1950), 48.

36. Mistinguett, *Toute ma vie* (Paris, 1954), 41.

37. Maurice Vaucaire, "Les Cafés-Concerts," *Paris Illustré* (Aug. 1, 1886): 134.

38. André Chadourne, *Le Café-Concert* (Paris, 1889), 231. See also *DC*, 14.

39. Charles Féré, "Baillements chez un épileptique," *Nouvelle iconographie de la Salpêtrière* 1 (1888): 164.

40. Augustin Galopin, *Les Hystériques des couvents, des églises, des temples, des théâtres, des synagogues, et de l'amour* (Paris, 1886), 126; hereafter abbreviated *H*.

41. Gustave Coquiot, *Le Café-Concert* (Paris, 1896), 17.

42. See Pierre Janet, *Les Obsessions et la psychasthénie*, 2 vols. (Paris, 1903), 2: 76. This series of movements can be seen in a Méliès film entitled *Jack Jaggs and Dum Dum*, also dating from 1903.

43. Vaucaire, "Les Cafés-Concerts," 130.

44. Coquiot, *Le Café-Concert*, 17.

45. Ernest Coquelin, *L'Art de dire le monologue* (Paris, 1884), 92; emphasis mine.

46. René Meizeroy, *Masques* (Paris, 1887), 105.

47. Coquelin, *L'Art de dire le monologue*, 92; emphasis mine. The absolute incarnation, according to Coquelin, of the "modern monologue" was Charles Cros's

Obsession. One could also cite Cros's *The Hanged Man* (who is afflicted with a nervous tic) and Félix Galipaux's *A Man Who Has a Tic.*

48. Félicien Champsaur, "Nina de Villars," *Paris: Le Massacre* (Paris, 1885), 103.

49. Jules Barbey d'Aurevilly, *Le Constitutionnel* and *Le Chat Noir*, June 1, 1882. Rollinat suffered from hallucinations and died insane in 1903. Several other cabaret personalities, André Gill (founder of Le Lapin Agile), Jules Jouy, and Nina de Villard among them, died insane.

50. Binet and Féré, *Recherches expérimentales sur la physiologie des mouvements chez les hystériques* (Paris, 1887), 326; hereafter abbreviated *R.*

51. Binet wrote that he had "observed a more or less accentuated feeling of doubling in all [his] patients" (*R*, 25).

52. In a footnote at the end of *Cinéma 2, l'image-temps*, Gilles Deleuze refers to Janet's work: "These are two extreme modes of thought, the spiritual automaton of logic, invoked by Spinoza and Leibniz, [and] the psychological automaton of psychiatry, studied by Janet" (Gilles Deleuze, *Cinéma 2, l'image-temps* [Paris, 1985], 344 n. 4). The correspondences between my study of automatisms here (see the conclusion of this essay) and Deleuze's discussion of the "automate spirituel" may be worth pursuing. The limits of this study dictate, however, that I focus solely on the psychological and physiological concept of automatisms current from the late 1880s into the 1920s.

53. Bergson, *Le Rire: Essai sur la signification du comique* (Paris, 1964), 22–38, 100. The popularity of puppets and marionettes—their strings pulled by an invisible force behind the scenes—in cabarets and theaters also coincides with the public's fascination with hysteria.

54. Louis Veuillot, *Les Odeurs de Paris* (Paris, 1867), 144, 146.

55. See T. J. Clark, *The Painting of Modern Life: Paris in the Art of Manet and His Followers* (Princeton, N.J., 1984), 231–33.

56. *Grotesque Dwarf* (a lost film of Méliès from 1897) offers a foregrounded example of deformity. Attractions like this one were not confined to sideshows but were featured in the music hall. The most famous midget comic of the period was Little Tich.

57. David Robinson is unfavorably comparing these comics to Max Linder. "Linder had the gift of naturalness [and] recognized that the rhythms of comedy could be varied, that films need not be unvaryingly frenetic from beginning to end" (David Robinson, "Rise and Fall of the Clowns: The Golden Age of French Comedy, 1907–1914," *Sight and Sound* 56 [Summer 1987]: 198–203). This, of course, is precisely my point: by 1910 the refutation of this explicit and crude mirror of the corporeal unconscious in all of its "wild" (= primitive, instinctual, savage) and "inhuman" (= mechanical, automatic) barbaric splendor had already begun.

58. Georges Sadoul, *Histoire générale du cinéma*, 6 vols. (Paris, 1977), 2: 192, 193.

59. Gunning has written a marvelous essay on the photographs of grimaces in the *New Iconography of the Salpêtrière* and the grimace film in early cinema. See his "In

Your Face: Physiognomy, Photography, and the Gnostic Mission of Early Film,"
Modernism/Modernity 4 (Jan. 1997): 1–29, reproduced in this volume, chap. 4.

60. Quoted in Sadoul, *Georges Méliès* (Paris, 1961), 229.

61. Freud's theory of the uncanny, like Bergson's theory of laughter, ties the double to the automaton. The automaton heads up the paradigm of inanimate objects that seem to come alive, arousing the feeling of the uncanny: other objects are waxwork figures, cataleptic bodies, dismembered limbs, severed heads, and feet that dance by themselves. All, of course, figure prominently in early cinema. The uncanny is the sensation we have of the "double" inside of us, our corporeal unconscious with its automatic gestures expressing an agenda about which we would prefer to know nothing. As Freud put it, we see in epilepsy and madness "the workings of forces hitherto unsuspected" and dimly perceived "in a remote corner of [one's] own being." The most frequent manifestation of the uncanny, an involuntary recurrence of a thing, can "call forth a feeling of the comic" (Sigmund Freud, "The Uncanny," trans. Alix Strachey, *On Creativity and the Unconscious: Papers on the Psychology of Art, Literature, Love, Religion*, ed. Benjamin Nelson [New York, 1958], 151, 154).

62. Maxim Gorky, "Gorky on the Films, 1896," trans. Leonard Mins, in *New Theater and Film, 1934 to 1937: An Anthology*, ed. Herbert Kline (New York, 1985), 229.

63. Quoted in Henry Jenkins, *What Made Pistachio Nuts? Early Sound Comedy and the Vaudeville Aesthetic* (New York, 1994), 56.

64. The notions discussed in this essay are further developed in my book *Why the French Love Jerry Lewis: From Cabaret to Early Cinema* (Stanford, Calif., 2001).

65. Émile Cohl, the creator of European film animation, was a caricaturist and a member of the literary-artistic groups Les Hydropathes and Les Incohérents before becoming a filmmaker.

66. Janet, *Les Obsessions et la psychasthénie*, 2: 101; emphasis mine.

67. See Jacques Lacan, *Les Psychoses*, vol. 3 of *Les Seminars de Jacques Lacan* (Paris, 1981), 201. This fantasy is due in part to the hysterical experience of anesthesia in members of the body; it also mirrors the mental phenomenon of "disaggregation," the dismemberment of the personality that, according to psychiatrists in the last half of the nineteenth century, characterized hysteria.

68. See, especially, Linda Williams's seminal "Film Body: An Implantation of Perversions," in *Narrative Apparatus Ideology: A Film Theory Reader*, ed. Philip Rosen (New York, 1968), 507–34, for a psychoanalytic reading of dismemberment and integration in Méliès, focusing on phallic objects and sexual difference in the "unprecedented illusion of film body" and a "celebration of the fetish function of the cinematic apparatus" (532). See also Lucy Fischer, "The Lady Vanishes: Women, Magic, and the Movies," *Film Quarterly* (Fall 1979): 30–40.

69. Quoted in Jacques Malthête, *Méliès: Images et illusions* (Paris, 1996), 51; emphasis mine.

70. Quoted in Madeleine Malthête-Méliès, *Méliès l'enchanteur* (Paris, 1973), 251.

71. Quoted in Sadoul, *Georges Méliès*, 136.

72. Méliès, letter to Maurice Druhot, *Ciné-Journal*, Jan. 17, 1930.

73. Donald Crafton, *Émile Cohl, Caricature, and Film* (Princeton, N.J., 1990), 110.

74. Quoted in René Jeanne and Charles Ford, *Histoire encyclopédique du cinéma*, 5 vols. (Paris, 1947–62), 1: 20.

75. Jules Romains, *Puissances de Paris* (Paris, 1919), 121.

76. Cendrars, *L'ABC du cinéma* (Paris, 1926), 8, 22–23.

77. The principal distinction between magnetism and hypnotism is that the former operates through the transmission of a universal "magnetic fluid" that, according to Mesmer, traverses all bodies, animate and inanimate. In the definition arrived at by the 1889 Congress of Physiological Psychology, hypnotism is an artificial sleep, induced by a hypnotist or a psychiatrist, and includes all of the phenomena produced by suggestion.

78. See Joseph-Rémi Léopold Delboeuf, *Magnétiseurs et médecins* (Paris, 1890), 42; hereafter abbreviated *MM*.

79. Eugène Azam, *Hypnotisme et double conscience* (Paris, 1893), 353.

80. Paul-Max Simon, *Hygiène de l'esprit au point de vue pratique de la préservation des maladies mentales et nerveuses* (Paris, 1877), 17; hereafter abbreviated *HE*.

81. See Pierre Briquet, *Traité clinique et thérapeutique de l'hystérie* (Paris, 1859), 371.

82. Parallels between prestidigitators' shows and cinema were often drawn: the sense of marvel and surprise experienced at the first film projections closely resembled "that which arises in a music-hall audience watching the exercises, more or less mysterious, more or less in contradiction to the apparent laws of nature, of a prestidigitator or an illusionist" (Jeanne and Ford, *Histoire encyclopédique du cinéma*, 1: 21).

83. Deleuze, *Cinéma 1, l'image-mouvement* (Paris, 1983), 76.

84. Gabriel de Tarde, *Les Lois de l'imitation* (1890; Paris, 1993), 82; hereafter abbreviated *L*.

85. As Jules Claretie wrote in the preface to his 1881 novel *Les Amours d'un interne* (Paris, 1883), "Nothing is more frequent in our modern society than those bizarre neuroses that produce either crazed women in society or in the theater. . . . Hysteria is just about everywhere at the present time. . . . these troubling manifestations, but which attract one as well, and these bizarre cases" (i–ii).

86. See, too, Joseph Roach's brilliant study on performance, doubling, detachment, and mimesis, *The Player's Passion: Studies in the Science of Acting* (Ann Arbor, Mich., 1993), for a sustained reflection on the relation of performance to bodily response in the actor.

87. Louis Haugmard, "L'Esthétique du cinématographe," *Le Correspondant*, May 25, 1913, 771.

88. Cited in Noël Burch, *In and Out of Synch: The Awakening of a Ciné-Dreamer*, trans. Ben Brewster (Aldershot, 1991), 214.

89. The fixed gaze on a brilliant object has inspired an analogy between hypno-

tism and film spectatorship from the writings of Yhcam (1912) to those of Jacques Brunius (1954). More recently, the analogy has been explored—quite differently—by Raymond Bellour.

90. Epstein goes on to explain why the film spectator develops a "hunger for [this] hypnosis"; it is because, as I've detailed and underlined here, film greatly "modifies the functioning of the nervous system" ("M," 2: 240).

91. Quoted in Rudolf E. Kuenzli, *Dada and Surrealist Film* (New York, 1987), 136. Similarly, Burch writes that the screen presence of actors in early cinema is solely corporeal, since they are almost never shot in close up; "they only have available a gestural language [*une écriture de gestes*]" (Burch, "Un Mode de représentation primitif," *Iris* 2, no. 1 [1984]: 120).

92. At the turn of the century, the café-concert, its program expanded to include acts often seen on British stages, was rebaptized the music hall.

93. Charles Keil, "The Story of Uncle Josh Told: Spectatorship and Apparatus in Early Cinema," *Iris* 11 (Summer 1990): 65.

94. Quoted by Crafton, *Émile Cohl, Caricature, and Film*, 321 n. 29.

95. Haugmard, "L'Esthétique du cinématographe," 768–69. In other words, the threat that film poses is the destruction of the higher faculties, bringing about an absolute domination of the lower faculties, and specifically the sensory regime. As we've seen, this disequilibrium in the two orders signals the onset of nervous illnesses, such as hysteria. But then again, perhaps this is a peculiarly French problem: Why do seven million people in France suffer from a disorder called *la spasmophilie*, a neuromuscular disorder that bears an uncanny resemblance to nineteenth-century hysteria? And why was a French law enacted on August 3, 1993 in response to thirty reported cases, requiring that on certain video games there be a label warning of the danger that prolonged focus on them could cause epilepsy?

96. Louis Aragon and André Breton, "Le Cinquantenaire de l'hystérie," *La Révolution Surréaliste*, Mar. 15, 1928, 22.

3. HACKING: AUTOMATISME AMBULATOIRE

This chapter previously appeared as "Automatisme Ambulatoire: Fugue, Hysteria, and Gender at the Turn of the Century," *Modernism/Modernity* 3 (1996): 31–44. It is reprinted here with the kind permission of Johns Hopkins University Press.

1. A. Pitres, *Leçons cliniques sur l'hystérie et l'hypnotisme faites à l'hôpital Saint-Andre à Bordeaux* (Paris: Doin, 1891), 2: 268. Fugue originated as a medical entity in Bordeaux, in Pitres's hospital. The curious name *automatisme ambulatoire* is due to Jean-Martin Charcot's Tuesday lecture of January 31, 1888, in his *Leçons du mardi* (Paris: Progrès médical, 1888), 1: 155–69. For a more medical account of fugue, with ample references, see my "Les Aliénés voyageurs: How Fugue Became a Medical Entity," in *History of Psychiatry* 7 (1996): 425–49.

2. I use the word 'prototype,' derived from cognitive linguistics, in a semitechni-

cal way. See my *Rewriting the Soul: Multiple Personality and the Sciences of Memory* (Princeton, N.J.: Princeton University Press, 1995), 33–35.

3. Théodore Flournoy, *Des Indes à la planète Mars: Étude sur un cas de somnambulisme avec glossolalie* (Geneva: Atar, 1900); *From India to the Planet Mars: A Case of Multiple Personality with Imaginary Languages*, intro. Sonu Shamdasani (Princeton, N.J.: Princeton University Press, 1994); also available as *From India to the Planet Mars: A Study of a Case of Somnambulism with Glossolalia*, trans. Daniel B. Vermilye (New York: Harper & Brothers, 1900).

4. *Diagnostic and Statistical Manual of Mental Disorders*, 4th ed. (Washington, D.C.: American Psychiatric Association, 1994), 484; hereafter abbreviated *DSM-IV*.

5. *The ICD–10 Classification of Mental and Behavioural Disorders: Clinical Descriptions and Diagnostic Guidelines* (Geneva: World Health Organization, 1992), 155; hereafter abbreviated *ICD–10*.

6. Philippe Tissié, *Les Aliénés voyageurs* (Paris: Doin, 1887). The case of Albert occupies half the published thesis, 55–108.

7. The papers delivered at the 1909 meeting of the Société de Neurologie (XIX Congrès des médecins aliénistes et neurologistes) appear in *La Revue neurologique* 17 (Aug. 30, 1909): 1013–76. I do not mean to imply that there was never again a French fugue study by psychiatrists. I mean that general interest disappeared and that thereafter fugues were taken to be mere symptoms of other problems.

8. Michael S. Roth, "Remembering Forgetting: *Maladies de la mémoire* in Nineteenth-Century France," *Representations* 26 (spring 1989): 49–68; and "Dying of the Past: Medical Studies of Nostalgia in Nineteenth-Century France," *History and Memory* 3 (spring/summer 1991): 5–29.

9. Richard J. Loewenstein, "Psychogenic Amnesia and Psychogenic Fugue: A Comprehensive Review," *Review of Psychiatry* 10 (1991): 189–222. The two references are Charcot's Tuesday lecture of January 31, 1888 (see note 1) and Pierre Janet's notes of a lecture given by Fulgence Raymond, Charcot's successor, in 1895 (see note 13).

10. Between 1980 and 1994 there was an intense debate among American psychiatrists who treat dissociative disorders as to whether amnesia should even be considered one of the defining conditions of multiple personality or fugue. It was first included, then excluded, and then reinstated as a condition for multiple personality. Such parochial infighting, which represents an unattractive internal power struggle, should not detain us here.

11. On gender and multiple personality, see my *Rewriting the Soul*, 69–80.

12. Hugh T. Patrick, "Ambulatory Automatism," *Journal of Nervous and Mental Disease* 34 (June 1907): 385.

13. Fulgence Raymond, "Les Délires ambulatoires ou les fugueurs," *Gazette des hôpitaux* 68 (July 2, 1895): 754–62; (July 8, 1895): 787–93. The lecture is by Raymond, but the notes published on it were taken by Pierre Janet. Patrick (see note 12) was still debating this question in 1907, but ambulatory automatism as a diagnostic category was fading away in France by that time.

14. Mark S. Micale, "On the Disappearance of Hysteria: A Study in the Clinical Deconstruction of a Diagnosis," *Isis* 84 (Sept. 1993): 496–526.

15. Michael Kenny, *The Passion of Ansel Bourne* (Washington, D.C.: Smithsonian Institute, 1986).

16. *William James on Exceptional Mental States: The 1896 Lowell Lectures*, ed. Eugene Taylor (New York: Charles Scribner's Sons, 1982), especially lecture four, "Multiple Personality," 73–92. There is internal evidence to suggest that in preparing these lectures James had been reading Janet's notes of Raymond's lectures, cited in note 13 above.

17. For example, as his wedding approached, an English remittance man in Rochester disappeared to Canada, where he probably traveled extensively, as far north as the great logging enterprises in Temagami, west to Winnipeg, and east to Montreal. See E. B. Angell, "A Case of Double Consciousness—Amnesiac Type, with Fabrication of Memory," *Journal of Abnormal Psychology* 1 (Oct. 1906): 155–69.

18. Jacques Donzelot, *The Policing of Families*, trans. R. Jurley (New York: Macmillan, 1979), 130.

19. Jean-Claude Beaune, *Le Vagabond et la machine. Essai sur l'automatisme ambulatoire. Médecine, technique et société en France, 1880–1910* (Seyssel: Champ-Vallon, 1987), 367. See also 63.

20. Gilles de la Tourette, "L'Automatisme ambulatoire au point de vue médico-légale," *Bulletin de médecine* 3 (1889): 344.

21. R. Benon and P. Froissart, "Conditions sociales et individuels de l'état de fugue," *Annales médico-psychologiques*, series 9, 10 (Sept. 1909): 290.

22. Ibid., 291; italics in original.

23. Henry Meige, *Études sur certains névropathes voyageurs. Le Juif errant à la Salpêtrière* (Paris: Bataile, 1893), 14. See also Jan Goldstein, "The Wandering Jew and the Problem of Psychiatric Anti-Semitism in Fin-de-Siècle France," *Journal of Contemporary History* 20 (Oct. 1985): 531–32.

24. Pitres, *Leçons cliniques*, 2: n.p. The plates are located at the end of the volume.

25. Jacqueline Carroy, "Entre mémoire et oublie: les deux vie de Félida," *Revue Internationale de Psychopathologie* 5 (Feb. 1992): 73–80; see also my *Rewriting the Soul*, 159–70.

26. Philippe Tissié, "Un Cas d'instabilité mentale avec impulsions morbides traitée par la gymnastique médicale," *Archives cliniques de Bordeaux* 3 (1894): 232–44. See also his *Hygiène du vélocipédiste* (Paris: Doin, 1889).

27. John J. MacAloon, *This Great Symbol: Pierre de Coubertin and the Origins of the Modern Olympic Games* (Chicago: University of Chicago Press, 1981), 109. I owe this reference to Brian Pronger.

28. Philippe Tissié, *La Fatigue et l'entrainement physique* (Paris: Alcan, 1897), 8.

29. Adrien Proust, "Automatisme ambulatoire chez un hystérique," *Bulletin de médecine* 4 (1890): 107–9.

30. Henri Ellenberger, *The Discovery of the Unconscious: The History and Evolution of Dynamic Psychiatry* (New York: Basic Books, 1970), 167.

31. Marcel Proust, *A la recherche du temps perdu* (Paris: Gallimard, Éditions Pléiade, 1954), 3: 716; and *Time Regained*, trans. Stephen Hudson (London: Chatto and Windus, 1931), 12: 25. I have, however, rendered Proust's *dédoublements de la personnalité* not as "duplications" but as "doublings," both French and English being derived from the original English medical label of double consciousness. "Scamp" is Hudson's somewhat old-fashioned rendering of *gredin*, a minor malefactor, which fits the historical Émile, who in real life was charged on his first arrest with *filouterie* (cheating), and on his second with *escroquerie* (swindling).

32. David Joravsky points out a literary use of fugue in Arthur Schnitzler's *Traumnovelle* (1926). There the hero contemplates becoming a *fugueur:* "He recalled certain strange pathological cases which he had read in books on psychiatry, so-called double-lives. A man living in normal circumstances suddenly disappeared, was not heard from, returned months or years later and didn't remember where he had been during this time" (*Dream Story*, trans. Otto P. Schinnerer [Los Angeles: Sun & Moon Press, 1990], 139). This is no simple case of a man considering whether to feign fugue as a way of absconding, because the hero is (ambiguously) already in a trance state.

33. Tissié, *Aliénés voyageurs*, 59–76, 83–103. For an extensive discussion of the case, see Ian Hacking, *Mad Travelers: Reflections on the Reality of Transient Mental Illness* (Charlottesville: University Press of Virginia, 1998), passim.

34. J. Grasset, "Les Maladies mentales dans l'armée et les fugues en psychiatrie. Histoire d'un deserteur voyageur," *L'Encéphale* 3 (1908): 370–85.

4. GUNNING: IN YOUR FACE

A version of this chapter previously appeared as "In Your Face: Physiognomy, Photography, and the Gnostic Mission of Early Film," *Modernism/Modernity* 4 (1997): 1–29. It is reprinted here with the kind permission of Johns Hopkins University Press. I would like to thank Lawrence Rainey, Mikhail Yampolsky, Yuri Tsivian, and Jan Holmberg for invaluable comments on this chapter.

1. Béla Balázs, *Theory of Film: Character and Growth of a New Art*, trans. Edith Boone (New York: Dover Books, 1970), 40. For insightful treatments of Balázs's concept of physiognomy in cinema, see Gertrude Koch, "Béla Balázs: The Physiognomy of Things," *New German Critique* 40 (Winter 1987): 167–78; Sabine Hake, *The Cinema's Third Machine: Writing on Film in Germany, 1907–1933* (Lincoln: University of Nebraska Press, 1993), 212–46; and especially Jacques Aurnont, *Du visage au cinéma* (Paris: Éditions de l'Etoile, 1992), 77–110. Aurnont's brilliant treatment of the face in silent film brings the concerns of this essay into the context of European film culture in the 1920s, especially in the work of Balázs and Jean Epstein.

2. Balázs, *Theory of Film*, 76.

3. Dziga Vertov, "The Writings of Dziga Vertov," in *Film Culture Reader*, ed. P. Adams Sitney (New York: Praeger Publishers, 1970), 367; Jean Epstein, "The Soul in Slow Motion," *Paris Midi Ciné* (May 11, 1928).

4. On these issues see my *D. W. Griffith and the Origins of American Narrative Film* (Champaign: University of Illinois Press, 1991).

5. Marta Braun, *Picturing Time: The Work of Étienne-Jules Marey (1830–1904)* (Chicago: University of Chicago Press, 1992), 176–80.

6. Good accounts of physiognomy can be found in Patrizia Magli, "The Face and the Soul," in *Fragments for a History of the Human Body: Part Two*, ed. Michael Feher (New York: Zone, 1989), 86–127; Jurgis Baltrusaitis, "Animal Physiognomy," in *Aberrations: An Essay on the Legend of Forms*, trans. Richard Miller (Cambridge, Mass.: MIT Press, 1989), 1–57; Graeme Tytler, *Physiognomy in the European Novel* (Princeton, N.J.: Princeton University Press, 1982); and Lynn Thorndike, *A History of Magic and Experimental Science* (New York: Columbia University Press, 1958), 8: 448–75.

7. Michel Foucault, *The Order of Things: An Archaeology of the Human Sciences* (New York: Random House, 1970), 26.

8. Charles Le Brun, *A Method to Learn to Design the Passions* (Los Angeles: University of California Press, 1980), 13. This is a reprint of a 1734 translation, including an abridgement of *Treatment of Physiognomy* by John Williams.

9. René Descartes, "Passions of the Soul," *The Philosophical Writings of Descartes* (Cambridge: Cambridge University Press, 1985), 1: 325–404.

10. Magli, "The Face and the Soul," 119; see her entire study, together with Baltrusaitis, "Animal Physiognomy," for treatments of animal imagery in Le Brun and reproductions of his illustrations.

11. See Tytler, *Physiognomy in the European Novel*, 35–81.

12. Ibid., 102.

13. See ibid., 57–59.

14. See ibid., 70.

15. Quoted in Judith Wechsler, *A Human Comedy: Physiognomy and Caricature in 19th-Century Paris* (Chicago: University of Chicago Press, 1982), 25–26.

16. Vachel Lindsay, "Hieroglyphics," in *The Art of the Moving Picture*, 199–216 (New York: Macmillan and Company, 1922).

17. See Wechsler, *Human Comedy*, 11–17, 20–31, 69–79, 93–95.

18. Ibid., 31–39.

19. Walter Benjamin, *Charles Baudelaire: A Lyric Poet in the Era of High Capitalism* (London: New Left Books, 1973), 32.

20. Wechsler, *Human Comedy*, 29–30.

21. Quoted in Sander Gilman, ed., *The Face of Madness: Hugh Diamond and the Origins of Psychiatric Photography* (New York: Brunner/Mazel, 1976), 15–16, hereafter cited as *FM* in the text.

22. On the concept of the medical gaze, see Michel Foucault, *The Birth of the Clinic: An Archaeology of Medical Perception*, trans. A. M. Sheridan Smith (New York: Vintage Books, 1975), 107–73.

23. G. B. Duchenne de Boulogne, *The Mechanism of Human Facial Expression*, ed. and trans. R. Andrew Cuthbertson (Cambridge: Cambridge University Press, 1990), hereafter cited as *MHFE* in the text.

24. Of course Duchenne was not the first to consider the mobile aspect of the face, even if he was the first to use technological means—photography—to capture it, and hence his crucial importance to my argument. Le Brun's distinction between the passions and physiognomy accentuated the difference between structure and expression, and Lavater's great critic Lichtenberg based himself in this distinction as well (Tytler, *Physiognomy in the European Novel*, 77). I thank Mikhail Yampolski for pointing this out to me, along with other oversimplifications of an earlier draft. Although Duchenne speaks of having taken some of the photographs himself, they were taken by Adrien Tournachon, the brother of Félix Tournachon, the famed photographer known by his pseudonym, Nadar. See Maria Morris Hombourg et al., *Nadar* (New York: Metropolitan Museum of Art, 1995), 223.

25. See *MHFE*, 102–3. It is interesting to note that Duchenne's work was part of a long tradition of writings by French physiologists that applied their discoveries to artistic practice. Other examples are Charcot's *Les Démoniaques dans l' art* (1887) and Marey and Demeny's *Du mouvement de l'homme* (1893), intended, as Marta Braun reports, to be "an artist's handbook," (Braun, *Picturing Time*, 268).

26. See Duchenne de Boulogne, *Mechanism of Human Facial Expression*, 101, 105.

27. Charles Darwin, *The Expression of the Emotions in Man and Animals* (Chicago: University of Chicago Press, 1965), 147, hereafter cited as *EEMA* in the text.

28. The importance of the construction of the individual body and identity for modern conception is traced in Foucault, *The Birth of the Clinic*, esp. 170; Alan Sekula's important article "The Body and the Archive," *October* 39 (Winter 1986): 3–64; and my essay "Tracing the Individual Body: Photography, Detectives, and Early Cinema," in *Cinema and the Invention of Modern Life*, ed. Leo Charney and Vanessa R. Schwartz (Berkeley: University of California Press), 42–71.

29. Georges Didi-Huberman, *L'Invention de l'hystérie: Charcot et l'iconographie photographique de la Salpêtrière* (Paris: Macula, 1982), 276, hereafter cited as *IH* in the text.

30. Sander Gilman quotes a contemporary review of the *Iconographie photographique de la Salpêtrière* that appeared in *Progrès médical* in 1879, declaring the camera as necessary to the study of hysteria as the microscope is to histology (Sander Gilman, "The Image of the Hysteric," in Gilman et al., *Hysteria Beyond Freud* [Berkeley: University of California Press, 1993], 352).

31. See also Ruth Harris, *Murders and Madness: Medicine, Law and Society in the Fin de Siècle* (Oxford: Clarendon Press, 1989), 165.

32. Quoted in Ulrich Baer, "Photography and Hysteria: Toward a Poetics of the Flash," *Yale Journal of Criticism* 7 (Spring 1994): 48.

33. Didi-Huberman, *L'Invention de l'hystérie*, 51. I might note here that photographic scientists have not fared well in recent discussions of hysteria by literary scholars. See Felicia McCarren, "The 'Symptomatic Act' Circa 1900: Hysteria, Hypnosis, Electricity, Dance," *Critical Inquiry* 21 (Summer 1995): 769, who describes Duchenne as Charcot's laboratory technician; Baer, "Photography and Hysteria," 48, 53, 64, who gives Londe's first name as "Alfred"; and Sander Gilman, "The Image of the Hysteric," 44, who reproduces a cropped version of André Brouillet's famous painting *Une Leçon clinique à la Salpêtrière* (1886)—a copy of it hung in Freud's office—but a version that omits Londe. (The error is presumably unintentional, since Gilman discusses other details of the painting that are also omitted in the cropped version.) In the complete painting, Londe sits in the foreground on the far left, his white apron and arms akimbo, differentiating him from the other auditors. See the engraving based on Brouillet's painting in Bernard and Gunthert, *L'Instant rêvé. Albert Londe*, 44.

34. Martha Noel Evans, *Fits and Starts: A Genealogy of Hysteria in Modern France* (Ithaca, N.Y.: Cornell University Press, 1991), 21.

35. See Baer, "Photography and Hysteria," 63–66.

36. See Didi-Huberman, *L'Invention de l'hystérie*, 197–200.

37. Ruth Harris, *Murders and Madness*, 58.

38. On Bertillon see Sekula, "Body and Archive," and Gunning, "Tracing the Individual Body."

39. See Bernard and Gunthert, *L'Instant rêvé*, 100.

40. See ibid., 112–13.

41. Denis Bernard and André Gunthert, *L'Instant rêvé. Albert Londe* (Nimes: Jacqueline Chambron-Trois, 1993), 111.

42. Ibid., 62.

43. Albert Londe, *La Photographie médicale. Application aux sciences médicales et physiologiques* (Paris: Gauthier-Villars, 1893).

44. See Bernard and Gunthert, *L'Instant rêvé*, 125–27.

45. See ibid. On the role of instantaneous photography in the development of the cinema, see my "'Animated Pictures': Tales of Cinema's Forgotten Future," *Michigan Quarterly Review* 34 (Fall 1995): 465–85.

46. See Bernard and Gunthert, *L'Instant rêvé*, 121–35.

47. See ibid., 153–54.

48. See Wechsler, *Human Comedy*, 153–54.

49. See Bernard and Gunthert, *L'Instant rêvé*, 144–45, 160.

50. Georges Demenÿ, "Deboires d'un inventeur," in *Intelligence du cinématographe*, ed. Marcel L'Herbier (Paris: Correa, 1946), 46.

51. See Braun, *Picturing Time*, 68–70.

52. See ibid., 175.

53. Ibid., 176.

54. Ibid., 180

55. Weschler, *Human Comedy*, 168.

56. See Braun, *Picturing Time*, 182–83. For Marey's attitude toward the *cinématographe* and projected motion pictures generally, see ibid., 195–96, and Wechsler, *Human Comedy*, 144. I discuss his lack of enthusiasm more extensively in "'Animated Pictures'" 476–79.

57. See Braun, *Picturing Time*, 182–86. Demenÿ's work as a chronophotographer and his apparatuses and business deals have been detailed by the exemplary scholar Laurent Mannoni in "Glissements progressifs vers la plaisir: remarques sur l'oeuvre chronographique de Marey et Demenÿ," 1895 18 (Summer 1895): 11–52. Mannoni proposes the audacious and fascinating theory that Demenÿ's negotiation with the Lumières may have culminated in the theft of certain of his technical ideas by the Lumières for the perfection of the *cinématographe* ("Glissements progressifs," 35).

58. Mannoni, "Glissements progressifs," 41. In his major work on early cinema, *Le grand art de la lumière et de l'ombre: archéologie du cinéma* (Paris: Nathan Université, 1994), 311, Mannoni reveals that Georges Demenÿ's brother, Paul Demenÿ, was the friend of Arthur Rimbaud and the person to whom the famous "Lettre au voyant" was addressed in 1871.

59. *The Confessions of St. Augustine*, trans. Rex Warner (New York: New American Library, 1963), 246.

60. Hans Blumenberg, *The Legitimacy of the Modern Age*, trans. Robert M. Wallace (Cambridge, Mass.: MIT Press, 1985), esp. 229–596.

61. See Bernard and Gunthert, *L'Instant rêvé*, 114.

62. Neil Harris, *Humbug: The Art of P. T. Barnum* (Chicago: University of Chicago Press, 1973), 57.

63. On the relation between the tradition of *curiositas* and the early film style that I term "the cinema of attractions," see my essay "An Aesthetic of Astonishment: Early Cinema and the (In)Credulous Spectator," in *Viewing Positions: Ways of Seeing Film*, ed. Linda Williams (New Brunswick, N.J.: Rutgers University Press, 1994), 114–33.

64. Rachel Low, *The History of the British Film*, vol. 1, 1896–1906 (London: George Allen and Unwin, 1948), 76.

65. *The Chap Book*, June 15, 1896, quoted in Terry Ramsaye, *A Million and One Nights: A History of the Motion Picture* (New York: Simon and Schuster, 1926), 259.

66. André de Lorde and Alfred Binet, *Une leçon à la Salpêtrière*, in André de Lorde, *Théâtre d'épouvante* (Paris: Charpentier et Fasquelle, 1909), 1–81. Binet is the famous neurologist who also recounts Lorde's anecdote about photographing Blanche Witmann cited above in this chapter.

67. Rae Beth Gordon, "Le Caf' conc' et l'hystérie," *Romantisme* 64 (Jan.–Mar. 1989): 53–66.

68. That the performer dressed as a woman in *Goo Goo Eyes* has sometimes been

identified as a man only increases our sense of the carnivalesque in these films, the ambiguous physiognomy of gender found in both popular entertainment and hysteria.

69. On these utopian dimensions in Benjamin, see Susan Buck-Morss, "Mythic Nature: Wish Image," in her *The Dialectics of Seeing: Walter Benjamin and the Arcades Project* (Cambridge, Mass.: MIT Press, 1989), 110–58.

70. Roland Barthes, "The Face of Garbo," in his *Mythologies*, ed. and trans. Annette Laver (New York: Hill and Wang, 1977), 56–57.

5. BRENKMAN: FREUD THE MODERNIST

1. Carl E. Schorske, "Politics and Patricide in Freud's *Interpretation of Dreams*," in *Fin-de-Siècle Vienna: Politics and Culture* (New York: Vintage, 1981), 181–207.

2. See my *Straight Male Modern: A Cultural Critique of Psychoanalysis* (New York: Routledge, 1993).

3. Sigmund Freud and Lou Andreas-Salomé, *Letters*, ed. Ernst Pfeiffer, trans. William and Elaine Robson-Scott (New York: Harcourt Brace Jovanovich, 1972), 47.

4. Sigmund Freud, *Introductory Lectures on Psycho-Analysis (Part III)* (1916–17), in *The Standard Edition of the Complete Psychological Works*, ed. and trans. James Strachey (London: Hogarth Press, 1961), 16: 456–57. Hereafter referred to as S.E.

5. Freud, "On the Beginning of Treatment (Further Recommendations on the Technique of Psycho-Analysis I)" (1913), S.E. 12: 131–32.

6. Ibid., 132.

7. Freud, "Observations on Transference-Love (Further Recommendations on the Technique of Psycho-Analysis III)" (1915 [1914]), S.E. 12: 164.

8. Freud, "On the Beginning of Treatment," 134–35.

9. Ibid., 135.

10. Freud, "The Handling of the Dream-Interpretation in Psycho-Analysis" (1911), S.E. 12: 93.

11. Freud, "The Dynamics of Transference" (1912), S.E. 12: 99–100.

12. Ibid., 101, 103, 108. See also "Remembering, Repeating and Working-Through (Further Recommendations on the Technique of Psycho-Analysis II)" (1914), S.E. 12: 147–56.

13. Freud, "Observations on Transference-Love (Further Recommendations on the Technique of Psycho-Analysis III)" (1915 [1914]), S.E. 12: 159, 166–67.

14. Ibid., 166.

15. Freud, *Introductory Lectures on Psycho-Analysis (Part III)*, 432–33.

16. Ibid., 434.

17. Ibid., 457.

18. Richard Rorty, "Freud and Moral Reflection," *Essays on Heidegger and Others: Philosophical Papers, Volume 2* (Cambridge: Cambridge University Press, 1991), 154, 155.

19. Freud, "The Future Prospects of Psycho-Analytic Therapy" (1910), S.E. 11: 146.

20. Freud, "Lines of Advance in Psycho-Analytic Therapy" (1919 [1918]), S.E. 17: 163.

21. Freud, "Analysis Terminable and Interminable" (1937), S.E. 23: 243.

22. Ibid., 244, 243.

23. Freud, Introductory Lectures on Psycho-Analysis (Part III), 331–32.

24. Freud, "On Narcissism: An Introduction" (1914), S.E. 14: 102.

25. Freud, Totem and Taboo (1913 [1912–13]), S.E. 13: 156–57.

26. Marie Balmary, Psychoanalyzing Psychoanalysis: Freud and the Hidden Fault of the Father, trans. Ned Lukacher (Baltimore, Md.: Johns Hopkins University Press, 1982); Maud Manonni, The Backward Child and His Mother: A Psychoanalytic Study, trans. A. M. Sheridan Smith (New York: Pantheon, 1972). I have commented on Balmary and Manonni in Straight Male Modern, 91–95, 204–22. See also my "Introduction" to Maud Manonni, Separation and Creativity: Refinding the Lost Language of Childhood, trans. Susan Fairfield (New York: Other Press, 1999), xvii–xxxi.

27. Freud, "Analysis Terminable and Interminable," 250.

28. Ibid., 251 n., citing Sándor Ferenczi, "The Problem of the Termination of Analysis."

29. Ibid., 251.

30. My argument here should not be taken as a wholesale criticism of Freud's concept of the castration complex. I am concerned with how he articulated (and disarticulated) castration and the social-political categories of gender and sexuality, especially in the theme of penis envy. Far-reaching reexaminations of the Oedipus complex, castration, and femininity have recently been undertaken by analysts in the Lacanian tradition. See, for example, Paul Verhaeghe, Does the Woman Exist? From Freud's Hysteric to Lacan's Feminine, trans. Marc du Ry (New York: Other Press, 1999), esp. 205–40. From a clinical as well as theoretical perspective, Verhaeghe reworks the whole of Freud's reflections on castration in order to show that when he interpreted the opposition between having-a-penis and not-having-a-penis as the fixed insignia of sexual difference he mistook a fantasy for reality. Castration enters psychic life as a multivalent fantasy: 1) "The idea of castration, as it arises in the infant's world, is first of all an interpretation of the female genitals, one that makes them disappear in such a way that they are never seen. The castration complex covers the mystery of femininity." 2) In the ordeal of separation, that is, in the child's crooked path toward pursuing its own desires and sensing its own autonomy, this idea of castration becomes a kind of defensive protection or bar against dependence on maternal omnipotence, against being swept up in, in Lacanian terminology, the enjoyment (jouissance) of the Other. 3) The threat of castration—which Freud's Oedipal theory made the origin and benchmark of the castration complex—is also a fantasy, indeed a derivative of the previous ones, which shifts the primordial anxiety

of being devoured in the maternal Other's enjoyment over onto a new, more "workable" anxiety in the face of the paternal Other's threatening "No"—more workable because its prohibitions also signify, and point the way to, unforeseen permitted pleasures. In Verhaeghe's account, castration is not, as in Freud's Oedipal theory or Ferenczi's gender therapy, a blueprint for the assumption of socially acceptable roles but rather the inner labyrinth of multilayered fantasy through which the individual is fated to seek his or her autonomy and desire.

31. Freud, "Analysis Terminable and Interminable," 252.

32. Ibid.

33. Jacques Lacan, "Kant avec Sade," in *Écrits* (Paris: Éditions du Seuil, 1966), 765–90.

6. RAINEY: SHOCK EFFECTS

1. F. T. Marinetti, "The Technical Manifesto of Futurist Literature," in *Let's Murder the Moonshine: Selected Writings / F. T. Marinetti*, ed. and trans. R. W. Flint (Los Angeles: Sun and Moon Press, 1991; 1st ed., New York: Farrar, Strauss, and Giroux, 1971), 92. Hereafter all references to the 1991 edition are given in the text with the abbreviation *LMM*. Whenever appropriate, I have altered the English translations in order to correct mistakes or underscore connotations pertinent to my discussion. The references to the edition by R. W. Flint are meant to help readers check the only available translation into English. For the text in Italian, see Luciano de Maria, ed., *Teoria e invenzione futurista*, 2d ed. (Milan: Mondadori, 1990), 46. Hereafter this edition is abbreviated *TIF*, and page reference are given in parentheses within the text.

2. For discussion of this terminology, see Josef Martin, *Antike Rhetorik: Technik und Methode* (Munich: Verlag C. H. Beck, 1974), 317–19, with references to the ancient sources.

3. See, for example, Filippo Bettini, "Forma e contenuto nel 'Manifesto Tecnico,'" paper presented at the conference "Parole in Libertà Futuriste: Futurist Literature," University of California at Los Angeles, Mar. 12, 1993. See also Marjorie Perloff, *The Futurist Moment* (Chicago: University of Chicago Press, 1986), 56–61. One discussion that focuses on the opening scene is the excellent essay by Jeffrey Schnapp, "Propeller Talk," *Modernism/Modernity* 1, no. 13 (Sept. 1994): 154–76.

4. See William Butler Yeats, "Preliminary Examination of the Script of E. R. [Elizabeth Radcliffe]," in *Yeats and the Occult*, ed. George Mills Harper (Toronto: Macmillan of Canada, 1975), 130–71. For Yeats's subsequent involvement with automatic writing, see George Mills Harper, ed., *Yeats's Notes for "A Vision"* (New York: Macmillan, 1992), 1: 1–55.

5. On Breton and Soupault, see Marguerite Bonnet's "Notice" in André Breton, *Oeuvres complètes*, ed. Marguerite Bonnet (Paris: Éditions du Pléiade, 1986), 1: 1121–48.

6. For a near-contemporary account of the Fox sisters, see [Epes Sargent], *Planchette; or, the Despair of Science* (Boston: Roberts Brothers, 1869), chap. 2. I also rely on R. Laurence Moore, *In Search of White Crows: Spiritualism, Parapsychology, and American Culture* (New York: Oxford University Press, 1977), 7–8, 12–13, 15, and 19. Also useful is the account of Blake McKelvey, *Rochester, the Water-Power City, 1812–1854* (Cambridge, Mass.: Harvard University Press, 1945), 289–90. The Fox sisters are discussed briefly by Janet Oppenheim, *The Other World: Spiritualism and Psychical Research in England, 1850–1914* (Cambridge: Cambridge University Press, 1985), 11; and in passing by Geoffrey K. Nelson, *Spiritualism and Society* (London: Routledge & Kegan Paul, 1969), 3–6.

7. [Sargent], *Planchette*, 33.

8. Ibid., 37. The Davenport brothers are also discussed by Moore, *In Search of White Crows*, 33 and 47, who reports that they were soon numbered among "the famous commercial mediums," together with the Fox sisters, Anna Fay, and J. V. Mansfield.

9. On the journey of Mrs. Hayden to England, see Oppenheim, *The Other World*, 11; and Nelson, *Spiritualism and Society*, 89–91. On the rise of spiritualism in France, see Christine Bergé, *La Voix des Esprits: Ethnologie du spiritisme* (Paris: Éditions Métaillié, 1990), 27–28; and Régis Ladous, *Le spiritisme* (Paris: Éditions Cerf, 1989), 27–30.

10. See Gustave Simon, ed., *Chez Victor Hugo: les tables tournantes de Jersey* (Paris: Éditions Stock, 1980; 1st ed., 1923).

11. Henry O'Reilly came to Rochester from New York in 1826 to be the editor of the *Daily Advertiser*. His papers are preserved at the Rochester Historical Society and are described by E. R. Foreman, "The Henry O'Reilly Documents," *Rochester Historical Society Publications Fund Series* 3 (1924): 125–26. His life is recounted in John Garraty, ed., *Dictionary of American Biography* (New York: Scribner, 1995), 14: 52–53; and in Dexter Perkins, "Henry O'Reilly," *Rochester History* (Jan. 1945). To be precise, it should be noted that the "first reports" of rappings actually took place in Hydesveille, New York, outside Rochester. The earliest is an anonymous pamphlet entitled *A Report of the Mysterious Noises Heard in the House of Mr. John D. Fox, in Hydesville, Aracadia, Wayne County, Authenticated by the Certificates, and Confirmed by the Statements of the Citizens of the Place and Vicinity* (Canandaigua, N.Y.: E. E. Lewis, 1848). All the subsequent documents appear *after* the Fox sisters gave their public performance at the Corinthian Hall in Rochester on November 14, 1849.

12. See McKelvey, *Rochester, the Water-Power City*, 332–33; and James D. Reid, *The Telegraph in America* (New York: J. Polhemus, 1886), 152–55, 300–316, and 462–70.

13. The telegraph and the railroad were components of a "machine ensemble" established by the modern railway system; on their linkage and their place within this ensemble, see Wolfgang Schivelbusch, *The Railway Journey: Trains and Travel in the*

19th Century (New York: Urizen Books, 1980, 1st ed., in German, 1978), chap. 2, "The Machine Ensemble."

14. Moore, *In Search of White Crows*, 13. The weekly newspaper was edited by Samuel Byron Brittan, a Universalist minister, together with Charles Patridge, a wealthy New York match manufacturer, from 1852 to 1860 in New York. Brittan was also the editor of a spiritualist quarterly called *Shekinah* during the period 1852–53. Moore terms Brittan "the leading publisher of works heralding the new movement" (13) and "the most important editor of the early movement" (289). He shows that Brittan and his colleagues were "strongly impressed by the sensation the Fox sisters created in New York City" and "eager to capitalize as best they could on the strong wave of popular interest in the rappings" (12–13).

15. [Sargent], *Planchette*, 2.

16. See Anonymous, "What Is Planchette?" *Scientific American* 19, no. 2 (July 8, 1868): 17–18; and Gina Covina, *The OUIJA Book* (New York: Simon and Schuster, 1979), 102–4. In 1966 the Fuld brothers sold their rights to the toy-manufacturing company Parker Brothers.

17. Allan Kardec, *Le Livre des mediums* (1857), quoted in Bergé, *La Voix des esprits*, 27.

18. Moore, *In Search of White Crows*, 22.

19. A full bibliography of Azam's writings on Félida appears in Ian Hacking, *The Rewriting of the Soul* (Princeton, N.J.: Princeton University Press, 1995), 298–99. Hacking also presents an exemplary discussion of her case, 159–70.

20. See Alan Gauld, *A History of Hypnotism* (Cambridge: Cambridge University Press, 1992), 363–69. Gauld summarizes, "As may be supposed, Azam holds that spontaneous and induced somnambulism (hypnosis) are essentially identical" (368).

21. "Every French case of *dédoublement* was described as hysteric" (Hacking, *Rewriting the Soul*, 162). For a comprehensive discussion of the vast scholarly literature that has accumulated around the study of hysteria in the last two decades, see Mark S. Micale, *Approaching Hysteria: Disease and Its Interpretations* (Princeton, N.J.: Princeton University Press, 1995). For scholars of English literature, the most familiar discussion is still that of Elaine Showalter, *The Female Malady: Women, Madness, and English Culture, 1830–1890* (New York: Penguin, 1987; 1st ed., 1985). Two works that have appeared since the publication of Micale's book are Janet Beizer, *Ventriloquized Bodies: Narratives of Hysteria in Nineteenth-Century France* (Ithaca, N.Y.: Cornell University Press, 1995); and Sander Gilman et al., *Hysteria Beyond Freud* (Berkeley: University of California Press, 1995).

22. See Esther Fischer-Homberger, *Die traumatische Neurose: Vom somatischen zum sozialen Leiden* (Bern: Verlag Hans Huber, 1972).

23. "Traumatic hysteria" was coined by Hermann Oppenheim in the late 1880s. See Schivelbusch, *The Railway Journey*, 142, and Fischer-Homberger, *Die traumatische Neurose*, 29–36.

24. Hacking, *Rewriting the Soul*, 184.

25. Janet's reputation has been rescued from unwarranted obscurity by the magisterial work of Henri Ellenberger, *The Discovery of the Unconscious: The History and Evolution of Dynamic Psychiatry* (New York: Basic Books, 1970), 331–417. See also Ellenberger's "Bibliography of the Writings of Pierre Janet," which takes up most of his brief essay on "Pierre Janet, Philosopher," in Mark S. Micale, ed., *Beyond the Unconscious: Essays of Henri F. Ellenberger in the History of Psychiatry* (Princeton, N.J.: Princeton University Press, 1993), 155–75. For studies of Janet in the last two decades, see Micale's excellent "Bibliographical Essay" in the same volume, 390–93.

26. C. M. Alan and H. Merksey, "The Development of the Hysterical Personality," *History of Psychiatry* 3 (1992): 157.

27. *Automatisme* was not a new term invented by Janet, however. It had a long history in French intellectual debates concerning the implications of Descartes's supposed materialism. For recent surveys of the term's history, see A. Gorceix, "La notion d'automatisme psychologique d'Aristote à Janet," and H. Maurel, "Approche historique de la notion d'automatisme en psychiatrie," both in *Annales Médico-Psychologiques* 147 (May 1989): 944–45 and 946–50.

28. Pierre Janet, "Les actes inconscients et le dédoublement de la personnalité pendant le somnambulism provoqué," *Revue philosophique* 22 (1886): 577–92.

29. Ibid., 592.

30. Pierre Janet, *L'Automatisme psychologique. Essai de psychologie expérimentale sur les formes inférieures de l'activité humaine* (Paris: Félix Alcan, 1889).

31. Ibid., 404.

32. Ibid., 405.

33. Ibid., 406.

34. Ibid.

35. Frederic W. H. Myers, [Part One] "On a Telepathic Explanation of Some So-called Spiritualistic Phenomena," *Proceedings of the Society for Psychical Research* 2 (1884): 217–37; [Part Two] "Automatic Writing—II," *Proceedings of the Society for Psychical Research* 3 (1885): 1–63; [Part Three] "Automatic Writing—III," *Proceedings of the Society for Psychical Research* 4 (1886–87): 209–61. In his first essay, Myers had proposed "to consider how far the already recorded phenomena of automatic writing and the like may be explained by telepathy" (218), a question quite alien to the psychological approach he adopted in the next two essays, and especially the third.

36. Myers, "Automatic Writing—III," 225.

37. Ibid., 227.

38. Ibid., 237–45.

39. Ibid., 223, 245, 254.

40. Ibid., 256–57.

41. Frederic W. H. Myers, "Automatic Writing, or the Rationale of Planchette," *The Contemporary Review* 47 (1885): 233.

42. William James, "Notes on Automatic Writing," in *Essays in Psychical Re-*

search, ed. Robert McDermott (Cambridge, Mass.: Harvard University Press, 1986), 37–38. The essay originally appeared in *Proceedings of the American Society for Psychical Research* 1 (Mar. 1889), 548–64. Needless to say, this was not James's only acquaintance with the work of Janet. He also wrote an extensive discussion of Janet's *L'Automatisme psychologique* in an essay titled "The Hidden Self," originally in *Scribner's Magazine* 7 (1890): 361–63, now more readily available in William James, *Essays in Psychology* (Cambridge, Mass.: Harvard University Press, 1983). See also the lectures "Exceptional Mental States" that James delivered at the Lowell Institute in Boston in 1896, collected and edited by Eugene Taylor under the title *Exceptional Mental States* (New York: Charles Scribner's Sons, 1983). As Taylor notes (21–22), "James was to draw heavily from Janet for the 1896 Exceptional Mental States Lectures, particularly from Janet's ideas on dissociation and the synthesizing capacity of consciousness." James's copy of Janet, which contains extensive marginalia, is housed in the Houghton Library at Harvard University. Further evidence of Janet's influence is found in the numerous citations of Janet that appear in James's *Principles of Psychology*.

43. James, "Notes on Automatic Writing," 40.

44. Ibid., 41.

45. For an informative survey of Janet's studies in spiritualism, see Pascel le Maléfan, "Pierre Janet, le spiritisme et les délires spirites," *L'Évolution psychiatrique* 58, no. 2 (Apr.–June 1993): 445–52. His principal works on hysteria are: *L'État mental des hystériques*, 2 vols. (Paris: Rueff et Cie., 1894); *Névroses et idées fixes*, 2 vols. (Paris: Félix Alcan, 1898); and *Les Obsessions et la psychasthénie* (Paris: Félix Alcan, 1903).

46. There have been many discussions of the intellectual and personal relations between Janet and Freud, as well as the differing reception histories of their work. A survey of the secondary literature is given in the "Bibliographical Essay" by Mark Micale (see note 25). More recently, Ian Hacking adds a perceptive comparison of the two men in *Rewriting the Soul*, 191–95.

47. On the early reception of Freud in France, see Jean-Pierre Mordier, *Les débuts de la psychanalyse en France, 1895–1926* (Paris: François Maspero, 1981), 54–86, who cites two 1907 essays on Freud by Alphonse Maeder, 56 n. 1. See also Elizabeth Roudinesco, *La Bataille de cent ans* (Paris: Éditions Ramsay, 1982), 1: 223–41, who discusses Maeder's essays on 222–27. On the reception of Freud in Italy, see Michel David, *La psicoanalisi nella cultura italiana*, 2d ed. (Turin: Editore Boringhieri, 1970; 1st ed., 1966), 140–86, who lists the earliest essays on Freud on 144 nn. 7, 8, 9.

48. Yves Le Lay translated the *Vorlesungen zur Einführung in die Psychoanalyse* in 1921 under the title *Origines et développment de la psychanalyse* for an edition that was issued in Geneva by the publisher Sonor; later the same year this translation was reissued under the title *Cinq leçons sur la psychanalyse* (Paris: Payot, 1921). Roudinesco, *La Bataille de cents ans: Histoire de la psychanalyse en France* (Paris: Éditions

Ramsay, 1982), contains an appendix listing all translations of Freud's works into French, 481–83.

49. On the foundation of these three societies, see, respectively, L. S. Hearnshaw, *A Short History of British Psychology, 1840–1940* (London: Methuen, 1964), 164; Jean-Pierre Mordier, *Les débuts de la psychanalyse en France*, 184; Michael David, *La psicoanalisi nella cultura italiana*, 168–69.

50. F. T. Marinetti, "Destruction of Syntax—Imagination Without Strings—Words in Freedom," in *Futurist Manifestos*, ed. Umbro Apollonio (New York: Viking, 1970), 95–106. Hereafter this is abbreviated as *FM*, and page references are given within the text.

51. Critics have not hesitated to tease out the phallic implications of this image and correlate it with other passages in Marinetti's writings that call for the "metallization" of man or otherwise exploit images of hardness with phallic undertones. In an exemplary study, Hal Foster cites this passage, among others, and correlates it with: 1) Freud's notion of the stimulation shield (a way to resist or filter shocking experience) from *Beyond the Pleasure Principle*, and 2) the distinction that the later Lacan draws between "having" versus "being" the phallus. See Hal Foster, "Prosthetic Gods," forthcoming in *Modernism/Modernity*. It should be noted that the fantasy of producing wings is also prominent in Marinetti's novel *Mafarka il futurista*, in which the protagonist gives birth to his winged son through parthenogenesis, a process once again described in terms that echo the medium's creation of new limbs. "Individual divinity and continuity of the mind which is animated by an omnipotent will that must be externalized in order to modify the world! . . . that is the only real religion!" Mafarka's entire speech is given in *TIF*, 255–64. For discussion of the misogyny that underlies this fantasy of parthenogenesis, see Barbara Spackman, "Mafarka and Son: Marinetti's Homophobic Economics," *Modernism/Modernity* 1, no. 3 (Sept. 1994): 89–107. For a more wide-ranging assessment of gender in Marinetti's oeuvre, see Cinzia Blum, *The Other Modernism: F. T. Marinetti's Futurist Fiction of Power* (Berkeley: University of California Press, 1996).

52. The paragraph containing this sentence is omitted in *LMM*, 97, though without indication of the editorial intervention.

53. Schnapp, "Propeller Talk," 168.

54. The net or network image (Italian *rete*) is used repeatedly by Marinetti in contexts that alter its implications. In the "Technical Manifesto," it is used as a figure for language, more specifically for the words-in-freedom, viewed as an instrument that captures reality: "To capture and gather whatever is most fugitive and ungraspable in matter, one must shape strict nets of images or analogies, to be cast into the mysterious sea of phenomena" (*LMM*, 94; *TIF*, 49). But this contradicts the motif that otherwise dominates the manifesto, which argues for a fusion of language and matter and hence denies the instrumental sense implied here. Elsewhere in Marinetti's writings of this period, the image of the net is associated not with a device that captures reality but with what has been captured.

55. See Peter Nicholls, *Modernisms: A Literary Guide* (Berkeley: University of California Press, 1995), 98.

56. Marinetti, "Response to Objections," in *Let's Murder the Moonshine*, 136–55.

7. CARROY: PLAYING WITH SIGNATURES

I would like to thank Professeur Gabriel Richet, Charles Richet's grandson, for granting me several interviews, for allowing me to consult the unpublished memoirs of his grandfather, and for kindly taking the time and trouble to respond patiently to my many questions. I should also like to thank Madame Pierrette Estingoy, who is working on a doctoral thesis at the University of Lyon III Jean Moulin, for presenting me her two memoirs, and for talking to me at length about her important and very interesting work on Charles Richet. Finally, I wish to thank Madame Lenoir, librarian of the Bibliothèque de l'Académie de Médecine, for permission to consult the Richet collection.

1. "Quand j'ai quitté le lycée Bonaparte, malgré un goût très vif pour les lettres et la philosophie, je ne savais trop quelle carrière choisir. Mon père, quoiqu'il ne m'en eut formellement jamais rien dit, désirait en secret me voir faire de la médecine. Alors je me dis: 'Pourquoi pas?'. La grande situation de mon père, professeur à la Faculté, chirurgien réputé, pouvait m'être utile dans cette noble profession médicale. Donc je me décidai à entrer comme étudiant à l'Ecole de Médecine."

2. Adèle Renouard's father was a member of the Académie des sciences.

3. Anaphylaxis (the word was invented by Richet) refers to hypersensitivity to substances whose introduction into the organism sets off a violent reaction. The term has been more or less completely superseded in current medical parlance by "allergy." For a more detailed analysis, see Wolf (1992), Estingoy (1992–93, 1993–94) and Richet (1993).

4. Contrary to what I had gathered from contemporaneous texts (Carroy 1993: 115), Richet was not Charcot's intern at the Salpêtrière but Moreau de Tour's.

5. "Du somnambulisme provoqué" (On induced somnambulism), published in 1875, is, to my knowledge, both Richet's first scientific publication and his first publication on hypnotism. Wolf is in error in dating "La suggestion mentale et le calcul des probabilités" (1884) to 1874 in his chronology. Indeed, *La Revue philosophique*, in which the article appeared, was not founded until 1876. Wolf is, however, quite right to highlight this text, which is probably Richet's first French publication on the "inexplicable" phenomena related to magnetism. For a survey of Richet's views on hypnotism, see Gauld (1992).

6. "C'est une histoire singulière, et qui démontre, mieux que toute théorie, le bizarre et inextricable enchevêtrement des effets et des causes."

7. Félix Alcan was, like the psychologist Ribot, a product of the Ecole Normale Supérieure; he became the prestigious publisher of all the major philosophers, psychologists, and sociologists of the period. Among those he published were Ribot,

Tarde, Binet, Janet, Bergson, and Durkheim. Around 1900, authors were liable to the condition of "Alcanitis," that is, they preferred to await publication by Alcan rather than publish immediately elsewhere.

8. "Pour en revenir à Beaujon, mes essais d'hypnotisme déterminèrent ma carrière. On a vu que j'étais incertain entre la médecine et la chirurgie. Après avoir goûté à l'expérimentation, je compris que c'était là ma voie; et je me résolus, sinon au début de l'année 1873, mais à la fin à être un physiologiste."

9. Paul Ollendorff was Fournier's and Richet's friend. He was at that time a well-known literary publisher.

10. In the indices of the *Revue des deux mondes* for 1886–93, "Charles Epheyre" and "Charles Richet" appear as two different authors. In those for 1893–1901, after the name "Charles Epheyre" we find "See Charles Richet."

11. "J'aurais, comme tout auteur, bien des pages inutiles à écrire sur mon livre. Le mieux est de n'en rien faire, et de laisser à ceux qui me liront le soin de me deviner ou de me comprendre. D'ailleurs en m'annonçant comme votre élève, j'indique assez que j'aime la vérité plus que tout au monde, et que je hais, comme la mort, ce qui est convenu et banal."

12. "Si je pris ce pseudonyme de Charles Epheyre, c'est qu'avec mon cher ami Paul Fournier, étant encore étudiants tous les deux, nous avons publié ensemble un volume de poésies (1874) heureusement introuvable aujourd'hui, portant la première lettre de nos deux noms F. et R. (Epheyre)."

13. The initial typed version of the manuscript kept in the Bibliothèque de l'Académie de médecine simply states "we published" ("nous avons publié") and "notre nom" in the singular, as French permits where a singular attribute is ascribed to each. In his corrections, Charles Richet adds "we together published" ("nous avons publié ensemble") to underline the collective aspect of the publication. He removes the ambiguous singular formulation "notre nom," replacing it with a plural and insisting on the duality: he crosses out "notre nom" and writes "nos deux noms" ("our two names") in its place.

14. Charles Richet and Paul Fournier read Greek very well. I would like to thank Chris Miller for his translation of this chapter, and for this suggestion.

15. I would like to thank Jacqueline Richou, Fournier's granddaughter, for information about Paul Fournier. "Palefroi" is an archaic French word meaning "horse for ceremonies."

16. There had, however, been one such previous case. Ribot had published passages from an anonymous letter written in 1878 by an unknown author. The author was in fact Gabriel Tarde, who was then an obscure provincial magistrate. He was later to abandon his anonymity and, like Richet, become an assiduous contributor to the *Revue philosophique* (see Milet 1970: 18).

17. "Nous nous produisons; et nous avons tort / Nous avons chanté l'amour et la guerre / La fatalité, le printemps, la mort, / Eh bien! Franchement! Mieux valait nous taire!"

18. "Ne nous indignons pas; il faut que chacun meure / Pour résoudre là-haut le problème inconnu."

19. It seems that *Possession* was published for the first time in 1887. The Bibliothèque nationale in Paris possesses only the second edition.

20. For a comprehensive study of spiritualist novels, see Nicole Edelman (1995).

21. "Peut-être trouvera-t-on bien anormale cette réunion dans le même individu de deux tendances contraires. Mais n'est-il pas avéré que l'être humain est complexe?"

22. In French, to speak of an "honnête femme" is to make a sexual judgment: "une honnête femme" is a chaste or faithful woman. An "honnête homme," by contrast, is a man with moral and intellectual qualities not necessarily connected with his sexuality. It is recorded that in the seventeenth century the courtesan Ninon de Lenclos was spoken of as an "honnête homme." In *Une conscience d'homme,* "honnête homme" is to be taken in the standard sense of "loyal and honest" as opposed to "scoundrel." But perhaps it also suggests chastity and faithfulness to the friendship of Léon, by analogy with the expression "une honnête femme." Similarly, the title *Une conscience d'homme* seems to refer to both "a human being" and "a male being."

23. "Les mots lui venaient aux lèvres, sans sa volonté, comme si un pouvoir magique les lui dictait. Chose étrange, en lui apparaissait un autre personnage, écoutant ses propres paroles, se rendant compte qu'elles dépassaient la mesure, mais impuissant à les arrêter.

Il ne parlait pas; il se laissait parler."

24. "C'est comme un acteur qui, pris de folie, s'imaginerait que le drame qu'il joue est une réalité, non une fiction, et qu'il a été transformé de corps et d'âme, dans le personnage qu'il est chargé de jouer."

25. "Sa mère tournait la tête; il arrachait la rose; mais alors, de la tige sortait un flot rouge comme du sang; sa mère poussait un grand cri, et soudain il se trouvait, tenant un poignard à la main, couvert de sang, les cheveux tout blancs, hérissés d'horreur devant le cadavre d'une femme dont la poitrine était traversée de coups de poignard. Les juges, assis en cercle autour de lui, le montraient du doigt. Sur la table, à côté du cadavre, était une rose. Et derrière le cercle des juges, à grands coups de maillet, on dressait la guillotine."

26. "Louise est là, à côté de lui! Et nul trouble-fête n'est à craindre. Personne ne viendra nous forcer à affecter l'indifférence."

27. "Non! Vous ne vous êtes jamais donné sans réserves, et, même aux premiers jours, vous pensiez à Léon plus qu'à moi. Vous aviez peur de vous compromettre. Peur, vous aviez peur et toujours peur. Peur de tout, peur du scandale, peur du remord. . . . Vos hésitations, vos faiblesses ont fini par me faire pitié."

28. "Ces évènements, dont je me suis fait le véridique historien, se sont passés il y a deux ans. Aujourd'hui l'oubli est venu; et son épais linceul a recouvert toute cette vieille histoire."

29. For a fuller analysis of the novel, see Beizer (1994) and Carroy (1993a).

30. Epheyre seems to like this first name. There were many men or children called "Georges" in Richet's family.

31. "Il a fait une grande découverte qui a bouleversé la science et ouvert un monde nouveau." "Parfois encore il se voit ministre tout-puissant." "Souvent aussi c'est une salle de théâtre, brillante de lumières. Les plus jolies femmes de Paris, les actrices les plus séduisantes s'empressent autour de lui, le rideau se lève, on écoute, on est stupéfait d'admiration."

32. "J'ai abandonné le roman, je n'ai pas abandonné la littérature." In *Suite de mes mémoires*, Charles Richet, however, reports having written only one further novel after 1896, which never saw the light of day.

33. About 1903, Charles Richet left his Masonic committment (personal communication with G. Richet).

34. "Souvent en cherchant ce qui m'aurait séduit le plus,—après le rôle d'explorateur, d'aventurier entrant dans des terres inconnues—ç'aurait été celui d'auteur dramatique."

35. This is a black notebook of 134 handwritten pages. Much of it is written in an unknown hand (Paul Fournier's?), sometimes corrected in Charles Richet's hand. Richet himself wrote certain passages, especially toward the end of the manuscript. The text is undated, but it was certainly written before 1914, as reference is made to the oppression of Alsace-Lorraine. It is difficult to say whether it was written before, during, or after the period of Richet's pacifist and Dreyfusard activities, or whether it dates from before, during, or after the writing of *La douleur des autres*, in which the character Olga replicates Katia. In Turgenev's short story "Après la mort," which probably inspired *Possession*, the heroine is called "Katia" by her family, refuses point-blank to marry, and goes so far as to slap the man intended by her family to marry her. *Katia* belongs to Richet-Epheyre's Russian vein. *Possession*, too, is set in Russia, and many of William Will's adventures take place there. Finally, Charles Richet, though he praises the genius of Tolstoy, nonetheless takes it upon himself to write a long preface in which he refutes Tolstoy's theses about luxury and diet.

36. "Hermann: . . . Un chimiste ne doit pas connaître autre chose que ses formules. Est-ce que j'ai lu Bakounine, et Tolstoï, et Spencer, et Nietzsche! . . . En dehors de son laboratoire, le chimiste ne doit connaître que le foyer famille [*sic*]. Et encore . . . En fait de politique il ne doit avoir d'autre opinion que celle de son gouvernement. Il est sûr ainsi de ne pas se tromper. Et quant aux grandes phrases sur la société et l'humanité, qu'il les laisse aux ignorants. . . .

Alexis: Alors! Les grands problèmes qui agitent le monde? . . .

Hermann: La science est une personne jalouse. Elle veut être aimée seule et elle n'accepte pas le partage. Là-dessus, allons voir nos cornues!"

"And Nietzsche" is added to the text in Charles Richet's hand. "Home and family" translates the phrase "le foyer famille" [*sic*], a mistake for "le foyer familial" in the manuscript.

37. "Ecoute-moi bien, Gretchen, et retiens cette parole triste et vraie, que j'ai

souvent méditée: même celui que nous aimons est pour nous un étranger . . . Celui-là surtout!" "Indeed, he above all!" is added in Richet's hand.

38. "Adieu! . . . Attends! Un mot encore! J'ai foi dans ton avenir! Et il ne faut pas qu'une femme entrave tes desseins. . . . Les femmes ne savent comprendre que l'amour. Tout le reste n'est rien! Rien! Rien! J'avais cru autrefois que des idées plus hautes . . . Mais non je m'étais trompée. Pour nous il n'y a que l'amour." This part of the text is all written in Richet's hand, to which he himself added "Nothing else counts! Nothing! Nothing!"

39. "J'ai conscience que je n'ai jamais rien écrit que je n'aie pensé et que je n'ai jamais été inspiré que par l'amour de la vérité, de la justice et des hommes."

40. For the text of these two protests, see Duclert (1994: 42–43).

41. Around two thousand signatures were published in January and February of 1898.

42. In a recent *Dictionnaire des intellectuels français* (Julliard and Winock 1996), Richet's commitment to Dreyfus's cause is not evoked, although Richet is mentioned. Wolf portrays Richet's commitments in somewhat anecdotal light. The figure of the French intellectual is, perhaps, somewhat alien to him. I believe, however, that it is important to cast light on Richet's stature as intellectual by referring to contemporary works of history about intellectuals and the Dreyfus Affair.

43. Leroy 1983: 156. For a more detailed analysis of the popularization and use of the noun *intellectuel* during the Dreyfus Affair, see J.-P. Honoré, "Autour d'intellectuel" (in Leroy 1983: 149–57).

44. In his *Mémoires* (V: 44–45), Richet rightly insists that he was among the first hundred Dreyfusards. He also gives an account of the network of connections through which he came to his conviction. Bernard Lazare, one of the first intellectuals to have publicly taken up Dreyfus's cause (which he did in 1896), came to Richet's laboratory with a photograph of the famous *bordereau* (note) and a specimen of Dreyfus's handwriting. Dreyfus had been sentenced in December 1894 because an anonymous document, called the *bordereau*, which offered to sell certain military secrets to the military attaché of the German embassy in Paris, had been identified as being written in his hand. Experts had begun the battle to contest or confirm this attribution in 1894. Like Binet and Tarde, Richet was interested in graphology.

45. Pace Charles (1990: 221), Richet's political activities as a scientist did not, like those of Duclaux, the *directeur* of the Institut Pasteur, begin in 1898; at that date he had already "come out of the laboratory."

46. "Puisque vous aimez avec raison la méthode scientifique, *cela ne compte pas*" (Jan. 24, 1899). "Je ne m'explique pas comment tous les honnêtes gens ne sont pas avec vous.—Hélas! Il y a beaucoup de très honnêtes gens parmi nos adversaires! Est-ce possible? Quel étrange mystère!" (Jan. 23, 1899). Like many other French people of the time, Richet had to face conflicts within his own family. In his *Mémoires*(V: 44), too, he turns his attention to the psychology of anti-Dreyfusism, speaking of a kind of "horrible collective suggestion" (*suggestion collective atroce*).

47. "Dès le début de la séance, M. Richet, professeur de physiologie, membre de l'Académie de médecine, s'est levé, et, au milieu d'un silence profond, a prononcé les paroles suivantes:
—Chaque fois qu'un de nos membres est honoré ou distingué, la Société lui adresse des félicitations. Un des nôtres, M. Grimaux, a été honoré par des mesures sur la nature desquelles je n'ai pas à me prononcer. Ce que nous pouvons faire, c'est d'assurer M. Grimaux de notre attachement et de notre estime pour sa personne.
Au milieu des applaudissements de tous les membres et du public qui assistait à la séance, M. Grimaux très ému et d'une voix tremblante a remercié ses confrères sur la marque d'estime qu'ils lui donnaient:
—La loi, a-t-il dit, a été violée en ma personne car on ne poursuit pas les témoins. Dans ma déposition, je n'ai écouté que la voix de ma conscience; et comme j'ai juré de dire la vérité, je l'ai dite.
Des applaudissements nouveaux ont éclaté et presque tous les membres ont signé une adresse de félicitation à M. Grimaux, victime de son honnêteté. Dr. R."

No mention of this mark of homage is made in the scientific proceedings of the Société de biologie. The evening paper *Le Temps* of the same date gives a slightly different version of the scene. The forty professors awaited the arrival of Grimaux and stood up as he entered. Then Richet began his speech. The paper gives the text of the letter of congratulation, which was approved unanimously with four abstentions: "My dear colleague, the members of the Société de biologie consider it a matter of honor to offer you their profound sympathy at a moment when you have suffered a cruel blow" ("Mon cher collègue, les membres de la Société de biologie tiennent à honneur de vous adresser leur profonde sympathie au moment où vous êtes durement atteint"). *Le Siècle* of February 28 offers a longer version of Grimaux's "improvised" reply.

8. MEYER: WRITING PSYCHOLOGY OVER

This chapter previously appeared as "Writing Psychology Over: Gertrude Stein and William James," *Yale Journal of Criticism* 8 (1995): 133–63. It is reprinted here with the kind permission of Johns Hopkins University Press.
1. Gerald Weissmann, in particular, argues that Stein's "revolution in words is based on [the] mechanistic conception of life" of Jacques Loeb, "the leader of the new, mechanistic school of American biology, the adherents of which tried to explain the phenomena of biology by the equations of physics" (88, 86); see Weissmann, "Gertrude Stein on the Beach," in *The Doctor With Two Heads* (New York: Knopf, 1990), 80–97, reprinted as "The Mechanistic Conception of Life: Loeb the Teacher, Stein the Student at the MBL," in *The Biological Century: Friday Evening Talks at the Marine Biological Laboratory*, ed. Robert Barlow, John Dowling, and Gerald Weissmann (Woods Hole: Marine Biological Laboratory, 1993), 5–20. Loeb, who served as the model for Max Gottlieb in Sinclair Lewis's Pulitzer Prize-winning novel *Arrowsmith*, published in 1925, spelled out his reductionist per-

spective in *The Mechanistic Conception of Life* (1911–12) and *The Organism as a Whole: From a Physico-Chemical Viewpoint* (1916); see J. P. Pauly, *Controlling Life: Jacques Loeb and the Engineering Ideal in Biology* (Oxford: Oxford University Press, 1987).

2. The use of the term "deconstruction" in relation to Stein's practice may not be as anachronistic as it no doubt seems. Mina Loy, in an essay on Joseph Cornell that dates from 1950, recalled that Stein had "explained the aim of Cubism to me as 'deconstruction preparatory to complete reconstruction of the objective.'" Loy's essay, "Phenomenon in American Art," is included in *The Last Lunar Baedeker*, ed. Robert L. Conover (Highlands, N.C.: Jargon Society, 1982), 300–302, and Carolyn Burke cites Stein's words in "Gertrude Stein, the Cone Sisters, and the Puzzle of Female Friendship," *Critical Inquiry* 8, no. 3 (Spring 1982): 560. "Deconstruction," it should be added, was a term with considerable currency in the early 1950s; thus Robert Duncan uses it in two works of 1953, "For a muse meant" as well as the charmingly titled "Deconstruction a Discussion," the topic of which is in fact Stein's writing. These pieces were first published, respectively, in *Letters* (Highlands, N.C.: Jargon Society, 1958) and *Notebook Poems: 1953* (San Francisco: The Press in Tuscany Alley / San Francisco State University, 1991).

3. That Stein recognized her affinities with Whitehead—at whose country home she and Toklas stayed during the first six weeks of World War I when they were temporarily trapped in England—is clearly displayed in her decision to have Toklas observe early in *The Autobiography of Alice B. Toklas* that "only three times in my life have I met a genius and each time a bell within me rang and I was not mistaken, and I may say in each case it was before there was any general recognition of the quality of genius in them. The three geniuses of whom I wish to speak are Gertrude Stein, Pablo Picasso and Alfred Whitehead. I have met many important people, I have met several great people but I have only known three first class geniuses and in each case on sight within me something rang." See Gertrude Stein, *The Autobiography of Alice B. Toklas* (New York: Vintage Books, 1990), 5 (hereafter cited as *Autobiography*). In aligning herself with *both* Picasso and Whitehead, Stein situates herself as a bridge between art (Picasso) and science (Whitehead). Whitehead's philosophy of science—a "philosophy of organism," in his terms—is most fully elucidated in his 1925 Lowell Lectures, "Science and the Modern World," and in the 1927–28 Gifford Lectures, "Process and Reality." For a discussion of Whitehead in relation to both William James and Stein, see Clive Bush, *Halfway to Revolution: Investigation and Crisis in the Work of Henry Adams, William James and Gertrude Stein* (New Haven, Conn.: Yale University Press, 1991), 281–91.

4. For a consideration of the lines of affiliation between Emersonian naturalism and Stein's experimental writing, see my "Stein and Emerson," *Raritan* 10, no. 2 (Fall 1990): 87–119.

5. Gertrude Stein, "The Gradual Making of The Making of Americans," in *Lectures in America* (Boston: Beacon Press, 1985), 156 (hereafter cited as "Gradual").

6. Ibid., 156–57.

7. Ibid., 154, 156, cited from Gertrude Stein, "A Long Gay Book," in *Matisse Picasso and Gertrude Stein with Two Shorter Stories* (Millerton, N.Y.: Something Else Press, 1972), 23, 114. Stein used the phrase "first manner" twice in this 1921 piece—in both the "first" and "second" persons. Several sentences into the work she writes, "Not in the form of games not in the way of repetitions. Repetitions are in your first manner and now we are in the South and the South is not in the North." The subsequent reference is similarly, if more appreciatively, dismissive: "I approach the wonder. I wonder why I have so many wishes. I wish to please and to be repeated. This is in my first manner. Thank you so much for your first manner. That is most kind of you." See Gertrude Stein, "A Sonatina Followed by Another," in *Bee Time Vine and Other Pieces* [1913–1927] (New Haven, Conn.: Yale University Press, 1953), 4, 15.

8. Stein, "Gradual," 157.

9. The fullest discussion of Stein's portraiture remains Wendy Steiner's *Exact Resemblance to Exact Resemblance: The Literary Portraiture of Gertrude Stein* (New Haven, Conn.: Yale University Press, 1978). Largely due to Stein's own compelling analysis in the 1934 lecture "Portraits and Repetition," the category of the literary portrait has remained central to considerations of her writing. More recent studies that complement, and in certain respects qualify, Steiner's include Jayne L. Walker, *The Making of a Modernist: Gertrude Stein from* Three Lives *to* Tender Buttons (Amherst: University of Massachusetts Press, 1984); Henry M. Sayre, "The Artist's Model: American Art and the Question of Looking Like Gertrude Stein," in *Gertrude Stein and the Making of Literature*, ed. Shirley Neuman and Ira B. Nadel (Boston: Northeastern University Press, 1988), 21–41; Jane Palatini Bowers, *"They Watch Me as They Watch This": Gertrude Stein's Metadrama* (Philadelphia: University of Pennsylvania Press, 1991); Stan Brakhage, "Gertrude Stein: Meditative Literature and Film," *Millennium Film Journal* 25 (Summer 1991): 100–107; and Karin Cope, "Painting After Stein," *Diacritics* 24, nos. 2–3 (Summer–Fall 1994): 190–203.

10. William James, *The Principles of Psychology* (Cambridge, Mass.: Harvard University Press, 1983), 216–17 (emphasis in original; hereafter cited as *Principles*). See Harriet Scott Chessman, *The Public Is Invited to Dance: Representation, the Body, and Dialogue in Gertrude Stein* (Stanford, Calif.: Stanford University Press, 1989), 156–60, on the related distinction between "knowledge" and "understanding" in what Chessman characterizes as "Stein's dialogue with William James."

11. Stein's *An Acquaintance with Description* was originally published in 1929 by Laura Riding's and Robert Graves's Seizin Press, in a limited edition of 225 copies; a newly edited version is included in *A Stein Reader*, ed. Ulla E. Dydo (Evanston, Ill.: Northwestern University Press, 1993), 504–34.

12. Many critics have discussed James's influence on Stein's writing, but those who argue for an ultimately nonmechanistic interpretation of her practice tend to do so in a manner that removes the writing from the realm of science. Donald Sutherland, author of the first extended study of Stein, demonstrates this process of abstraction in exemplary fashion: Stein's "persuasion" that "present thinking is the

final reality," he observes, "is neither validated nor invalidated by what happens . . . in philosophy or psychology. . . . As with the theory of humors to the Elizabethans, any philosophical or scientific theory is to an artist a working articulation of the universe, a language or an alphabet, with which to express experience. Everything depends on the eloquence, completeness, and exactitude with which the living experience is expressed by the language used." See Sutherland, *Gertrude Stein: A Biography of Her Work* (New Haven, Conn.: Yale University Press, 1951), 7. Insofar as Stein produces works of art, the truth-value of the "philosophical or scientific theory" upon which her writing is based is irrelevant; that the writing may itself function as science after she moves beyond her "deterministic theories of personality" (Hoffman, 207) is hardly conceivable. For additional considerations of the relation between Stein and James, see Michael J. Hoffman, *The Development of Abstractionism in the Writings of Gertrude Stein* (Philadelphia: University of Philadelphia Press, 1965), 199–215; Clive Bush, *Halfway to Revolution*, passim, esp. 264–65, in which Stein's practice is examined in terms of its relation to "social psychology"; and Lisa Ruddick, *Reading Gertrude Stein: Body, Text, Gnosis* (Ithaca, N.Y.: Cornell University Press, 1990), 12–41, 95–98, which offers an analysis of Stein's writing largely in relation to the deterministic operations of the Freudian unconscious.

13. William James, "Does 'Consciousness' Exist," in *Writings 1902–1910* (New York: Library of America, 1987), 1141, also cited in Sutherland, *Gertrude Stein*, 210.

14. In 1893–94, her freshman year, Stein took "Philosophy 1: General Introduction to Philosophy," which was divided into logic (taught by George Herbert Palmer), metaphysics (taught by George Santayana), and psychology. Although the Harvard General Course Catalogue merely lists "Mr. — " for the psychology segment, James had returned to teaching in 1893 after a yearlong sabbatical and, according to the editors of his *Manuscript Lectures*, taught the introductory course that year along with Palmer and Santayana. See "Introduction," *Manuscript Lectures* (Cambridge, Mass.: Harvard University Press, 1988), li–liii.

15. James, "Does 'Consciousness' Exist," 1144–45. One might compare the "verifiable and concrete" dualism that James attributes here to the experience of a painting with Stein's 1934 description of Cézanne's "pictures": "The apples looked like apples . . . and it all had nothing to do with anything because if they [the apples] did not look like apples . . . they were apples. . . . They [the apples] were so entirely these things that they [the apples] were not an oil painting and yet that is what the Cézannes were they [the paintings] were an oil painting. They [the paintings] were so entirely an oil painting that it was all there whether they were finished, the paintings, or whether they were not finished" (Stein, "Pictures," in *Lectures in America*, 76–77). Bob Perelman discusses these lines in *The Trouble With Genius: Reading Pound, Joyce, Stein, and Zukofsky* (Berkeley: University of California Press, 1994), 148–49.

16. "Does 'Consciousness' Exist" serves as the lead essay in the posthumously published *Essays in Radical Empiricism*, the title of which recalls *The Will to Believe*

where James first used the term "radical empiricism." In light of the discussion below concerning James's psychical research and its relation to Stein's writing practice, it may be noted that *The Will to Believe* concludes with James's 1896 presidential address to the British Psychical Research Society, "What Psychical Research Has Accomplished."

17. See James's 1908 Hibbert Lectures on "The Present Situation in Philosophy," published the following year as *A Pluralistic Universe*.

18. Ralph Waldo Emerson, "Experience," in *Essays and Lectures* (New York: Library of America, 1983), 480–81.

19. James, "Does 'Consciousness' Exist," 1145.

20. Two pages after this description of his reader James cited a comparable passage from the *Grundzuge der Psychologie* of his colleague Hugo Munsterberg: "'I may only think of my objects,' says Professor Munsterberg, 'yet, in my living thought they stand before me exactly as perceived objects would do, no matter how different the two ways of apprehending them may be in their genesis. The book here lying on the table before me, and the book in the next room of which I think and which I mean to get, are both in the same sense given realities for me, realities which I acknowledge and of which I take account. If you agree that the perceptual object is not an idea within me, but that percept and thing, as indistinguishably one, are really experienced *there, outside*, you ought not to believe that the merely thought-of object is hid away inside of the thinking subject.'" See James, "Does 'Consciousness' Exist," 1149, emphasis in original, quoting Munsterberg, *Grundzuge der Psychologie* 1: 48.

21. James, "Does 'Consciousness' Exist," 1151.

22. For self-styled "pragmatic" accounts of literary interpretation that follow James here, see Stanley Fish, *Is There a Text in This Class? The Authority of Interpretive Communities* (Cambridge, Mass.: Harvard University Press, 1980), and *Doing What Comes Naturally: Change, Rhetoric, and the Practice of Theory in Literary and Legal Studies* (Durham, N.C.: Duke University Press, 1989); Steven Knapp and Walter Benn Michaels, "Against Theory," *Critical Theory* 9 (1982–83): 723–42, along with the series of defenses of their position that they have published over the last decade, most recently "Reply to John Searle," *New Literary History* 25, no. 3 (1994): 669–75; and, in a less "literary" context, Richard Rorty, "Inquiry on Recontextualization: An Anti-Dualist Account of Interpretation," in *Objectivity, Relativism, and Truth* (Cambridge: Cambridge University Press, 1991), 93–110, vol. 1 of his *Philosophical Papers*. For a quite different—and considerably more Emersonian—account of "pragmatism as a form of literary skepticism" (4), see Richard Poirier, *Poetry and Pragmatism* (Cambridge, Mass.: Harvard University Press, 1992), as well as Ross Posnock's review, "Reading Poirier Pragmatically," *The Yale Review* 80, no. 3 (July 1992): 156–69.

23. James, "Does 'Consciousness' Exist," 1151.

24. About writing, Emerson was genuinely a mystic and could talk about it no

more directly than any mystic might address a central mystery or, in Stevens's technical term, "a supreme fiction." In relation to the immediate reality of his writing Emerson was exactly what he said he was, a "transparent eyeball": the writing he was looking at was the writing he was. James, on the other hand, exhibited few mystical tendencies. He was instead sympathetic, reserving judgment, a researcher. He had no trouble talking about writing; at the same time, he had no particular interest in talking about his own.

25. Stein, *Autobiography*, 211.

26. John Hyde Preston, "A Conversation," *Atlantic Monthly* 156 (Aug. 1935): 192 (emphasis in original).

27. On Emerson's "passion" for writing, see O. W. Firkins, *Ralph Waldo Emerson* (Boston: Houghton Mifflin, 1915), 227–73; B. L. Packer, *Emerson's Fall: A New Interpretation of the Major Essays* (New York: Continuum, 1982); Julie Ellison, *Emerson's Romantic Style* (Princeton, N.J.: Princeton University Press, 1984); Richard Poirier, *The Renewal of Literature: Emersonian Reflections* (New York: Random House, 1987); and Stanley Cavell, *In Quest of the Ordinary: Lines of Skepticism and Romanticism* (Chicago: University of Chicago Press, 1988), *This New Yet Unapproachable America: Lectures after Emerson after Wittgenstein* (Albuquerque, N.M.: Living Batch Press, 1989), *Conditions Handsome and Unhandsome: The Constitution of Emersonian Perfectionism* (Chicago: University of Chicago Press, 1990), and "What Is the Emersonian Event? A Comment on Kateb's Emerson," *New Literary History* 25 (1994): 951–58.

28. See Ralph Waldo Emerson, "Circles," in *Essays and Lectures*, 401–14. Although such concentration serves to distinguish Stein and Emerson from James, it is certainly not unique to them. The late novels of William's brother, Henry, for example, possess it in abundance, and, from another angle, it forms the basis for I. A. Richards's conjectures on Coleridge's literal imagination and, more generally, on "the interinanimation of words." See Richards, *Coleridge on Imagination* (New York: Harcourt, Brace and Co., 1935), passim.

29. Empson's distinction between the word as "solid tool" and as "a member of the language" clearly parallels, even if it doesn't exactly correspond to, Ferdinand de Saussure's structuralist distinction between *parole* (in the sense of "speech") and *langue* ("the language" or "linguistic system"). Roy Harris offers helpful analysis of the *parole/langue* distinction in the annotations he provides to his translation of Saussure's *Course in General Linguistics* (La Salle, Ill.: Open Court, 1983), as well as in *Reading Saussure: A Critical Commentary on the* Cours de linguistique generale (La Salle, Ill.: Open Court, 1987), and in *Language, Saussure and Wittgenstein: How to Play Games with Words* (London: Routledge, 1988).

30. See William Empson, *Seven Types of Ambiguity* (New York: New Directions, 1947 [1930]), 6–7.

31. Stein's first experiments with automatic writing were in fact directed by Hugo Munsterberg during her sophomore year; but it was James who, according to Stein,

originally suggested that a planchette be used in these experiments. I cite the passage in question below.

32. William James, "The Confidences of a 'Psychical Researcher,'" *Essays in Psychical Research* (Cambridge, Mass.: Harvard University Press, 1986), 372 (hereafter cited as "Confidences").

33. The letter, postmarked December 17, was written to Lindley Hubbell and is now in the Yale Collection of American Literature. Hubbell was a young writer whose verse tribute, "A Letter to Gertrude Stein," had been published in *Pagany* 1, no. 1 (Spring 1930) and is reprinted in *A Gertrude Stein Companion: Content with the Example*, ed. Bruce Kellner (New York: Greenwood Press, 1988), 115–16. The spelling of "experiments" as "xperiments" was customary for Stein; she tended to drop the *e* in words that began with *ex-*.

34. B. F. Skinner, "Has Gertrude Stein a Secret?" in *Critical Essays on Gertrude Stein*, ed. Michael J. Hoffman (Boston: G. K. Hall, 1986), 67–68 (hereafter cited as "Secret"). For additional considerations of Skinner's article, see Hoffman, *The Development of Abstractionism in the Writings of Gertrude Stein*, 201–3, and Weissmann, "Gertrude Stein on the Beach," passim.

35. Skinner, "Secret," 68. Skinner's concept of the "inferential author" clearly links up with the notion that Wayne Booth would develop thirty years later of the "implied author" who "chooses, consciously or unconsciously, what we read; we infer him as an ideal, literary, created version of the real man; he is the sum of his own choices." See Wayne C. Booth, *The Rhetoric of Fiction*, 2d ed. (Chicago: University of Chicago Press, 1983), 74–75. The connections between scientific psychology and literary theory, which I am examining here in the particular case of Stein and James, constitute an important secret history of twentieth-century thought, and they certainly don't travel in just one direction; for a consideration of Skinner's literary aspirations and an analysis of their role in his life and work, see Alan C. Elms, "Skinner's Dark Year and *Walden Two*," in *Uncovering Lives: The Uneasy Alliance of Biography and Psychology* (New York: Oxford University Press, 1994), 85–100. Although Skinner criticizes Stein on account of the way her "inferential author" falls short of the "ideal," behind this critique lies a more substantial one that has been expressed by many readers: namely, that in her experimental writing Stein seems to have forcibly removed the reader from the picture. The implied author may be immature, but "the implied reader," to use Wolfgang Iser's term, has apparently been killed off. For considerations, *pace* Skinner, of the very real place—and active role— of the reader in Stein's texts, see Neil Schmitz, *Of Huck and Alice: Humorous Writing in American Literature* (Minneapolis: University of Minnesota Press, 1983); Ulla Dydo, "*Stanzas in Meditation*: The Other Autobiography," *Chicago Review* 35, no. 2 (Winter 1985): 4–20; and Chessman, *The Public Is Invited to Dance*, passim.

36. Skinner, "Secret," 71.

37. Stein, *Autobiography*, 77–78. Stein studied with Munsterberg both her freshman year, 1893–94, taking Philosophy 7 (normally "The Content of Christian Faith," but the Harvard Course Catalogue for that year gives Munsterberg's name in the slot,

without listing the title of his course), and her sophomore year, in Philosophy 20a ("Psychological Laboratory"—"primarily," according to the catalogue, for graduate students). Returning to Germany after the 1894–95 school year was over, Munsterberg, in a letter written from aboard a ship, praised Stein for having been an "ideal" student: "I thank you above all for that model-work you have done in the laboratory and the other courses wherever I met you. My contact with Radcliffe was in every way a most charming part of my Cambridge experience. But while I met there all types and kinds of students, you were to me the ideal student, just as a female student ought to be, and if in later years you look into printed discussions which I have in mind to publish about students in America, I hope you will then pardon me if you recognize some features of my ideal student picture as your own." See *The Flowers of Friendship*, ed. Donald Gallup (New York: Farrar, Straus and Giroux, 1979), 4. For a consideration of Munsterberg's later work on a "scientific" social psychology in relation to Stein, see Bush, *Halfway to Revolution*, 275–79.

38. James, *Principles*, 201.

39. Gertrude Stein, *Everybody's Autobiography* (London: Virago Press, 1985), 231.

40. Gertrude Stein and Leon Solomons, *Motor Automatism* (New York: Phoenix Book Shop, 1969), 28. For further considerations of these articles, see Sutherland, *Gertrude Stein*, 1–3; Hoffman, *The Development of Abstractionism in the Writings of Gertrude Stein*, 199–207; Bush, *Halfway to Revolution*, 279–80; and Weissmann, "Gertrude Stein on the Beach," passim.

41. Stein and Solomons, *Motor Automatism*, 21.

42. Stein, *Autobiography*, 78.

43. Skinner, "Secret," 70, 71. See Gerald Weissmann's article "Gertrude Stein on the Beach" for a recent interpretation of Stein's writing that follows Skinner's account in most of its details. Weissmann is careful to distinguish Stein's "automatic writing," however, from her later experimental writing.

44. The linkage, especially in the second half of the nineteenth century, of women with hysteria—etymologically, "hysteria" derives from the Greek *hustera*, or "womb"—has been the subject of much recent academic study. See Carroll Smith-Rosenberg, "The Hysterical Woman: Sex Roles and Role Conflict in Nineteenth-Century America," in *Disorderly Conduct: Visions of Gender in Victorian America* (New York: Alfred A. Knopf, 1985), 197–216; Charles Bernheimer and Claire Kahane, ed., *In Dora's Case: Freud—Hysteria—Feminism* (New York: Columbia University Press, 1985); Martha Noel Evans, *Fits and Starts: A Genealogy of Hysteria in Modern France* (Ithaca, N.Y.: Cornell University Press, 1991); Janet Beizer, *Ventriloquized Bodies: Narratives of Hysteria in Nineteenth-Century France* (Ithaca, N.Y.: Cornell University Press, 1994); Ulrich Baer, "Photography and Hysteria: Toward a Poetics of the Flash," *Yale Journal of Criticism* 7, no. 1 (Spring 1994): 41–77; and Mark S. Micale, *Approaching Hysteria: Disease and Its Interpretations* (Princeton, N.J.: Princeton University Press, 1995).

45. The letter, tentatively dated February 1934, is now in the Yale Collection of American Literature. Although, as noted above, Stein customarily left out the *e* when

a word was spelled *ex-*, in this case it appears from the manuscript that she originally spelled "excess" without the initial "e" and only added it as an afterthought—perhaps as an immediate example of the sort of "[e]xcess" consciousness she had in
mind.

46. James, *Principles*, 166, 172.

47. Sigmund Freud, *The Psychopathology of Everyday Life* (New York: W. W.
Norton, 1989), 346 (emphasis in original).

48. Ibid., 345.

49. Ibid., 330.

50. For a very different account of Stein's understanding of the unconscious, and
of the relation her analysis of the psyche bears to Freudian psychoanalysis, see
Ruddick, *Reading Gertrude Stein*, esp. 93–99.

51. Stein, *Everybody's Autobiography*, 229.

52. Stein, *Motor Automatism*, 28–29.

53. Stein, *Autobiography*, 83.

54. Gertrude Stein, *Fernhurst, Q.E.D., and Other Early Writings* (New York:
Liveright, 1983), 144.

55. Stein, *Autobiography*, 84.

56. The earliest example cited by the *Oxford English Dictionary* for the use of
"hysteria" in the "transferred" or "figurative" sense of "Morbidly excited condition;
unhealthy emotion or excitement" is in fact a line of Poe's: "'an evidently restrained
hysteria in his whole demeanor.'" "Women [are] much more liable than men to this
disorder," the compilers of the dictionary observe of the term in its principal, pathological sense; the example's masculine pronoun ("*his* whole demeanor") may well
have signaled for them the "figurative[ness]" that they attributed to Poe's usage. For
recent considerations of "male hysteria," see Neil Hertz, "Medusa's Head: Male
Hysteria under Political Pressure" (together with responses by Catherine Gallagher
and Joel Fineman), in *The End of the Line: Psychoanalysis and the Sublime* (New
York: Columbia University Press, 1985), 160–215; Mark S. Micale, "Charcot and the
Idea of Hysteria in the Male: Gender, Mental Science and Medical Diagnosis in
Late Nineteenth-Century France," in *Medical History* 34 (Oct. 1990): 363–411; Mark
S. Micale, "Hysteria Male / Hysteria Female: Reflections on Comparative Gender
Construction in Nineteenth-Century France and Britain," in *Science and
Sensibility: Essays on Gender and Scientific Enquiry, 1780–1945*, ed. Marina
Benjamin (London: Basil Blackwell, 1991), 200–242; and Jan Goldstein, "The Uses
of Male Hysteria: Medical and Literary Discourse in Nineteenth-Century France,"
Representations 34 (Spring 1991): 134–65.

57. Gertrude Stein, *Picasso: The Complete Writings*, ed. Edward Burns (Boston:
Beacon Press, 1985), 47.

58. Peter Neagoe, ed., *Americans Abroad: An Anthology* (The Hague: Servire
Press, 1932), 418.

59. Skinner, "Secret," 68.

60. Letter from Stein to Lindley Hubbell, postmarked December 17, 1932, in the Yale Collection of American Literature.

61. Stein, "A Transatlantic Interview," in *A Primer for the Gradual Understanding of Gertrude Stein*, ed. Robert Bartlett Haas (Los Angeles: Black Sparrow Press, 1971), 18.

62. Stein, *Autobiography*, 50.

63. Ibid., 79.

64. Stein, *Everybody's Autobiography*, 230.

65. Emily Dickinson, "My Life Had Stood—a Loaded Gun—," in *The Complete Poems of Emily Dickinson*, ed. Thomas H. Johnson (Boston: Little, Brown & Co., 1976), 369. See Susan Howe, *My Emily Dickinson* (Berkeley, Calif.: North Atlantic Books, 1988), passim, for an extended reading of this poem. The first part of Howe's study begins: "In the college library I use [as it happens, the library at Yale University, where Stein's papers are housed] there are two writers whose work refuses to conform to the Anglo-American literary traditions these institutions perpetuate. Emily Dickinson and Gertrude Stein . . ." (11).

66. Eugene Taylor, in *William James on Exceptional Mental States*, ed. Taylor (New York: Charles Scribner's Sons, 1983), offers the following definition of a planchette: "an automatic writing device consisting of a heart-shaped disc with three legs, one of which is a pencil; one or both hands resting on the disc will record, on a piece of paper, involuntary muscle movements as well as unconscious writing" (43).

67. Stein, *Everybody's Autobiography*, 230.

68. James, "Confidences," 372. One might compare James's description of this "subconscious region" with Bruno Latour's characterization of the "new actor" who in the mid-seventeenth century "intervenes," as Latour puts it, in Robert Boyle's report of his experiments with the air pump: "inert bodies, incapable of will and bias but capable of *showing, signing, writing, and scribbling on laboratory instruments* before trustworthy witnesses. . . . Endowed with their new semiotic powers, [these nonhumans] contribute to a new form of text, the experimental scientific article, a hybrid between the age-old style of biblical exegesis—which has previously been applied only to the Scriptures and classical texts—and *the new instrument that produces new inscriptions*. From this point on, witnesses will pursue their discussions around the air pump in its enclosed space, discussions about the meaningful behaviour of nonhumans. The old hermeneutics will persist, but it will add to its parchments *the shaky signature of scientific instruments*." See Bruno Latour, *We Have Never Been Modern* (Cambridge, Mass.: Harvard University Press, 1993), 23–24 (emphasis added). It is as if Latour has extended the realm of the phenomena James is describing from psychical research to all experimental science. Are laboratory instruments, then, as Latour seems to suggest, in essence complex writing instruments: pen and paper writ large?

69. "Matisse, Pablo and I," Stein observed, "do not do ours with either brains or character, we have all enough of both to do our job but our initiative comes from within a propulsion which we don't control, or create." See Stein, *Picasso*, 107.

70. Ralph Waldo Emerson, "Spiritual Laws," in *Essays and Lectures*, 309.

71. Stein, *Autobiography*, 119.

72. Ibid., 156.

73. Ibid., 119.

74. Ibid., 210.

75. Ibid., 211.

76. James, "Confidences," 374.

77. Ibid., 375.

78. Gerald Myers thus observes that although "according to most commentators, James was chronically introspective . . . there are two important respects in which he was not. . . . First, he did not try to manage negative feelings by paying them introspective attention. Whereas some therapists contend that troublesome feelings are best handled by intense scrutiny, James counseled otherwise. . . . Negative states of consciousness, he claimed, are more effectively dissipated by strategic behavior than by introspective scrutiny. Second, James did not practice introspective self-diagnosis or self-analysis as Freud did, for example, in *The Interpretation of Dreams*. One of the most remarkable aspects of James's numerous references to his own problems is that he never attempted a sustained introspective analysis of their underlying causes. . . . James was to an extent an introspectionist in psychology, but he seldom used introspection to discover the causes of his own psychic states, nor did he advocate any systematic method by which people could locate the causes of their psychological troubles." See Gerald E. Myers, *William James: His Life and Thought* (New Haven, Conn.: Yale University Press, 1986), 47–48.

79. John Dewey, "The Development of American Pragmatism," in *The Later Works, 1925–1953: Nineteen Twenty-Five to Nineteen Twenty-Seven*, ed. Jo Ann Boydston and Bridget Walsh (Carbondale: University of Southern Illinois Press, 1984), 2: 15.

80. James, *Principles*, 244.

81. Ibid., 238 (emphasis in original).

82. Gertrude Stein, "Poetry and Grammar," in *Lectures in America*, 213.

83. Stein, "Gradual," 147.

84. James, *Principles*, 245. For an extended consideration of "James' idea that the thought is already complete at the beginning of the sentence," as Ludwig Wittgenstein put it, see Wittgenstein, *Remarks on the Philosophy of Psychology* (Chicago: University of Chicago Press, 1988), 1: 35e–36e, ff.

85. Gertrude Stein, *The Making of Americans* (Normal, Ill.: Dalkey Archive, 1995), 504 (emphasis added). This procedure is central to what David Lodge calls Stein's "experimental metonymic writing," in which the "natural emphasis on syntagmatic continuity" of prose is replaced by an "emphasis on paradigmatic similarity" that is more appropriate to lyric poetry; see David Lodge, *The Modes of Modern Writing: Metaphor, Metonymy, and the Typology of Modern Literature* (Ithaca, N.Y.: Cornell University Press, 1977), 155. Lodge draws on the linguistic distinction between a paradigm ("a set of words with the same grammatical function") and a syn-

tagm (a combination of "linguistic entities" into a "linguistic unit . . . of a higher degree of complexity") as well as on the distinction between metonymic language ("association by contiguity") and metaphoric language ("association by similarity") that Roman Jakobson employs in his essay "Two Aspects of Language and Two Types of Aphasic Disturbances" (Lodge, 73–75). (In this 1956 essay Jakobson proposes that different forms of the language disorder known as aphasia may be understood as involving difficulties, respectively, with the selection and the combination of language: language as metaphor and as metonymy. See Jakobson, "Two Aspects of Language and Two Types of Aphasic Disturbances," in *Language and Literature*, ed. Krystyna Pomorska and Stephen Rudy [Cambridge, Mass.: Harvard University Press, 1987], 95–114.) There is nothing wrong with characterizations like Lodge's per se, but they run the risk of creating the illusion that something has been *explained* whereas what has really been provided is a new *description*. Thus, when Lodge observes that Stein's writing "oscillated violently between the metonymic and metaphoric poles, pushing out in each direction to points where she began to exhibit symptoms of Jakobson's two types of aphasia" (144), all that he has actually accomplished — despite the appearance of having *explained* Stein's writing (as exhibiting "symptoms of aphasia") — is a *redescription* of the writing (as oscillating "violently between the metonymic and metaphoric poles").

86. James, *Principles*, 266.

87. Ibid., 243.

88. Although repetition plays a key role in Stein's writing, she never merely repeats herself, as she explains when she distinguishes between repetition and *insistence* in her lecture "Portraits and Repetition": in "expressing any thing there can be no repetition because the essence of that expression is insistence, and if you insist you must each time use emphasis and if you use emphasis it is not possible *while anybody is alive* that they should use exactly the same emphasis. . . . Anybody can be interested in a story of a crime because no matter how often the witnesses tell the same story the insistence is different. *That is what makes life* that the insistence is different, no matter how often you tell the same story *if there is anything alive in the telling* the emphasis is different. . . . No matter how often what happened any time any one told anything there was no repetition. This is what William James calls *the Will to Live. If not nobody would live*." See Stein, *Lectures in America*, 167, 169 (emphasis added). Although Stein is discussing self-expression and narration here, her repeated invocation of "life" is not merely rhetorical; rather, she is describing a feature of discourse that links it quite directly with biological evolution, which also takes the form of repetition with a difference.

89. Gertrude Stein, "Picasso," in *Portraits and Prayers* (New York: Random House, 1934), 17.

90. Northrop Frye, in an important essay on what he calls "generic seeds or kernels, possibilities of expression sprouting and exfoliating into new literary phenomena" (123), distinguishes riddle from charm as follows: "the rhetoric of charm is dissociative and incantatory: it sets up a pattern of sound so complex and repetitive that

the ordinary processes of response are short-circuited. . . . [T]he riddle is essentially a charm in reverse: it represents the revolt of the intelligence against the hypnotic power of commanding words. In the riddle a verbal trap is set, but if one can 'guess,' that is, point to an outside object to which the verbal construct can be related, the something outside destroys it as a charm, and we have sprung the trap without being caught in it. . . . Charms and riddles, however, are psychologically very close together, as the unguessed or unguessable riddle is or may be a charm." See Northrop Frye, "Charms and Riddles," in *Spiritus Mundi: Essays on Literature, Myth, and Society* (Bloomington: Indiana University Press, 1976), 126, 137–38 (emphasis added). Frye goes on to observe that "in modern times, at least, a poet interested in charm techniques is likely to be interested in riddle techniques also," and offers Stein as his principal example: she "came to be thought of as the very type of dissociative writer, was often ridiculed or caricatured on that basis, and of course it is true that she was greatly interested in dissociative techniques. . . . But many of the vignettes of *Tender Buttons* are riddles of a fairly conventional type, with the solution, as often happens, provided in the title" (142). The portrait of Picasso would similarly seem to be charm and riddle in one.

91. For a description of Basic English—which consisted of approximately a thousand words that could be used in combination to replace all other English words—see Reuben Brower's interview with Richards in *I. A. Richards: Essays in his Honor*, ed. Brower, Helen Vendler, and John Hollander (New York: Oxford University Press, 1973), esp. 33–36, as well as the essay by William Empson in the same volume. Empson's essay, "The Hammer's Ring," is reprinted in his collection, *Argufying: Essays on Literature and Culture*, ed. John Haffenden (Iowa City: University of Iowa Press, 1987), along with several other pieces that he wrote on the subject. "There are three chief reasons why Basic is important," he observes in one of these: first "as an 'auxiliary' international language . . . secondly as a first step in the direction of full English which gives the right feeling about the words . . . thirdly as a test of a bit of writing for the Englishman himself, a way of separating statement from form and feeling." "But for a word or two in 'quotes,'" Empson adds, "this [particular] bit of writing is in Basic, and the better for its limits" (230–31).

92. Although not entirely impossible. Much recent criticism of Stein, beginning with Richard Bridgman and William Gass, has been concerned with developing such personal associations; see Bridgman, *Gertrude Stein in Pieces* (New York: Oxford University Press, 1970), and Gass, "Gertrude Stein and the Geography of the Sentence," in *The World Within the Word* (Boston: David Godine, 1979), 63–123. The point that needs to be made is that this is exactly what Stein was *not* doing. She was rigorously, ruthlessly, trying to make these associations irrelevant, inoperative—trying to make their operations irrelevant. Decoding her compositions is certainly not pointless, but it unavoidably misses the point of writing this way at all.

93. Stein, "A Transatlantic Interview," 26. For an account of Stein's early writing as a progressive identification with "the dirt"—from "Melanctha" (etymologically,

"black earth") to "the solid dirt" of *The Making of Americans* — see Ruddick, *Reading Gertrude Stein*, esp. 5, 99–102.

94. Myers, *William James: His Life and Thought*, 247. According to Myers, James "retained his faith in association while rejecting the atomistic ideas of British empiricism . . . That a specific thought or feeling seems to arouse another involuntarily is explained by the law of association of cerebral events . . . At the same time, James characteristically believed that some thinking is voluntary and not mechanical; what and how we think can result not only from cerebral causes, but also from our deliberately attending to one mental item rather than another in the thought process. . . . James denied that we can spontaneously create thoughts and argued that we are limited to emphasizing or reinforcing one thought over another among those that have already been put before consciousness by the associative machinery of the brain. Through such emphasis we introduce our interests and values into the causal chain, redirecting and rearranging the train of associations and thus exhibiting the capacity of thinking to influence indirectly its own cerebral conditions" (245); see also James's chapter on "Association" in *Principles*, 519–69. On Coleridge's anti-associationism, see Richards, *Coleridge on Imagination*, esp. 67–71; M. H. Abrams, *The Mirror and the Lamp*; and Jerome Christensen, *Coleridge's Blessed Machine of Language* (Ithaca, N.Y.: Cornell University Press, 1981).

95. In *The Mirror and the Lamp*, M. H. Abrams distinguishes between Coleridge's notions of the "mechanical fancy" and "organic imagination" (167–77). See also Samuel Taylor Coleridge, *Biographia Literaria*, ed. James Engell and W. Jackson Bate (Princeton, N.J.: Princeton University Press, 1983), I: esp. 89–128.

96. J. Laplanche and J.-B. Pontalis note in *The Language of Psycho-Analysis* (New York: W. W. Norton, 1973) that "the free-association method is meant to bring out a determinate order of the unconscious," and cite Freud to the effect that "'when conscious purposive ideas [*Zielvorstellungen*] are abandoned, concealed purposive ideas assume control of the current of ideas'" (170).

97. As Jerome Christensen suggests in *Coleridge's Blessed Machine*, "the foremost difficulty confronting a rigorously necessitarian theory of association is to account for its own writing" (28).

98. Alfred North Whitehead, *Science and the Modern World* (New York: Free Press, 1967), 80, 75. "I would term the doctrine of these lectures," Whitehead observes, "the theory of the *organic mechanism*. In this theory, the molecules may blindly run in accordance with the general laws, but the molecules differ in their intrinsic characters according to the general organic plans of the situations in which they find themselves" (80, emphasis in original). Such a "philosophy of organism" contrasts with "the extreme doctrine of materialistic mechanism," "which holds that each molecule blindly runs. The human body is a collection of molecules. Therefore, the human body blindly runs, and therefore there can be no individual responsibility for the actions of the body." As Whitehead notes, "if you once accept that the molecule is definitely determined to be what it is, independently of any determina-

tion by reason of the total organism of the body, and if you further admit that the blind run is settled by the general mechanical laws, there can be no escape from this conclusion" (78).

99. Arthur Danto makes a similar suggestion when he comments in a recent essay that if "we are structured as texts, then criticism is preemptive psychology and even now the strategies evolved for addressing literary texts have application to us" (382). Supposing that "texts, as literary artifacts, are projections and extensions of the unifying structures of a self or of a life," and that "the principles, whatever they are, that enable us to tell and follow stories, to construct and read poetry, are the principles that bind lives into unities," then criticism—as "the theory of texts"—would be "the paradigm of human science" and "the matrix for understanding the physiology and ultimately the molecular biology of human cognition" (384, 381, 385). See Arthur Danto, "Beautiful Science and the Future of Criticism," in *The Future of Literary Theory*, ed. Ralph Cohen (New York: Routledge, 1989), 370–85.

9. JORAVSKY: BETWEEN SCIENCE AND ART

1. Freud, *The Standard Edition of the Complete Psychological Works* (London: Hogarth, 1953–74) (hereafter *S.E.*), 4: xxiv; and *Gesammelte Werke* (London: Imago, 1940–52) (hereafter *G.W.*), 2: viii.

2. See especially Adolf Grünbaum, *Foundations of Psychoanalysis: A Philosophical Critique* (Berkeley: University of California Press, 1984); and Jürgen Habermas, *Knowledge and Human Interests* (2d ed., London: Heinemann, 1978), part 3. Neither gives serious attention to fiction as an approach to knowledge of ourselves.

3. Brentano, *Psychologie vom empirischen Standpunkt* (Leipzig: Duncker, 1874), vi. The 1924 reprint has a crucial misprint: "psychic realm" is "physical realm." For Freud's "academic bliss" in Brentano's course, see William J. McGrath, *Freud's Discovery of Psychoanalysis: The Politics of Hysteria* (Ithaca, N.Y.: Cornell University Press, 1986), 122ff.

4. I have used the common names—expressive understanding versus scientific explanation—for the kinds of psychology that Brentano called "descriptive" and "genetic." See Lucie Gilson, *La Psychologie descriptive selon Franz Brentano* (Paris: Vrin, 1955), 73 and passim. The shift in Brentano's views after 1875, when Freud took his course, can be denied—in metaphysics. See A. C. Rancurello, *A Study of Franz Brentano: His Psychological Standpoint and His Significance in the History of Psychology* (N.Y.: Academic Press, 1968), 75 and passim.

5. I quote early Foucault, as he denied that Freud's stories are of that sort, which he discerned in pre-Freudian psychiatry, in the clinician's *"regard"* or "view" of the patient. ("Gaze," the usual translation, obscures the meaning.) See Foucault, *The Order of Things: An Archaeology of the Human Sciences* (New York: Random House, 1973), 377, translation of *Les Mots et les choses* (Paris: Gallimard, 1966), 388. Later Foucault, while conceding that Freud did, after all, belong to the tradition of the

clinician's *"regard,"* the "episteme" of *"pouvoir/savoir,"* expressed such criticism of Freud much less vividly than he had the praise. See Foucault, *Power/Knowledge: Selected Interviews and Other Writings, 1972–1977* (New York: Pantheon, 1980), esp. chaps. 3, 10, 11; and *The History of Sexuality,* vol. 1 (New York: Pantheon, 1978), translation of *La Volonté de savoir* (Paris: Gallimard, 1976), passim.

6. See Bruce Thompson, *Schnitzler's Vienna: Image of a Society* (London: Routledge, 1990); Reinhard Urbach, *Arthur Schnitzler* (New York: Ungar, 1973); Renate Wagner, *Arthur Schnitzler; eine Biographie* (Wien: Molden, 1981).

7. See Heinrich Schnitzler et al., *Arthur Schnitzler: sein Leben, sein Werk, seine Zeit* (Frankfurt: Fischer, 1981), 108–9, 342–44; A. Schnitzler, "Über Psychoanalyse," *Protokolle* 2 (1976): 277–84; Gail Finney, *Women in Modern Drama: Freud, Feminism, and European Theater at the Turn of the Century* (Ithaca, N.Y.: Cornell University Press, 1989), chap. 1; Michael Worbs, *Nervenkunst: Literatur und Psychoanalyse im Wien der Jahrhundertwende* (Frankfurt: Europäische, 1982), 225–58; M. L. Perlmann, *Der Traum in literarischen Moderne; Untersuchungen zum Werk Arthur Schnitzlers* (Munich: Fink, 1987). For Schnitzler's most important fictive presentations of the mind-doctor, see his play *Paracelsus* (1897) and his novellas *Traumnovelle* (1926) and *Flucht in die Finsternis* (1931).

8. See H. F. Ellenberger, *The Discovery of the Unconscious: The History and Evolution of Dynamic Psychiatry* (New York: Basic Books, 1970), 460, 834–37; and Susan Suleiman, "Surrealism," in *Feminism and Psychoanalysis: A Critical Dictionary,* ed. Elizabeth Wright (Oxford: Blackwell, 1992), 417–20.

9. See Justin Miller, "Interpretations of Freud's Jewishness, 1924–1974," *Journal of the History of the Behavioral Sciences* 17 (1981): 357–74. Note especially the works he cites by Max Schur, David Bakan, Henri Ellenberger, John Cuddihy, Marthe Robert, Philip Rieff, and Reuben Rainey. See also Sigmund Diamond, "Sigmund Freud, His Jewishness, and Scientific Method: The Seen and the Unseen as Evidence," *Journal of the History of Ideas* 4 (1982); 613–34; Peter Gay, *Freud, Jews and Other Germans: Masters and Victims in Modernist Culture* (New York: Oxford, 1978); Sander Gilman, *The Case of Sigmund Freud: Medicine and Identity at the Fin de Siècle* (Baltimore, Md.: Johns Hopkins University Press, 1993); Sander Gilman, "Freud, Race and Gender," in *Psychoanalysis in Its Cultural Context,* ed. Edward Timms and Ritchie Robertson (Edinburgh: Edinburgh University Press, 1992); Sander Gilman, *Jewish Self-Hatred, Anti-Semitism, and the Hidden Language of the Jews* (Baltimore, Md.: Johns Hopkins University Press, 1986); Moshe Gresser, *Dual Allegiance: Freud as a Modern Jew* (Albany: SUNY, 1994); Susann Heenen-Wolff, *"Wenn ich Oberhuber hiesse—": die Freudsche Psychoanalyse zwischen Assimilation und Antisemitismus* (Frankfurt: Nexus, 1987); Dennis B. Klein, *Jewish Origins of the Psychoanalytic Movement* (New York: Praeger, 1985); McGrath, *Freud's Discovery of Psychoanalysis;* Emanuel Rice, *Freud and Moses: The Long Journey Home* (Albany, N.Y.: SUNY, 1991); James L. Rice, *Freud's Russia: National Identity in the Evolution of Psychoanalysis* (New Brunswick, N.J.: Transaction, 1993); Y. H. Yerushalmi,

Freud's Moses: Judaism Terminable and Interminable (New Haven, Conn.: Yale University Press, 1991); Benedict Anderson, *Imagined Communities: Reflections on the Origin and Spread of Nationalism* (London: Verso, 1987).

10. See Hannah Decker, *Freud, Dora, and Vienna* (New York: Free Press, 1991); Lisa Appignanesi and John Forrester, *Freud's Women* (New York: Basic Books, 1992), 165–66.

11. See especially Peter Pulzer, *The Rise of Political Antisemitism in Germany and Austria* (New York: Wiley, 1964); George Mosse, *Toward the Final Solution: A History of European Racism* (New York: Fertig, 1978); Stephen Wilson, *Ideology and Experience: Antisemitism in France at the Time of the Dreyfus Affair* (Rutherford, N.J.: Fairleigh Dickinson University Press, 1982); and Sander Gilman, *The Jew's Body* (New York: Routledge, 1991).

12. *A Psychoanalytic Dialogue: The Letters of Sigmund Freud and Karl Abraham, 1907–1926* (New York: Basic Books, 1966), 34. The same day Freud wrote to Jung confessing a distaste for Ernest Jones: "He gives me a feeling of, I was almost going to say racial strangeness." *Freud/Jung Letters* (Princeton, N.J.: Princeton University Press, 1974), 145.

13. See James Rice, *Freud's Russia*.

14. Gay, *Freud: A Life for Our Time* (New York: Doubleday, 1989), 647–48 and passim.

15. See the dismay of Salo Baron, the great historian of the Jews, in *American Journal of Sociology* (Nov. 1939): 471–77.

16. Welsh, *Freud's Wishful Dream Book* (Princeton, N.J.: Princeton University Press, 1994).

17. Ellenberger, *The Discovery of the Unconscious*, 303–11.

18. Thorough reduction to biology entails dismissal of the dream's content, as in explanation of delirium by malarial fever, or alcoholic poisoning, or pellagra. Dream content can also be ignored in behaviorist studies, in which it is limited to twitching limbs and muted sounds in sleeping dogs or eyeball movement in sleeping humans.

19. Freud, *S.E.*, 4: xxiv; and *G.W.*, 2: viii.

20. See Mann, "Die Stellung Freuds in der modernen Geistesgeschichte," a 1929 speech to the Club of Democratic Students at the University of Munich; and "Freud und die Zukunft," a 1936 celebration of Freud's eightieth birthday. Reprints in Mann, *Leiden und Grösse der Meister* (Frankfurt am Main: Fischer, 1982); *Past Masters and Other Papers* (New York: Knopf, 1933); and *Essays of Three Decades* (New York: Knopf, 1947).

21. *S.E.*, 4: 442. *G.W.*, 2: 444. Other translations: "they might move freely across frontiers," or "become liberal minded." The *Oxford-Duden German Dictionary* defines *freizügig*: "1. Free in choice of place to live, . . . not bound to a place. . . . 2. Grand, broad-minded, liberal . . . not in accord with bourgeois [*bürgerliche*] moral notions." For rich analysis see A. Grinstein, *Sigmund Freud's Dreams* (New York: International Universities, 1980), chap. 13.

22. Grinstein, *Sigmund Freud's Dreams*, 72–73. Freud's censored report is in *S.E.*, 4: 195.

23. Sander Gilman, *Difference and Pathology: Stereotypes of Sexuality, Race, and Madness* (Ithaca, N.Y.: Cornell University Press, 1985), 175–90. See also Gilman, *The Case of Sigmund Freud: Medicine and Identity at the Fin de Siècle* (Baltimore, Md.: Johns Hopkins University Press, 1993).

24. W. E. B. Du Bois, *The Souls of Black Folk* (New York: New American Library, 1982), 45. Thanks to Sterling Stuckey for calling this to my attention.

25. *S.E.*, 8: 49ff. For the dirty beard joke see 72.

26. William McCagg, *A History of Habsburg Jews, 1670–1918* (Bloomington: Indiana University Press, 1989), passim.

27. *S.E.*, 8: 81; *G.W.*, 6: 86–87. Freud says that pain causes "primitive nature to break through all the layers of education." "*Ai waih!*" is Freud's version of "*Oi weh!*"—to exaggerate the ludicrous difference between "primitive" jargon and standard German?

28. Leo Rosten, *The Joys of Yiddish* (New York: Simon & Schuster, 1970), xii, calls such jokes a "ploy of deflation." There are many in his collection.

29. *S.E.*, 8: 80. Cf. 112 for Freud's belated attempt to characterize the mentality expressed in this joke—"the democratic mode of thinking of Jews"—without reference to gentile scorn. *G.W.*, 6: 86 and 123. Freud's version of the Yiddish is "*Aesoi.*"

30. There are many studies of the Jew in literature. See, e.g., Herbert A. Strauss and Ch. Hoffmann, *Juden und Judentum in der Literatur* (Munich: Deutscher Taschenbuch, 1985); Edgar Rosenberg, *From Shylock to Svengali: Jewish Stereotypes in English Fiction* (Stanford, Calif.: Stanford University Press, 1961). Note the usual disregard of Yiddish literature, which broke the stereotypes before Schnitzler.

31. Schnitzler, *Der Weg ins Freie* (Berlin: Fischer, 1908), 189. There are two English versions, which I have used with some alteration: *The Road to the Open* (Evanston, Ill.: Northwestern University Press, 1991)—a reissue of a 1922 translation by Horace Samuel—and the translation by Roger Byers (Berkeley: University of California Press, 1992).

32. I have run together phrases from the letter and an autobiography, quoted in Emanuel Rice, *Freud and Moses*, 95, 104. The full text of the letter is in Albrecht Hirschmüller, *Joseph Breuer* (Paris: PUF, 1991), 289–96.

33. Schnitzler, *Der Weg ins Freie*, 186–87.

34. Claudio Magris, *Weit von wo? Verlorene Welt des Ostjudentums* (Vienna: Europa Verlag, 1974). The book was originally published in Italian, in 1971, and republished in 1977. Magris cites multiple sources for the joke. Cf. Albert Memmi, *The Liberation of the Jew* (New York: Orion Press, 1966), 295; and Th. Reik, *Jewish Wit* (New York: 1962), 51. Thanks to Stuart Strickland for calling my attention to Novalis' aphorism.

35. Kafka, *Gesammelte Werke: Briefe, 1902–1924* (Frankfurt am Main: Fischer,

1958), 337. I have tried to get closer to the concrete German than the translation by Richard and Clara Winston in Kafka, *Letters* (New York: Schocken, 1977), 288–89.

36. See W. H. Auden, "Psychology and Art Today," in *The English Auden* (London: Faber, 1977), and "In Memory of Sigmund Freud," in *Collected Poems* (New York: Faber, 1976), 215–18. For Freud's exchanges with Arnold and Stefan Zweig, see Ernest Jones, *The Life and Work of Sigmund Freud*, 3 vols. (New York: Basic Books, 1957), passim.

37. See Schnitzler, "Über Psychoanalyse," and the quotations from Schnitzler in this chapter's Appendix.

38. Virginia Woolf, *Contemporary Writers* (New York: Harcourt, 1965), 152–54. Cf. Elizabeth Abel, *Virginia Woolf and the Fictions of Psychoanalysis* (Chicago: University of Chicago Press, 1989), 17–19, for more of Woolf's mocking responses to Freud's ideas, before Abel turns to a psychoanalytic reading of Woolf.

39. See Jeffrey Berman, *The Talking Cure: Literary Representations of Psychoanalysis* (New York: New York University Press, 1987), 22: "The bitterness in Woolf's tone reflects the dominant attitude among writers, who regard psychotherapy as a threat to free will, creativity, spiritual belief and individuality."

40. Cf. Emanuel Berman, ed., *Essential Papers on Literature and Psychoanalysis* (New York: New York University Press, 1993), for a recent sampling distinguished by recognition of "the ambivalent interaction of the two domains" (16).

41. Musil, *Precision and Soul: Essays and Addresses* (Chicago: University of Chicago Press, 1978), 111.

42. Musil uses a punning compound metaphor that defies translation: "*Denn man hatte ihnen einen Floh ins Ohr gesetzt, und sie glaubten das Gras der Zeit wachsen zu hören.*" Musil, *Der Mann ohne Eigenschaften* (Hamburg: Rowohlt, 1981), 1: 193. The Sophie Wilkins translation omits it: "because it was they who through their admiration had first created Arnheim's image as a great man, though they did not realize how much he was their own creation." Musil, *The Man Without Qualities* (New York: Knopf, 1995), 1: 207. The Eithne Wilkins and Ernst Kaiser translation tries to keep it, with "a bee in their bonnet," whose "buzzing deceives" the journalists into believing they "could hear the grass of time growing." Musil, *Man Without Qualities* (London: Picador, 1954), 1: 227. Perhaps two clichés of today's media would work: "Buzzwords had been put in their heads and they believed they heard the march of time."

43. David S. Luft, *Robert Musil and the Crisis of European Culture, 1880–1942* (Berkeley: University of California Press, 1980), 59–60 and passim.

44. *Mann* (1981), 1: 90–91; *Man* (1995), 1: 91–92; *Man* (1954), 1: 102–3.

45. See *Mann* (1981), 1: 34; *Man* (1995), 1: 30.

46. In the later parts, which Musil was still working over when his heart stopped—in Swiss exile during World War II—the man without qualities retreats with his sister to seek authentic personhood in love and mental creativity.

47. See David Midgley, "The Word and the Spirit: Exploration of the Irrational

in Kafka, Döblin and Musil," in *Modernism and the European Unconscious* (New York: St. Martin's, 1990), 119. Also see the quotation from Kafka in this chapter's Appendix.

48. See Benedict Anderson, *Imagined Communities: Reflections on the Origin and Spread of Nationalism* (London: Verso, 1987), for keen analysis of historians' and political scientists' views.

49. *G.W.*, 14: 569. I have changed the translation in *S.E.*, 13: xv.

50. See Frank J. Sulloway, *Freud, Biologist of the Mind: Beyond the Psychoanalytic Legend* (New York: Basic Books, 1979).

51. See, e.g., Emanuel Rice, *Freud and Moses*, and Yerushalmi, *Freud's Moses*.

52. See his review essay cited in note 15. Another Austro-German-Jewish intellectual, born in 1895, Baron sought a "scientific" (*wissenschaftlich*, scholarly) understanding of Jewishness in social history. He introduced the subject to U.S. universities at Columbia.

53. See John McClure, *Kipling and Conrad: The Colonial Fiction* (Cambridge, Mass.: Harvard University Press, 1981); Patrick Brantlinger, *Rule of Darkness: British Literature and Imperialism, 1830–1914* (Ithaca, N.Y.: Cornell University Press, 1988), 255–74; Edward Said, *Culture and Imperialism* (New York: Knopf, 1993), 19–31. Note the effort to counter Achebe's argument that Conrad's critique of European identity excludes Africans from authentic humanity.

54. Schnitzler, *Briefe* (Frankfurt am Main: Fischer, 1981–84), 2: 35–38.

55. Ibid., 2: 35–36.

56. Kafka, *Briefe an Milena* (Frankfurt am Main: Fischer, 1983), 292–93. I have adapted the translation of Philip Boehm, in *Letters to Milena* (New York: Schocken, 1990), 216–17.

57. Musil, *Tagebücher, Aphorismen, Essays und Reden* (Hamburg: Rowohlt, 1955), 796–99.

58. Ibid., 435.

10. TOEWS: REFASHIONING THE MASCULINE SUBJECT

This chapter previously appeared as "Refashioning the Masculine Subject in Early Modernism: Narratives of Self-Dissolution and Self-Construction in Psychoanalysis and Literature, 1900–1914," *Modernism/Modernity* 4 (1997): 31–67. It is reprinted with the kind permission of Johns Hopkins University Press.

1. For a survey of the early Weininger reception see Jacques Le Rider, *Der Fall Otto Weininger: Wurzeln des Antifeminismus und Antisemitismus* (Vienna and Munich: Loecker Verlag, 1985), 220–42. This is an expanded and revised (and translated) version of a study originally published in French in 1982.

2. Aside from Le Rider's study, analysis of Weininger's impact on central European and Italian modernism is demonstrated in some detail in the anthology *Otto Weininger: Werk und Wirkung*, ed. Jacques Le Rider and Norbert Leser (Vien-

na: Österreichisches Bundesverlag, 1984), especially parts 1, 2, and 3 (71–105). See also Ursula Heckmann, *Das Verfluchte Geschlecht: Motive der Philosophie Otto Weiningers im Werk Georg Trakls* (Frankfurt am Main: Peter Lang, 1992); Gisela Brude-Firnau, "Wissenschaft von der Frau? Zum Einfluss von Otto Weininger's 'Geschlecht und Charakter' auf den deutschen Roman," in *Die Frau als Heldin und Autorin: Neue Kritische Ansaetze zur deutschen Literatur,* ed. Wolfgang Paulsen (Bern: Francke verlag, 1979), 136–48; and Émile Delavenay, "D. H. Lawrence, Otto Weininger, and a Rather Raw Philosophy," in *D. H. Lawrence: New Studies,* ed. Christopher Heywood (Houndmills, Basingstoke, Hampshire: Macmillan, 1987).

3. I use the word "home" here and throughout to designate a conception of community in which individual identity is perceived as rooted in and integrated into social being. In the German tradition the term "Heimat" has developed strong connotations of nostalgic and utopian longing, which are also clearly present in my usage. Among my three authors only Schnitzler uses the term self-consciously.

4. Otto Weininger, *Geschlecht und Charakter. Eine prinzipielle Untersuchung* (Munich: Matthes & Seitz, 1980), 12. This is a reprint of the first edition of 1903. Translations are my own, but I have made use of an English translation of the sixth edition, Otto Weininger, *Sex and Character* (London: William Heinemann, 1906).

5. *Geschlecht,* 456; *Sex,* 344.

6. Weininger dismissed the movement for women's emancipation as an attempt to emancipate femininity. He claimed to support attempts by individual women to become "masculine." Cf. *Geschlecht,* 79–93. Similarly Weininger despised as an excess of femininity in men what he perceived as effeminate homosexuality, but praised a type of Greek homoeroticism in which masculinity was attracted to masculinity in a process that promoted sexual renunciation and spiritualization.

7. Ibid., 91.

8. *Geschlecht,* 407; *Sex,* 303.

9. *Geschlecht,* 409; *Sex,* 306.

10. Overviews of the controversy about priority and plagiarism can be found in Peter Heller, "A Quarrel over Bisexuality," in *The Turn of the Century: German Literature and Art, 1890–1915,* ed. Gerald Chapple and Hans H. Schulte (Bonn: Bouvier, 1981), 87–115; and Le Rider, *Der Fall Otto Weininger,* 78–101.

11. Freud to Fliess, July 23, 1904, in *The Complete Letters of Sigmund Freud to Wilhelm Fliess, 1887–1904,* trans. and ed. Jeffrey Moussaieff Masson (Cambridge, Mass.: Harvard University Press, 1985), 464.

12. *Complete Letters,* 450.

13. Hannelore Rodlauer, "Fragmente aus Weininger's Bildungsgeschichte," in Otto Weininger, *Eros und Psyche: Studien und Briefe, 1899–1902,* ed. Hannelore Rodlauer (Vienna: Verlag der Österreichischen Akademie der Wissenschaft, 1990), 39, 41–42.

14. Freud, "Zur Geschichte der psychoanalytischen Bewegung" (1914), in Freud, *Gesammelte Werke,* 19 vols. (London: Imago, 1940–47), 10: 95–102.

15. For a detailed presentation of the ways in which "Dora" can be read as a textual site for the fashioning of Freud's masculine identity, see my "Fashioning the Self in the Story of the 'Other': The Transformation of Freud's Masculine Identity between 'Elisabeth von R' and 'Dora,'" in *Proof and Persuasion: Essays on Authority, Objectivity, and Evidence*, ed. Suzanne Marchand and Elizabeth Lunbeck (Princeton, N.J.: Shelby Cullom Davis Center, 1996).

16. "Fragment of an Analysis of a Case of Hysteria," in Sigmund Freud, *Collected Papers*, trans. Alix and James Strachey, 5 vols. (New York: Basic Books, 1959), 3: 72–73.

17. "Analysis of a Phobia in a Five-Year-Old Boy, 1909," in *Papers*, 3: 179, n. 1.

18. The connection between a successful sublimation of infantile homoeroticism and the social interest or communal identification runs through the case studies of the prewar period, and finds its political conceptualization in the essays of *Totem and Taboo* of 1912–13.

19. "Eine Kindheitserinnerung des Leonardo da Vinci" (1910), in Sigmund Freud, *Studienausgabe*, 10: 153, 156.

20. *The Correspondence of Sigmund Freud and Sandor Ferenczi*, vol. 1: 1908–1914 (Cambridge, Mass.: Harvard University Press, 1993), 239–40; *The Freud/Jung Letters: The Correspondence between Sigmund Freud and C. G. Jung*, ed. William McGuire (Princeton, N.J.: Princeton University Press, 1974), 377.

21. *Freud/Jung Letters*, 368, 311.

22. "Psychoanalytic Notes Upon an Autobiographical Account of a Case of Paranoia (Dementia Paranoides)," in Freud, *Papers*,3: 440; "Psychoanalytische Bemerkungen ueber einen Autobiographisch Beschriebenen Fall von Paranoia (Dementia Paranoides), in Freud, *Studienausgabe*, vol. 7; Freud, *Zwang, Paranoia und Perversion* (Frankfurt am Main: Fischer, 1982), 180.

23. "Psychoanalytic Notes," 429–30; "Psychoanalytische Bemerkungen," 171.

24. Freud had first used the term "narcissism" to account for homosexual object-choice in the second edition of his *Three Essays on the Theory of Sexuality* (1910). The Schreber case was the first text in which he specifically used the term to describe a stage of childhood development between autoeroticism and object-love. See "Psychoanalytic Notes," 446; "Psychoanalytische Bemerkungen," 183–84.

25. Freud to Ferenzci, Oct. 10, 1910, in *Correspondence*, 221. See also *Freud/Jung Letters*, 199.

26. "Psychoanalytic Notes," 465–66; "Psychoanalytische Bemerkungen," 200.

27. Freud's selective reading on these two issues has been pointed out by Jay Geller, "Freud v. Freud: Freud's Readings of Daniel Paul Schreber's *Denkwuerdigkeiten eines Nervenkranken*," in *Reading Freud's Reading*, ed. Sander Gilman et al. (New York: New York University Press, 1994), 180–210.

28. A good summary of the materials covering various aspects of the relationship, including a discussion of the first two quoted phrases, can be found in Michael

Worbs, *Nervenkunst: Literatur und Psychoanalyse im Wien der Jahrhundertwende* (Frankfurt am Main: Europäische Verlagsanstalt, 1983), 179–258. Schnitzler's self-perception as Freud's twin is from an interview with George Viereck published in Viereck, *Glimpses of the Great* (New York: Macaulay, 1930), 333.

29. Schnitzler suffered tolerantly through a rather schematic reading of his own work in Freudian categories in Theodor Reik's *Arthur Schnitzler als Psycholog* (Minden: J. C. C. Bruns, 1913).

30. Arthur Schnitzler, *Tagebuch 1903–1908* (Vienna: Verlag der Österreichschen Akademie der Wissenschaften, 1991), 177 (Jan. 6, 1906).

31. Ibid., 123 (Feb. 25, 1905) and 337 (June 6, 1908).

32. See Michaela L. Perlmann, *Der Traum in der literarische Moderne: Zum Werk Arthur Schnitzlers* (Munich: Wilhelm Fink, 1987), 133. There are also striking parallels in father/son relations.

33. Arthur Schnitzler, *Der Weg ins Freie: Roman*, vol. 4 of *Gesammelte Werke in Einzelausgaben; Das Erzaehlerische Werk* (Frankfurt am Main: Fischer Taschenbuch, 1978), 8; Arthur Schnitzler, *The Road into the Open*, trans. Roger Byers (Berkeley: University of California Press, 1992), 4. I have used the Byers translation as a basis for my own translations throughout.

34. *Weg ins Freie*, 328; *Road into the Open*, 295.

35. *Weg ins Freie*, 53; *Road into the Open*, 44.

36. *Weg ins Freie*, 166; *Road into the Open*, 148.

37. *Weg ins Freie*, 236; *Road into the Open*, 211

38. *Weg ins Freie*, 240; *Road into the Open*, 215.

39. *Weg ins Freie*, 102; *Road into the Open*, 90.

40. *Weg ins Freie*, 80; *Road into the Open*, 69.

41. *Weg ins Freie*, 94; *Road into the Open*, 82.

42. *Weg ins Freie*, 9, 12; *Road into the Open*, 5, 8.

43. *Weg ins Freie*, 34; *Road into the Open*, 27.

44. *Weg ins Freie*, 56; *Road into the Open*, 47.

45. *Weg ins Freie*, 42; *Road into the Open*, 34.

46. One could see the fictional relationship between these two types of artists as Schnitzler's attempt to work through the dichotomy of modernist art constructed by his friend Hugo von Hofmannsthal in an essay published in 1893: "Today two things seem to be modern; the analysis of life and the flight from life. . . . One engages in the anatomy of one's own psychic life or one dreams. Reflection or fantasy, mirror-image or dream-image" (Hugo von Hofmannsthal, *Gesammelte Werke*, vol. 1: *Prosa* [Stockholm: Bermann Fischer, 1956], 149).

47. *Weg ins Freie*, 50; *Road into the Open*, 41.

48. *Weg ins Freie*, 48–49, 261, 330; *Road into the Open*, 40, 235, 296.

49. *Weg ins Freie*, 330; *Road into the Open*, 296.

50. *Weg ins Freie*, 214; *Road into the Open*, 191.

51. *Weg ins Freie*, 262; *Road into the Open*, 235–36.

52. Robert Musil, "Ueber Robert Musils Buecher" (1913), in Robert Musil, *Tagebuecher, Aphorismen, Essays und Reden*, ed. Adolf Frise (Hamburg: Rowohlt, 1955), 776. A description of the biographical materials reworked in the novel can be found in Uwe Bauer, "Zeit und gesellschaftskritik in Robert Musils' Die Verwirrungen des Zoeglings Toerless," in *Vom 'Toerless' zum 'Mann ohne Eigenschaften': Musil-Studien* IV, ed. Uwe Bauer and Dietmar Goltschnigg (Munich: Wilhelm Fink, 1973), 19–45.

53. Robert Musil, *Die Verwirrungen des Zoeglings Toerless* (1906), in Robert Musil, *Saemtliche Erzaehlungen* (Hamburg: Rowohlt, 1957), 15–16. My translations often depart from but were constructed in consultation with the standard translation by Eithne Wilkens and Ernst Kaiser (Robert Musil, *Young Toerless* [New York: Random House, 1964], 15).

54. *Verwirrungen*, 12, 48; *Young Toerless*, 10, 56.

55. *Verwirrungen*, 18; *Young Toerless*, 18.

56. *Verwirrungen*, 14; *Young Toerless*, 13.

57. Musil's description of unconscious and conscious dimensions of psychic structure and the role of sexual desire in articulating this structure has provoked an extensive literature on both the possible influence of Freud on Musil and on analogies between Freudian theories and Musilian constructs. The problems of identity formation involving the relationship between masculinity, autonomy, and narration, on which I focus, are not, as far as I know, discussed in this literature. A summary of the debate and a discussion of Musil's constructions of sexual desire from the Lacanian perspective can be found in Andrew Webber, "Sense and Sensuality in Musil's *Toerless*," *German Life and Letters* 41, no. 2: 106–30.

58. *Verwirrungen*, 19; *Young Toerless*, 20.

59. *Verwirrungen*, 26–27; *Young Toerless*, 29.

60. *Verwirrungen*, 32; *Young Toerless*, 36.

61. *Verwirrungen*, 34–35; *Young Toerless*, 39–40.

62. *Verwirrungen*, 104; *Young Toerless*, 128.

63. *Verwirrungen*, 52, 99; *Young Toerless*, 61, 122.

64. *Verwirrungen*, 87; *Young Toerless*, 106.

65. *Verwirrungen*, 32; *Young Toerless*, 36.

66. *Verwirrungen*, 42; *Young Toerless*, 48.

67. Freud's judgments on the heresies of Adler and Jung are contained in the last section of his "Zur Geschichte der psychoanalytische Bewegung," 84–123. Musil later saw his construction of the cultural types of Beineberg and Reiting as prophetic anticipations of the political mass leaders of the 1920s and 1930s.

68. *Verwirrungen*, 140; *Young Toerless*, 173.

69. *Verwirrungen*, 136–37; *Young Toerless*, 169.

70. *Verwirrungen*, 125, 137; *Young Toerless*, 154, 170.

71. *Verwirrungen*, 140; *Young Toerless*, 173.

72. *Verwirrungen*, 112; *Young Toerless*, 137.

73. A masterful analysis of the historical conditions of Musil's intellectual project can be found in David S. Luft, *Robert Musil and the Crisis of European Culture, 1880–1942* (Berkeley: University of California Press, 1980).

74. *Tagebuecher,* 788.

11. MATZ: HULME, BERGSON, AND PSYCHOLOGISM

1. See Michael Levenson, *A Genealogy of Modernism: A Study of English Literary Doctrine 1908–1922* (Cambridge: Cambridge University Press, 1984), 37–47, 80–102. These influences are of course subject to some doubt: Ezra Pound, for example, claimed of "Imagisme" that he "made the word—on a Hulme basis," but then he spoke dismissively of "this Hulme business" years later (Hugh Kenner, *The Pound Era* [Berkeley: University of California Press, 1971], 178. See also Ethan Lewis, "'This Hulme Business' Revisited, or Of Sequence and Simultaneity," *Paideuma* 22, nos. 1–2 (Spring-Fall 1993): 255–65.

2. T. S. Eliot, "A Commentary," *Criterion* 2, no. 7 (Apr. 1924): 231; Alun R. Jones, *The Life and Opinions of T. E. Hulme* (London: Victor Gollancz, 1960), 13.

3. For a more extensive discussion of psychologism and its relation to modernist culture see Martin Jay, "Modernism and the Specter of Psychologism," in this volume. My essay offers a case study of the problem Jay more broadly explains and is indebted to his map of its territory. For more general discussions of psychologism as a concept and problem see, as Jay suggests, Martin Kusch, *Psychologism: A Case Study in the Sociology of Philosophical Knowledge* (London: Routledge, 1995), particularly pp. 1–16, which survey the range of definitions.

4. T. E. Hulme, "Notes on Bergson," in *The Collected Writings of T. E. Hulme,* ed. Karen Csengeri, 125–53 (Oxford: Oxford University Press, 1994), 126. All subsequent citations of Hulme's works will refer to this volume.

5. For recent accounts of Bergson's influence among the moderns see Richard Lehan, "Bergson and the Discourse of the Moderns," in *The Crisis in Modernism: Bergson and the Vitalist Controversy* (Cambridge: Cambridge University Press, 1992), 277–305, and Mark Antliff, *Inventing Bergson: Cultural Politics and the Parisian Avant-Garde* (Princeton, N.J.: Princeton University Press, 1993).

6. By our contemporary standards Bergson's theories seem to comprise a philosophy more than a psychology, but as Judith Ryan points out in the preface to her *The Vanishing Subject* (Chicago: University of Chicago Press, 1991), such disciplinary distinctions did not obtain at Bergson's moment (and it was partially the reaction against psychologism that created them).

7. For an excellent English-language overview of Bergson's career and its reception see Sanford Schwartz, "Bergson and the Politics of Vitalism," in *The Crisis in Modernism: Bergson and the Vitalist Controversy,* ed. Frederick Burwick and Paul Douglass (Cambridge: Cambridge University Press, 1992), 277–305; for a famous effort to encourage a return to Bergson, see Gilles Deleuze, *Bergsonism,* trans. Hugh Tomlinson and Barbara Habberjam (New York: Zone Books, 1988).

8. Refuting determinist psychology, Bergson's early work was itself, ironically, an early attack on psychologism. See my conclusions for a description of the pattern that such ironies reveal.

9. Henri Bergson, *Time and Free Will: An Essay on the Immediate Data of Consciousness*, trans. F. L. Pogson (London: George Allen Unwin, 1910), 100.

10. Henri Bergson, *An Introduction to Metaphysics*, trans. T. E. Hulme (New York: Macmillan, 1955), 23–24.

11. In her 1922 study of Bergson, Karin Stephen reflects upon the problem of the connection between Bergson's popularity and his alleged irrationalism: "The immense popularity which Bergson's philosophy enjoys is sometimes cast up against him. . . . It has been suggested that Bergson's writings are welcomed simply because they offer a theoretical justification for a tendency which is natural in all of us but against which philosophy has always fought, the tendency to throw reason overboard and just let ourselves go" (*The Misuse of Mind: A Study of Bergson's Attack on Intellectualism* [London: Kegan Paul, Trench, Trubner and Co., 1922], 9).

12. Bergson later applied the theory of the "two selves" to the realm of ethics as well, but his *Two Sources of Morality and Religion* (1932)—which distinguishes between the "closed" morality that preserves but limits social forms and the "open" morality that would enable progress toward human solidarity—fell on ears deafened by the anti-psychologism that triumphed years before.

13. Russell, "Bergson," in *A History of Western Philosophy* (New York: Simon and Schuster, 1945), 791–810 (originally published in the *Monist* in 1912).

14. Most prominent of those who criticized Hulme's inconsistencies were Murray Krieger, *The New Apologists for Poetry* (Minneapolis: University of Minnesota Press, 1956), 31–45, and Frank Kermode, *Romantic Image* (London: Routledge and Kegan Paul, 1961), 119–37. A more recent effort to prove that "Hulme is philosophically something else than the mere Bergsonian propagandist he is typically portrayed to be" (559) is Richard Shusterman, "Remembering Hulme: A Neglected Philosopher-Critic-Poet," *Journal of the History of Ideas* 46 (Oct.–Dec. 1985): 559–76.

15. Levenson, *A Genealogy of Modernism*, 39; and see Karen Csengeri, "The Chronology of T. E. Hulme's *Speculations*," *Papers of the Bibliographical Society of America* 80 (1986): 105–9.

16. See Karen Csengeri, "Introduction," in *The Collected Writings of T. E. Hulme*, xvi–xxiv.

17. Csengeri and Levenson differently distinguish the terms of this progression: Csengeri thinks that Levenson is "wrong in claiming that Hulme's 'anti-humanism' is different from his 'classicism,' but the evidence that Hulme's final position required movement beyond the thinkers who inspired his classicism (Husserl and Moore) suggests that Levenson is correct after all (Csengeri, "Introduction," xxxiv n. 17).

18. Hulme quotes Lasserre's explanation of his opposition to Bergson: "'I have lectured on Bergson,' [Lasserre] said, 'because I think that from the point of view I rep-

resent he constitutes a real danger. Put very briefly, the attitude of L'Action Française is this: At the back of our position there is a certain intellectual discipline. We think that the only road to sanity in these matters is to take as a guide for the theory and practice the natural and necessary relation of things. We believe, then, in the existence of laws which express what we know of the necessary and permanent characteristics of any social and political order . . . . Our side . . . can claim all the intellectual, if not the material victories. Nothing serious has been opposed to us by the "progressives." . . . But now . . . they have endeavored to cut the ground out from under us [by superseding] our assertion that there are such things as necessary laws governing societies, and more particularly that these laws can be discovered from past history. . . . If we ask why, we are told that Bergson has now proved that *Time is real*—that is, that the present moment is a *unique* moment and can be paralleled by nothing in the past. . . . If we point out that history does or does not show us any prosperous, strong, and conquering nation, which was at the same time a democracy, they retort, history would not be history if it were not change itself and a perpetual novelty. To our judgments on politics in the name of reason interpreting experience, the Bergsonians oppose to us what they call "Life"—life which is always creation and always incalculable'" ("Balfour, Bergson, and Politics," in *Collected Writings*, 164–65).

19. Patricia M. Rae, "T. E. Hulme's French Sources: A Reconsideration," *Comparative Literature* 41, no. 1 (Winter 1989): 88; Miriam Hansen, "T. E. Hulme, Mercenary of Modernism, or, Fragments of Avant-garde Sensibility in Pre-World-War-One Britain," *ELH* 47, no. 2 (Summer 1980): 365.

20. See Eschbach, *The Higher Education of Women in England and America 1865–1920* (New York: Garland, 1993), particularly chap. 9, "Continuing Hope and Struggle" (180–208); and Kent, *Sex and Suffrage in Britain, 1860–1914* (Princeton, N.J.: Princeton University Press, 1987), particularly chap. 6, "Sex War" (157–83). Surrounding Hulme's turn against Bergson were two events likely to dramatize women's encroachments: "Black Friday" (Nov. 18, 1910), when police attacked suffragists in Parliament Square, and the events of March 1, 1912, when Mrs. Pankhurst and her fellow agitators broke windows all over London (see Kent, *Sex and Suffrage*, 173–74, 201).

21. Antliff refers to a drawing by René Vincent, "La Leçon de philosophie dans les fleurs," in *La Vie heureuse* (Mar. 5, 1914), 99.

22. In this Hulme falls in with a tradition of elitist distinction making, one that extends, as Terry Eagleton suggests, far back into the history of the aesthetic, which has direct precedents in the orientations of Stéphane Mallarmé, Henry James, Oscar Wilde, and a host of others, and which arguably extends to form the basis for much of modernist posturing. See Eagleton, *The Ideology of the Aesthetic* (Oxford: Blackwell, 1990); Jonathan Freedman, *Professions of Taste: Henry James, British Aestheticism, and Commodity Culture* (Stanford, Calif.: Stanford University Press, 1990); and Peter Bürger's landmark argument about modernism in his *Theory of the Avant-Garde* (Minneapolis: University of Minnesota Press, 1984).

23. Rita Felski, *The Gender of Modernity* (Cambridge, Mass.: Harvard University Press, 1995), 62; and see also Lisa Rado, ed., *Rereading Modernism: New Directions in Feminist Criticism* (New York: Garland, 1994).

24. Martin Jay in this volume likewise notes the connections among modernism, psychologism, and misogyny, noting that the anti-psychologist trend developed in part due to "the challenge to traditional gender roles" that "created anxieties about the domination of masculine conceptions of cultural value." Jay cites Andreas Huyssen's discussion of this problem, to recognize the fact that "modernism . . . often defended itself against a feminized version of mass culture, which it stigmatized as debased kitsch." Hulme's response to Bergson's female followers is a good example of the trend Huyssen describes when he writes, for example, that "the fear of the masses in this age of declining liberalism is always also a fear of woman, a fear of nature out of control, a fear of the unconscious, of the loss of identity and stable ego boundaries in the mass" (*After the Great Divide: Modernism, Mass Culture, Postmodernism* [Bloomington: Indiana University Press, 1986], 52).

12. JAY: MODERNISM AND PSYCHOLOGISM

This chapter previously appeared as "Modernism and the Specter of Psychologism," in Martin Jay, *Cultural Semantics: Keywords of Our Time* (Amherst: University of Massachusetts Press, 1998), 165–80. It is reprinted with the kind permission of the University of Massachusetts Press.

1. Judith Ryan, *The Vanishing Subject: Early Psychology and Literary Modernism* (Chicago: University of Chicago Press, 1991).

2. Carl E. Schorske, *Fin-de-Siècle Vienna: Politics and Culture* (New York: Knopf, 1980).

3. Ryan, *The Vanishing Subject*, 224.

4. Louis A. Sass, *Madness and Modernism: Insanity in the Light of Modern Art, Literature, and Thought* (Cambridge, Mass.: Harvard University Press, 1994), 13.

5. The most recent and complete account of the debate over "psychologism" can be found in Martin Kusch, *Psychologism: A Case Study of the Sociology of Philosophical Knowledge* (New York: Routledge, 1995). He notes that the term itself was coined by Johann Eduard Erdmann in his *Grundrisse der Geschichte der Philosophie* (Berlin: W. Hertz, 1866). A Hegelian, Erdmann introduced the term to describe the work of Friedrich Eduard Beneke, but did not actively criticize it (Kusch, *Psychologism*, 101).

6. It would also be possible to make a case based on musical examples, beginning with Eduard Hanslick's defense of "absolute music," continuing through the post-Wagnerian rejection of Romanticism, and culminating in Schoenberg's twelve-tone row. If Ortega y Gasset is right in his well-known analysis of the modernist "dehumanization of art," the pivotal figure was Debussy. For a recent discussion of anti-psychologistic impulses in Stravinsky, see Richard Taruskan, "A Myth of the Twentieth

Notes to Jay: Modernism and Psychologism

Century: The Rite of Spring, the Tradition of the New, and 'The Music Itself,'"
Modernism/Modernity 2 (Jan. 1995): 1–26.

7. Immanuel Kant, *Logic*, trans. Robert S. Hartman and Wolfgang Schwarz
(Indianapolis, Ind.: Bobbs Merrill, 1974), 16. The origins of what was later called psy-
chologism can perhaps be put in the late seventeenth century, with the rise of British
empiricism. It had an impact in Germany through such figures as Johann Nicolaus
Tetens, whose *Philosophische Versuche über die menschliche Natur und ihre Ent-
wicklung*, 2 vols. (Leipzig: bei M. G. Weidmanns Erben, 1777), was a spur to the first
Critique. For a discussion of Kant on psychology, see Gary Hatfield, "Empirical,
Rational, and Transcendental Psychology: Psychology as Science and as
Philosophy," in *The Cambridge Companion to Kant*, ed. Paul Guyer (Cambridge:
Cambridge University Press, 1992). In Germany, psychologism was revived by the
post-Kantians Jakob F. Fries and Friedrich E. Beneke in the early nineteenth century. See the discussion in John Fizer, *Psychologism and Psychoaesthetics: A Historical
and Critical View of their Relations* (Amsterdam: J. Benjamins, 1981), introduction.

8. For a discussion of the growth of experimental psychology and the philosophers' defensive response, see Mitchell G. Ash, *Gestalt Psychology in German Culture, 1890–1967: Holism and the Quest for Objectivity* (Cambridge: Cambridge University Press, 1995), esp. chap. 3.

9. Gottlob Frege, *The Foundations of Arithmetic*, 2d rev. ed., trans. J. L. Austin
(Evanston, Ill.: Northwestern University Press, 1980).

10. For a recent account of the psychologizing imperative in Nietzsche, see
Graham Parkes, *Composing the Soul: Reaches of Nietzsche's Psychology* (Chicago:
University of Chicago Press, 1994).

11. Gottlob Frege, "Review of E. G. Husserl, *Philosophie der Arithmetik I*," in
Gottlob Frege: Collected Papers on Mathematics, Logic, and Philosophy, ed. Brian
McGuinness (Oxford: B. Blackwell, 1984), 195–209. For an assessment of the review
and its implications, see Jitendranath N. Mohanty, *Husserl and Frege* (Bloomington:
Indiana University Press, 1982), chap. 2. He claims that Husserl was already moving
beyond psychologism by 1891 and that Frege's attribution of a strong version of it to
him was mistaken. Also see Claire Ortiz Hill, *Word and Object in Husserl, Frege, and
Russell: The Roots of Twentieth-Century Philosophy* (Athens: Ohio University Press,
1991).

12. See David F. Lindenfeld, *The Transformation of Positivism: Alexius Meinong
and European Thought, 1880–1920* (Berkeley: University of California Press, 1980),
chap. 5; Thomas E. Willey, *Back to Kant: The Revival of Kantianism in German
Social and Historical Thought, 1960–1914* (Detroit, Mich.: Wayne State University
Press, 1978), 108ff.; and Gillian Rose, *Hegel Contra Sociology* (London: Athlone,
1981), chap. 1. It should be noted that Heidegger's initial critique of psychologism,
Die Lehre vom Urteil im Psychologismus: Ein kritischpositiver Beitrag zur Logik
(Leipzig: J. A. Barth, 1914), was written when he was a student of the neo-Kantian
Heinrich Rickert.

13. "Energeticism" was an attempt to subsume all phenomena under the category of energy, "matter" being merely an anthropomorphic projection onto a world of flux.

14. Although Durkheim's sociology, echoing that of Auguste Comte, was more resolutely hostile to methodological individualism than Weber's, even the latter insisted that a proper sociological explanation of behavior was irreducible to psychological states of mind. Dilthey's attitude toward psychologism was intensified by his reading of Husserl's *Philosophical Investigations*, but he showed signs of skepticism as early as 1860. See the discussion in Michael Ermarth, *Wilhelm Dilthey: The Critique of Historical Reason* (Chicago: University of Chicago Press, 1978), 182ff.

15. Kusch, in *Psychologism*, shows how loose and amorphous the debate was, with almost every figure on both sides of the fence, including Husserl himself, being accused of some variety of psychologism. He situates the debate in the context of the institutional challenge to philosophy presented by the rise of experimental psychology, exemplified by Wilhelm Wundt, Hermann Ebbinghaus, Georg Elias Müller, and Carl Stumpf, in the 1880s.

16. It is important to note, as Dagfinn Follesdal was perhaps the first to underline in his "Husserl's Notion of Noema," *Journal of Philosophy* 66 (Oct. 16, 1969): 680–87, that both the analytical and phenomenological traditions shared a common root in anti-psychologism (although Frege was more important for the analytical tradition and Husserl for the continental). Here the celebrated gap between Anglo-American and continental philosophy yawned far less widely than is normally assumed. This is not to deny, of course, that some later philosophers in these traditions reopened the question of the links between psychology and philosophy, e.g., Maurice Merleau-Ponty, whose debts to Gestalt psychology are evident.

17. Cora Diamond, *The Realistic Spirit: Wittgenstein, Philosophy, and the Mind* (Cambridge, Mass.: MIT Press, 1991). Also see Nicholas F. Gier, *Wittgenstein and Phenomenology: A Comparative Study of the Later Wittgenstein, Husserl, Heidegger, and Merleau-Ponty* (Albany, N.Y.: State University of New York Press, 1981), 204–6, for a discussion of Wittgenstein's complicated debt to Frege's anti-psychologism.

18. Lucien Goldmann, to take one example, was hostile to psychologism only when it referred to the individual, libidinal psyche. But he supported the idea of a collective, cognitive psyche and derided neo-Kantians for their attempt to deny any human origins to the objects of knowledge. See his *Immanuel Kant*, trans. Robert Black (London: NLB, 1971), 153–56. In general, Marxist critics of psychologism refused the absolutizing of logic evident in Frege, the neo-Kantians, and Husserl, which they saw as the acceptance of reification. Their anti-psychologism only meant a resistance to understanding the subject of knowledge in psychological rather than transindividual, social terms.

19. Frege, "Thoughts," in *Collected Papers*, 369.

20. For a typical anti-psychologistic elaboration of this distinction, see Ralph Eaton, *General Logic: An Introductory Survey* (New York: C. Scribners Sons, 1931), 16ff.

21. For comparisons of Husserl and Frege, see Mohanty, *Husserl and Frege*, and Robert Hanna, "Logical Cognition: Husserl's Prolegomena and the Truth in Psychologism," *Philosophy and Phenomenological Research* 53 (June 1993): 251–75.

22. Frege, *The Foundations of Arithmetic*, vi.

23. See, for example, J. Meiland, "Psychologism in Logic: Husserl's Critique," *Inquiry* 19 (Autumn 1976): 325–39; and John Aach, "Psychologism Reconsidered: A Re-evaluation of the Arguments of Frege and Husserl," *Synthese* 85 (Nov. 1990): 315–38. Aach claims that Skinnerian behaviorism can avoid the pitfalls of the associationist psychology that Frege and Husserl mistakenly identified with psychology *tout court*.

24. Kusch argues that the war itself, at least in Germany, produced a general intellectual consensus that stilled the battle over psychologism, leaving phenomenology the winner. The war also provided a new role for experimental psychology as an applied discipline, which took its practitioners away from philosophical disputes. Those who remained in philosophy departments in a general atmosphere that was anti-scientific and anti-atomistic made their peace with the reigning orthodoxy. See Kusch, *Psychologism*, chap. 8.

25. Theodor W. Adorno, *Aesthetic Theory*, ed. Gretel Adorno and Rolf Tiedemann, trans. C. Lenhardt (London: Routledge and K. Paul, 1984), 12. Adorno, to be sure, goes on to challenge Kant's contrary denial of any interest, any desire in allegedly autotelic works of art. "In contrast to the Kantian or Freudian views on the matter," he argues, "works of art necessarily evolve in a dialectic of interests and disinterestedness" (*Aesthetic Theory*, 17). Earlier, Adorno provided an equally dialectical treatment of Husserl's one-sided anti-psychologism. See Theodor W. Adorno, *Against Epistemology: A Metacritique*, trans. Willis Domingo (Cambridge, Mass.: MIT Press, 1983), chap. 1.

26. Peter Bürger's controversial distinction between modernism and the avant-garde in his *Theory of the Avant-Garde*, trans. Michael Shaw (Minneapolis: University of Minnesota Press, 1984), is useful in this context. Those artists who most feared psychologistic pollution conform to his definition of modernist, whereas those who were less anxious, for example the Surrealists, were members of the avant-garde that sought to reconcile life and art.

27. Renato Poggioli, *The Theory of the Avant-Garde*, trans. Gerald Fitzgerald (Cambridge, Mass.: Belknap Press of Harvard University Press, 1968), 201. For another discussion of the modernist fetish of purity, see Frederick R. Karl, *Modern and Modernism: The Sovereignty of the Artist 1885–1925* (New York: Atheneum, 1985), 162–69. He claims that the demand for purification ultimately means that "authority of style was based not on the assimilation of other styles but on the expression of honest feeling which is then transformed into individuality of style" (*Modern and Modernism*, 153). Such an argument underestimates the modernist desire to purify the work of psychological and emotional residues.

28. See, for example, H. Stuart Hughes' classic study *Consciousness and Society: The Reorientation of European Social Thought 1890–1930* (New York: Knopf, 1958).

29. Andreas Huyssen, *After the Great Divide: Modernism, Mass Culture, Post-modernism* (Bloomington: Indiana University Press, 1986). He points to the links between certain misogynist theories of psychology during this period, such as Nietzsche's and Freud's, and modernist elitism, but he neglects the opposite connection, which ties anti-psychologism with misogyny. By isolating works from the contexts of their production and reception, anti-psychologism furthered the fiction that they were timeless, universal creations undisturbed by issues of gender.

30. See, for example, Sanford Schwartz, *The Matrix of Modernism: Pound, Eliot, and Early 20th-Century Thought* (Princeton, N.J.: Princeton University Press, 1985); and Michael H. Levenson, *A Genealogy of Modernism: A Study of English Literary Doctrine 1908–1922* (Cambridge: Cambridge University Press, 1984). On the vexed notion of "impersonality," see in particular Brian Lee, *Theory and Personality: The Significance of T. S. Eliot's Criticism* (London: Athlone Press, 1979).

31. For persuasive accounts, see Levenson, *A Genealogy of Modernism*, chap. 6; Richard Shusterman, "Remembering Hulme: A Neglected Philosopher-Critic-Poet," *Journal of the History of Ideas* 46 (Oct.–Dec. 1985): 559–76; and Richard Shusterman, *T. S. Eliot and the Philosophy of Criticism* (New York: Columbia University Press, 1988), 30ff. These works are directed against the earlier claims by Murray Krieger, *The New Apologists for Poetry* (Minneapolis: University of Minnesota Press, 1956), and Frank Kermode, *Romantic Image* (London: Routledge and Kegan Paul, 1961), that Hulme was actually in the Romantic tradition, even Coleridgean, because of his debts to Bergson.

32. For an argument about the importance of analytical philosophy for Hulme and then T. S. Eliot, see Shusterman, *T. S. Eliot and the Philosophy of Criticism*.

33. T. E. Hulme, *Speculations: Essays on Humanism and the Philosophy of Art*, ed. Herbert Read (London: K. Paul, Trench, Trubner & Co., 1924).

34. Among certain German neo-Kantians, most notably the Heidelberg School around Windelband and Rickert, a search for objective values (*Werte*) rather than mere validity (*Geltung*) had also been conducted. But Hulme does not seem to have been influenced directly by their work.

35. Wilhelm Worringer, *Abstraction and Empathy: A Contribution to the Psychology of Style*, trans. Michael Bullock (New York: International Universities Press, 1953). As his subtitle indicates, Worringer was actually interested in providing a psychological explanation for the stylistic dispositions of different artists and periods of the kind Hulme disdained. For recent analyses of the complicated reception of Worringer's work, see Neil H. Donahue, ed., *Invisible Cathedrals: The Expressionist Art History of Wilhelm Worringer* (University Park: Pennsylvania State University Press, 1995).

Aesthetic empathy, it should be noted, had been most extensively defended by the German philosopher Theodor Lipps. As Levenson notes, "Lipps also appeared in Husserl's *Logical Investigations*, where he is criticized as a proponent of psychologism. Indeed, Worringer's argument against Lipps and on behalf of abstraction bears notable similarities to Husserl's defense of 'pure logic,' and although I know of no evidence of any contact or influence, the theories of the two figures meet in Hulme's enthusiastic embrace" (A Genealogy of Modernism, 96).

36. A similar argument, with a far less positive evaluation, was famously made in 1925 by José Ortega y Gasset, The Dehumanization of Art and Other Essays on Art, Culture, and Literature, trans. Helene Weyl (Princeton, N.J.: Princeton University Press, 1968).

37. Hulme, Speculations, 118. Romanticism blundered by trying to realize perfection, which belongs only to the religious sphere, in human affairs. Modern art wisely sought its perfection only in the sphere of art and eschewed the Romantics' redemptive hope of transfiguring life as well.

38. For one attempt to underscore his political influence, see John R. Harrison, The Reactionaries (London: Gollancz, 1967).

39. For a discussion of Woolf, which shows her links to the work of Russell and the technique of "speakerless sentences" pioneered by Flaubert, see Ann Banfield, "Describing the Unobserved: Events Grouped Around an Empty Centre," in The Linguistics of Writing: Arguments Between Language and Literature, ed. Nigel Fabb et al. (Manchester: Manchester University Press, 1987). Banfield provides a useful corrective to Judith Ryan's claim in The Vanishing Subject, chap. 15, that Woolf provides another example of the influence of impressionistic psychological empiricism, with a touch of psychoanalysis.

40. See Joseph Frank, "Spatial Form in Modern Literature," in The Avant-Garde Tradition in Modern Literature, ed. Richard Kostelanetz (Buffalo, N.Y.: Prometheus Books, 1982), 72–76.

41. T. S. Eliot, "Tradition and the Individual Talent," in Selected Prose of T. S. Eliot, ed. Frank Kermode (New York: Harcourt Brace Jovanovich, 1975), 43. It is even cited in Sass's Madness and Modernism as an example of the impersonal aesthetic of early modernism, which replaced the Romantic concern with inner experience and the unique self. He then goes on to say, however, that in the latter's place was soon put a fetish for innovation that "placed, if anything, even more emphasis on novelty of perspective" (Madness and Modernism, 135).

42. Schwartz, The Matrix of Modernism, 166–67.

43. On Eliot's debt to F. H. Bradley, see, for example, Lewis Freed, T. S. Eliot: The Critic as Philosopher (West Lafayette, Ind.: Purdue University Press, 1979).

44. Schwartz, The Matrix of Modernism, 166.

45. For another analysis of the subjective moment in Eliot's criticism, see Shusterman, T. S. Eliot and the Philosophy of Criticism, chap. 3.

46. Charles Altieri, Painterly Abstraction in Modernist American Poetry: The Contemporaneity of Modernism (Cambridge: Cambridge University Press, 1989), 38.

47. According to Hulme, poetry "is not a counter language, but a visual concrete one. . . . It always endeavors to arrest you, and to make you continuously see a physical thing, to prevent you gliding through an abstract process" (Speculations, 134).

48. Jonathan Crary, Techniques of the Observer: On Vision and Modernity in the Nineteenth Century (Cambridge, Mass.: MIT Press, 1990).

49. Heinrich Wölfflin, *Principles of Art History: The Problem of the Development of Style in Later Art*, trans. M. D. Hottinger (New York: Dover, 1932), 229. As we have noted, Worringer also sought a psychology of style.

50. Norman Bryson, *Vision and Painting: The Logic of the Gaze* (London: Macmillan, 1983). Crary explores the impact of the new models of visuality on Impressionism, most notably Manet, in "Unbinding Vision," *October* 68 (Spring 1994), 21–44.

51. Ryan, *The Vanishing Subject*, 17ff.

52. Maurice Merleau-Ponty, "Cézanne's Doubt," in *Sense and Nonsense*, trans. Hubert L. Dreyfus and Patricia A. Dreyfus (Evanston, Ill.: Northwestern University Press, 1964).

53. For a selection of Cézanne's remarks about returning to nature and leaving cultural conventions behind, see Herschel B. Chipp, ed., *Theories of Modern Art: A Source Book by Artists and Critics* (Berkeley: University of California Press, 1975), 16–23.

54. Ibid., 15.

55. Altieri, *Painterly Abstraction in Modernist American Poetry*, 178ff.

56. Thierry de Duve, *Pictorial Nominalism: On Marcel Duchamp's Passage from Painting to the Readymade*, trans. Dana Polan (Minneapolis: University of Minnesota Press, 1991), 77–78.

57. One might see certain Surrealist paintings in this light.

58. As Antoine Compagnon writes, "initially, in the mind of the first abstract painter, abstraction was supposed to make individual psychology extinct, to explore a world of meanings and energies, and to produce images with which we would all be able to commune spiritually" (Antoine Compagnon, *The Five Paradoxes of Modernity*, trans. Franklin Philip [New York: Columbia University Press, 1994], 67).

59. Another philosophical lineage for the impersonality and universalism of modernist abstraction culminating in Mondrian has been suggested by Donald Kuspit, *The Cult of the Avant-Garde Artist* (Cambridge: Cambridge University Press, 1993), 45ff. He sees Spinoza as the great predecessor of this visual flight from the messiness of human emotions.

60. Clement Greenberg, "Modernist Painting," in *The New Art: A Critical Anthology*, ed. G. Battcock (New York: Dutton, 1973), 67.

61. See, for example, John McGowan, *Postmodernism and Its Critics* (Ithaca, N.Y.: Cornell University Press, 1991), 9.

62. Robert Storr, "No Joy in Mudville: Greenberg's Modernism Then and Now," in *Modern Art and Popular Culture: Readings in High and Low*, ed. Kirk Varnadoe and Adam Gopnik (New York: Abrams, 1990), 169ff. Noting Greenberg's Jewish anxiety about assimilation, he compares it with Eliot's Anglo-Catholicism, and concludes that "Greenberg's similar insistence on the aesthetic extinction of personality, and his determination to purge from art all traces of mundane existence, for which kitsch became the shorthand term, reflect not so much a political or even art historical perspective as they do a fundamentally religious one. Located against the

backdrop of Jewish emigration from the shtetl and the ghetto, the opposition of purity and impurity stands as a metaphor for the perilous choices imposed by cultural assimilation in the New World" (Storr, "Greenberg's Modernism," 175). Situated in the context of the anti-psychologistic tradition as a whole, however, Greenberg's values seem less quirkily reflective of his own personal predicament. For a comparison between Greenberg and Adorno, see Compagnon, *The Five Paradoxes of Modernity*, 47. Adorno's position was less internalist than Compagnon suggests, although he was a critic of vulgar Marxist reductionism.

63. See Shusterman, *T. S. Eliot and the Philosophy of Criticism*, for comparisons with Gadamer and Rorty.

64. See de Duve, *Pictorial Nominalism*. See also his essay, "Echoes of the Ready-made: Critique of Pure Modernism," *October* 70 (Fall 1994): 61–98.

65. Nor was he attracted to Cézanne's project of revealing a primordial ontology of visuality, prior to the split between subject and object. See Jean-François Lyotard, *Les transformateurs Duchamp* (Paris: Éditions Galilée, 1977), 68.

66. Werner Hofmann, "Marcel Duchamp and Emblematic Realism," in *Marcel Duchamp in Perspective*, ed. Joseph Masheck (Englewood Cliffs, N.J.: Prentice Hall, 1975), 61.

67. An account of Duchamp's lecture in Houston at the conference "The Creative Act" and the discussion that followed is contained in *Marcel Duchamp: Work and Life*, ed. Pontus Hulten (Cambridge, Mass.: MIT Press, 1993), under the listing for April 5, 1957; he liberally cites Eliot. The remark was made to Lawrence D. Steefel, Jr., and is cited in his "Dimension and Development in The Passage from the Virgin to the Bride," in Masheck, ed., *Marcel Duchamp in Perspective*, 97.

68. For an analysis of Duchamp's function as the paradoxical (male) master of a tradition that eschews father figures, see Amelia Jones, *Postmodernism and the Engendering of Marcel Duchamp* (Cambridge: Mass., Cambridge University Press, 1994).

69. See, for example, Rosalind E. Krauss, *The Optical Unconscious* (Cambridge, Mass.: MIT Press, 1993), chap. 3, in which Duchamp is presented as introducing carnal desire rather than cerebral reflexivity into his art. She explicitly contrasts his work to the ascetic, contemplative aesthetics of Bloomsbury theorists such as Robert Fry, which she claims was derived from G. E. Moore's anti-psychologistic ethics. A very different account, which nonetheless also stresses the psychological sources of his work, can be found in Jerrold Seigel, *The Private Worlds of Marcel Duchamp* (Berkeley: University of California Press, 1995). According to Seigel, "behind Duchamp's claim to have devoted his career to destabilizing his personality, countering the pull of taste and habit with an aesthetic of indifference and avoiding the trap of fixed identity by his various stages of self-contradiction, there lurked an uncompromising exaltation of the self" (206). This self, however, was less a sovereign maker than a chooser, who worked with the "givens" provided by chance or the debris of the culture around him.

70. The German philosopher Odo Marquard has argued that a "second psychologism" can be discerned as early as the dissemination of psychoanalysis almost a century ago. See his *Transcendentaler Idealismus, Romantische Naturphilosophie, Psychoanalyse* (Cologne: Verlag für Philosophie J. Dinter, 1987).

71. Pierre Bourdieu, *Distinction: A Social Critique of the Judgment of Taste*, trans. Richard Nice (Cambridge, Mass.: Harvard University Press, 1984); John Guillory, *Cultural Capital: The Problem of Literary Canon Formation* (Chicago: University of Chicago Press, 1993).

72. See, for example, the essays in *The Institution of Philosophy: A Discipline in Crisis?* ed. Avner Cohen and Marcelo Dascal (Lasalle, Ill.: Open Court, 1989).

73. See, for example, Wilhelm Wundt, "Psychologismus und Logizismus," in his *Kleine Schriften*, vol. 1 (Leipzig: Wilhelm Engelmann, 1910), 511–634.

74. Richard Rorty, *Philosophy and the Mirror of Nature* (Princeton, N.J.: Princeton University Press, 1979), 168.

75. Shusterman, *T. S. Eliot and the Philosophy of Criticism*, chap. 8. In an earlier essay, "Remembering Hulme: A Neglected Philosopher-Critic-Poet," Shusterman tries to do the same for the figure who has been taken as the quintessential anti-psychologist. His evidence, however, is basically limited to one aphorism in the unfinished collection entitled *Cinders*, included by Herbert Read in *Speculations*, which begins "The truth is that there are no ultimate principles, upon which the whole of knowledge can be built once and for ever as upon a rock" (Hulme, *Speculations*, 233–34). On this basis, Shusterman claims Hulme was close to Rorty in his anti-foundationalist stress on the priority of Weltanschauungen to absolute truth. Putting aside the performative contradiction entailed in a sentence against absolute truth that begins "the truth is . . . ," Hulme, it seems to me, was attacking the humanist pretension to combine cognitive, ethical, and religious knowledge in one grand system, not the possibility of foundations in separate spheres. His appeal for strict discontinuity between those spheres and belief in the authority of revealed religion in value questions makes his views a far cry from Rorty's philosophy of relativist edification.

76. Jacques Derrida, *Speech and Phenomena and Other Essays on Husserl's Theory of Signs*, trans. David B. Allison (Evanston, Ill.: Northwestern University Press, 1973), 12ff.

77. On Paul de Man's reaction to New Criticism in these terms, see Lindsay Waters, introduction to *Paul de Man, Critical Writings, 1953–1978*, ed. Lindsay Waters (Minneapolis: University of Minnesota Press, 1989), xl–lix.

78. See, for example, Roman Ingarden's essay "Psychologism and Psychology," *New Literary History* (Winter 1974): 215–23, for an attempt to distinguish between reductionist psychologism and the subtle use of psychological insights that respect the relative integrity of the work.

79. Mohanty, *Husserl and Frege*, 115.

80. It is for this reason that many commentators see Surrealism in certain of its guises as an anticipation of many postmodernist positions. See, for example, Hal Foster, *Compulsive Beauty* (Cambridge, Mass.: MIT Press, 1993).

81. For example, Mohanty, *Husserl and Frege*.

82. See Alasdair MacIntyre, *After Virture* (Notre Dame, Ind.: University of Notre Dame Press, 1981).

83. For Derrida on Marx, see his *Specters of Marx: The State of the Debt, the Work of Mourning, and the New International*, trans. Peggy Kamuf (New York: Routledge, 1994).

Index

Index

Index

Rigoli, Juan, 368
Robin, Charles, 223
Robinson, David, 388
Rollinat, Maurice, 105
"roman à l'hystèrie," 72–74, 83ff
Rorty, Richard, 183, 185, 363–64
Ross, Dorothy, x
Rousseau, George, 367
Russell, Bertrand, 357
Ryan, Judith, x, 3, 8, 16, 352, 360, 368, 377, 436

Sade, Marquis de, 195
Salpêtrière hospital, 94–95, 157–59, 386
Sass, Louis, ix, 3, 91, 352, 368, 383
Schnitzler, Arthur, 8, 277–97, 301, 311, 312–25, 331–35, 434
Schoenberg, Arnold, 298
Schopenhauer, Arthur, 5
Schorske, Carl E., 172, 174, 352
Schwartz, Sanford, 347, 358
Schwartz, Vanessa, 384–85
Scriabin, Alexander, 13
Sengoopta, Chandak, 372
Seurat, Georges, 15, 17
Shakespeare, William, 5, 189, 199
Shamdasani, Sonu, 5, 9, 12, 373, 375–76
Shaw, George Bernard, 340
shock (of modernity), 208
Silverman, Debora, 73, 372
Skinner, B. F. (and Gertrude Stein), 257, 259–60, 263–64, 418–19
Snow, C. P., vii, 368
somnambulism, 10–13, 117, 245, 407
Sorel, Georges, 339
Soupault, Philippe, 198
Spencer, Herbert, 341
spiritualism, 10, 13–14, 202–4
Society for Psychical Research, 13
Souriau, Pierre, 119
Spencer, Herbert, 9
Stein, Gertrude, 8, 15, 250–74, 377
Steiner, Rudolf, 13

Stekel, Wilhelm, 307
Stevenson, Robert Louis, 217
Stravinsky, Igor, 13
Strindberg, August, 298, 301
Surrealism, 8, 92, 171
Symbolism, 205
syphilis (and hysteria), 83

Taine, Hippolyte, 6, 78–79, 223
Tarde, Gabriel de, 118, 120, 218
Taylor, Eugene, 10, 373
telegraph, 402
Terrien, Firmin, 73
theosophy, 13
therapeutics, 9
Third Republic (in France), 86ff, 217–49 passim
timeline, of dates, 21–68
Toews, John, 18, 298–335
trauma (and modernity), 205, 403
Turgenev, Ivan, 231, 410
two cultures (the concept of), vii, 368

unconscious, theories of, 9

Van Eeden, Frederik, 8
Vienna, city of, 9, 12, 71, 277, 298–335 passim, 311, 313
Vorticism, 18

Wagner, Richard, 301
wandering Jew, 133
Weber, Max, 174, 354
Wegman, Jesse, timeline of dates by, 21–68
Weininger, Otto, 8, 298–99, 302–5, 432–33
Whitehead, Alfred North, 251, 413, 425–26
Wiene, Robert, 124
Wilde, Oscar, 78
Winter, Alison, 11
Winter, Jay, 377
Wittgenstein, Ludwig, 298, 354